# PERSPECTIVES ON RADIO AND TELEVISION

## TELECOMMUNICATION IN THE UNITED STATES

LEA's COMMUNICATION SERIES

**Jennings Bryant/Dolf Zillmann, General Editors**

Select titles include:

Abelman • *Reaching a Critical Mass: A Critical Analysis of Television Entertainment*

MacFarland • *Future Radio Programming Strategies: Cultivating Listenership in the Digital Age, Second Edition*

Moore • *Mass Communication Law and Ethics*

Smith/Wright/Ostroff • *Perspectives on Radio and Television: Telecommunication in the United States, Fourth Edition*

Sterling/Bracken/Hill • *Mass Communication Research Resources: An Annotated Guide*

For a complete list of other titles in LEA's Communication Series, please contact Lawrence Erlbaum Associates, Publishers.

# PERSPECTIVES ON RADIO AND TELEVISION

## TELECOMMUNICATION IN THE UNITED STATES

### Fourth Edition

F. Leslie Smith
John W. Wright II
David H. Ostroff

*University of Florida*

 LAWRENCE ERLBAUM ASSOCIATES, PUBLISHERS
1998   Mahwah, New Jersey                           London

Lawrence Erlbaum Associates, Inc., Publishers
10 Industrial Avenue
Mahwah, NJ  07430


**Library of Congress Cataloging-in-Publication Data**

Smith, F. Leslie, 1939–
    Perspectives on radio and television : telecommunication in
the United States / F. Leslie Smith. —4th ed.
        p.  cm.
    ISBN 0-8058-2092-2
    1. Broadcasting—United States.  I. Title.
    HE8689.8.S63 1998
    384.54'0973—dc21                          98–26812
                                                    CIP


Books published by Lawrence Erlbaum Associates are printed on
acid-free paper, and their bindings are chosen for strength and
durability.

Printed in the United States of America
10  9  8  7  6  5  4  3  2  1

*For Cindy Smith, Pam Wright, and Arnall Downs*

# CONTENTS IN BRIEF

# Contents

# PREFACE

The three previous editions of this book set forth these objectives—(a) to describe the field of radio–TV in the United States, (b) in a manner the reader could grasp and enjoy, and (c) in a form the classroom teacher could use. Judging by your warm response, these were good objectives. Our sincerest thanks to the critics, radio–TV executives, teachers, and students (especially the students) who made the 1979, 1985, and 1990 *Perspectives* such a success; because of your kind endorsement, we have aimed this fourth edition at those same three goals.

## FIRST GOAL: BREADTH

In working toward the first goal, we found that the scope of *Perspectives* would have to be broad. After all, "radio and television" is a field that covers subjects ranging from the *A&P Gypsies* to Zworykin, Vladimir K., and encompasses areas as diverse as churn and charlatans, static and statistics. If the reader were to get a complete picture of the field, the book had to include not only the usual areas but also subjects such as ethics, careers, and rivals to U.S. commercial radio and TV.

## SECOND GOAL: TO THE STUDENT

You will find *Perspectives* easy to understand at first reading—whether you are a beginning radio–TV major or a nonmajor elective student. Terms are defined as they occur in the narrative. In-text notes refer to sections that contain explanatory information. Boldface type indicate words and concepts that are especially important. A short, selective list of books for further reading follows every chapter.

## THIRD GOAL: TO THE INSTRUCTOR

*Perspectives* was written to adapt to *your* teaching situation. The book is divided into logical chapter divisions by subject matter, and you can assign them in the order appropriate for your course and students. Each chapter stands by itself. If you feel that technical aspects should come first in the course, then make chapters 10, 11, and 12 the initial reading assignments. Want to start with career opportunities? Put chapter 21 first on your syllabus. But *Perspectives* is also an integrated whole. If you are new at teaching radio–TV survey, you may wish to rely heavily on the text and use it straight through, as written.

Whether or not you are experienced in teaching the survey course, please read chapter 1. That is where the rationale of the book is laid out; it "sets up" the remaining 26 chapters.

## ACKNOWLEDGMENTS

The following supplied information or suggestions, information, or illustrative material, without which revision would be incomplete: Ron Carney, Ron Carney Graphic Design; Bill F. Chamberlin, Brechner Center for Freedom of Information, University of Florida; Bob Clarke, Harry Guscott, and Tom Krynski, WRUF-AM and WRUF-FM; Jimmy Cromwell, formerly with WCJB, now with Cable Rep Advertising; Jill Davidson, Cable Rep Advertising; Dolores Jenkins, University of Florida library; Rick Lehner, Rick Schneider, and Greg Smith, WUFT-TV; Laura Kendall Smith, WVEC-TV; Hallie Teitelman, HST Design Studios; and Priscilla West, Neuharth Reading Room, University of Florida.

Most academic authors do not thank administrators, but then, most authors do not work under leadership that is enlightened, effective, and equitable. We do, and we deeply appreciate the encouragement and support of Paul Smeyak, former chair of our department and now director of Oklahoma State University's School of Journalism; and Ralph Lowenstein, Terry Hynes, and James L. Terhune, dean emeritus, dean, and associate dean, respectively, of Florida's College of Journalism and Communications.

The folks who teach the telecommunication survey course at Florida have used *Perspectives* as the required text and provided valuable feedback for improving the fourth edition. We are grateful to Jeanne Chamberlin for creating the bar-none best index of any survey text in print. Linda Kilgore has, among other attributes, a persuasive telephone demeanor; her help tracking down and convincing copyright holders was invaluable. Thanks go to Pam, John III, and Lindsey Wright for putting up with missed dinners, missed bicycle rides, missed family outings, and a father weary from missed sleep, and for their wonderful support and understanding throughout the project. Thanks also to Arnall Downs for her patience and willingness to put up with unmowed lawns, dull weekends, and the many other things necessary to finish this work. Cindy Smith did research, proofread copy, and made suggestions for rewriting. Without her help and encouragement, you would not be holding this volume in your hands today. Responsibility for any problems, weaknesses, or inadequacies herein fall, of course, solely on the authors.

## KEEP THOSE CARDS AND LETTERS COMING. . .

Les started requesting direct reader response in the first edition and continued that in the second and third editions. The suggestions so generated proved invaluable in revising and improving, and others have since picked up on the idea. We continue to solicit comments from you, the reader—student, instructor, radio–TV employee or executive, interested member of the public. Contact us directly (our e-mail addresses are at the end of this preface) or through the publisher, and describe what you like or do not like about the book, what you think its strong and weak points are, what errors you find, what you had trouble understanding, and—most importantly—what you think could be done to improve future editions. This is a complete revision, and as you will see, we took previous comments and recommendations to heart.

*—Les Smith*
LeSmith@ufl.edu

*—John Wright*
JWright@jou.ufl.edu

*—Dave Ostroff*
DOstroff@jou.ufl.edu

# 1

## PREVIEW

Instant communication—telephone, television, cable, the Web: It is our accepted reality. But not so long ago, just a generation or two, the choices in use of distance communication, person-to-person as well as mass, seem by today's standards limited, even primitive. Not only has communication changed, but the *rate* of that change has increased dramatically.

### 1.1 FROM QUILL PEN TO THE WORLD WIDE WEB

With the perspective of history, we realize that many recent changes are not so earth-shaking as they are incremental; real, far-reaching communication changes are usually tied to changes not only in scientific knowledge but also in culture, marketplace, transportation, population, and many other elements. A sample of one family's communication experiences illustrates these points.

### 1.1.1 1822: Probated Message in Abbeville

The day was miserable. Freezing rain and sleet had stolen down from the north and were now turning piedmont clay into raw, red slush. Huge oak and pine logs blazed in every one of the house's many fireplaces, but their brave heat could push only a few feet into the massive cold that seeped into the large, rambling wooden structure. All rooms were for the most part uncomfortably, numbingly cold, but none more so than that which served as plantation office. Seated at the desk, lost in thought, apparently oblivious to the cold, a man of about 74 years idly played with a quill pen as he stared at the sleet falling outside the window. Finally he sighed, took a sheet of paper out of the desk drawer, dipped his pen in a small inkwell, focused his thoughts and began to write. He dated the paper January 19, 1822, and penned, "I, William Lesly, of the district of Abbeville, and State of South Carolina, being in good health and of perfect mind and memory, do make and ordain this my last will and testament." Then he specified how his property should be divided among his heirs. He frowned as he considered what to do about his oldest surviving son, the profligate John Harris Lesly. William decided that his son would not inherit the estate. Instead, he wrote that he forgave all debts his son had incurred and bequeathed John "a Shorter Catechism, to be bought by my executors and should he study it well, and particularly the 84th and 85th questions,[1] it may do him more good at the day of judgment than all my estate."

William died that December. The will, carefully scribed on hand-made paper, would survive in the Abbeville County Courthouse. But the message, the moral lesson he hoped to send his son through the will, probably never reached its intended recipient, because by the time William penned his will, John Harris Lesly had traveled westward over the trails and traces that served as roads in early 19th-century America. He was last seen heading to Indiana in the company of abolitionists.

### 1.1.2 1910: Postcard Near Madison

Nineteen-year-old Lillian Leslie, great-granddaughter of John Harris Lesly (her grandfather had changed the spelling of the family name), walked down the wagon path. She breathed in the fresh morning air, perfumed by corn and tobacco growing lush on either side. A mockingbird sang from a nearby live oak, insects and other birds murmured in the background, and a slight breeze rustled leaves of the crops. Lillian was off to get the day's mail. The postal box was planted on a short pole at the edge of the property by the county road, about a 15-minute walk down this two-rut track. Rural free delivery of mail had started when Lillian was only 3, and she took its convenience for granted. She reached in the box—a few letters for Papa, a catalog from Sears and Roebuck, and a picture postcard addressed to her. Mr. Sheppard had written again. Among Lillian's many beaus, Walter Sheppard, an apprentice pharmacist, seemed to court her most seriously. The card was manufactured by the Grant Company, and the tinted picture on its front showed a mockingbird, in full song, perched on a live oak limb. The back of the card, postmarked Madison, Florida, and dated May 20, 1910, carried the message. "Dear Miss Leslie," it began, "There is going to be a tent revival in Monticello this Saturday. I would very much like to take you there, if your father would permit." It was signed, "Your good friend, Walter B. Sheppard."

### 1.1.3 1924: Election Report in Apopka

The long wooden drugstore was full of men. The noise and talk they created made it impossible to study. And the stink—They all smoked: the younger men, cigarettes; the older ones, huge, foul-smelling cigars. The large, lazy overhead fans did little to disperse the smell. Beatrice Sheppard, daughter of Lillian Leslie Sheppard, finally gave up, closed her math book, and shoved it to one side of the small, round marble-top table. Her father, Walter, was installing a radiobroadcasting receiver in his place of business, the Apopka Drug Company. Orlando (or at least the radiobroadcasting station there) had promised to transmit returns from the presidential election this evening as they came in by telegraph to the local newspaper. Earlier in the day, her two younger brothers had helped string the aerial wire between the chimney on the roof of the drugstore and a nearby tree, and now her father was doing the last-minute tuning and fiddling needed to bring in the station as clearly as possible.

Walter had bought the device as both public service and a means to attract customers. And attract them, it did. This was one of the area's first receivers, and most people had never seen one before. Folks from all over town and the surrounding orange-grove countryside flocked to the drugstore that evening. The crowd was predominantly male, and they bought tobacco, fountain drinks, and—for those lucky enough to have a physician friend during these years of prohibition—prescription-only whiskey (strictly for medicinal purposes; please drink *off* the premises).

The receiver itself was in a polished wooden box slightly smaller than an orange crate. Attached to it were a large hornlike structure that produced the sound, the wire from the aerial, and connections to several wet-cell batteries to power the whole thing. This was November, way past the daily thunderstorm season of the central Florida summer, so static should not have been much of a problem. Nonetheless, the speaker horn had emitted only noises and squawks, and the men crowded into the store took great delight in giving Walter "advice," mostly in the form of raucous comments. Suddenly music floated over and silenced the crowd. Walter stepped back, grinning. "That'll do it," he announced, "They should start giving the returns in about a half-hour." Beatrice, as fascinated as any of the customers, listened to the music—mostly a not-very-good soprano with piano accompaniment—and the interspersed announcements. It all sounded sort of tinny, but nonetheless—talking and music captured out of the air by a box: Now that was really something! She telephoned her friend Emily to get down here right away.

### 1.1.4 1944: News Bulletin in Plymouth

"How much longer, now?" asked Leslie Smith.

"About a minute less than the last time you asked," replied Avey, the lady who "helped out" and took care of Leslie while his mother taught school. Avey was usually there just during the day, but Leslie's mother had to attend some special school function that Sunday evening. His father had joined the Army shortly after the attack on Pearl Harbor and was somewhere around the Philippine Islands. So here was Avey in the Smith's kitchen on a Sunday night, doing her best both to press clothes in the evening heat and to keep 5-year-old Leslie informed about how much longer before his mother, Beatrice Sheppard Smith, returned.

Avey suddenly remembered something the boy's mother had mentioned. "Say, don't you have some radio program you like to listen to on Sunday nights?" she asked.

His eyes lit up. "*Blondie and Dagwood!* It's my favorite show." The Smiths lived in a house on a country road outside the village of Plymouth. Orange groves surrounded the house on three sides, and neighbors were few and far between. Nonetheless, people living in Plymouth could pick up all four Orlando radio stations clearly, and Leslie loved listening to the radio. He never missed *Let's Pretend* on Saturday mornings, and he had already received several "premiums"—rings and compasses and other toys obtained by mailing cereal box tops and 15 cents to an address in Battle Creek, Michigan—from radio shows featuring the Lone Ranger and Sky King. But tonight *Blondie* came on. This weekly radio comedy series was based on Chic Young's newspaper comic strip, and Leslie did not want to miss a minute of it.

Avey turned back to her ironing. "Well you better turn that radio on then. Your show will be on in a few minutes." Leslie rushed into the living room and turned the volume knob of the tabletop radio until it clicked on. The dial lighted, and he could hear a slight hum as the radio's vacuum tubes warmed up.

The sound finally came up in the middle of a sentence. ". . . terrupt this program to bring you this bulletin," intoned the announcer, "The Allies have captured Rome. Today, June 4, 1944, elements of the United States Fifth Army entered the Eternal City at . . . ." Leslie grimaced; that war news stuff had interrupted and even displaced his favorite radio shows ever since he could remember. But the news bulletin ended quickly, and the regularly scheduled Columbia Broadcasting System program started on time. "Ah-ah-ahhhh," warned the announcer, "It's time for . . . ," and the voice of Arthur Lake playing Dagwood Bumstead cut in with his weekly anguished howl, "Blondie?!?"

### 1.1.5 1952: Campaign Commercial in Sanford

Mike Smith, aged 4½ years old, slipped into the darkened living room. In spite of the warm, humid July evening, the place was crowded with family and neighbors. There was no light save the small rectangular screen at which they all stared, its bluish glow reflected in their faces. No one spoke. All were fascinated, mesmerized. Astounding: Moving pictures available in a living room with just the flick of a switch! This was the first television set most of those people had ever seen.

Mike's father ran a store downtown that sold hardware and appliances, and his family was one of the first in Sanford, Florida, to get a TV set. There were just two TV stations in the entire state. One was in Miami, far too distant to ever pick up a decent signal. The closer one was in Jacksonville, but at more than 110 air miles, still not close enough for even fairly decent fringe reception. There was no cable system in Sanford (in fact, there were very few cable systems anywhere). In an attempt to pull in a signal, Mike's father and older brother, Leslie, had put a receiving antenna on a tall mast on the roof of the house. Lead-in wire took the signal from the antenna to the TV set. Special eyehooks held this flat, brown, plastic-covered cable away from the mast, the roof, and the wall until it reached the window nearest the TV set, then it was squeezed between the screen and window frame and attached to the TV set. Even so, the picture was snowy most of the time. Yet, people would stare at the tube just to catch a glimpse of a barely discernable picture.

Sometimes, when weather conditions were just right, a beautiful clear, snow-free picture would boom through. This was one of those nights. Mike had gone into his bedroom to put on his cowboy outfit "just like Hopalong Cassidy," one of TV's first cowboy heroes. As he wandered back into the living room, a TV ad supporting Dwight D. "Ike" Eisenhower for President was closing with the slogan, "I like Ike." Mr. Reese, a neighbor, spotted Mike just at that time and announced, "And I like Mike!" Everyone laughed, and Mike, pleased with the idea, adopted that as his own slogan for the next few months. Years later, as an adult, Mike could not remember a time when there was no TV.

### 1.1.6 1997: Weather Report in St. Croix

This layout for an advertisement on the World Wide Web was really giving Hallie problems. After hours of experimentation using the most sophisticated design program available, she decided that she literally could not get onto one page all the copy, pictures, animation, and sounds the client wanted and still have it look good. She could do either one ugly crowded page that would attract no one but include everything, or a subtle and tasteful layout that branched and led to other pages, each of which would feature just one or two items but would catch the eye of the casual browser. Well, that was the client's choice; she would set up examples of both alternatives on her website tomorrow morning and notify the client by e-mail to try them out.

Hallie Smith lived on St. Croix. A graphic designer, she did most of her work on computer. She also used the Internet to communicate with her mainland clients. Her home, the Virgin Islands, was an idyllic place to live and work—tropical weather, beautiful beaches—but the islands were vulnerable to hurricanes. Earlier in the week, the National Weather Service had spotted a tropical depression in the Atlantic that seemed to gather strength as it headed east, so as she worked, Hallie had keyed the Weather Channel into a window in the upper right corner of her computer screen. She saved to the hard disk the best of her several designs, then enlarged the Weather Channel window and turned up the sound. The depression had apparently stalled; it was now just blustering and blowing, not going anywhere.

That reminded her that she needed to call her father in Florida. Hallie was doing some illustrations for a book he was writing. She opened the e-mail program, inserted the code that would route the completed note to Leslie Smith in Gainesville, Florida, and typed in the message area, "We need to talk about your figure 9-14. I don't quite understand some of your sketches. I'll use the Web to call you tonight at 9 p.m. Love, Hallie."

Just before 9 that evening, her father logged onto his computer. He and Hallie used special hardware and software on their respective computers to speak with each other over the Internet, bypassing the telephone company completely. Hallie was worried about the sketches, but her father was worried about the hurricane.

## 1.2 CHANGES

From quill pen to satellite-delivered computer communications in less than 200 years—and that is just part of the story. We have also seen during that period first a divergence and then a convergence of communication. For most of that period, mass communication grew more specialized and different from private communication. More recently, however, we have seen the computer used increasingly for both private and mass communication. The impact of readily available communication is one of the basic elements in the evolution of human society.

In the short history of electronic mass media, we have experienced one of the most exciting periods in communication. Since the first edition of this book was published in 1979, as consumers of media we have enjoyed a rapid expansion of options. For the first time ever, many can choose from a number of programming alternatives—not simply which situation comedy, but true alternatives. As students of media, we have watched as the very structure of radio and television has begun to change. New technology and fresh thinking have challenged the "givens," concepts that once seemed cast in bronze and sunk in cement, concepts as basic as broadcast stations, advertising support of programming, and public ownership of the airwaves.

Technology has ignited much of the change. By 1979, some new technology had already appeared; still, broadcast radio and television were the primary electronic media. Today, some of what were "new media" in 1979 have grown, expanded, and diversified—cable television, cable networks, pay cable, wireless cable, videocassette recorders (VCRs), video games, corporate video, and home computers. Others, not yet widely available, seem about to grow and expand—interactive cable, video-on-demand (VOD), digital broadcasting, and various forms of electronic text. Yet other technology has emerged since 1979—the low-power television service, C-band direct, direct broadcast satellite, high-definition television, pay-per-view, digital audio and video, stereophonic television sound, video graphics generators and animators, the charge coupled device (in effect, a tubeless video pickup tube), continuing developments in solid state electronics (particularly miniaturization), the World Wide Web and its ability to carry sound and motion.

## 1.3 BROADCASTING

The movers and shakers seemed convinced these new media would stay, spread, and compete. Naturally, they would compete at the expense of broadcasting, particularly the broadcast television networks.

Some early returns from the marketplace indicated that such predictions were not all "blue sky." Cable networks captured some programming that would previously have run on the broadcast networks, particularly sports. By the late 1990s, cable had spread to over 65% of U.S. television homes. VCR penetration had reached that level years before. National advertisers had invested increasing amounts in cable networks—over $2.4 billion by 1997—most of which came from money that would otherwise have been spent on the broadcast networks. In 1978, the total share of television audience that all three commercial networks drew was 93%. Nearing the end of the century, it had dropped below 60%. Advertising agency personnel projected this trend could continue, and the percentages would bottom, according to some predictions, in the 50% range. The broadcast business no longer had a monopoly in radio and television.

Commercial broadcasting is not quite ready to lie down quietly and wait for the undertaker. It is still the dominant form of radio and television, and the broadcast business is still viable. However, other media, other delivery systems, and other means of economic support challenge that dominance.

### 1.4 RADIO AND TELEVISION

The field of radio and television has expanded far beyond commercial network broadcasting, that which we had called "the norm" since 1930. As consumers and students of radio and television, we must study these new uses of radio and television, as well as the old.

Like previous editions of *Perspectives on Radio and Television,* this edition takes advantage of the generic terms in its title. Its framework for analysis is radio and television, of which broadcasting is but one use. On the other hand, because it is by far the most popular and widespread form of radio and television, broadcast-ing—particularly commercial broadcasting—receives the lengthiest, most detailed coverage.

Academics and others have adopted the term *electronic mass media* to refer to this framework. Most devices and practices included under electronic mass media are actually new or supplementary uses to which the technology of radio and (particularly) television have been put. To consumers, TV is TV, and it does not matter where the programming comes from or how it is delivered. Even for media such as video games, computer software, and teletext, the display vehicle is often the screen of a TV receiver. So this volume retains "radio and television" in the main title and "electronic mass media" in the subtitle.

Why study radio and television? The facts and figures cited previously demon-strate that radio and television constitute a major factor in our lives, our society, and our economy. Their size, nature, pervasiveness, and ubiquity all indicate the necessity to study radio and television. The important question then is what radio and television are. That is what we answer in this book.

## 1.5 FORMAT

What are radio and television? The question is not only important, but complex as well, even for a book with 27 chapters and more than 680 pages. Thus, this question—What are radio and television?—has been broken down into a number of smaller questions.

- How did radio and television come about?
- What are the messages of radio and television, and how are these messages formed?
- How are the messages sent?
- Within what kind of legal and ethical framework do they operate?
- How do they generate the revenues that allow them to exist?
- What are some of the alternatives to the profit-driven U.S. model of radio and television?
- What relationships exist among radio and television, the individual, the group, and the society?

Each of these smaller questions represents a different way of looking at, or perspective on, radio and television.

This book is written to answer these questions and thus the title, *Perspectives on Radio and Television.* Each of the seven main sections reflect a different perspective—historical, creative and informational, physical, legal and ethical, economic, comparative, and sociopsychological. Each perspective is further broken down into a number of different major topics, which are the chapters within each section. Especially important names, words, phrases, and other information are printed in **boldface** type. When you come across a new or unfamiliar word, you will find either an explanation in context or a reference to another section of the book (e.g., *PRT* 1.4) that contains the explanation.

You will find the writing style in the following pages informal, its function primarily to describe and explain the concepts as completely and simply as possible. The subject of radio and television is intrinsically interesting; the aim of the writing is to let it emerge that way from the pages of this book.

## NOTES

1. Question 84: What doth every sin deserve? Answer: Every sin deserveth God's wrath and curse, both in this life, and that which is to come.

Question 85: What doth God require of us, that we may escape his wrath and curse, due to us for sin? Answer: To escape the wrath and curse of God, due to us for sin, God requireth of us faith in Jesus Christ, repentance unto life, with the diligent use of all the outward means whereby Christ communicateth to us the benefits of redemption. (Westminster Shorter Catechism)

## FURTHER READING

The volume that you are now reading is a survey book. The term *survey*, in this usage, means that the author or authors present a comprehensive examination of a particular field. In *Perspectives on Radio and Television,* we survey the field of electronic mass communication. There are other fine books that survey the same field, and each presents the material from a different point of view. The following are particularly worthwhile and deserve your attention to compare and help put *Perspectives* into perspective.

Bittner, John R. *Broadcasting and Telecommunication: An Introduction.* 3rd ed. Englewood Cliffs, NJ: Prentice-Hall, 1991.

Gross, Lynne Schafer. *Telecommunications: An Introduction to Electronic Media.* 6th ed. Dubuque, IA: Brown, 1997.

Head, Sydney W., Christopher H. Sterling, and Lemuel B. Schofield. *Broadcasting in America: A Survey of Electronic Media.* 7th ed. Boston: Houghton, 1994.

Keirstead, Phillip O., and Sonia-Kay Keirstead. *The World of Telecommunication: Introduction to Broadcasting, Cable, and New Technologies.* Boston: Focal, 1990.

Orlik, Peter B. *The Electronic Media: An Introduction to the Profession.* Needham, MA: Allyn, 1992.

Whetmore, Edward Jay. *American Electric: Introduction to Telecommunications and Electronic Media.* New York: McGraw, 1992.

Willis, Edgar E., and Henry B. Aldridge. *Television, Cable, and Radio: A Communications Approach.* Englewood Cliffs, NJ: Prentice-Hall, 1992.

Following are some principal sources, although others exist. Your reference librarian can help you find various periodicals and books on specific media.

*Broadcasting & Cable.* New York: Cahners. Weekly. Probably the single most important periodical for the business aspects of electronic mass media.

*Broadcasting & Cable Yearbook.* New Providence, RI: R.R. Bowker. Annual. This compilation contains much information about broadcasting, cable, and other electronic mass media, including a short history and status report, important FCC rules, state-by-state listings of outlets with descriptions, and many other directories of organizations and various people involved in radio and television.

*Cablevision.* Denver: Titch. Biweekly. Reports on the cable television business.

*Television Digest.* Washington, DC: Television Digest. Weekly. This publication describes itself as "the authoritative service for broadcasting, cable, consumer electronics, and allied fields."

*Television Factbook.* Washington, DC: Television Digest. Annual. This compendium is similar to *Broadcasting & Cable Yearbook* but focuses on video media and contains additional data.

# I

# HISTORICAL PERSPECTIVE

All of us view our world in the "now." But just a moment back from today so many of the things we take for granted did not exist. Radio and television are primary examples. It took bright, adventurous, and creative people who developed ideas and inventions to turn their future into our present.

To understand radio and television as they are now, we have to look back to see the amazing and often unlikely chain of events that got us from Heinrich Hertz to Home Box Office, from Sarnoff to satellites, from De Forest to digital technology. Our perspective in this section is historical, and the four chapters answer the question, "How did it all happen?"

In chapter 2, we look at the technical and industrial origins of radio and television. We start before the middle of the 19th century and, as we travel forward in time, meet the devices and the companies on which modern electronic mass media were founded, focusing on the development of radio broadcasting. In chapter 3, we pick up late in the nineteenth century and survey the history of television broadcasting. In chapter 4, we begin in 1949 and trace the rise of cable television. In chapter 5, we start with 1948 and examine the development of solid-state, digital, and other technologies that have impacted electronic mass media.

# 2

## Radio Broadcasting: From 1842

How to send messages over long distances—dreamers have sought solutions to this dilemma since the torch fires of the ancient world. It was not until more recent history that significant inventions changed the technology of communication. The technological predecessors of broadcasting date from at least 1842, the patent year of the electromagnetic telegraph. Broadcasting itself originated almost by accident. Although the first radio broadcasting stations signed on about 1920, the business structure that would provide radio's financial support did not fully develop until about a decade later. *Broadcasting*—all broadcasting—was radio. And *radio*—all radio—was AM radio.

By the time of the Great Depression, radio had begun to develop the program genres that are still in use today. Dramas, game shows, situation comedies, musical and variety shows, news commentary, sports play-by-play: Radio networks developed and programmed them, and local stations broadcast them. Radio broadcasting became the primary entertainment medium for many U.S. homes in the 1930s. Most programs lasted 30 or 60 minutes, and family members would gather in the living room around their one radio receiver to listen.

Radio flourished during World War II and the later 1940s. During the 1950s, however, television spread and grew into the dominant glamour medium. Radio, in turn, lost its huge network audiences and had to remake itself to survive. It was a radical and sometimes painful transition. In the 1960s FM radio emerged. Throughout the 1970s more AM and FM stations went on the air, intensifying competition. Many radio stations lost money. By the 1990s, radio, with many stations still struggling to find a profitable niche, faced the possibility of even more competition from new over-the-air aural media.

This, then, is radio's story—from its earliest days through the 1990s. We begin with the discovery of the unseen—radio waves.

### 2.1 DEVELOPMENT OF RADIO AND THE BROADCASTING BUSINESS

The prehistory and history of U.S. commercial radio unfolded in seven stages—radiotelephonic communication, industrial firms with interest in communications,

**13**

broadcast stations, audience, advertising as financial support, networks, and comprehensive federal regulation. All developed over time through trial and error, sometimes by sheer coincidence.

### 2.1.1 Stage 1: Origins of Radiotelephonic Communication

The first stage in the development of broadcasting was achievement of **radiote-lephony**—transmission and reception of sound by radio waves. Like broadcasting itself, radiotelephony is not one device, unique unto itself, but rather the combination of a series of discoveries and inventions—electricity, telegraphy, telephony, and wireless telegraphy.

Scientific interest and research in **electricity** began in earnest during the Renaissance and reached its peak in the 18th and early 19th centuries. In the 1880s **Thomas Edison** began to wire New York City, the first step in what would become the electrification of America.

**Telegraphy**—relaying messages from one point to another—had been around for centuries. The ancient Greeks employed beacon fires and torches to convey information over distances. Various visual signaling devices had been used through the years, but these were cumbersome, time consuming, and subject to problems from bad weather and human error. In the 19th century several persons worked on a totally different idea—development of an *electrical telegraph*. It was an American, **Samuel F. B. Morse,** who was credited as the first to succeed. Morse had worked on his electromagnetic telegraph system for more than a decade when he finally patented it in 1842.

Congress appropriated $30,000 for Morse to build an experimental electrical telegraph line between Washington, DC, and Baltimore. In May 1844 the words "What hath God wrought!" were transmitted as the first message. The experiment was successful; a message had been sent over wire via electricity.

Thirty-two years later, electricity was used to send voice communication by wire. **Alexander Graham Bell** filed formal application to patent his telephone (Fig. 2.1) on March 7, 1876. Three days later, Bell operated his telephone successfully for the first time.

In the meantime a group of scientific discoveries had begun that would lead to signals sent through the air with no wires at all, **wireless telegraphy.** Beginning in 1864 **James Clerk Maxwell** wrote a series of theoretical papers showing that energy passed through space as waves traveling at the speed of light. He said light waves were electromagnetic, but there were probably other electromagnetic waves, too, invisible because they differed in length from light waves. In other words, Clerk Maxwell predicted the existence of something that could not be seen, felt, heard, or smelled, something that today we call **radio waves.**

Maxwell's predictions were soon proved correct. In 1887 the German scientist **Heinrich Hertz** demonstrated the existence of radio waves. He constructed a device that included two coils or hoops of wire, one of which was an oscillator, a device that produced radio waves. He found that the oscillating coil excited

**FIG. 2.1. Invention of the telephone.** Bell's device, the 1876 liquid telephone. (Photo courtesy of AT&T Archives. Used by permission.)

electrical current in the other coil. When he moved the two coils farther and farther apart, the results were the same; the current was moving along an invisible connection between the two coils (Fig. 2.2). This was the first transmission and reception of radio waves. Others started experimenting with these mysterious **Hertzian waves,** as they came to be called.

Scientists had predicted wireless telegraphy for years, and in the 1880s American and English scientists developed some crude devices to that end. Most, however, were based on electrical induction[1] and therefore limited in range. Interestingly, no one had thought of using Hertzian waves to carry information. Transmission and reception of these waves remained a laboratory stunt, pure science. It took a nonscientist to bring all elements together. **Guglielmo Marconi,** a young Italian, put together Hertz's oscillating coil, a Morse telegraph key, a coherer (a radio wave detection device), and grounded transmitting and receiving antennas of his own design (Fig. 2.3). In 1895, at the age of 21, Marconi succeeded in sending a message in telegraphic code over a distance of 1¼ miles using electricity without wires.

The final step was to combine wireless transmission and reception with voice. **Reginald Fessenden,** a University of Pittsburgh electrical engineering professor, felt that a high-frequency generator was needed to transmit speech. He contracted

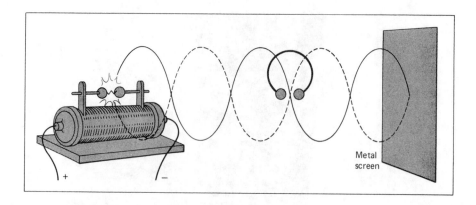

**FIG. 2.2. Hertz's device.** The wires led to a power source. The power source caused electrical sparks to oscillate between two metal balls. These sparks sent out waves of high-frequency alternating current. The waves hit a metal screen that reflected them. When properly positioned between the spark gap and the metal screen, an open copper wire loop would spark in resonance with the metal balls.

**FIG. 2.3. Guglielmo Marconi.** Marconi and his apparatus for "telegraphy without wires" shortly after his arrival in England in 1896. (Photo courtesy of GEC-Marconi. Used by permission.)

to have General Electric (GE) build one. GE shipped the great 50,000-cycle machine to Fessenden's wireless station at Brant Rock on the Massachusetts coast. Combining the generator with a telephone and his recently patented high-frequency arc, Fessenden made the first wireless voice transmission on Christmas Eve 1906.

Momentous as Fessenden's achievement was, his technology was eclipsed just 1 week later. On December 31, 1906, another American scientist transmitted and received code by use of radio waves from one side of his laboratory to the other. The scientist was **Lee De Forest** (Fig. 2.4), and his method of reception was based on his invention, the **Audion**—immediate forerunner of the triode vacuum tube, ancestor of the transistor, the integrated circuit, and the "chip."

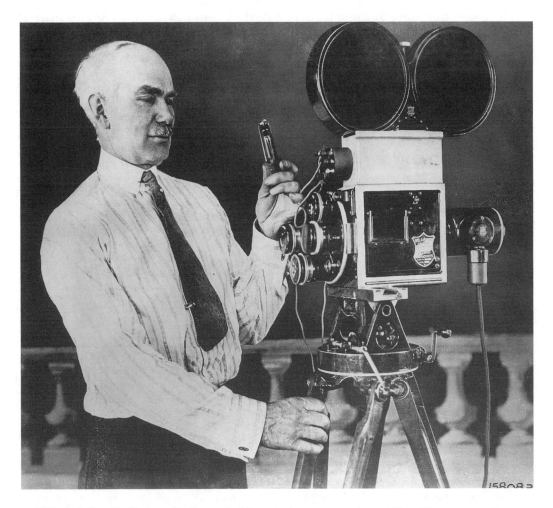

**FIG. 2.4. Lee De Forest.** De Forest holds an early vacuum tube used in a film camera, about 1926. De Forest had earlier developed a system for film sound, but it had little success, primarily because the film business felt it had no use for sound. Ultimately film sound succeeded because of De Forest's invention, the Audion. (Photo courtesy of AT&T Archives. Used by permission.)

The Audion's origin dated from 1879 when Edison invented the electric light. Four years later, Edison noted that when a metallic plate was put in a bulb along with the light filament, current flowed from the filament to the plate. No immediate application was seen for this "Edison effect," although later James A. Fleming, a fellow worker of Marconi, used it to develop the two-element valve (tube) in improving wireless communication. What De Forest did, however, was to insert in the bulb, between the filament and the plate, a third element, a tiny grid of fine wire. The grid carried a weak electric current. By varying the charge on the grid, he also varied the higher voltage current that flowed through it from the filament, or negative element, to the plate, or positive element (Fig. 2.5). In other words, the Audion could take a weak electric signal and magnify it. Put multiple Audions in tandem, and the result was increased amplification.

The invention of the Audion launched the electronic age, the second industrial revolution. Thus the full implication of the Audion extends far beyond the realm of wireless transmission. But for our purposes, in one stroke De Forest had developed a device that would eventually perform all four **basic operations of radiotelephony—generation, modulation, detection, and amplification.** There would be further refinements in equipment and circuitry for transmission and reception, but all the basic devices necessary for broadcasting had now been developed. However, broadcasting itself had not yet developed. Radio was still used almost exclusively for point-to-point communication.

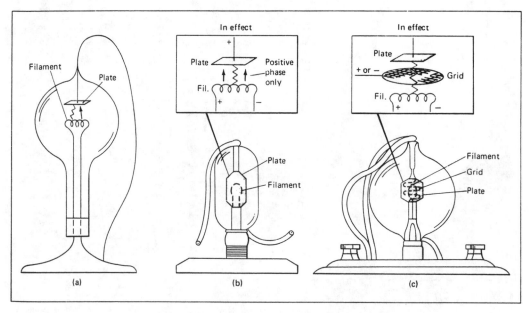

**FIG. 2.5. Development of the Audion.** (a) In 1883 Edison noted that current flowed from the filament to a plate. (b) Fleming connected the plate to an antenna. Incoming waves made the plate alternate rapidly from positive to negative, attracting and repelling current from the filament and reproducing incoming radio signals as current in the earphones. (c) De Forest put a grid between the plate and the filament. Weak current from the antenna went to the grid and controlled the higher voltage passing from filament to plate.

## 2.1.2 Stage 2: Formation of Communications Business Firms

Many new inventions remain only interesting science unless business brings them to the marketplace. The devices and discoveries described earlier led to the formation of five important corporate entities: American Telephone and Telegraph, General Electric, Westinghouse Electric and Manufacturing Company, Marconi Telegraph Company of America, and Radio Corporation of America. These five organizations, along with other companies, held different patents necessary to the development of radiotelephonic communication (the mass use of which would eventually be named *broadcasting*). Eventually this patent situation would reach the point that none of the companies could work and develop without access to the patented inventions of the others. This would make for interesting times.

In July 1877, Alexander Graham Bell and six close associates formed the Bell Telephone Company. By 1880, however, the company had passed into other hands. In 1881, Bell Telephone purchased a manufacturing rival, Western Electric Company, and in 1885 it formed a subsidiary to manage long-distance operations, **American Telephone and Telegraph Company** (AT&T). In 1899, after Machiavellian battles with corporate rivals, AT&T became the parent company of the Bell system.

In October 1878, Edison was well on his way to development of the incandescent light. He persuaded a syndicate of financiers to underwrite his research. This group formed the Edison Electric Light Company. Edison later sold his interest, but from this beginning emerged the **General Electric Company** (GE). During World War I, GE researched and developed advances in wireless transmission for the United States and its allies.

George Westinghouse, who received the first of many patents on a railway air brake in 1869, also developed an interest in the generation of electric power. He founded the forerunner of the **Westinghouse Electric and Manufacturing Company** in 1886 but left the company in 1911. The firm retained his name and got involved in radio early in World War I when it accepted a contract from the British government to do research in wireless transmission. After the United States entered the war, the Westinghouse Company manufactured wireless equipment for the armed forces.

Guglielmo Marconi, who first put together all the elements of wireless transmission, offered his invention to the government of his native Italy. Italy refused it, so in 1896 the 22-year-old Marconi went to England where he patented his device. In 1897 he and others formed a company to promote his wireless apparatus, the Marconi Wireless Telegraph Company, "British Marconi." Soon after, British Marconi formed the Wireless Telegraph Company of America, "American Marconi," to further Marconi interests in the United States. The combined companies led the world in marine communication through World War I.

***2.1.2.1 Patent Problems.***    After De Forest patented the Audion in 1906 and successfully tested its wireless transmission abilities in his laboratory, he started the De Forest Radio Telephone Company. He ran transmission tests over wider distances. He equipped a fleet of 24 U.S. Navy ships for a cruise around the world, transmitted phonograph records of music from the Eiffel Tower in Paris that were heard all over Europe, and transmitted performances from the stage of the Metropolitan Opera.

Meanwhile AT&T had concluded that coast-to-coast long-distance telephone was not possible without a "repeater" (amplifier). Repeaters used three-element tubes. Irving Langmuir, a GE scientist, had improved the Audion by expelling all gases from the bulb, creating the **vacuum tube**. Harold D. Arnold of AT&T had also made improvements. However, De Forest's patent—the first to involve the third element—was essential.

De Forest, meanwhile, was fighting a court battle. He had been arrested in 1912, charged with using the mails to defraud by selling stock in his company. He was acquitted in 1913. Desperate for money, however, he had sold his patent rights on the Audion to AT&T for $50,000. With this patent, the telephone company was able to stretch its long-distance reach to the West Coast in 1914 and, soon after, overseas.

At this point, as mentioned earlier, a number of different companies owned a number of different patents that collectively were vital to further development of wireless transmission. But individually these companies were blocking this same development. Almost any attempt to build or use equipment for commercial purposes infringed on several patents. For example, suppose a vacuum tube were used. The vacuum tube involved patents on devices and improvements developed by Fleming for Marconi, by De Forest but now owned by AT&T, by Arnold for AT&T, by Langmuir for GE, and by others. The United Wireless Company, for a time the most extensive U.S. company in wireless telegraphy, was caught in the patent bind. Found guilty in the courts of infringing on Marconi patents, United was so weakened that American Marconi was able to absorb United, thereby attaining a monopoly on radio communications in the United States.

When the United States entered World War I, the government closed all civilian wireless stations and ordered the pooling of patents. This government-enforced **patent pool** allowed war contractors—including Westinghouse, GE, and AT&T's Western Electric—to manufacture tubes and circuits for military radios without regard to patent infringement. As a result, wireless equipment developed, improved, and standardized. However, when the war ended, so did the patent pool. No one company could manufacture and market the improved equipment because it would infringe on the patents of others.

The end of war contracts caused other problems. Westinghouse, for example, had made great progress in the development of wireless transmitters and receivers and had geared up production to supply military needs. Now there was no stable market for this equipment. GE had turned out expensive equipment such as the Alexanderson alternator.[2] Without government contracts GE would be obliged to dismiss many skilled employees.

The end of World War I in 1918 left the U.S. government in control of the nation's wireless communications facilities. The Alexander Bill, introduced in Congress in November, would have perpetuated government monopoly of radio. The U.S. Navy favored the bill, but it was bitterly opposed by civilian wireless interests and voted down in committee, reaffirming the principle of private ownership of electronic communication facilities.[3]

### 2.1.2.2 Creation of Radio Corporation of America.

About this time, British Marconi tried to buy rights to the Alexanderson alternator from GE. The offer supposedly set off two trains of thought in the administration of President Woodrow Wilson. First, if British Marconi got the alternator, Great Britain could gain a worldwide monopoly in wireless communications. Second, national security demanded that no foreign-controlled corporation be permitted to dominate U.S. wireless communications.

**Owen D. Young,** GE general counsel, solved both problems. He implied that he had the backing of the Wilson administration and the Navy to set up a new firm, **Radio Corporation of America** (RCA). RCA purchased controlling interest in American Marconi from the British firm, and in November 1919 all assets, patents, and good will of American Marconi were transferred to RCA. Individuals who held stock in American Marconi received shares of RCA. British Marconi, convinced that the U.S. government strongly opposed foreign control of U.S. communication facilities, welcomed the sale. Young chaired the board of directors; Edward J. Nally of American Marconi became president.

The formation of RCA was only part of the plan. GE, RCA, AT&T, and Western Electric (an AT&T subsidiary), the major companies holding patents in wireless devices, agreed to pool their patents, with RCA serving as the enabling vehicle. In return, GE and AT&T received stock in RCA. Later Westinghouse, which had recently acquired Edwin H. Armstrong's critical patents, joined the pool and received RCA stock. The United Fruit Company[4] group, including the Wireless Specialty Apparatus Company and the Tropical Radio Telegraph Company, added their wireless assets to the pool and received RCA stock.

These agreements were not limited to patents. Under the agreements, GE and Westinghouse had exclusive rights to use the pooled patents to manufacture radio receivers, and RCA would sell large percentages of them. AT&T was to control all toll (paid for by the customer) radiotelephonic communication, including exclusive rights to manufacture radio transmitters for sale or lease to others. (GE and Westinghouse could make transmitters for themselves, but not for others.) Also, AT&T and Western Electric could now use the pooled patents in telephone equipment.

This series of agreements linked the corporations into two groups—the **Telephone Group** (AT&T and Western Electric) and the **Radio Group** (General Electric, Westinghouse, and RCA). They had pooled their patents and divided the communications world, including point-to-point radio communication, among themselves. All eventualities had been foreseen and provided for—except one. It arose even as the agreements were being drawn up, and it rendered them all but worthless. It was called broadcasting.

### 2.1.3 Stage 3: First Broadcast Stations

**Frank Conrad** worked as a chief technician at the Westinghouse plant in East Pittsburgh. Conrad was an amateur radio enthusiast and had a receiver and a transmitter licensed as **8XK** (Fig. 2.6) in the garage of his Wilkinsburg, Pennsylvania, home. In spring 1920 Conrad began to transmit music from phonograph records. He soon received mail requests from enthusiastic listeners to play specific records at specific times.

Conrad tried to comply with requests, but mail became so heavy that he finally announced he would transmit music 2 hours twice a week at 7:30. His two sons added live instrumental and vocal talent. As the summer wore on, the Conrads began nightly transmissions, and their concerts' popularity continued to grow. Several local newspaper articles mentioned the concerts. On September 29, 1920, the *Pittsburgh Sun* carried an advertisement for a local department store (Fig. 2.7), noting that receiving sets for those who wished to listen to the Conrad radio concerts were available for purchase in the store's west basement.

**FIG. 2.6. Conrad's transmitter for 8XK.** (Photo courtesy of Westinghouse Electric Corporation. Used by permission.)

## Air Concert
## "Picked Up"
## By Radio Here

Victrola music, played into the air over a wireless telephone, was "picked up" by listeners on the wireless receiving station which was recently installed here for experiments. The concert was heard Thursday night about 10 o'clock, and continued 20 minutes. Two orchestra numbers, a soprano solo—which rang particularly high and clear through the air—and a juvenile "talking piece" constituted the program.

The music was from a Victrola pulled up close to the transmitter of a wireless telephone in the home of Frank Conrad, Penn and Peebles avenues, Wilkinsburg. Mr. Conrad is a wireless enthusiast and "puts on" the wireless concerts periodically for the entertainment of the many people in this district who have wireless sets.

Amateur Wireless Sets, made by the maker of the Set which is in operation in our store, are on sale here $10.00 up.

--*West Basement*

FIG. 2.7. The inspiration for KDKA.

By chance Harry P. Davis, a Westinghouse vice-president, saw the ad and realized that the Conrad transmission pattern had marketing potential. He knew that Conrad's audience had been people who had the technical knowledge to put together their own radio receivers. However, reasoned Davis, the concerts would probably be popular with almost everyone if there were simple-to-operate radio receivers, complete in one unit. Westinghouse had developed and manufactured just such receivers during the war. The company could probably develop a civilian market for these receivers, concluded Davis, if it were to operate a radio transmitting station that would supply transmissions on a regular schedule announced in advance. The next day Davis called in Conrad and a few others, told them his idea, and said he wanted a Westinghouse radio station ready for the November 2, 1920, presidential election. That was just 33 days away.

Conrad and his crew installed a transmitter in a shack on top of the East Pittsburgh Westinghouse plant. They connected the transmitter to the antenna, a wire strung between a steel pole on the roof and a nearby smokestack. The U.S. Department of Commerce licensed[5] the station to operate on 360 meters (833.3 kHz[6]) and awarded it the call letters **KDKA**. On election night (Fig. 2.8) returns were telephoned to the station from the offices of the *Pittsburgh Post.* A recruit from the plant's information office read them over the air. Between returns the microphone was pushed up to the speaker horn of a hand-wound phonograph. Conrad was in his garage in Wilkinsburg, ready to transmit with 8XK in case of problems with the hastily installed KDKA transmitter. But KDKA stayed on the air. Warren G. Harding won the election over James M. Cox, and broadcasting was on its way. (Cox's family would later own a media firm with major investments in broadcasting and cable television.)

**FIG. 2.8. KDKA and its opening-day staff.** (Photo courtesy of Westinghouse Electric Corporation. Used by permission.)

### 2.1.4 Stage 4: Audience—Who Invented Broadcasting?

KDKA was not necessarily the first broadcasting station. KCBS in San Francisco (formerly KQW in San Jose, California), WHA in Madison, Wisconsin, WWJ in Detroit, and probably others all have some claim to being the first. However KDKA was assuredly one of the first. Its story typifies what happened elsewhere around the country—technically minded tinkerers like Frank Conrad built transmitters and found themselves programming in response to comment from listeners on a regular basis.

Who were these listeners? Certainly they consisted in part of other people engaged in amateur radio transmission. But another type of **radio hobbyist** was also in the audience. This hobbyist, spiritual ancestor of today's shortwave listener, was interested in **reception**—how many stations could be received, from how far away could stations be received, and how clearly could they be received.

For the most part, the "listen-in" hobbyists had to be content with receiving the conversations of others, usually in Morse code. Naturally, these early listeners responded enthusiastically when Conrad and others transmitted voice and music. The content seemed aimed at the listeners, elevating their status from eavesdroppers to audience. As mail came in from listeners, the pioneer station operators responded by setting up regular schedules of transmissions, programming for a general audience. They evolved from station operators into radio broadcasters. At the beginning of the 1920s radio ceased being just point-to-point communication and *broadcasting* was born.

Who invented broadcasting? As much as anyone could be said to have "invented" it, the audience did.

As the months passed, the early stations experimented with program types. They broadcast the first play-by-play sports, the first radio dramas, the first religious services, and so on.

The number of radio broadcast stations increased. The Department of Commerce had issued 30 licenses by the end of 1920. In 1921 the department issued 28 more licenses. But in 1922 the rush began, and by the end of July 430 more licenses were issued. On the other hand a high percentage of these stations were short-lived. Some were started by individuals as a hobby, but others were launched by businesses as promotional vehicles, and some by colleges as science projects. They had no means of self-support, and they often consisted primarily of junklike collections of wires and tubes.

### 2.1.5 Stage 5: Advertising—Who Invented Commercial Broadcasting?

The more successful stations improved their facilities. They increased transmitter power. They added studios—rooms for performers, separate from the transmitter. These studios, unlike those of today, usually had heavy drapes on ceilings and walls to cut down on reverberation. They were sometimes furnished in the style of middle-class hotel lobbies or living rooms of the day, complete with potted palms, pianos, and bird cages.

Announcers and performers were often employees from other departments of the firm that operated the station. The programs were mostly musical, with some recitations, some talks for children, and a sprinkling of "remotes" from ballrooms where dance bands played, from church services, and from sports events. Occasionally, a star from another entertainment medium would perform free before the microphone of a station to experience the novelty of broadcasting, but much of the programming still came from phonograph records. Programs, as such, were rare.

As the novelty of appearing before the microphone began to wear off, fewer people volunteered to perform. In need of programming, some stations began to pay their performers. This created a problem. The stations cost money to operate but did not bring in direct revenue. They were serious financial drains on their owners—primarily radio manufacturers and dealers, newspapers, educational institutions, and department stores. How could owners pay the costs of operating their radio stations? Various methods were suggested to pay for broadcasting—wealthy individuals should endow stations, cities and states should operate stations out of tax revenues, a common fund should be established to receive contributions that would then be distributed to the stations, or receivers or tubes should be taxed or licensed. However, none of these was to be the answer.

In 1922, AT&T opened radio station **WEAF** in New York based on a novel concept—**toll broadcasting**. AT&T saw WEAF's service as parallel to telephone service. The company would provide no programs, only facilities. Whoever wished to address a message to the radio audience would pay a toll or fee to use the station. It was to be a telephone booth of the air. The telephone company soon found that it had to provide programming on a **sustaining** (unsponsored) basis when there were no messages. A regular schedule of programming was needed to create and hold an audience if people were expected to pay tolls to broadcast messages.

On August 28, 1922, at 5:00 a.m., WEAF aired its first toll broadcast. A Mr. Blackwell of the Queensboro Corporation spoke for 10 minutes on Hawthorne Court, a condominium in the Jackson Heights section of Long Island, New York. The toll was $50. The first commercial had been broadcast.

Shortly thereafter, WEAF did away with such talks. Radio came into people's homes, and the station felt the public would not accept the intrusion of direct advertising. Instead, the advertiser was allowed to sponsor a program, elements of which would reflect that sponsorship. For example Browning King, Inc. sponsored a program but could not mention that the firm sold clothing. Instead, the program featured the "Browning King Orchestra," which was mentioned frequently.

Similar programs (Fig. 2.9) included the *Eveready Hour* (battery company), the *Cliquot Club Eskimos* (ginger ale), the *Ipana Troubadours* (toothpaste), the *Gold Dust Twins* (cleanser), the *Silvertown Cord Orchestra* and its "Silver Masked Tenor" (Goodrich tires), the *Lucky Strike Orchestra* (tobacco company), the *A&P Gypsies* (food store chain), and the *Happiness Boys* (candy store chain). Most were musical

(a)

(b)

FIG. 2.9. Radio performers of the 1920s. (a) Browning King Orchestra. (b) Cliquot Club Eskimos. (Used by permission of the National Broadcasting Company.)

(c)

FIG. 2.9(c). Joseph M. White, the "Silver Masked Tenor." (Used by permission of the National Broadcasting Company.)

programs, primitive and corny by today's standards. Nonetheless, they were significant because, first, they were **programs**—individually presented units of the broadcast schedule, complete in themselves—and, second, they were deemed **suitable for sponsoring** by advertisers.

The *Eveready Hour* was one of the best. The sponsor's advertising agency took an active hand in production. Scripted and rehearsed—rarities in those days—the *Eveready Hour* went on one of AT&T's ad hoc network hookups in 1924, making it one of the first successful network series.

The choice of advertising as financial support for all broadcasting, however, was still not a fait accompli. Other financial support models had been proposed, and many broadcasters, business leaders, and members of the public felt that radio should not carry advertising.

### 2.1.6 Stage 6: Formation of Networks

Under the intraindustry cross-licensing agreements, AT&T had been granted all rights for toll radiotelephonic communication. In AT&T's opinion, (a) they now held exclusive rights to the manufacture and sale of all radio transmitters, and (b) because toll broadcasting was just another form of toll radiotelephonic communication, only AT&T-licensed stations could charge tolls or fees for announcements by advertisers. Committed to toll broadcasting, AT&T sold its stock in RCA and removed its directors from the RCA board in 1923.

Westinghouse had put WJZ on the air in 1921. Licensed to Newark, New Jersey, WJZ had studios in New York City. RCA bought WJZ in mid-1923 and made it the main rival to AT&T's WEAF. WJZ epitomized the broadcasting philosophy of the Radio Group—operation of a station by one company such as Westinghouse to stimulate sales or promote that company. WEAF epitomized the philosophy of the telephone group—operation of a station as a service paid for by many different companies that wished to present advertising messages designed to stimulate sales.

AT&T's interpretation of the cross-licensing agreements prohibited WJZ from toll broadcasting. Unable to sell advertising, WJZ began to persuade other companies to share the cost of programming expenses in exchange for free time and publicity. By having other companies help pay for its programs in that manner, WJZ was giving away that which WEAF was trying to sell. Naturally, this upset AT&T. And WJZ still lost money.

***2.1.6.1 AT&T's "Network."***   AT&T's master plan for toll broadcasting included live interconnection of stations. A small number of transmitters across the country would be leased to local corporations. These local stations could sell advertising and run local programs, but they would also be tied into AT&T's long lines for occasional live interconnection when an advertiser wished to reach a multicity audience.

AT&T ran the **first permanent network line** from New York to WMAF in South Dartmouth, Massachusetts, in June 1923. Stations had been linked previously for simultaneous broadcasts, but no permanent hookups had been made. The special line to WMAF ran through Providence, Rhode Island, so that by late summer, WJAR in Providence became the third station on the network. Network technology and programming improved. At the end of 1923, six stations were on the chain. By the end of 1924, the number was 26, and the AT&T network reached from coast to coast.

Denied use of AT&T telephone lines, GE and RCA attempted to put together a network fed by WJZ and connected by telegraph lines. Even though the telegraph wires were technically unsuited for broadcast-quality voice transmission, the WJZ network built up to some 14 stations by the end of 1925.

Under the cross-licensing agreements, AT&T contended it had the sole right to manufacture and to sell or lease transmitters to radio stations, and because of its plans for toll broadcasting, AT&T limited those sales and leases. However, many stations had signed on the air using transmitters from other sources—building them, importing them, and so on. AT&T filed suit against one such station in 1924, and the station settled out of court. Meanwhile, the nation's press depicted the suit in terms of a big, bad corporate bully picking on poor, struggling radio stations, causing AT&T to worry about public opinion. The telephone company decided to change policy and license all stations that applied, regardless of the origins of their transmitters. An AT&T license would also allow a station to charge tolls or fees for use of its time and to interconnect over telephone lines. Hundreds of stations paid AT&T's license fees.

AT&T also wanted to market radio receivers. The Radio Group argued this would violate the 1919 agreements. Binding arbitration between the two sides favored the Radio Group. Then AT&T produced an influential, convincing legal opinion that said the agreements were probably unlawful in the first place, a violation of the antitrust laws. It was time to renegotiate.

### 2.1.6.2 David Sarnoff and the National Broadcasting Company.   RCA Board Chair Owen Young opened negotiations with AT&T, but key discussions involved RCA's vice-president and resident expert on broadcasting, **David Sarnoff**. Sarnoff had emigrated from Russia to the United States in 1900 at age 9. At 15 he went to work for American Marconi. Through hard work and good impressions on the right people (Box 2.1), Sarnoff rose steadily through company ranks: office boy, junior wireless telegraphy operator, operator, telegraphy instructor at the Marconi Institute, chief inspector and assistant chief engineer, and commercial manager.

---

### BOX 2.1. SARNOFF AS LEGEND

David Sarnoff was an effective and far-seeing executive. He was also excellent at self-promotion and ensuring his place in history. Two oft-told stories illustrate.

(Photo courtesy of RCA Corp. Used by permission of General Electric Co.)

---

In one, the 21-year-old Sarnoff was said to have made 1912 headlines as the wireless operator in contact with the sinking S.S. *Titanic,* not leaving his station for 72 hours. In the second, Sarnoff supposedly wrote a 1915 memo to his superiors at American Marconi suggesting development of what he called a "radio music box," describing in essence the system of broadcasting that would not develop for another 5 years.

With respect to the *Titanic* story, Sarnoff was apparently neither the first nor the only operator to receive messages about the sinking ship, nor did he remain at his post for 3 days and 3 nights.[1] He was, instead, one of three people at the Marconi station in New York's Wanamaker store who passed wireless messages about the disaster on to Hearst's New York *American.* When the Sarnoff-as-hero version of the story arose, Sarnoff himself encouraged it.

Concerning the 1915 radio music box memo, Louise M. Benjamin made the case that the most-quoted version was actually written 5 years later.[2] Sarnoff's 1920 memorandum to Owen Young (*PRT,* 2.1.6.2) included several pages devoted to the "radio music box" plan. These pages constitute the oldest statement of the plan still extant; no trace of a 1915 version has been found. By 1920 there had already been articles and experiments involving the concept that would become known as broadcasting, so its possibilities were not too hard to see. On the other hand, a full-blown music radio box plan set forth in a 1915 memo, had it existed, would have earned its author the reputation as a farsighted prophet of the electronic world, so Sarnoff allowed that story to develop.

---

[1] See, for example, Kenneth Bilby, *The General: David Sarnoff and the Rise of the Communications Industry* (New York: Harper, 1986) 30–35; and Tom Lewis, *Empire of the Air: The Men Who Made Radio* (New York: Harper, 1991) 105–107.

[2] "In Search of the Sarnoff 'Radio Music Box' Memo," *Journal of Broadcasting & Electronic Media* 37 (1993): 325-335.

When RCA was formed, Sarnoff moved to the new company as commercial manager and proceeded to make himself invaluable. In early 1920 Sarnoff wrote a long memorandum to Young on the radio business in which he championed, among other things, a use for radio that was very much like the system of broadcasting that would soon develop. Shortly after this memo, KDKA made its debut, and RCA radio receivers began moving into stores. Sarnoff became RCA general manager in 1921. In 1922 he wrote to an RCA board member suggesting formation of an RCA-controlled company to specialize in broadcasting. RCA took no immediate action, but once negotiations with AT&T were underway, his idea began to seem attractive. In January 1926, RCA's board decided to form a new company, owned by RCA, GE, and Westinghouse—a company that would specialize in broadcasting. Nine months later this company went into business as the **National Broadcasting Company** (NBC).

After intricate negotiation, representatives from the Telephone and Radio groups reached an agreement. AT&T, changing its corporate mind on the matter of toll radio transmissions, would get out of broadcasting entirely. RCA would carry on all commercial networking activity, for which it would use, and pay for, AT&T's long lines. AT&T and Western Electric would not market receivers. AT&T would not manufacture and market transmitters, but Western Electric and RCA could. AT&T sold its broadcasting activities, including WEAF, to RCA.

On September 9, 1926, NBC was formed, and shortly thereafter the NBC board of directors voted to buy out RCA's broadcasting assets. The word *toll* was quietly dropped, but the idea of radio advertising as a means of support was retained.

NBC inaugurated network service on November 15, 1926 (Fig. 2.10), with a 4½-hour special program aired coast to coast on 25 stations. On January 1, 1927, NBC set up two separate national networks. The **Red Network,** derived primarily from the Telephone Group hookups, had 25 stations based on WEAF. The weaker **Blue Network,** derived from the Radio Group, had only six stations based on WJZ. The colors, according to one story, came from the red and blue pencils used by engineers to draw in the stations and connections of the two networks on their maps. Also in 1927, NBC adopted a three-tone chime that became familiar to nearly every American as the network's audio identification signal. On December 23, 1928, NBC began regular, coast-to-coast service with 58 affiliates.

***2.1.6.3 Columbia Broadcasting System.***  Even before NBC got well underway, a rival network was developing. **George A. Coats** and **Arthur Judson** formed

FIG. 2.10. **NBC goes on the air.** NBC's engineers put on the air the network's first show, November 15, 1926. (Photo courtesy of the National Broadcasting Company, Inc. Used by permission.)

the Judson Radio Program Corporation in September 1926 as an organization to provide programming for radio. They asked David Sarnoff for help; he refused, and Judson swore that he and Coats would set up their own network. They formed the United Independent Broadcasters network in January 1927 and signed 12 stations as affiliates beginning with WCAU in Philadelphia. However, they found that station compensation[7] and AT&T line charges would cost so much that they would need greater financial resources. Judson and Coats convinced the Columbia Phonograph Company to invest in the venture. The network now became the Columbia Phonograph Broadcasting System.

On September 19, 1927, the Columbia Phonograph Broadcasting System aired its first program, *The King's Henchman,* performed by artists from the Metropolitan Opera. The Columbia Phonograph Company, losing heavily in the new network, withdrew from the venture. Oddly, the infant chain was allowed to keep "Columbia" in its name. Coats and Judson persuaded some Philadelphia residents to invest in the network. In the process the name was changed to the **Columbia Broadcasting System** (CBS). But the money continued to drain away with no sign of any return, and soon the new stockholders also wanted out.

Meanwhile, **William S. Paley,** who at age 27 was production and advertising director for his family's Congress Cigar Company in Philadelphia, had sponsored a program on the new network and been impressed with the results. He learned that CBS was for sale, persuaded his family to join him in buying controlling interest, and took over the network in September 1928. Paley purchased a station in New York and brought Paramount Pictures in as a partner. The network lost over $330,000 in 1928 but showed a profit thereafter. Within a few years, CBS had grown into a serious rival to NBC.

We have now seen the origins of NBC and CBS. As they were developing, the legal structure of broadcasting was changing.

### 2.1.7 Stage 7: Congressional Enactment of Regulation

Congress passed the **Wireless Ship Act in 1910.** This law required certain classes of ocean vessels to carry wireless apparatus and an operator. Two years later, as a direct result of the S.S. *Titanic* disaster, Congress passed the **Radio Act of 1912,** spelling out exactly how and why radio would be used on ships. It specified that the Secretary of Commerce and Labor would assign wavelengths and issue licenses and that it was illegal to operate without a license. These laws all pertained, of course, to radio as point-to-point communication.

Then, broadcasting was born. Unlike point-to-point stations that operated intermittently and for brief periods, broadcast stations operated continuously, thereby enormously increasing the potential for interference. At first, the Commerce Department assigned all broadcast stations to one wavelength. As the number of stations increased, a second channel was opened. However, more and more broadcast stations signed on.

The transmitters in use then were often unstable, causing them to drift off assigned wavelengths. The result was **interference,** and the Commerce Department seemed unable to solve the problem. Some broadcasters took matters in their own hands. If station A's signal interfered with that of station B, B changed frequency, time of operation, power, or even location to overcome the interference—without, of course, consent of the Commerce Department. Inevitably, the result was that B now interfered with stations C, D, and E, which then proceeded to take the same action that B had taken. The result was interference raised to intolerable levels. Finally, the Commerce Department opened a whole band of wavelengths, 550–1350 kHz, the basis of today's 540–1700 kHz AM radio band.

Despite the increased number of wavelengths, interference problems continued. Both the public and the broadcasters complained. Commerce Secretary **Herbert Hoover** (Fig. 2.11) called four **radio conferences,** one each in 1922, 1923, 1924, and 1925, attended by leaders of the radio industry. Conferees recommended that Congress pass legislation to regulate broadcasting and that Hoover take interim

FIG. 2.11. **Herbert Hoover.** In 1926 Commerce Secretary Hoover found that the 1912 Radio Act did not grant him power to regulate radio. In 1927 the comprehensive Radio Act passed, and Hoover took part in the first public demonstration of intercity (Washington to New York) TV. The box at the extreme left is the camera; a telephone provided sound. (Photo courtesy of AT&T Archives. Used by permission.)

action to straighten out the problems. But Congress would not act, and Hoover found that he could not act.

The Radio Act of 1912, enacted some 8 years before KDKA signed on the air, had been written with no provision for discretionary action to enforce it. In a series of legal decisions—*Hoover v. Intercity Radio Co.* (1923),[8] *United States v. Zenith Radio* (1926),[9] and an Attorney General's Opinion in 1926[10]—the Commerce secretary found that under existing law he had to issue a license when application was made, he had to assign a frequency to a station, and he could make no regulations or restrictions on the operation of broadcast stations. In other words, Hoover had no power to straighten out the mess.

To complicate matters further, there were characters and charlatans on radio. "Doctor" John Brinkley used KFKB in Milford, Kansas, to peddle patent medicines and to advertise his sexual rejuvenation operations. Norman Baker used KTNT in Muscatine, Iowa, to attack what he called the "radio trust" (network broadcasting) and later to advertise a cancer clinic. Reverend Robert "Fighting Bob" Shuler used KGEF in Los Angeles, California, to muckrake and battle corruption in Los Angeles officialdom. Evangelist Aimee Semple McPherson used KFSG, also in Los Angeles, to propagate her brand of the gospel. Her station constantly deviated from assigned frequency, causing interference. When Commerce Secretary Hoover ordered an inspector to close down KFSG, she wired Hoover to call off his "minions of Satan" because he should not "expect the Almighty to abide by your wavelength nonsense." She said she had to "fit into His wave reception" when she prayed. There were other such broadcasters.

With the Radio Act of 1912 useless for broadcast regulation and the public clamoring over the interference problem, Congress finally acted. It passed the **Radio Act of 1927,** creating a five-member **Federal Radio Commission** (FRC) and giving it appropriate discretionary powers to carry out its duties. The FRC was to regulate all radio, including point-to-point, but a large part of its time was spent straightening out broadcasting. The FRC first worked to control interference. It assigned frequencies to stations and imposed operating limitations; in some cases, the Commission forced nearby stations to use the same frequency on a share-time basis, one transmitting while the others were off the air awaiting their "turns" to transmit. The FRC also looked into programming problems—the Brinkleys, the Shulers, and all the rest. The 1927 Act also contained the first reference to the granting and transferring of broadcast licenses based on the "public interest, convenience, and necessity." That phrase would become the foundation of broadcast regulation.

Seven years later, Congress passed the Communications Act of 1934. This superseded the 1927 law but included most of the same provisions. The Communications Act replaced the FRC with a seven-member (reduced to five in 1983) Federal Communications Commission (FCC) and gave it interstate wire communication to regulate along with radio.

## 2.1.8 Broadcasting's Conversion to an Advertising Medium

In the past, most historical accounts have told the story of broadcasting as though advertising support was firmly established by about 1926.[11] Implicit in most such histories are a number of assumptions: suggestions for other means of financial support were quaint and cute but not practical, advertising was the natural and only possible means to pay for broadcasting in the United States, broadcasting would have failed and gone extinct without advertising support, and everyone accepted advertising as a fair exchange for the free programming broadcasting carried.

During the late 1980s and the 1990s, however, some scholars began to question those assumptions. Cultural historian Susan Smulyan,[12] for example, said that even as late as 1928, a number of decision makers both in and out of broadcasting felt that radio should be financed by means other than advertising. According to Smulyan, a key element in converting the consensus to advertising support may have been NBC's decision on national program distribution. When RCA bought AT&T's broadcasting interests, NBC fell heir to AT&T's telephone-line-based distribution and interconnection concept. Other, less expensive means existed and had been proposed, yet NBC opted to keep the wired service and finance it with sponsored programs aimed at national audiences. The network marshaled an elaborate public relations campaign to convince all concerned to accept advertising support as the "American system of broadcasting."

Mass communication historian Robert W. McChesney has assembled evidence to show that an organized reform movement opposed the commercialization of broadcasting.[13] Nonprofit broadcasters whose frequencies had been appropriated, thanks to malignant FRC regulation, by aggressive commercial broadcasters formed the nucleus of this early-1930s movement. Joined by intellectuals, civic activists, and elements of the labor movement and the press, they attempted to generate public and congressional support to establish a countervailing force, a significant nonprofit, noncommercial broadcasting presence. Commercial broadcasters opposed this effort. They pushed for passage of legislation that would solidify advertising-supported broadcasting as the status quo. Congress passed that legislation, and the president signed it into law as the Communications Act of 1934. Shortly thereafter, according to McChesney, the reform movement collapsed. Commercial interests had won, and advertising would supply the means for broadcasting's financial support.

## 2.2 COMMERCIAL RADIO'S GROWTH AND DOMINANCE

During the Great Depression of the 1930s, many businesses suffered, lost money, and even dissolved. One exception was commercial broadcasting. Although profits dropped and a few stations gave up licenses, generally speaking, broadcasting emerged from the 1930s strong and stable. The 1940s were pure profit, up to a point.

## 2.2.1 Building the Mass Audience

In 1925, only 10% of U.S. homes had radio receivers. Still, radio was leaving the hobby stage. Receiver design changed for the better—manufactured sets were available for those who did not wish to build their own; loudspeakers replaced earphones; superheterodyne circuitry improved the audio signal; AC current operation made it possible to "plug in" to home electric outlets and eliminate messy, short-lived batteries. Just 5 years later, 46% of all homes had radios.

The stock market crashed in 1929, and the economic depression set in. Most families had little money, and that went for food, clothing, and shelter. But radio, after an initial investment for the receiver, brought hours of entertainment at little cost. People saved pennies to buy radios and keep them in good repair.

Receiver prices dropped (Fig. 2.12). Production of radios fell in 1930, 1931, and 1932. In 1933, sales increased, especially for small, inexpensive table models. By 1935, radio penetration reached 67%. People also began to put radios in their cars.

As the economy recovered, ominous events took place in Europe, events that would lead to World War II. Radio reported these events, often with on-the-spot coverage. The public listened to and relied on radio for the latest news, and the percentage of radio-equipped homes continued to climb. War production priori-

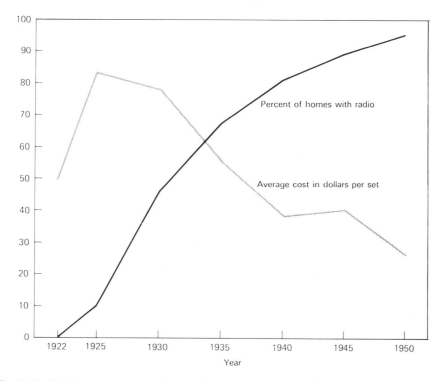

**FIG. 2.12. Radio set penetration and cost per set: 1922–1950.** Generally, as prices dropped, more and more people bought radios. (*Sources*: U.S. Department of Commerce and *Broadcasting Yearbook 1977*. Washington, DC: Broadcasting, 1977.)

ties halted manufacture of civilian radios, but after the war the public went on a buying spree. By 1950, 95% of all homes in the United States had at least one working radio receiver.

### 2.2.2 Growth of Commercial Radio Stations

At first the U.S. Department of Commerce had managed to keep the number of broadcast stations down (Fig. 2.13). At the beginning of 1926, 528 stations were transmitting, but when the Department found it had almost no power to regulate broadcasting (*PRT* 2.1.7), that number increased nearly 40%. With regulation by the new FRC, the number decreased 16% by 1929 and showed a slight decline during the early 1930s and the depth of the economic depression. After 1934 the number of stations grew steadily, leveling off somewhat during World War II to reach 956 by the end of 1945.

Stations grew in other ways (Box 2.2). Most increased transmitter power and coverage. WLW in Cincinnati, received special FCC authorization to use "superpower"—500,000 watts—during the period between 1934 and 1939. The number of stations having to share time on a single frequency decreased.

Broadcasting grew increasingly commercial. By the end of the 1920s, 9 out of 10 stations sold commercial time; most did not make enough to meet expenses.

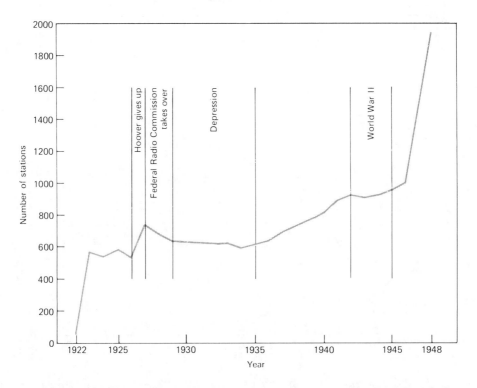

FIG. 2.13. Total AM stations authorized: 1922–1948. (*Sources*: FRC, FCC, U.S. Department of Commerce.)

## BOX 2.2. FROM SHACK TO TENT TO "LIVE WALL"

When KDKA started, the shack on the right (a), on the roof of the East Pittsburgh Westinghouse plant, housed the entire station. Figure 2.8 shows the interior. After about 6 months, the station decided to broadcast large musical groups. The first band and orchestra programs originated from the plant auditorium, but its acoustics were more than the primitive microphones of the day could handle. So the station pitched the tent seen here and originated its musical programs from the tent. Because there were no walls or other hard surfaces off which the sound could bounce, music broadcasts had more clarity. In the fall, a wind blew the tent down. The tent had worked so well that when the station built its first permanent studio, its walls were draped with hangings (b)—in effect, a tent inside the studio! As years passed, both microphones and studio design became more sophisticated. By the late 1930s, many studios had a "live wall"—one without acoustical deadening (c)—in order to enhance the sound of programming.

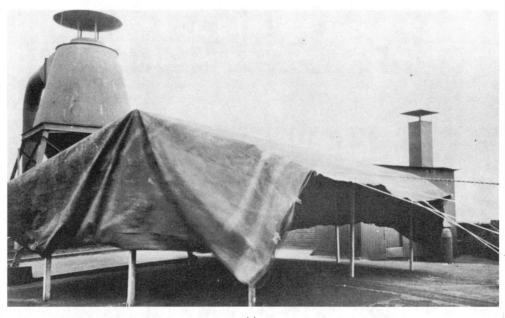

(a)

(Photographs a and b used by permission of the National Broadcasting Company, Inc. Photograph c from John S. Carlile, *Production and Direction of Radio Programs.* New York: Prentice-Hall, 1939.)

**BOX 2.2 (cont'd.)**

(b)

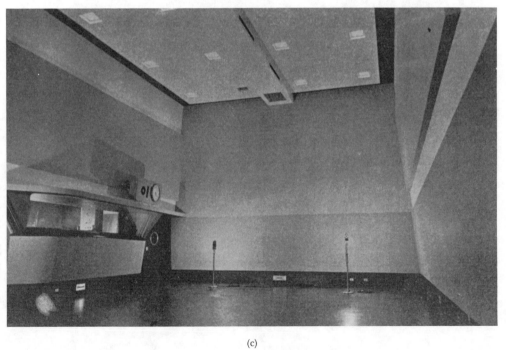

(c)

Then radio listenership shot up. More advertisers put more money into the new medium. From 1935 to 1940, radio advertising billings jumped 96% (Fig. 2.14). Although half was in network advertising, local and national spot advertising (national advertising placed with individual stations) accounted for increasing shares. Still, about one third of all stations operated at a loss.

The Japanese attack on Pearl Harbor in 1941 plunged the United States into World War II. Raw materials and assembly lines were diverted to the war effort. Many manufacturers ceased production of consumer goods and had little or nothing to sell to the public. Even so, companies continued to advertise. They had defense contracts and earned profits, but they also planned to return to the manufacture and marketing of consumer goods after the war. Institutional advertising would keep the names of these companies before the public. Besides, the

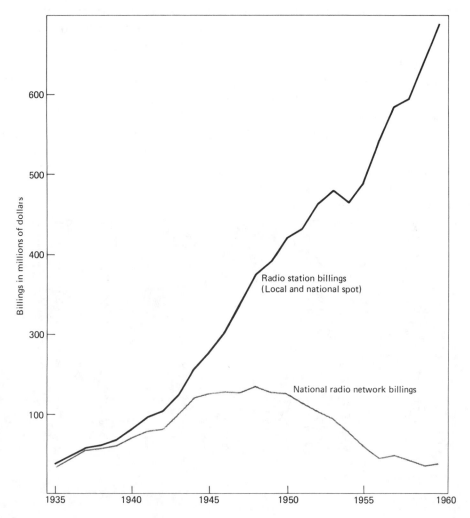

FIG. 2.14. **Radio station and network gross advertising revenues: 1935–1960.** After a decade of growth, network billings leveled off in 1945 and began a long decline in 1949. Station revenues continued to climb except for one dip in 1954. (*Source*: FCC.)

federal excess profits tax took a huge bite out of corporate earnings, but the tax could be reduced by deducting for business expenses, such as advertising. Because the war caused a shortage of paper, the amount of advertising these companies could place in newspapers and magazines was limited. They turned to broadcasting. From 1940 through 1945, radio advertising billings increased by 99.4%. At the same time, the number of stations increased by only 17.4%. A few more stations shared a lot more money, and over 95% earned a profit.

### 2.2.3 Growth of Commercial Radio Networks

The networks took a large share of this prosperity. They earned profits even during the economic depression, dipping to their lowest point in 1933 but recovering well thereafter. NBC had a slight head start on CBS, had two networks (which meant two affiliates in many cities), and enjoyed the corporate backing of RCA. NBC got the largest audiences, the best programs, and the established performers. Yet, the shrewd management of CBS's president William Paley (Fig. 2.15) usually earned that network a healthy profit, too.

Paley developed the **network option.** It worked like this: An **affiliate** (a station that contracted to carry the network's programs) could carry any or all network sustaining (unsponsored) programs for free (NBC charged for sustaining programs), in return for which the affiliate gave CBS an option on (advance permission to use) all nonnetwork time during its broadcast day. When a new sponsored program series started, CBS could order the affiliate to **clear** time for it; that is, cancel local programming and broadcast the network series. The network paid the affiliate to carry the sponsored series. Under the option plan,

**FIG. 2.15. Opening of the CBS building, 1929.** The young network's young president, Bill Paley, is in the center. (CBS Photo Archives. Used by permission.)

written into each affiliation contract between network and station, the station received revenue and programming with no effort and the network could guarantee station clearance to an advertiser.

With the option in place, CBS added affiliates. From 16 in 1927, CBS went to 112 in 1940, versus 53 for NBC Red and 60 for NBC Blue. In 1935, NBC adopted its own version of the option.

Paley made another shrewd move in 1948. A number of popular programs and stars incorporated themselves and moved to CBS—*Amos 'n' Andy,* Jack Benny, Edgar Bergen, Red Skelton, and others. At NBC, the comedians had been highly paid employees and so had to pay taxes at the personal income rate. At CBS, as incorporated entities, they paid taxes at the lower capital-gains rate. CBS had suggested the idea to Music Corporation of America, agent for many of the comedians, and the exodus became known as Paley's **talent raid.** The move quickly paid off, putting CBS solidly ahead of NBC in the critical 7 p.m. to 8 p.m. time period as early as January 1949. This gave CBS a programming lead that it kept, took into television, and never really lost for years.

The networks had expanded in other ways. Both formed **artist management bureaus** and **concert booking companies.** This guaranteed a ready reserve of performers for their programs and income from the personal appearance tours of the talent they represented. Both networks were affiliated with **phonograph record companies.** RCA had bought the Victor Talking Machine Company in 1929, and CBS purchased its former owner, Columbia Records, in 1938. NBC and CBS each owned and operated profitable **broadcast stations** in a number of large cities.

David Sarnoff became president of RCA in 1930 and continued to build that company's communications empire. In 1933, NBC moved into its Radio City home in New York's Rockefeller Center. The next year Sarnoff assumed the chair of the NBC board. GE and Westinghouse withdrew from ownership of both RCA and NBC in 1932 after threat of an antitrust suit, leaving RCA a separate corporate entity and NBC its wholly owned subsidary (GE would buy RCA outright 53 years later). Also in 1932, William Paley bought out Paramount's 49% share of CBS.

The **Mutual Broadcasting System** (MBS) started in 1934. It was to be mutual in practice as well as name. Member stations were to pool resources, each contributing program material. This would eliminate the expense of a network program department. The network would own no stations.

Initially, Mutual consisted of four cooperating stations—WOR in Newark; WGN in Chicago; WLW in Cincinnati; and WXYZ in Detroit. MBS eventually did acquire a staff to coordinate the cooperative programming activities. Most powerful, large-city stations had already affiliated with CBS or one of the NBC networks, so MBS became the network of small-town and lower powered stations. MBS attempted to make up in numbers of network stations the coverage it lacked from its affiliates' low power. By 1940, MBS had 140 affiliates; in 1945 it had 384.

The **American Broadcasting Company** (ABC) grew out of NBC Blue. NBC had made the Red Network the stronger of its two chains. The Blue network had less popular programs, smaller audiences, and fewer sponsors. In 1943 RCA formed the Blue Network into a separate corporation and sold it. The buyer was Edward J. Noble, Lifesavers candy manufacturer. On its sale, the network became the third strongest, as its affiliates had more power than Mutual's. In 1945, the network became ABC.

### 2.2.4 Development of Commercial Programming Forms

During the 1930s, radio presented reformers and rogues, messiahs and maniacs, saints and sinners. In 1932, the United States inaugurated a president who promised a "new deal" to a citizenry burdened with economic depression. Franklin D. Roosevelt was the first president to use radio to talk directly to the American people. Two bizarre characters in the political limelight used radio effectively as well—Huey Long and Father Charles Coughlin—each with his own idea of how to save the nation. John Brinkley still peddled patent medicines by radio, now from Mexico. A whole breed of "outlaw" stations developed in the Southwest, especially Texas and Oklahoma. They operated without licenses because their owners said they transmitted intrastate only and so were not liable to FRC jurisdiction.

But when most people speak of "old-time radio," they mean the mainstream, network entertainment programs. Radio developed its program formats in the 1930s. They stayed popular through the 1940s and into the 1950s. Most program types transferred successfully to television.

Radio played somewhat the same role for the American public that television did later. Radio ran a full schedule of entertainment programs. Most were live, 30 or 60 minutes long, and performed before studio audiences. Millions of Americans listened; families would gather around the radio—usually the only radio in the home and usually in the living room—in the evening to listen to their favorite network programs. The years 1930 through about 1953 have been called **radio's golden age.** This probably better describes the financial success of the networks than the average quality of their programming. Nonetheless, the programming was unique, and it did achieve a high degree of development as popular culture.

Radio could also report news. The foundations for broadcast news were laid in the 1930s. After a few false starts, the networks assembled personnel and techniques that would be needed to report the biggest story yet, World War II.

*2.2.4.1 Network Radio Programs and Performers.* National advertisers began using radio heavily in the 1930s. Both advertising and radio were developed into big business. In 1931, for example, American Tobacco Company spent $19 million during the Depression to advertise Lucky Strike cigarettes. A sponsor paid up to $500,000 per year for production costs alone on a program series; airtime might cost another $4,000 per week. The sponsor controlled programming. The sponsor's advertising agency produced the program; the network was all but a common carrier, merely renting facilities and selling airtime.

One program type that developed in the early 1930s was **comedy-variety.** A comedian acted as master of ceremonies to introduce and bridge the acts and guests on the program. Often the comedian came out of vaudeville. This program type initiated the radio careers of Eddie Cantor, Al Jolson, George Burns and Gracie Allen, Ed Wynn, Fred Allen, and Jack Benny—all performers who earned near-legendary status in radio (Fig. 2.16).

**Drama** became popular. During the 1920s some efforts were made to broadcast drama by putting microphones on the stage of Broadway plays. There were also attempts to write and perform drama especially for radio. However, the birth of true radio drama came in the 1930s, when writers and performers learned to create for the ear, for a **"blind" audience.** Radio drama's **sound effects** staff (Fig. 2.17) came into its own. Technicians used odds and ends that—when clopped, crumpled, rubbed, tinkled, opened, or closed near a microphone—sounded like what the script called for. Dramatic dialogue defined the sound—"Listen to that rain!"; "Wasn't that a shot?"; "Here come two men on horses!" Through sound effects and dialogue, the listener's imagination created settings and characters. It was a **theater of the mind.**

Radio drama comprised several program types. These included continuing series, anthology series, mystery and adventure series (often using characters

(a)                                    (b)

**FIG. 2.16. Husband–wife radio comedy teams.** (a) Jack Benny and Mary Livingston. (b) Fred Allen and Portland Hoffa. (Photo a CBS Photo Archives; photo b courtesy of the National Broadcasting Company, Inc. Used by permission.)

**FIG. 2.17. Radio sound effects technician.** (Photo courtesy of the National Broadcasting Company, Inc. Used by permission.)

developed in comics or film), and experimental dramatic series. Writers and directors on the experimental series raised the level of radio drama to an art form. Orson Welles' experimental *Mercury Theater of the Air* (Fig. 2.18) produced the scariest radio drama of all, the Halloween 1938 production of H. G. Wells' *War of the Worlds*. Thousands panicked, believing Martians had invaded Earth.

Some of the longest lived dramas were serialized into 15-minute segments presented each weekday. Aimed at housewives and often sponsored by detergent manufacturers, this dramatic genre acquired the name **soap opera**. NBC broadcast the first soap opera in 1932. By the end of 1938, the networks broadcast 38 sponsored daytime soap operas daily, and the number was growing. The programs were slow moving, emotionally charged, and humorless. They contained none of the racy plot and character elements that would characterize their TV descendants. Yet, they appealed to millions, prompting social scientists to investigate the relationship between these serials and their loyal audiences.

In the early 1930s, radio brought together a mixture of drama and news. News events from the preceding week were put into script form and reenacted before network microphones. The result was the *March of Time*. First broadcast in 1931, it changed networks several times and went off the air in 1945. The *March of Time* spawned several imitators.

FIG. 2.18. *Mercury Theater of the Air.* Orson Welles directs. (CBS Photo Archives. Used by permission.)

Radio broadcast many other program types—contests and games; children's shows; public interest programs; and classical, light classical, Western, and popular music (and remember that most music on radio came from actual musicians, not recordings). There were programs for persons with special interests, for example, in gardening, cooking, and march music. There were sports broadcasts, religious programs, country music programs, disc jockey programs, and every kind of dramatic and music program you could think of.

Program ratings were developed. Based on audience surveys, these ratings showed the public preferred comedy. During the 1930s, the favorite evening programs were those of *Amos 'n' Andy,* Eddie Cantor, Rudy Vallee (musical variety), *Maxwell House Showboat* (variety), Burns and Allen, Fred Allen, Major Bowes' *Original Amateur Hour,* and Bing Crosby (musical variety). In 1950, preferences had not changed much. Comedians were still the favorites—Jack Benny, Edgar Bergen, Bob Hope, and Burns and Allen. Bing Crosby hosted the favorite variety hour. Arthur Godfrey had replaced Major Bowes as the best liked amateur-hour host. *Lux Radio Theater* was the favorite dramatic series. *Amos 'n' Andy* was still among the top 10 rated programs.

Many radio series were long lived. In 1950, the networks were running 108 series that had been on the air 10 years or more; 12 of them, for 20 years.

***2.2.4.2 Early Radio News.*** News reporting was part of broadcasting from the birth of radio. KDKA's first transmission reported results of the Harding–Cox election. Some stations broadcast news reports on a daily basis in the early 1920s.

**H. V. Kaltenborn** (Fig. 2.19), one of radio's first reporters, went on the air in 1923 at WEAF. Later he worked for CBS and then NBC. Other well-known commentators of the early 1930s included Boake Carter, Gabriel Heatter, Edwin C. Hill, Floyd Gibbons, and **Lowell Thomas** (Fig. 2.20). Thomas stayed with network news for 46 years, retiring from his CBS Radio commentary program in 1976.

Radio established a reputation for on-the-spot coverage. One example was Herbert Morrison's report of the ***Hindenburg* disaster.** On May 7, 1937, Morrison of WLS in Chicago, was in Lakehurst, New Jersey, recording a description of the arrival of the German passenger dirigible, *Hindenburg*. Suddenly the ship burst into flames. Morrison, horrified, described the scene as his engineer continued to record. That night, NBC broke its rule barring broadcast of recordings to use Morrison's description.

***2.2.4.3 Radio Covers World War II.*** As the 1930s wore on, the world groaned closer to war. Worldwide interest focused on Europe. The radio networks increased news activities. Correspondents reported and tried to make sense of the senseless. Listeners heard the voices of Hitler, Mussolini, Chamberlain, and other European political leaders.

FIG. 2.19. Paul White and H. V. Kaltenborn. (CBS Photo Archives. Used by permission.)

FIG. 2.20. **Lowell Thomas: News and commentary.** (CBS Photo Archives. Used by permission.)

**Paul White** (Fig. 2.19), head of CBS News, organized a team of correspondents that would become the model for broadcast reportage. Each member combined objective reporting with compassion and an eye for the telling detail. Their names became legend in broadcast news—William L. Shirer, Eric Severeid, Larry Lesueur, Howard K. Smith, Charles Collingwood, Robert Trout, Richard C. Hottelet, Bill Downs, Winston Burdett, Ned Calmer, Cecil Brown, and John Daly. The other networks also fielded teams of outstanding reporters, individuals who risked and sometimes lost their lives to keep the American public informed.

Perhaps more than anyone else, it was **Edward R. Murrow** (Fig. 2.21) on whom the public relied to explain the whys and hows of a distant and ominous war. CBS had sent Murrow to Europe in 1937 to arrange for broadcasts of special events and to report the news. But as Hitler began marching, Murrow devoted all efforts toward news reporting. At 8:00 p.m. eastern standard time on March 3, 1938, he broadcast his first report from Vienna as that beautiful, historic city awaited Hitler's arrival. The same broadcast included reports from correspondents in London, Paris, Berlin, Rome, and New York. This was radio's first world news roundup. Later based in England, Murrow opened broadcasts with the words, "This—is London," and Americans heard him report from a rooftop while bombs fell in that blacked-out city, from an Air Corps C-47 headed toward Holland, from London streets smashed by German bombs in the Battle of Britain, and from the North African front.

On December 7, 1941, radio reported that the Japanese had attacked Pearl Harbor, Hawaii. The next day, 79% of all U.S. homes listened to radio as President Roosevelt asked Congress for a declaration of war. Radio stepped up its already heavy reporting activities, and news was reported every hour.

FIG. 2.21. Edward R. Murrow in London. (CBS Photo Archives. Used by permission.)

As U.S. industries were mobilized for the war effort, so was radio. Unlike World War I, operation of radio stations was left in civilian hands. The government formed an **Office of War Information** (OWI) to coordinate propaganda and information services to the American people. The advertising industry organized the **War Advertising Council** and worked with OWI to create and schedule war-related public service campaigns—war bond purchase appeals, "careless talk costs lives," forest fire prevention, promotion of victory gardens, and many others.

One spectacular success in war bond appeals involved the radio singer, Kate Smith. In a marathon drive in February 1944, she urged listeners to buy bonds. They did—$108 million worth.

Entertainment programming continued more or less unchanged. Most programs promoted the win-the-war theme in some way. A number of government-created propaganda and meet-your-armed-services programs were broadcast. Some programs originated from armed forces bases and hospitals; Bob Hope, well-known radio and film comedian, was a leader in this. Care was taken that broadcasts did not contain information the enemy could use, such as weather reports.

Overseas, **Tokyo Rose** used Japanese government radio to broadcast popular music, propaganda, and sweet talk to American soldiers in the Pacific. **Axis Sally** was her German counterpart.

Inspired by an unauthorized station built and operated by service personnel in Alaska, the War Department created the **Armed Forces Radio Service** (AFRS). AFRS grew to a network of stations in the Pacific and European war theaters that provided entertainment and information for U.S. troops.

Commercial radio's greatest achievements during World War II were in news and public affairs. Reporters began to use voice recording machines to record actual events for later broadcast. Special radio series combined journalism and drama—the first step toward development of the radio documentary. Eyewitness accounts were broadcast as events occurred—Murrow's description of the London air raids, the Japanese attack of Manila, the Allied invasion of Normandy on D-Day, American troop landings on Japanese-held Pacific islands, the surrender of Germany, and the Japanese signing of surrender documents aboard the *U.S.S. Missouri* in Tokyo Bay.

### 2.2.5 Problems for Commercial Radio

The golden age of radio was not without occasional spots of tarnish. Some of these involved newspaper publishers, fraudulent medical advertising, music, editorials, network business arrangements, and public service.

*2.2.5.1 Press–Radio War.*    Before radio, newspapers had a monopoly on news, using their various editions to get out fast-breaking stories. Now radio could air a story immediately, beating the next newspaper edition by hours. The *extra*, a special edition that rushed important news to the public, was doomed by 1929. Publishers, seeing readers and advertisers turn to radio, decided to act. In 1933 the major news wire services—United Press (UP), Associated Press (AP), and International News Service (INS)—announced they would no longer provide news to radio networks.

The networks had no formal news gathering operations. Now, if they wished to continue to broadcast news, they would have to gather their own. NBC's effort was small, based on the long-distance telephoning efforts of A.A. Schechter. Each day Schechter managed to gather enough news for the Lowell Thomas program. CBS organized a full-fledged news department headed by Paul W. White. White established correspondents around the country and exchange arrangements with overseas news agencies. The **press–radio war** had begun.

The newspaper publishers forced a showdown. In December 1933, they met with representatives of CBS and NBC at New York's Hotel Biltmore. The two sides agreed to creation of a **Press–Radio Bureau.** Beginning March 1, 1934, the Press–Radio Bureau would provide a restricted diet of news to broadcasters for restricted use on the air. As a result, radio would not be able to report news before the newspapers. CBS was to disband its news service; NBC was not to build one.

There were ways around the restrictions. Radio could offer all the "comment" and "interpretation" it wanted; so radio's newscasters became "commentators" or "analysts." Most radio *stations* did not even join the Press–Radio Bureau and did not feel bound by the Biltmore agreements.

By mid-1935 the restrictions were falling apart. First, rival news services were formed to provide news to radio stations. Then UP and INS offered news to stations. By the end of the decade, even AP provided news to stations. In 1940 the Press–Radio Bureau went out of business, and radio went on to report World War II.

### 2.2.5.2 Quelling Radio's Quacks.

In 1935, the brand new FCC launched its first campaign to ensure that broadcasters programmed in the public interest. The FCC's law department ran the campaign, focusing on the elimination of fraudulent medical radio advertising. While the FCC and the FRC had removed the charlatans—John Brinkley, Norman Baker, and all the rest—from the airwaves, this was the FCC's first general criticism of "mainstream" broadcasters. Eighteen stations underwent hearings for airing such medical advertising; one station lost its license. The campaign, which took place during a protracted congressional battle over tougher controls for medicine and cosmetics, alarmed broadcasters and advertisers. It also involved the Food and Drug Administration, the Federal Trade Commission, and several other government departments. After 8 months, President Roosevelt, a particular friend of commercial broadcasters, invited FCC Chair Anning Smith Prall to the White House for a talk. The very next week, the FCC shut down the campaign and disciplined the staff people who ran it. Nonetheless, this 1935 campaign helped establish a continuum from the FRC to the FCC with regard to programming regulation; it served notice that the new agency, like its predecessor, would examine past programming content (including advertising) in making public-interest determinations.

### 2.2.5.3 Radio Music Troubles: ASCAP and AFM.

Problems with music had started early. Under the 1909 copyright law, copyrighted music could not be performed in public for profit without permission of the copyright holder. The **American Society of Composers, Authors and Publishers** (ASCAP) had organized to grant permission to music users and to collect and pay royalty fees to copyright-holder members.

In 1922 ASCAP demanded that station owners pay royalties. Broadcasters were outraged; after all, the stations brought in no revenue and were, in fact, financial drains. A test suit was brought against WOR, Newark, and the court ruled[14] that because a large department store ran WOR for publicity (stations did not carry advertising, yet), the station's use of music was "for profit." Stations had to pay ASCAP annual fees starting at $250. Broadcasters, still angry, formed an anti-AS-CAP organization that eventually became the trade group, National Association of Broadcasters (NAB). By 1936 the license fee was 2⅓% of a station's advertising income.

In 1937 ASCAP announced a sharp increase to take effect in the early 1940s. Broadcasters resolved to fight. They funded formation of a rival licensing organization, **Broadcast Music, Incorporated** (BMI). Finally, the showdown came. ASCAP raised its rates; broadcasters refused to pay and relied on music from BMI and the public domain (music on which there was no copyright or the copyright had expired). This period in 1941 became known as the era of "Jeannie With the Light Brown Hair," since that song, no longer under copyright, was used on the air so often.

The broadcasters won the battle when ASCAP reduced its demands. Then musicians stopped making records. James C. Petrillo, president of the American Federation of Musicians (AFM), said that sound films, jukeboxes, and the use of records on radio stations had put musicians out of work. At its 1942 convention, AFM decided to stop making recordings until their demands for fees were met. The major record companies yielded to AFM demands in 1943 and 1944.

**2.2.5.4 Editorials Discouraged.**    The license of WAAB in Boston was up for renewal. Mayflower Broadcasting Corporation filed an application with the FCC to build a new station in Boston to operate on WAAB's frequency. The FCC held hearings on the matter in 1939. Mayflower's application was denied; WAAB's license was renewed.[15] But the proceedings revealed that WAAB had editorialized during 1937 and 1938. In its decision the FCC said "the broadcaster cannot be an advocate." This **Mayflower doctrine** effectively discouraged broadcast editorials until the FCC reversed itself in 1949.[16] Leaders in the radio trade denounced the doctrine; to most stations it made little difference because they had no desire to air editorials.

**2.2.5.5 Network Case.**    CBS and NBC affiliation contracts deprived affiliated stations of control over their own programming. Under the option clause, for example, both networks could require that affiliates broadcast sponsored network shows even if local programming had to be canceled. The FCC launched an investigation in 1938.

Three years later, the commission issued its findings as the *Report on Chain Broadcasting.* At the same time, the FCC adopted regulations to deal with matters described in the report. The report said that, through affiliation contracts, NBC and CBS controlled the programming of their affiliated stations, stations that accounted for 85% of the total nighttime broadcast transmitter power of all stations in the country. Network control violated federal law, which put responsibility for programming on the individual station licensee. Such control also smacked of monopoly.

The new regulations aimed at breaking this illegal control. CBS would have to eliminate the network option plan and NBC would have to relinquish one of its networks. The regulations limited the term of affiliate contracts to 3 years, gave affiliates the right to reject programs, gave networks the right to offer rejected programs to nonaffiliated stations, limited network station ownership to one per city, and prohibited networks from controlling affiliate advertising rates. The report also mentioned the networks' artist bureaus: How could a network artist bureau represent the best economic interests of both performers, as their agent, and the network, as their employer?

CBS and NBC got rid of their artist bureaus immediately. However, they contended that the other regulations would end network broadcasting, even commercial broadcasting itself. The networks and other broadcasters mounted a full-scale attack on the FCC. A congressional committee investigated the commission.

NBC and CBS both challenged the regulations in court. The case wound its way up the judicial ladder to the U.S. Supreme Court. On May 10, 1943, the High Court announced its ruling in *NBC v. U.S.,*[17] **affirming constitutional validity of the Chain Broadcasting Regulations**. NBC sold the Blue Network, and CBS modified its network option requirements.

***2.2.5.6 Blue Book.***    Released in 1945, the publication's official title was *Public Service Responsibility of Broadcast Licensees.* It had a blue cover and hence was called **the Blue Book**.

The Blue Book reported on programming by a group of licensees. These licensees had broadcast excessive numbers of commercials, had not carried local public interest programs, had not aired network public affairs programs, and generally had not fulfilled promises made on their license renewal applications. Quoting statements by broadcasting business leaders, the Blue Book argued that stations should observe certain broad guidelines to ensure their programming met public interest obligations. The guidelines suggested that stations avoid advertising excesses and devote time to sustaining programs, to local live programs, and to discussion of public issues. The FCC, in turn, should examine a station's past record at license renewal time to see how well the station had met these guidelines.

The Blue Book's suggestions represented a departure from previous FCC policy. Station license renewals had been passed routinely as long as all technical requirements were met. Now, the FCC proposed to look at the past programming of each broadcaster at every renewal time.

The NAB launched an attack, attempting to discredit the Blue Book. According to the NAB, any FCC decision based on programming would violate the First Amendment to the U.S. Constitution and the prohibition against FCC censorship in the Communications Act. The trade press joined the battle on the side of the NAB. Invective targeted the commissioners and the FCC consultants and staff members who had prepared the book. They were likened to communists and fascists. Members of Congress joined the criticism. Interestingly, amidst all the ad hominem attacks, no one argued over the content of the Blue Book.

The FCC, surprised and uneasy over reaction to its publication, did not follow its own new standards. By the end of 1946 it was clear that the Blue Book was to be unused. Although never officially repudiated, neither was it enforced. The FCC did, however, adopt some Blue Book recommendations, such as using license renewal applications to compare programming promises to actual performance. Continued concern with Blue Book issues also eventually led to other regulatory reforms.

## 2.3 COMMERCIAL RADIO'S METAMORPHOSIS

The profits earned by AM radio stations during World War II had not gone unnoticed. After the war, hundreds of persons applied to build stations. The FCC licensed many to transmit with directional antennas, low-power, daylight-only operation, or some combination of these. Such limits were designed (a) to allow more stations to be built (b) by controlling the amount of interference new stations caused existing stations. Many communities got their first local radio service during this postwar period. In mid-1945, 933 AM radio stations were on the air. Thirty-six months later, the number was 1,621, with another 341 authorized.

Total station sales of advertising time climbed from $176.5 million in 1945 to $275.6 million in 1948. However, the number of radio stations on the air had grown so large that average annual advertising time sales per station actually dropped from $180,000 to $133,000 (Fig. 2.22).

At the same time, national radio network sales slowed (Fig. 2.23). The yearly increase of network sales billings dropped from 22.5% in 1944 to 0.8% in 1947. The last good year for network sales was 1948, with a 4.5% increase over 1947. This was followed by 12 years of shrinking sales, with the pattern of yearly decrease interrupted only once. By the end of the decade-plus sales slump, network radio billings were down $100 million from their 1948 total.

One problem was television. Television began its meteoric rise in popularity in 1948. People bought television receivers and deserted radio in droves. They peered at tiny screens, often through the all-but-obliterating snow of distant station reception. They saw poor imitations of the same program types that radio already did so well, but that did not matter: There were pictures.

It was simply a bad time for radio. Average station billings were falling, network audiences were falling, network billings were falling, and the nation was entering an economic recession. Radio had undergone radical change once before; some two decades earlier it had "commercialized" its program structure in order to accommodate advertising. Now, if it was to survive television's usurpation of its

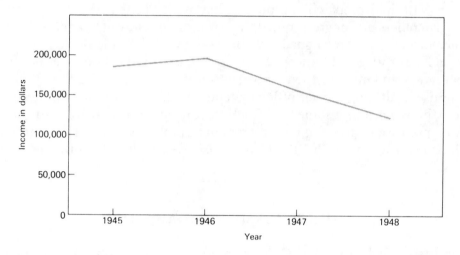

**FIG. 2.22. Average radio station compensation: 1945–1948.** Radio station billings climbed (Fig. 2.14), but station numbers increased (Fig. 2.13) so average compensation fell. (*Source*: FCC.)

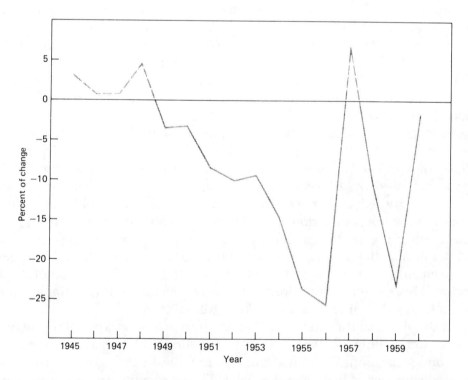

**FIG. 2.23. Annual change in national radio network gross advertising revenues: 1945–1960.** Radio networks billed less each year by increasing percentages. (*Source*: FCC.)

audiences and viewing patterns, radio would have to change again. But change how?

### 2.3.1 Radio Stations Specialize

The answer lay in a programming form as old as radio itself, the **disc jockey** or DJ show. Independent stations had featured music-and-talk DJ programs at least as far back as 1935. Now, some stations converted to a total DJ format, using it to **specialize.** In effect, these stations decided not to compete with television for a general audience. Instead, they tailored programming to reach a specific segment of the audience, then sold advertising time to companies that wished to reach that segment.

One such programming specialization spread between 1948 and 1952—the so-called **Negro radio** station. These stations used Black DJs, played rhythm 'n' blues and gospel music, and programmed news and features for the Black community.

About 1950, another specialization evolved and spread—the **top-40 radio** station. Pioneered by group station owners **Todd Storz** and **Gordon McLendon**, top-40 stations targeted an audience in its teens and early 20s. The top-40 format called for emphasis on the most popular single recordings, a rapid-fire pace, and heavy promotion, both on-air (contests, singing station identifications, etc.) and off-air, in other media.

About this time, a form of popular music arose that became known as "rock 'n' roll" (Fig. 2.24). Top-40 radio was the perfect setting for this music. As the 1950s ground on, city after city fell under the spell of raucous, razzle-dazzle, rocking top-40 stations, and their near-fanatic youth audiences pushed the stations to the top of the ratings in nearly every market.

Naturally, there were imitators. Larger cities acquired two, three, or even four top-40 stations. After some failed, radio managers realized that the lesson of top-40 success was not top 40 itself, but specialization. In the 1960s and 1970s, radio formats diversified—country music, beautiful music, rock music, all-talk, all-news, ethnic.

While this programming change occurred, another took place in sales and advertising. Stations persuaded local retail outlets to buy radio commercials, and income from local advertising sales climbed.

### 2.3.2 Radio Networks Accommodate

Network radio's adjustment to the age of television was more difficult than that of local stations. At first the radio networks tried to economize and compete with television for the mass audience. They dropped their ban on recordings and even ran a few disc jockey shows. They added telephone quiz shows, offering money and prizes to those who could answer the questions posed by long-distance telephone. Audiences continued to dwindle. In the 1950s network radio programs of long standing went off the air and were not replaced.

**FIG. 2.24. Alan Freed.** In the early 1950s he became one of the most popular and important disc jockeys in the new top-40 radio format. Supposedly, he coined the name "rock 'n' roll." His confession of involvement in payola before a congressional committee effectively ended his career. (CBS Photo Archives. Used by permission.)

The importance and vitality of radio shifted from networks to local stations. Network affiliation was a hindrance. If radio networks were to stay in business they would have to adjust to the changing needs of the stations.

One need was network programming designed for the change in how people listened to radio. Pretelevision radio had forced the public to develop a plan-ahead, time-block audience pattern. However, that pattern had shifted almost entirely to the visual medium. Now, people did not plan ahead to listen to radio; they listened when they had time and usually while doing other things. NBC responded with *Monitor*, a very different kind of network radio program. Launched in 1955 under NBC's innovative president, Pat Weaver, *Monitor* represented a novel attempt to adjust network programming to the audience's tune-in/tune-out listening patterns. *Monitor* ran on weekends, 40 hours (later 25), covering many areas of interest with short capsules of information. This allowed listeners to tune in briefly and still hear a complete feature. Following *Monitor's* success, ABC and CBS began their own versions.

MBS and ABC reduced their network services to capsule news and features, usually on the hour and the half hour, giving the rest of the hour to affiliates. First NBC, then CBS adopted this pattern for weekday programming.

### 2.3.3 Radio Scandals in the 1950s

Radio's transitional years were unsettling. In addition to the competition from television and the proliferation of radio stations, the radio business was jolted by several serious scandals. The most troubling were McCarthyism, planted news, and payola.

*2.3.3.1 McCarthyism Invades Radio.*   McCarthyism, a bleak period in U.S. history characterized by political "witch hunts" and paranoia, transcended the field of broadcasting, pervading all aspects of American life. Joseph McCarthy, junior senator from Wisconsin, did not invent the mass paranoia that bears his name. He did profit by it, however, building a career on finding and purging from the U.S. government people he accused of being or having been communists.

McCarthy's tactics, fed by a growing public fear of atomic attack and internal subversion by communists, created an aura of universal suspicion and accusation. People and ideas were labeled *communist* just because they were different. An accusation by itself of being a communist or communist sympathizer—whether true or not—was cause enough for the accused to be summarily fired. The careers of many innocent people were ruined.

McCarthy was a master at using news media to publicize his activities and thus to build his power base among the public. Few opposed him because McCarthy had the perfect defense—he would simply brand the opposition "un-American," synonymous in those days with communist or traitor.

One of McCarthyism's more virulent forms was **blacklisting** (Box 2.3). It worked like this: Self-appointed protectors of the public weal, who professed concern that communist agents were gaining control of the nation's communications channels, would supposedly investigate the background of creative personnel in stage, screen, and broadcasting. The blacklisters circulated names of performers, writers, directors, and others alleged to be communists or communist sympathizers to producers, sponsors, and studio heads. Blacklisted individuals lost their jobs and could not get new ones, often without knowing why; few employers would admit to being influenced by the blacklisters. The accused were presumed guilty based on allegations alone. Some never got entertainment work again. Some went through humiliating blacklister-specified rituals of "clearing," usually by publicly

---

**BOX 2.3. HOW THE BLACKLISTERS WORKED**

Leading blacklisters in broadcasting included three ex-FBI agents who publish-ed *Counterattack: The Newsletter of Facts on Communism* and *Red Channels: The Report of Communist Influence in Radio and Television,* and Aware, Inc., publisher of periodical bulletins listing supposed communists. The blacklists were by no means nonprofit activities. Vincent Hartnett, who formed Aware in 1953, checked names for a fee on request by sponsors and producers. He also prescribed means by which blacklisted individuals could "clear" them-selves—again for a fee. He was backed by Laurence Johnson, owner of a Syracuse, New York, supermarket chain. If broadcast programs persisted in using persons blacklisted by Aware, Johnson pressured the sponsors with tacit threats to prevent his customers from buying the advertised products. Agencies, networks, sponsors, stations—all ran scared, bowing to the whims of Aware because of the possibility of economic recrimination by Johnson.

---

admitting they had been communists (whether or not they actually had been) and vowing to take a militant anticommunist attitude from then on. Some committed suicide. The blacklisters' power, however, was successfully broken by humorist and storyteller John Henry Faulk (Box 2.4) who won a lawsuit against Aware, Inc., a leading blacklisting organization.

***2.3.3.2 News Planting.***    This involved MBS being paid to run favorable news items on a foreign country. In January 1959, MBS President Alexander Guterma

---

**BOX 2.4. JOHN HENRY FAULK TAKES ON AWARE**

John Henry Faulk, radio personality for WCBS in New York, spoke out against Aware's influence in the New York Chapter of the American Federation of Television and Radio Artists, the performers' union. In 1956, Faulk helped draft a noncommunist, anti-Aware slate of candidates for election to office in the union. He was one of the candidates. Aware struck back, blacklisting Faulk as a communist sympathizer. Although Faulk had no communist connections, advertisers still dropped sponsorship of his radio program, intimidated by the Aware blacklisting. Faulk brought suit against Aware's Hartnett and Johnson for libel. In less than its finest hour, WCBS fired Faulk, saying his ratings were poor. He hired Louis Nizer, a famous trial lawyer. In June 1962 Faulk's libel case went to trial. The jury found Hartnett and Johnson guilty of libel and awarded Faulk more damages than he had asked—an unprecedented $3.5 million (subsequently scaled down to $550,000 by an appellate court).

Faulk's victory signaled the end of blacklisting in broadcasting but opened no doors for the victor. In 1974 a Dallas radio station broke the blacklisters' curse and hired Faulk as a telephone call-in show host. This was his first regular job in broadcasting in almost 18 years.

---

made a secret agreement with representatives of Rafael Trujillo, Dominican Republic dictator. Under this agreement, MBS would broadcast a monthly quota of news and commentary about the Dominican Republic. None of the news was to be negative. In exchange for this publicity disguised as news, Guterma received $750,000. But the month after he had made the agreement, Guterma became involved in legal and business problems, and the stories were never run. The Dominican Republic sued to get its money back, and the suit exposed the shady deal. Broadcasters and the public alike were astounded that a news organization could be so easily corrupted.

*2.3.3.3 Payola.*   Since the beginning of radio's top-40 stations, record companies had paid or otherwise bribed disc jockeys under the table to promote records. The theory was that a top disc jockey on a big market top-40 station could play and push a record enough to make it become popular. Dubbed **payola**, this practice constituted advertising for which the station received no revenue; even worse, it deceived the public because it was not labeled as advertising. The story came out in 1959, and testifying before Congress, some of the nation's best-known DJs were caught in this scandal admitting they had taken payola. Congress amended the Communications Act in 1959 to prohibit payola. However, despite efforts by both government and broadcasters to curb the practice, payola scandals recurred sporadically in the ensuing years.

## 2.4 RISE OF FM RADIO

During the 1960s frequency modulation (FM) radio, previously suppressed by the industry's corporate giants and ignored by the public, began to move and shake the radio business. The increased popularity of FM hastened the trend toward specialization and helped sharpen competition for audiences among radio stations. So now we catch up on the story of FM.

FM is almost as old as radio itself; the first patent was issued in 1902. FM broadcasting did not become practical, however, until the work of **Edwin H. Armstrong** during the period between 1928 and 1934. RCA opposed advancement of FM on grounds it might detract from the development of television, in which the electronics giant had a vested interest (*PRT,* 3.1). Undaunted, Armstrong promoted FM. He showed that FM had inherent advantages over AM—higher fidelity reproduction, less static, and not so subject to fading and interference from other stations. By March 1940, 22 experimental FM stations were on the air. The FCC authorized commercial FM operation, establishing 42 to 50 MHz as the FM band. During World War II, the FCC stopped granting applications for new FM stations.

In 1945 the FCC moved the FM band to 88 to 106 MHz.[18] With this decision, the FCC rendered obsolete all transmitters at the existing 46 FM stations and all 400,000 FM receivers owned by the public.

RCA's opposition, the wartime freeze, and now a major frequency shift—this should have killed any chance for development that the new aural medium had. In the long run, however, the 1945 frequency shift turned out to be a good move; it lessened chances of FM suffering from interference, and it increased the number of FM channels from 40 to 100. Additionally, the FCC reaffirmed the principle of reserved channels for education. In setting up the 1940 FM band, the FCC had set aside five channels for noncommercial educational use. Now, in the 1945 move, the commission reserved the first 20 of the new band's 100 channels for noncommercial educational stations.

FM radio was being touted as the coming medium, perhaps even replacing AM radio. In spite of the 1945 frequency shift, just 3 years later the FCC had authorized over 1,000 new FM stations (Fig. 2.25). But FM's time had not yet come. Audiences did not find FM attractive. The receivers manufactured at the time were expensive and did not sound much better than AM receivers. In many cases, FM programming was exactly the same as AM; AM–FM licensees would duplicate AM programming on the FM station. Audiences were content with AM radio and fascinated with a new broadcast medium, television. Advertisers put their money in AM and TV. FM stations lost money almost without exception. From 1949 through 1952, over 350 FM station owners voluntarily returned licenses to the FCC.

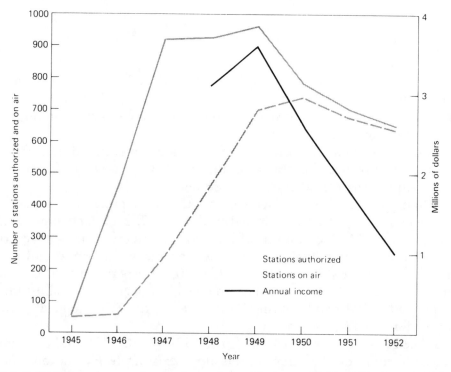

FIG. 2.25 FM stations authorized, on air, and income: 1945–1952. (*Source*: FCC.)

In the 1950s, a small coterie of "hi-fi" enthusiasts discovered the technical delights of FM. They also enjoyed the classical music that some independently programmed FM stations featured. Then stereophonic reproduction hit the consumer market. In 1961 the FCC adopted a system of stereophonic FM transmission and authorized stations to **broadcast stereophonically.**

In 1963, the commission adopted the **FM nonduplication rule.** This rule required licensees of AM–FM combinations in all but the smallest cities to program the FM stations separately from AM most of the time. Such stations had to look for formats—preferably formats that did not duplicate those already in the market and that would show off FM's technical advantages. Many chose "beautiful music." Others took an entirely different direction.

Rock 'n' roll evolved into rock, which, in turn, evolved and divided into increasingly esoteric forms. Large-market FM stations specialized and appealed to the fragmented audiences generated by these new rock music forms. Many new recordings were longer than normal and relied on electronic gimmickry that AM could not reproduce adequately. These were a natural fit for FM radio.

At the same time, rock fans discovered stereophonic reproduction. A new mass market, they bought stereo discs, tapes, turntables, tape decks, amplifiers, speakers, and, of course, FM tuners. They put stereo in their cars. The stereo explosion boosted FM radio, and FM boosted stereo.

FM stations competed in formatting, also. Programmers discovered that contemporary popular music could thrive in quieter, less frenetic surroundings than the original top-40 format of the period. Audiences appreciated long, uninterrupted stretches of similar music. FM stations instructed announcers to stop screaming, to play two or more selections at a time, even to **track** albums (play them in their entirety without interruption).

These strategies succeeded. By 1970, FM stations successfully competed for shares with AM stations in some large markets. FM programmers continued to refine techniques. More listeners discovered the superior technical quality of FM. Stereo receivers dropped in price. In 1979, for the first time, FM passed AM in overall market shares and, in succeeding years, increased its lead. FM, once the unwanted, ill-treated sibling of AM, had become the desired, admired, and more popular medium.

## 2.5 RADIO COMPETITION INCREASES

From 1950 to 1980, the number of stations increased markedly, about 276%. During the 1970s, the FCC made proposals that would have further increased the number of stations. One proposal reduced the area in which dominant stations on AM clear channels were protected from interference by other stations; the commission put this into effect and created room for some 125 new AM stations.

Another proposal would have reduced AM channel width from 10 kHz to 9 kHz. Such a move required cooperation from neighboring countries, and the FCC proposed the reduction at the international level. Most U.S. licensees, however, did not want the expense of changing frequencies, feared technical problems, and did not look forward to the hundreds of new AM-station competitors the 9 kHz spacing would create. They fought the move, and in 1981 the FCC recommended that the United States stay with 10 kHz spacing.

However, the FCC did pave the way for hundreds of new FM stations. In 1980 the FCC proposed changes in FM; the proposal became known by its FCC file number, **docket 80-90.** Three years later the Commission approved most docket 80-90 changes; modification of station and channel classifications made room for up to 1,000 new FM stations. In 1989 the FCC changed the FM station classification system, a move that would allow yet another 200 stations to sign on.

Even before docket 80-90, there were a lot of radio stations. On January 1, 1980, broadcasters operated nearly 8,800 radio stations. During the period 1950 to 1980, radio advertising sales had increased tenfold, from $321 million to $3.4 billion. But by the late 1990s, the number of stations had increased to 12,000, 85% of which were commercial, and radio advertising revenue exceeded $11.4 billion. Despite increases in station numbers and expenses, there was money to be made, especially in medium and large markets. Competition increased.

### 2.5.1 Impact on Radio Station Operation

The increase in competition and the success of FM led to three basic changes. First, the **programmer grew in importance.** The successful programmer used statistically based **quantitative research.** Research helped to define the station's target audience, to tailor content to capture that audience, and to spot trends in audience tastes and habits—all critically important in marketing a station to potential advertisers. Research helped make stations in competitive markets **highly formatted.** Research helped select records to play, news to report, jingles to insert, things to say, commercials to run, and times to do all these things—even the talent to do them.

The second change involved **decreasing reliance on local programming resources.** Successful radio programmers sometimes syndicated their services. A station could hire such a programmer to come into the market, study the competitive situation, and make programming recommendations. Or the station could automate and subscribe to a programmer's service—large reels of tape that contained all music and announcements. In the late 1970s some syndicators went to satellite distribution for their programming.

The third change involved overall programming trends in AM and FM. **FM stations tended to program formats that featured music,** any kind of music in which reproduction of sound was important to the listener—rock, beautiful, country, jazz, classical, and ethnic. **AM stations tended to program formats in which the range of frequencies reproduced was not as important**—talk, news, nostalgia music (which featured many prestereo recordings), and newer nonmusic formats such as sports.

By the end of the 1980s, AM faced stiff competition for advertising dollars. For many, nationally **syndicated talk radio** provided the answer. Although some programs were informational in format, most talk shows were controversial, confrontational, and mean spirited. Other programs purposely shocked listeners with prurient content. To some these shows brought back unpleasant reminders of radio's early charlatans, but for many AM stations, talk radio shows also brought back listeners and advertisers.

### 2.5.2 Technology and Regulatory Policy

By the 1980s, the tables had turned; FM was the dominant aural medium, and AM was struggling. Channel congestion and interference had increased dramatically in the AM band. Radio receiver manufacturers attempted to lessen interference by building AM radios so they picked up narrower and narrower bands of frequencies—which, in turn, resulted in a decline in fidelity. AM radio, once a vital service, could not compete in the marketplace. By the 1990s, FM radio had about three quarters of all radio listening. Two thirds of all AM stations were in financial trouble.

The FCC had helped in FM's long uphill battle, and now it would do the same for AM. In 1991, after 4 years of working on and studying AM's problems, the Commission adopted a strategy of **rule and policy changes designed to help AM radio.** These actions aimed to reduce interference, improve the quality of the transmitted signal, reduce the number of interfering stations, and encourage the production of better quality AM receivers. As part of this package, the FCC added 100 kHz to the AM band and, by encouraging existing stations to move to these 10 new channels, used them to relieve congestion in the older part of the band.

Many had also believed that AM stereo had the potential to help in the competition with FM, and in 1982 the FCC authorized AM licensees to transmit in stereo but without selecting a specific transmission system. Therefore, no preferred marketplace standard emerged. For 10 years AM stereo languished. Congress finally directed the FCC to make a choice. In 1993 the FCC designated the Motorola C-Quam system, which had the largest installed base among stations, as the **national standard for AM stereo broadcasting.** However, stereophonic reproduction did not particularly enhance AM's programming formats so listeners saw little reason to invest in AM stereo.

Some AM broadcasters competed outside the limits of their broadcast programming. They **contracted with local cable companies to provide programming**—channels for the cable audio service, even video programming such as local newscasts. Others explored new revenue-producing uses of their carriers (*PRT,* 11.6.2).

Technological advances were not limited to AM, however; digital technology also strengthened FM's claim to superior sound reproduction. Equipment manufacturers included **digital** (*PRT,* 10.3.1) circuitry in the various devices and "black boxes" radio stations used to process their signal. This allowed the audio signal to travel within the station—from source to transmitter—without picking up the distortion and extraneous signals normally acquired from even the finest nondigital equipment. Some radio networks digitally encoded their signals for satellite distribution; these signals arrived at the station as clear as they left the network. Record companies used digital technology, too, for cleaner, purer recordings. The standard aural playback medium changed from vinyl records to the **compact disc.**

### 2.5.3 Impact on Network Programming

The heightened competition among stations showed up at the network level as well. ABC started a trend toward **format-specific networks.** In 1968, ABC announced the launch of four separately programmed networks. Each offered brief newscasts; each was tailored to a different type of station format. None of the ABC networks dominated a station's weekend as did *Monitor.*

MBS followed ABC's lead 4 years later, adding a network for stations whose audiences were predominately African American and another for Spanish-language stations. MBS dropped the Mutual Spanish Network after 7 months but continued the Mutual Black Network (MBN) until 1979, when MBS sold its interest to Sheridan Broadcasting Corporation. MBN was then renamed Sheridan Broadcasting Network.

Mutual itself had passed through the hands of a number of owners. In 1978, the Amway Corporation, door-to-door marketer of home and personal products, bought the network. While under Amway, Mutual purchased two radio stations, the first Mutual had ever owned. These were later sold.

In 1973, a brand new organization, the National Black Network (NBN), signed on, originating hourly 5-minute newscasts aimed at Black stations across the country. NBN soon added sports and features.

NBC changed *Monitor* and finally dropped it in 1975. NBC retained what had become conventional network service—brief newscasts and features. In mid-1975, NBC added the News and Information Service (NIS), a program service separate from the NBC Radio network. Designed for stations with all-news formats, NIS fed news, reports, and features throughout the hour, giving affiliates the opportunity to insert local news and advertising. Stations paid a monthly subscription to use NIS. NBC could not attract enough subscribing stations to make it pay and took NIS off the air in 1977.

National Public Radio (NPR) was formed in 1970 as a network to serve noncommercial educational radio stations. Numerous commercial state networks signed on to feed state, farm, and other special-interest news and features to affiliated stations. In the 1980s, American Public Radio formed to supplement NPR.

The late 1970s and early 1980s marked a renaissance in national networking. More stations, driven by increased competition, saw networks as a way to help them grab a greater share of the audience. Most new network activity involved format-specific programming, a trend accelerated by both increased numbers of stations and development of domestic satellite distribution. ABC added additional networks. CBS and NBC both launched youth-oriented networks. MBS used multiple satellite audio channels to deliver various types of programming to affiliates. Sheridan and NBN expanded program offerings. AP and UPI had both operated news program services for a number of years; now AP cooperated in a country-music radio programming service and UPI started a Spanish-language news service.

A number of new networks started during this late 1970s through early 1980s period; some failed. The successes included American Public Radio, Turner Broadcasting System's (TBS) CNN Radio, RKO Radio Networks, Satellite Music Network, Transtar Radio Networks, and United Stations.

All told, radio networking seemed to be on the rise, and even some state and regional networks went to satellite distribution. Most of these newer networks paid no compensation, operating instead on some form of barter basis.

## 2.6 RADIO COMPETITION DECREASES

Dramatic changes, however, started a trend toward lessening competition. Historically, the FCC had encouraged diversification of, and localism in, broadcast station ownership. Its regulations encouraged integration of ownership with management (the owner actually participates in the day-to-day operation of the station) and limited the number of stations in which one individual could hold financial interest. During the late 1970s and the 1980s, however, the FCC began to **deregulate** (remove regulatory controls from) the various media businesses for which it was responsible, one result of which was that the Commission raised its station ownership limits. Licensees discovered and used loopholes in the regulations to enter into local marketing agreements, contractual arrangements by which one individual could operate two or more stations in the same market.

In the mid-1980s, electronic mass media businesses began to combine in a series of major corporate and financial transactions. Of course, radio networks were affected. In 1985, Capital Cities Communications, Inc., bought ABC; United Stations bought RKO Radio Networks; and GE bought RCA, parent company of NBC. The two most historically notable radio network purchases were made in the mid-1980s. In both cases, the buyer was Westwood One, Inc., a producer and distributor of sponsored radio programs. In 1985 Westwood One acquired MBS from Amway; 2 years later, it bought the NBC Radio network. GE had decided that the nation's senior network—the business that had started NBC—was expendable. NBC sold all its radio stations in 1988.

Consolidation of radio network ownership continued. In 1989 Transtar and United Stations merged to form Unistar. In 1993 Infinity Broadcasting gained control of both Westwood One and the Unistar Radio Networks, forming a programming service that rivaled ABC Radio in size and revenue. In 1995 the Walt Disney Corporation acquired ABC. That same year Westinghouse bought CBS, and in 1996 it purchased Infinity.

Sheridan Broadcasting and NBN combined to form American Urban Radio Network in 1992. American Public Radio changed its name to Public Radio International in 1994. And by the late 1990s the array of Spanish-language networks included Cadena Radio Centro, CNN Radio Noticias, UPI Radio Noticias, Spanish Information Service, and Spanish Broadcasting System.

## 2.7 RBDS, DIGITAL RADIO, AND THE TELECOMMUNICATIONS ACT OF 1996

The radio business began discussing the **radio broadcast data system** (RBDS) about 1990. RBDS, already widely used in Europe, took advantage of radios with special circuitry and liquid crystal displays (LCDs). At the same time an RBDS-equipped station broadcast its regular programming, it could also use RBDS to transmit to the LCDs on listener receivers information such as its call letters, slogans, and format. An RBDS radio in a car could scan for a station with a particular format or network and then, when the car drove out of that station's range, automatically switch to another station with a similar format or the same network. When fully implemented, RBDS could deliver emergency information, even to the point of turning on a switched-off receiver! A U.S. RBDS standard was established in 1993, and many stations began installing RBDS transmission equipment. Some receiver manufacturers built RBDS circuitry into their more expensive radios.

RBDS, however, did not have nearly the potential to change the basic structure of U.S. radio as did two other late-20th-century developments. One of these was **digital radio**. Digital radio (also called **digital audio broadcasting** and **digital audio radio service**) would apply digital technology to the very transmission system and could provide audio reproduction with a quality as high as that produced by the compact disc. The problem was that the switch to a digital system would require replacement of every existing radio station transmitter and consumer receiver. In other words, no present radios—not Walkmans, not boom boxes, not FM stereo tuners, not clock radios, not expensive automotive systems that annoy people as you drive down the street rattling windows—none of them could pick up a digital signal. Radio stations would have to buy digital transmission gear, and listeners would have to buy digital-reception-capable radios. Most plans for digital radio included, however, some phase-in scheme. A station would broadcast both a digital signal and its AM or FM analog signal for a number of years but eventually end the analog transmission. Because all stations would convert to digital, all stations could sound equally good. There would be no more AM–FM sound-quality differential because there would be no more AM or FM stations. This led to quite a bit of jockeying for position among various segments of the radio business.

The other development that promised fundamental change in the structure of radio was passage of the Telecommunications Act of 1996. That law directed drastic **relaxation of ownership rules.** One individual could now own as many as eight radio stations in the same town; that same individual could own an unlimited number of radio stations nationally.

A recession at the beginning of the 1990s had stalled station sales, but with the economy starting to recover in 1993, the buying and selling of stations had resumed. The 1996 law served to increase both the rate and prices of station trading. Large radio station group owners took advantage of these rules and began "bulking up" and "clustering"—buying more stations in markets where they were already strong, and selling off stations where they were weak. The result was that more and more stations fell into fewer and fewer hands, the number of outlets for different views and ideas was reduced, and the number of absentee owners unfamiliar with the needs and interests of the communities in which their stations were located was increased. Some in the business predicted that the single-station owner and the small group owner would disappear except in small markets and that radio would evolve into a structure somewhat like cable television—a few large companies owning most of the local outlets.

The broadcasting business—its structure, its business practices, its relationships, its programming, almost everything—was formed when broadcasting was only radio. When television came along, it adopted the procedures that had been developed in radio. For years, NBC and CBS radio revenues financed their TV ventures. Then when television caught on, radio had to adjust and adapt to survive. We have examined the changes in radio wrought by television. Now it is time to focus directly on the history of the visual medium itself.

## NOTES

1. When a conductor (a substance capable of carrying current, such as copper wire) carries a voltage (current), a magnetic field is built up around it. A second conductor has a voltage induced in it when moved through this field. This is known as *induction*.

2. Ernst F. W. Alexanderson, a Swedish emigrant and electrical engineer at GE, had worked with Fessenden on development of the alternator then later perfected it "working along different lines from Fessenden." Christopher H. Sterling and John M. Kittross, *Stay Tuned: A Concise History of American Broadcasting*, 2nd ed. (Belmont, MA: Wadsworth, 1990) 28.

3. This was at least the second time the government had refused a monopoly on some form of electromagnetic communication. Morse wanted to sell the telegraph to the government, but Congress took no action on the matter.

Also as a result of World War I, the federal government took over control of all telephone and telegraph systems in the United States in July 1918. During the period in which the postmaster general controlled these systems, rates for local telephone service increased, long-distance telephone charges went up by 20%, and, for the first time, an installation fee was levied for new telephone service (which is still with us). Subscribers and the state regulatory commissions complained, but the U.S. Supreme Court upheld all increases. Congress ended this experiment in government ownership effective August 1919.

4. United Fruit Company used ships to get products from its Latin American plantations to its North American markets. The company used radio to direct movement of these ships.

5. The Westinghouse transmitter was licensed as a limited commercial station. This referred to its use by a private firm, not to permission to sell advertising time. Broadcast advertising would not develop until 1922. The Commerce Department did not license the Westinghouse operation as a broadcast station because there was no such category; the department started licensing broadcast stations as such in 1921.

6. The letters kHz are an abbreviation for *kilohertz,* meaning a thousand cycles per second; MHz, for *megahertz,* a million cycles per second.

7. A network pays an affiliated station for carrying network programming containing advertising; this payment is compensation for the network's use of the station's time.

8. 286 F. 1003 (1923).

9. 12 F.2d 614 (1926).

10. 35 Ops. Att'y Gen. 126 (1926).

11. Previous editions of *Perspectives on Radio and Television,* for example, declared that radio had, by 1928, "passed successfully through a critical and formative stage" (e.g., F. Leslie Smith, *Perspectives on Radio and Television: Telecommunication in the United States,* 3rd ed. [New York: Harper & Row, 1990] 25). They cited research showing that radio had met all requirements needed to serve national advertisers by 1928 and concluded that "the foundations . . . were laid" for "American commercial broadcasting."

12. *Selling Radio: The Commercialization of American Broadcasting, 1920–1934* (Washington, DC: Smithsonian, 1994) 165–166.

13. *Telecommunications, Mass Media, & Democracy: The Battle for the Control of U.S. Broadcasting, 1928–1935* (New York: Oxford University Press, 1993).

14. Witmark v. Bamberger, 291 F.776 (1923).

15. In the Matter of Mayflower Broadcasting Corporation and the Yankee Network, Inc. (WAAB), 8 F.C.C. 333 (1941).

16. In the Matter of Editorializing by Broadcast Licensees, 13 F.C.C. 1246 (1949).

17. 319 U.S. 190 (1943).

18. The frequencies 106 to 108 MHz, originally reserved for broadcast facsimile, were later used by FM broadcasting.

## FURTHER READING

Aitken, Hugh G. H. *The Continuous Wave: Technology and American Radio 1900–1932.* Princeton, NJ: Princeton University Press, 1985.

Bannerman, R. LeRoy. *Norman Corwin and Radio: The Golden Years.* University of Alabama Press, 1986.

Banning, William P. *Commercial Broadcast Pioneer: The WEAF Experiment 1922–1926.* Cambridge, MA: Harvard University Press, 1946.

Barnouw, Erik. *A Tower in Babel.* New York: Oxford University Press, 1966.

Barnouw, Erik. *The Golden Web.* New York: Oxford University Press, 1968.

Barnouw, Erik. *The Image Empire.* New York: Oxford University Press, 1970.

Baudino, Joseph E., and John M. Kittross. "Broadcasting's Oldest Station: An Examination of Four Claimants." *Journal of Broadcasting* 21 (1977): 61–83.

Bilby, Kenneth. *The General: David Sarnoff and the Rise of the Communications Industry.* New York: Harper & Row, 1986.

Brown, James A. "Selling Airtime for Controversy: NAB Self-Regulation and Father Coughlin." *Journal of Broadcasting* 24 (1980): 199–224.

Cantor, Louis. *Wheelin' on Beale: The Story of the Nation's First All-Black Radio Station.* New York: Pharos, 1992.

Carson, Gerald. *The Roguish World of Dr. Brinkley.* New York: Holt, 1960.

De Forest, Lee. *Father of Radio: The Autobiography of Lee De Forest.* Chicago: Wilcox, 1950.

Douglas, George H. *The Early Days of Radio Broadcasting.* Jefferson, NC: McFarland, 1987.

Douglas, Susan J. *Inventing American Broadcasting: 1899–1922.* Baltimore: Johns Hopkins University Press, 1987.

Ely, Melvin Patrick. *The Adventures of Amos 'n' Andy: A Social History of an American Phenomenon.* New York: Free Press, 1992.

Erickson, Hal. *Religious Radio and Television, 1921–1991: The Programs and the Personalities.* Jefferson, NC: McFarland, 1992.

Faulk, John Henry. *Fear On Trial.* Rev. ed. New York: Grosset, 1983.

Fessenden, Helen. *Fessenden: Builder of Tomorrow.* New York: Coward, 1940.

Frierson, Meade, III, and James F. Widner. *Science Fiction on Radio: A Revised Look.* Birmingham, AL: A.F.A.B., 1995.

Garay, Ronald. *Gordon McLendon: The Maverick of Radio.* Westport, CT: Greenwood, 1992.

Glick, Edwin L. "The Life and Death of the Liberty Broadcasting System." *Journal of Broadcasting* 23 (1979): 117–135.

Glick, Edwin L. "WBAP/WFAA—570/820: Til Money Did Them Part." *Journal of Broadcasting* 24 (1977): 473–486.

Godfrey, Donald. "Radio Comes of Age, 1900–1943." In *The Media of America, A History,* 3rd ed. David Sloan and William Startt, eds. Northport, AL: Vision, 1996.

Harmon, Jim. *Radio Mystery and Adventure and Its Appearances in Film, Television, and other Media.* Jefferson, NC: McFarland, 1992.

Havig, Alan. *Fred Allen's Radio Comedy.* Philadelphia: Temple University Press, 1990.

Hay, Peter. *Canned Laughter: The Best Stories from Radio's Golden Years.* New York: Oxford University Press, 1992.

Hijiya, James A. *Lee De Forest and the Fatherhood of Radio.* Bethlehem, PA: Lehigh University Press, 1992.

Hilliard, Robert L., and Michael C. Keith. *The Broadcast Century: A Biography of American Broadcasting.* Boston, MA: Focal, 1992.

Hoffer, Thomas W. "TNT Baker: Radio Quack." In *American Broadcasting: A Source Book on the History of Radio and Television.* Lawrence W. Lichty and Malachi C. Topping, Eds. New York: Hastings, 1975.

Jolly, W. P. *Marconi.* New York: Stein, 1972.

Koch, Howard. *The Panic Broadcast.* New York: Avon, 1971.

Lamb, Edward. *No Lamb for Slaughter: An Autobiography.* New York: Harcourt, 1963.

Lessing, Lawrence. *Man of High Fidelity: Edwin Howard Armstrong.* New York: Lippincott, 1956.

Lewis, Tom. *Empire of the Air: The Men Who Made Radio.* New York: HarperCollins, 1991.

MacDonald, J. Fred. *Don't Touch That Dial! Radio Programming in American Life from 1920 to 1960.* Chicago: Nelson-Hall, 1979.

Maclaurin, W. Rupert. *Invention and Innovation in the Radio Industry.* New York: Macmillan, 1949.

McChesney, Robert W. *Telecommunications, Mass Media, & Democracy: The Battle for the Control of U.S. Broadcasting, 1928–1935.* New York: Oxford University Press, 1993.

Orbison, Charley. "'Fighting Bob' Shuler: Early Radio Crusader." *Journal of Broadcasting* 21 (1977): 460–472.

Paley, William S. *As It Happened: A Memoir.* Garden City, NY: Doubleday, 1979.

Paper, Lewis J. *Empire: William S. Paley and the Making of CBS News.* New York: St. Martin's, 1987.

Schiffer, Michael Brian. *The Portable Radio in American Life.* Tucson: University of Arizona Press, 1991.

Sklar, Rick. *Rocking America: An Insider's Story: How the All-Hit Radio Stations Took Over.* New York: St. Martin's, 1984.

Smulyan, Susan. *Selling Radio: The Commercialization of American Broadcasting, 1920–1934.* Washington, DC: Smithsonian, 1994.

Spalding, John W. "1928: Radio Becomes a Mass Advertising Medium." *Journal of Broadcasting* 8 (1964): 31–44.

Sperber, Ann M. *Murrow: His Life and Times.* New York: Freundlich, 1986.

Sterling, Christopher H., and John M. Kittross. *Stay Tuned: A Concise History of American Broadcasting,* 2nd ed. Belmont, CA: Wadsworth, 1990.

Vane, John Mac. *On the Air in World War II.* New York: Morrow, 1979.

Weaver, Pat. *The Best Seats in the House: The Golden Years of Radio and Television.* New York: Knopf, 1994.

Wertheim, Arthur Frank. *Radio Comedy.* New York: Oxford University Press, 1992.

# 3

# TELEVISION BROADCASTING:
# FROM 1884

Born in an experimenter's first startling idea of sending pictures through the air, broadcast television has changed society as radically as Gutenberg's invention of the printing press 500 years before. In this chapter, we explore how broadcast television grew from an idea to an institution. We see how the key TV process of scansion evolved; how business, politics, and economics helped to shape technical standards; and how programming evolved. We see how commercial networks rose to dominate television, just as they had radio; how broadcast television was affected by scandal and corruption; and how regulatory and citizen groups worked to reform television. We see how commercial broadcasting began to get what it had wanted for years—less regulation—and how less regulation also had a few surprises for commercial broadcasting—more competition and structural and financial changes in the TV business itself.

## 3.1 TECHNICAL STANDARDS AND GROWING PAINS

### 3.1.1 Scansion and the NTSC

Both television and radio originated as broadcast media. The development of over-the-air transmission, therefore, is the common history of both media—up to a point. That point derives from the major difference between radio and television: Whereas radio transmissions consist primarily of audio information, television transmissions must carry not only audio but also huge and complex amounts of video information. The need to develop a method of visual trasmission marks the point at which the histories of radio and television diverge.

The crucial technical process on which modern television is founded is **scansion.** Scansion is the systematic and continuous translation of minute parts of an image into specific electrical charges suitable for transmission and retranslation into a series of pictures that give the illusion of motion. In 1884, **Paul Nipkow,** a German, developed a device that would scan a picture (Box 3.1).

## BOX 3.1. THE NIPKOW SCANNING DISK

The Nipkow pickup device ("camera") consisted of a flat spinning disc (a) with a ring of small holes at increasing distances from the edge. When the disc was spun, each hole allowed, in its turn, a separate bit of picture information—light reflected from a part of the physical scene being scanned—to reach a phototube. This phototube generated a current that varied with the amount of light falling on it. Thus each bit of picture information was translated by the phototube into a specific electrical charge. These charges could be fed by wire to another scanning disc (b) that acted as a viewer. The electrical charges illuminated the viewer glow lamp or discharge lamp, and the viewer disc spun in synchronization with that of the pickup device. Someone facing the viewer scanning disc at eye level with the glow lamp would then see a rough image of the scene being scanned.

The photograph (c) shows an early research apparatus based on the scanning disc. The viewing disc is at the left; the pickup at the right.

(Photograph courtesy of AT&T Archives. Used by permission.)

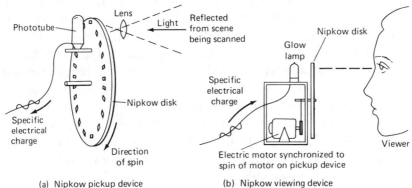

(a) Nipkow pickup device
(b) Nipkow viewing device

(c)

Nipkow's **scanning disc** set off a whole line of research based on **mechanical scansion**—television systems that required spinning discs. Among the researchers were E. E. Fournier, C. F. Jenkins, and John Baird. Fournier, a French scientist, experimented with the idea in the early 1900s. Then, Jenkins, an American, transmitted motion pictures over radio waves in June 1925. Only 6 months later in England, Baird demonstrated the first true live television picture on January 26, 1926 (Box 3.2). Baird began broadcasting in 1929. The British Broadcasting Corporation took over Baird's transmissions 3 years later and began regularly scheduled telecasts in 1936.

The future of television lay in **electronic scansion**, not mechanical. Dr. **Vladimir K. Zworykin** (Fig. 3.1), a Russian-born American, was a research scientist for Westinghouse in Pittsburgh. In 1923 Zworykin demonstrated a crude but working all-electronic TV system based on a camera tube that he named the **iconoscope**. Three years later, he developed a TV receiver using a form of cathode ray tube that he called a **kinescope**.

**FIG. 3.1. Dr. Vladimir K. Zworykin.** Dr. Zworykin holds an early model of his iconoscope. (Photo courtesy of RCA Corporation. Used by permission of General Electric Co.)

## BOX 3.2. JOHN BAIRD'S TELEVISION SYSTEM

Baird developed an intermediate film scanner television process. A film camera shot the scene. The film was not wound on a spool in the camera. Instead, it moved out of the camera immediately and directly into a film processor. As soon as it was developed, the film exited the processor and went into a video pickup, the primitive equivalent of today's telecine unit (*PRT,* 12.2.5).

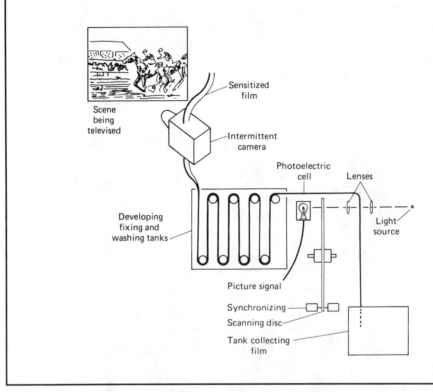

Television was still technically primitive by today's standards. The resolution (amount of picture information) was only 30 horizontal lines, as compared to the eventual U.S. standard of 525 lines. The picture was not sharp.

In 1930 the television research activities of Westinghouse, GE, and RCA were consolidated in **RCA's Electronic Research Laboratory,** Camden, New Jersey. This brought Zworykin together with some 40 other engineers. Work proceeded apace on the iconoscope, the cathode ray receiver, resolution, and other elements required for an electronic television system. In 1936 RCA signed on experimental television station W2XF in New York, and continued developmental work. By 1939 RCA achieved 441-line resolution, and that year the company inaugurated a limited but regular schedule of programming, including a live telecast of President Franklin D. Roosevelt opening the New York World's Fair.

At the same time, others had been active in electronic television's development—AT&T, CBS, Allen B. DuMont Laboratories, and Philco Radio and Television Corporation. By 1937, 17 experimental TV stations were operating.

Like Zworykin, **Philo Farnsworth** played a pivotal role in television research. He outlined a system of all-electronic television as early as 1922, when he was a high school student. Farnsworth filed a patent application for his system in 1927, demonstrated a working model of his **image-dissector camera** (Fig. 3.2) to financial backers in 1928, and by 1932 had built up his own strong patent structure in electronic television. Farnsworth did so much important basic research in the field that he was able to force RCA to break its tradition of never paying royalties, of buying patent rights instead. After Farnsworth refused to sell his patents outright, RCA, in 1939, entered into a licensing agreement for their use.

The issue of television transmission standards was controversial. In 1938, the Radio Manufacturers Association (RMA) recommended a set of standards to the FCC. The FCC soon found that the broadcasting business was really divided on the matter of standards. In 1940 the FCC, with the RMA, formed the **National Television System Committee** (NTSC) composed of engineers from various companies and interests. The NTSC drew up standards for television, and in April 1941 the FCC adopted them and authorized the start of commercial television on July 1, 1941.

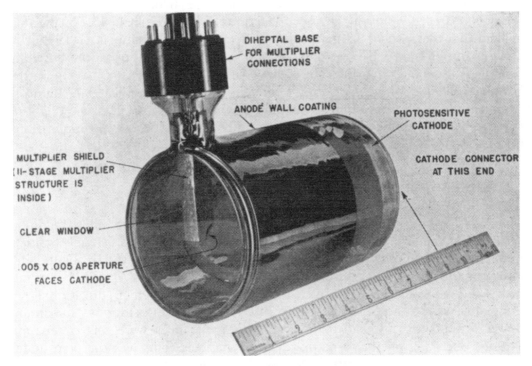

**FIG. 3.2. Farnsworth's all-electronic television system.** This diagram shows an image dissector. (*Source*: William C. Eddy, *Television: The Eyes of Tomorrow*, 1945.)

NTSC standards called for 18 channels located between 50 and 295 MHz in the very high frequency (VHF) band. Five years later the FCC reduced the number of channels to 13, then to 12 in 1948 by deleting channel one. Except for the number of channels, those 1941 standards were still in force over 50 years later:

- Each channel is 6 MHz wide.
- Amplitude modulation of video and frequency modulation of audio.
- Resolution of 525 horizontal lines.
- Thirty frames (complete pictures) per second.

In 1945 the FCC adopted its first table of assignments, allotting television channels among 140 cities for a total of 500 stations.

### 3.1.2 Freeze: 3½ Years

In 1942, just a year after the start of commercial television, the U.S. government imposed a wartime stoppage on station and receiving set construction. Of the 10 pioneer television stations, only six continued through the war. They broadcast 4 hours per week to the 7,000 or so sets in existence. Even after the stoppage was lifted in 1945, shortages of materials continued. Station and TV set construction did not resume for almost 2 years.

In 1947 television began to grow at a phenomenal rate (Fig. 3.3). Sales of receivers soared. TV station license applications flooded the FCC. It soon became evident that there would be many more applications than channels. In 1948, the commission ordered a **freeze** (halt) on processing station applications to allow time to work something out. The freeze was supposed to last 6 to 9 months. However, the issues involved were so complex that the freeze lasted 42 months. After a series of hearings, conferences, and negotiations, the FCC issued the *Sixth Report and Order*[1] on April 14, 1952, and in July, resumed processing applications for new stations. The freeze was over.

### 3.1.3 Thaw: Sixth Report and Order

The *Sixth Report and Order* was a new plan for U.S. television. Under the order, existing VHF channels 2 through 13 were to remain. Seventy additional channels numbered 14 to 83 were opened in the ultrahigh frequency (UHF) band. The table of assignments was revised to provide for 2,053 stations in 1,291 communities; 242 of these assignments were reserved for noncommercial educational use. Standards were established to reduce interference among stations—maximum power outputs were specified, and minimum distances were set to separate stations operating on the same or adjacent channels. This was the plan under which the television broadcast service would continue to operate for years.

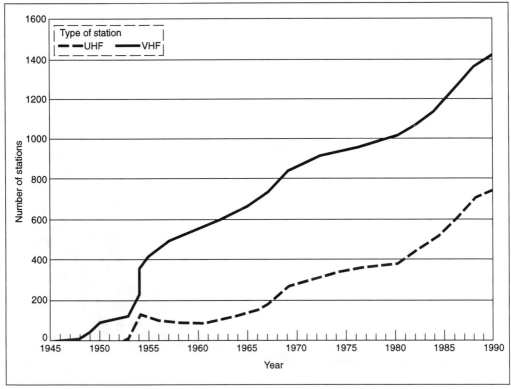

FIG. 3.3. **Growth of television stations.** The distance from the top curve to the baseline indicates total number of TV stations; that from the top curve to the second curve, number of VHF stations; and that from the second curve to the baseline, number of UHF stations. (*Source: Television and Cable Factbook.*)

### 3.1.4 Postfreeze Growth of Television

The freeze had limited the number of television stations to the 108 authorized prior to the halt on construction. During the 30 months following the end of the freeze, 308 television stations signed on the air. There were two good reasons for the rush to obtain television licenses—audiences and money. In 1948 there were 190,000 television sets in use in the United States. In 1955 the number was 32,500,000; in just 7 years, 65% of all homes had acquired at least one TV receiver.

This sudden growth in television caused a significant change in U.S. society. It had begun with radio. In centuries before the advent of the electronic mass media, people sought entertainment in the company of others. People gathered in varied groups whether in ancient coliseums or 19th-century medicine shows. Now, television brought entertainment into our homes on a day-to-day basis, often isolating us from the larger community. As we turned into "couch potatoes" settled in front of the TV, we became something even more important to broadcast television—an easily reached mass market. In 1948, total television station advertising revenue was $6.2 million; in 1955, station advertising revenue had multiplied over 6,000% to $372.2 million (Fig. 3.4).

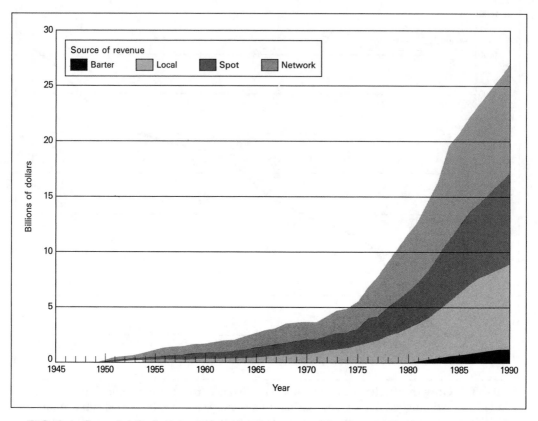

**FIG. 3.4. Growth of television advertising revenue.** The distance from top curve to base line indicates total amount of money spent on TV broadcast advertising; distances within each horizontal segment indicate amount spent in each of four categories. (*Sources*: McCann Erickson and TvB.)

The networks also grew rapidly. ABC, CBS, and NBC bought television stations and signed up affiliates. DuMont also formed a television network and looked for affiliates.

Network distribution required the broadband capacity of coaxial cable. One television channel was nearly six times wider than the entire AM broadcast band, much too wide for the limited capacity of normal telephone wire at the time.[2] Therefore, the networks expanded their reach as the telephone company extended its coaxial cable—from New York to Washington, DC, in 1946, to Boston in 1947, to the Midwest in early 1949, and to the West coast on September 10, 1951. Affiliated television stations that were not yet on the cable received network programming in the form of **kinescope film,** a prevideotape recording medium that involved making a filmed recording from a television screen as a program was telecast live.

By 1955, CBS and NBC had developed strong, nationwide lineups of affiliates in major markets. ABC had many fewer affiliates. Over three times as many stations carried the DuMont network as carried ABC, but DuMont had trouble getting affiliates in large cities and the network lost money. Additionally, the other three companies had radio networks whose earnings offset the losses of their TV networks; DuMont had no radio network. The year 1955 was DuMont's last as a TV network.

As the networks expanded, so did their advertising billings. In 1948 total network billings were $2.5 million; in 1955 they were $308.9 million, up 12,300%. Gradually, the growth slowed, but it did not stop, and overall television billings increased every year except during the early 1970s, when a legal ban on broadcast cigarette advertising went into effect.

### 3.1.5 Rise, Fall, and Rise of UHF Television

Many would-be broadcasters applied for the new UHF channels, but the cards were stacked against them. First, all other things being equal, **UHF signals do not travel as far** as VHF signals. The FCC, in an effort to compensate, purposely allowed an inequality. Transmitter power affects coverage area, so the commission allowed UHF stations to operate with 5 million watts, 16 times the maximum for any VHF station. However, no UHF transmitters were available to operate with such high power.

Second, **few receivers could pick up UHF channels.** The 108 stations that were on the air during the freeze were all VHF stations. During the 3½ years of the freeze, the number of homes with television sets had gone from 1.6 million in 1949 to 17.3 million in 1952. Naturally, the television sets were equipped to pick up VHF television stations only. When UHF stations went on the air, no one owned UHF-capable sets, so no one was able to watch the new stations. Advertising income, therefore, was difficult to obtain.

Third, **many of the UHF stations were independents,** not affiliated with a network. The major networks had grabbed most of the big-city VHF television stations as affiliates. The public, primarily interested in receiving network fare, did not buy the converters that were needed to adapt existing television sets to pick up both VHF and UHF stations. Manufacturers continued to build VHF-only television sets. They offered UHF capability as an extra-cost option on some models; few buyers of new sets were interested.

UHF licensees found it nearly impossible to compete with VHF stations. Most lost money (Fig. 3.5), and many let their stations go dark and turned licenses back to the FCC. By 1956 the pattern of UHF television station failure was clear, and the FCC became concerned.

First, the Commission tackled the transmitter problem. Transmission tests were conducted in 1961 and 1962. The FCC found that high-power transmission was feasible and did extend a UHF signal to a distance comparable to that of VHF.

The Commission could not force networks to affiliate with UHF stations, but it could do something about the lack of UHF-capable receivers. At the FCC's request, Congress adopted a law that empowered the Commission to require all-channel tuning. Starting April 30, 1964, every new TV set sold in the United

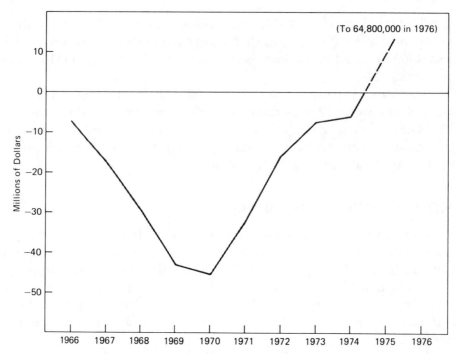

FIG. 3.5. UHF television station income: The long climb toward profitability. (*Source*: FCC.)

States had to be able to receive all VHF and UHF channels. Six years later, the commission adopted rules to make UHF tuning comparable to that of VHF; receiver design now had to be such that UHF channels were as easy and convenient to select as VHF.

The FCC took other steps, dealing with both transmitter and receiver, to make the quality of the UHF signal comparable to VHF. The cable must-carry rule (*PRT*, 3.5.2.1) helped, too. Cable systems had to carry all local stations, including UHF stations, and the systems usually placed VHF and UHF stations next to each other on the dial, making one as easy to tune as the other. Eventually, FCC efforts to make commercial UHF television viable paid off. During the 1970s UHF TV stations as a group lost less money each year until 1975, when they finally showed a profit.

### 3.1.6 Color Television and Compatibility

Color television experimentation began as early as the late 1920s. Subsequently, various companies worked on and promoted different systems of color TV, but the main rivalry was between **RCA's dot sequential system** and **CBS's field sequential** system.

In 1949, as a result of a petition by CBS to the FCC, the major television interests demonstrated their color television systems. CBS's system was **mechanical.** Largely the work of Peter Goldmark, the CBS field sequential system used three filters—red, blue, and green. The filters rotated past the camera pickup tube in rapid succession. When the filters were synchronized with similar filters on the receiver picture tube, the viewer's eye would see the full range of natural colors. Originally, the field sequential system needed an 18 MHz channel, but CBS refined it to operate in the 6 MHz width of existing channels. The field sequential system, despite its excellent color reproduction, was incompatible; monochrome (black-and-white) receivers displayed a distorted picture when tuned to a field sequential color transmission. However, existing monochrome television sets could be adapted to receive black-and-white versions of color transmissions for about $10, and to receive color pictures for about $45! Further, CBS contended that the system could eventually be refined to be completely electronic, eliminating the mechanical color disc.

The FCC adopted the CBS color system effective November 20, 1950. The television business was unhappy because the system was mechanical and incompatible. Before the FCC order could go into effect, RCA filed suit against its adoption. A number of manufacturers and service companies did the same. The suit delayed implementation of the order for 6 months while the case worked its way up the federal court system. In May 1951 the Supreme Court upheld the FCC.[3]

In October, color receiver production was halted because of the Korean War. CBS had broadcast the first network color program with the new system in June and continued technical development. Congress questioned the delay in introduction of color television, and in March 1953 the war ban was lifted.

Meanwhile, RCA and its allies had been busy. Another NTSC was formed to study and recommend standards for an electronic, compatible color television system. By mid-1953, NTSC had completed its work, and RCA petitioned the FCC to adopt NTSC standards. In December, the FCC approved the NTSC all-electronic system and thus rejected the CBS mechanical system.

The first RCA color sets were expensive. RCA's basic color television receiver with a 15-inch screen retailed for $1,000 in 1954. (Remember the now-rejected CBS system would have cost only $45 to convert a black-and-white set to color!) In addition, very few stations were equipped for color telecasting. The public did not rush out to trade in old monochrome receivers for new color sets. In 1955 there were only 5,000 color sets in use in the entire United States (Fig. 3.6). Even 10 years later, less than 5% of all television homes were equipped for color. In 1953, CBS and NBC each carried over 22 hours of color programming weekly. Both cut back, and by 1958 only NBC still broadcast a regular schedule of color programs.

In the mid-1960s, prices of color receivers dropped somewhat, and sales picked up. Sales of color sets for the first 9 months of 1965 doubled those of the same period in 1964. The lead oxide vidicon camera tube was introduced, resulting in better color cameras. Networks increased color telecasting and, in September 1966, began full-color programming in prime time. Stations installed color equipment; national advertisers demanded it. By 1967 it was clear that color

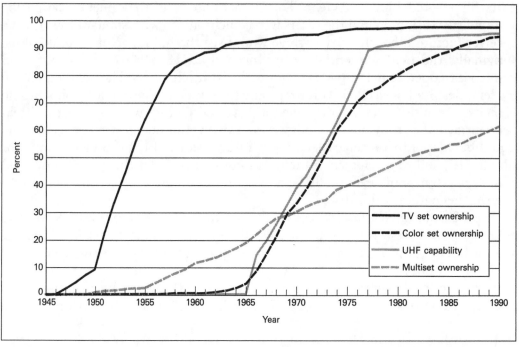

**FIG. 3.6. Growth of American homes with television.** The top curve indicates the percentage of all U.S. households equipped with at least one working television receiver; the other curves show households that can receive UHF stations, that have at least one color receiver, and that have two or more working receivers. (*Sources*: Arbitron, NBC, and Nielsen.)

television was an unstoppable trend. By 1969, one third of all television homes in the United States were equipped for color, and 30 years later virtually all TV sets being sold were color.

## 3.2 TELEVISION PROGRAMMING EVOLVES

### 3.2.1 Early TV Station Programming

In the earliest days of television, there was no large backlog of syndicated programs to fill a station's schedule. For much local programming, stations used old feature films. These were the only films Hollywood had made available to its young rival medium, so television acquired an **old-movies** reputation. Some stations even ran silent films, adding narration and sound tracks. Some stations used **short musical films**—well-known bands, vocalists, and singing groups—and put them together in the form of a visual disc jockey show, anticipating a video format that MTV would reinvent 30 years later. Most stations ran lots of film **travelogues.**

However, when the network was not feeding programs and all the old movies and travelogues had been aired, a station had little choice other than to devise and air its own programs. There was no videotape, so local programs were all **live.**

The stations tried **local production** of all types of shows—soap operas; cooking programs; interview shows; the man/lady who played the piano/organ/both and sang/recited poetry; local talent shows; and children's programs, hosted by Captain/Uncle Somebody-or-other, featuring old black-and-white movie cartoons of Farmer Alfalfa or Felix the Cat.

### 3.2.2 Development of Television Network Entertainment Programming

At the network level there was much experimentation, attempts to find programming suitable for the visual medium. These efforts, however, had to await the spread of AT&T's coaxial cable. In June 1946 the Joe Louis–Billy Conn fight for the heavyweight boxing championship was broadcast on an ad hoc network to four East Coast cities. Sponsored by the Gillette Safety Razor Company, the broadcast reached an estimated 100,000 viewers and was reported to have convinced skeptics that television was here to stay.

Bristol-Myers became the first advertiser to sponsor a network television series. It was called *Geographically Speaking,* consisted of travel films taken and narrated by Mrs. Carveth Wells, and started in October 1946 on NBC. Two months later Mrs. Wells ran out of film, and the series ended. At that time, NBC was a two-station network.

In the early days a network sometimes took a radio series and made an **adaptation** of it for television. Some series were **simulcast**; that is, aired concurrently on both radio and television. Soon, the first prime-time hit programs emerged (Fig. 3.7). In 1948, the *Texaco Star Theater,* a comedy-variety show, went on the air, launching the television career of Milton Berle. "Uncle Miltie" was so popular that he became known as "Mr. Television." That same year, *Toast of the Town* began, produced and hosted by Ed Sullivan. This variety program was almost straight vaudeville. Later renamed the *Ed Sullivan Show,* it ran for 22 years; for 10 of those years, it was one of the 20 most popular programs. Sid Caesar and Imogene Coca first teamed up in 1949 on the *Admiral Broadway Revue,* carried by the combined NBC and DuMont networks. They moved to NBC's new *Your Show of Shows* in 1950, and people deserted restaurants, theaters, and parties on Saturday nights to watch their comedy.

There was some reliance on film programming, but much network television was **live and produced in New York.** As today, most early dramatic programs were episodic series—a complete story each week, evolving out of the same situation, with the same main characters.

*3.2.2.1 Live Anthology Drama.*   During the early 1950s, another type of dramatic program developed, the **anthology series.** Here, the program title remained the same, but each program featured a completely different play—different characters, different actors, different stories, and different situations. The programs included *Philco Playhouse* (which later alternated with *Goodyear Playhouse*), *Kraft Television Theater, Playhouse 90,* and *Studio One.* The plays they produced

(a)

(b)

(c)

**FIG. 3.7. The first network superstars.** (a) Milton Berle. (b) Ed Sullivan. (c) Sid Caesar and Imogene Coca. (Photos a and c courtesy of the National Broadcasting Company, Inc. Photo b, CBS Photo Archives. Used by permission.)

catapulted their young authors into prominence—Paddy Chayefsky, Rod Serling, Reginald Rose, Tad Mosel, Horton Foote, and others. Some of the plays were subsequently made into fine motion pictures—*Requiem for a Heavyweight, Marty, Dino, Twelve Angry Men,* and *Patterns.*

The anthology series reached their peak in 1953. By 1956 they were all but gone, victims of changing audience taste, sponsor script interference, and the economics of syndication. This brief period of live anthology series drama is often referred to as the **golden age of television drama.** This may overstate the case; much—perhaps most—of the writing was mundane. But the plays were live, they were theater, and they were peculiarly television. When they were good, they had a quality that transcended their time, which is still evident today.

**3.2.2.2 Trends and Synthesis.**    Trends in network programming emerged in the early and mid-1950s. CBS had benefited in radio from Bill Paley's 1948 talent raid (*PRT,* 2.2.3). When the time came to beef up its prime-time TV schedule, CBS stuck with success. Its TV forms and formats were those of radio, **fully sponsored, regularly scheduled programs.** Its programming nucleus was its stable of big-name comedians. CBS's strategy worked, and by 1953 it had captured the lead in prime-time network ratings. CBS held that lead year after year, almost continually.

NBC's programming reflected the thinking of **Sylvester L. "Pat" Weaver** (Fig. 3.8). Weaver, a former advertising executive, joined NBC in 1949 as vice-president in charge of television. In December 1953 he became president of NBC. Control of network programs by sponsors and their advertising agencies, a practice that developed in radio, had transferred to television; Weaver now worked to shift control to the network. He pushed for what he called the **magazine concept**—the network would own and control programs, advertisers could buy time for commercial messages within programs, and each program would have a number of different advertisers. Using this concept, NBC started the *Today* and *Tonight* shows, which are both still in existence.[4]

Another Weaver idea was the **spectacular.** Spectaculars were one-time programs made with extra care and money. Preceded by greater-than-normal publicity, they were designed to stand out from the usual programming, to create talk and excitement.

ABC, the weakest of the three major radio networks, began video operations in 1948 as an even weaker television network. In 1951 ABC entered into negotiations for a merger with United Paramount Theaters, the former exhibition arm of Paramount Pictures. The merger was completed in 1953, bringing Paramount's working capital and former Paramount executive **Leonard Goldenson** to ABC. Goldenson used his Hollywood contacts to get the major studios interested in program production.

Using themes and formulas popular with movie audiences—cowboys, cops-and-robbers, detective stories—ABC played a catch-up game. Its first big successes were *Cheyenne,* produced by Warner Brothers, and *Disneyland,* produced by the

(a)

(b)

(c)

**FIG. 3.8. Pat Weaver's programming innovations.** (a) Dave Garroway, first host of *Today*, and J. Fred Muggs. (b) Betty Hutton in *Satins and Spurs*, first NBC "spectacular." (c) The first *Tonight* cast: Gene Rayburn, Steve Allen (host), Eydie Gorme, and Steve Lawrence (at piano). (Photos courtesy of the National Broadcasting Company, Inc. Used by permission.)

Walt Disney organization. ABC-TV based its programming strategies on action-adventure dramatic series—*The Untouchables, 77 Sunset Strip, The Rebel, The Rifleman,* and *Hawaiian Eye.* All were produced on film instead of live. All were violent, but all attracted audiences.

ABC made a major commitment to sports coverage. Starting in 1959, the network acquired television rights to numerous sporting events. It also acquired Sports Programs, Inc., a production company. One of the company's young producers was **Roone Arledge.** Originally hired to produce football telecasts, Arledge brought flair and imagination to all types of sports coverage; under his leadership ABC Sports helped push the network closer to its competitive goals.

Despite having weaker affiliates in large markets and fewer affiliates overall, ABC-TV managed to close the ratings gap between itself and the other networks. In the 1975–1976 season, ABC-TV took the lead in overall prime-time ratings and did not lose it until the early 1980s. However, by this time, ABC had picked up stronger affiliates, and its days of running fourth in a three-network race seemed to be over.

Each of these trends influenced the overall shape of network programming. Regularly scheduled programs formed the basis of the prime-time schedule. Over the years, all three networks telecast **specials** (the successor term to *spectacular*) and *Today* and *Tonight*-style programs. Film production displaced live production of prime-time programs (although economics resulting from rising production costs later forced emphasis on videotape production). The television production center shifted from New York to Hollywood, and the action-adventure series became a staple of network prime-time programming.

Finally, few programs were completely sponsored. The networks had moved purposefully to take control of programming, as urged by Pat Weaver (and spurred at least in part by the quiz-show scandals; *PRT,* 3.3.3). At the same time, the cost of program production—already many times that of radio—had risen so much that most advertisers could not afford to pay for an entire program. In addition, Procter and Gamble, television's largest advertiser, adopted a policy of spreading commercials throughout a number of programs. The result was participation sponsorship—the network controlled the programs, and advertisers bought commercial positions within them.

### 3.2.2.3 *Compared to Radio.*    Most of radio's major program types proved successful in television. Some that were long-running features on network radio, however, were not regularly scheduled on television and appeared only sporadically as specials after the 1950s—for example, experimental drama, fine arts programs, and programming for minority interests such as the old NBC radio program for farmers, *National Farm and Home Hour.*

Prime-time television series proved to be, on the average, much shorter lived than radio series. A television series was a veteran if it survived 5 years (Fig. 3.9), but many prime-time radio series ran 10 or 15 years or even longer.

(a)

(b)

FIG. 3.9. Long-running TV programs. (a) *The Red Skelton Show,* 1951–1971. (b) *I Love Lucy,* 1951–1971: Vivian Vance, William Frawley, Desi Arnaz, Lucille Ball. (Cont'd.)

(c)

(d)

FIG. 3.9. (cont'd.) (c) *The Jackie Gleason Show*, 1952–1970. (d) *Bonanza*, 1959–1973: Dan Blocker, Lorne Greene, Pernell Roberts, Michael Landon. (Photographs a, b, and c, CBS Photo Archives. Photograph d courtesy of the National Broadcasting Company, Inc. Used by permission.)

Because its program turnover was higher, television was more cyclical than was radio. A theatrical film or a new program type became popular, and it spawned a host of imitators. Situation comedies and dramas multiplied by means of the spin-off—secondary characters from one series would become the basis upon which new series were built. *All in the Family* spawned *Maude* in 1972 and *The Jeffersons* in 1975; *Maude* spun off *Good Times* in 1974. *Dallas* spun off *Knot's Landing* in 1979. The 1981 theatrical film *Raiders of the Lost Ark* inspired at least two prime-time 1982 series, *Bring 'Em Back Alive* and *Tales of the Gold Monkey.* Jake left *Beverly Hills 90210* in 1992 for *Melrose Place.* When *Cheers* went off NBC in 1993, it left behind *Frasier.* And Fox's *The X-Files* gave birth to *Millennium* in fall 1996.

Television, on the other hand, popularized program forms that did not exist on radio, such as children's animated cartoons and feature films. First introduced on network prime-time television in 1961, feature films proved to be extremely popular. They also captured and held audiences for long periods of time. This inspired the networks to lengthen other prime-time programming to 1 hour, 90 minutes, and even up to 4 hours on special occasions. Sports events proved much more popular on television than on radio, from the early *Friday Night Boxing* and wrestling programs to sophisticated coverage of football, baseball, golf, tennis, Olympic games, and other sports.

### 3.2.3 Development of Television Network Informational Programming

Forerunners of the early evening network news programs began in the late 1940s (Fig. 3.10). CBS's *Douglas Edwards With the News* went on first in 1948. NBC's *Camel News Caravan* with John Cameron Swayze began the next year, and ABC and DuMont soon followed with their own newscasts. These newscasts were 15 minutes long, and the networks contracted with theatrical newsreel companies and other film organizations for news film.

The networks strengthened their news operations during the 1950s (Fig. 3.11), adding newscasts at other times during the broadcast day as well as resources and personnel. CBS and NBC increased the length of their evening newscasts to 30 minutes in 1963; ABC followed 4 years later. Polls revealed that the public saw television as the most relied-on news medium as early as 1959 and as the most believable news medium by 1961. Polls continued to show the same reliance and believability in succeeding years.

In 1976 all three commercial television networks prepared to lengthen evening newscasts to 1 hour. Affiliates protested, saying expanded newscasts would take away 30 minutes of valuable, salable local time. Four years later, the networks again announced plans to expand their evening newscasts; again the affiliates protested. Although not able to lengthen the early evening newscasts, network news organizations did eventually expand their program offerings in other ways. Short summary newscasts—no longer than 60 seconds—were added during prime time as well as long-form news programs. These were all in addition to other regular news programming, such as *Today, 60 Minutes,* and *Good Morning America.*

(a)                                                    (b)

FIG. 3.10. **Early network news programs.** (a) *Douglas Edwards with the News.* (b) John Cameron Swayze on *Camel News Caravan.* (Photo a, CBS Photo Archives. Photo b courtesy of the National Broadcasting Company, Inc. Used by permission.)

Broadcast news also expanded in two other areas—the documentary and on-the-spot coverage. Edward R. Murrow, along with Fred Friendly, began network television's first news documentary series, *See It Now,* in 1951 and established standards by which television documentaries are still measured (Box 3.3). NBC broadcast its *Victory At Sea* series in 1952, recounting U.S. naval operations in World War II. ABC's documentary efforts began in the late 1950s. By 1961 all three networks produced stimulating, vital news documentaries. Many local stations produced documentaries, too.

Some of television's finest work was live coverage of various events—national political conventions; elections; presidential inaugurations; the Kefauver Crime Committee Hearings in 1951; the Army–McCarthy Hearings in 1954; the debates between presidential candidates in 1960 (the so-called "great debates") and then, starting in 1976, every 4 years; the deaths and funerals of President John F. Kennedy, Senator Robert Kennedy, and Reverend Martin Luther King, Jr.; U.S. space efforts; the Watergate and Iran–Contra hearings; the Grenada and Panama expeditions; and the Persian Gulf War.

During the 1970s and 1980s, the networks lost impetus in long-form documentary production and live coverage. First, they cut back on frequency of full-length documentaries. Later, they gave up extended, live coverage almost completely, allowing Cable News Network (CNN) and C-SPAN to fill the void.

(a)

(b)

**FIG. 3.11. Network news stars.** (a) After doing well during the 1956 political convention telecasts, Chet Huntley and David Brinkley took over the evening news spot from John Cameron Swayze. Highly popular with viewers, NBC's *The Huntley–Brinkley Report* ran for 14 years. (b) In 1962 Walter Cronkite replaced Douglas Edwards as the CBS evening newscaster. Cronkite would remain in that job for two decades, helping move CBS past NBC in the news ratings. (Photo a courtesy of the National Broadcasting Company, Inc. Photo b, CBS Photo Archives. Used by permission.)

## BOX 3.3. DOCUMENTARY AND LIVE COVERAGE IMPACT: SENATOR JOSEPH MCCARTHY

Even in television's earliest days, documentaries and live coverage had the power to enhance the public weal, to help citizens keep a check on their government and uncover rogues and wrongdoing, hype and hypocrisy. Such was the case with Senator Joseph McCarthy.
(Photo Source: UPI/BETTMAN.)

In 1953–1954, Ed Murrow and Fred Friendly did what others in television news could not or would not do. They focused the journalistic eye of several *See It Now* programs on McCarthy-inspired accusations of guilt by association. As discussed in *PRT,* 2.3.3.1, McCarthyism was founded on a fear of communist subversion that had grown, cancerlike, into a national paranoia. Its basic structure was (a) a presumption (b) of guilt (c) by association; its mechanism, simple—you were guilty if accused. It had a built-in defense; those who opposed the methods of Senator McCarthy and his allies were themselves branded "un-American" or worse. The accused lost their jobs and could not find work. They included people in radio and television, as well as other areas of entertainment.

**BOX 3.3** (cont'd.)

On March 9, 1954, Murrow and Friendly did a program on McCarthy himself, juxtaposing excerpts of various speeches the senator had made to show the inconsistencies and illogic of McCarthy's rhetoric. Messages flooded into CBS, overwhelmingly favorable toward the program. Senator McCarthy's rebuttal, a personal attack on Murrow, was broadcast by CBS on April 6. However, McCarthy's reply was such that it inadvertently proved Murrow's points, and the mail ran two-to-one in favor of Murrow.

Two weeks later, ABC and DuMont televised hearings before the Senate Permanent Subcommittee on Investigations over a dispute between McCarthy and the U.S. Army. The hearings ran 36 days, exposing the real, live McCarthy to many for the first time. On the 30th day, McCarthy launched a vicious, unprovoked, and irrelevant attack on a junior member of the Boston law firm of Joseph N. Welch, the Army's lawyer. The hastening of McCarthy's fall seemed to date from that point. The Senate voted to censure him later that year. In May 1957, he died.

## 3.3 TELEVISION PROBLEMS AND SCANDALS IN THE 1950s

Television, like radio, suffered its share of problems. Many involved questionable ethics and occurred during the 1950s—so many problems that the 1950s may have been the most shameful, scandal-ridden 10 years in the short history of radio and television. Television's share included plugola, FCC corruption, and the quiz show scandals. As we will see, reaction to these problems would eventually lead to an era of reform and activism.

### 3.3.1 Plugola: Nonadvertising Advertising

**Plugola** was discovered a few years before radio's payola revelations (*PRT,* 2.3.3.3). If a certain product was used on camera in a television program, the publicity agent for the product would pay the program's writers and directors. This constituted, in effect, advertising. However, the audience did not realize it was advertising, nor was it so informed, a clearly deceptive and unethical practice. The Communications Act required that licensees inform the audience when their stations broadcast program material provided or paid for by others, but that requirement apparently did not apply to the TV creative community, those who made, produced, and distributed programming.

### 3.3.2 Government Corruption

In 1957 the Committee on Interstate and Foreign Commerce of the U.S. House of Representatives decided to look into the performance of regulatory agencies under its jurisdiction. One of these was the FCC. Bernard Schwartz, a professor from New York University, was hired as chief counsel. When Schwartz produced embarrassing findings, Commerce Committee members tried to impede his investigation. The committee finally fired him in 1958, but Schwartz released his findings to the press.

Schwartz found several pieces of damning information:

- FCC commissioners were reimbursed for the same trip by both government and broadcasters.
- Commissioners received gifts from broadcasters—television sets and vacation trips.
- One commissioner, Richard A. Mack, had sold his FCC vote to an applicant for a contested Miami television channel.
- Representative Oren Harris, who chaired the House Commerce Committee, had paid a cash total of just $500 for a one-quarter interest in an Arkansas television station. The FCC had previously denied the station's application for an increase in power. After Harris acquired his equity, the station again applied, and the FCC approved the increase.

Schwartz's revelations led to the resignation of FCC Chair John C. Doerfer and Commissioner Mack. Harris, however, went on to a federal judgeship.

### 3.3.3 Quiz Show Scandals

Then there were the **quiz show scandals** (Fig. 3.12). *The $64,000 Question*, first of the big-money quiz shows, started on CBS-TV in 1955. The amount of prize money, the difficult questions, the suspense of the game itself and the gimmicky setting all helped make *The $64,000 Question* popular. Naturally, it spawned imitators. By July 1955, 3 of the top 10 programs in audience ratings were big-money quiz shows.

Four years and several government investigations later, the truth came out. The shows had been rigged—contestants given answers in advance—on a regular basis to enhance, said the producers, their "entertainment value." Ten people pleaded guilty to perjury for lying during the investigations, and the careers of a dozen or so other people were ruined. The networks canceled the shows and tightened program control.

### 3.4 TELEVISION REFORM AND ACTIVISM IN THE 1960S AND 1970s

Reaction to the problems and scandals of the 1950s was broadly based. It was characterized by activism—activism on the part of regulators to see that broadcasters served the public interest, and activism on the part of educators and others to provide an alternative television service, activism on the part of citizen groups to ensure that stations responded to the needs and interests of the communities to which they were licensed.

**FIG. 3.12.** *The $64,000 Question.* Host Hal March and a guest. (CBS Photo Archives. Used by permission.)

### 3.4.1 Regulators "Discover" the *Public* Interest

The FCC started it. Beginning in 1960, there was to be a **new approach to regulation**; the public interest would come before the broadcasters' private interest. There would be no more back scratching between the regulators and the regulated. The FCC issued the "1960 Programming Policy Statement"[5] defining what was needed in programming to meet the public interest. Licensees were to ascertain (find out with certainty) the needs of the communities they served, and then program to meet those needs. An FCC Complaints and Compliance Division was created to receive and investigate complaints from the public. The Commission developed a license application form that required detailed information on public-interest programming. Congress amended the Communications Act to make payola and plugola illegal and to prohibit rigged quiz shows.

In 1961 Newton N. Minow (Fig. 3.13) was appointed to chair the FCC. He told broadcasters their programming was "a vast wasteland" and warned they would have to live up to their promises regarding programming on license renewal applications. The FCC subsequently stepped up disciplinary actions against erring broadcast stations.

### 3.4.2 Noncommercial Broadcasting Goes "Public"

Noncommercial broadcasting began to develop into a **viable alternative to commercial broadcasting.** Congress passed the Educational Television Facilities Act in 1962 to build and improve stations. The Carnegie Commission on Educational Television, a blue-ribbon citizen panel, issued an influential report on funding and improvement of programming in February 1967. In the same year Congress, acting on recommendations of the Carnegie Commission, passed the Public Broadcasting Act which created the Corporation for Public Broadcasting (CPB). CPB was to serve as the funding agency for programming. Two years later, the Public Broadcasting Service was formed to distribute television programming. In 1970 NPR was set up to produce and distribute radio programming.

**FIG. 3.13. Newton N. Minow, III.** Minow chaired the FCC from March 1961 to June 1963. (*Source*: UPI/CORBIS-BETTMAN.)

As a result of these changes, noncommercial broadcasting improved and increased facilities and programming, attracted audiences, and even began to influence the programming of commercial broadcasters. In the process, the generic term changed from educational broadcasting to **public broadcasting.**

### 3.4.3 The Public Impacts Broadcasters

Citizen groups forced the FCC and broadcast licensees to deal with them directly. In the 1966 and 1969 **WLBT cases**[6] a federal court of appeals ruled that the FCC had to allow representatives of the public to participate in license renewal proceedings and had to give weight to their testimony in arriving at decisions. The court's ruling in the WLBT cases touched off a rash of citizen-group challenges to station license renewals. Stations entered into negotiations with the groups, discussing policies, soliciting suggestions, and making agreements; in this way, the public could directly influence programming. In the 1970s the FCC adopted rules, the net effect of which was to encourage the public to take a more active interest in license renewal proceedings.

*3.4.3.1 Use of the Fairness Doctrine.*   Citizen groups filed fairness doctrine complaints about commercials and other aspects of broadcast programming. According to a 1949 FCC statement,[7] a broadcast licensee whose station aired one side of a controversial public issue had to ensure that the other side was presented, too; this was the **fairness doctrine.** Now citizen groups attempted to use this requirement in a variety of situations and, thus, expand the types of issues to which the fairness doctrine applied.

*3.4.3.2 Pressures on Programming.*   Some groups functioned on the national level. They noted research that showed increasing evidence of links between exposure to televised violence and aggressive behavior in the viewer. There had been concern over violent content for decades. Recent anecdotal evidence, including attempts on the life of a president of the United States, seemed to illustrate the legitimacy of such concern.[8]

These national groups also took note of changes in TV programming. Cable TV, particularly premium channels, had fewer content restrictions than did broadcasters and could schedule more "daring" programming. With respect to feature-length theatrical films, for example, Home Box Office (HBO) could run a movie intact, whereas broadcasters would have to make cuts for reasons of language, nudity, and other such taboos. During the mid-1970s, cable programmers also started attracting audiences away from broadcasting in what would soon become significant numbers. It was about this time that the NAB suspended the programming standards of its Television Code (*PRT,* 16.2.1). The broadcast networks said they would continue to screen their own programming and apply to it their own standards, which were supposedly higher than those of the Code. Nonetheless, *All in the Family* and other so-called "social consciousness" situation comedies had, for several years, been dealing with previously banned themes. And now the sexual content of network programming seemed to increase. So while prime-time network audiences saw the lead on *Maude* get an abortion and go through menopause, they also watched as *Three's Company* and *Soap* increased the level of sexual innuendo.

Citizen groups, worried over the impact of such programming, worked to curb the sex-and-violence trend. They used publicity, complaints to the FCC, and meetings with network officials. The groups themselves were varied, ranging from the American Medical Association to the PTA and Action for Children's Television.

**3.4.3.3 Mobilization of the Religious Right.**   Activism came to broadcasting in a quite different form also. During the 1970s Christian evangelists turned to television to reach audiences. They packaged video ministries in slick, often star-studded productions and paid stations to carry them. Their audiences were small but intensely loyal. Audience contributions financed not only the programs but also ancillary organizations such as colleges, broadcast stations, and theme parks. Most television evangelists professed fundamentalist theology and conservative social values. Some took advantage of a trend toward political conservatism and "born-again" faith that swept the country to increase their influence. They played active roles in politics and they also joined an increasing number of voices that called for the television networks to eliminate gratuitous depictions of sex from programming.

## 3.5 TELEVISION'S RETRENCHMENT IN THE 1980s

Despite all this reaction, television prospered. Costs, particularly programming costs, climbed alarmingly, but so did audience levels and advertising billings. Advertising rates went up every year, and advertisers had little choice but to pay the increases. After all, television pulled in the people. There was no lack of advertisers; networks came close to selling every prime-time commercial position, and stations adopted rate cards that encouraged advertisers to bid against each other for time. If you wanted video advertising, broadcast television—primarily network broadcast television—was the only game in town.

However, the winds of change had already begun to blow. By 1990, it was apparent that these winds had caused at least two radical alterations in the structure of commercial television broadcasting. First, new competitive elements had begun to whittle away network dominance of audiences and advertising dollars. Second, Wall Street had discovered broadcasting. That, too, affected the networks.

A major factor that cleared windbreaks and so made possible these alterations was a series of FCC actions. For years the broadcast business had continually and repeatedly requested these same actions—the lifting of government regulation.

### 3.5.1 Deregulation: Good and Bad

As the years passed, the FCC had made more and more regulations. The regulated businesses complained of hours and money spent on FCC requirements—checking equipment, filling in forms, completing reports, and establishing and updating files. Broadcasters began to feel relief in the 1970s. U.S. President Jimmy Carter announced plans to lift regulation on transportation businesses—trucking, railroads, and airlines. The FCC, in turn, started proceedings to do the same for communications media. The first major achievement of FCC deregulation came in 1981, when the Commission deleted certain requirements for commercial radio broadcasters; 3 years later, similar requirements were lifted from commercial TV.

Deregulation signaled the end of public-interest reform in the FCC, at least for a time. The Commission even eliminated some of their 1960s industry cleanup provisions. For example, the FCC did away with formal community ascertainment procedures. In a general reorganization, the Commission replaced the Complaints and Compliance Division, which had been established to accept comment from the public, with a lower level complaints branch. The FCC adopted a "postcard-size" license renewal form and, in the process, eliminated the requirement for licensees to provide information on the public-interest aspects of their programming.

Among the FCC's many deregulatory actions, the most conspicuous had to be its elimination of the fairness doctrine. The fairness doctrine ensured that, when a station's broadcasts dealt with significant controversial issues, the public had opportunity to hear opposing viewpoints. Mark Fowler, appointed by President Ronald Reagan to chair the Commission in 1981, accelerated the process of deregulation. Fowler made the deletion of fairness a primary goal. Although fairness remained intact (if somewhat unused) during his tenure, the Commission did lay the groundwork for its deletion. In August 1987, 3 months after Dennis Patrick had succeeded Fowler to the chair, the Commission voted to cease enforcing the 46-year-old doctrine. Several citizen groups filed court appeals, and powerful congressional leaders vowed to turn fairness into law. None succeeded.

For years, broadcasters had argued for less regulation. They based their arguments on First Amendment grounds and asked for the same freedom from regulation that newspapers enjoyed. They said that competition—the marketplace—should determine programming, not "some Washington bureaucrat's" idea of the public interest.

In theory, deregulation seemed the answer to broadcasters' prayers, but they found that in practice it went further than they wished. The FCC agreed with the marketplace concept and applied it across the board. After all, if broadcasters were to be free to compete in the marketplace, there had to be an open marketplace in which they could compete. If there was to be a marketplace, the Commission had to lift regulatory barriers to make entry easier and more available, to allow more people a chance to compete. Therefore, the FCC used the marketplace concept as rationale to reduce regulation, to add more stations, and to authorize new electronic mass media that would compete with broadcasting for audiences and advertising dollars.

Under the marketplace concept, electronic mass media outlets were simply businesses. If an outlet produced a product (in most cases, the audiences, which they attracted with programming) that others would buy (in this case, advertisers who paid to have their messages exposed to the audiences), it would generate enough revenue to exceed expenses, and it would survive. If not, it would die and go out of business. Communications Act requirements for licensing in the "public interest" were either redefined in marketplace terms or ignored. It was the antithesis of a philosophy of regulation, dominant for a half-century and approved by the federal court system, that recognized radio frequencies as scarce natural resources in the public domain—resources that justified an agency of the "government of the people" to ask licensees what programming, in addition to that designed primarily to make money, would they provide solely to enlighten and inform the public. Those days had passed. Regulatory dialogue would move away from the common weal (i.e., the good of all) to the bottom line.

### 3.5.2 Development of New Competition

Broadcasters now faced less regulation but more competition. Seven elements in this competition directly impacted the development of traditional broadcasting: cable television, independent programming, increasing numbers of stations, program availability, subscription programming, home video, and new broadcast networks.

*3.5.2.1 Competition from Cable Television.*    The cable business first developed as **community antenna television** (CATV) systems during the 1948 to 1952 freeze on new television construction. These first systems brought television broadcast signals to communities where stations could not be picked up directly off the air. They carried only the signals of broadcast stations.

At first, television licensees thought cable was a good idea. They were glad to see their signals extended to new audiences and improved in areas with poor reception. As cable evolved, however, it added services and moved into areas that could already receive television stations directly off the air. At that point, cable had introduced competition to broadcast television and, according to broadcasters, not very fair competition at that.

Broadcasters complained of **signal importation** from distant stations. Local stations found themselves competing for local audiences with stations miles away. Even worse was **leapfrogging,** when a cable system carried the signal of a distant station instead of a local station.

Broadcasters were partially mollified when a number of legal requirements were imposed on cable systems. These included **syndicated exclusivity** (syndex), **network nonduplication,** and **must-carry** rules. Syndex required systems to blank out the signals of distant TV stations when those stations carried the same syndicated programs as local stations; network nonduplication did the same thing for current network programs. Must-carry required cable systems to carry the signals of local television stations.

But, broadcasters complained, that still did not relieve what they felt to be the basic injustice in the whole system: cable television was founded on the signals of television stations. The product that comprised the very heart of a cable system's service was the group of broadcast signals it carried. The entities that created these signals, the broadcasters, had to pay for the programming they transmitted. Yet, the cable system got this programming at no charge, then sold it to subscribers. In effect, television licensees actually financed and created the vital component of the competition's product—for which the competition received payment. To make things worse, cable operators added more and more nonbroadcast networks to their systems, networks such as USA Network and MTV, which the operators paid to carry.

The 1992 cable act added a new wrinkle that responded to the issue of cable use of broadcast TV signals, **retransmission consent.** Under the 1992 law, a local full-power commercial TV station had to choose the status it wanted with respect to cable TV and other multichannel video systems (such as satellite master antenna television [SMATV] and wireless cable; *PRT,* 4.4 and 5.2). The choices were must-carry and retransmission consent. If a station chose retransmission consent, then a cable system (and any other multichannel video system) could carry the signal of that station only with the permission of that station. CBS had championed this arrangement, the idea being that the cable system would have to pay such a station in order to carry that station's signal, just as the system had to pay to carry USA Network and MTV.

Most anticable rhetoric centered on the operator's role as **carrier and gate- keeper of broadcast signals**—the ability to allow and deny access to the local audience. Implicit in these arguments was the realization that **cable subscribers constituted a significant percentage of the total television audience.** For the most part, however, such rhetoric ignored the two factors with greatest ultimate potential to impact broadcast television:

1. Cable television offered a large number of **competing programming serv- ices.**
2. Cable television also **competed with broadcasters for advertising.**

Historically, the three major TV broadcast networks together had a 90% share of the television viewing audience. Programming competition, however, started to affect viewing patterns as early as the late 1970s (Fig. 3.14). By the late 1990s, three-network prime-time audience shares had dropped below 60%. Cable caused at least part of this **share erosion** by offering expanded choices for viewers.

Competition also affected program content. For example, the networks de- creased their use of theatrical films (those originally shown in theaters). Once a staple of prime-time network programming, theatrical films increasingly reached

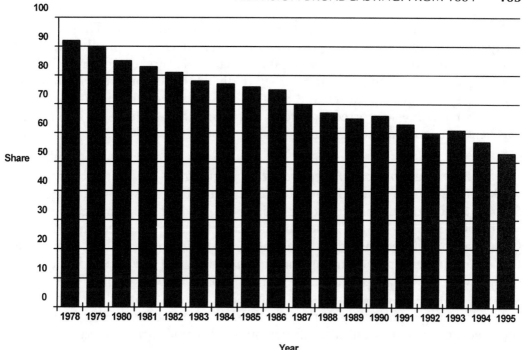

**FIG. 3.14. Three-network share erosion, 1978–1995.** (*Source*: Nielsen.)

audiences through other media. In fact, home video and pay cable got them before the networks. In response, the networks scheduled more made-for-TV films and loosened standards to compete with the so-called adult programming that cable offered.

Cable did not pose the same immediate threat in advertising, however. During the 1980s, cable systems depended on subscriber fees for 95% of their revenues; cable's total advertising revenue was less than 4% of that of broadcast television. Still, cable entities sold advertising at both system and network levels, and their advertising income increased every year. Cable continued to expand its share of the advertising dollar at the expense of broadcasting.

In addition to complaining, broadcasters reacted to cable by competing and joining. Responding to the 24-hour cable news channels, all three networks added additional news programming. By 1990, nearly one third of all cable systems had ownership ties with broadcast-related facilities; some of the biggest station group owners were also some of the largest multiple system operators (MSOs, cable system operators with franchises in more than one community). Broadcasters, including the networks, invested in cable programming ventures. NBC, for example, had ownership stakes in CNBC, Bravo, American Movie Classics (AMC), and some half-dozen regional cable networks. ABC held equity in Lifetime and ESPN. NBC and ABC both had interest in Arts & Entertainment (A&E). Licensees of a few independent television stations profited from cable directly, becoming nationally distributed "superstations" (*PRT*, 7.4.2.2).

Many commercial broadcasters, however, still felt threatened. They launched campaigns to enlist public support for their very survival. Typically, such campaigns attempted to convince the populace that cable threatened "free TV," was draining off programming, and threatened to divide the nation's television service into one system for the haves and another for the have-nots. Free TV was, of course, advertising-supported broadcast television that, at least by implication, was being threatened with extinction by the "not-free" variety, cable television.

### 3.5.2.2 Competition From Independent Programming.

At least part of the networks' share erosion resulted from competing broadcast television programming. Sources included independent stations and independent programmers.

The FCC put the **Prime Time Access Rule** (PTAR) into effect in 1971. The Commission believed that the three commercial television networks controlled the entertainment programming market and designed the rule to encourage competition. One main provision of the rule forbade network-affiliated television stations in the 50 largest markets from broadcasting more than 3 hours of entertainment programming during the 4 hours of prime time. This prohibition included not only new but also off-net material—syndicated programming and movies that had run on the network.

At first, most affiliates affected by PTAR programmed this newly vacated slot poorly. They aired the relatively few first-run (not previously on the networks) programs available—game shows, cheap action-adventure series, and other equally unappealing programs whose main virtue was low cost. However, PTAR did not apply to independent television stations.

The independents competed by programming this "access" time slot with popular syndicated off-net series. This tactic paid off. The independents' ratings improved, not only during this one particular time period but also overall, as audiences discovered they offered entertaining alternatives to current network fare. Meanwhile, the networks themselves, through continuous competitive schedule shuffling, kept audiences confused—canceling new programs before they had time to gather audiences, moving older programs around the schedule, and constantly substituting specials for regular programming.

### 3.5.2.3 More Stations: UHF and Low-Power Television.

PTAR helped independent television stations to experience growing financial success. The message seemed to be that a television station had the potential to make money in almost any market. Would-be broadcasters applied for the remaining vacant channels in large and medium markets. Most VHF assignments were already in use, so unused **UHF channels became attractive to prospective licensees.** As the remaining channels were snapped up, applicants competed for vacant UHF assignments even in smaller markets. By the 1980s, it became common to read that three, four, or more parties had applied for channels and locations no one would have wanted just a few years before.

In 1982 the FCC adopted rules for a completely new class of broadcast service, **low-power television** (LPTV). Licenses for LPTV stations were awarded on a demand basis similar to AM radio stations. This meant they could be put anywhere so long as they did not interfere with existing stations. Because they operated with low power, their signals did not reach nearly as far as those of full-power stations. On the other hand, LPTVs operated with few of the programming restrictions and requirements that applied to full-power stations.

The number of applications for LPTV stations quickly reached 8,000. The FCC announced it would accept no more new applications until it could deal with the backlog. After revising procedures, the FCC ended the freeze and began licensing LPTV stations in 1987. Many LPTV stations programmed highly specialized content and targeted narrowly defined audiences. For the most part, LPTV stations did not compete for audiences and advertising dollars to the same degree as full-power independent television stations and cable networks. During the 1990s, wireless cable operators started using LPTV stations in addition to, or even in place of, the omnidirectional microwave services they had used previously to transmit digitally compressed, scrambled signals.

### 3.5.2.4 Higher Off-Net Prices; More First-Run Programming.

The number of television stations increased, and so did the competition to acquire good programming. **Syndicators were able to demand and get outrageously high prices for off-net series** that had proved popular on the networks. Some independents bought more than they could afford.

PTAR and the increased number of stations also encouraged production and syndication of new programming directly for stations. Once the market opened, **producers turned out first-run syndicated programming**. Advertisers and advertising agencies got back into the programming business through barter syndication (*PRT*, 7.3.2.1). The stations themselves created programming and syndicated their better efforts. Groups of stations cooperated to produce programming, some of which was designed to compete directly with prime-time network offerings.

### 3.5.2.5 Short-Term Competition: Subscription Television.

During the late 1970s and early 1980s, traditional television had competition from yet another source—subscription television (STV). Similar to a pay cable channel such as HBO, an STV station offered commercial-free programming in scrambled form. Subscribers paid monthly to use a decoder that unscrambled the signal. The difference lay in the transmission medium—the STV station broadcast the signal, rather than sending it by cable.

Subscription broadcast systems had been tested as early as 1950. The first full-scale public tryout was launched in 1962 at WHCT, channel 18 in Hartford, Connecticut. The **Hartford STV experiment** lasted 7 years. In 1968, despite bitter opposition from commercial television interests and motion picture theater owners, the FCC authorized regular STV service. The response was not exactly overwhelming. Even 7 years after the Hartford experiment, no station offered subscription programming.

Cable television actually gave STV its big boost. In 1975 HBO began satellite distribution, becoming the first nationally distributed pay cable (premium) channel. It was a success. Cable customers signed up in droves to pay a monthly fee for (primarily) uncut movies. Most big cities did not have cable, but TV stations could provide similar service by STV.

The STV boom started in 1977. Wometco Enterprises, owner of movie theaters and previously one of STV's major opponents, bought a New Jersey UHF station and began subscription programming. Wometco's move seemed to signal the beginning. Five years later, some 30 stations offered STV programming and subscription broadcasters formed their own trade group.

As STV grew, so did its problems. Few operations were profitable. A whole underground industry developed around signal piracy; nonsubscribers bought illegal decoders and viewed without paying. Several group broadcasters who owned STV stations ceased subscription programming, citing lack of subscribers. In some markets, two or more stations started STV service and competed with each other for subscribers.

Ultimately, however, it was cable television—the medium that had inspired the STV boom—that killed off subscription television. An STV station transmitted only one channel; cable offered multiple channels—for about the same price as an STV subscription fee. STV subscribership dropped as pay cable penetration increased. By the end of the 1980s, most stations had converted to advertising-supported, unscrambled programming.

*3.5.2.6 Competition From Home Video.*    Although it posed negligible competition for the TV broadcast advertising dollar, home video threatened to develop into a competitor for audiences even more formidable than cable. The real worry for broadcasters and advertisers was the ability of the VCR to **rearrange programming** and **eliminate commercials!** Using a VCR, a viewer could do all of the following:

- **Time shift**—capture otherwise ephemeral television programming broadcast at odd hours, even when asleep or not at home, and view that programming at a convenient time.
- **Double view**—watch programming on one channel while recording that on another.
- **Zip** commercials—fast-forward past them during playback.
- **View prerecorded cassettes**—watch material that had never been broadcast.

*3.5.2.7 Competition From New TV Broadcast Networks.*    New networks went on the air and competed with ABC, CBS, NBC, and their affiliates for audience and advertising. During 1986 and 1987, no less than four commercial networks signed on the air. **Univision,** a full-service Spanish-language network, had actually originated years earlier as Spanish International Network. In 1986, however, it reorganized into Univision and began expanding. That same year **Home Shopping Network,** the successful direct marketing cable programmer, bought stations and formed a broadcast network. In 1987 **Telemundo,** another Spanish-language network, formed and began operation.

The fourth network began when **Rupert Murdoch,** Australian media tycoon, purchased 20th Century Fox Film Corporation and Metromedia's six independent television stations for a total of $2.5 billion. Murdoch, who became an American citizen so that the FCC would approve transfer of the Metromedia licenses to his company, formed a television network, the **Fox Broadcasting Company.** Fox recruited a lineup of independent stations as affiliates and launched its prime-time programs in 1987. This was to be a real English-language, advertising-supported ABC-CBS-NBC-style network.

Fox failed to register significantly on the ratings scale at first, but Murdoch stuck with the project. He hired excellent staff, encouraged them to innovate, and continued to pour money into what must have seemed like a financial black hole. Fox executives looked at what other networks were doing and decided to do the opposite. They adopted a strategy of counterprogramming by audience. While the big three—CBS, NBC, and even once-famed-for-its-own-young-audience-strategy ABC—tended to attract an older demographic, Fox went after younger folks. It attracted them with programming that, for the most part, was sophomoric—irreverent and brash with much adolescent humor. Critics and the big three panned it. In fact, no one liked Fox programming except the audience at whom it was aimed. The Fox audience grew, and the other three networks, seeing the success of their junior competitor, introduced more in-your-face programming into their own schedules. This resulted in the overall quotient of prime-time sexual innuendo, comedy-club-sounding laugh tracks, negative intellectual content, and general poor taste ratcheting upward another couple of notches with highly popular programs such as *Married . . . With Children, Roseanne,* and *The Simpsons.*

### 3.5.3 Structural and Financial Changes During the 1980s

*3.5.3.1 Evolution: The Old Order Passeth.*    Evolutionary changes continued in television broadcasting. At the most visible level, the networks made key personnel changes. One by one, the founders and "older generation" bowed out. David Sarnoff retired as head of RCA in 1969 and died 2 years later. Sarnoff had groomed his son Robert to be his successor, and the latter did take over the reins of the company in 1969 but was fired in 1975. Following the end of the Sarnoff dynasty, RCA suffered under poor leadership until 1981 when the company tapped Thornton F. Bradshaw as chair. Bradshaw's first act as head of RCA was to hire Grant A. Tinker as chief executive of NBC. Tinker had founded the highly successful production firm MTM Enterprises, and under his direction the programming fortunes of NBC slowly began to improve. NBC-TV finally won the prime-time ratings battle for the first time in the 1985–1986 season.

Early in 1983, Frederick S. Pierce was made president of ABC, apparently confirming his role as heir apparent to ABC Chairman Leonard Goldenson. At CBS, William Paley went through several candidates to take over as chair. In 1980 CBS brought in Thomas H. Wyman as president. Three years later, Wyman succeeded Paley as chair.

### 3.5.3.2 Revolution: Money and Trafficking.

These evolutionary changes, however, pale beside the revolution that was brewing. It started about 1983. Before it was over, in addition to a new network having been formed (*PRT,* 3.5.2.7), all of the "big three" major broadcast networks would be under new ownership or control and scores of TV stations would change hands. These were only the most obvious of the many changes this revolution caused in the television business. It was television's financial revolution, and—bromidic though the term may be—it was, indeed a true revolution. Wall Street and the banking business had discovered broadcasting, and the result was a **frenzy of station purchases, buying and selling at ever-increasing prices.**

The trigger was the gradual **recovery of the national economy** and a **decline in interest rates.** The cost of borrowing money had dropped from record highs to a level within the reach of most people in business. This included broadcasters.

This was the year, too, in which media analysts and bankers realized that broadcasting would survive, despite cable television. Predictions that cable TV would fractionalize broadcast television's audience right away had not come true, and such predictions seemed to become more unlikely all the time.

Regional banks took an interest in underwriting the purchase of broadcast stations. Traditionally banks had little interest in lending money for broadcast ventures because stations had few fixed hard assets—inventory, machines, real estate—with which to secure (i.e., guarantee) loans. Now, with economic recovery loosening the money available to lenders, **banks looked at broadcast stations in terms of the amount of money they made**—specifically, the amount available to pay off long-term debt. The banks set up communications departments and solicited business from prospective buyers of broadcast properties, encouraging them to borrow against the stations' future earnings.

Station purchasers discovered creative financing. Various financial devices were used to supplement money available from banks and other traditional sources. Two popular devices—the limited partnership and the leveraged buyout—were basically means of using other people's money to buy control of a business.

Deregulation also helped spur the financial revolution. The FCC had **repealed the antitrafficking rule** in 1982; a licensee no longer had to own a station at least three years before selling it. Two years later, the Commission **raised the number of stations a licensee could control.** The limit went from 7 in each service (AM, FM, TV) to 12. Station group owners at or near the previous seven-station limit now looked for additional stations to acquire.

Group owners were not the only companies to acquire stations. Management teams put together financing packages and bought out the stations and station groups for which they had worked. Individuals and companies who had no experience in the business saw financial opportunities in broadcasting and looked for properties to buy. This rash of acquisitions drove up station prices drastically (Box 3.4).

When a company found a likely target for acquisition, it could try a number of tactics. It could buy the target company outright, it could merge with the company, or it could attempt a **takeover.** Here, the target company was usually publicly traded (i.e., anyone could buy and sell shares of the company on the open market). In this tactic, the company attempting the takeover would try to buy up enough stock to get control of the target company. If the target was willing, the takeover was said to be friendly; if unwilling, hostile.

Critics expressed concern at the changes in the business. How could someone who planned to buy a television station, they asked, possibly have in mind to serve the public interest (as required by law) when the deal was so structured that it put the station deep into debt and when the aim was to resell the station as quickly as possible so as to realize a fast profit? Demands came from all directions—public interest groups, the U.S. Congress, even a few broadcasters—to stop what was seen as the damage done by deregulation, to reinstate some sort of antitrafficking rule.

*3.5.3.3 Hostile Takeover Attempt: CBS.* The most prominent acquisition activities were those involving the TV networks. CBS was first to make news. In 1985 both Fairness In Media (FIM) and Ted Turner tried to gain control of the network. FIM, a group associated with U.S. Senator Jesse Helms, urged political conservatives to buy stock in and "do something" about what they perceived as a "liberal bias" in CBS News. Turner owned superstation WTBS and CNN, and

---

**BOX 3.4. 1980S STATION TRADING: WHEELER DEALERS AND RISING PRICES**

The sale of television station KTLA illustrates. In 1982, Kohlberg, Kravis, Roberts & Co. (KKR), a private investment banking firm, put together a complicated leveraged buyout to purchase KTLA, a Los Angeles independent television station on channel 5. This was KKR's first station. The deal included investments from two limited partnerships, participation by members of the KTLA management team, and a loan underwritten by a group of banks. The purchase price was $245 million. Just 2 years later, KKR sold the station to Tribune Broadcasting Co. for $510 million, twice the original purchase price. KKR, however, had continued to put together station deals and by the end of 1985 was one of the top 10 TV group owners in terms of percentage of population covered by its station's signals. Ten years later, KKR was not even on the top 50 chart.

he wanted to add the network to his growing electronic mass communication empire.

The FIM effort failed, and CBS successfully fought off Turner's takeover attempt. In October CBS management announced that it had found a "guardian angel" to help fend off future takeover attempts. Loews Corporation, a New York-based conglomerate, had acquired a 11.7% interest in CBS, and the chair and chief executive officer (CEO) of Loews, **Laurence A. Tisch,** had been asked to join the network's board of directors. Loews subsequently increased its CBS holdings to just under 25%, becoming the network's largest stockholder. In September 1986 CBS Chairman Thomas Wyman was forced out, as were other top executives. Tisch was named CEO, the person in charge of the company. He brought William Paley back in the company as chair, a largely honorary position. The network founder held that title until his death in 1990, at which point the board elected Tisch as chair and CEO. The FCC ruled that the Loews/Tisch takeover was not a change of control. Nonetheless, the fact remains that CBS management had fought and won a costly battle with Turner, only to be ousted and replaced by a third party, Lawrence Tisch.

CBS also had a $1 billion debt to pay off, the result of a stock buy-back tactic it had used in fighting the Turner takeover bid. The network peddled subsidiaries and laid off employees. CBS even sold the division that had given the company its original name (*PRT,* 2.1.6.3, note 7, and 2.2.3); CBS Records (formerly Columbia Records) was purchased by Sony Corporation in 1987. By 1988 CBS had a cash surplus of some $3.4 billion. By this time, however, hundreds of CBS employees had been released and numerous activities had been closed down. Almost all departments lost personnel, several hundred from the CBS News Division alone.

*3.5.3.4 Ownership Changes: ABC, NBC.*   Even in a period characterized by financial and structural change, 1 year stands out: 1985. *Broadcasting* magazine called 1985 a "30 billion-plus year . . . a record 12 months of mergers, sales and acquisitions."[9] It counted 108 deals that involved $10 million or more, seven worth over $1 billion each. Some of these deals constituted historic changes of ownership.

In March, while CBS was still fighting FIM, **American Broadcasting Companies, Inc., was acquired by Capital Cities Communications, Inc.,** for $3.5 billion. Capital Cities was a group station owner that also had publishing and cable properties. This was the first acquisition of a television network since ABC had merged with Paramount Theaters 32 years previously. Leonard Goldenson retired; **Thomas S. Murphy,** Capital's chair and CEO, took on those same roles in the new company, Capital Cities Communications/ABC, Inc. After a reorganization, Frederick Pierce resigned.

In December, even the ABC acquisition was dwarfed. A $6.3 billion deal was struck, and history came full circle; **RCA was acquired by GE,** the company largely responsible for its creation 66 years before. GE, a co-owner of NBC in the network's earliest days (*PRT,* 2.1.2.2), had sold off its own station group several years before. Now, with one deal, GE was back in both the network and the station-group business. In 1986 **Robert Wright,** a GE executive who at one time had served as president of Cox Cable, was named president of NBC.

Despite new ownership, the big three (ABC, CBS, and NBC) continued to suffer share erosion (Fig. 3.14). This limited their ability to increase advertising rates. Yet programming and other costs rose steadily. Network executives sought ways to cut expenses and tap alternative income sources. Both ABC and NBC laid off hundreds of employees; the latter sold its radio stations and networks (*PRT,* 2.6).

***3.5.3.5 Bad Times Coming.***   The **religious broadcasters** were first. Pat Robertson's Continental Broadcasting Network sold stations, laid off workers, and canceled programming. In 1987 a sexual scandal broke concerning Reverend James O. Bakker, president of the PTL Television Network. An investigation of the PTL ministry revealed severe mismanagement, including huge back payments due cable and broadcast outlets for carrying the programming. Some outlets canceled PTL programming. The next year, yet another sexual scandal broke, this time involving a second TV preacher, Reverend Jimmy Swaggart.

The buy–sell syndrome continued to the end of the decade, but the bloom had started to rub off the boom. Licensees of independent television stations seemed to be having financial problems. Many found themselves beset with burdensome financing as a result of limited partnerships and crippling payments for extensive programming purchases. Dozens of **independents filed for bankruptcy.** This was just a hint of what was to come, because the country's economy was about to lurch into recession.

## 3.6 TELEVISION'S RECESSION AND RECOVERY IN THE 1990s

The financial recession hit in 1990 and impacted television broadcasting almost immediately. The buying-and-selling frenzy finally ended. Advertising revenues and station values dropped. The money supply was tight. Borrowing became almost impossible. Many who had invested in television stations were left with staggering debts. Some lost their stations. Others successfully renegotiated the terms of their loans and cut expenses so that the station could cover financial obligations.

The economy began to recover in 1993. Advertising revenues increased, and the revolution proceeded: Station values went up, money became available, station trading resumed, two more new TV broadcast networks started, two old networks were sold (again), broadcasters increasingly got into the cable business, and new technologies offered both promise and challenge.

### 3.6.1 Deleting, Downsizing, and Deterioration

The tough economic times of the recession made second and third independent stations unprofitable in all but the largest markets. In order to boost revenues, group owners with economically strong independents began deleting the competition. They did this using a number of tactics—paying the competing station to simulcast the strong station's programming; contracting to handle sales, programming, and other functions for the competing station; even buying the competing station to shut it down or sell it to a noncompeting broadcaster, such as a home shopping or nonprofit licensee. This continued even when the economy recovered. By 1995 there were more than 30 **local marketing agreements**, contracts whereby one broadcaster managed two separately owned stations in the same market.

One means by which broadcasters attempted to cut expenses during the recession was to get rid of nonessential operations (those operations they could eliminate and still function) and lay off employees. The polite term for this was **downsizing**. It occurred at both station and network levels and in many other businesses besides broadcasting. Network affiliates, for example, cut news staffs but increased the amount of programming expected from news departments. This resulted in savings in two areas—a smaller news staff meant less money paid out in salaries, and the increase in news-department-produced programming meant less money paid out for syndicated shows.

ABC, CBS, and NBC, too, cut news staffs and demanded increased programming from their news departments. Network news, long regarded as a prestige loss leader, had to start making money. Foreign bureaus were shut down. Reporting specialists (e.g., on law, the economy, or medicine) were released. Senior staffers, both on- and off-air, got pink slips. Automation and simpler procedures replaced people wherever possible; NBC was first to automate production of its nightly newscasts, using robotics mechanisms instead of human camera and video playback operators.

At the same time, however, the networks further increased the amount of on-air time for which their news departments were responsible. This resulted in programming such as CBS's overnight news feeds and ABC's *Nightline*. Additionally the documentary form made a comeback of sorts. The networks did schedule some long-form documentary programs, such as CBS's *48 Hours,* but most were variations of CBS's *60 Minutes,* an attempt to repeat some of that series' extended success: a magazine format, usually featuring two or three minidocumentaries, their subjects often unrelated, linked together with regularly appearing on-camera talent. NBC, for example, had such success with *Dateline,* that it ran the magazine show four nights a week during the mid-1990s.

Documentary presentation style had changed, however. Whether long or short, documentaries often reflected the influence of entertainment-oriented **reality programming**, such as the syndicated series *Entertainment Tonight, A Current Affair,* and *Inside Edition.* Reality programming often used news production techniques because of its low cost, relative to that of producing drama and comedy. Critics questioned the wisdom of making entertainment shows that looked like news programming, and of making news look like entertainment. What, they asked, were the implications for society of this blurring of the boundaries between news and entertainment?

Networks also attempted to cut expenditures by reducing compensation, the money they paid to affiliates for carrying the commercials in network programming. The affiliates, already frustrated by a lackluster economy and network ratings decline, fought this attempt to reduce their revenues. Eventually the networks were able to **make some adjustment in their compensation schedules.** However, the affiliates now felt freer to preempt (i.e., not broadcast) some network programming. In place of selected (usually low-rated) network shows, they would air their own programs, sell the commercial positions within those programs to their own advertiser clients, and thereby make more money than they could get from compensation. With the end of the recession, the compensation issue seemed to subside.

### 3.6.2 Networks New and Old

During the summer of 1993, two new TV broadcast networks were announced. Paramount said that it would team with the Chris Craft station group to form an advertising-supported network, and Warner Brothers (WB) said that it would join Tribune Broadcasting to do the same. Both **United Paramount Network** (UPN)[10] and **The WB Television Network** began recruiting affiliates. Both launched a prime-time schedule in January 1995. Fox, UPN, WB, local marketing agreements, Univision and Telemundo affiliates—by the late 1990s, with all these networks operating, there were very few true independent TV stations left.

In the meantime, Fox Broadcasting continued to grow. The fourth commercial network had earned a reputation for surprise, for planning creatively, and for being able to move quickly. It confirmed that reputation in 1994. **New World Communications,** a group owner, had 12 VHF TV stations. One was affiliated with NBC; three, with ABC; the other eight, with CBS. In return for a programming deal and some $500 million in stock and interest-free loan money, New World agreed to affiliate all 12 stations with Fox. This set off a nationwide scramble among the four networks, a **chain reaction of affiliation switches** that, before it ended, affected nearly 70 stations across the country. In the process, Fox gained over 15 VHF stations as affiliates, and more than 20 stations moved from big-three affiliations to Fox. Fox bought the New World stations outright in 1996.

Fox also had ownership problems. The FCC, after looking into the matter of who owned Fox Broadcasting (and thus the stations Fox owned), found that the company had violated national foreign ownership limits. Under FCC regulations foreigners and foreign companies could hold no more than 25% interest in the ownership of a U.S. broadcast station. News Corporation, an Australian-chartered company, held 99% of the stock in Fox. Although controlled by Rupert Murdoch, a naturalized U.S. citizen, News Corporation was still a foreign company. Fox petitioned the FCC for a waiver of the ownership limitation based on the company's public interest role in fostering competition to ABC, CBS, and NBC, and the Commission granted the waiver.

CBS and NBC, despite the relative newness of their ownership, were still viewed as takeover targets. During the early 1990s various interests attempted to buy out the two senior networks. GE had admitted that NBC was for sale, but CBS seemed particularly vulnerable. It had lost a number of strong affiliates, a result of the Fox–New World deal. Then in overall ratings for the 1994–1995 prime-time TV season, CBS wound up in third place behind ABC and NBC. That was bad enough, but in the adults 18–49 audience demographic category, highly desired by advertisers, Fox Broadcasting actually beat CBS.

Sources both inside and outside CBS put much of the blame on Laurence Tisch's leadership. They faulted what they saw as his inability to realize how truly different broadcasting is from other businesses (a result, said his critics, of Tisch's lack of experience in broadcasting) and for failing to have a cohesive long-term game plan for CBS. Affiliates were said to hope that CBS would be sold to a broadcaster, someone with a clear vision of how to turn the network around.[11]

They got their wish in 1995. Pioneer broadcaster **Westinghouse Electric Co.** would **buy CBS, Inc.**, for $5.4 billion. Westinghouse would raise most of the money through sale of several subsidiaries including its defense electronics business. After nearly 60 years of control by one person, Bill Paley, CBS had now changed hands twice within a decade. The next year Westinghouse purchased Infinity Broadcasting, one of the country's largest radio network firms, then announced that it would split into two companies, one with its broadcasting operations, the other with everything else. (Also in 1995 a one-time suitor of CBS—the company that had helped kick off the train of events 10 years before that resulted in Larry Tisch controlling CBS—was itself taken over by another company: Turner Broadcasting agreed to a merger with Time Warner.)

But the purchase of CBS was almost overshadowed by the sale of another of the big three (and it was not, as some had predicted, NBC). The day before Westinghouse made its announcement, the **Walt Disney Company** disclosed that it would **buy Capital Cities/ABC** for $18.5 billion, the second-highest price ever paid for a U.S. company.[12] With revenues of Disney and ABC totaling $19 billion a year, this purchase made Disney the largest media firm in the world. This would be the fourth time that ABC had changed control in its 68-year history.[13]

### 3.6.3 Radical Technological and Regulatory Change

Even without all the corporate moving and shaking, the decade of the 1990s would prove significant in the history of electronic mass media for at least two reasons. First, an FCC industry advisory committee **recommended fundamental changes in the technology of over-the-air television.** In 1995, after extensive testing, the committee advised the Commission to adopt a new TV system for the United States. The system would feature **high-definition television** (HDTV), with higher resolution and a wider raster (the viewed portion of the TV screen) than NTSC's existing 525 lines and 3:4 aspect ratio.

Almost overshadowing the HDTV aspect, however, was the recommendation that the system be **digital.** Just as with radio (*PRT*, 2.7), the switch to a digital system would involve temporary use of a second channel during a years-long phase-in period. But again, just as with radio, digital represented a completely different technology from the existing analog system. Digital television would allow much greater flexibility in manipulating the TV signal at both the receiver and the transmitter. A digital TV set, for example, could function as the ultimate channel surfing tool, simultaneously displaying almost any number of different channels on the screen. Many TV station licensees planned to use digital technology, at least initially, not for HDTV but to transmit as many as four different program services on one broadcast channel. Eventually the time would come when all broadcast TV stations would transmit only digital signals, and only TV sets equipped for digital reception would be able to pick up those signals.

The second 1990s event that had the potential for long-range, fundamental change in electronic mass media was passage of the Telecommunications Act of 1996. One of the most comprehensive amendments ever to the Communications Act of 1934, this law lowered the amount of restrictions on a number of regulated services and allowed everybody to get into everybody else's business. Certainly the 1996 law would impact broadcast TV by strengthening and encouraging competing video programmers. It freed cable from certain types of regulation and permitted telephone companies to own and deliver video programming. However, there were major provisions that aimed specifically at broadcasters—ownership limitations, for example, were lifted or eased, local marketing agreements were recognized, license terms were extended, the chances of a station successfully getting a license renewed were increased, and all TV broadcast programming was to be closed captioned (*PRT*, 5.5.2).

Another provision of the 1996 law, one that broadcasters did not like, required programmers to develop a ratings system. The system would alert viewers concerning violent and other indecent material in upcoming programming. If TV broadcasters failed to develop a ratings system within 1 year, the law directed the FCC to develop a system based on recommendations of an appointed advisory board. The rating system was tied to another of the law's requirements, this one aimed at television receiver manufacturers: new TV sets with a screen size of 13 inches or larger sold in the United States had to have the capability for viewers to block such programming for themselves or their minor children. Broadcasters grumbled about this V-chip (the V stood for violence) legislation, and threatened to take it to court on First Amendment grounds. As usual, their professed concern, freedom of expression, masked their real concern, freedom to attract large audiences and make money. (Some critics commented that if TV sets had not originally developed with on–off switches but were instead later mandated by law, TV broadcasters would have challenged the requirement in court, contending such switches violated their First Amendment rights!) Nonetheless, the networks and production houses acquiesced and developed the ratings.

### 3.6.4 Other Media: Even More Competition

Broadcasters' plans to charge cable systems for carrying station signals under the retransmission consent option did not work out as envisioned. The large MSOs vowed not to pay for the broadcast station signals they carried, and for the most part these cable system owners kept to their vows. Except for some small systems in small markets, almost no cable operators agreed to pay cash. The best retransmission consent agreements most broadcasters could get was to **create special cable programming** (a) on which the broadcasters would sell advertising and (b) that the systems would pay for and carry. The programming in these deals ranged from local news inserts done by individual TV stations to entire 24-hour programming services provided by broadcast networks and large group owners—Fx, for example, from Fox; ESPN2 from ABC; and America's Talking from NBC.[14]

These deals also suggested the seriousness with which **broadcasters had invested in the cable business.** Cox Communications, for example, owned broadcast stations and cable systems and held equity in cable networks and broadcast program production firms. The Walt Disney Company, long a producer of broadcast TV programming, owned both The Disney Channel and ABC. ABC, in turn, and GE's NBC both owned TV broadcast stations and major cable networks. Time Warner, a primary producer of broadcast programming, owned cable systems, cable networks, and a broadcast TV network, as well as Ted Turner's extensive cable programming holdings. Viacom, one of the chief syndicators of broadcast programming, owned both cable networks and Paramount, a leading producer of programming for TV networks and syndication. Tele-Communications, Incorporated (TCI), the country's largest MSO and owner of extensive cable programming interests, and News Corporation, parent company of Fox Broadcasting and its program production and syndication firms, were partners in a number of foreign and domestic programming and direct broadcast satellite enterprises. With heavy hitters like these having substantial investments in both the broadcasting business and the cable business, it was no wonder that the love–hate relationship between these two media was so convoluted.

Despite cable's growth in audience share and advertising revenue, however, broadcasters now had other worries. Additional media had sprung up, media such as **wireless cable, direct broadcast satellite,** and **telephone company video services.** Even the **Internet's World Wide Web** began to steal discernible amounts of time from TV viewing. More and more people bought personal computers and discovered that increasingly sophisticated technology and software allowed the Web to provide graphics, audio, and real-time telephone service and to move ever closer to full-motion video. These were not "someday" media, laboratory models that appeared on the cover of *Popular Science* as possibilities that might be available some day. These media actually existed. Large, well-known companies had invested in them, offered them as consumer services, and had every intention of grabbing audience share and earning a profit from them. That being the case, these media were challenges that cablecasters faced as well as broadcasters.

## NOTES

1. 41 F.C.C. 148.

2. Advances in digital compression techniques during the 1990s would allow a telephone line to carry multiple 6-MHz television channels (see *PRT,* 10.3.2).

3. RCA v. U.S., 341 U.S. 412.

4. Pat Weaver also had a daughter, Sigourney, who later went into motion pictures and earned a reputation as a fine actress.

5. Report and Statement of Policy re: Commission en banc Programming Inquiry, 25 Fed. Reg. 7291, 29 July 1960.

6. Office of Communication of the United Church of Christ v. Federal Communications Commission, 359 F.2d 994 (1966); and 425 F.2d 543 (1969).

7. In the matter of Editorializing by Broadcast Licensees, 13 F.C.C. 1246 (1949).

8. See, for example, Daniel Schorr, "Go Get Some Milk and Cookies and Watch the Murders on Television," In *Impact of Mass Media,* 2nd ed. Ray Eldon Hiebert and Carol Reuss, Eds. (New York: Longman, 1988) 132–143.

9. "Fifth Estate's $30 billion-plus year," *Broadcasting* 30 Dec. 1985: 35.

10. When UPN actually launched, neither Viacom nor its Paramount subsidiary had ownership interest in the new network. BHC Communications, the TV broadcasting subsidiary of Chris Craft Industries, controlled UPN. Paramount did, however, have an option to buy in.

11. Steve McClellan, "The Meeting of Their Discontent," *Broadcasting & Cable* 29 May 1995: 12.

12. RJR Nabisco's $25 billion merger with KKR (Box 3.4) in 1989 held the record. Don West, "The Dawning of Megamedia: Broadcasting's $25 Billion Week," *Broadcasting & Cable* 7 August 1995: 4. The difference in purchase price between ABC and CBS had to do with the amount of "other businesses" held by each. CBS had, during the Tisch years, sold off almost every asset it owned except for its station and network operations. CapCities/ABC owned, in addition to its broadcasting and cable businesses, extensive publishing holdings.

13. NBC set up the Blue Network in 1927 (*PRT,* 2.1.6.2). RCA formed the Blue Network into a separate corporation and sold it to Edward J. Noble in 1943, who renamed it the American Broadcasting Company (*PRT,* 2.2.3). ABC merged with United Paramount Theaters in 1953 (*PRT,* 3.2.2.2). Capital Cities Communications acquired ABC in 1985 (*PRT,* 3.5.3.4). Disney completed its acquisition in 1996.

14. NBC eventually sold part ownership of America's Talking to computer software giant Microsoft. America's Talking was then converted to a news and information network, renamed MSNBC, and linked to a new, joint NBC–Microsoft-funded online news service.

## FURTHER READING

Abramson, Albert. *Zworykin: Pioneer of Television.* Urbana: University of Illinois Press, 1995.

Adir, Karin. *The Great Clowns of American Television.* Jefferson, NC: McFarland, 1990.

Allen, Steve. *Hi-Ho, Steverino: My Adventures in the Wonderful Wacky World of Television.* New York: Barricade, 1992.

Anderson, Kent. *Television Fraud: The History and Implications of the Quiz Show Scandals.* Westport, CT: Greenwood, 1978.

Auletta, Ken. *Three Blind Mice: How the TV Networks Lost Their Way.* New York: Random, 1991.

Barnouw, Erik. *The Image Empire.* New York: Oxford University Press, 1970.

Barnouw, Erik. *Tube of Plenty: The Evolution of American Television.* 2nd rev. ed. New York: Oxford University Press, 1990.

Bergreen, Laurence. *Look Now, Pay Later: The Role of Network Broadcasting.* Garden City, NY: Doubleday, 1980.

Block, Alex Ben. *Marvin Davis, Barry Diller, Rupert Murdoch, Joan Rivers, and the Inside Story of America's Fourth Television Network.* New York: St. Martin's, 1990.

Boddy, William. *Fifties Television: The Industry and Its Critics.* Champaign: University of Illinois Press, 1990.

Brooks, Tim, and Earle Marsh. *The Complete Directory of Prime Time Network TV Shows, 1946–Present.* 5th ed. New York: Ballantine, 1992.

Browne, Nick, Ed. *American Television: New Directions in History and Theory.* Langhorne, PA: Harwood, 1994.

Erickson, Hal. *Religious Radio and Television in the United States, 1921–1991: The Programs and Personalities.* Jefferson, NC: McFarland, 1992.

Erickson, Hal. *Syndicated Television: The First Forty Years, 1947–1987.* Jefferson, NC: McFarland, 1989.

Erickson, Hal. *Television Cartoon Shows: An Illustrated Encyclopedia, 1949 Through 1993.* Jefferson, NC: McFarland, 1995.

Everson, George. *The Story of Television: The Life of Philo T. Farnsworth.* 1949. New York: Arno, 1974.

Frank, Reuven. *Out of Thin Air.* New York: Simon & Schuster, 1991.

Goldenson, Leonard. *Beating the Odds: The Untold Story Behind the Rise of ABC: The Stars, the Struggles, and the Egos That Transformed Network Television by the Man Who Made It Happen.* New York: Scribner's, 1991.

Hollis, Tim. *Cousin Cliff: Forty Magical Years in Television.* Birmingham, AL: Campbell's, 1991.

Inglis, Andrew F. *Behind the Tube: A History of Broadcasting Technology and Business.* Boston: Focal, 1990.

Kearton, Fran. *Waiting for the Banana Peel: We Did It Live, the Early TV Shows of Dick Van Dyke & Fran Adams.* San Jose, CA: R&E Publishing, 1993.

Kisseloff, Jeff. *The Box: An Oral History of Television: 1920–1961.* New York: Viking, 1995.

Lebow, Guy. *Are We on the Air: The Hilarious, Scandalous Confessions of a TV Pioneer.* New York: Sure, 1991.

MacDonald, J. Fred. *Blacks and White TV: African Americans in Television Since 1948.* 2nd ed. Chicago: Nelson-Hall, 1992.

MacDonald, J. Fred. *One Nation Under Television: The Rise and Decline of Network TV.* Updated, enlarged ed. Chicago: Nelson-Hall, 1994.

Marling, Karal Ann. *As Seen on TV: The Visual Culture of Everyday Life in the 1950's.* Cambridge, MA: Harvard University Press, 1994.

Mazzocco, Dennis. *Networks of Power: Corporate TV's Threat to Democracy.* Boston: South End, 1994.

Murray, Mike. "The Contemporary Media, 1974–Present." In *The Media in America, A History.* Wm. David Sloan and James Startt, Eds. 3rd ed. Northport, AL: Vision, 1996.

Murray, Michael, D., and Donald G. Godfrey. *Television in America: Local Station History From Across the Nation.* Ames, IA: Iowa State University Press, 1997.

Paley, William S. *As It Happened: A Memoir.* Garden City, NY: Doubleday, 1979.

Papazian, Ed. *Medium Rare: The Evolution, Workings, and Impact of Commercial Television.* New York: Media, 1991.

Powers, Ron. *Supertube: The Rise of Television Sports.* New York: Coward, 1984.

Quinlan, Sterling. *The Hundred Million Dollar Lunch.* Chicago: O'Hara, 1974.

Ritchie, Michael. *Please Stand By: A Prehistory of Television.* Woodstock, NY: Overlook, 1994.

Rosteck, Thomas. *See It Now Confronts McCarthyism: Television Documentary and the Politics of Representation.* Tuscaloosa: University of Alabama Press, 1994.

Shapiro, Mitchell. *Television Network Daytime and Late-Night Programming, 1959–1989.* Jefferson, NC: McFarland, 1990.

Shapiro, Mitchell. *Television Network Prime-Time Programming, 1959–1989*. Jefferson, NC: McFarland, 1989.

Shapiro, Mitchell. *Television Network Weekend Programming, 1959–1990*. Jefferson, NC: McFarland, 1992.

Shawcross, William. *Murdoch*. New York: Simon & Schuster, 1992.

Slide, Anthony. *One Nation Under Television: The Rise and Decline of Network TV*. Chicago: Pantheon, 1990.

Slide, Anthony, Ed. *The Television Industry: A Historical Dictionary*. Westport, CT: Greenwood, 1991.

Sterling, Christopher H. *Electronic Media: A Guide to Trends in Broadcasting and Newer Technologies, 1920–1982*. New York: Praeger, 1984.

Sturcken, Frank. *Live Television: The Golden Age of 1946–1958 in New York*. Jefferson, NC: McFarland, 1990.

Sullivan, Neil. *The Captain Video Book: The Dumont Television Network Story*. Monroe, LA: Loosestrife, 1992.

Tinker, Grant. *Tinker in Television: From General Sarnoff to General Electric*. New York: Simon & Schuster, 1994.

Williams, Huntington. *Beyond Control: ABC and the Fate of the Networks*. New York: Atheneum, 1989.

Winans, Christopher. *The King of Cash: The Inside Story of Laurence Tisch*. New York: Wiley, 1995.

# 4

## CABLE TELEVISION: FROM 1949

Throughout history, new ideas and inventions have changed the marketplace in unexpected ways. Cable television, the first electronic mass medium to emerge and compete with television broadcasting, is an excellent illustration. The first primitive cable systems started shortly after the end of World War II when a few entrepreneurs pulled in a few TV broadcast signals for residents of small towns. Over the years the medium underwent changes in technology, marketing, and regulation. Those changes transformed cable television into huge horizontally and vertically integrated conglomerates encompassing both cable systems and programming and providing myriad services to millions of subscribers mainly in big cities. In this chapter we examine cable's transformation and organization—the process and forces behind the changes. We also look at cable television's close relative, satellite master antenna television.

### 4.1 CABLE AS COMMUNITY ANTENNA TELEVISION: 1948–1966

For its first two decades of existence, cable television operated primarily as a small-town business, an ancillary to broadcast television. The typical system offered relatively few channels, and those were used only to carry the signals of otherwise locally unavailable broadcast television stations. There were no premium channels and no cable-only channels of any kind. The growth rate during this period was steady but slow, from 70 systems serving 14,000 subscribers in 1952 to 1,500 systems and 1.5 million subscribers in the mid-1960s.

#### 4.1.1 Origins of Cable Television

**Cable television originated during the 1948–1952 freeze** (*PRT,* 3.1.2) imposed by the FCC on the construction of new TV broadcast stations. These were the very years that television "caught on" among consumers, the number of TV-equipped U.S. households rising from 1.6 million in 1949 to 17.3 million in 1952. Yet, there were relatively few stations on the air,[1] and most were in the largest cities.

122

Many people who lived outside the coverage area of any TV station bought television receivers. If the terrain to the closest TV station was not too hilly, a distant set owner could erect a tall pipelike mast (often on top of the house), attach a special outside TV receiving antenna at the top of the mast, and connect the antenna to the TV set with "lead-in" wire.[2] However, in areas far beyond any station's coverage area or where mountains blocked TV signals, few people could afford the equipment and structures necessary to overcome such television reception problems. It was in such areas that cable television was born.

The earliest systems began in 1948 and 1949 in the mountainous areas of Pennsylvania and Oregon.[3] The **sole purpose of these and other early systems was to deliver the signals of TV broadcast stations to their subscribers** (cable customers). An entrepreneur—often an appliance store or radio repair shop owner—would erect a tower atop a tall building or mountain. Antennas on the tower could pick up signals from the nearest stations. These signals were amplified and sent by cable to TV sets of residents who paid the entrepreneur for the service.

Cable systems functioned only as substitutes for individual receiving antennas, so the business called itself **community antenna television** (CATV). The number of systems grew steadily, but the basis of CATV remained to provide subscribers with higher quality, and usually a greater number of, television station signals than they could normally receive on their own.

The primary trade association for cable television organized early on in response to a federal tax. In September 1951 community television executives from a number of towns, mainly in Pennsylvania, met in Pottsville, Pennsylvania, to discuss Internal Revenue Service attempts to levy an 8% excise tax on two systems. The group decided that what they really needed was a permanent national organization to look out for the best interests of the business. They met several times as the National Community Television Council. Then in January 1952 they held an organizational meeting and adopted the name, National Community Television Association. Years later the group changed its name to the **National Cable Television Association** (NCTA).

### 4.1.2 Cable as Fill-In Service

More stations signed on the air. Whereas most prefreeze stations had been in the largest cities, many newer stations went into not-quite-so-large and medium-sized cities. The CATV business adjusted to meet the change. The first CATV systems, which had the technical capacity to carry no more than two or three channels, originated in small, relatively remote towns to bring the first TV service to homes that could pick up no stations over the air. Now, with technological improvements that allowed 5 to 12 channels, CATV moved into larger towns and offered **fill-in service.** If, for example, the homes in a city could receive over the air only a local CBS affiliate, the CATV system would offer service that included signals not only from the CBS station but also from more distant affiliates of ABC and NBC.

### 4.1.3 Regulation of Cable Systems

Local governments were first to regulate cable systems. The cable itself was strung in the public right-of-way, and for that the operator needed permission from the local government. So the operator applied to the city council, the county commission, or whatever the governing body for a **franchise** was, that would allow the operator to wire the area. This governmental body, the **franchising authority,** also controlled rates the operator charged system subscribers. In many cases, the franchising authority made demands on the operator in return for granting the franchise—for example, to pay a fee to the government, limit subscriber fees, or dedicate a channel for community use. The franchise itself was not permanent but instead granted for a set period, say 10 to 15 years. The franchising authority could therefore use the possibility of franchise renewal or nonrenewal, carrot-and-stick style, in dealing with the system operator.

But what about the FCC? The Communications Act of 1934 said nothing about cable television. A system used no over-the-air transmitter to distribute its programming and so needed no federal license to operate. There were cable systems, however, that imported signals of distant stations by microwave relay. Microwave uses radio frequencies and thus is covered directly by the Communications Act and licensed by the FCC. So in 1962 the Commission began to apply carriage and nonduplication requirements (*PRT,* 3.5.2.1) to CATV systems that used microwave. At first the FCC worked on a case-by-case basis, but in 1965 it formally asserted jurisdiction over microwave-fed systems.[4]

The FCC then reconsidered the matter of CATV regulation. The agency concluded that the Communications Act, despite lack of specific reference to CATV, conferred broad authority over interstate communication, so the FCC did have the power to regulate cable. **In 1966 the FCC asserted full jurisdiction over all cable systems** and adopted new rules.[5] These rules reflected a change of emphasis. TV licensees in small markets had begun the fight for FCC regulation of CATV in the mid-1950s. Now in 1966 the FCC placed severe restrictions on carriage of distant signals in the 100 largest markets. The Commission reasoned that CATV would most likely hurt UHF television stations (which were as a group struggling for their financial lives), and new UHF stations would most likely be built in large markets.

### 4.2 CATV EVOLVES INTO CABLE TELEVISION: 1967–1983

During the next decade and a half cable technology improved, increasing the number of channels that one system could offer. As cable operators upgraded their systems, their newly expanded channel capacity often exceeded the number of broadcast signals they wanted to carry, so they programmed these "extra" channels themselves. At the same time the next obvious move for the business was to go into larger markets.

Upgrading existing systems, creating cable-original programming, wiring big cities—all required money, much more money than the small operators who started the business could afford. But there was also the potential to earn a lot of money, so **large investors moved in.** This signaled the beginning of the end of cable as a group of small, locally owned businesses. By the mid-1980s, the new shape of cable had begun to emerge: a few big companies that held ownership interest in both lots of cable systems and in the major cable programming firms.

Cable's rate of growth also increased during this period, a product of moving into larger markets and offering original programming. In 1967 some 1,700 systems operated and 2.1 million homes subscribed. Sixteen years later the number of systems had risen to 5,600, subscribers to 28.3 million, accounting for one third of all TV homes.

### 4.2.1 Cable Channel-Capacity Increases

As cable amplifier technology improved, it allowed coaxial cable to carry ever greater numbers of channels. For years the only distribution medium used in CATV systems was **coaxial cable.** This cable is literally *coaxial*—a conductor and a metal sheath share the same axis. *PRT,* 12.9, explains the workings of coaxial cable in detail; for this discussion, we need only know that the coaxial configuration allows this cable to carry more frequencies than the unsheathed conductor could by itself. As with all wired communication, however, as signals pass through coaxial cable, they attenuate; that is, they lose strength. About every one-third mile of cable, therefore, a cable system must boost the signals by passing them through an **amplifier.**

In the earliest days, each CATV channel required its own amplifier, limiting system capacity to three to five channels. Later, development of **broadband technology** allowed one amplifier to boost multiple channels, first 5, then 12. During the 1960s and 1970s, cable equipment makers made the transition from vacuum tubes to solid-state technology. With each new generation of amplifier, channel capacity increased—20 channels, 30 channels, 35 channels. Technology would continue to improve until eventually one cable would carry more than 50 channels.

Cable system channels 14 and higher do not operate on the same frequencies as corresponding broadcast TV channels. This meant that regular over-the-air-only TV sets (the only ones in use at that time), when hooked up to a cable system, could not tune these higher cable channels. Therefore, when cable systems first offered more than 12 channels, they had to supply **converters** so subscribers could view them. These converters usually took the form of set-top boxes; the cable fed into the box, and a short cable fed the output of the box to the television receiver. Set-top box technology improved, too, adding capabilities to handle features such as scrambling and unscrambling for premium channels, remote control, and eventually even pay-per-view and video-on-demand (*PRT,* 4.3.1).

## 4.2.2 Cable Business Strategy

As cable television grew (Fig. 4.1) and the technology evolved, investors and system operators looked toward larger cities. Large populations would lead to more subscribers and higher revenues. Most city dwellers, however, already received multiple TV broadcast signals. How could they be sold on cable? Cable operators came up with four answers.

1. **Signal improvement.** The nature of a city degrades broadcast TV signals. The many electrical devices cause interference, and tall buildings create shadow areas and ghosting (Box 10.1). A cable system, on the other hand, could provide consistently strong, interference-free signals.

2. **Additional broadcast signals.** A cable system could **import** signals from stations in distant cities, giving subscribers a wider range of broadcast viewing alternatives; for example, the few independent and noncommercial television stations that operated in some markets.

3. **Cable-only basic programming.** A cable system could offer programming available only on cable. Some might be produced by the system itself. Some might come from other sources. Most would be supported by advertising. The operator could bundle this programming with the system's broadcast signals and market it as **basic service,** that is, the service provided for the system's lowest monthly rate.

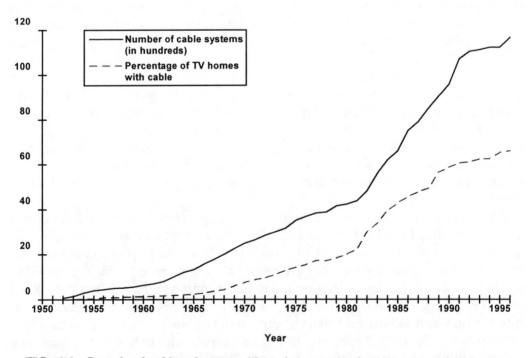

**FIG. 4.1. Growth of cable television.** Note that growth of cable systems is shown in hundreds of cable systems, whereas growth in cable subscribers is shown as the percentage of television homes with cable. (*Sources*: Nielsen Media Research; *Television and Cable Factbook.*)

4. **Premium channels**. An operator could charge extra for some cable-only programming. This programming would have to be special or exclusive—recent feature films, uncut and without commercial interruption; sports events not covered by broadcast TV; specially commissioned programs; or stage performances and nightclub acts. Channels carrying such programming would be electronically scrambled. Subscribers would pay extra to receive the signals unscrambled.

The cable business, which had begun as mom-and-pop operations, continued to consolidate and to take on more of a regional and even national aspect. The large companies that had begun moving into the business sought new franchises in a number of cities. They also continued to buy out small entrepreneurs who had started existing systems but faced expensive equipment upgrades. A firm that operated cable systems in more than one city became known as a **multiple system operator** (MSO).

### 4.2.3 Cable and the "Wired Nation"

Compared to other forms of wired media at the time, coaxial cable had the potential to carry huge amounts of information. With proper equipment, signals could move not only *downstream* (to subscribers) but *upstream* (from subscribers) as well. Cable signals could also be sent to a specified destination. Such capabilities gave rise to conjecture about a "wired nation" based on a **broadband communications network.**

The **wired nation concept** got its big boost in the late 1960s. As envisioned, a grid or network of coaxial cables would cover the entire country. Each home and business would contain a communications center connected to the grid. This communications center would be **interactive**; that is, it could be used to both send and receive information by audio, video, and facsimile. The all-cable system could carry 20, 30, or more channels of television programming simultaneously. With so many channels, the potential for program diversity would increase greatly. All programming and all audiences would be on the cable. Broadcast stations, therefore, could be eliminated. Broadcast frequencies could be released for other uses and thus lessen crowded conditions in the radio frequency spectrum.

The communications center would include a visual telephone that could be used in all kinds of business dealings, from shopping for groceries at home (then having choices delivered) to face-to-face conferences, with conferees scattered all over the country. On request, police and fire departments could monitor your home while you vacation. You could take all types of courses in your home yet still enjoy personal interaction with instructors. Facsimile would make possible near-instantaneous delivery of mail, magazines, newspapers, books, and photographs. You could dial into a central computer for anything from help with personal income taxes to sophisticated data storage and analysis.

Such a system would reduce need for travel. Small group conferences, fiscal transactions, meter readings, exchange of letters and documents, and polling all could be accomplished through transmission of electrical impulses by wire. You could work at home, contacting associates, retrieving materials from central files, initiating and responding to correspondence, and doing sundry other duties through the interactive communications center and the coaxial network. With so much physical travel eliminated, traffic congestion would be reduced in air, interurban rail, truck, and automotive transportation.[6]

### 4.2.4 Cable Versus Broadcast TV

Cable's change in strategy helped the business grow and spread into larger markets. It also marked cable as a competitor to existing media, particularly TV broadcast licensees. Broadcasters in small markets complained about cable signal importation as early as the mid-1950s. Now cable was moving into larger cities by actually **marketing itself as an opportunity to watch TV programs from sources other than local stations.** That did not make TV licensees very happy, nor did they find talk about a wired nation very reassuring, especially the part about elimination of broadcast stations. As discussed in *PRT,* 3.5.2.1, by the late 1960s cable operators and broadcasters argued over issues such as signal carriage, signal importation, and copyright.

### 4.2.5 New Cable Regulations

In June **1968 the U.S. Supreme Court affirmed the FCC's authority to regulate CATV.**[7] In 1969 the Commission issued rules allowing cable systems to interconnect, originate programming,[8] and carry advertising.[9] However, the FCC had concerns about concentration of ownership, too. With cable evolving into big business—and particularly because the cable operator serving any given area almost inevitably had a monopoly—the FCC in 1970 adopted rules that restricted cable system ownership by TV stations and networks and telephone companies.[10]

As a result of its 1966 rules (*PRT,* 4.1.3), however, the Commission was swamped with papers—cable operators seeking relief from carriage and nonduplication rules, prospective cable operators seeking permission to begin operation, and broadcasters seeking protection from cable competition. It became clear that the 1966 rules were not working. From 1968 to 1971 the FCC initiated a series of rule-making proceedings. In the process the commissioners learned much about CATV. They read statements, heard testimony, and listened to discussion. They were exposed to the whole spectrum of opinion on regulation, from unrestricted cable growth to absolute protection for broadcast television.

On February 3, **1972, the FCC adopted a comprehensive set of CATV rules.** They eliminated the 1966 prohibition against signal importation and provided for growth of cable in cities. At the same time, they gave protection to broadcasters, particularly small stations, with provisions for carriage and nonduplication. In retrospect, these 1972 rules actually aimed to restrict cable's growth and protect existing broadcast television stations, and in ensuing years, the FCC eliminated most of them. Nonetheless, cable operators felt they could live with them, and broadcasters were at least partially satisfied, so these 1972 rules represented a landmark for the cable trade.

Then there was the question of copyright. When a cable system picked up a broadcast program, processed the signal, and relayed it to the subscriber for pay, did the system first have to obtain permission from the holder of the program's copyright; that is, did the system have to pay copyright fees? Cable operators said no; the system was passive and simply substituted for a viewer's own antenna. Broadcasters and copyright owners said yes; signal processing and subscriber payments made cable carriage another performance of copyrighted material. The matter batted around the courts for years. The bottom line in two principal cases was that CATV systems were not liable for copyright fees.[11] In **1976**, however, **Congress passed a comprehensive copyright law making cable systems liable for royalty payments.** Under this law a cable operator received a **compulsory license** to carry broadcast stations' signals in exchange for a small percentage of gross receipts that the government then distributed to copyright holders.

### 4.2.6 Cable's Slump and "Blue Sky Talk"

Meanwhile serious internal issues struck cable television hard. Many centered on **Teleprompter Corporation,** at that time the nation's largest MSO. In 1971 Teleprompter and its CEO, Irving B. Kahn, were convicted of bribing city officials to keep the cable franchise in Johnstown, Pennsylvania. By 1973 Teleprompter also faced serious financial trouble. Three years earlier the company had won a franchise for New York's borough of Manhattan, but the company found the city difficult to wire, encountering problems that ranged from high installation costs and low sign-up rates to vandalism and piracy (hooking up without subscribing). By the end of 1973, Teleprompter had invested $30 million in the franchise without showing a profit. The company undertook a major cost-cutting program, and officials announced Teleprompter might have to write off $62 million in 22 uncompleted cable systems. The U.S. Securities and Exchange Commission investigated the company for possible wrongdoing.

Shock waves spread through the cable business. Financial investors **viewed cable as capital intensive,** that is, a cable system required a lot of money to start and a long time to pay off. **Cable operators found money harder to get to build new systems in the cities.** The U.S. economy lurched into recession. Profits were up, but stock prices were down, investment money scarce, and interest rates high. Several proposed mergers by large MSOs were called off because of adverse market conditions. The wired nation, now known as **blue sky talk,** disappeared as financial realities set in. The NCTA (*PRT,* 4.1.1) asked the FCC to ease regulatory controls, which would reduce the equipment investment needed to meet technical requirements.

### 4.2.7 Premium Services Boom

Some cable operators had already devised a way to generate additional revenues without additional capital outlay. They would scramble a channel and program it with special material, often uncut movies without commercial interruption, that was shipped to the systems on videotape. The operators marketed these channels as **premium services**. They were also called **pay cable** because a premium-service subscriber paid an extra monthly fee over and above that for basic service. In return the operator would unscramble the signal by means of a set-top box with special descrambling circuitry, and the premium-service subscriber could tune in to the special programming at any time.

These early premium services had not been a big business, did not use satellite distribution (or any type of simultaneous network arrangement), and were not offered by many cable systems. However, the NCTA was particularly interested in loosening the FCC's rules on premium services.

The Commission had adopted pay cable rules in 1970. These rules aimed to protect commercial broadcast television from pay cable competition by restricting programming, particularly with respect to movies and sports. Cable interests felt the rules limited pay cable's ability to attract programming and thus prevented the medium from growing. In 1975 the FCC adopted new rules. Cable owners believed the new rules were still too restrictive, and broadcasters said they were lax. However a 1977 federal appeals court overturned the FCC's rules, thus freeing pay cable from most restrictions.

The real pay cable boom started in 1975. More than anyone else, it was **Home Box Office**, Inc. (HBO) that launched the boom in 1975 when it announced plans for a **satellite-interconnected national pay cable network**. The cable business reacted with enthusiasm. Within days large MSOs signed up for the new service and acquired receive-only dishes to pick up HBO's signal. Cable stocks climbed, and the trade began to crawl out of its slump.

To cable operators, pay cable represented a source of revenue without the high investment required to expand a system's physical plant; in other words, low investment and fast return. To subscribers, pay cable represented a chance to see programming—primarily uncut feature films but sometimes nightclub acts, stage performances, concerts, sports events, or original made-for-cable material—without the annoyance of commercial interruption.

HBO's success inspired others. The key seemed to be satellite distribution, a relatively low-cost means to network on a national basis. Myriad companies tried to emulate HBO or become "the CBS of cable" with satellite-delivered programming.

### 4.2.8 Basic Services Multiply

National satellite-delivered nonpay services developed and proliferated. The majority did not follow the HBO premium-channel model but instead sold advertising time. Unlike the network–affiliate relationship in broadcasting (*PRT,*

2.2.3), however, cable operators usually had to pay to carry these advertising-supported networks, generally something like 10 or 15 cents per subscriber per month. The ad-supported cable networks intended for their programming to be offered along with local broadcast signals for the system's lowest monthly rate; for this reason they were often called **basic services**. Many system operators, however, scrambled the signals of some of the more attractive networks and bundled them together as a separate **tier** of service. Subscribers paid extra for this tier.

Most cable networks programmed more like radio stations than like broadcast TV networks; they **specialized**. They had much smaller audiences than ABC, CBS, or NBC. This small-audience factor prevented the cable networks from competing for national advertising on the basis of numbers, so they attempted to make their medium an efficient tool for marketing. They **looked for an audience "niche"** then programmed to that niche, targeting, for example, older people, or people who spoke Spanish as a first language, or African Americans, or young popular music fans.

To find a niche, cable programmers were **willing to experiment** and to attempt new programming forms. Among others, they developed two highly successful genres, music video and home shopping. MTV, launched in 1981, targeted pop music programming at persons in their teens and 20s, an age group highly susceptible to the blandishments of advertising. Four years later, Home Shopping Network combined continual advertising with direct marketing to become both programmer and retailer. These format innovations led to financial success, were copied by other cable programmers, and spread to broadcast television.

Some cable networks did program to a broad, general audience. Two of these, USA Network and Turner Broadcasting System's Superstation WTBS, were particularly successful in attracting cable affiliates.

### 4.2.9 Ancillary Services Offered

Some of the "blue sky" actually came to pass. In 1977 Warner Cable began testing **Qube**, an interactive service in its Columbus, Ohio, cable system. Using a special home terminal, Qube subscribers participated in cable programming—playing interactive games, testing knowledge, and registering opinions. In 1981 Warner–Amex (American Express had gone into partnership with Warner the year before) started building Qube in other systems. There were even plans to interconnect local Qube systems into an interactive national network. Qube failed to pay for itself, however, and the company terminated production and distribution of interactive programming in 1984.

Other companies offered cable-based home security systems. Subscribers could get police and fire surveillance of their homes while away. With a few systems, subscribers could do some transactions at home (shopping, banking, bill paying, etc.) and utilize information and scheduling services (such as news, stock prices, and airline schedules).

## 4.2.10 Cable Shakeout

Despite its wide acceptance by subscribers and its myriad services, cable still did not make much money in the late 1970s and early 1980s. MSOs competed for big-city franchises and found them expensive to win. Smaller firms, unable to get the financing needed to apply for major franchises, merged or sold out to larger companies. At least one company that won franchises with big promises later encountered financial difficulties.

Piracy and churn also ate into cable profits. **Piracy** had spread to the pay channels. Subscribers constructed or purchased decoders that allowed them to view premium channels without paying the added fee. **Churn** was continual turnover of pay-cable subscribers. Many homes would sign up for premium service then, after a short time, drop it.

National cable programmers faced an uphill climb toward profitability. Scores of ad-supported cable networks started or announced plans to launch in the future, so many that even the largest, most advanced cable systems did not have enough channels to carry them all. One major problem for these networks was getting cable systems to carry them. Even the older, better known, ad-supported services, the successful ones, did not reach high numbers of persons—at least relative to broadcast television networks. Advertisers and agencies included them in media buys only reluctantly or experimentally. Most pay services also ran in the red. Unable to find cable space or audience or advertising dollars, several cable network ventures delayed signing on or even went out of business. CBS Cable, for example, ambitious and critically acclaimed, folded in 1982 after losing an estimated $30 million that year alone. The Entertainment Channel, a pay service, closed in 1983 after operating for less than a year. Satellite News Channel, having failed to overtake rival CNN, was sold to CNN owner Turner Broadcasting and closed in 1983 after 16 months of operation. The next year, Turner Broadcasting shut down Cable Music Channel after just 36 days. Few of the many Home Shopping Network clones survived. In the wake of the PTL scandal (PRT, 3.5.3.5) many cable operators stopped carrying that network. Pay-cable subscriptions declined as home video penetration and videocassette rentals increased. Cable operators responded with pay-per-view (PPV) services in which the audience paid by the program. Some of those PPV ventures failed, too.

## 4.3 REGULATION, CONSOLIDATION, AND MORE BLUE SKY: 1984–PRESENT

The growth rate for cable television had accelerated in the early 1980s. By the late 1990s over 11,000 systems served 60.5 million homes.

### 4.3.1 Cable, Newer Technologies, and Competing Media

For years cable TV itself was a new technology. Even as late as the 1980s discussions of new technology would include cable, and publications, both popular and scholarly, would refer to "cable and other new technologies."[12] By the mid-1990s, cable TV, having originated 50 years earlier and now serving two thirds of all TV homes, hardly qualified as a new technology. However, more recent technological developments helped enhance the cable business. Among these were addressability, PPV, optical fiber, and digital compression.

Many operators rebuilt their systems to include **one-way addressability.** This allowed the cable operator to send a signal downstream so that it went to one subscriber or one group of subscribers and to no others. The most common use of one-way addressability was for PPV service. Once a PPV subscriber "ordered" a PPV event (i.e., notified the operator, usually by telephone, of willingness to pay to see the event), the operator would send a signal so that the event was unblocked or descrambled for that particular viewer. In 1992, NBC and Cablevision Systems Corporation offered several packages of the summer Olympic games as the **Pay-Per-View Olympics Triplecast.** The project was a financial failure for the two partners, but because a system needed three-PPV-channel capability in order to carry the Triplecast, operators all over the country had upgraded their facilities. As a result, the cable business as a whole increased its capacity to offer PPV service.

Some systems opted for **advanced one-way addressability.** This allowed for even greater "remote control." When a subscriber changed service (say, adding a tier or dropping two pay services) or even dropped service, the operator could make the changes or cancel the service without dispatching an installer to the subscriber's home.

With **two-way addressability,** a subscriber could send a signal upstream to the headend and ultimately to any other point on the system (such as another subscriber). This would allow cable systems to offer interactive services (including telephone) complete with sophisticated video. That, however, required a switched network, a technical capability that telephone companies had and that most cable companies viewed as prohibitively expensive to build themselves. One way to achieve this interactive capability would be to combine the resources of telephone companies and cable systems, which is what began to occur in 1993. Most such ventures were short-lived, however, as large MSOs began to consider the possibility of buying their own switches and offering telephone service themselves.

Optical fiber and digital compression would change the cable marketplace as well. During the 1980s many cable operators began to install **optical fiber** as a replacement for coaxial cable in parts of their systems. Among the advantages of optical fiber over coaxial cable were clearer video, lower maintenance costs, and much greater bandwidth. Toward the end of the 1980s and the beginning of the 1990s, technological developments made **digital compression** practical for use. Digital compression reduced the amount of video information that needed to be transmitted to produce a picture and thereby increased channel capacity. With optical fiber and digital compression, the number of channels one system could offer was almost unlimited.

People began to talk about the **500-channel universe** and what it would bring. Cable operators viewed this expanded capacity as a way to provide **video-on-demand** (VOD) service or **near-video-on-demand** (NVOD). In VOD, the cable system sent to your home programming (say a currently popular movie) that you could choose to see at the time you want to see it. In NVOD, also called **multiplexing,** the cable system devoted a number of channels to continuous repeat plays with staggered start times of the same program (again, perhaps that movie you wanted to see) so that no subscriber would have to wait more than 15 or 20 minutes before that program started on one of the channels.

One of the first companies to offer true VOD was Time Warner. It launched **Full Service Network** (FSN) in 1994, offering subscribers in Orlando, Florida, VOD and home shopping services. Video news and sports services were to be added later. The VOD aspect used a sophisticated, costly set-top box. When a subscriber ordered programming, a file server at the headend downloaded that programming to the box. The box stored the programming, allowing the subscriber to pause, fast forward, and rewind. FSN cost Time Warner a great deal of money, and the company eventually curtailed the service.

Cable systems looked forward to transmitting **HDTV,** to providing high-speed access to **computer networks,** and to myriad **interactive services.** In the 1990s, when the U.S. Congress considered legislation to establish an **information superhighway,** a nationwide communications connector that would enhance the creation and combining of new technologies and communications services and would be available to companies and individuals, the cable business saw itself as the perfect vehicle for such a venture. Shades of "the wired nation"!

But such technology benefitted competing media, too. Telephone companies. direct-broadcast satellites, and wireless cable (*PRT,* 5.2)—all were multichannel video media that competed with cable. Even TV stations had figured a way to "go multichannel" (*PRT,* 3.6.3).

### 4.3.2 Cable Programming Proliferations

During the 1980s the older, larger cable networks turned the corner toward profitability. Cable penetration approached 50%. In cable homes, cable-only programming captured increasing audience shares at the expense of broadcast network affiliates. MSOs concluded that continued growth lay in **original programming.** They underwrote programming development by purchasing equity in (thus providing funds for) various satellite cable networks.

Despite technological advances, most cable systems still had limited channel capacity. By the time a system had loaded on all broadcast TV signals, mandated channels (such as access), C-SPAN, several of the most popular premium channels, and must-have ad-supported networks (such as CNN, ESPN, and MTV), there were very few channels left to carry new networks, even on a system with 50-plus channels. Many companies starting new networks offered equity at very low prices to MSOs as means to get on their cable systems. During the 1990s, some new cable networks actually began using FCC-mandated leased-access channels, paying cable systems to squeeze onto crowded channel lineups.

Even in this highly competitive environment, two factors during the 1990s seemed to spur formation of even more cable program sources. One was the **retransmission consent** option for TV stations spelled out in the 1992 Cable Act. Although few cable systems actually wound up paying to carry the signals of TV broadcast stations (*PRT,* 3.6.4), retransmission consent did result in a number of TV stations and networks creating programming that the cable systems carried.

The second factor was talk of "the 500-channel universe" (*PRT,* 4.3.1). Entrepreneurs felt sure that with such an abundance of channel capacity there would be room for many more advertising-supported networks. Networks formed focusing on every interest and seeking every audience niche imaginable, from betting and gaming to Filipino Americans, from horses to women's sports—and lots of channels featuring home shopping, various stripes of popular music, and infomercials (program-length commercials). As in the past, many—perhaps most—of these programming ventures would fail, but enough would succeed that the idea of hitting it big with cable would continue to lure people with new ideas or new twists on old ideas.

### 4.3.3 Cable and Congress

Congress waited nearly 40 years to deal head on with cable TV. It had previously written law that impacted cable on a peripheral basis; the 1976 copyright act, for example, included provisions that applied to cable (*PRT,* 4.2.5). When Congress did finally address cable directly, it wrote three laws in relatively rapid succession. Each treated the medium quite differently.

*4.3.3.1 1984: Deregulation of Cable.*    As the cable business had grown bigger and moved into larger markets over the years, the nature of franchising created friction between cable system operators and the cities. Cities awarded franchises on a competitive basis and, according to cable operators, made exorbitant demands for facilities and payments. To win big-city franchises, would-be operators felt forced to promise fantastic systems. Their investment was long range at best. Capital outlay was so large that profit depended on subscribers opting for extra-charge tiers, multiple pay channels, and expensive ancillary services. Churn and piracy lowered earnings. Further, contended the cable operators, the cities used their rate-regulation power primarily to refuse cable system requests for needed increases in subscriber charges.

The cities, on the other hand, looked on operators as opportunists. Here were a bunch of outsiders (with maybe a few local people included to make it look good) requesting permission to use city easements and rights-of-way to lay cable. They would have a monopoly to sell TV signals—something citizens really did not need and could already get for free. With demands for municipal services outstripping city resources, cable operators should be happy to provide some of those services and pay a franchise fee in exchange for an exclusive franchise.

The FCC had little authority to deal with franchising. Congress would have to address this problem directly. After several years of attempts, the NCTA, the National League of Cities, and the U.S. Conference of Mayors agreed on a proposal for legislation. Congress enacted this legislation as the **Cable Communications Policy Act of 1984,** its first comprehensive cable law.

The 1984 Cable Act added a few requirements to the business of cable system operation, but for the most part it was **deregulatory.** A cable operator could, for example, set subscriber rates for basic service and adjust program services relatively free of governmental restrictions or requirements. The act ended piecemeal local regulation of cable. It specified obligations of the cable operator to the franchising authority, and it limited demands the authority could make on the operator. Among the more welcome provisions for cable were those that made denial of franchise renewal more difficult, limited the franchise fee, and, of course, allowed an operator to raise subscriber rates for basic service without first getting permission. The 1984 Cable Act assured a profitable, predictable rate of return and thus made cable more attractive to investors.

*4.3.3.2 1992: Reregulation of Cable.*   Cable operators took advantage of every break offered by the 1984 act. The provision permitting unlimited basic-rate increases clicked into effect in 1987, and the MSOs made liberal and frequent use of it. Average monthly basic rate rose from $11 in 1986 to $21 in 1993. The operators explained to irate customers that the increases were only a means to make up for the years that local regulation had artificially depressed rates, and besides, the increases would result in expanded channel capacity, more programming, and additional ancillary capabilities. Subscribers only saw that their rates had gone up faster than the rate of inflation, and they screamed to their elected representatives in Congress.

Critics accused cable of wielding undue market power and contended that the cable business was anticompetitive. Many cable networks (which were often owned in whole or in part by large cable operators) refused to make programming available to competing technologies such as home satellite and wireless cable services. Cable conglomerates began to acquire large numbers of local franchises. There were suggestions that cable's alleged abuses should be corrected through legislation. The National League of Cities and the U.S Conference of Mayors both adopted resolutions urging that telephone companies be allowed to provide video services that would compete with established cable systems.

Complaints led Congress to pass its second major cable legislation. The **Cable Television Consumer Protection Act of 1992 reregulated** cable. Among other things, the act reimposed subscriber rate regulation, ensured that programming would be available for competing technologies, and instructed the FCC to set limits on various forms of cable ownership. The net result of the 1984 and 1992 acts was that federal law now impacted almost every area of cable operation, including programming.

*4.3.3.3 1996: Deregulation of Cable—and Everybody Else.* The 1992 act made those in the cable business very unhappy. They contended that the law would result in their losing money and that it violated their First Amendment rights. They immediately challenged it in court and worked on Capitol Hill to repair what they saw as the legislative damage.

Two years later the tide began to turn. U.S. voters put Republican majorities in Congress, and these new majorities made deregulation a major thrust of their legislative program. At the same time they deregulated, Congress wanted to **increase competition** so that the marketplace would keep consumer prices down. The result was the **Telecommunications Act of 1996.**

As discussed previously, this law affected both radio (*PRT,* 2.7) and television broadcasting (*PRT,* 3.6.3) and was one of the most extensive amendments ever to the Communications Act. However, the 1996 act had its greatest impact on cable and telephone companies. The cable business got its wish: Subscriber rate regulations were eased. However, in writing this law, Congress recognized the fast-blurring boundaries between media. For example, it **allowed telephone companies to provide video programming.** It eliminated a previous law that had prohibited telephone companies from getting into the cable business, so now cable systems faced the possibility of competition from the local telephone company. But the law also **allowed cable systems to offer telephone service!** Among other major provisions aimed specifically at cable were the following:

- Operators were required to scramble programming that subscribers deemed unsuitable for children.
- Cable operators were empowered to refuse access programs they considered obscene or indecent.
- Cable programmers, like broadcast TV programmers, were required to develop a ratings system (*PRT,* 3.6.3).
- A cable operator could not acquire an existing telephone company within the system's franchise area.[13]
- An operator could (through elimination of a statutory antitrafficking provision) sell a cable system without first having to own it at least 3 years.

### 4.3.4 Structural and Financial Changes

During the 1980s some of the same buy–sell fever rampant in broadcasting (*PRT,* 3.5.3.2) impacted cable. During the 1990s the **cable business began to consolidate,** the midsized MSOs selling out to the big MSOs.

Ted Turner (Box 4.1), after failing to take over CBS (*PRT,* 3.5.3.3), turned his attention elsewhere. In 1985 Turner made a deal to buy MGM/United Artists Entertainment Co. for $1.5 billion, primarily for MGM's huge library of films, television series, and cartoons (he spun off United Artists as a separate company and later sold the MGM production and distribution businesses). The next year, he lost money on coverage of the Goodwill Games, an expensive cooperative effort

---

**BOX 4.1 TED TURNER: ATLANTA'S COMMUNICATIONS GADFLY**

Robert E. Turner took a shaky family outdoor advertising business and parlayed it into a communications empire. In 1970 Turner bought WTCG, a money-losing UHF television station in Atlanta, programmed it with sports and movies, and made it available by satellite to cable systems all over the country. He bought Atlanta professional baseball and basketball teams to guarantee access to sports programming and formed Southern Satellite Systems to guarantee nationwide distribution for his station. Turner thus converted his UHF television investment from a 98-pound weakling into superstation WTBS. He used WTBS as the cornerstone for TBS, CNN, Headline News, Turner Network Television, and various other broadcast and cable enterprises. His competitive tactics and his critical comments on broadcast networks made trade press headlines and upset the broadcasting establishment. He sold a minority share of TBS to cable operators in 1987 but for all intents and purposes continued to run the organization. Eight years later he merged TBS into the giant Time Warner media conglomerate. Time Warner CEO Gerald Levin engineered the deal and continued as head of the merged firm, while Turner came in as a vice chair and also directed certain major operations.

---

with the Soviet Union. This loss presented a problem; if unable to make payments on his MGM debt, he would gradually lose control of TBS. In 1987 a group of MSOs agreed to pump $575 million into TBS in exchange for a 35% share of the company and 7 of the 15 seats on the TBS board. This diluted Turner's control over the company that bore his name. Nonetheless, the board subsequently approved major purchases of program resources such as the Hanna-Barbera animation library, Castle Rock Entertainment, and New Line Cinema. It also approved launch of new cable programming ventures such as Cartoon Network, Turner Classic Movies, SportSouth Network, Turner Network Television, and several widely distributed international program services.

Several other cable programmers changed ownership, too. National Amusements, Inc., a film-theater operator, acquired Viacom International, part owner of Lifetime and owner of Showtime and The Movie Channel. Viacom, in turn, acquired Paramount Communications after a long, expensive bidding war with QVC, then sold its interest in the Lifetime network and put its cable systems up for sale. Viacom was, nonetheless, still a major player in cable television. It held controlling interest in FLIX, The Movie Channel, MTV, Nickelodeon, Showtime, VH-1, and the MSG Network regional sports service, and half interest in Comedy Central, SciFi Channel, and USA Network.

**Tele-Communications, Inc.** (TCI), **the nation's largest MSO,** pursued an aggressive program of investment and acquisition during the 1980s and 1990s. It bought out a number of cable operators of various sizes. In the programming area, TCI acquired equity, either directly or through its Liberty Media programming subsidiary, in the following networks and services: American Movie Classics, Black Entertainment Television, La Cadena Deportiva, Encore, Family Channel, AMC, The Box, Home Shopping Network, MacNeil/Lehrer Productions, NewSport, Prime Time Tonight, QVC, Starz!, and various regional sports networks.

In 1989 Time, Incorporated, and Warner Communications merged. This merger united the second and sixth largest MSOs. It brought together the largest pay-cable programmer (Time's HBO and Cinemax) and a leading producer of motion pictures and TV programming. It also created **Time Warner,** Incorporated. Time Warner, a huge firm from its very creation, bought Turner Broadcasting System in 1995. That purchase assured Time Warner's ranking as the world's largest media and entertainment company.

Some of these companies intensified the trend toward system consolidation in 1994. Large MSOs bought out medium-sized MSOs as means to **cluster** cable systems, to own a number of adjacent or nearby systems that collectively served a large number of subscribers. By clustering, the MSOs improved growth prospects for their cable business. They also accumulated a critical mass of customers and service areas for telephone, interactive services, and other businesses they might launch. MSOs Telecable and Viacom, for example, sold systems to TCI, bringing the latter's subscriber count to 17 million households. Time Warner entered into a joint venture with Newhouse, bought Summit Communications, and bought systems from Cablevision Industries. The media group of telephone company U.S. West bought Continental Cablevision in a merger priced at $10.8 billion. The latter deal brought the number of U.S. cable customers managed by U.S. West and its partner, Time Warner, to 16.2 million.

Other MSOs expanded their cable holdings during this period. By 1996 *Broadcasting & Cable*[14] reported that, through ongoing consolidation, the four largest MSOs controlled 60% of all cable systems, and the 100 largest operators controlled 95% of all systems.

Cable companies also expanded in other areas. Both MSOs and programmers invested in foreign and international ventures. Among the networks that established Latin American services, for example, were Canal de Noticias, Discovery, ESPN, Gems, HBO, MTV, TeleUno, Turner, and USA. Among those programming to Europe were QVC, TCI, Turner, and Viacom. Several networks began to draw on their programming for direct sales of videocassettes and as a source for creating multimedia CD-ROM products. TCI invested as a minority partner in Microsoft's online computer network, bundled with the Windows 95 computer graphical user interface.

## 4.4 SATELLITE MASTER ANTENNA TELEVISION

About the same time that the first primitive cable systems were built, **Milton Shapp,** founder of Jerrold Electronics, designed a similar method of TV signal distribution. In 1949 at the National Electronics Distributors Association in

Chicago, Shapp displayed his specialized TV signal distribution system. The system was a master antenna that TV dealers could use in their stores to demonstrate a number of TV sets at the same time. In 1950, Shapp broadened his vision from electronics stores to apartment houses. Early that year, he installed a master antenna system in a New Jersey apartment house.[15]

In the 1950s television set ownership boomed. Most multiunit dwelling facilities, however, did not allow residents to erect their own individual outside antennas. So apartment houses, condominiums, mobile home parks, planned unit developments, and others solved the problem with Shapp's idea. They installed **master antenna television** (MATV) systems. A typical MATV system consisted of a TV receiving antenna, distribution amplifiers, cable to each of the individual dwelling units, and a connection tap of some type to which the resident's TV set could be attached. It was, in other words, a great deal like early CATV systems except it was **installed on private property and did not use the public right-of-way.** Fees for the service were either included as part of the rent or billed separately to residents who subscribed.

During the 1970s some entrepreneurs began offering one- or two-channel satellite service for MATV systems. The C-band receiving dishes of the day were large and expensive, so a firm offering such service would buy one receiving dish to serve many housing facilities. The signal received from the satellite would feed to a multipoint distribution service (MDS; *PRT,* 5.2) transmitter that would "broadcast" it in all directions over the microwave frequencies. MDS receiving antennas at each of the housing facilities with which the firm had a contract would pick up the signal and feed it into the MATV system. The satellite programming services thus distributed (there were few at the time) were generally some variation of the HBO theme, uncut movies without commercial interruption.[16]

Communication firms began to put more powerful satellites in orbit. Dish manufacturers were able to reduce the size and price of their product commensurately, the number of satellite-delivered program services increased, and eventually each building that wanted satellite service on its MATV system could have its own TV receive-only ground station (dish and associated electronics). This was the beginning of **satellite master antenna television** (SMATV; usually pronounced SMAT-vee).

There was still one block to widespread SMATV: The FCC required that all receiver dishes be licensed. In 1979, however, the Commission ended that requirement, and the service began to proliferate. Additionally, in 1991 the Commission opened 73 point-to-point microwave channels for use by SMATV, allowing operators to serve multiple locations with multiple channels rather than building a separate headend for each.

A SMATV operator would contract with the owner of a multiunit dwelling or private housing development to provide cable-type service. Because SMATV operated on private property, it was free from regulation—it needed no franchise, had none of the local regulations that usually accompany a franchise, and paid no franchise fee. Further, most SMATVs did not meet the FCC's definition of a cable system, so they were, for the most part, exempt from federal regulation, too. These advantages made SMATVs attractive to entrepreneurs and helped these systems to be successful members of the TV distribution business.

## NOTES

1. By the end of the freeze there were just 108 stations on the air; all had been authorized before the freeze. Robert Pepper examined these influential stations in "The Pre-Freeze Television Stations," In *American Broadcasting: A Source Book on the History of Radio and Television.* Lawrence W. Lichty and Malachi C. Topping, Eds. (New York: Hastings, 1975) 139–147.

2. Even with all that, the picture often consisted of "snow." When a TV set that is not hooked up to a cable system is tuned to a channel where there is no local station, the screen fills with a random pattern of white and gray dots that looks something like a blizzard; this is **snow**. If the set receives a weak signal from a distant station transmitting on that channel, the viewer may be able to discern a snowy picture. But on good nights, when weather conditions are just right, the distant viewer can pick up a nearly snow-free picture.

During the late 1940s and early 1950s there might be just one or two families in an area that owned television receivers. On good nights, the set owner's darkened living room would fill with "TV-less" neighbors and relatives, all peering at the small screen—a 12-inch tube was considered huge—of this box that brought moving pictures into the home. The future as predicted in science fiction was here at last.

3. E. Stratford Smith, "The Emergence of CATV: A Look at the Evolution of a Revolution," *Proceedings of the IEEE* 58 (1970): 967–982.

4. First Report and Order, 38 F.C.C 683 (1965).

5. Second Report and Order, 2 F.C.C. 2d 725 (1966).

6. Although this concept of the wired nation eventually fell by the wayside (*PRT*, 4.2.6), some of its ideas would reappear in the 1990s concept popularly known as the information superhighway (*PRT*, 5.14). However, its most practical and popular realization has been the computer-based Internet (*PRT*, 5.6.3).

7. United States v. Southwestern Cable Co., 392 U.S. 157 (1968).

8. In fact, the new rules required systems with more than 3,500 subscribers to originate programming. This requirement was, however, challenged in court (United States v. Midwest Video Corp., 406 U.S. 649, 1972) and as a result was in effect for only a short period before the FCC rescinded it in 1974.

9. First Report and Order, 20 F.C.C. 2d 201 (1969).

10. Second Report and Order, 23 F.C.C. 2d 816 (1970), and Final Report and Order, 21 F.C.C. 2d 307 (1970).

11. Fortnightly Corp. v. United Artists Television, 392 U.S. (1968); and Teleprompter Corp. v. Columbia Broadcasting System, 415 U.S. 394 (1974).

12. Chapter 5 of the third edition of this volume, for example, was titled "Cable and Other Nonbroadcast Technologies." In addition to cable television, discussions in that chapter dealt with topics such as direct broadcast satellite, computers, and videotex.

13. The reciprocal of this prohibition was that a telephone company could not buy an existing cable system within the telephone company's service area. The cable operator could, however, build a new telephone system in its franchise area, and the telephone company could start a new video delivery system in its service area.

14. Michael Katz, "Cable Trading: A Big Deal," 11 Mar. 1996: 42.

15. The history of SMATV and cable television actually intersect here. Robert J. Tarlton, owner of Panther Valley Television Company in Lansford, Pennsylvania, used Jerrold products and had Shapp's cooperation in constructing one of the very first cable systems in 1950. Mary

Alice Mayer Phillips, *CATV: A History of Community Antenna Television* (Evanston, IL: Northwestern University Press, 1972) 35–39.

16. This is another intersection-of-technologies point; this use of MDS would lead eventually to development of the medium with the oxymoronic name wireless cable (*PRT,* 5.2).

## FURTHER READING

Bartlett, Eugene R. *Cable Television Technology and Operations: HDTV & NTSC Systems.* New York: McGraw-Hill, 1990.

Bibb, Porter. *It Ain't As Easy As It Looks: Ted Turner's Amazing Story.* New York: Crown, 1993.

Bruck, Connie. *Master of the Game: Steve Ross and the Creation of Time Warner.* New York: Simon & Schuster, 1994.

Clurman, Richard M. *To the End of Time: The Seduction and Conquest of a Media Empire.* New York: Simon & Schuster, 1992.

Crandall, Robert W., and Harold Furchtgott-Roth. *Cable TV: Regulation or Competition?* Washington, DC: Brookings Institute, 1996.

Engelman, Ralph. *The Origins of Public Access Cable Television, 1966–1972* (Journalism Monographs 120). Columbia, MO: Association for Education in Journalism and Mass Communication, 1990.

Garay, Ronald. *Cable Television: A Reference Guide to Information.* Westport, CT: Greenwood, 1988.

Goldberg, Robert, and Gerald Jay Goldberg. *Citizen Turner: The Wild Rise of an American Tycoon.* New York: Harcourt, 1995.

Heeter, Carrie, and Bradley S. Greenberg. *Cableviewing.* Norwood, NJ: Ablex, 1988.

Johnson, Leland L. *Toward Competition in Cable Television.* Cambridge, MA: MIT University Press, 1994.

Johnson, Leland L., and Deborah R. Castleman. *Direct Broadcast Satellites: A Competitive Alternative to Cable Television?* Santa Monica, CA: Rand, 1991.

Jones, Glenn R. *Jones Cable Television and Information Infrastructure Dictionary.* 4th ed. Englewood, CO: Jones, 1994.

Mair, George. *Inside HBO: The Billion Dollar War Between HBO, Hollywood, and Home Video Revolution.* New York: Dodd, 1988.

Many, Kevin. *Megamedia Shakeout: The Inside Story of the Leaders and the Losers in the Exploding Communications Industry.* New York: Wiley, 1995.

Nance, Scott. *Music You Can See: The MTV Story.* Las Vegas, NV: Pioneer, 1993.

National Cable Television Association. *A Cable Television Primer.* Washington, DC: NCTA, 1990.

Ostroff, David H. "A History of STV, Inc. and the 1964 California Vote Against Pay Television." *Journal of Broadcasting* 27 (1983): 371.

Picard, Robert G., Ed. *The Cable Networks Handbook.* Riverside, CA: Carpelan, 1993.

Raugust, Karen. *Merchandise Licensing in the Television Industry.* Boston: Focal, 1996.

Reed, Robert M., and Maxine K. Reed. *The Facts on File Dictionary of Television, Cable, and Video.* New York: Facts on File, 1994.

Reymer & Gersin Associates and National Association of Broadcasters. *Building Bridges With Cable: A Survey of Local Cable System Operators and MSO Executives.* Washington, DC: National Association of Broadcasters, 1990.

Wasko, Janet. *Hollywood in the Information Age: Beyond the Silver Screen.* Austin: University of Texas Press, 1994.

# 5

# OTHER ELECTRONIC MASS MEDIA
# TECHNOLOGIES: FROM 1948

The history of radio and television did not end with broadcast or cable television. More happened, much more. Electronic technology continued to evolve. This evolution led to (a) additional electronic media that competed for advertising and audience and (b) devices and concepts that affected or became part of radio and television. Ultimately the separate components were seen as parts of a national information infrastructure that was at the center of the U.S. economy.

This chapter begins with developments in electronics, the enabling technology for the media subsequently discussed. Then we examine delivery systems—wireless cable (multichannel TV), satellite distribution and relay, direct broadcast satellite, and electronic text. We follow with home devices—personal computers, video games, VCRs, videodisc players, and advances in receiver technology. We look at changes in broadcast television reproduction—HDTV and multichannel television sound. We also look at changes in the tools of the trade and the uses of those tools—miniaturization of production equipment and growth of small-format production. We end with common carrier developments and the federal government's efforts to create a national information infrastructure (NII).

## 5.1 SOLID-STATE AND DIGITAL ELECTRONICS

Solid-state and digital electronics did more than displace tubes and wires. They were revolutionary developments, such a departure from their predecessors that they gave rise to Promethean advances in the ability to manipulate and process electronic information. All phases were affected—production, distribution, transmission, and reception. Pretransistor media such as broadcasting and cable were changed and improved. Newer media, including many discussed in this chapter, were created.

### 5.1.1 Transistors

The vacuum tube, long at the heart of electronic communications, had limitations. It was expensive to make because many of the glass bulbs had to be hand blown. It was fragile and bulky, consumed a great deal of power, and generated heat. It changed temperature and, thus, operating parameters of the equipment of which it was part. It burned out. Despite these problems, the vacuum tube represented the state of the art in electronics for 40 years.

Then in 1948, three Bell scientists developed a simple, solid device that performed the same chores as the vacuum tube, except better. The scientists were John Bardeen, Walter H. Brattain, and William Shockley. Their device consisted of a sandwich of semiconducting materials, primarily germanium crystals, and later silicon. A weak current entered the sandwich and, because of the arrangement of the crystals, controlled a stronger current—just like a vacuum tube. However, it was smaller and worked faster than a vacuum tube, failed infrequently, gave off little heat, and was cheap to make. It was called the *transistor.*

### 5.1.2 Chips

The next step was to manufacture electronic circuits including all components in one device and in one process. Two engineers working independently developed variations of this idea in 1959—Jack Kilby and Robert Noyce. As finally developed, the construction process produced a silicon bead or chip that had been treated in several stages to create an integrated circuit—a tiny printed circuit that incorporated transistors, diodes, resistors, capacitors, and connections. A chip could be programmed to do more than one task—play a video game, guide a space vehicle, or operate a video effects unit. The chip made possible the personal computer and other digital electronic devices. Further advances in solid-state technology increased the numbers of components on a single chip.

Solid-state technology changed the concept of electronic equipment manufacture and repair. No longer was there a circuit. Now, equipment consisted primarily of circuit boards filled with, first, transistors and other electronic components and, later, chips. If a piece of equipment malfunctioned, technicians did not look for and replace the specific resistor or condenser at fault; they tested and replaced entire circuit boards.

### 5.1.3 Development of Digital Technology

The chip was a digital electronic circuit. It did not measure the size of an electronic signal; it simply looked for the presence or absence of a signal—that is, on or off. The chip utilized various combinations of on (or 1) and off (or 0) to represent and manipulate any number. This was digital calculation, using the binary system of numbers (based on 2), the type of processing done by most modern computers.

Alec Reeves, an English scientist, demonstrated that digital techniques could apply to information other than pure mathematics. In 1938, Reeves patented pulse code modulation, conversion of a telephone signal into varying combinations of 1 and 0. Years later, solid-state technology paved the way to apply this same principle to radio and television. An audio or video signal that had been digitized (converted into binary code) could be processed, altered, transmitted, or copied multiple times, then reconverted into audio or video with no loss of fidelity. Digital equipment could even create signals. Such capabilities led to advances in the transmission of radio and television signals, audio and video effects, networking, video graphics and animation, production and postproduction, and consumer electronic products.

### 5.2 RISE OF WIRELESS CABLE

Wireless cable, also called multichannel television, emerged in 1983. It consisted of channels from the **instructional television fixed service** (ITFS), the operational fixed service (OFS), and the **multipoint distribution service** (MDS). All transmitted signals omnidirectionally (360°) in the microwave frequencies (*PRT*, 12.8). Special antennas picked up the signals.

The FCC established the ITFS in 1963. Originally ITFS had 31 channels; 3 were later reallocated to OFS. Only educational institutions could get ITFS licenses; the channels were to be used to distribute televised instructional programming.

The three OFS channels were used mainly by cities and oil companies. In 1981, the FCC amended its rules to allow OFS licensees to supply pay television programming to apartments, hotels, and other multiunit dwellings.

The MDS began in the early 1970s. A common-carrier service, MDS consisted of two channels. Licensees leased channel time to users who provided televised material to be transmitted to specific points.

MDS proved ideal to distribute pay programming to multiunit dwellings. At first, receiving antennas cost too much for home use, but prices dropped over the years, and as early as 1978, entrepreneurs offered MDS service to homes. By March 1980, the FCC had authorized 131 MDS systems; 2 years later the figure had gone over 350. As a home subscription programming service, however, MDS was handicapped by a limited number of channels. Cable television could offer a greater variety of channels for the money. Whenever cable penetrated a market, the MDS subscriber count dropped.

In 1983, the FCC reallocated eight channels from ITFS to MDS, thereby creating two new four-channel television services (**multichannel MDS**; MMDS). The FCC also permitted ITFS licensees to lease "excess" capacity (time when ITFS channels carried no instructional programming) to others. Theoretically, programmers in a given market might now be able to lease as many as 15 channels full time (2 MDS, 3 OFS, and 8 MMDS) plus as many as 20 part time (ITFS channels), for a total of 33 channels. That could surely compete with cable.

Some 16,000 applications for MMDS channels flooded the FCC. The Commission decided to select applicants by lottery. Nearly 2 years passed before the lottery awarded the first licenses. In the meantime, investor interest had flagged. Would-be multichannel programmers had difficulty finding start-up money and getting distribution rights to popular cable services, such as HBO and Showtime. Nonetheless, by 1990, wireless cable had appeared in a number of large markets.

The 1992 Cable Act mandated fair access to programming for the competitors of cable television. With new programming available, the number of wireless cable subscribers increased from 200,000 in 1992 to about 750,000 by 1994, served by 170 systems. Investments by communication companies such as Bell Atlantic and Pacific Telesis helped fuel growth and provided economic stability. Wireless cable systems also operate in more than 60 nations, and the system in Mexico City has more than 450,000 subscribers.[1] Some entrepreneurs have begun using LPTV channels for wireless cable. **Subscription LPTV** services use digitally compressed signals to provide multiple programs to viewers.

Proponents of a new **local multipoint distribution service** (LMDS) wanted to share the 28 GHz band with some satellite services. Others advocated using the 41 GHz band for the service. Such high frequencies would restrict signals to a short distance—no more than a few city blocks—but in densely populated areas LMDS could prove to be a profitable business.

## 5.3 SATELLITE RELAY AND DISTRIBUTION

As we ponder the recent revolution in the electronic media, perhaps no technology has had a greater impact than the communication satellite. New program services, live news from anywhere in the world, and specialized training programs for employees are all made feasible by communication satellites.

### 5.3.1 Impact of Satellite Relay

Communication satellites broke the bottleneck that existed when AT&T's terrestrial facilities were needed to create radio and television networks. AT&T's coaxial cable and microwave transmission facilities were expensive, and newcomers were required to pay significant up-front tariffs.

Communication satellites meant anyone who could afford a few hundred dollars an hour could distribute programming to broadcast stations, cable systems, or directly to the home. Networks could easily be put together for a one-time or occasional basis.

Communication satellites also enabled local stations to increase their news coverage. The news department must consider how long it takes a reporter and crew to travel to an event, cover it, and return to the station in time to prepare the package for the newscast. With **satellite news gathering** (SNG), a feed (live or taped) can be made even during the newscast. Consortia, such as **Conus** and

Florida News Network enabled affiliates and independents to present national and international news to local audiences without having to rely on the major broadcast network news departments.

More news sources allowed stations to increase the length of their newscasts. Where local news had consisted of 30-minute programs leading to the network newscast, in many markets 90-minute, and even 2-hour, local newscasts became common.

Finally, in such areas as live sports, the communication satellite allowed expanded coverage. "Whiparounds" from one collegiate basketball tournament game to another, or split-screen telecasts of two baseball playoff games have become common. Prior to the advent of communication satellites, such programming was economically and technically more complicated.

### 5.3.2 History of Satellite Communication

Arthur C. Clarke first proposed using satellites for communications in 1945. Although Clarke is best known as the author of such works as *2001: A Space Odyssey*, what he proposed was not science fiction. Writing in the British journal *Wireless World*, Clarke noted that three satellites in geostationary orbit above the earth could relay signals to all points of the earth. Clarke's idea proved highly workable; in fact, the only problem was demand for satellite capacity. We long ago exceeded the need for only three satellites. In recognition of Clarke's proposal the space 22,300 miles above the equator, where all geostationary satellites must be placed into orbit is known as the **Clarke Belt.** Other communication satellites, placed in **low earth orbit,** required tracking by receivers.

The United States launched its first active communications satellite in late 1958. In 1962, AT&T launched a satellite that relayed television programming between Europe and the United States. That same year, Congress passed the **Communications Satellite Act.** This act created the **Communications Satellite Corporation** (Comsat), a private corporation that launched **Early Bird,** the first commercial communications satellite in 1965. Comsat became the U.S. representative in **Intelsat,** the **International Telecommunications Satellite Organization.** All international commercial satellite traffic, except for the then-Soviet bloc, went through Intelsat satellites and ground stations. American users accessing Intelsat first had to use Comsat facilities. Comsat became a highly profitable company, and many complained about the Comsat monopoly.

Early Bird and its successors provided international and long-distance commercial service for all types of communication, including radio and television programming. As time passed, satellite communications proved superior to most other forms of relay—more reliable, less distortion and noise, and less expensive.

In 1972, the FCC revised its rules to encourage satellite relay for domestic use (domsats). Various companies launched satellites and offered service. Perhaps the most important push came from Ted Turner and Gerald Levin. Both men were interested in delivering programming nationally to cable systems: Turner's "Superstation," WTBS, and Levin Home Box Office. Each offered to deliver programming to any cable system with receiving capability. For cable systems looking for specialized programming in urban markets, the unique services proved a boon.

Soon, other services looked at satellite distribution of programming. Most of the early efforts were by pay services, such as Showtime and The Movie Channel, but soon such basic services as CNN and ESPN created networks of cable systems linked by communication satellites.

The broadcast networks used satellites for news, and to backhaul programs from remote sites to network control centers. However, the broadcast networks were slower to switch to satellite distribution to affiliates. An important reason was that under the affiliation agreements then in place, the networks paid for the terrestrial AT&T links to the affiliates. The networks said their affiliates would have to pay for their own receiving equipment. The networks also feared that once the affiliate had a dish it could be used to receive competitive programs from syndicators or ad hoc networks.

The first network to switch to satellite networking was PBS. The lower costs of delivering programs, compared to the terrestrial networks, were highly attractive to the struggling noncommercial services. PBS switched to satellite distribution in 1978.

Another key player was RCA, then the parent company of NBC, and a satellite manufacturer. NBC offered its affiliates a price break if they would purchase an RCA earth station. Eventually, every major cable and broadcast network converted from land lines to satellite.

In 1984, Hubbard Broadcasting opened the door to SNG. Hubbard organized Conus, a satellite-based news distribution service. Stations picked up video by satellite from truck-mounted uplink dishes at remote locations. Conus coordinated the stations' satellite use. Subsequently, other organizations followed Hubbard's lead, including the commercial broadcast networks and CNN.

## 5.4 DIRECT BROADCAST SATELLITE

The first equipment to receive satellite signals was expensive—$75,000 and more for the simplest dish and electronics receivers, or ground stations, called **television receive only** (TVRO). However, prices dropped, the necessary dish size shrunk, and reception technology improved. With mass production, surely ground stations were possible for every home. Then a national programmer could transmit directly to home ground stations through a **direct broadcast satellite** (DBS), a dedicated service intended for individual subscribers.

### 5.4.1 High- and Medium-Power DBS

Comsat proposed the DBS idea in August 1979. The following June, Comsat set up **Satellite Television Corporation** (STC) as its DBS subsidiary. In December 1980, STC applied to the FCC to construct a pay-supported DBS system for the

United States. The system would utilize new high-power satellites whose radio and television signals could be received with roof-mounted dish antennas 1 to 2 feet in diameter. The DBS satellites would operate in the Ku frequency band rather than the lower frequency C band used by most existing satellites, and would deliver programming directly to customers.

The FCC accepted STC's application and invited others. Broadcasters fought the idea of DBS. After all, if a programmer could transmit directly to the public, what would happen to the local station? Nonetheless, the Commission authorized some applicants to construct DBSs, the first of which would be in orbit no earlier than 1986. A trade group was formed, the **Direct Broadcasting Satellite Association** (DBSA).

Several companies decided to get a jump on the competition. They secured FCC permission to use existing medium-power Ku-band satellites. This would require a slightly larger dish but allow DBS service to begin immediately. **United Satellite Communications, Inc.** (USCI) was first, commencing its multichannel DBS pay service in Fall 1983. USCI opened marketing efforts in Indianapolis, then rolled out the service eastward. The venture proved the technology would work, and eventually USCI signed up some 10,000 subscribers. However, the company did not attract enough subscribers and revenues to cover its high overhead and could not attract investors to underwrite continued operation. USCI, the only operating DBS venture, went under in 1985. Most other companies abandoned their DBS projects, including Comsat.

In other parts of the world, however, DBS-type services were more successful. In countries lacking cable television infrastructure, satellites became a practical means of delivering programs. By the end of the 1980s Europe had launched its first DBSs. Rupert Murdoch's Sky Channel in Europe and Star Channel in Asia delivered movies, original programming, and such familiar fare as the international versions of MTV, CNN, and HBO. NHK, Japan's national network, also had a high-power system operating. In the United States, only two of the original eight applicants still had active plans to go into high-power DBS. Other firms, however, had taken note of foreign DBS efforts and the growth of backyard TVRO. Talk of U.S. DBS heated up again.

### 5.4.2 Home TVRO Develops

Even when earth stations were still expensive, a few individuals—mainly the very wealthy and those who lived in remote areas beyond the reach of cable and broadcast signals—invested in dishes and picked signals off satellites for their private enjoyment. In 1979 the FCC further deregulated communication satellites, including removal of the requirement that individuals needed a license for a receiving station. This started the TVRO or home satellite dish trade. The satellite-delivered cable networks argued that these dish owners were illegally intercepting private transmissions meant only for cable systems.

Retail businesses specialized in sales of backyard earth stations. Home dish prices dropped, eventually dipping below $2,000. As prices fell, more people bought. The Cable Communications Policy Act of 1984 sanctioned home reception of unscrambled signals; none were scrambled at the time. The number of home dishes rose from 4,000 in 1980 to 1.3 million in late 1985 and sales hit 45,000 per month.

This was where the cable operators stepped in. According to one estimate, one third of all new home dishes went into cable franchise areas; people bought dishes and viewed all satellite-delivered networks for free rather than paying the local cable company to view only those networks carried by its system. Early in 1985, cable operators demanded that satellite-delivered networks scramble programming (the Cable Act provided stiff penalties for unauthorized reception of scrambled signals).

TVRO interests objected and vowed to fight any move toward scrambling. Manufacturers and dealers objected because they saw their business going down the drain. Home dish owners objected because they could no longer receive free programming. There was a certain irony to such objections as satellite programming had not been intended for direct reception in the first place. The cable networks used satellites to relay programming to cable systems and had never given permission for direct reception.

### 5.4.3 TVRO Legitimized

Satellite-delivered program services needed access to cable's large subscriber base. They acceded to the cable operators' demand to scramble. HBO was first. It began full-time scrambling in January 1986.

The 1984 Cable Act had also provided for the marketing of satellite cable programming for private viewing. The Videocipher II scrambling system provided the means for that marketing. Signals could be transmitted that turned on and off individual home descramblers, allowing sale of satellite programming on a subscription basis.

The transition to scrambling was not easy. The many problems included the following:

- At first, no one was able to put together a comprehensive package of signals to sell to home dish owners. This was just as well, because there was a shortage of descramblers.
- Home dish sales dropped precipitously; manufacturers and retailers went out of business.
- By 1986, technically adept spoilers had developed illegal descrambler modifications to decode without payment.
- When program packages were made available, TVRO interests objected that the cable business controlled most programmers and discounted packages to dish owners in their franchise areas. Noncable firms that tried to put together a package faced refusals and high prices from the cable networks.

To TVRO interests, theirs was a business on the verge of collapse, and they sought help from Congress. To the cable trade, TVRO was thriving and needed no governmental interference.

Congress passed the **Electronic Communications Privacy Act** in 1987. This law safeguarded private satellite feeds from unauthorized interception and interference. It protected broadcast television **backhauls**—relay of raw programming to network headquarters for insertion of commercials and other material before distribution to affiliated stations. Some motels and bars had used dishes to provide patrons with commercial-free sports backhauls.

Despite the problems, TVRO seemed to be evolving into a full-time business. By 1988, about 2.2 million homes had dishes, and about 12,000 more were sold each month.

Meanwhile, the sale of illegal descrambling boxes flourished. Electronic countermeasures shut down many illegal boxes. Congress stiffened penalties for piracy and directed the FCC to consider encryption standards (*PRT,* 15.2.3.3). Several estimates, however, put the proportion of pirate boxes as high as half the total decoders.

## 5.4.4 Digital Satellite Services

In 1994 Hughes Communication and Hubbard Communication each began DBS program services, **DirecTV** and **USSB**, respectively. The services came from three colocated high-powered satellites, one of which was shared by the two services, and the other two exclusively used by DirecTV.

The new satellite services used digital compression techniques to increase to more than 100 the number of signals (i.e., programs) that could be transmitted to subscribers. During its first year, DirecTV signed up about 1 million subscribers, with hopes to reach 10 million by the year 2002.[2]

The services avoided many of the errors that had doomed earlier DBS services. First, the home receiving equipment was cheaper and easier to operate than earlier systems. Digital transmissions allowed the services to use small, 18-inch dishes. Because all of the services were carried on colocated satellites, the receiving dish could be installed and left in a fixed position.

Second, both companies offered a large number of existing program services. There was no effort to create original programming. The Cable Act of 1992 had removed barriers to access to cable networks, and Hughes and Hubbard reached agreements to carry the most popular of those networks on their DBS services. They offered multiple channels of pay-per-view programming, and contracted with professional sports leagues to carry packages of NFL football and NBA basketball, available to subscribers for an additional fee.

Broadcast network–affiliate contracts prevented DirecTV and USSB from carrying broadcast network programs into locales covered by the signal of network affiliates. However, in areas not receiving a broadcast network signal, the DBS services could deliver selected network affiliates.

Finally, the services combined media advertising with retail sales outlets like Sears and discount electronic stores to sell their DBS programming packages. The receiving dishes, electronics, and other components were manufactured by companies such as RCA and Sony and originally sold for $700 to $900, depending on the features of the package. Manufacturers conducted their own consumer advertising campaigns, giving additional exposure to digital satellite services. By 1996 dish prices were under $200.

**Primestar** was a digital service owned by TCI and other cable MSOs. Primestar used a medium-powered satellite to deliver about 100 program services also delivered to cable subscribers. In many cases local cable television systems marketed and installed Primestar equipment, primarily in areas outside of the cable franchise area. Unlike DirecTV and USSB, Primestar leased equipment to subscribers.

In 1996 the FCC auctioned spectrum that would allow one additional DBS operator to deliver 170 channels to the entire United States. The long-distance carrier, MCI, in partnership with Rupert Murdoch's News Corporation, won the auction, bidding more than $680 million. The organization planned to offer video entertainment and business information services. Later, MCI merged with British Telecom, raising doubts about its further participation. News Corporation said it would go forward with its American Sky Broadcasting (ASkyB).

ASkyB sought satellite carriage by attempting a merger with Echo Star (Dish TV). The agreement soon fell apart, and ASkyB entered into discussions with Primestar about a merger.

One other impediment to the growth of satellite television services was removed by the Telecommunications Act of 1996. Some communities had restricted or prohibited receiving dishes in yards or on the roofs of homes. Congress directed the FCC to preempt state or local restrictions with federal rules to ensure reception of DBS signals. Local or state restrictions on the use of the larger C-band dishes were not affected by the new law.

## 5.5 ELECTRONIC TEXT

Electronic text appeared about the time cable systems entered larger markets. It consisted of text and, sometimes, illustrations supplied apart from or in addition to normal video programming. Four primary forms developed: rotatext, closed captioning, teletext, and videotex.

### 5.5.1 Rotatext

Many persons first noticed electronic text as **rotatext**. "Pages" (screens) of news, weather, sports, announcements, and advertisements were created and stored electronically. These screens were then televised in a repeating cycle on one or more automated television channels. Most commonly these services were offered by cable systems with excess channel capacity. Some broadcast stations used rotatext during the hours after more conventional programming ended.

### 5.5.2 Closed Captioning

In the early 1960s, British broadcasters developed closed captioning to serve hearing-impaired viewers. Viewers with special decoders saw printing superimposed over the regular picture. Other viewers saw only the regular picture. PBS and ABC worked on a U.S. version in the early 1970s, and the FCC approved regular transmission of closed captioning in 1976. In 1980 the National Captioning Institute began captioning selected network programming.

The Telecommunications Act of 1996 required the FCC to inquire into the extent of closed-captioned programming, and to report its results to Congress. By 1997 the FCC had new regulations in place ensuring that equipment manufacturers and program providers made closed captioning fully accessible to hearing-impaired viewers.

The 1996 Act also required the FCC to conduct an inquiry into **video description**. This service for the sight-impaired uses a portion of the television signal and home decoder to transmit an audio description of the action taking place on the screen. The FCC would study the methods and time frame required to bring video description to the marketplace, the technical standards, and the types of programming appropriate for the service.[3]

### 5.5.3 Teletext

Like rotatext, **teletext** presented electronic pages. Like closed captioning, teletext required a decoder and could be transmitted by TV stations along with normal programming. Unlike rotatext, teletext viewers could select specific pages. Unlike closed captioning, teletext content was unrelated to and completely displaced program video.

In 1975, British broadcasters transmitted teletext on an experimental basis. Soon after, the British Broadcasting Corporation and Independent Television used teletext to offer newspapers over the air—**Ceefax** and **Oracle**, respectively.

U.S. interests began to experiment with teletext in 1978. Two incompatible systems developed—**World System Teletext** and the **North American Broadcast Teletext Specification** (NABTS). Of the two, NABTS produced better graphics but required a more complex decoder. In 1983, the FCC said broadcasters could transmit teletext using any standard so long as it did not interfere with their broadcast signal.

In 1981, Field Enterprises, Inc., launched **Keyfax** on WFLD-TV in Chicago, using British technology. Keyfax went national in 1982 with satellite distribution on Superstation WTBS but ceased in 1984.

CBS's Extravision and NBC Teletext started in 1983. Both used NABTS. A few affiliates promoted the service and inserted local material. However, decoders were scarce and expensive (models for less than $300 did not reach the market until 1986). In late 1984, NBC discontinued its service and CBS followed suit in 1986.

Teletext could generate additional revenues for a station. Should many persons buy and use decoders, advertisers would pay to place messages on the information pages, as with print media. On the other hand, teletext also could turn a station into its own competitor. After all, television viewers would most likely check the teletext service during the most important (to the station) part of program schedule—the commercials.

Cable systems could also offer teletext service. A cable system could dedicate an entire channel—no programming, only teletext—that allowed it to carry thousands of pages (broadcast teletext was limited to about 200 pages) and a wide variety of information.

Cable teletext, however, was no more successful than broadcast teletext. Time, Inc., after testing a 5,000-page service for about 1 year, shut it down. Westing-house Corp. launched Request Teletext, a 1,500-page system, on its Buena Park, California, cable system in 1984. In 1985, having decided to sell its cable systems, Westinghouse phased out Request.

### 5.5.4 Videotex

Like rotatext and teletext, **videotex** provided information with electronic pages or frames. And—again, like rotatext and teletext—videotex frames could be displayed on the screen of a TV receiver. However, videotex was telephone based and interactive; a user operated a home terminal to transmit inquiries, requests, and directions and to receive responses. Unlike rotatext and teletext, videotex could offer encyclopedic information resources.

Videotex, too, originated in England. Developed in the late 1960s to eliminate the need for live operators to take postal orders and train reservations, the British post office named the service **Prestel**. In the 1980s, France gave telephone subscribers free terminals and electronic directory service to replace printed telephone books. Software allowing personal computers to use the **Minitel** services was also available. Minitel was a success. By 1994 there were 6.5 million Minitel terminals in France, and another 600,000 computers also had access. More than 20 million users had access to some 25,000 online services.[4] However, the growth of the Internet led commentators in France, and elsewhere, to question the viability of the closed Minitel system.

Videotex ventures in the United States were unsuccessful. One of the biggest U.S. videotex ventures was **Viewtron**, launched in 1983. This south Florida system was operated by Knight-Ridder, Inc., a newspaper and broadcasting group owner. Viewtron featured color graphics and services such as shopping, banking, news, reference, education, stock quotations, and e-mail. Telephone lines connected home terminals to the central computer. A subscriber paid initial and monthly fees, plus $600 for an AT&T Sceptre terminal. The service did not attract enough use to provide adequate revenue. Viewtron was gradually restructured. The subscriber base began to build, but the operation closed in 1986.

**Gateway** opened in 1984. This Orange County, California, service was created by the Times Mirror Co., owner of newspapers, magazines, broadcast stations, and cable systems. In 1986, with some 3,000 subscribers and after 15 months of operation, Gateway shut down.

In 1984, the Keyfax name was revived and offered as a videotex service in Chicago by Keycom Electronic Publishing. Keycom was owned by Centel, a telephone company, in partnership with Honeywell. Keyfax lasted until mid-1985, about 6 months. It had attracted 800 subscribers.

Failure of systems in three large markets raised questions. Was there really demand for consumer videotex service? The answer was yes, but delivered through the home computer, not the television set (*PRT,* 5.6.2).

## 5.6 COMPUTERS

The concept of a device to perform calculations dated back at least 2,500 years to development of the abacus in China. As early as the 1930s, computers used the binary system of numbers, now standard in digital computers. The first electronic computers used relays—electromechanical on–off switches that physically clacked open and shut to represent combinations of 1 and 0. Vacuum tubes, however, eventually replaced relays and greatly speeded calculations. These early computers were large—taking up one or more entire rooms. They were weak by today's standards, with the computing power of a modern pocket calculator.

The silicon chip marked a major breakthrough in computer construction. Using these miniaturized integrated circuits, designers could make computers more powerful (i.e., make them do more in a shorter time), smaller, and more reliable. As chips improved, so did the capabilities of computers.

### 5.6.1 Personal Computers

The first microcomputers (personal computers) appeared about 1975. Many owners used television receiver screens for computer display. Most purchased peripherals, devices that connected to, and operated in conjunction with, the computer. Entrepreneurs wrote and marketed application programs, or software. Software allowed consumers and businesses to use computers without having to write programs.

In 1980, two dozen computer firms sold just under 750,000 units for $1.8 billion. The next year, 20 more companies sold personal computers, and consumers spent almost $3 billion for 1.4 million units. The rush was on. By 1994 there were almost 30 personal computers for every 100 U.S. inhabitants. By contrast, the 100-year-old telephone was distributed at about 60 per 100 inhabitants.[5]

### 5.6.2 Online Computer Services

One intriguing 1990s development was growth of online computer services. These subscription-based services provided customers with special software and local or toll-free long-distance telephone connections for access. After years of unsuccessful efforts to develop dedicated information services such as videotex, and news services such as Viewtron, the spread of personal computers and low-cost modems made possible commercial services providing news, entertainment, and bulletin boards. Modems *mo*dulate and *dem*odulate telephone or broadband frequencies to allow computers to send and receive data.

CompuServe, one of the first of the commercial online services, was originally a business-oriented service. Two newer services, America Online (AOL) and Prodigy, also attracted a large number of subscribers, with each claiming more than 1 million users. **Bulletin board systems** (BBS) were accessed by local and long-distance users.

There were controversies and growing pains associated with the online services. All of the companies tried different pricing policies to attract subscribers. Both AOL and Prodigy made extensive use of free 1-month trial subscriptions, but the companies were criticized for using the trial subscribers to inflate the number of actual users. The growth of the World Wide Web (*PRT*, 5.6.3) also threatened the online services. Many of the services and information providers that made the services unique opted to make themselves directly accessible through the Internet (*PRT*, 5.6.3). Sears, partner with IBM in Prodigy, announced in 1996 that it would sell its interests in the company. Later that year the company was purchased by a group of Prodigy executives and managers, ending its direct connection to its retail and computer parents.

The new owners turned Prodigy into a Web-based service. In 1996 AOL restructured itself into a content provider and an Internet service provider. It changed its pricing formula from an hourly charge to a flat monthly rate.

Other problems arose from the linkage of the commercial online services to the Internet. Longtime users complained that AOL and Prodigy subscribers were invading Usenet news groups without understanding the behaviors ("netiquette") considered proper for board users (*PRT*, 5.6.3). Others used the Prodigy or AOL connections to "spam" the network with commercial messages sent indiscriminately to thousands of unrelated news groups.

Another problem was the alleged use of the commercial services to distribute child pornography and the alleged use of computer services by adults to entrap minors into sexual encounters. The Telecommunications Act of 1996 included criminal penalties for transmission of obscene or indecent content. Many computer network users protested, arguing that the ban violated the First Amendment. Further, they argued, policing content on a decentralized, international system would be a practical impossibility. In 1997, the Supreme Court overturned the rules.

### 5.6.3 Internet

In the 1960s the U.S. Department of Defense began studying ways to maintain effective communications in the event of a nuclear war. From these plans came **ARPAnet**, a computer network in which links were established from one computer center, or **node**, to the next. If the network was disrupted, a new pathway could be quickly created to reform the distribution. Only sites directly connected to the node would be disrupted.

**NSFnet** came a few years later. A computer network funded by the National Science Foundation, a government agency, linked research institutions. The **Internet,** an international network of computer networks, grew from ARPAnet and NSFnet.

The growth in the number of Internet users was explosive in the 1990s. A. C. Nielsen estimated almost one quarter of the population of the U.S. and Canada used the Internet.[6] Different definitions and the fluid nature of some user groups, such as university students, made accurate estimates virtually impossible.

The Internet allows rapid and widespread communication among computer users around the world. Two examples are **Usenet** news groups and **listservs**. Usenet groups are bulletin board-like entities that allow for the public posting of information and opinions on topics ranging from the serious to the purely entertaining. Listservs are mailing lists and discussion groups distributed to subscribers through e-mail.

The **World Wide Web** (WWW) became the most popular use of the Internet. The Web was developed by scientists at **CERN**, the European High Energy Physics lab, to make research materials more easily available to other scientists. Text documents were linked electronically to other documents located at any other computer on the network. Activating the link (most commonly by using a computer mouse) transfers the user to the computer server on which the desired document is located. As users explored the capabilities of the Web, and its **hypertext markup language** (HTML), they realized that the same technology could also link other types of files. Soon, text was joined by graphic files, then by sound, and even moving pictures. Technologies such as RealAudio (Fig. 5.1) allowed for worldwide computer distribution of radio programs as they were being broadcast.

The Web became a popular place for traditional electronic media to promote themselves and their programs. The websites were publicized in programs and network promotions. Some organizations, such as CNN and ESPN, created online services using the content created by the on-air services, including text, video, and sound clips. On election night in 1996, the CNN website recorded 50 million visits.[7] Services attempted to generate revenue both from advertisers and from subscribers given access to special stories, statistics, and other material. The major broadcast networks, cable program services, and production companies maintained websites to promote their programs and services.

Some people suggested that the Web was the precursor to video-on-demand services touted by cable and other industries as a means of allowing subscribers to select any content for playback at a time of their own choosing. Others called the Web a fad. Interestingly, similar arguments about the long-term prospects for radio had occurred in the early 1920s.

Welcome to The Broadcast Network on the Internet

*The* Broadcast Network on the Internet℠

**Help**
**E-Mail**
**Newsletter**
**About Us**

**Music**
CD Jukebox
RA3.0 Jukebox
Concerts

**Events**
Upcoming Events
Current Events
Greatest Hits
Archives

**Shows**
Netcasts
Seminars
Computers
Internet
Sports
Music
Archives

**Sports**
Collegiate
NFL, NBA, ABL
High School
Snow Report
USA TODAY TOP

**Radio**
RA3.0 Radio
Special

**Search The AudioNet Site**
**The AudioNet Programming Guide**
**Hot Software Deals**
**RealAudio 3.0 Users ... Click, Hear.**

**Featured Events**

**This Weekend's College Football Action**
**Saturday, Dec. 7th**

Army vs. Navy - 11am CST
The Big 12 Championship Game - Noon CST
The WAC Championship Game - 3:30pm CST
The SEC Championship Game - 7pm CST

**Today's Shows & Events**

Live Network News Broadcasts - 5 Times Daily
*The Ken Hamblin Show* - 2pm CST
 Political Talk With *"The Black Avenger"*
*The Michael Reagan Show* - 5pm CST
 Conservative Political Commentary
*CyberLine* With Mick Williams - 7pm CST
 Breaking The Mold of Boring Computer Shows
*The Dan & Scott Show* - 8pm CST
 An Outrageous Comedy Talk Show
Dallas Police Dept. Scanner Radio - 24 Hours A Day
Listen to D/FW Area Air Traffic Control - 24 Hours A Day
 Brought to you by: *SimuFlite*
Click Here For A Complete Listing of Today's Live Shows & Events

**Today's Live Sports**

**FIG. 5.1 World Wide Web.** The hypertext-based computer technology made the Internet an international phenomenon. AudioNet feeds stations to users around the world, redefining the concept of local broadcasting. Some producers created programming distributed by AudioNet, rather than a broadcast station. (Used by permission of AudioNet.)

Television
Talk
Sports
News
Country
Classical
Dance
Rock
Classic Rock
Urban
Alternative
Business
Jazz
Christian
Classics
Top 40 / Pop
College
Contemporary
International
Mix
Old Time
Public

**Interviews**
Celebrity
Sports
Music
General
Political

**AudioBooks**
New Books
Publishers
Book List

Best Experienced With

Click Here To Start.

See Our Live College Basketball Schedule - Over **10** Games Today!
*Sports Talk* (Kansas) - 5:15pm CST
*Gator Hotline* With Steve Spurrier (Florida) - 6pm CST
*The Bobby Bowden Show* (Florida St.) - 6pm CST
*Carolina Calls* With Eddie Fogler (So. Carolina) - 6pm CST
*Carolina Blueline* With Dean Smith (UNC) - 6pm CST
New England Blizzard vs. San Jose Lasers - 6pm CST
Women's Pro Basketball Action From The American Basketball League
*Coach Kevin Stallings Show* (Illinois St.) - 6pm CST
See This Weekend's Live College Football Schedule
Click Here For A Complete Listing of Live Games & Coaches Shows

## Upcoming Live Events

NRK 94.7's 2nd Annual Snowball Concert - Dec. 8
  Featuring Republica, Stabbing Westward, Luscious Jackson & More...
  Tune Into NRK 94.7 For More Details
A Public Address From UNICEF's Carol Bellamy - Dec. 12
  Live From The JFK School of Government At Harvard
The Bears-Packers Showdown - "Insanity, hilarity, stupidity, and
  terrific coverage of the greatest rivalry in pro sports!"
Click Here For A Complete Listing of Upcoming Events

## New Radio Stations

KRNB 105.7 FM - Urban, Dallas
WTAE 1250 AM - Sports, Pittsburgh
KSDO 1130 AM - News, San Diego
WLVE FM - Jazz, Miami
Grateful Dead Radio - 24-Hour Grateful Dead
WRXQ 96 FM - Alternative, Memphis
WMTX 95.7 FM - Mix, Tampa
KRBE 104 FM - Alternative, Houston
Click Here For Our Complete List of Over **80**
  Live Radio Stations

## The CD Jukebox

Listen To The New George Winston CD *"Linus &
Lucy - The Music of Vince Guaraldi"* In 28.8
Stereo*.

This Is Just One Of Over **725** CDs In Our Jukebox.
Click Here To See & Hear The Rest!

*\* Requires The RealAudio 3.0 Player*

**159**

The growth in the number of Internet users frustrated scientists and others who had lost exclusive use of the computer networks. A new Internet 2, comprised of major research universities and scientific centers was announced in 1997. Access and uses of Internet 2 will be more restricted than with the Internet.

## 5.7 VIDEOCASSETTE RECORDERS

Ampex introduced the first commercially available **videotape recorder** (VTR) in 1956. That machine used 2-inch-wide tape and four video recording heads. Later, helical-scan VTRs were developed using 1-inch tape, fewer heads, and a different principle for recording. Cassette versions of these machines reached the marketplace by the early 1970s.

Sony Corporation first marketed its **Betamax** VCR in 1975, thereby launching the VCR or home video revolution. Two VCR formats evolved, Beta and **VHS**. Eventually, VHS overtook Beta in the consumer market. Competition dropped prices. Sales climbed steadily until 1979 when they soared; home VCR ownership went from less than 500,000 in 1979 to over 2 million in 1981. Six years later, Arbitron and Nielsen reported that VCR penetration of U.S. homes had surpassed that of cable television. In 1993, 73% of U.S. homes had VCRs.[8]

Viewers used VCRs for time shifting, double viewing, and zipping. They also used VCRs for programming not available on cable or broadcast. They could rent or purchase videocassettes. Their favorites were feature films, but they also viewed tapes made especially for the home market, such as how-to, self-improvement, physical fitness, and music videos. In 1994 videocassette rentals were a $16.1 billion market in the United States.[9]

## 5.8 VIDEODISCS, LASER DISCS, CDs, DVDs, AND DATs

About the time Betamax hit the market, N.V. Philips Co. developed the videodisc system. The videodisc player converted information from a digital "record" into video and stereophonic audio for playback on a TV receiver.

MCA-Universal teamed up with Philips to market **DiscoVision** in the United States. Philips launched sales of the players through its Magnavox subsidiary during the 1978 Christmas season; MCA sold movies on discs. In 1981, RCA introduced its **SelectaVision** analog videodisc system, and Japan's Matsushita Co. (Panasonic) announced it would market yet a third system. CBS, IBM, and GE formed partnerships with the various videodisc pioneers to get in on the action. Sales of players, however, fell far short of projections, and by 1983 most videodisc plans and operations had closed down. Pioneer Electronics continued to market players in the United States and even sold discs.

Consumers rejected videodiscs for at least two reasons. First, owners of videodisc players complained that too few interesting discs were available. Second, the videodisc could not record. On both counts, the videodisc suffered in comparison with the VCR.

The videodisc had advantages, however, for business and education. By 1987, the marketplace success of the compact disc suggested a revival of the consumer videodisc, now dubbed the laser disc. Films looked and sounded better on the digital laser disc than on even the best videocassettes. Consumers found laser disc players easier to use than VCRs, and newer models played both compact discs and laser discs.

Digital technology also improved consumer audio. In 1983, the Sony Corporation launched the **compact disc** (CD), on which the very recording itself was digitally encoded. CDs were capable of clean, distortion-free reproduction of sound, loud or soft, at almost any audible frequency.

Although the recording industry adapted to the CD quickly, it was less enthusiastic about another audio development, the **digital audiotape** (DAT) recorder. The Recording Industry Association of American (RIAA) threatened lawsuits to block Japanese and European companies from retailing DATs in the United States. The RIAA said that the digital recorders, with their ability to make perfect copies of a CD, represented a threat to copyrights of recording artists. In 1989, however, the two sides agreed on a compromise that would allow the sale of DATs.

The **CD-ROM** (read-only memory) brought multimedia—video, sound, and still images—to the home computer. Many young people found interactive games more compelling than traditional television programs.

The next major advance was **DVD**, the **high-density videodisc** format. Major developers Toshiba, Sony, Philips, Pioneer, and Thomson agreed on a standard before engaging in consumer battles such as had occurred with the home VCR. Initially DVD players cost $500 or more, but the technology could carry video, audio, or computer data. Most importantly the DVD, 5 inches in diameter, could hold as much as 9 hours of broadcast quality video.[10]

## 5.9 ADVANCES IN RECEIVERS

In the 1980s, manufacturers began using digital technology on expensive models to add multiple-image screens (to view two or more programs at once), on-screen time readouts, zoom capability (to allow the viewer to enlarge a portion of the picture), voice-actuated controls, built-in telephone answering devices, and improved sound.

**Multichannel television sound** (MTS) sets were equipped to receive stereophonic and second-audio-program (SAP) channel (e.g., foreign language) television sound transmissions. **Cable-ready sets**, capable of receiving 100 or more cable channels, connected directly to the cable system drop line (*PRT,* 12.9.3), eliminating the need for a converter to pick up basic cable service. The cable television receiver had only two channels (3 and 4) and required a converter to pick up all channels on the cable system.

**Component television systems** allowed consumers to buy separate elements of the television system—video monitor, stereo amplifier, and speakers, and source selector (which fed the system from various sources, such as a personal computer, a broadcast TV tuner, a videotex decoder, and a VCR). Most early large-screen receivers projected a picture on a reflective screen; because they simply blew up what was already there, imperfections and all, the picture often looked blurry.

In the 1990s large-screen **home theater** systems became widespread. Advances in picture tube technology allowed the manufacture of 32-inch sets selling for less than $1,000 and 52-inch projection systems were available for about $2,000.

Tiny microminiature receivers used electronic chips and the **liquid-crystal display** (LCD). LCD technology, used for pocket calculator readouts and digital watch faces, was adapted for high-resolution video applications such as screens for laptop computers and pocket television sets; Seiko even marketed a "wrist watch" TV receiver. Miniature hand-held units were introduced capable of playing small videocassettes or 3-inch CDs. This technology also seemed to hold the key for development of the flat, hang-it-on-the-wall color TV screen.

## 5.10 PICTURE AND SOUND IMPROVEMENTS

Various groups worked to better the video signal delivered to the viewer. Proposals ranged from improving the existing NTSC system to creating a new wide-picture, high-resolution system (*PRT*, 12.5). Most would require new television receivers especially designed to pick up the improved signals. An industrywide committee was formed in 1983 to study the various proposals and subsequently generated several recommendations for new standards. In 1996 the FCC received the recommendations of the advisory committee. The computer industry argued for a system based on its technology. Eventually the two industries agreed to let the market decide. The FCC went along, choosing not to adopt any standard.

Traditionally, television sound had received secondary consideration at best. The few telecasts that featured two-channel sound required viewers to tune in a cooperating FM station for the full stereophonic effect. Japan's NHK network launched regular MTS (*PRT*, 12.3.3) service in 1978, and U.S. manufacturers started considering standards in 1979. In 1984 the FCC established an MTS system developed by Zenith and by dbx, Inc., as the industry standard for stereophonic and second-audio program (SAP) TV sound transmissions.

## 5.11 PRODUCTION EQUIPMENT

Video production equipment increased in sophistication. Digital technology made possible advances in special video effects, audio and video editing, and video graphics and animation. Miniaturization, a result of solid-state electronics, led to greater flexibility in nonstudio production—smaller, more rugged video equipment, including the self-contained camera and recorder. By the mid-1990s, cameras that recorded digital sound and images directly on computer disks improved the technical quality of video and reduced editing time.

Important changes in postproduction effects and editing came from the development of digital, computer-based technologies. **Nonlinear editing systems** became a staple in the mid-1990s. Videotaped signals were digitized and transferred to a computer hard drive. Any video or audio segment could be moved from one part of the program to another in the same way that word processing programs can move blocks of text from one location to another. Segments could be quickly edited, and graphics and transitions between scenes added at the same session. Nonlinear editing systems, consisting of video and computer hardware, and accompanying software initially sold for about $50,000; they allowed producers to accomplish work that would have required 10 times the expenditure a few years earlier.

### 5.12 SMALL-FORMAT VIDEO

In 1968, Sony introduced a low-cost, portable video camera in the United States. That camera, combined with helical-scan videotape recorders, made possible small-format video—use of compact equipment for nonbroadcast production. Later formats included **Hi-8,** which used 8mm-wide tape, and **s-vhs,** a format that could meet the technical quality required for broadcasting. Consumer versions were easy to use and provided good quality. The single unit **camcorder** became a common household device, ubiquitous where parents videotaped the activities of their young children or where tourists wanted a record of their travels. Low-cost computer-based editing and special effects systems enabled students to produce video "yearbooks," and made the wedding video a popular successor to the photo album.

Small-format video attracted notice in education, business, and industry. During the 1950s and 1960s, school systems purchased video gear for closed-circuit use. Many schools successfully used television receivers in the classroom for instructional programs transmitted by the local educational station or by the ITFS facility (*PRT,* 12.8).

As nonbroadcast video gear improved, businesses and industries of all kinds discovered that television could serve many purposes. They hired video specialists and equipped small studios. They took advantage of the small, less expensive, more rugged video equipment to create their own in-house production facilities for training, sales, information, and myriad other intracompany uses (*PRT,* 24).

Low-cost computer-based video special effects and editing systems allowed these video producers to turn out work comparable to their broadcast and filmmaking colleagues. In the early 1990s the Commodore Amiga computer system became a popular tool. Combined with a hardware and software package called a **Video Toaster,** the Amiga system could be used for professional-looking editing and special effects; the system could be put together for about $10,000. Less sophisticated configurations were available for about $5,000. Soon other computer "platforms" like Macintosh and IBM-compatibles were built for use in video production.

## 5.13 COMMON CARRIER DEVELOPMENTS

Common carriers provide service on a nondiscriminatory, first-come, first-served basis. All customers pay the same rates for the same class of service. The best known common carrier is the telephone company. Telephone companies have made significant contributions to the development of the electronic media and, as reflected in the Telecommunications Act of 1996, there is growing convergence between these two industries.

### 5.13.1 Technical Developments

From the earliest days of electromagnetic communication, technical innovation had come from ongoing research by common carriers. Their research yielded a number of devices and concepts that utilized or had the potential to affect radio and television.

A flexible strand of glass about the size of a human hair, an **optical fiber** could carry dozens of TV signals. Charles Kao and George Hockham of ITT undertook the first industrial research in 1966. Corning Glass marketed optical fibers as early as 1970. Experimental communications links were set up in 1976. During the 1980s, optical fiber supplanted some telephone lines, replaced coaxial cable supertrunks in a few cable systems, and connected New York and Washington on an experimental basis for ABC.

By the mid-1990s, most terrestrial long distance traffic was carried over fiber networks. The first optical fiber transatlantic cable was built between Europe and North America in 1988, and later cables were placed in the Pacific Ocean and Mediterranean Sea. Cable television systems deployed fiber in the trunk lines of their plants and considered extending the fiber network to curbside terminals. Optical signals still required conversion into electrical pulses to be used by consumer equipment, and the high cost of that equipment made "fiber-to-the-home" too expensive for full deployment until at least the first decade after 2000.

The FCC paved the way for **cellular radio** in 1982. Cellular radio used multiple transmitter and receiver units to increase the number of automobile telephones that could operate in an area. As callers moved about an area, computers transferred callers from cell to cell, enabling them to maintain contact with cellular and wireline telephone users.

With the development of digital technologies, the common carriers began to introduce new systems with the potential to revolutionize communications. **Integrated services digital networks** (ISDN), and **asynchronous transfer**

**mode** (ATM) were two examples (*PRT,* 12.10.2). Although most of these technologies made use of optical fiber, experiments also demonstrated the ability of traditional copper "twisted pair" to carry more signals than previously thought possible.

### 5.13.2 Legal and Regulatory Developments

For more than 100 years the telephone industry was dominated by one company, AT&T. Although such "independent" telephone companies as GTE and United Telephone operated in many parts of the country, to most people, "Ma Bell" was the telephone company. With roots in Alexander Graham Bell's original telephone patent, AT&T was the largest corporation in the world. It provided long-distance services, enjoyed monopoly status in local telephone through its regional operating companies, its Western Electric subsidiary manufactured equipment, and its Bell Labs was considered by many to be the finest research organization in the world.

AT&T's growth was periodically challenged by the government. In a **1956 consent agreement,** AT&T agreed to stay out of such businesses as cable and broadcast television and computer services. In the following years a series of FCC and court decisions allowed competitors to enter businesses in which AT&T had previously enjoyed a monopoly. The opening of long-distance services to competition was most visible to the public, but AT&T also faced new entrants in data and other computer-related businesses. Still affected by the 1956 consent agreement, seeking to enter new lines of business, and facing new federal inquiries into its operations, AT&T entered new negotiations with the Department of Justice.

*5.13.2.1 Breakup of AT&T.*　In 1984, under the supervision of federal district court **Judge Harold Greene,** the giant firm divested itself of its seven **regional Bell operating companies** (RBOCs). Each former Bell System telephone company now offered local telephone services in its operating area (Fig. 5.2) and competed with the other six and with AT&T in such sectors as equipment manufacturing. AT&T retained its long-distance business, and part of Bell Labs became **Bellcore,** serving the RBOCs. All were allowed to enter new businesses—computer manufacturing, cellular telephony, joint ventures with foreign companies, and various innovative services—and to pursue aggressive marketing and product development strategies.

Four years later, the court gave the RBOCs permission to establish videotex gateways. These telephone-computer systems would provide links between **information service providers** (ISPs) and users. ISPs could include companies ranging from newspapers to legal research firms to travel bureaus. Users would include anyone—individuals, businesses, or institutions. In connection with these gateways, the RBOCs could also offer certain electronic services—voice messages, mail, and "white-pages" directories. Within 6 months after receiving court permission, the telephone companies had gateway services up and running on a test-market basis.

**FIG. 5.2 Regional Bell operating companies.** In 1984 AT&T agreed to divest itself of its local telephone operations. The regional companies became separate entities, each serving geographic regions of the United States. Following passage of the Telecommunications Act of 1996, Bell Atlantic and NYNEX agreed to merge, and SBC and Pacific Telesis also entered into a business partnership.

The telephone companies wished to expand into video delivery, although legal restrictions prevented such expansion (*PRT,* 19.3). Nonetheless, RBOCs invested in cable systems outside their telephone areas and lobbied for unrestricted ownership. They also developed technologies that employed digital compression techniques for the transmission of video over regular twisted pair telephone lines (*PRT,* 12.10.1).

The RBOCs could carry information, but they could not provide it and neither could AT&T. The 1982 court judgment that led to the breakup of the telephone company prohibited the eight resulting firms from entering the field of electronic publishing for at least 7 years. The RBOCs requested that their ban be lifted. The court refused, and the regional companies appealed the decision. In 1989, AT&T asked that its ban be allowed to expire on schedule and not be renewed.

Marketplace advocates within the government urged further freedom for RBOCs. They argued that the telephone companies could provide **universal information service** for consumers, an optical-fiber delivery system that would handle telephone service, data transport, videotex, and cable television programming. However, the telephone companies earned huge revenues. Each RBOC had higher revenues than the entire cable television industry. Publishers, cable operators, and many broadcasters feared that the RBOCs would use their overwhelming financial resources to crush or control existing newspaper and television media. The first two groups fought telephone company entry into their areas of endeavor. Television broadcasters also worried that they would have to pay for telephone company carriage of station signals.

In the early 1990s court decisions and FCC actions allowed the regionals to enter the video delivery business outside their telephone service area. In 1992 the FCC declared that telephone companies could offer a **video dialtone** in their service area. This meant that the telephone company could transmit video signals over its system, but not own the programming. In 1994 the FCC authorized Bell Atlantic to offer video dialtone services, and later authorized other RBOCs and the independent telephone company GTE to begin video dialtone trials. Subsequently Bell Atlantic and US West withdrew their applications, saying they wished to test alternative technologies.

Some of the RBOCs bought existing cable systems, whereas others, such as US West, invested in such media giants as Time Warner (this alliance was later threatened by Time Warner's purchase of Turner Broadcasting, a move opposed by US West). Some telephone companies invested in cable television systems outside the United States. For example, in 1991 TCI, the largest MSO, and US West combined operations into a 50–50 partnership to own and operate European cable and telephone operations.

In 1993 the proposed merger of Bell Atlantic with the largest cable MSO, TCI made headlines. Eventually the merger fell apart but the potential for multimedia organizations became clear.

Bell Atlantic created Bell Atlantic Video Services, and began testing an interactive video-on-demand service called "Stargazer" in Virginia. Another group of telephone companies, including RBOCs Ameritech, BellSouth, and SBC (Southwestern Bell) and independent GTE, and entertainment giant Disney, created Americast. The telephone companies had responsibilities for technical and marketing functions, while Disney would license programming to the venture, and act as a liaison to other program suppliers.[11]

It was almost impossible to keep up with the rush of technical, regulatory, and business events. The Communications Act of 1934 seemed ill-suited to cover the changes. After years of false starts, in 1996 Congress finally acted to adapt the law to the new realities.

### 5.13.2.2 Telecommunications Act of 1996 and Common Carriers.

The Telecommunications Act changed the environment entirely.[12] The new law removed most entry barriers into the business of being a **local exchange carrier,** meaning cable television systems, wireless services, long-distance carriers, and even gas and electric utilities would be able to enter the local telephone business. Major cable MSOs and RBOCs soon entered **interconnection** agreements, allowing telephone customers of one service to call customers of the other. NYNEX and Bell Atlantic announced merger plans, as did Pacific Telesis and Southwestern Bell (SBC).

The RBOCs and other local exchange carriers were also allowed to enter the long-distance telephone business outside of their own service area. However, before providing long-distance service, an RBOC had to receive certification from the FCC that the company faced competition in its local phone area.

Two other aspects of the law are of significance. These deal with video delivery, and the provision of universal telecommunication services.

*Video Delivery.*    The new law allowed telephone companies to provide video delivery services within their service areas. Although there were restrictions on the extent to which telephone companies could control their local video markets, within weeks of the law's passage US West purchased Continental Cable, then the third-largest MSO with 4.2 million subscribers. The purchase, for $10.8 billion, included Continental's share of such programming services as E! and TBS as well as the Primestar satellite service. US West originally intended to combine fiber and coaxial networks into a hybrid system to deliver video, voice, and data. Later, US West cited technological and regulatory developments in deciding to separate the cable operations from the telephone, data, and wireless company.

Finally, the law replaced the FCC's video dialtone concept with one called **open video systems** (OVS). Operators can choose to act as traditional cable systems, and comply with the cable rules. However, telephone companies are limited to a 10% financial interest in cable systems in their service area, and may not participate in system management. Or, the telephone company (or other public utility or even a cable system) can choose to be an OVS.

OVS systems would operate more like common carriers than cable systems. They are expected to provide channel capacity to program providers on a nondiscriminatory basis. OVS operators may provide their own programming on their channels as long as channel capacity does not exceed demands from other programmers. The OVS is also subject to must-carry and retransmission consent requirements, as well as franchise-area requirements for public, educational, and government access channels.[13]

*Universal Service.*    The new Telecommunications Act also redefined and reiterated the concept of **universal service**. Historically, U.S. laws and policies regarding broadcasting, telephone, and other telecommunications services have sought to ensure that as much of the population as possible receive those services. This universal service philosophy was first espoused by AT&T president **Theodore Vail** in the early 1900s. Although ensuring that everyone has telecommunication services serves public safety and public information goals, it is also in the interests of a monopoly provider that can spread the costs among its customers.

Universal service is less attractive to providers in a competitive market. Because of the expense of building infrastructure in some areas, or the uncertainty of sufficient customers in others a provider might opt to "allow" its competitor to undertake the expense. The new law mandated that the FCC develop mechanisms to ensure that services would be provided to as many people as possible.

Schools, health care providers, and libraries were singled out for special attention. Schools and libraries would receive services at discounted rates, and rural health facilities would receive telecommunication services at rates comparable to those charged in urban areas. The FCC developed regulations to enhance access to advanced telecommunication and information services by public and nonprofit schools, health care providers, and libraries.[14]

The increasing sophistication of communication technologies highlighted the growing economic importance of information. In 1980, Americans spent almost 20% of their personal expenditures for food and about 10% for "information" (defined as communications, education, recreation, and culture). By 1992 the ratio had changed to 16.5% for food and 12.5% for information.[15] The government began speaking of a national information infrastructure.

## 5.14 NATIONAL INFORMATION INFRASTRUCTURE

In 1993 the Clinton administration unveiled its strategy to weave all of the communication elements into one interconnected "information superhighway." Like the interstate highway system built during the 1950s and 1960s, the **national information infrastructure** (NII), was expected to remake the cultural and economic foundations of the country. The NII was described as "a wide and ever-expanding range of equipment including cameras, scanners, keyboards, telephones, fax machines, computers, compact disks, video and audio tape, cable, wire, satellites, optical fiber transmission lines, microwave nets, switches, televisions, monitors, printers, and much more."[16]

These physical components were only part of the NII. Other elements included information, such as video programs, business databases and library archives; applications and software to allow access and use of the information; network standards and transmission codes to allow interconnection and interoperation between networks; and people to create information, develop applications and services, build facilities, and train others.

Although the interstate highway system was built largely with federal tax monies, the economic and political realities of the 1990s meant that much of the NII would be built and operated by the private sector. The federal government's role was to facilitate and encourage cooperation among the competing industries, coordinate standards, and provide funding for demonstration projects.

Finally, the NII was seen as part of a larger **global information infrastructure** (GII). The idea of a worldwide system won support from the G7 group of major democratic industrial powers (the United States, Canada, Japan, United Kingdom, France, Germany, and Italy). The European Union also undertook activities to create an Information Society linked to the GII.

## NOTES

1. Wireless Cable Association, "What is Wireless Cable," http://www.cais.com/wca/whatis.html.

2. "Directly to You: New TV Systems Bypass Cable," CNNfn, 14 December 1995, http://www.cnnfn.com/news/9512/14/dbs/index.html.

3. Robert Emeritz, et al., Eds., *The Telecommunications Act of 1996: Law and Legislative History* (Bethesda, MD: Pike & Fischer, 1996) 40.

4. France Telecom, "Overview of Minitel in France" http://www.minitel.fr/English/Minitel/overview.html, 8 March 1996.

5. International Telecommunications Union, *World Telecommunication Development Report 1995*, online version, Overview, http://www.itu.ch/WTDR95/ov.htm, 6 February 1996.

6. August Grant, Ed., *Communication Technology Update*, http://tfi.com/ctu/cturedev.html, 21 October 1997.

7. "Online Services Survive Election Night," *Gainesville Sun Work/Life* 11 November 1996:4.

8. International Telecommunications Union, *World Telecommunication Development Report 1995*, online version, Chapter 1, "The Information Society," http://ITU.ch/WTDR95/c1.htm, 6 February 1996.

9. International Telecommunications Union, *World Telecommunication Development Report 1995*, online version, Chapter 1, "The Information Society," http://ITU.ch/WTDR95/c1.htm, 6 February 1996.

10. Becky Waring, "DVD is Coming to Town," *New Media* 19 February 1996: 17.

11. Drew Smith, "Frequently Asked Questions About Telephone Companies Video Networks," January 1996, http://www.vipconsult.com/~ipi/vipc/tlvidFAQ.html.

12. As this is written some provisions of the Act and elements of the FCC's implementation were being challenged in court.

13. Emeritz 34; Federal Communications Commission, *Second Report and Order: Implementation of Section 302 of the Telecommunications Act of 1996*, Open Video Systems, adopted May 31, 1996.

14. Emeritz 14.

15. International Telecommunications Union, *World Telecommunication Development Report 1995*, online version, Chapter 1, "The Information Society," http://www.itu.ch/WTDR95/c1.htm, 6 February 1996.

16. National Institute for Standards, "What is the NII," http://nii.nist.gov/whatnii.html, 24 February 1996.

## FURTHER READING

Burstein, Daniel, and David Kline. *Road Warriors: The High-Stakes Battle to Build the Information Highway*. New York: Dutton, 1995.

Dholakia, Ruby Roy, Norbert Mundorf, and Nikhilesh Dholakia, Eds. *New Infotainment Technologies in the Home*. Mahwah, NJ: Lawrence Erlbaum Associates, 1996.

Ernst, Martin L., Anthony G. Oettinger, Anne W. Branscomb, Jerome S. Rubin, and Janet Wikler. *Mastering the Changing Information World*. Norwood, NJ: Ablex, 1993.

Krol, Ed. *The Whole Internet User's Guide and Catalog*. Sebastopol, CA: O'Reilly, 1992.

Lebow, Irwin. *Information Highways & Byways: From the Telegraph to the 21st Century*. New York: IEEE Press, 1995.

Mosco, Vincent. *Pushbutton Fantasies: Critical Perspectives on Videotex and Information Technology*. Norwood, NJ: Ablex, 1982.

Negroponte, Nicholas. *Being Digital*. New York: Random, 1995.

Oslin, George P. *The Story of Telecommunications*. Macon, GA: Mercer University Press, 1989.

Pavlik, John V. *New Media Technology: Cultural and Commercial Perspectives*. Boston: Allyn, 1996.

# II

# CREATIVE AND INFORMATIONAL PERSPECTIVES

Chances are good that you will think this section is the real meat of this book, the part that really matters.

And you may be right.

The glamour and excitement of radio and television definitely grow out of programming and program creation. There is a feeling of creativity and accomplishment and vitality in programming that stretches from the disc jockey shift at the local cable radio station to the highest paid directing positions for network television.

It's fun. It's hard. It's long hours, crises, and heartbreaks. You have to want to do it—more than pay, pride, or privacy. And if you don't, you had better choose something easier for your life's work, such as brain surgery or corporate accounting.

End of sermon.

At any rate, this is the section in which you find out how it all works—how programs are put together in chapter 6, how programmers operate in chapter 7, how news works in chapter 8, and how commercials are created in chapter 9. But watch out! It's addictive.

# 6

## Production, Programs, and Performance in Electronic Mass Media

A program can be examined from many different angles. At this point, we are interested in its structure, the program as a creative endeavor. Thus we focus on five of the facets—audio and video production, types of programs, procedures for getting programs "on the air," talent, and critical review.

### 6.1 AUDIO PRODUCTION PROCESS

The production process in almost any medium can be divided into three phases. **Preproduction** includes activities necessary to prepare for broadcast or recording; **production**, actual broadcast or recording; and **postproduction**, creative treatment after production to put the production into final form for the audience. We look at the production process for audio—radio and other aural-only media—in these terms.

#### 6.1.1 Audio Preproduction

The exact procedures covered by the term *preproduction* vary with medium and intended finished product. In a radio station, preparation for broadcast includes a variety of activities, from choosing the overall programming specialization and devising the format to selecting recordings for airplay and preparing newscasts. Preproduction for a radio program or a commercial often involves preparation of a script or rundown sheet, selection of talent, and acquisition of special music and other creative components. In the recording industry, preproduction may cover selection of artists, music, backup musicians, and the recording facilities themselves.

### 6.1.2 Audio Production

Audio production usually centers on the **mixing** process. Audio from several sources is fed to a central point for selection, control, and amplification, then sent on to broadcast or recording. Audio sources may include microphones and playback devices, such as tape machines and CD players. Mixing takes place at an audio control board (*PRT,* 11.3.2.1).

Titles and duties of audio production personnel vary—in radio broadcasting, they even vary from one station to the next. In a fairly common arrangement, one person makes on-the-spot creative decisions and supervises (but does not actually manipulate) the audio control board operation. Board operators are usually given the title **audio technician** or **audio engineer.** In the recording industry, the supervisor is a **producer.** In radio, the supervisor is a **director**; however, more times than not, the same person is both technician and director and is called the **producer.** On most local disc jockey programs the technician works alone, combining two jobs—talent and audio technician. This is called **combo** (combination) operation.

Radio stations that broadcast live telephone call-in programs use a special production technique, **audio delay,** to retain control over content. (The term *delay* is also used to refer to an audio technique, the effect of which sounds similar to echo or reverberation.) A delay device picks up the audio signal coming from the audio console and holds it up a specific number of seconds. If someone utters an objectionable remark during a program, the station has those several seconds in which to react and cut the remark before it actually goes over the air.

The recording industry strives for absolute control of audio quality. When a studio makes a record of a musical group, it sets up a **separate microphone** for every section, often every performer. In popular music the studio may even **record each component separately.** The band may record one day, the special rhythm section the next, the background voices on the third day, and the soloist on the fourth. The result is a **multitrack recording**; each signal records on a separate track or channel (horizontal section) on the same special wide audiotape. (So it is entirely possible that the musicians on your favorite music CD have never even met each other!) Production houses sometimes use this same technique for radio commercials, sound tracks for television commercials, and some radio programs.

Sounds can also be created by computer. The **musical instrument digital interface** (MIDI) allows engineers to synthesize sounds approximating any musical instrument or effect.

### 6.1.3 Audio Postproduction

For ongoing radio station programming, any postproduction processing is normally passive. A station may put electronic devices in the line that **process** the audio signal before transmission. The usual aim of such processing is to make the average audio level louder so radio receivers will pick up and reproduce the transmitted signal "loud and clear." Some devices, however, add effects such as echo.

Radio programs and commercials produced on audiotape often require post-production **editing.** The producer or director (or an editor under supervision) edits the tape. The editing process involves cutting out, adding, or rearranging segments of the taped material or splicing together two or more tapes. Typical motivations for editing include time (to lengthen or shorten) and continuity (to append, delete, or restructure material).

Increasingly, audio postproduction makes use of digital, nonlinear technologies. In these computer-based systems, sounds are digitized and converted to computer files. The file output is displayed as a **waveform** indicating amplitude and duration. The editor can select all or portions of files and manipulate them, rearrange files, add such effects as reverberation, change pitch and tone, and mix sound segments more precisely than possible with traditional tape editing.

In preparing a popular music recording for final release, the studio adds **effects** to the various channels, making some louder than originally recorded, some softer, some in echo, and sundry other electronic gimmicks. After such effects have been added, the multichannel recording is **rerecorded** down to two channels. Again, production houses may do the same for commercials and other elaborate audio projects.

## 6.2 TELEVISION PRODUCTION

An entertainment television program begins as someone's idea. Most production companies do not accept unsolicited program ideas from an individual. Instead, a recognized **agent** deals with the company on behalf of the individual.

Two main outlets for TV programs are syndication and networks. A production company that aims a program idea at the syndication market makes its pitches to local outlets and, often, to advertisers. If the pitch draws enough commitments to pay for the program, production goes forward. If the company pitches an idea to network executives, the network may commission (contract for) an elaboration of the idea, ranging from a **treatment** (simple outline or description of a sample show) to a **pilot.** A full pilot is a sample program, sometimes in the form of a made-for-TV movie, and is generally produced only for proposed prime-time broadcast television network shows. Pilots are often tested before audiences that respond to questions about characters, casting, and other program elements. Many pilots are rejected by the networks after this testing phase, but some receive a positive reaction from test audiences or when broadcast. The network may then commit to a limited number of episodes, in which case the program goes into production.

By the time it hits the production stage, the original program concept has gone through the hands of agents, production company executives, network people, and others. Sometimes the finished product resembles the creator's first idea only in the most general manner. The script, for example, will be changed continuously, even during production.

The **producer** is in overall charge of the program. The producer first shepherds the program through preproduction—has the script written, cost estimates and budgets made, personnel hired, sets built, and so on. Then the producer oversees production as the **director** chooses various camera shots to translate the written script into visual images. Finally, the producer supervises postproduction, in which the visual images are turned into a finished program. Writers or directors, to retain creative control of their material, may take on the role of producer. They are called **hyphenates** because of the hyphens in their job titles—for example, producer-writer.

We can divide television production techniques into two types. In electronic production, the result—the output of the production process that carries the picture information—is video, an electronic signal. Video may be immediately transmitted or stored on videotape. In film production, the output is exposed and developed motion picture film.

### 6.2.1 Electronic Production Techniques

The following paragraphs describe electronic production. Three electronic production techniques are most commonly used—multicamera, multivideotape, and single-camera.

#### 6.2.1.1 Multicamera.
As the name implies, multicamera production involves two or more cameras. During production, every camera produces a picture different from that of every other camera, and all cameras produce pictures at the same time. Only one picture, however, is "used"—broadcast or recorded (although that one may be a combination of several that are available). Multicamera production involves a series of on-the-spot, as-it-happens answers to the question, "What one best picture should be the ultimate video product of this production right now?" Multicamera production is traditionally used in many studio and location productions—for example, news programs, sports remotes, and comedy and variety shows.

For a dramatic program, the **director** blocks (plans) all performer and camera movement in advance. Television studio time is expensive, so the director rehearses performers elsewhere, perhaps in an empty rehearsal hall. When they move into the studio, sets have been erected, dressed (props put in place), and lighted. Only then are cameras and performers rehearsed together.

When the program is finally telecast or taped, the director usually works in the control room (Fig. 6.1). There, the director has two principal tasks, **selection** (editing) and **instruction** (directing).

Selection involves the decisions already discussed, the ongoing choices of video for inclusion in the production from among the varied sources available—sources such as studio and remote cameras, videotape playback, and character generators.

**FIG. 6.1 Control room preparation.** On the left the graphics operator prepares the text information to be inserted over pictures during the telecast. The director, in the center, discusses the readiness of the engineering staff in the tape room elsewhere in the station.

The control room contains video monitors (television screens), each showing the picture or output from one video source. The director observes these monitors and "calls the shots," that is, instructs which picture or combination of pictures are to be selected. A technical director (TD), also in the control room, operates the mixing controls and other devices to carry out the director's commands.

The director's second task, instruction, consists of issuing directions to production crew members. Most crew members are located outside and away from the control room, so the director communicates through use of two-way headsets. Each studio and remote camera has an **operator,** and the director tells the operator what camera shot to get. Similarly, the director gives other instructions to the production assistants and technicians that comprise the rest of the crew. Thus, the director **simultaneously directs** (tells the camera operators what shots to get) **and edits** (tells which, of the several available, shots to use and in which order).

Television **audio** uses basically the same equipment and follows the same principles as audio-only production. Unlike audio-only production, however, the performer in television is often in motion. Therefore, TV sound pickup (the capture of sound by microphone) requires some specially adapted equipment and techniques.

The postproduction phase includes videotape editing. The amount of editing varies with the program. For example, many local public affairs programs use **live-type videotaping**. Here the VTR begins recording, and the program is done as though it were being televised live. The tape is later broadcast with little or no editing. At the other extreme is a program produced in segments and assembled afterward, almost like editing a film (*PRT,* 6.2.2). Somewhere in between is the videotaped situation comedy. Typically, the program is recorded several times all the way through, then separate scenes or shots are recorded again as needed. The best of each is edited together to make one complete program.

### 6.2.1.2 Multivideotape.

Multivideotape production also employs two or more cameras. In this technique, however, all pictures are "used"—that is, recorded for postproduction editing.

Each of a number (say, four) of electronic cameras feeds a separate VTR, all operating simultaneously. The result is four complete videotapes of the same scene, each from a different angle or shot. Online switching is completely eliminated, and the director works in the studio with the performers. After production, an editor selects various shots and angles from the four videotapes and edits them together into the finished production. Thus all editing is done in the postproduction phase, motion picture style.

### 6.2.1.3 Single-Camera/Electronic Field Production.

Single-camera production uses one camera. Through stop-and-go taping, the camera records every scene and sequence in the script one shot at a time. The various shots may even be taped out of sequence, just as in film production (*PRT,* 6.2.2.3). However when well done and skillfully edited, the shots go together to form a unified whole that looks as slick as the best standard multicamera production. The single-camera technique works well in situations where the program creator wants hands-on control of production or must work with less than a full production crew.

When used out of the studio, the single-camera technique is called **electronic field production** (EFP). It is particularly well suited for production of commercials and documentaries, and independent video documentary makers and corporate television producers often use it.

## 6.2.2 Film Production

Much television program material is produced on film. This section focuses on the feature film technique, film and computer animation, and film postproduction.

### 6.2.2.1 Feature Film Production.

The majority of television dramas and many commercials are produced using feature film production techniques. One camera is used. Each time the camera moves, it is a new **setup**, and often the lights and microphones must be reset, as well. A setup takes anywhere from a few minutes to most of a day, according to its complexity.

Scenes are filmed **out of sequence**; that is, they are not filmed in the order they appear on the program. In the finished program, a particular section might open on a close-up of a performer speaking the first line, cut to a reaction shot of another performer as the original performer speaks the second line, then cut to a long shot as the third line is spoken. In filming, however, the entire section is first filmed in one or a series of long shots. These **master shots** correspond to the scenes as written in the script. Then the director films supplementary scenes—first, medium shots; then close-up shots; and finally, reaction shots and cutaway shots. By the time the director has filmed the section from all angles and views, much more film has been shot than will be used. On the average, 10 feet of film are shot for every 1 foot used in the program.

To confuse matters further, the sections of the program are also filmed out of sequence. The script may call for the first section to take place in an office, the second in a house, the third in the office again, the fourth in a bar, the fifth in the house, the sixth in the office, and the seventh back in the bar. In filming the program, the first, third, and sixth sections will be filmed one after the other in the office set; the second and fifth, in the house set; and the fourth and seventh, in the bar set. This filming method saves time and money by reducing major camera movements from one set to another, thus cutting soundstage rental and location (at someone's actual office, house, and bar) usage fees.

Dialogue is recorded at the same time as the picture, but separately. While the camera records the picture, sound is recorded on audiotape. In many cases audio is recorded separately and **synched** (synchronized) to the movement of lips and action. Crude mechanical systems used to result in the out-of-synch style often seen in "Kung Fu" movies. Today, digital technologies allow for precise postproduction matching of sound and picture. In some cases dialogue is rerecorded on a soundstage to replace segments recorded during the original filming. Sound effects are also added during postproduction.

The **director** supervises the entire production, directs performers in rehearsal and during filming, and decides how to film each scene and section. The **director of photography** is in charge of the camera crew, advises the director on the best use of the camera in filming a scene, and designs and directs the setup of lighting. The film production crew consists of individuals or teams that handle properties, sets, lighting, heavy equipment, sound, clerical functions, logistics, and transportation.

*6.2.2.2 Film Animation.* Technology has changed the procedures for creating animation. Traditional film animation begins with a series of drawings, or **cels**, and each second of screen time may require at least 24 separate drawings. These drawings are photographed using special cameras that film one frame at a time, stopping after each frame to allow the drawing to be changed.

Highly articulated, lifelike film animation, such as that used in the Walt Disney classics, is very expensive compared to live action filming. Computer animation, on the other hand, allows the artist to draw the basic shapes once and then animate them electronically. This saves a great deal of time and, thus, money. Despite high initial costs for equipment and software, computer animation is replacing cel animation in film and television. In 1995 Disney released *Toy Story,* the first feature-length film created entirely with computer animation.

   ***6.2.2.3 Film Postproduction.***   Each day, exposed film is delivered to the processing laboratory. The next day the processed film is viewed as **dailies** or **rushes** to determine whether any scenes need to be refilmed.

   The film next goes to the **editor.** The editor chooses scenes, sets them in the order that will best tell the story, and edits the dialogue to match the picture. Other sound is added—sound effects, music, and voice-over narration (if used). Finally, picture and sound are put together on one film, the completed program.

### 6.2.3 Electronic Production Versus Film Production

We have described two different types of television production. In traditional electronic production the program is largely produced in sequence and in real time. There may be some postproduction editing, but for the most part the shots have gone together in the proper, finished order at the time of production. In film production, on the other hand, the program is produced out of sequence and is edited after production. The director films, then the editor assembles.

   There is a difference, too, in quality of picture. As viewed by audience members on home receivers, electronic cameras result in brighter, sharper pictures, more intense colors, better color reproduction, and a greater feeling of simultaneity—of watching a performance as it happens. Film programs seem less alive than electronic productions (and remember, we mean here only quality of picture, not program content) chiefly because of their intermedium nature.

   On the other hand, many producers favor the "film look," which tends to have richer color and softer images. However, comparable results can be accomplished using video with careful lighting, and even with postproduction effects.

   **Intermedium nature** simply means that a program is produced on film and played back on television. Film stores information through photochemical means; television transmits information using electrons. Each medium has its own limitations on amount and types of information it can reproduce. The combination of these two sets of limitations makes for a picture that is not as crisp as a direct, electronic picture. Videotape, on the other hand, is actually part of the electronic production medium. Videotape avoids loss of crispness because it stores signals from electronic cameras, reproducing them with nearly total fidelity on demand. In fact, unless the viewer is so informed, it is impossible to tell whether a production is live or on videotape.

   Film production, however, is still the method that allows greatest flexibility in production—scheduling performers, crews, and sets—and moving from location to location. Hollywood, California, is the home of most major production companies, and film is the medium with which they are most experienced.

Although videotape production is slightly less costly, initial investment for equipment is much higher than for film production.

A sort of trichotomy has evolved based on live, videotape, and film production characteristics. Programs in which the element of time is important—to get it on the air as soon as possible—are produced live using electronic techniques. These include news, sports play-by-play, on-the-spot coverage, local church services, and, occasionally, informational and public affairs programming.

However, the majority of television programs are produced on either videotape or film. Both allow some degree of flexibility in production scheduling and postproduction editing. Perhaps more important from an economic standpoint, both allow the program to be syndicated.

Videotape is used for programs in which the illusion of aliveness and simultaneity is thought to be important. Film production is used for programs in which production flexibility is important, whereas time and apparent simultaneity are not. Most film sizes are also compatible all over the world, an advantage in international production and syndication.

### 6.2.4 Electronic Production and Film Production

The boundaries among various media have become blurred. Film uses production techniques once associated only with video, and vice versa.

Also, film crews routinely use video equipment. They strap a video camcorder onto the film camera. When they film a scene, they switch on both the film camera and the camcorder. Immediately afterward, they play back the tape and determine whether or not the shot was good—without having to wait for the next day's rushes. In postproduction the tape becomes a video work print, and the editor uses a video editing console to assemble a tape version of the completed production. Finally, the editor physically cuts and splices the film to match the tape. This saves time and work.

**High-definition television** (HDTV; *PRT,* 12.5.1) opens even more possibilities. HDTV differs from conventional television in at least one respect, perhaps two—resolution and aspect ratio. **Resolution** refers to the amount of picture elements or information in the frame, and HDTV features such high resolution that it can be projected onto a motion picture screen and look as sharp as film. **Aspect ratio** refers to the height of the picture as compared to its width. HDTV includes a wider television screen so that its shape more closely matches that of the motion picture screen. Thus, a director could make a movie using HDTV video cameras and record it on videotape. The completed movie would then go to the theaters in two ways. For some theaters, the studio would transfer the tape to film to be shown in the traditional method, on a film projector. For other theaters, the studios would play the taped "movie" and relay it by satellite to the theaters. The theaters would feed the satellite signal directly to large video projectors to show the movie on their screens.

## 6.2.5 Computers and Production

Nothing has had a greater impact on film and electronic production than the computer. Computers have become important tools for the creation of animation, graphics, and special effects. Increasingly, postproduction activities and editing are computer-based (Fig. 6.2).

*6.2.5.1 Graphics and Special Effects.* News programs, commercials, and instructional videos use graphics to convey important information. Computer systems make creation of graphics so simple that even home videos include titles and identifying graphics. Systems used in professional production environments provide a selection of text styles and easy placement of graphics on the screen. Eye-catching techniques bring the graphics to the screen, such as flips or "flying" them in from off screen.

These computer systems allow live action to be combined with animated sequences. Thus, a professional basketball player can appear to play against a cartoon martian in a television commercial or feature film.

*6.2.5.2 Postproduction and Editing.* Computer-based **nonlinear editing systems** are rapidly replacing traditional videotape editing. These systems combine computer hardware and sophisticated software to allow one person to edit and

**FIG. 6.2 Offline editing.** Segments of a news package or program edited in an offline session have no special effects; transitions are only cuts. A more complex online session uses computer editing to add special effects and transitions. Offline segments are used as is, or to make decisions about elements to be included in the online session.

add special effects, titles, and transitions. The acquired video is digitized and stored on computer hard drives (new cameras can record video directly in digital form, and the data can be copied directly into the editing software). The editor selects sequences and places them in a time line. Transitions, titles, and other effects can be added. All of the elements can be moved around quickly, similar to a word processing program that allows for the cutting and pasting of paragraphs, inclusion of fonts, and so forth. Once the program is edited, the digitized data can be converted to a video signal and recorded on tape.

## 6.3 RADIO PROGRAMS

Most radio stations emphasize programming as a whole (PRT, 7.2.1), not individual programs. Radio audiences tend to listen to rock radio stations, not rock radio programs; to country music stations, not country music programs. However, many stations air individual programs, and even an ongoing programming format is a program. Therefore we examine types, scripting, and syndication of radio programs.

Live programming at most radio stations consists of the disc jockey, the telephone call-in, or the news format. Except for some commercial copy (script) that must be read live, the disc jockey and call-in formats do not use a script in the formal sense of the term. Even a public affairs program often takes the form of extemporaneous discussion, with the moderator's list of questions being the only written script. News programs, sports programs, and weather reports are fully scripted, and sports play-by-play broadcasts use partial scripts. For the most part, scripted network- and station-produced programs are commentary, editorials, documentaries, and (rarely) dramas and comedy.

A great variety of scripted, recorded radio programs is available from syndication sources. The term *syndication* implies production, sale, and distribution of programs designed primarily for the station to attract and interest an audience. There are firms that produce such programs, and the programs themselves range from 1 minute to several hours in length and from commentaries and features to drama and musical anthologies. Syndicated music services offer automated stations literally weeks of music programming.

Programs are available that promote the opinion or stand of the producing organizations. These organizations include churches and church-related groups, various levels and branches of government, educational institutions, political organizations, industry and trade groups, labor unions, and other special-interest groups. Sometimes stations are asked to air these programs for free; other times they are paid rate card prices (the amount charged to advertisers) to run them.

## 6.4 TELEVISION PROGRAMS

Television programming consists of individual programs. Some cable and satellite programmers, independent television stations, and low-power television (LPTV) outlets have adopted ongoing programming formats, such as those based on music videos. However, for the most part, discrete units of entertainment and information comprise television schedules. In this section, television programs are divided into eight broad categories—entertainment, information, sports, advertising, special audience, cultural, educational, religious, and miscellaneous.

## 6.4.1 Entertainment

The first concern of any TV programmer is attracting and keeping an audience. To a certain extent, this holds true even for television news (*PRT*, 8.1.5). Most TV programming consists of pure entertainment—it has no other purpose but to hold our attention so as to bring us pleasure (and, of course, to expose us to the advertising messages contained within). Nearly every electronic media network and outlet telecasts the various entertainment program types; these may be categorized as drama, comedy, music, variety, talk, game, and reality.

*6.4.1.1 Drama.*    The weekly **dramatic series** is a continually popular program type, especially in prime time. A program in a dramatic series is generally 1 hour in length. Each program in the series features a complete and different play, although some programs feature story lines that extend beyond a single episode. Some series occasionally extend a drama over two or three episodes. The same performers play the same main characters every week; only supporting characters change.

The **daily serial,** also called the **soap opera** or simply "soap," runs 30, 60, or 90 minutes per daily episode. Usually, several main plots unfold at once in a soap. Dramatic pacing is slow, and plot and characters carry over from one program to the next. Soaps generally air during the day; however, themes and characters in some popular prime-time network weekly series bear a strong resemblance to those in the daytime soaps and are even called **prime-time soaps.**

The **miniseries** combines elements of both the dramatic series and the soap. The miniseries is finite; the series will run for a specific number of episodes and then end. Individual episodes have continuing characters, and each program is a complete story. However, the series also tells an overall story—for example, a family evolving with the times or an individual going through a particularly critical phase of life. There may be a trace of the soap's cliff-hanging element in the miniseries; an individual episode, although complete in itself, may close with a tacit question concerning the fate of a major character or endeavor.

The broadcast networks have reduced the number of miniseries they telecast because few of these programs seem to attract sufficient audiences in second runs or syndication. They can also cause ratings problems if they do not attract large audiences because the network has committed to carry them for a number of nights. Still, compelling miniseries like *Roots* and *Lonesome Dove* can capture very large audiences.

The **docudrama** re-creates an actual incident, situation, or individual, usually in the form of a made-for-television film. The docudrama is scripted to highlight dramatic elements, uses professional actors, and is produced as an entertainment program. Historical facts are often altered or ignored to meet dramatic requirements.

### 6.4.1.2 Comedy.

Comedy programs may feature a funny person, the humor that derives from putting certain types of people in certain types of situations (the situation comedy), or a string of seemingly unrelated funny lines and situations.

Situation comedies have been part of television programming since the medium's origins. *I Love Lucy, Father Knows Best,* and *The Life of Riley* were among the popular comedies of the 1950s. In the early 1980s dramatic programs were ratings successes and viewers found few half-hour situation comedies on the network schedule.

Influenced by the dominance of *The Bill Cosby Show* in the 1980s, the situation comedy returned as a staple of the broadcast networks' prime-time schedules. *Cheers, Roseanne, Seinfeld, Home Improvement,* and *Friends* became ratings successes. Comedy Central, a 24-hour cable and satellite program service carried all varieties of comedy: movies, series, and prerecorded stand-up comedy routines.

### 6.4.1.3 Music and Variety.

In pure form, **musical programs** would feature only music, and **variety programs** would feature various changing acts and performers. Early in television's history, there were such pure forms; later, however, music and variety were usually combined. In the 1990s musical variety TV shows were seldom seen on the major broadcast networks. However, they could be found on niche networks, such as The Nashville Network, and as specials on pay services such as HBO and Showtime. Comedy programs sometimes still contain music and variety; *Saturday Night Live* is an example. Even some dramatic programs may include musical numbers.

Two musical program forms really qualify more as television disc jockey shows. One, the dance program, dates from the 1950s. A host introduces each recording, and the video accompanying the music shows the dancing of a studio full of audience participants. The other program form is the music video show, a product of the 1980s. Inspired by the success of MTV, this program features "videos"—videotapes of visual interpretations of popular music—often introduced by a "video jockey." Cable programmers and TV stations put such programs in their schedules; a few devoted their entire program day to music videos, becoming, in effect, television radio stations.

### 6.4.1.4 Talk.

The basic talk show format features a moderator who converses with one or more guests. Talk shows may have elements of comedy, music, and variety as well. In another variation, the moderator also calls for studio audience participation.

The most successful program of this type is NBC's *Tonight Show.* On the air since the mid-1950s, its most famous host was Johnny Carson, who dominated late-night television for 30 years. In the mid-1980s a former television station weatherman, David Letterman appeared on NBC immediately following *Tonight.* Letterman's show was popular with college students and others who stayed up late. Many people expected Letterman to replace Carson when he retired from *Tonight.* Instead, in 1992 comedian Jay Leno was named the new host, and Letterman moved to CBS as host of *Late Night,* a direct competitor to *Tonight.*

By the end of the 1980s, personality-based, audience-participation talk shows had emerged as one of the staples of so-called "reality" programming (*PRT,* 6.4.1.6). By the mid-1990s the form was ubiquitous on daytime and late-night television.

The ratings leader was *The Oprah Winfrey Show.* In 1996, Phil Donahue retired after more than 20 years as host of his syndicated program. Other successful hosts included Geraldo Rivera, Sally Jessy Raphael, and Rosie O'Donnell. The genre came under heavy criticism for the nature of many of the programs. Many involved perverse topics and publicity-seeking guests. Perhaps the most notorious situation involved the *Jenny Jones* program after which a male guest murdered another male guest after the victim revealed a secret attraction to the first man.

**6.4.1.5 Game.** Game shows use a host who sets up the game situation or asks the questions, and include one or more contestants who try to win the game and collect a prize. This theme seems to have endless variations, and television broadcast schedules nearly always include game shows. Beginning in the late 1980s and continuing well into the 1990s, one company, King World, distributed the three most popular syndicated shows—*Wheel of Fortune* and *Jeopardy!,* both game shows, ranked one and two, and *Oprah Winfrey* was third.

**6.4.1.6 Reality.** In the early 1980s, programming interests in the trade began to use the term **reality programming** to cover a number of different types of programs. By the latter part of the decade, a two-part distinction had emerged. **Reality programming** featured nonactors dealing with issues of personal concern (e.g., *The People's Court*). By the mid-1990s, talk shows replaced this genre on many schedules. In **reality-based programming,** paid talent dealt with nonfictional material (e.g., the syndicated *A Current Affair* and NBC's *Unsolved Mysteries*).

These programs resembled both fiction and news or public affairs but were neither. Most were strictly entertainment fluff yet left the viewer with the impression of "having learned something." Some TV news personnel condemned them as **trash TV** and worried that they blurred the line between journalism and entertainment for TV audiences.

**6.4.1.7 Miscellaneous.** Into this subcategory go those entertainment programs that do not easily fit into the other slots. For example, various exercise and aerobics shows might conceivably be construed as educational, because they supposedly aim at how-to and self-help needs. On the other hand, most such programs feature well-developed, attractive people clad in skin-tight clothing who bounce around energetically to popular music—more than a little entertainment even for the most unathletic voyeur. Similarly, *Entertainment Tonight* and its clones are not categorized readily.

### 6.4.2 Information

Information programs include news, discussion, documentaries, on-the-spot coverage, and commentary and editorials. *PRT,* 8.4 deals with these at some length. Cable networks such as CNN and CNBC have greatly expanded the availability of information programming. On the other hand, there are cable networks and television stations that broadcast little or no informational programming.

### 6.4.3 Sports

Sports programs divide into two categories—sports reports and play-by-play. A **sports report** is structured much like a newscast. An anchor reads sports news—who won, who got hired, what stadium is nearing completion, and so on. Sometimes the sports report includes an interview with a prominent sports figure. In broadcast television, local stations do most of the regularly scheduled sports reports. In cable television, however, several national networks telecast daily sports reports. ESPNnews and CNN-SI are full-time sports news services.

**Play-by-play** is a remote telecast of an entire sports event—a football game, a horse race, a golf tournament, and so on. Several sports announcers offer commentary, statistics, explanations, and interviews during the event.

In addition to reports and play-by-play, there are **documentaries** on sports personalities or events, program **series** devoted to a single sport (such as fishing or hunting), and **sports magazine** programs (spot coverage of various events on one show, sometimes live, sometimes recorded and edited for time).

The major broadcast networks and some independent stations carry sports programming. In cable, ESPN and ESPN2, among others, provide national sports coverage. Several regional networks specialize in sports and telecast extensive play-by-play programming. Superstations and some general programming cable networks, such as Time Warner's TNT, also carry sports programming. Various pay television outlets occasionally offer full play-by-play coverage of individual sporting events on a pay-per-view basis. The professional sports leagues and some colleges and universities offer sports programming for a per-package or per-view fee.

### 6.4.4 Advertising

This category comprises programs designed solely to sell things (*PRT,* 9.1.2.1). An advertising program may contain elements of entertainment, information, or instruction, but these are incidental to the advertising message.

### 6.4.5 Special Audience

Special-audience programs are designed to appeal to a particular segment of the public. Common special-audience programs include those for women, children, farmers, and specific ethnic groups. This program category overlaps others somewhat; many of these programs could also be classified as entertainment or information.

In recent years, stations have done less and less locally produced programming for women and children and have relied more and more on network and syndication sources. Cable systems, however, have begun to provide **women's programs.**

The Public Broadcasting Service (PBS) runs some of the finest **children's programming** in existence. Cable networks also offer good children's programming; Nickelodeon, in fact, aims its entire daytime program schedule at children. By contrast the broadcast networks have eliminated such daily programming as *Captain Kangaroo.* The **Children's Television Act of 1990** required broadcast stations to carry some educational programming aimed at children, but critics questioned whether the act achieved its goals. Licensees cited syndicated and network programs as evidence of their efforts to comply, but some observers questioned the inclusion of programs such as *The Jetsons* and the *3 Stooges* as meeting the educational needs of children. In 1996 broadcasters agreed to provide a minimum of 3 hours per week of children's educational programming.

Stations and cable systems produce programs for **farmers.** Such programs occur particularly in agricultural areas, usually in the early morning.

Programs for **special ethnic groups** originate from local stations, cable systems, cable networks, and PBS. Some cable networks target racial and ethnic minorities; for example, Black Entertainment Television and Univision (Spanish language).

### 6.4.6 Cultural

Cultural programs focus on arts, letters, and scholarly pursuits. This is, perhaps, the broadest of all program categories, the one that offers the most diversity. Whereas most programs must focus on the "now," the current, and the popular or are otherwise limited as to content, cultural programs select subjects from the whole range of human achievement and study, from the past as well as the present. They range from films to plays to symphony concerts to dramatizations of lives and literature to documentaries of wildlife and archaeological explorations. Public television broadcasts much cultural programming. Among the cable and satellite program services that focus all or most programming on cultural subjects are A&E, Discovery, and Bravo. Advertising-supported broadcast stations rarely carry cultural programs.

### 6.4.7 Educational

Educational programs are designed to teach or to supplement the teaching process. Many focus on conventional educational goals, particularly those dealing with schools and the teaching of children. They may take the form of for-credit lessons for classroom or home use. They may supplement or offer assistance in formal school instruction; these range from PBS shows that have been integrated into school curricula to local "homework hotline" programs. They may teach the same concepts taught in a classroom but do so through informal, less traditional instruction, as does *Sesame Street.* They may teach more abstract concepts, such as self-esteem and positive social values offered by another perennial favorite, *Mister Rogers' Neighborhood.*

The educational category also includes programs that focus on self-improvement, health, and how-to instruction, subjects that often have little to do with schools or children. Subjects range from beauty and makeup hints to home repair, from fitness and health to landscape painting and cooking.

Not all educational broadcast programs are telecast by public television sources. The Learning Channel, a national cable and satellite network, specializes in educational programming, and The History Channel, as its name suggests, features documentaries and other programs of a historical nature. Some cable systems carry instructional programming originated by local school systems. Self-improvement and how-to programs, once the nearly exclusive domain of public television, have grown in popularity, appearing on local commercial stations, on cable and satellite networks, and in home video stores.

### 6.4.8 Religious

Religious programs are telecast chiefly on commercial and religious broadcast stations and religious networks. They originate locally, from networks, or from religious syndication sources, such as a denominational radio-TV-film agency or an evangelistic association. The programs themselves range from local worship services to slick, star-studded productions of major evangelists, from children's programs that teach moral lessons to intellectually stimulating, professionally produced dramatic presentations.

**6.5 ON THE AIR**

Somehow, programs must be transmitted. They must be strung together into some sort of whole, then embedded into the proper channel and dispersed to the intended audience. The decisions that go into that stringing together are called **programming,** the subject of the next chapter. In this section, we are concerned with the procedures by which those decisions are translated into the material you hear and see on your receiver, how it gets on the air (or cable or whatever).

### 6.5.1 Program Log

In the United States, radio and TV programs begin and end at exactly the time they are supposed to, and every second during the programming day is accounted for. Most broadcast stations (and many other media outlets) achieve this precision with the program log (Box 6.1). The log lists in chronological order information such as the following: each program and announcement, its length, when it begins and ends, the type of program material (such as news, religion, or entertainment), whether it is recorded, the source of the audio and (in television) the video, and sponsor and advertiser information.

In a broadcast station the **traffic department** publishes the log. The staff maintains and constantly updates records concerning the program elements that are to go on the air. Program elements are all individually scheduled items, such as programs, commercials, and public service announcements; relevant information includes when and how these items will run, and for how many days, weeks, or months they will run. Each day, the traffic department uses its records to compile information about the next day's programming and to generate the log, ready for the sign-on crew the next morning.

## 6.5.2 Program Sources

To understand how the log is translated into ongoing programming, you must know about the physical places from which the programs originate. We call these places of origin *sources,* although it must be understood that this is a special use of the term. Sources of programs here means where the programs come from when they are actually transmitted, not who produced or distributed them. The term *program* is also used here in a special sense to refer to anything listed on the program log and thus includes commercials, station identifications, and other such elements, as well as those productions we normally think of as programs. With that understanding, programs originate from four main sources—studio, network, remote, and recordings.

*6.5.2.1 Live From the Studio.*    Most programs that originate in the studio also have input from other sources. For example, a disc jockey radio program includes disc recordings and audiotaped commercials and jingles. A television news program includes film and tape reports and commercials.

*6.5.2.2 Network Sources.*    Here we include interconnected program services as well as networks. For example, a radio station may subscribe to a satellite-delivered music program service and, at the same time, be affiliated with a national radio network, a network to broadcast major league baseball games, a network to broadcast the state university's football games, and a farm news network. Even an independent (not affiliated with one of the three major commercial networks) TV station may occasionally carry programs from a network of one kind or another.

*6.5.2.3 Remote.*    In a remote, the program is relayed live to the studio from a distant location. The transmission of a local high school football game, the weekly service at a local house of worship, the Fourth of July parade—all are examples of remotes.

## BOX 6.1. DECIPHERING THE PROGRAM LOG

The program log provided is used to control and keep track of programming content. Most stations use a computerized system to schedule programming elements and to generate the log. The page pictured here is the 10 a.m. to 11 a.m. segment of a computer-generated log for a radio station.

Abbreviations are defined across the top. The Sponsor-Program-Title-Product column lists programming elements that will run during the hour. Entries under Scheduled Time indicate when each element is to be aired; those under Length specify how long each lasts in hours, minutes, and seconds (HMS); and those under Source and Type show the origin and classification of the element, respectively. The remainder of the columns apply to commercials. The numbers under INST (instructions) indicate audiotape cartridges that contain the recorded commercials; Reference No. entries refer to the client contract and the affidavit (the certification that the commercials have run); Ordered time shows the daypart during which the commercial is to run. An entry under Make Good for Date indicates a commercial scheduled for a previous broadcast that had not run correctly or had not run at all. This station originates its own AOR format (Quality Rock n' Roll), so the first entry is marked LIV (live) under Source. The U.S. Army entry lists NBC as the source, indicating that it comes from the NBC radio network. (Log courtesy of WRUF-FM. Used by permission.)

| TIME<br>@ EXACT (ALL<br>OTHERS APPROXI-<br>MATE)<br>A - AM<br>P - PM<br>N - NOON<br>M - MIDNIGHT | SOURCE/NETWORK<br>CBS<br>NBC<br>ABC<br>MUT - MUTUAL<br>NET - OTHER NETWORK<br>REC - RECORDED<br>LOC - LOCAL | PROGRAM TYPE<br>A - AGRICULTURE<br>E - ENTERTAINMENT<br>I - INSTRUCTIONAL<br>N - NEWS<br>O - OTHER<br>P - PUBLIC AFFAIRS | R - RELIGIOUS<br>S - SPORTS<br>ET - EDITORIAL<br>ED - EDUCATIONAL<br>PL - POLITICAL<br>ID - STATION<br>IDENTIFICATION | TYPE<br>COMMERCIAL MATTER OR ANNOUNCEMENT TYPE<br>CM - COMMERCIAL MATTER<br>MRA - MECHANICAL REPRODUCTION<br>ANNOUNCEMENT<br>PRO - PROMOTIONAL ANNOUNCEMENT<br>PSA - PUBLIC SERVICE ANNOUNCEMENT<br>(✓) - ANNOUNCED AS SPONSORED | FCC - LOCAL NOTICE ANNCT.<br>OSC - GENERAL SYSTEMS CUE<br>NCA - NON COMMERCIAL ANNCT. |

**PROGRAM LOG**     **WRUF 103.7 FM**

EST    33    WRUF-FM GAINESVILLE, FL                TUESDAY

**PAGE**    13

| SCHEDULED TIME | SPONSOR-PROGRAM-TITLE-PRODUCT | LENGTH<br>HMS | SOURCE | TYPE | INST | REFERENCE NO. ||| MAKE GOOD FOR DATE | ORDERED TIME |
| | | | | | | CONTRACT LINE NUMBER | SPOT NUMBER | | | |
|---|---|---|---|---|---|---|---|---|---|---|
| 1100.00A | QUALITY ROCK 'N' ROLL | 1 00 00 | LIV | E | | | | | | |
| 1120.00A | PIZZA HUT/SPRING BRK | 60 | | CM | 146 | 2128 | 02 | 158 | | 10-3P |
| 1121.00A | ALLSTATE INSURANCE/INS | 30 | | CM | 079 | 2158 | 01 | 138 | | 6A-7P |
| 1121.30A | FLA LOTTERY/JACKPOT | 30 | | CM | 031 | 2080 | 04 | 129 | | 6A-7P |
| 1122.00A | ABC ROCK NEWS | 1 30 | ABC | N | | | | | | |
| 1123.30A | WEATHER | 15 | | N | | | | | | |
| 1137.00A | GODFATHER'S PIZZA | 30 | | CM | 114 | 2229 | 01 | 214 | | 10-1230P |
| 1137.30A | ORKIN/ESTERMINATOR | 60 | | CM | 061 | 2205 | 02 | 178 | | 10-3P |
| 1145.00A | RECORD ABC NEWS @45 | | | | | | | | | |
| 1150.00A | DELTA COMAIR/COMAIR | 60 | | CM | 086 | 2179 | 02 | 151 | | 10-3P |
| 1151.00A | CHESNUTS/OFFICE SUP | 30 | | CM | 081 | 2213 | 01 | 185 | | 6A-12M |
| 1151.30A | GATOR SUBARU/AUTOS | 30 | | CM | 098 | 2177 | 01 | 197 | | 10-3P |
| 1153.00A | PSNACK NETWORK SPOT | 60 | WWO | | | | | | | |
| 1154.00A | PSYCHEDLIC PSNACK | 5 50 | WWO | | | | | | | |

*6.5.2.4 Recordings.* These may be syndicated programs or locally produced programs. Most syndicated radio material arrives at stations on tape or disc; the stations, in turn, usually **cart** (transfer to tape cartridges) for easy handling and instantaneous cuing those programs not already in cartridge form. Recorded television programs are on film or videotape. Short program material is often transferred to videotape cartridges for ease of handling. Television audio and video can originate from separate sources; a news story, for example, might consist of a silent film narrated live by the newscaster.

## 6.5.3 Gatekeepers: People and Machines

The **operator** at a radio station (usually the announcer or disc jockey on duty) sits at the audio console and feeds the programs to the transmitter as prescribed by the log—originating some live, throwing the switch to bring in the remote, loading and playing back taped programs, opening the microphone in the booth for the newscaster, and bringing in the network on time.

The **duty** or **residue director** is in charge of getting TV programs on the air on time and in correct order. The duty director starts and stops videotape playbacks, joins the network, cues the booth announcer, signals directors of live programs when to begin, and goes into and out of various program sources.

In many cases no person actually throws switches or pushes buttons. Instead, technicians program sophisticated automation devices to choose sources and get programs on. These devices can operate at varying levels of automation. For example, all television switching functions can be funneled to a limited number of simple control devices; an operator watches clock and log to punch the button at the correct time, and the automation system programs that one button to punch up a VTR playback, punch out of the VTR playback, join the network, cut away from the network, punch up an identification frame, cut away from the frame, and so forth. Or, the system can handle the whole routine, with no human intervention. In this case, the logging information can go directly into the system, without first having to be printed out. Listen to a good automated radio station (the good ones do not sound automated), or watch certain pay cable services. They are smooth, they never make mistakes, they do exactly what they are told, and they work literally for pennies.

## 6.6 TALENT: CREATORS AND PERFORMERS

The two major production centers for nationally distributed television programs are New York and Hollywood. People who wish to write, direct, and perform in "the big time" congregate around these two cities. Although the pay is high and the life seems glamorous, the work is hard and long, and job security is low. To put together an hour-long television film show every week is all-involving and demanding, requiring early-morning to late-evening production schedules and, for the director, producer, and other key creative personnel, 7-day work weeks for most of the year. Programs using electronic production techniques take just as much time; taped half-hour situation comedies are usually produced on a 7-day per week schedule.

The foregoing discussion of hard work applies only to the few—the very few—who stay employed. Bit parts, small supporting roles, commercial work—such jobs are not glamorous, do not qualify you as one of "the beautiful people," and do not grant you automatic entry into the current fad nightspot. However, they do bring in paychecks, and that equates with success.

## 6.7 CRITICISM

A play in the theater runs for a number of performances. A motion picture plays for days or even weeks at theaters around the country. A book remains on sale in bookstores over a period of time. A painting or sculpture exists for the ages. Critics of theater, motion pictures, literature, and other fine arts report on what they see as good, bad, or indifferent and can influence future attendance and sales. A television critic cannot do this. A television program is here and gone in an instant, to be repeated rarely and at widely spaced, unannounced intervals as reruns or in syndication, making it difficult for the TV critic to influence future attendance.

What is criticism? You have probably heard some people say they never watch television because it is so bad, so violent, so immoral, or so commercial. That is criticism, but it is not the type we mean here. Usually, the I-never-watch-TV criticism implies (a) use of critical standards from other media such as literature or painting to judge television, and (b) judgment of the medium as a whole, rather than its individual parts. After all, few people have stopped reading books because there is so much "trash" in the bookstores; why then should television be judged by such an inclusive standard? To condemn television out of hand is to condemn the consistently high standards of network news organizations, the occasional presentation of outstanding drama, music, dance, and film, and the entire schedules of PBS and the arts cable services, much of which qualifies as fine art by any standards.

Aside from its presentation of journalism and fine art, one should be able to distinguish between good and bad television, even among the more popular entertainment programs. This is the job of professional critics, who review programs and other aspects of television, in newspapers and syndicated columns. These critics look at a television program and, recognizing the limitations of the medium—it has to draw a large audience, has to fit within a time slot, has to be sponsorable, and all the rest of the "has-to's"—judge the worth of the program. They look at its overall premise or theme or idea, the writing, the directing, the acting, the opening and closing titles and credits, the music, and the setting. They judge these elements on originality, cleverness or quality, depth, and taste. Based on prior experience and their individual, absolute standards, they distinguish between good and bad programs.

Critics pay particular attention to the new broadcast network programs each September and January. The repetitive nature of television series allows a critic to look at the first one or two programs and to make fairly accurate judgments about the entire series. If the initial judgment is wrong, the critic can reexamine and rereview the series later in the season.

Unlike their colleagues in art, music, drama, and literature, television critics are expected to comment on nonprogram aspects of their medium. Therefore you read in their columns information and observations on business developments, laws and regulation, station and network personnel changes, and advertising practices.

## FURTHER READING

Alten, Stanley. *Audio in Media.* 4th ed. Belmont, CA: Wadsworth, 1994.

Anderson, Gary. *Video Editing and Post-Production: A Professional Guide.* 3rd ed. Belmont, CA: Wadsworth, 1993.

Armer, Alan A. *Directing Television and Film.* 2nd ed. Belmont, CA: Wadsworth, 1990.

Benford, Tom. *Introducing Desktop Video.* New York: MIS, 1995.

Boden, Larry. *Mastering CD-Rom Technology.* New York: Wiley, 1995.

Breyer, Richard, Peter Moller, and Michael Schoonmaker. *Making Television Programs: A Professional Approach.* 2nd ed. Prospect Heights, IL: Waveland, 1991.

Burrows, Thomas D., Lynne S. Gross, and Donald N. Wood. *Television Production: Disciplines and Techniques.* 6th ed. Madison, WI: Brown, 1995.

Ford, Ty. *Advanced Audio Production Techniques.* Newton, MA: Focal, 1993.

Gross, Lynne S., and Larry W. Ward. *Electronic Moviemaking.* 2nd ed. Belmont, CA: Wadsworth, 1994.

Hausman, Carl, Philip Benoit, and Lewis O'Donnell. *Modern Radio Production.* 4th ed. Belmont, CA: Wadsworth, 1996.

Honthaner, Eve Light. *The Complete Film Production Handbook.* Newton, MA: Focal, 1996.

Jarvis, Peter. *The Essential Television Handbook.* Newton, MA: Focal, 1996.

Mamer, Bruce. *Film Production Technique: Creating the Accomplished Image.* Belmont, CA: Wadsworth, 1996.

McLeish, Robert. *Radio Production.* 3rd ed. Newton, MA: Focal, 1994.

Millerson, Gerald. *Effective TV Production.* 3rd ed. Newton, MA: Focal, 1993.

Nelson, Mico. *The Cutting Edge of Audio Production and Audio Post-Production.* Newton, MA: Focal, 1994.

Ohanian, Thomas A. *Digital Nonlinear Editing.* Newton, MA: Focal, 1993.

Rapping, Elayne. *The Movie of the Week: Private Stories/Public Events.* Minneapolis: University of Minnesota Press, 1992.

REBO Studio with Clay Gordon. *The Guide to High Definition Video Production: Preparing for a Widescreen World.* Newton, MA: Focal, 1996.

Schmidt, Rick. *Feature Filmmaking at Used-Car Prices.* New York: Penguin, 1995.

Wasko, Janet. *Hollywood in the Information Age: Beyond the Silver Screen.* Austin: University of Texas Press, 1995.

Whittaker, Ron. *Video Field Production.* 2nd ed. Mountain View, CA: Mayfield, 1995.

Whitver, Kathryn Shaw. *The Digital Videomaker's Guide.* Studio City, CA: Wiese, 1995.

Wollen, Tana, and Philip Hayward, Eds. *Future Visions: New Technologies of the Screen.* London: British Film Institute, 1993.

Zettl, Herbert. *Television Production Handbook.* 5th ed. Belmont, CA: Wadsworth, 1992.

# 7

## PROGRAMMING BY ELECTRONIC MASS MEDIA

We sell *you* the way we sell soap. It's as cold blooded as that, huh? What's so cold blooded about it? I'm sick of people talking about the industry as an art form. It isn't. It's a business. It's no less ethical, and it's just as hard-boiled as any other business. We're selling time to sell personalities that in turn sell products. Simple as that.

—Philip Carlton (Dean Jagger),
Amalgamated Broadcasting System head,
in *The Great Man,* directed by Jose Ferrer, 1956.

In the United States, our economy is based on the buying and selling of products and services to one another. McDonald's makes a hamburger, its product, and you buy it. In commercial radio and television, the product that is sold is the audience. You listen to and view stations, cable channels, and networks; they, in turn, sell your listening and viewing (along with that of everyone else who is tuned in) to advertisers to air commercial messages. In exchange, you receive elements of entertainment and information put together in a particular way. This is programming. Programming that attracts few listeners or viewers results in low prices for commercial messages, few advertisers, and low profit. Ultimately then, success in commercial programming is measured in terms of profit, and commercially successful programming is vital to a commercial radio or television operation.

In this chapter we look at the various elements that make up programming on U.S. radio and television. We start with the daypart concept and radio programming. Then we look at television programming—local and network, broadcast and nonbroadcast. Finally, we examine outside constraints on and audience promotion of programming.

### 7.1 AUDIENCES AND DAYPARTS

The radio–TV business divides the programming day into standard time periods—**dayparts** (Table 7.1). Much planning and evaluation in radio and television

195

**TABLE 7.1**

Dayparts

| Television[a] | | Radio[a] | |
|---|---|---|---|
| Early morning | 6–9 a.m. | Morning | 6–10 a.m. |
| Daytime[b] | 9 a.m.–4 p.m. | Mid–day | 10 a.m.–3 p.m |
| Morning | 9 a.m.–12 Noon | Afternoon | 3–7 p.m. |
| Afternoon | 12 Noon–4 p.m. | Evening | 7 p.m.–12 Midnight |
| Early fringe | 4–6 p.m. | Overnight | 12 Midnight–6 a.m. |
| Early evening | 6–7 p.m. | | |
| Access hour | 7–8 p.m.[c] | | |
| Prime time | 7–11 p.m. (8–11 p.m.) | | |
| Late fringe | 11–11:30 p.m. | | |
| Late night | 11:30 p.m.–2 a.m. | | |
| Overnight | 2–6 a.m. | | |

[a]Times given for Eastern time zone. Daypart groupings differ slightly depending on time zone. Saturdays and Sundays are divided into fewer and different dayparts. [b]Defined and used primarily by networks. [c]The necessity for an "access hour" ended with the fall 1996 demise of the PTAR.

revolves around the concept of the daypart. Programmers, sales personnel, advertisers, and audience research firms all deal in dayparts.

For the most part, audience levels and patterns define dayparts. For example, during television's daytime daypart, homemakers, preschool children, and, later, school-age children do most television viewing. During the early fringe daypart, audience composition and size change as wage earners return home. Radio's audience patterns differ from those of television, so it also has different dayparts. Radio and television schedule programming by dayparts so advertisers can target their messages to particular segments of the audience. Depending on the size and composition of the audience, different dayparts command different prices for commercial time.

## 7.2 RADIO PROGRAMMING

Listening to radio is so commonplace, so easy, we cannot really imagine a world without our favorite station. Physically, broadcast radio is portable, more so than any other medium. As listeners, we turn on the radio primarily when we are doing something else. The radio audience is the commuter driving to work, the student doing homework, the counter people scooping ice cream at Baskin-Robbins, and the teenager washing the car. Most listeners in the radio audience tune in and tune out; they do not listen for extended periods. Yet, radio reaches over 95% of all persons 12 years and older every week.

Radio draws its largest audience during the period between 7 a.m. and 9 a.m. (Fig. 7.1). Audience levels decline gradually until early afternoon, then build to a secondary peak between 5 p.m. and 6 p.m. Radio audiences abate as television sets light up.

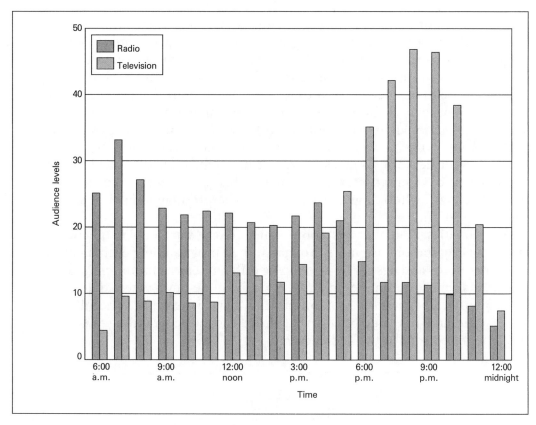

**FIG. 7.1 Radio and television audience levels.** Radio's audience patterns are almost exactly opposite those of television. (Based on Radio Advertising Bureau data.)

The implication for the programmer is clear. Program elements must be arranged so that audience members may **tune in and tune out** and not feel they have missed anything. This usually means that program elements will be short—music, 2½ to 3½ minutes; news, 1 to 4 minutes; commercial messages, no longer than 60 seconds. It also means there will be repetition; if you do not hear the news or your favorite popular song while getting dressed in the morning, then listen as you drive to work, and you will probably hear both. Stations and networks have designed most radio programming around these concepts.

## 7.2.1 Radio Station Programming: Specialization and Consistency

Most radio stations specialize. Rather than attempting to program for the general public, a radio station chooses a target audience then devises a programming **format**—that is, content the station uses to attract that audience. The format is often built around music that appeals to the target audience, and a disc jockey host alternates among records, commercials, and self-contained information capsules. Most likely, then, format is what makes you decide which station to listen to.

Essential to format programming is consistency—insurance that the listener can hear the expected programming at any time. With the advent of format programming in the 1950s and 1960s, programmers developed a clock chart (Fig. 7.2) to control for consistency. The clock specified which program elements were to be aired at what time during each hour. A news station's clock chart, the news wheel, indicated when to run the various types of hard news (local, state, national, international), sports, weather, business news, headlines, traffic reports, time checks, features, station identifications (IDs), and commercials. A music station's clock chart, the hot clock or music wheel, stipulated types of music, when and for how long the disc jockey was to speak, when to air commercials, when to give time checks, when to play a musical station ID jingle, and so on.

In larger cities, a number of stations aimed for the same target audience. Here, the competing stations attempted to match their programming even more closely to listener needs and desires by developing different clocks for different dayparts. A news station, for example, might use a drive-time news wheel that called for traffic and weather reports more often than news wheels for other dayparts; a music station might use hot clocks that varied the music according to time of day and types of persons in the audience.

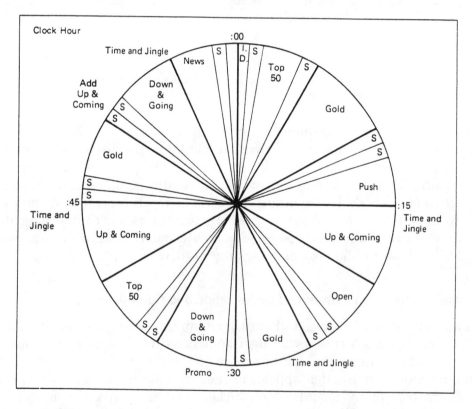

**FIG. 7.2 Radio format clock.** The large "S" stands for "spot," indicating a commercial or a public service announcement. (*Source*: KNTU-FM.)

Since the introduction of computer technology into station operation, the principles behind the clock chart have been built into radio programming software. This is especially handy for music formatted stations. A computer generates a play list, embodying the station's clock chart and specifying exactly which recordings are to be played (Fig. 7.3). Many stations that use computer-generated play lists, however, still post a clock chart so that on-air personnel can see what goes where at a glance.

```
********************************
*           WRUF-FM            *
*  2 PM  Monday     08-26-96   *
********************************
        ARTIST              TITLE          C   SOURCE    TIME
================================================================================
--------------------------------------------------------------------------------
    00:00 WRUF-FM LEGAL ID CART                                     :05
--------------------------------------------------------------------------------
BUSH                     COMEDOWN             H   CD B-40    5:26
        SIXTEEN STONE         95

POLICE                   ROXANNE              I   CD P-40    3:12
        OUTLANDOS D' AMOUR       79

SOUNDGARDEN              BURDEN IN MY HAND     A   CD S-3     4:00
        DOWN ON THE UPSIDE    96

AEROSMITH               THE OTHER SIDE        F   CD A-20    4:03
        PUMP                  89

--------------------------------------------------------------------------------
    16:46 :17 BREAK--LINER/COMMERCIALS                              4:30
--------------------------------------------------------------------------------
SEMISONIC               IF I RUN              D   CD S-415   3:22
        GREAT DIVIDE          96

COLLECTIVE SOUL          SHINE                E   CD C-1     5:05
        HINTS ALLEGATIONS AND TH 94

NEIL YOUNG              SOUTHERN MAN          J   CD Y-110   5:41
        AFTER THE GOLD RUSH    70

RED HOT CHILI PEPPERS    MY FRIENDS           H   CD R-33    4:03
        ONE HOT MINUTE        95

SCORPIONS               NO ONE LIKE YOU       I   CD S-36    3:55
        BLACKOUT              82

PEARL JAM               ALIVE                E   CD P-25    5:41
        TEN                   91

--------------------------------------------------------------------------------
    49:03 :48 BREAK--LINER/COMMERCIALS                              4:00
--------------------------------------------------------------------------------
REM                     E-BOW THE LETTER      D   CD R-417   5:22
        NEW ADVENTURES IN HI FI  96

--------------------------------------------------------------------------------
    58:25 OPTION RECORD (PLAY ONLY IF NEEDED)                       :05
--------------------------------------------------------------------------------
SIMPLE MINDS            (DON'T YOU) FORGET ABOU  I   CD S-47    4:27
        BREAKFAST CLUB SDTRK    85

Total Time for Hour is 62:57                             WRUF-FM
```

**FIG. 7.3 AOR play list.** In the WRUF-FM control room, air personnel use printed play lists instead of a music wheel. The programming department issues the lists, which specify the selections to play and the order in which they are to be played. WRUF features an AOR format and consistently places first in ratings in the Gainesville market. (*Source*: WRUF-FM. Used by permission of WRUF-AM/FM.)

*7.2.1.1 Major Commercial Radio Formats.*    Table 7.2 shows many of the major formats in use in the late 1990s. Radio formats, especially music formats, vary over time and with changes in taste. No firm definitions exist for most formats. One station calls its music mix *adult contemporary*; another using the same mix calls it *soft rock*. At any given time, however, the radio business uses a group of labels, target audiences, and play lists that denotes the current major or mainstream formats.

*7.2.1.2 Radio Format Evolution and Niches.*    During the 1980s large numbers of new radio stations signed on. As a result, competition for audiences increased greatly. At the same time, some music formats, developed 20 years before to attract the huge numbers of young people who comprised the post-World War II population bulge, went through **identity crises**. The music of these formats had changed and evolved, and eventually the now-middle-aged baby boomers who formed the core audiences of these stations no longer identified with many of the recordings they heard. The stations faced a choice: Play more "agreeable" and older recordings to keep the large older demographic but lose younger audiences, or keep current musically, which would constantly renew the audience by attracting younger listeners but would also "flush through" older fans, starting with the large core audience. The result was often a **split** in the format.

Developments in the album-oriented rock (AOR) and adult contemporary (AC) formats illustrate this splitting process. AOR originated during the 1970s and targeted men 18 to 34 years old. In the 1980s, some AOR stations went after aging baby boomers by playing more album selections from the late 1960s and 1970s. This eventually gave rise to yet another format, **classic rock**. Stations programming classic rock targeted an audience 25 to 54 years old, focusing on older recordings. AC, on the other hand, developed in the late 1960s and aimed at a predominantly female 24- to 45-year-old audience. During the 1980s, AC evolved into three variants:

1. *Hot AC* (current AC hits, no hard rock or rap, mixed with popular music from the preceding few years) targeting the 18- to 34-year-old demographic.
2. *Classic AC* (AC standards and any newer music that fit the format, often featuring personalities and news during drive times) aimed at the 25- to 49-year-old age group.
3. *Soft AC* (noncurrent, soft-rock originals and some standards and softer jazz recordings programmed in a less-talk-more-music setting; actually a cross between easy listening and AC) went after a 35- to 54-year-old audience.

Meanwhile radio programmers in competitive markets also combined, fine-tuned, and shaded music formats, hoping to carve out more and more discrete target audiences. Stations began describing their formats in terms such as alternative AC, alternative top 40, contemporary hit radio (CHR)-dance hybrid, CHR-leaning dance-urban, CHurban, hot AC, hot top 40, the mix, progressive

**TABLE 7.2**

Major Radio Formats in the 1990s

| Format | Target Audience | Origins | Variants | Notes |
|---|---|---|---|---|
| Adult contemporary (AC) | Predominantly women, age 24–45 | Developed during 1960s to reach baby boomers who outgrew top-40 | Hot AC, Classic AC, Soft AC | Most listened-to format until 1992; second since then |
| Adult standards | 49-plus | Originated in early 1950s as middle-of-the-road (MOR) | Nostalgia, Big band, MOR | One of four most widely programmed formats. Pop and jazz standards from big-band era and compatible recent music |
| Album-oriented rock (AOR) | Men, 18–34 | Developed during late 1960s to reach male baby boomers who outgrew top-40 | Classic rock | Stations played album cuts (even whole albums) of distinct variant of popular, rock-oriented music |
| Contemporary hit radio (CHR) | Young (12–24) audience. | Revival of top-40 format developed in late 1940s and early 50s | Top-40 | Consistently one of any market's most popular formats |
| Country | Men and women, 25–64 | Originated as country-and-western in 1940s | Hot, adult, or classic country | Most listened-to music format |
| Dance | Women 18–34 | Evolved from 1970s disco format and dance-club music | Often mixed into other formats | Stations with another format (e.g., CHR) may add dance to play list to broaden audience |
| Easy listening | Upscale 35–64 | Evolution of 1950s beautiful music format | Beautiful music | Once highly popular; lost audience to similar formats (e.g., soft AC, New Age) |
| Full service | Varies; generally 25–54 | Outgrowth of concept of radio as a local service | Most full-service stations program another format but add information elements | For example, full-service AC station adds news-and-information during morning and afternoon drive, personalities, features, even sports play-by-play |
| New age | Upscale baby boomers | Late 1980s West Coast development | "Yuppie jazz"; new AC | Light instrumental jazz/fusion music in a relaxed setting |

**TABLE 7.2** (cont'd.)

| Format | Target Audience | Origins | Variants | Notes |
|---|---|---|---|---|
| Information | 35–64; news audience tends upscale | 1960s; outgrowth of concept of radio as a local service | News, Talk, News/talk, Conversation | Foreground formats; that is, people actually listen to them |
| Oldies | 35–54 | Came to prominence during 1970s nostalgia for 1950s top-40 rock-'n'-roll hits | Golden oldies | Top-40 rock hits of 1950s, 1960s, and 1970s; 1990s variant: formats focusing on music of one decade |
| Religious | 18–64; primarily 35–64 | Number increased dramatically in 1970s–1990s; many use noncommercial educational FM channels, but often program continuing pleas for money | Christian, Gospel | Mostly operated by fundamentalist Christian groups. Often feature religious music, talk, advice, preaching, and worship services |
| Spanish | Hispanics, 18–64, depending on specific format | As the percentage of Spanish speakers in the U.S. population increased during the 1980s and 1990s, so did the number of Spanish-language stations | Ranchera, Nortena, Chicano, Tejano, la Caliente, Banda, Salsa, Meringue, Contemporary international hits, Soft international hits, Spanish top 40, Spanish news/talk | As competition increased, Spanish-language stations tailored their formats to target the heritage and interest of Hispanic listeners in their market |
| Black radio | African Americans, 18–64 | Some stations programmed "Negro radio" in the 1940s. | Urban contemporary (UC), Rhythm 'n' blues, Soul, Black gospel | Music (from gospel to rhythm 'n' blues to jazz), news, features, for African-Americans; UC music is a form of rock-based pop music |

AC, rhythmic top 40, rock AC, soft AC, soft urban contemporary (UC), smooth jazz, and urban AC.

At the same time, contemporary music continued to generate esoteric variations. These included genres with names such as hip-hop, grunge, and punk, each of which influenced station programming. Modern rock (also called alternative or new rock), for example, seemed at last ready to emerge from its decades-long hatchery, the college radio station. Commercial rock stations increasingly picked up the format that featured young, relatively unknown bands playing for young audiences.

Some commercial stations still did **block** programming, primarily in small, one-station markets. Block or diversified programming offered something for everyone, changing format every 2 or 3 hours according to who was in the audience—for example, farmers in early morning, homemakers during the day, and teens at night.

Classical and fine arts, ethnic, and jazz were primarily large-market commercial formats. Classical and fine arts audience members were few, well-educated, had high incomes, were fiercely loyal, and used the format for foreground listening. Ethnic stations broadcast to minority ethnic or nationality groups, often in their own languages. On the West Coast, for example, a number of stations broadcast part or full time in Mandarin, Hunan, Korean, and other Asian languages, whereas stations in the upper Midwest aired programming in French, German, and Scandinavian languages. Some commercial jazz stations did very well, although they frequently competed for audiences with noncommercial and new-age music stations.

Starting in the 1980s, AM programmers spearheaded the search for new formats. Hoping to regain lost listeners (*PRT*, 2.5.2), AM stations tried highly targeted formats—all sports, all business, all weather, all comedy, and all children's programming. One station even focused on traffic reports. AM talk stations got a big boost from the 1988 success of *The Rush Limbaugh Program*. Airing at noon Eastern time, this national program usually generated top ratings; it demonstrated conclusively that a talk station did not have to program locally during the entire day, that it could save money with a barter-syndicated[1] program and still do very well competitively.

*Educational radio* is used here as a generic term to mean no advertising. The largest number of educational stations were in the reserved part of the FM band, but some were AM stations or on commercial FM channels. Frequently programmed formats on NPR affiliates included fine arts/classical, jazz, and news/information. Some combined two formats into a dual format, targeting, say, the classical music audience during the day and early evening and the jazz audience at night. Many programmed an eclectic format, a form of block programming that combined a variety of programming types into one format—for example, jazz overnight, an extended news block in the early morning, classical music until noon, discussion programs at noon, and so on. A few took the eclectic idea one step further and operated almost entirely with volunteers as a **community station,** a sort of "do-your-own-thing" approach to programming. Campus-licensed student-controlled stations usually programmed alternative music, AOR, UC, CHR, or some variation of the "do-your-own-thing" approach.

Table 7.2 and this discussion do not cover all formats. What about, for example, show tunes/light classical, reggae, and Southern gospel? With over 12,000 radio stations, one short listing could hardly be inclusive. Even among the categories discussed here, permutations are legion. The larger and more diverse the community, the more format variations are broadcast. Categorization is confused, too, by **crossover records.** The popularity of a recording made by a country music performer may, for example, spread beyond country music fans and show up on other types of stations.

### 7.2.1.3 Programming Competition Among Radio Stations.
Various elements can be manipulated in the competition for audience. A station will improve methods to determine locally popular records. It will shade and fine-tune the format, adding, perhaps, dance music into a CHR format or jazz into a UC format. It will adjust play lists and clock hours, seeking just the right mix of current top-10 hits, golden oldies, and hit-bound records. It will change on-air personnel—shift them to different time periods, hire new ones, or remove those who have lost rating points. The station will alter, juggle, add, or delete various nonmusic elements—news, sports, and features. It will upgrade weather and traffic reports with new equipment, personnel, and services. It will change production gimmicks, air personalities' deliveries, and musical station IDs.

Some stations hire **programming consultants.** The consultant studies the market, listens to the client station and the competition, lays out a competitive strategy, alters the format of the client station, and may even conduct research to construct the station's play list. The consultant is sometimes highly successful, pushing a station low in the ratings to one of the 10 most popular in just one or two rating periods.

Some radio programming firms offer **syndicated music services.** Used mainly in automated or semiautomated programming situations, they give even a small-market station a big-market sound. The more costly syndicators function much like a consultant; they customize their services for each situation and can help a station's ratings. Some syndicators deliver their product by recording—big reels of tape, compact discs, or some combination of the two. Others use satellite transmission and deliver a "live" service, much like a full-time music network.

### 7.2.1.4 Cable Audio Services.
Cable television systems usually offer audio services. These services frequently take three forms—cable radio stations, audio basic services, and audio premium services. Outfit a studio for radio production, feed the output to a cable system, and you have a **cable radio station** (Fig. 7.4). Station operation may take three forms—**local origination** (the system does the programming; *PRT,* 7.4.1.1), **access** (programming comes from the public or public institutions; *PRT,* 7.4.1.2), and **leased-channel** (programming comes from a third-party operator who pays the system; *PRT,* 7.4.1.3). Access operation often parallels that of a community station or a college's student station; the others, a commercial station.

Cable subscribers receive audio services by attaching the drop line (cable lead-in) to an FM receiver. Cable operators often charge just a modest fee for **audio basic service** or even include it as part of their basic cable TV service. Typically, the audio basic service includes signals from cable stations, local radio broadcast stations, and radio superstations (*PRT,* 7.2.2). Subscribers pay a substantial extra fee for **audio premium service.** Premium service frequently

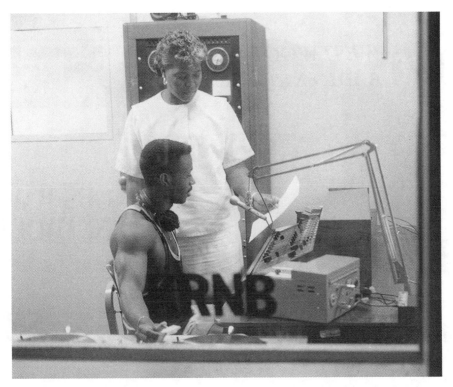

**FIG. 7.4 Cable radio station**. A cable radio station needs no license from the FCC and is not subject to broadcast regulation, not even call-letter requirements. Many cable stations, however, adopt and use call letters for promotional reasons—for example, "KRNB: Kable Rhythm 'N' Blues." Further, the actual operation of a successful commercial cable radio station often parallels that of a successful commercial broadcast radio station—right down to control room checks by the general manager to ensure that commercials for a new advertiser are aired properly.

consists of commercial-free national services and special audio channels, such as stereophonic sound for the MTV cable network.

### 7.2.2 National Networks and Program Services

By the late 1990s, any listing of major national radio programmers would include at least the following (Fig. 7.5). Still predominant were the traditional networks, those that programmed news, features, and entertainment scattered throughout the hour aimed at a general audience—several of the ABC "line" networks, CBS Radio Network, USA News, and Westwood One's CNN Radio News, CNN Headline News, NBC Radio Network, and Mutual News. ABC, USA, and Westwood One (WWO) also offered extended talk programming and 24-hour satellite-delivered music formats.

**FIG. 7.5 National radio networks and services.** These are logos for a few of the national radio programmers.

A number of radio networks packaged news and information for specific segments of the national audience. Young adults, for example, were targeted by WWO's The Source and by several ABC networks, African Americans by American Urban Radio Networks, and Hispanics by UPI/CBS Americas. Radio program networks offered various types of content: business news and information from Business Radio Network and The Wall Street Journal Radio Network/Dow Jones Radio Network; entertainment talk formats from Chancellor Broadcasting Company; Spanish language content from CRC/Cadeno Radio Centro Radio Network and SIS Notisat Radio Network; religious programming from Family Stations, Moody Broadcasting Network, and WLIR Jewish Radio Network; general news and sports from GBI/Gear Broadcasting International; and music formats and programs from Jones Satellite Networks, Superadio Satellite Network, TNNR/The Nashville Network Radio, and WFMT Fine Arts Network. The two leading public radio services were NPR and Public Radio International.

National firms also distributed cable system audio services. Several offered multiple channels, each carrying a different format. Some offered specialized programming—reading service for the sight impaired, background audio for text channels, or religion. Some offered radio superstations such as WFMT in Chicago (fine arts, music), and KKGO in Los Angeles (jazz).

## 7.3 BROADCAST TELEVISION PROGRAMMING

Unlike most modern radio programming, television programming typically demands blocks of time and full attention from its audience. Despite miniaturization, television is not a mobile medium. We sit down to watch at home, and we usually watch in blocks of half or whole hours. These blocks of time are available to most of us in the evening after dinner. Audience levels (Fig. 7.6) build rather gradually until 7 p.m. Eastern time, when they shoot up, far out of proportion to previous levels. The levels stay up until bedtime, and after 11 p.m. they drop dramatically. This 7 p.m. to 11 p.m. period is **prime time** for getting large audiences.

### 7.3.1 Broadcast TV Network Programming

Broadcast television programming aims to attract and hold large, general audiences. Therefore, the dominant programming in television, in terms of audience drawing power, is that produced by and for the broadcast networks—ABC, CBS, Fox, and NBC. The networks, through their affiliated stations, draw huge, nationwide audiences for which they charge advertisers the sums necessary to finance programming as well as make a profit. Despite competition from cable and other media, those audiences are still huge. There are no other four places that an advertiser can use to reach 70% of the viewing audience.[2]

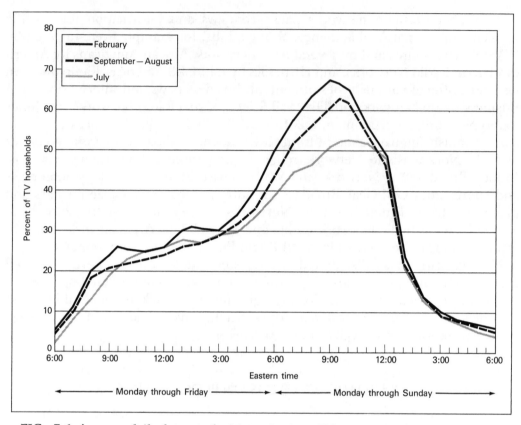

**FIG. 7.6 Average daily home television viewing.** Television viewing levels increase gradually through the day. They climb sharply starting about 5 p.m. as people arrive home from work, peak between 8 p.m. and 10 p.m., then drop rapidly at bedtime. During the winter, when many people stay indoors a good part of the time, viewing levels are high. In summer, more persons go out and viewing levels are lower, particularly in late afternoon and early evening. (*Source*: Nielsen Media Research. Used by permission.)

An affiliated television station benefits from its network's audience-pulling power. Network programming draws high audience levels that allow the station to charge more for its own advertising. Whereas in radio the emphasis in programming rests with stations, in television it rests with networks.

***7.3.1.1 Costs and Control.***   Prime-time program production is expensive, and it gets more expensive every year. By the 1990s, one episode of a half-hour situation comedy could cost up to $1 million; hour-long action shows could cost up to $1.4 million.

The networks changed the system of pilot programs for prospective series in order to mitigate program costs. They used more extended treatments (*PRT*, 6.2) and scripts and fewer pilots to make decisions on proposed series. In some cases they ordered partial pilots—two or three scenes—rather than a finished program. Even when a project reached the full-pilot stage, the network might order it as a television movie; if rejected as a series, the pilot could still run as a movie.

Early on, the high per-episode cost of prime-time series programming led to two developments—**repeats** of an episode and the increasing importance of syndication. In most cases, advertising revenue from one broadcast does not cover cost. A repeat, however, generates enough additional revenue to yield a profit. Over the years, the networks ordered fewer new episodes for each series. By 1979, the norm for successful, veteran series was 22 or less a year; most were repeated. A decade later, however, competing media had lured away so much prime-time audience, that the networks increased new-episode orders to 25 or 26, 28 to 30 for prime-time soap operas. Not so for new shows, however; a network's standard order for a new series is 13 episodes. If successful, additional episodes may be ordered to fill out that first season. On the other hand, if the show bombs in its first few broadcasts, the network may cancel the order for the remaining episodes. Further, CBS in 1993 started contracting for only 6 or 8 episodes of many new shows. This appeared to be a trend.

With demise of the fin-syn rules (*PRT,* 14.1.3.2), "the big three" (ABC, CBS, and NBC) could produce and own their own prime-time entertainment programming. However, broadcast TV networks (including the big three) get most such programming from independent producers. The networks purchase exclusive rights—to air the program first and to air it a designated number of times—that last a specified period of time. Network payment often covers only about two thirds of the huge production costs already mentioned. In other words, the producers may take a loss in making prime-time network programs. This is **deficit production.** When series episodes have completed their run on the network, they are put into **syndication** (made available at a price for use by local stations, cable programmers, or other media). This is where the producers hope to recoup their investment and make a profit.

***7.3.1.2 Competitive Tactics.***    So far, this discussion of programming has applied primarily to the four major networks. However, many of the concepts presented in the paragraphs that follow pertain to other networks and to individual stations as well. Specialized networks such as Univision and Telemundo (Spanish language) use these scheduling practices and, insofar as they vie for a targeted segment of the general audience, may even counterprogram the big three. (Highly specialized programmers such as HSN and MTV do not schedule in quite the same way; they counterprogram with format—that is, their entire programming concept—instead of individual programs.)

The networks **strip program** (Fig. 7.7) during every weekday daypart except prime time. This means they schedule series programs Monday through Friday, the same series at the same time each day. Traditionally, ABC, CBS, and NBC have scheduled informational "magazines" to start the day, game shows and dramatic serials in daytime to capture homemakers, and major newscasts in early evening. They program weekends and prime time individually. Children's shows air Saturday morning. Saturday and Sunday afternoon sports lineups target men.

| Monday through Friday | | | | |
|---|---|---|---|---|
| | *Station A*<br>*(ABC affiliate)* | *Station A*<br>*(PBS affiliate)* | *Superstation*<br>*(Independent)* | *Discovery Channel* | *Family Channel* |
| 10:00 a.m | Montel Williams (Talk) | Instructional programming | Who's the Boss (Situation comedy) | Home Matters | 700 Club (Religion) |
| 10:30 | ↓ | ↓ | Three's Company (Situation comedy) | Start to Finish | ↓ |
| 11:00 | Caryl & Marilyn (Talk) | ↓ | Beverly Hillbillies (Situation comedy) | House Smart | ↓ |
| 11:30 | ↓ | ↓ | Andy Griffith (Situation comedy) | Lynette Jennings Home | Fit TV (Exercise) |
| 12:00 noon | News | ↓ | Matlock (Action adventure) | Graham Kerr's Kitchen | Rescue 911 (Action Adventure) |
| 12:30 | The City (Serial) | ↓ | ↓ | World Class Cuisine | ↓ |
| 1:00 | All My Children (Serial) | ↓ | Afternoon Movie | Great Chefs | Home & Family (Talk) |
| 1:30 | ↓ | ↓ | ↓ | Home Matters | ↓ |
| 2:00 | One Life to Live (Serial | ↓ | ↓ | Start to Finish | ↓ |
| 2:30 | ↓ | ↓ | ↓ | Easy Does It | ↓ |
| 3:00 | General Hospital (Serial) | Mister Rogers (Children) | Flintstones (Children) | Lynette Jennings Home | Highway to Heaven (Drama) |
| 3:30 | ↓ | Barney & Friends (Children) | ↓ | Graham Kerr's Kitchen | ↓ |
| 4:00 | Oprah Winfrey (Talk) | Sesame Street (Children) | Scooby-Doo (Children) | World Class Cuisine | Punky Brewster (Situation comedy) |

**FIG. 7.7 Strip programming.** During weekdays, stations and networks generally program the same shows at the same time, Monday through Friday.

In other words, they schedule programs that appeal to the group most prevalent in the audience during any given daypart. This is **dayparting** (*PRT,* 7.1, 7.3).

Within each daypart, the commercial television networks compete for audiences. Network competition for audiences is greatest during prime time, and we use this 8 p.m. to 11 p.m.[3] period to illustrate broadcast network program competition at its sharpest.

The aim of a network is to capture a large share of audience and to keep it throughout the evening. This is **audience flow.** One way to achieve audience flow is to schedule **long-form** programming. All other things being equal, an hour program gives a viewer only half the opportunity to switch networks as do two half-hour programs. Over the years, networks have lengthened many program slots from the historic norm of 30 minutes to 60 and even 90 minutes, with regularly scheduled slots for movies of 2 hours and more.

More vital than length, however, is the strength of individual programs. If one program has high ratings, then the following program has a built-in advantage because it "inherits" the **lead-in** (the audience level). If the following program is strong, it will maintain or improve the rating; if weak, it will "waste" the lead-in by losing audience and may even reduce audience levels for a stronger third program.

A network attempts to capture and keep its audience (positive audience flow) on any given night through **block programming.** It schedules—one after another—either similar programs (e.g., all comedy and musical variety) or different types of programs that have proven individually strong. If block programming is successful, the network could win the ratings race for the entire evening.

ABC introduced the idea of **seamless programming** to broadcast networking in 1989. In its simplest mode, seamless programming means that one network program ends and another begins with no interruption. Under seamless programming, network program formats include internal positions for local breaks and station identifications, so the audience gets little chance to tune away before the next program begins. In its most sophisticated form, seamless programming also means that commercials air in clusters, with fewer breaks throughout the evening. The broadcast networks, for the most part, have not adopted seamless programming tactics. Some cable networks, on the other hand, have wholeheartedly embraced it.

At any given time, total prime-time audience levels for ABC, CBS, NBC, and increasingly Fox are fairly constant. One gains audience at the expense of the others. In planning its schedule, a network will try to **counterprogram.** There are many different ways to counterprogram. In addition to those discussed in Box 7.1, another counterprogramming tactic involves length of program, as when one network starts a strong hour-long program 30 minutes before a competitor's popular half-hour situation comedy; this is **bridging.** Other tactics that attempt to use programs with high ratings to build audience for weaker shows include the **tent-pole**—putting a strong program between two weak ones—and the **hammock**—putting a weak or new show between two strong ones. These various strategies do not always pay off. In some cases, ratings actually fall.

In January or February, network executives begin planning schedules for the following fall. They use a scheduling board, a graphic display of days and time slots. Programs that rival networks are expected to offer are placed in their proper slots, each rival represented by a different color. The executives then enter programs of their own network, in yet another color, in an attempt to program competitively. They must determine which programs to keep and which to drop, what the other networks will do at each time slot, what programs are needed to maintain successful audience flow and to counterprogram on those evenings that are not so successful, and what is available as new programming.

In most cases, the factor that determines whether a series is continued is its **share**—the percentage of all homes using TV that tune to the series. Network competition for ratings is keen—so keen that a network will often cancel a new series with a low share even before the end of the season. The practice of canceling some series and adding others at midseason began in the late 1960s. ABC gave

---

## BOX 7.1. MIKE HARDING ON COUNTERPROGRAMMING

*Michael T. Harding is founder, president, and chief executive officer of Millennium Media, Inc., a group owner of TV stations across the country. Harding has worked in a variety of television broadcasting positions, among them director of marketing, operations manager, news anchor, and chief assignment manager. He was a general manager for 13 years and held that title at three TV stations. Harding has a BS degree in broadcasting from the University of Florida and an MS degree in broadcast administration from Boston University.*

The traditional broadcasting concept of counterprogramming, the one the most people think of when they hear the term, is *counterprogramming by genre.* At a particular time, two broadcast networks program drama, so a third programs sitcoms. The hope is that the other networks will fragment the audience, leaving the greatest share to the counterprogrammer. Another classic example is the independent TV station that counterprograms the network affiliates' early evening newscasts with entertainment programming. Right now, sitcoms and *Star Trek: The Next Generation* work best.

National cable networks have successfully done *narrowcasting,* in which they counterprogrammed by demographic *niche.* Fox, when it first went on the air, decided to go after an age niche, those in the demographic category 18 to 34 years of age. Therefore, Fox scheduled programming primarily to reach that group, and it worked. Fox perfected the concept of *counterprogramming by age.*

Another successful Fox innovation was *counterprogramming by launch date.* The big three networks had traditionally launched most of their new programming at the fall start of the new TV "season." Fox, on the other hand, announced that it would launch new programming—both new series and new episodes for ongoing series—at any time during the calendar year. This was the *52-week programming year.* The real success story for this tactic involved a weekly dramatic series about a bunch of young people who lived in Southern California. Fox premiered the show in fall 1990, and it was an instantaneous nonsuccess. According to the ratings it was one of TV's least-watched shows, and cancellation seemed likely. Production of the series was actually running ahead of schedule, and rather than wait until fall to debut the show's second season, Fox decided to air the new second-season episodes starting July 11. ABC, CBS, and NBC all scheduled reruns, of course, so Fox was counterprogramming with new episodes. Again, it worked. The series attracted a huge audience across all advertiser-friendly demographics, especially among the core demos sought by Fox. Viewers, hungry for something other than summer reruns, got an opportunity to sample the program, something they probably would not have done if Fox had saved the new episodes for fall where they would have been lost among the glut of new programming options. The program was *Beverly Hills 90210,* and without a doubt that tactic saved the series, which continued to be a mainstay of Fox's Wednesday night lineup for years.

(Cont'd.)

---

**BOX 7.1** (cont'd.)

A network may *counterprogram by ratings*. In fall 1994 Fox launched a new series, *Party of Five*, airing it at 9 p.m. Mondays with the well-established *Melrose Place* as its 8 p.m. lead-in. On Wednesday nights Fox scheduled the popular *Beverly Hills 90210* as the 8 p.m. lead-off, followed by *Models, Inc.*, a program that had premiered just the previous June. In January 1995 Fox switched nights for the 9 p.m. shows, the idea being that the more cunning *Models* was a better match with *Melrose*, whereas the more wholesome, family-oriented *Party* made for a better audience and genre match with *90210*. *Models* did not succeed. If *Party* had stayed on Monday nights, it would probably have been canceled, too. But it was moved to Wednesdays, and enough of *90210*'s audience got into the habit of "staying tuned" that *Party* remained on the schedule. This was literally a textbook example of successful **lead-in placement.**

---

these January changes the name **second season.** By the end of the 1970s, the second season had evolved into near-continuous programming changes.

### 7.3.2 TV Station Programming

Stations affiliated with ABC, CBS, Fox, and NBC receive highly promoted, big-audience programming for relatively little effort. As a result, in most markets

---

**BOX 7.2. WHAT QUALIFIES AS A HIT?**

When ABC, CBS, and NBC attracted 90% of all viewing, a program was a hit with a 30 share—about one third of the audience. When competition from other nonbroadcast services caused a drop in network viewing, the share needed to qualify a hit dropped also. By the 1990s criteria for a hit were as follows:

- The show earns at least a 20 share.
- The show wins its time period.
- The show retains 80% or more of the lead-in program's audience share.

A share in the 15 to 19 range put the show in the "toss-up" category (could be kept; could be canceled). Any show with less than a 15 share was a "miss" and sure to be canceled. Those figures were adjusted to 65% to 75% for Fox because of its smaller station lineup—at least until the New World round of affiliate changes (*PRT*, 3.6.2).

*Source*: Morrie Gelman, "The Hits, Misses and Maybes for Fall," *Broadcasting* 10 August 1992: 15; Morrie Gelman, "Madison Ave. [*sic*] Predicts Prime Time," *Broadcasting & Cable* 19 July 1993: 18; and Morrie Gelman, "Agencies Pick ABC for Fall, *Broadcasting & Cable* 1 August 1994: 19.

---

affiliates of these networks usually draw the highest overall ratings and earn the greatest revenues. Rarely can an independent or a station affiliated with one of the newer networks achieve first overall place in market ratings. However, it can win in certain dayparts and among certain segments of the audience, and when the network is dark (not feeding programming), the affiliate and the independent compete head to head.

### 7.3.2.1 Competitive Programming Elements.

*7.3.2.1 Competitive Programming Elements.*   A key element in competitive programming is syndicated material. **Syndicated programming** is classified according to origin: (a) **off-net,** that which ran previously on networks (Fig. 7.8), and (b) **first-run** original material prepared especially for syndication. A station looks for programming that will be popular in its market, then buys the rights to that programming. Typically, these rights allow the station exclusive use of the programming in the market for a stated period—say 2 years—during which time the station may broadcast it a specified number of times, frequently two or three. FCC rules limit the geographical extent of this exclusivity.

There is no set or "catalog" price for a syndicated program. The price varies with factors such as success of the program (on the network or in other markets), size of the market in which it will be run, and the number of stations in the market that want it. Buying and selling television programming resembles the proverbial

**FIG. 7.8 Off-net syndication.** *Love Boat* made its debut on ABC in 1977 then went into syndication several years later. It ran on the network for nine seasons. (Photo provided by Worldvision Enterprises, Inc. Copyright © 1981 Aaron Spelling Productions.)

"Persian marketplace"—the price paid represents a compromise between all the syndicator can get and as little as the station can pay.

The larger the market, the more television stations it contains and the greater the competition for successful programming. A station may buy and **shelve** (not use) a series; this keeps the series off the market and out of the competition's schedule until the buyer is ready to use it. Stations sometimes buy **futures** on hit network series (pay for first off-net rights in its market), an investment of which they may not be able to take advantage for years. Syndicators even have stations **bid** on futures, one market at a time, for an especially desirable off-net series. This can drive prices very high.

Before the widespread availability of satellite communications, syndicators avoided topical programming. It went out of date quickly—even while being shipped—and could not be stored and used again. The advent of domestic communication satellites, however, made TV program distribution both instantaneous and relatively inexpensive. In the 1980s, distributors successfully began to offer topical programming by satellite. Time-dated, one-run series, from *Oprah*, *Jeopardy*, and *Wheel of Fortune* to *Entertainment Tonight* grew into a major force in the syndication world.

Some syndicated programming is offered on a **barter** basis. The station pays no money for rights to air such programming. The syndicator makes its money by selling some of the availabilities (slots for commercials) within the programming to national advertisers. A station that airs the barter programming must air the commercials within (those the syndicator has sold) but may sell the remaining availabilities. In the **time banking** variation, the program contains no commercials; the station may sell every availability locally. Availabilities are, however, "banked" by the syndicator, often an advertising agency or independent media-buying firm. This means the station "owes" the syndicator a specified number of commercials, which the syndicator will use at a later time.

Yet another wrinkle in the distribution of syndicated programming is **cash-plus-barter**. Here, the program contains some syndicator-sold commercials that the station must air (plus availabilities that it can sell), and the station must pay a fee. Syndicators contend that such an arrangement helps pay for better production and allows higher quality shows without raising the price to the station. In the past, most programming distributed on a barter or cash-plus-barter basis has been first-run. Viacom, however, started the practice for off-net syndication in the 1988–1989 season when it offered the immensely popular off-NBC *Cosby Show* for top dollar and withheld a minute for advertising.

Another source of programming is the **stations themselves**. In the 1995 Partner Stations Network venture, for example, a consortium of cooperating station-group owners provided financing for production of a half-hour reality strip, *Lifeguard*. Group-owned stations sometimes cooperate to produce programming for use among themselves; if successful, this programming may be syndicated to other stations. Large-market stations occasionally put their production efforts into syndication.

A second key element in successful competitive programming is **feature films.** Films need not be new to attract large audiences. For example, local station showings of the film *Casablanca* have often given network fare heavy competition for ratings. Widespread conversion of black-and-white films to color began in 1986 when Turner Broadcasting colorized a number of old MGM movies. Film buffs decried the practice, but in a generation raised on color television, many who would tune away from the original monochrome version watch these colorized movies.

A third element—perhaps first in importance for affiliates—is **local news programming.** A strong news department takes time, money, and effort, but local news, effectively done, draws high audience levels, good advertising rates, and enough revenue to pay for itself and turn a profit.

Local productions can be assets or liabilities in overall programming strategy. Well-planned and slickly produced local programs—discussion programs, cooking shows, children's programs, community magazines—can augment local news efforts in building a positive public image and high circulation for the station. Poorly done programs drive audiences away.

Stations use many of the same programming tactics discussed in *PRT*, 7.3.1.2. Dayparting, audience flow, counterprogramming, lead-in programs, and block programming are all concerns of the station programmer. In 1986 and 1987, a few stations revived a tactic from earlier days. They used checkerboard programming (Fig. 7.9)—a different series (of the same type and length) each weekday at the same time. Most tried five half-hour first-run situation comedies in access time.

*7.3.2.2 Network Affiliated Stations.*    By the late 1990s ABC, CBS, and NBC supplied nearly two thirds of a station's program schedule; Fox, about one third. With affiliation providing such a large proportion of the broadcast day, a station's programming burden is significantly reduced. On the other hand, network affiliation can cause problems with **positioning**—making the station stand out in the minds of the audience. As you have probably noticed, the big TV networks program very much alike. Differences exist in program titles and specific performers, but basically all run the same type of programming. That means the affiliates,

| | Source | Time | Program Type | Programs | | | | |
|---|---|---|---|---|---|---|---|---|
| | | | | *Monday* | *Tuesday* | *Wednesday* | *Thursday* | *Friday* |
| A | NBC owned and operated stations | 7:30 P.M. (Eastern) | Situation Comedies* | Marblehead Manor | She's the Sheriff | You Can't Take It with You | Out of This World | We've Got It Made |
| B | Public Broadcasting Station | 12:30 P.M. | Sewing | Sewing Today | Sewing with Nancy | America Sews | Quilting from the Heartland | Kaye's Quilting Friends |
| C | Nostalgia Channel | 2:30 P.M. | Cooking | Flavors of Philadelphia | Monterey's Cookin' Pisto Style | It's Cooking but It Ain't | Monterey's Cookin' Pisto Style | Health Smart Gourmet Cooking |

FIG. 7.9 Checkerboarding.

too, look very much alike. An affiliate often puts great effort into overcoming this sameness, into convincing viewers that it really does differ from the other affiliates in town. Such effort focuses on promotion (*PRT,* 7.7) and on local programming, primarily news. A station advertises its helicopters, or its satellite news capability, or its pretty, chatty anchor reporters, or the nightly "weather school" question its weather reporter asks, or whatever to convince the public that it is unique.

With local news programming filling part of the schedule, an affiliate of ABC, CBS, NBC, or, increasingly, Fox has relatively few hours to fill with syndicated programming. Often, too, affiliated stations are financially the strongest in the market. In other words, a network affiliate usually has more money and fewer slots to spend it on than a station that is independent or affiliated with one of the newer part-time networks. So the affiliate, when playing the game of programming, should hold the winning hand at every deal. Programmers at competing stations, however, take the opposite view: Affiliates are most vulnerable during those few key times when they use syndicated entertainment to compete directly against independents and affiliates of newer networks.

The FCC actually created one of these direct-competition times. The Commission's prime-time access rule (PTAR; *PRT,* 14.1.3.2) had the effect of prohibiting ABC, CBS, and NBC from programming during the period 7 p.m. and 8 p.m. Eastern and Pacific time, and 6 p.m. and 7 p.m. Central and Mountain time. Even before PTAR, the three networks had not programmed the first half-hour of prime time, so they actually gave up only 30 minutes. This first hour of prime time became **access time,** a 25-year programming arena that pitted affiliates against independents in a battle of syndicated entertainment. With the FCC's repeal of PTAR, however, access time ended in 1996.

### 7.3.2.3 Independent Stations and Affiliates of an "Emerging" Network.    Fox Broadcasting, UPN, and The WB all launched operations by feeding just a few hours of prime-time programming a week. Fox, which had an 8-year lead on the other two, began 7-nights-a-week scheduling in 1993. It had, over the years, carefully built and nurtured a certain network image and had encouraged affiliates to program and promote in other dayparts so as to reinforce that image. Nonetheless, for major segments of the broadcast day, Fox, UPN, and The WB affiliates found themselves in the same situation as independent stations; they had to rely on their own resources to program against ABC, CBS, and NBC. We use the term *independent programmer* to mean the chief programmer not only for an independent TV station but also for an affiliate of one of the newer networks, particular during those extended periods when the affiliate must program on its own.

An independent station **builds its schedule from scratch** and can usually position itself more easily than an ABC/CBS/NBC-type affiliate. It might, for example, program and promote as "the more movies station." Some independents target particular audiences with specialized programming. Most, however, compete for a general audience; they counterprogram the local big-three affiliates and, therefore, the networks.

The **chief programmer plays a more crucial role** in an independent situation than at a big-three affiliate. The independent programmer must literally match wits against "the best programming minds in New York and Los Angeles," the network gurus. A programmer who can utilize research, gauge audience taste, purchase series rights on favorable terms, and effectively package and promote programming is a living profit center.

In pursuing these goals, successful independents have **perfected the art of counterprogramming**. When networks schedule game shows in the morning, the independent may counter with movies or situation comedies. Later, when networks run soap operas, the independent airs situation comedies, musical variety programs, children's shows, and feature films. During early fringe time, affiliates aim for adults with syndicated courtroom, game, and talk shows and off-net action adventure; the independent targets children. In early evening, the independent can do particularly well, capturing a large number (often a plurality) of persons who would rather watch situation comedies or *Star Trek* reruns than news (Box 7.1). Competition is more difficult against network prime-time programming; however, an independent may get enough tune-in/tune-out audience to raise average ratings to respectable levels. At 10 p.m. Eastern time, the independent begins to recapture audiences and often puts the station's major news effort at this time. Then, while network affiliates run news at 11 p.m., the independent is back to entertainment programming.

Independents achieve success through **creative packaging and marketing of feature films and off-net series**. They group old and familiar films into thematic packages—for example, "The Films of Bogart," "The Charlie Chan Series"—and draw respectable ratings. With regard to off-net series, they look for programs that have been hits on the network, earning shares in the 20s—which means, of course, that nearly 80% of the viewing audience has not seen them!

Some independents have gone heavily into local production. They produce talk shows, interview programs, children's shows, and community magazines. Some broadcast play-by-play of local sports events.

Independents occasionally carry programming from one of the big three networks. If an affiliate decides not to run a particular network program, the network offers the program to another station in the market, often an independent. Independents may also broadcast programs from special networks, such as the ad hoc chain Mobil put together in 1983 to broadcast *The Life and Adventures of Nicholas Nickleby*. Some specialty networks even offer programming primarily for independent stations; Conus Communications, for example, provides the 24-hour All News Channel, a fully anchored newscast service, to broadcast stations as well as to DBS and regional cable news channels.

***7.3.2.4 Narrowcast Stations.***    Some television stations narrowcast—they target particular segments of the general audience with special programming. Examples include religion, ethnic, and home shopping. By the late 1990s most ethnic stations programmed for the burgeoning Hispanic population; most religious stations, primarily for conservative Christians.

Narrowcast station programmers often took advantage of existing networks. For example, a number of the Spanish-language broadcasters were actually Univision or Telemundo affiliates. The religious stations frequently aired programs from the cable religious networks. Home shopping stations took the majority of their programming from a special broadcast feed of the HSN.

Many narrowcast programmers actually broadcast a variety of program types. Hispanic stations, for example, may schedule Spanish-language programming that includes everything from comedy to news to sports play-by-play. Others operate much more like radio stations, programming a continuous schedule of basically the same type of content, such as home shopping. Most of the narrowcast stations are licensed to big cities. Full-service (that is not low-power) narrowcast stations tend to be in the UHF band; many narrowcast stations, however, are low-power.

*7.3.2.5 LPTV Stations.*   Most of the nearly 1,800 LPTV stations operate as translators, automated repeaters of other TV stations. Some educational institutions use LPTV stations to transmit cultural enrichment and instructional programming. Religious groups may use LPTV stations as "satellators," transmitting programming received from a satellite-delivered religious network. Many locally programmed LPTV stations narrowcast, and the range of LPTV ethnic programming includes Hispanic, African American, Native American, Hunan, and Korean. Some LPTVs operate much like full-power, full-service TV stations, airing entertainment programming from syndication sources and national networks; broadcasting local news, sports, and public affairs programs; and selling local advertising. In some cases, the newer networks have used LPTVs as building blocks. Fox, UPN, and WB, when they first signed on, all turned to LPTVs to fill in areas where full-power affiliates did not reach or cable had not yet penetrated. The networks have even "grouped" LPTVs; a network will feed its program to multiple LPTVs in a given market area to ensure its programming reaches all parts of the area.

The one major key to success for an individual LPTV station is **cable carriage**. Cable systems do not have to carry LPTV stations, so low-power station licensees often strike deals with cable operators. An LPTV licensee, for example, might agree to air programs that promote the local cable system in exchange for being carried on the system.

By the late 1990s some entrepreneurs had began to use LPTV licenses to compete with cable. They would license a group of LPTVs serving the same area and offer **subscription low-power TV** (SLTV) service, a multichannel subscription service similar to wireless cable (*PRT,* 5.2).

## 7.4 NONBROADCAST TELEVISION PROGRAMMING

The size of the marketplace for nonbroadcast television programming has exploded with continued advances in the technology of delivering video to the home.

All kinds of services, networks, and programmers are competing for a share of the nonbroadcast audience. In this section, we focus on these alternatives to the programming of full-service, advertising-supported broadcast stations, to include local production, satellite-delivered basic services, satellite-delivered pay services, TVRO packagers, and what we call unconventional services.

Locally produced programming is created in the area served by, and often using the facilities of, the local outlet. Our "unconventional" category embraces several disparate programming options. They may be locally originated or national.

Satellite-delivered services ordinarily program for national audiences. Local outlets receive them by satellite and put them on local channels for relay to homes in the community. Most originated to serve cable systems and are called *national cable programmer services, satellite networks,* or *cable networks.* Other media, however, also distribute them. Hotel and motel TV, wireless cable, satellite master antenna television (SMATV) systems, TVRO satellite packagers, and DBS services carry them. Some LPTV stations carry them, particularly in areas without cable.

### 7.4.1 Locally Produced Programming

Cable system practices have evolved three types of locally produced programming. **Local origination** is programming produced by the cable system's staff; **access programming** is that produced by others for which the cable system neither pays nor receives direct payment; and **leased-channel content** is that produced by others, and which the cable system is paid to carry.

LPTV stations that have production capability may also originate programming. Hotel and motel systems usually include a locally programmed, mainly text channel that lists the guest-oriented events for the day and the video offerings on the system's other channels. Some SMATV systems may include a locally produced community channel. Other video distribution systems rarely have the capability or desire to produce their own programming.

*7.4.1.1 Local Origination Programming.*   Local origination efforts by cable systems range from electronic text bulletin boards and "video classifieds" with still frames of houses for sale to feature films, high school and college sports, and live telecasts of city council meetings. Some systems and LPTV stations operate their own studios and produce a daily schedule of newscasts, discussions, children's shows, educational materials, commercials, and other programming.

*7.4.1.2 Access Programming.*   Access programming is cable program material provided by groups or individual members of the community. If your community's cable system has an access channel, you can probably use it to cablecast your own TV program. The choice of subject and presentation is yours. You can do a roundtable discussion on competitive macramé, play-by-play coverage of a chess game, your own dramatic efforts, political commentary, or whatever else you want.

Access channels have other uses. They may carry meetings of governmental bodies—city commissions, county planning boards, or school boards. They may run programming for the school system or community college—supplementary and enrichment material, courses, and announcements. For this reason, access channels are often called **PEG** (public, educational, government) **channels.**

*7.4.1.3 Leased-Channel Content.* A cable system may lease channels to others on a full-time or part-time basis. Possible uses for these **leased-access channels** vary. Some lessees might offer regular programming—advertising-supported or pay. Others might offer part-time programming or even single programs—for example, program-length commercials disguised as entertainment to sell cosmetics or exercise devices or car wax or whatever. Still others might use leased channels to provide home-security service or to exchange computer data among several locations; home subscribers would not, of course, have access to such content. Some new cable networks, when they encountered large-market cable systems that had no room for additional channels, made use of leased-access channels in order to get their programming (and their commercials) on the systems. In other words, they paid the operators for carriage (instead of the normal arrangement in cable programming in which the operator pays the network).

### 7.4.2 Satellite-Delivered Basic Service Programming

Companies planned and launched many more cable networks (Fig. 7.10) than the typical cable system could carry. This went on continually, almost from the very beginning of domestic satellite distribution of programming. The number of new networks announced increased during the 1990s, a result of technological and regulatory developments. Many that were announced did not launch, and many that launched did not survive. Therefore any description of cable networks risks being dated as soon as it is published. Some patterns, however, have emerged. Satellite-delivered basic services, for example, divided into **advertiser-supported, superstations, advertising-only,** and **noncommercial.** They were basic services because most were designed to run on a cable system's basic tier (*PRT,* 4.2.8). Most cable operators, in reacting to the Cable Television Consumer Protection Act of 1992 (*PRT,* 4.3.3.2), stripped most such channels off their lowest-cost tier of service and put them on an extra-cost tier. The networks nonetheless retained their designation as **basic services.** Following are some examples of the various networks in each of these four areas.

*7.4.2.1 Programming by Advertiser-Supported Services.* In some ways, **advertiser-supported satellite services** resemble broadcast networks. They program nationally and earn money from the advertising they carry. They also increasingly schedule original (not previously seen on other channels) programming. In other ways, ad-supported services resemble modern radio and magazines. Most focus their content on a particular theme or interest.

**FIG. 7.10 Satellite-delivered national program services.** During the 1990s dozens of services operated, fought for niches and carriage, and tried to survive. Even more were proposed. All aimed for channel space on multichannel programmers such as cable systems, wireless cable systems, and DBS services. These are the logos for some of those networks, both operating and proposed.

Programming of ad-supported services can be divided into seven broad categories. One group includes services that program **horizontally**. Like the broadcast networks, they aim for a general audience, and some of the better known of these general and consumer services are listed in Fig. 7.11. The other groups comprise the majority of ad-supported services, those that program **vertically**. Like radio stations and magazines, these networks aim for specificity. Some do this by offering just one type of content, although they may attract a broad audience. The Weather Channel, for example, programs exactly and only what its name implies, but many different types of people tune it in (although usually for short periods). Others achieve specificity through the audience to which they appeal. Telemundo and Univision (which are also broadcast networks) program a wide variety of programming, but because they transmit only Spanish-language content they attract primarily people who speak Spanish as a first language. These services can be categorized as informational, music (Fig. 7.12), racial and ethnic and non-English, and religious, as exemplified in Fig. 7.11, sports as in Table 7.3, and special interest as in Fig. 7.13.

### 7.4.2.2 Superstation Programming.

A superstation is a television broadcast station whose signal is distributed by satellite to many cable systems. A firm picks up the station's programming and utilizes satellite relay for national distribution. A cable operator that takes the station's programming off the satellite and puts it on a system must pay the distribution firm.

The most popular superstations are independents. Like the majority of full-service independents, the superstation programs to a general audience. Beyond this, however, its "superstation" appeal—the reason this station attracts audiences across the country—is usually its heavy schedule of professional sports and movies.

As a broadcast station, the superstation must serve the market to which it is licensed. If the station does not actively promote its "super" status, that may be as far as it goes—it is a good independent that serves its market and its national audience can take it or leave it. Two factors, however, may alter that. First, the firm that distributes the signal may change the programming of the satellite-delivered signal. In 1988 the FCC adopted the syndicated exclusivity rule (syndex; *PRT,* 14.1.1.9), requiring cable systems to blank out certain programs that duplicate those on local TV stations. The distribution firms reacted by **syndex-proofing** the superstation programming they carried. They acquired their own programs that were not subject to the syndex rule. When the superstation aired shows that were subject to syndex, the distribution firms did not carry those shows on the national feed but instead ran their own programs.

Second, a TV station may actually seek superstation status and program with its national audience in mind. For years, Atlanta's WTBS was the only such **willing superstation**. It counterprogrammed the broadcast networks around the clock but, because of time-zone differences, not specific stations in specific markets. Instead, WTBS scheduled in such way as to provide alternative program

## General and Consumer Programming Services

The Family Channel: Family entertainment; also carries religious programming

fX: General entertainment

The Nashville Network: Music, comedies, game and variety shows, sports with a country flavor

Turner Network Television: Major programming events, plus a regular schedule with increasing amounts of original (made-for-TNT) programming

USA Network: Focus on entertainment

## Informational Services

Cable News Network: Frequent general news updates, informational features and material, often continuous live coverage of breaking news

CNBC: Business, finance, and business-consumer programming

CNNfn: Business and financial reports

CNN International: World news

Court TV: Reports on U.S. legal and judicial systems; extended, "gavel-to-gavel" coverage of court trials

Fox News Channel: General news and news interviews

Headline News: Tightly formatted half-hour news cycle

MSNBC: General news and information; also provides programming through the Microsoft Network on-line computer service

The Weather Channel: Weather information, forecasts, and features

## Music Services

BET on Jazz: Jazz

The Box: Allows viewers to choose from a menu of music videos by dialing a 900 number; caller pays; all other viewers on the system see the video for free

Country Music Network: Country

Fish TV: Christian

MOR Music TV: Pop music with 800 number to order music

MTV: Pioneered and still focuses on music-video programming, but has developed other types of adolescent-appeal programs

VH-1: MTV stablemate; uses more inclusive popular-music play list

Z-Music: Christian music and direct marketing from Lake Helen, FL

## Racial/Ethnic and Non-English Services

Black Entertainment Television (BET): African-American family programming

La Cadena Deportiva: Spanish-language sports

Canal de Noticias NBC: General news in Spanish

Chinese Channel

CineLatino: Movies

Eco: Spanish language news

The Filipino Channel

Galavision: Entertainment and news

GEMS: Aimed at Hispanic women

HTV: Spanish-language all music

International Channel: programs to almost anyone who speaks a language other than Spanish or English

Jewish Television Network

Korean Channel

MTV Latino: Spanish-language all music

National Jewish Television: Programming for the Jewish community

RitmoSon: Spanish-language all music

Sur-Canal de Canales: Spanish language news

Telenovelas: Spanish-language drama

Telhit: Spanish-language all music

Telecompras Shopping Network: Spanish-language home shopping

Telemundo: Spanish-language family programming (for cable, other multichannel systems, and affiliated TV stations)

TeleNoticias: All news

TV-Japan

Univision: Spanish-language family programming (for cable, other multichannel systems, and affiliated TV stations)

VivaTelevision: Spanish-language entertainment, culture, and education

## Religious Services

Christian Broadcasting Network: Produces Evangelist and CBN founder M.G. "Pat" Robertson's *The 700 Club* which runs on the Family Channel as well as other outlets

Faith and Values Network: Much original programming including worship services, children's programs

The Inspirational Network

Trinity Broadcasting Network

Worship Channel: Nature scenes with inspirational Christian music; callers used 800, 900 telephone numbers to confide in counselors, hear Bible passages and sermons by pastor-and-network head James West

FIG. 7.11 Advertising-supported programming services: General and consumer, informational, music, racial/ethnic and non-English.

(a)

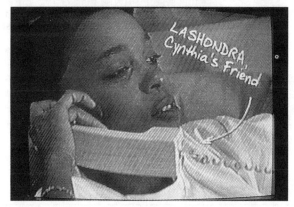

(b)

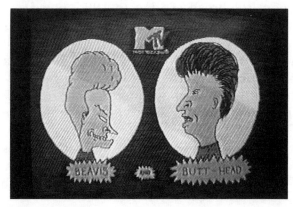

(c)

**FIG. 7.12 MTV programming.** (a) MTV's "Kennedy" hosts a Saturday lineup of music videos from outside MTV's Motel California. (b) A scene from MTV's *The Real World*. (c) The lead characters from MTV's *Beavis & Butt-head* animated series. (Photographs provided courtesy of MTV: MUSIC TELEVISION. © 1997 MTV Networks. All rights reserved. "MTV: MUSIC TELEVISION," "MTV's Motel California," "MTV's Real World," and "MTV's Beavis & Butt-head" and all related titles, characters, and logos are trademarks owned by MTV Networks, a division of Viacom International, Inc.

**225**

TABLE 7.3

Advertising-Supported Programming Services: Sports

| Type of Service | Programming | Examples |
|---|---|---|
| National sports services | Some, such as Entertainment and Sports Programming Network (ESPN), one of the most successful networks of any type, feature professional, amateur, and collegiate sports events of all types; others focus on one sport or one type of sport. | Classic Sports Network, ESPN, ESPN2, The Golf Channel, The Outdoor Life Channel, Prime Sports Showcase, Women's Sports & Entertainment Network. |
| Regional sports services | Typically based on a large market; features play-by-play of professional and college teams identified with the market. Feeds by satellite to cable systems in the market and surrounding area. Most cable systems put these ad-supported service on extended basic tier, although some put them on a separate tier. | The many regional sports channels bear names like Empire Sports Network (western and central New York State), Home Sports Entertainment (Texas), Home Team Sports (Washington/Baltimore), MSG Network (New York), SportsChannel Chicago, and Sunshine Network (Florida). |
| Sports supplementary services | Most regional sports channels also carry material from Prime Sports or NewSport. Prime offers a variety of sports programming, whereas NewSport carries sports news, information, and talk. Rainbow Program Holdings manages both, and they are available on DBS as well as cable. | |

choices throughout the broadcast day. In 1995, however, the trade press began mentioning plans to change WTBS from a cable superstation to a cable network.[4]

Ted Turner put his WTBS (then WTCG) on the satellite in 1976 to become the first superstation. By the early 1980s, three firms relayed the signals of six independent TV stations: Eastern Microwave distributed WWOR from Secaucus, New Jersey (New York City); Tempo Enterprises carried WTBS; and United Video distributed KTLA from Los Angeles, WGN-TV from Chicago, and WPIX from New York.

Some firms distributed the signals of other stations, mostly network affiliates. They marketed these to small cable systems that did not carry a full complement of broadcast TV signals and to the television receive-only (backyard) dish market (*PRT,* 7.4.4).

### 7.4.2.3 Programming by Advertising-Only Services.    Advertising-only services use most of their program time to sell things. Their predominant programming consists of sales messages, content to which, when it appears on other channels, viewers object to as intrusive, loud, and interruptive. Yet, paradoxical as it may

**Special Interest Services**

Arts & Entertainment (A&E): Fine arts; has broadened its appeal until similar to a general network
Cable Health Club: Health and fitness
Cartoon Network: Programs to children; has huge library of animation from Hanna-Barbera (e.g., *The Jetsons*, *The Flintstones*, *Top Cat*, *Yogi Bear*, *Scooby Doo*), MGM (*Tom and Jerry*, *Popeye*), and Warner Brothers
CelticVision: The Irish Channel: Celtic culture
Comedy Central: Funny and humorous material both old and new
The Crime Channel: Crime
The Dating Network: Relationships and lifestyles
Discovery Channel: Science, nature, history, technology, adventure, world exploration (night); crafts, home improvement, cooking (day)
E! Entertainment Television: Information on movies, TV, recordings, and other entertainment media; mainly short-form (interviews, previews, and other material) using an hourly news-network-like cycle
Fashion and Design Television: Fashion
Game Show Network: Game shows
Gay Entertainment Television: Relationships and lifestyles
Health and Fitness Network: Health and fitness
The Health Network: Health and fitness
The History Channel: History
Home & Garden Television: Home improvement
Home Improvement Channel: Home improvement
Independent Film Channel: Independent filmmakers
Intro TV: Introduces new cable networks
Jones Computer Network: Computers
Kaleidoscope: Serves individuals who have some type of disability
The Learning Channel: Documentaries and factual programs; focuses on ideas and intellectual creation; during daytime: crafts, home improvement, and cooking
Lifetime: Drama, movies, talk aimed at women
The Lottery Channel: State lotteries
The Military Channel: The military and war
National Empowerment TV: Conservative politics
Nick at Nite: Various older series for the family
Nickelodeon: Targets children with various types of programs
Nostalgia Channel: Targets an older demographic with older movies and series
Ovation: The Fine Arts Network: Music, art, literature, drama
Parent Television: Parenting and child rearing
The Popcorn Channel: Movie previews
Recovery Network/The Wellness Channel: Focuses on long-term illness
Sega Channel: Video games
Television Food Network: Food
Total Communication Network: Programs for the hearing impaired
The Travel Channel: Travel

FIG. 7.13 Advertising-supported programming services: Special interest services.

seem, these services, which carry little or no strictly entertainment or information content, attract loyal national audiences.

Most advertising-only programmers fall into one of two types based on predominant content—home shopping and program-length commercials (for which the business has coined the euphemism *infomercials*). This latter group, the **infomercial services,** run commercials that last as long as, and often try to look like, regular programs. Advertisers pay the service to carry their program-length commercials. National infomercial programmers up and running during the 1990s included, among others, Consumer Resource Network, Product Information Network, and DRAGnet (Direct Response Advertising Group Network).

**Home shopping services** retail goods directly to their audiences. Programming consists of pitches for the various items. Viewers are encouraged to call toll-free telephone order lines and make credit-card purchases. Because these services generate revenue directly from viewers, they normally do not need to sell advertising time to others or pay heed to ratings.

Home shopping developed as full-time cable programming during the 1980s, thanks largely to the success of HSN. The idea of these services seemed great—the ultimate merger of show business and marketing. Skip the programming costs; let us get down to business and sell full time with low investment and high return. Many tried it, and many went under. They could not get cable systems to carry them. Even large-capacity systems resisted carrying more than one or two specimens of such a specialized service.

In researching the previous edition of this volume, one count showed eight national services—two HSN channels, America's Shopping Channel, Cable Value Network, Fashion Channel, QVC Network, Shop TV, Telshop, and Video Mall Network. By this edition, all but QVC and one HSN channel had either gone under or merged with other networks. Meanwhile, other shopping channels had launched, among them BET Shop (BET-Home Shopping Network, aimed at African Americans), Catalog 1, Q2, Telecompras Shopping Network (aimed at Hispanic Americans), Valuevision, and Video Catalog Channel. Additionally, a number of advertising-supported networks had added home-shopping segments to their schedules; MTV, VH-1, and Nick at Nite, for example, all tested 30- and 60-minute shopping shows.

***7.4.2.4 Programming by Noncommercial Services.***    Noncommercial services carry no paid advertising. The best known is Cable Satellite Public Affairs Network (C-SPAN). C-SPAN consists of two channels that normally carry coverage of the U.S. House of Representatives and Senate. When Congress is not in session, they carry other public affairs programming. C-SPAN is financially supported by cable system operators.

This noncommercial category does include some entertainment programmers. Several began as premium channels. American Movie Classics, for example, which features older movies that have been critically acclaimed or otherwise made their mark, converted to a basic service during the late 1980s. Bravo started as a pay service focusing on feature films and the performing arts. It converted to a basic service in 1990 and started accepting corporate underwriting sponsors in 1992. The Disney Channel, which uses family entertainment from its own studios and other sources, operated for years as a pay service but converted to a basic service on many cable systems in 1995.

Another type of program service that often carries no advertising is the religious network. The programming of such networks may, however, include appeals for donations. Eternal Word Television Network, a Roman Catholic service, originates from Birmingham, Alabama, and features spiritual-growth programming. The Trinity Broadcasting Network offers Christian religious programming. The National Jewish Television Network features informational, cultural, and religious material, and the Jewish Television Network, which sells sponsorships in some of its programs, schedules material in the areas of news, arts, Israel, religion, and features.

### 7.4.3 Satellite-Delivered Premium Programming

For those who can afford them, satellite-delivered premium or pay services add another level of entertainment to the programming menu of cable and other multichannel video systems. These premium services are either **subscription** or **pay-per-view.** Cable subscribers who opt for such channels are normally charged fees over and above the cost for basic service.

*7.4.3.1 Programming by Subscription Services.*    A subscription service customer pays a monthly fee for the service.[5] This allows the customer to tune in to the service at any time, for as long as the customer wishes, and for as many times as the customer wishes. Most subscription services offer three inducements to potential subscribers. First, they offer material that is **uncut.** A subscription service generally does not cut programming to eliminate objectionable content or to squeeze it into a time slot. Second, they offer **uninterrupted** material. A subscription service may declare a recess in the middle of a long presentation to give viewers a break, but it does not insert commercials or promos.

Third, they offer **unique** material. The subscription services acquire some original material. You see it either first on subscription or nowhere else but on subscription. They also acquire much material that is not original—movies, for example, that have shown in theaters—but they acquire it on an exclusive basis. Networks and stations may not program such material while a subscription service has it.

Subscription services look at cumulative ratings for the month, rather than per-program or daypart ratings. They try to run a variety of material so that, over a month's time, they appeal to both sexes and diverse age groups. Viewers usually turn to most subscription channels to watch a particular offering, rather than for continuous viewing. Nonetheless, subscription services do make some attempt to counterprogram the broadcast networks and establish audience flow.

In the development of subscription services, **movies** played a key role. They figured large in the initial success of the services. Because the services made money directly from viewers, they had the financial resources to outbid broadcasters for first TV rights, rights that allowed them to show recent films long before their release to broadcasting.

By the mid-1980s, however, so many consumers owned VCRs that the home video business could outbid subscription services. Films were released on video-cassette before they went to cable. The novelty of premium movie channels wore off. Subscribers complained of repetition (not enough good new films) and duplication (the various services all showed the same films). The services responded in several ways. First, they produced more original programming. Second, they signed contracts with film studios to get exclusive rights for movies during the cable window (the time during which they can be shown on cable); this strategy involved primarily archrivals HBO and Showtime/The Movie Channel.

Subscription services attempt to position themselves through programming and promotion. HBO and Showtime compete head to head. Each promotes the variety on its programming schedule—movies, specials, documentaries, sports, comedy series, music, and original programs. Cinemax, HBO's companion service, aims at a young adult audience with select and broad-appeal films and with music and comedy original programming.

One 1990s development in subscription programming was **channel multiplexing**. Typically, this took the form of a subscription programmer adding additional channels. In some cases the programmer used these channels for **time shifting**, to schedule its existing programming at different hours for the convenience of its viewers. HBO/Cinemax and Showtime both added channels for time shifting.

In other cases the programmer used the additional channels to create **minipay services**. These were separately programmed channels, usually created from relatively inexpensive content (such as older movies), and retailed at very low prices. They were often used as a kind of value-added low-cost upgrade for those who already subscribed to premium channels. Liberty Media, for example, expanded its Encore older movies subscription service to eight channels—Encore and Starz! plus channels that specialized in westerns, romances, mystery, action-adventure, true stories and drama, and children's movies. All were low cost; existing pay subscribers paid as little as $1 per month per channel. Showtime set up a graduated rate for its Flix! minipay: The more premium channels a subscriber had, the less the subscriber paid for Flix!; subscribers with three or more premium channels received Flix! for free. Turner Classic Movies, which was also designed as a minipay, carried motion pictures from the period of the 1920s through the 1980s.

*7.4.3.2 Pay-Per-View Programming.*    A pay-per-view (PPV) service customer pays only for the programs (usually called *events*) actually viewed.[6] The PPV customer who wishes to view a particular event so notifies the system in advance (usually by calling a special telephone number). The system then sends a special coded signal down the line to the special addressable set-top box connected to the customer's TV set, instructing the box to unscramble the video for the selected event. The customer then gets billed for the cost of the event.

Movies, sports events (often, championship boxing matches and wrestling matches), rock concerts, hit plays and revues are the types of material that PPV services program. With respect to feature-length films, the release window for PPV is usually shortly after that for the VCR market (which is next after theatrical showings). PPV audiences can see new movies sometimes 6 months before they reach the subscription services.

By the 1990s, several satellite-delivered services provided PPV programming for cable systems and other pay outlets. To provide PPV service, a cable system had to make addressable converter boxes available to subscribers, and at least some subscribers had to be willing to pay the extra monthly charge for use of the converter. In 1992 the number of addressable converters nationwide rose by nearly 3 million to 20.1 million, partially attributable to the Olympic Triplecast (*PRT,* 4.3.1). Technical systems had improved; some advanced and experimental cable systems even offered true **impulse technology** (permitting the viewer to watch simply by pressing a button). Still, relatively few cable subscribers had the necessary equipment, so overall PPV audience figures were low compared to those for basic cable.

Pioneer PPV services included Viewer's Choice, Request TV, and Cable Video Store. Viewer's Choice and Request TV both operated multiple channels. Viewer's Choice, for example, provided programming on six channels—Viewer's Choice, which scheduled first-run movies and live events such as wrestling, boxing, and concerts; Hot Choice, which carried action-adventure material; and four Continuous Hits channels, each playing a different recent-release film on a continuous basis. Both firms planned to expand eventually, through digital compression, to 40 or more channels of PPV.

Ring sports accounted for the greatest amount of PPV revenue—boxing, wrestling, "tough-man" competitions, and martial arts. Action-oriented material was also popular, but much PPV growth during the 1990s came from sexually oriented so-called "adult services." The best known of these was the Playboy Channel; its parent company was the longtime publisher of *Playboy,* an "adult" magazine. Playboy TV, which expanded from nighttime-only to a 24-hour service in 1994, used mature-audience feature films and made-for-Playboy original programming. In 1995 Playboy launched AdultVision TV, featuring "harder edged" films, to compete directly with Graff Pay-Per-View's Spice adult service. Graff also operated the Adam & Eve Channel.

### 7.4.4 DBS and TVRO Programming Packagers

DBS and TVRO packagers retail groups of programming services to subscribers. Instead of a cable system, individuals use satellite receiving dishes and pay a monthly fee to pick up the satellite services. Most of the channels in the packages consist of the satellite-delivered program services surveyed in *PRT,* 7.4.2 and 7.4.3, and most of these services scramble their signals to prevent unauthorized reception. The DBS firms use ground receiving stations to pick up the satellite signals of the program services they will retail, digitize the services' signals, and then beam them back up to their own satellites. These DBSs contain high-powered transponders (receiver/transmitters) that transmit a digital signal back to earth. The signal is strong enough that subscribers can pick up the DBS program packages on dishes as small as 18 inches in diameter. Electronic circuitry converts the received signal to analog form and routes it to the subscriber's TV set. Firms that offer DBS service include DirecTV, EchoStar, Primestar, and United States Satellite Broadcasting.

TVRO packagers, on the other hand, provide the legal means for backyard dish owners to pick up and unscramble directly the satellite-delivered program services described in *PRT*, 7.4.2 and 7.4.3. The packager must get permission from and make arrangements with the individual program services. The satellites used by the program services contain medium- or low-powered transponders. The signals they send back to earth are weak enough that an individual who wishes to subscribe to a TVRO package must use a large dish, 6 meters in diameter. The dish owner must also buy a descrambler and then contact the TVRO packager. Once the dish owner has signed up, the packager activates the descrambler for the services in the package. The dish owner can pick up satellite signals other than those of the services in the package, but those that are scrambled remain so.

TVRO packagers retail through local cable systems or directly to the customer. Their ranks include some well-known company names, among them cable MSOs (e.g., Cox Satellite Programming, Jones Satellite Programming) and programmers (The Disney Channel, Playboy, Turner Home Satellite, Showtime Satellite Networks). However, TVRO dish owners do not have to deal with any of the packagers. Although most of the better known satellite-delivered services have scrambled their signals, some 150 programmers have not. Among those unscrambled as of this writing were the Canadian Broadcasting Corporation, C-SPAN, Fox network, Fox's fX cable network, The Learning Channel, NBC's eastern feed, Nostalgia Channel, PBS, scores of cable audio services, and dozens of "wild feeds" (occasional transmissions) of first-run and off-net syndicated TV programs such as *Oprah, Jeopardy!, Seinfeld,* several *Star Trek* series, and *Wheel of Fortune.* Some individual satellite-delivered services have been launched specifically to serve the TVRO market.

### 7.4.5 Programming in Unconventional Services

Most of us think of television programming in terms of "shows"—formal, fixed presentations by people for a relatively large audience who normally cannot affect the nature of the presentations. This has been the convention in TV since its beginnings. By extension, content that does not fit this mold is unconventional, and that is the subject of this section.

We discussed **electronic text** at some length in *PRT*, 5.5. Cable systems commonly use rotatext to program a channel with news, weather, announcements, advertising, and even cable channel program listings. Several firms provide satellite-delivered text services of various types—news, sports, and financial information; customized (to the local system) electronic program logs, some of which also promote programming on the system's premium services (**barker channel**); and even specialized services a cable system could feed to its subscribers' personal computers.

By contrast, none of the 1980s attempts at teletext and videotex service succeeded. Still, both seemed to have had the potential for success, given the right combination of equipment, cost, and, most important, content. On the other hand, CompuServe, AOL, Prodigy, and other commercial telephone-based interactive information services not only succeeded, they also upgraded their offerings. The growth during the 1990s of the Internet, and particularly its World Wide Web, was phenomenal. Broadcasters, cable MSOs, networks, program producers, syndicators, and others in the radio–TV business established their presence on these computer networks, designing and maintaining their own pages. Some outlets even used them to feed programming, both audio and video.

The key here is **interactivity.** Broadcasting, by its nature, is one way. Attempts to establish over-the-air return channels have resulted in technologically awkward solutions. However, programmers in broadcasting as well as cable and other media have, for years, offered a form of interactive programming involving the telephone. Viewers watch a program and then interact by making a phone call. According to the specific program, they can ask for more information or order advertised merchandise, call in opinions for polls, and participate in talk and game shows. Advertising-only program services (*PRT,* 7.4.2.3) consist almost entirely of such telephone-interactive programming.

Cable systems, on the other hand, have experimented with true same-medium interactivity. Warner-Amex, a partnership of Warner Cable and American Express, operated Qube for 7 years before shutting it down in 1984 (*PRT,* 4.2.9). Just a little over 10 years later, Warner launched yet another interactive system, the Full Service Network. Other cable systems have experimented with or operated other types of interactive services, particularly those involving PPV programming and advertising channels. By the late 1990s, however, cable operator interest in interactivity seemed to have shifted to Internet service. Cable systems could utilize their broadband connectivity capabilities coupled with extremely high speed modems to offer subscribers fast connections to the Internet, many times faster than those available by telephone line. MSOs planned to enter the Internet access business, promising near instantaneous picture build-up from World Wide Web sites.

## 7.5 MULTICHANNEL VIDEO SYSTEM PROGRAMMING

A multichannel video system (MVS) is one that delivers two or more channels of full-motion video. Probably the most familiar MVS we think of is our local **cable system.** Other media capable of providing multivideo service include **wireless cable systems, direct broadcast satellites,** and **telephone companies.**

### 7.5.1 Cable System Programming

Like broadcast stations, cable systems choose the programming they carry. However, the decisions can be far more complicated because of the sheer numbers of possible programming choices. Most cable systems offer four distinct types of services—the signals of local broadcast television stations, local productions, satellite-delivered basic networks, and satellite-delivered premium services. Many also program rotatext channels; a few, home security and other ancillary services. These can add up to a lot of channels. For example, a market may have seven or more full-service broadcast television signals, and the cable system carries them. Big cable systems—particularly newer systems in large markets—may carry a large number of local origination and access channels. According to when and how you count, there are some 65 nationally distributed basic and pay services.

Certain requirements and restrictions apply to cable system programming. The franchise agreement, for example, may call for access programming and put curbs on obscenity. Federal regulation includes the network nonduplication rule, the syndicated exclusivity rule (*PRT*, 3.5.2.1), and the political candidate equal-opportunities requirement (*PRT*, 14.1.1.4).

Reacting to the 1992 cable act (*PRT*, 4.3.3.2), most cable systems have reconfigured their service and now market it using a scheme called **tiering**. The law requires that cable operators offer a **basic service tier**. This tier must contain at least the signals of all broadcast TV stations the system carries and all franchise-required access channels. Cable operators generally put on their basic service tier only those channels required by law, plus, perhaps, C-SPAN, a barker channel, their own local origination channel, and maybe a home shopping channel.

Subscribers pay a certain monthly sum for the basic service tier. They may then, if they wish, subscribe to any other service or combination of services the system offers. Most subscribers, for example, also opt for the system's **extended basic tier**, the service on which the operator puts most of the satellite-delivered basic services it carries. Other tiers may consist of premium services, especially desirable (for the particular market) and separately available basic networks, and packages featuring varying combinations of services at discounted (as compared to buying them individually) prices.

Cable systems use various marketing ploys to convince subscribers that they need to pay for additional channels. They may, for example, name their basic service tier something like "Limited Basic," but call the combination of basic-service and extended-basic tiers "Standard Service." The implication, of course, is that the basic service tier by itself is somehow limited and incomplete. As mentioned earlier, the operator may also skim off some of the more desirable basic services and put them onto tiers other than extended basic. In a college town, for example, the cable system might charge extra for a new history-oriented program service for which subscribers have been asking, a regional sports channel that covers the college's intercollegiate athletic competitions, and a comedy network the students all like. Most subscribers have already opted for extended basic; those who want one of these three advertising-supported networks would be willing to pay an additional fee to receive them, which means more revenue for the operator.

### 7.5.2 Nonwired Multichannel System Programming Services

Ever since the mid-1970s, one of cable's major selling points has been the variety of programming it offers. For years, cable television was the only multichannel video provider. As the 20th century wound down, however, cable no longer had the monopoly on multichannel video service. Wireless cable systems, DBSs, and telephone companies all threatened to challenge cable television's dominance in the field of multichannel television. Further, they faced fewer regulatory requirements than did cable and so were freer to program their channels. They had no obligation, for example, to carry the signals of local TV stations. They needed no franchise to operate and so had no franchise-imposed obligations such as access channels.[7] Video delivery systems based on a telephone company's plant also had the advantage of operating in a switched network (*PRT,* 4.3.1); this arrangement would allow easy, flexible two-way interactivity.

Cable television, on the other hand, did seem to have the advantage in channel capacity. When MSOs rebuilt their systems, they often put in optical fiber trunks. This meant that no matter how many channels over-the-air systems such as DBS and wireless cable could squeeze into existence through the latest digital compression technology, modern cable systems could use the same technology to squeeze in even more channels—many more. As for the telephone companies' switched-network advantage, MSOs wanted to get into the business of providing local telephone service, too, which meant that they would install switches in their cable systems. The fight was just beginning. And how would the consumer benefit? Some looked forward to the greater choice of service, but most consumers hoped increased competition would end the local cable system's monopoly and thus result in lower subscriber rates.

### 7.6 CONSTRAINTS ON PROGRAMMING

Certain limitations affect programming. Some are set by law or federal regulation. Various government bodies and elements of the court system restrict coverage of their own activities. For years the National Association of Broadcasters (NAB) codes influenced programming. However, the NAB eliminated its code operations in 1983. The personal values of individual radio and TV outlet operators affect, and may act as a constraint on, programming. Factors outside law, regulation, and ethics also affect programming. Two of these are the reality of advertising support and the activities of some pressure groups.

### 7.6.1 Advertising Pressures

Advertisers today rarely attempt to dictate policy to programmers. Occasionally an advertiser will try to influence programming or news coverage, threatening to withdraw advertising unless the programmer takes some specific action. Several advertisers in 1995, for example, withdrew their commercials from various television series, particularly syndicated talk shows, which critics had labeled "trash TV." However, for the most part, the decline of single-sponsor programs caused a parallel decline of direct advertiser control of content.

On the other hand, **advertising support**—the fact that advertising revenue pays for programming—affects content directly. Consider the major TV broadcast networks, for example. The larger the audience, the more money the networks can charge for advertising time. Therefore, they attempt to maximize audiences by programming material that **appeals to the broadest spectrum of the public**, that **does not strain intellectual ability**, and that **avoids themes and depictions that might alienate** major segments of the audience. Such programming ordinarily precludes that which challenges or might offend prevailing established political beliefs, economic systems, social norms, standards, or customs.

There is a school of thought among network TV programmers that the "best" show, even when considering only "straight entertainment," is not the show that elicits strong reactions among its viewers. They reason that a show that generates a strong liking by some in the audience will also generate a strong disliking among others. Network prime-time programming aims to draw the largest audience possible, not the most satisfied audience. So a "lesser" show—one that most people like (but not too strongly) and no one hates—may actually serve programming aims better. Former NBC programmer Paul Klein called this the **least objectionable programming** (LOP) theory. According to Klein, viewers watch TV, not individual programs. Therefore most of the audience is composed of people who have tuned in to watch something, not to see a particular show. Among all channels available, they choose that which has programming least offensive to the viewers. Only when that channel presents something they do not like will they change to another.

Critics contend that the practice of maximizing audience limits not only range and treatment of subjects within programs, but also the amount of certain types of programs, that it results primarily in lip service to the statutory public interest requirement. Programming that draws relatively small audiences—usually documentaries, public affairs programs, educational or prosocial children's programming, drama and music with intellectual content above the comic-book level—is aired rarely or at odd hours, and when programming changes are made, these programs are first to be cut. Truly original content does not even make it to the program proposal stage. A new program is often sold based on how unoriginal it is and how much it resembles existing programs. One syndicator, for example, in hawking to stations a program designed for a teen audience, described it as *"Beverly Hills, 90210* meets MTV's *The Real World* meets *The Mod Squad.*"[8]

Defenders say that networks give the audience what it wants, that the consistently high ratings for entertainment programming prove it. The question then arises: How does the audience know it does not want more quality programming if it rarely has access to it? Still, ratings are relatively low even for the finest public television programs and for serious artistic and public-interest programs[9] from the commercial networks. Yes, the broadcast networks lost audience in the 1980s and

1990s, but most was lost to entertainment—on independent stations, cable, and home video—not culture and public affairs.

Another question that arises: On what stone tablet is it engraved that electronic mass media have to seek the largest possible audience at any given time? At the national level some media have successfully demonstrated that an outlet can achieve success by focusing on narrowly drawn interests and attracting advertisers who wish to reach individuals with those interests. Certainly print media have done that. Consumer periodicals range from *Yachting* to *Metropolitan Home* to *Wired* and beyond. Cable may have done the same thing if some of the minority-interest cable program services that have sprung into existence actually succeed. Media diversity is not so successful, however, at the local level. Radio stations, for example, seem to offer diverse formats but in reality duplicate each other from city to city. Listeners searching for programming other than the standard—news, talk, country music, "oldies" of various stripes, religion, sundry and esoteric shadings of contemporary music—usually do so in vain.

Finally, a third question arises: Why does electronic mass media programming have to be advertising supported? That question, commercial media apologists would say, is radical and subversive. Nonetheless, critics over the years have argued against advertising, and their criticisms are reviewed in other sections of this book (e.g., *PRT,* 9.5 and 17.1.3).

### 7.6.2 Pressure Groups

Occasionally, outside groups attempt to influence programming. One example is the blacklists of the 1950s, discussed in *PRT,* 2.3.3.1. Another is the continuing efforts of Action for Children's Television to improve programming for youngsters. Still another is the fight against excessive or gratuitous depictions of violence and sexual activities. As mentioned in *PRT,* 3.4.3.2, several organizations have opposed overuse of sex and violence on television programming. Often they attempt to organize consumer boycotts of products advertised on the programs to which they object.

In many cases the opinions and demands of these groups do not represent those of the majority of citizens and viewers. Because the total membership of such a group is miniscule when compared to the total consumer population of the United States, a boycott threat usually rings hollow. Nonetheless, these groups can be effective, and they can force advertisers to apply pressure for changes in program content. This is because advertisers want to avoid any hint of controversy concerning their products, as controversy could lead to a drop in sales. It is also because advertisers worry that such a group actually could, indeed, represent the feelings and opinions of a sizable percentage of the population, and companies that depend on mass consumer sales for revenues are peculiarly sensitive to the opinions, real or perceived, of "the buying public."

Among groups that made headlines for using the boycott were the following:

- Moral Majority, headed by TV preacher Jerry Falwell, opposed what its leader considered gratuitous sex on network prime-time programming in the early 1980s.[10]
- American Family Association, headed by Reverend Donald Wildmon, objected to nudity and language on ABC-TV's *NYPD Blue* (Fig. 7.14) in that series' first two seasons, 1993–1994 and 1994–1995.
- Empower America, headed by former U.S. Secretary of Education William Bennett, worked to get TV talk shows to stop featuring topics the group felt ran counter to the nation's moral grain.[11]

Some saw certain provisions included in the Telecommunications Act of 1996 as a triumph for the program-control crowd and a defeat for creative freedom. Among the provisions of that law that seemed to limit programming content were the following:

- Requirements for a TV program rating system and the so-called V-chip (*PRT,* 3.6.3 and 16.2.2).
- Requirements that cable operators scramble both audio and video on any channel dedicated primarily to sexually oriented material.
- Requirements that a cable operator scramble programming a subscriber finds unsuitable for children.
- Empowerment of cable operators to refuse leased-access programs they consider indecent or obscene.

The 1996 law also placed restrictions on Internet material, restrictions subsequently struck down in court.

## 7.7 ROLE OF AUDIENCE PROMOTION

Effective as a programming strategy may be, it does no good unless the potential audience knows about it. Networks and stations cannot rely on audience dial switching and newspaper schedule listings to inform the public of new programs and time changes in old ones. **Audience promotion** draws the audience. Programming, of course, must keep the audience. No amount of clever promotion can hold an audience for poor programming.

A broadcast medium's most effective promotional tool is its own airwaves. On-air promotion includes contests, promotional announcements (promos) for upcoming programs, call letters ("KBIV—Best In Viewing"), thematic graphic designs (to create an easily recognized symbol or **logo** of the station) worked into local production, clever station ID devices (special musical signature or animation), and even public service ("The KBIV Action Line Ombudsman").

Off-air promotion may include advertisements in other media (newspapers, magazines, billboards [Fig. 7.15], even other electronic mass media outlets); stunts

**FIG. 7.14 Pressure group target.** ABC-TV's *NYPD Blue,* whose episodes contained nudity and strong language, developed into one the network's most popular programs despite attempts by the American Family Association's Donald Wildmon to keep it off the air. (Photo courtesy of Steven Bochco Productions. Used by permission.)

and personal appearances by station personalities; display of the logo on station vehicles, equipment, and jackets; and giveaways, such as bumper stickers and

**FIG. 7.15 Promotional materials.** When WOGX-TV was an independent station, it used outdoor advertising along a busy street to promote its collection of movies and syndicated programs as "The Great Entertainer." Signs in other parts of the WOGX coverage area promoted individual programs on its schedule. WOGX-TV has since affiliated with Fox, and many of its extensive promotional activities, including outdoor advertising, now promote that affiliation. (Used by permission of WOGX-TV.)

program guides. In many promotional activities, the station seeks additional publicity through a printed **release.** The release contains information on the station, its personnel, or its programs and is intended for newspapers and trade publications to run as news stories.

Good programming and good promotion are year-round requirements. During ratings surveys, however, stations want to maximize audiences, so promotion efforts intensify. Some stations even run promotional contests. Broadcasters refer to such practices as **hypoing** the ratings and, over the years, have come to tolerate it as part of the promotion game. (Ratings distortion, however, is another matter; see *PRT,* 18.3.2 and 18.3.3.)

Promotion has grown in importance for broadcasters. TV stations, for example, faced increasing competition during the 1970s and 1980s on at least four fronts.

First, affiliates' local news efforts developed into fierce rivalries. Second, independent stations made audience gains in all dayparts. Third, many more TV stations signed on. Fourth, rival video media developed. Stations responded by increasing promotional activities. They started promotion departments or expanded existing ones, budgeted additional money for promotion, and, in general, moved promotion from a sideline to a major activity.

Cable and other media use some of the same promotional activities as broadcasting—promos, catchy logos, musical and animated IDs, advertising, and program guides. They use others that are quite different. Cable systems, for example, use door-to-door and telephone sales to sell services. They may offer special limited-run "packages" as inducements (e.g., no installation fee for new subscribers, or three pay services for the price of one for 1 month). At the national level, a subscription service may offer a free week of programming. It will urge affiliated cable systems to run the service's programs unscrambled so all subscribers can see it; then it will schedule "commercials" that urge subscribers to sign up for the service.

By 1990 broadcast and cable TV networks had tried promotional tie-ins with national retailers and marketers. For example, certain Sears 1989 customer mailings included a contest designed to familiarize viewers with new NBC shows for the upcoming prime-time season. CBS had a similar tie-in with K-Mart. ABC planned to give away a million promotional videocassettes through the Pizza Hut chain. Showtime Networks, Inc. worked out a tie-in with Beatrice Hunt Wesson, marketer of Orville Redenbacher Gourmet Popping Corn; HSN with Maxwell House Coffee. The idea of advertiser and promotional tie-ins strengthened and expanded during the 1990s.

## NOTES

1. In barter syndication, the station pays no cash for use of the program. See *PRT,* 7.3.2.1.

2. Steve Coe, "Network Share Average Drops," *Broadcasting & Cable* 2 October 1995: 28. Fox Broadcasting accounts for about 9% of the viewing audience. Steve McClellan, "Big Three Post Record Share Slide," *Broadcasting & Cable* 10 April 1995: 8.

3. Prime time is actually the 4 hours from 7 p.m. to 11 p.m. However during the years of the FCC's prime-time access rule (*PRT,* 7.3.2.2), that regulation had the effect of banning network programming during the 7 p.m. to 8 p.m. portion of prime time. This first hour of prime time therefore gained the label *access hour* or *access slot* and the status of another daypart, so that for the networks, prime time was 8 p.m. to 11 p.m.

4. Rich Brown, "Turner Takes Movies Directly to Cable," *Broadcasting & Cable* 6 November 1995: 99.

5. There may be, however, initial one-time charges, such as fees for hookup and set-top decoder box.

6. In addition to a monthly charge for the addressable set-top box, there may be, again, initial one-time fees on first acquiring the service.

7. With respect to video delivery systems operated by telephone companies, however, there were proposals to impose must-carry and retransmission consent provisions and to require

those systems to obtain franchises. There were also proposals to impose public interest requirements on some point-to-multipoint communication services, especially DBS.

8. Cynthia Littleton, "Syndicators Search for Elusive Teens," *Broadcasting & Cable* 15 January 1996: 122.

9. The exception was the news magazine program. CBS's *60 Minutes* started the trend. *60 Minutes* began to earn ratings in the top 10 programs in 1976 and, by the 1980s, often placed first. ABC and NBC successfully introduced their own news magazines, *20/20* and *Dateline NBC,* respectively. Eventually, however, even these shows degenerated to the point that much of their content was tabloid journalism at best.

10. The networks had discovered sex in 1977 and started the "T'n'A" programming fad as exemplified by series such as *Charlie's Angels.* This fad was characterized by camera shots of women's bottoms and what the business called "jiggle"—bouncing female breasts. Themes and dialogue were often suffused with sexism, leering innuendo, and suggestive language, usually unrealistic and unmotivated. (It was pretty tame stuff, however, compared with the tastelessness of later programs, such as *Married . . . With Children.*)

Falwell's Moral Majority had taken an active role in the 1980 election of Ronald Reagan to the U.S. presidency before turning its attention to television. Detractors said that Moral Majority's very name epitomized its tactics, the implication being that those who did not agree with its stand were not moral and, by extension, not Christian. Thus, many who might also have objected to the T'n'A fad did not join Falwell's campaign. A rival group organized to counter the Moral Majority's stand on television programming. This group, People for the American Way, included a number of mainstream religious leaders and was organized by Norman Lear, producer of television series including *All in the Family.* They used TV spots and other publicity vehicles to fight the Moral Majority philosophy.

11. Among the topics Bennett cited as examples: the mother who ran off with her daughter's fiancé on *Jenny Jones,* "I'm Marrying a 14-year-old Boy" on *Sally Jessy Raphael,* and "Women Who Marry Their Rapist" on *Geraldo.* Christopher Stern, "Backlash Against TV Talk Shows," *Broadcasting & Cable* 30 October 1995: 18. Some in the business called this "nuts 'n' sluts" TV. Cynthia Littleton, "Talk TV Toughs It Out," *Broadcasting & Cable* 15 January 1996: 59.

## FURTHER READING

Abelman, Robert, and Stewart M. Hoover. *Religious Television: Controversies and Conclusions.* Norwood, NJ: Ablex, 1990.

Anderson, Robin, *Consumer Culture and TV Programming.* Boulder, CO: Westview, 1996.

Butler, Jeremy A. *Television: Critical Methods and Applications.* Belmont, CA: Wadsworth, 1997.

Cantor, Muriel G. *Prime-Time Television: Content and Control.* 2nd ed. Newbury Park, CA: Sage, 1992.

Carroll, Raymond L., and Donald M. Davis. *Electronic Media Programming: Strategies and Decision Making.* New York: McGraw-Hill, 1993.

Clift, Charles E., Joseph C. Ritchie, and Archie M. Greer, Eds. *Broadcast and Cable Programming: The Current Perspective.* Dubuque, IA: Kendall-Hunt, 1993.

Eastman, Susan Tyler, and Klein, Robert, Eds. *Promotion & Marketing for Broadcasting & Cable.* 2nd ed. Prospect Heights. IL: Waveland, 1992.

Eastman, Susan Tyler, and Douglas A. Ferguson, Eds. *Broadcast/Cable Programming: Strategies and Practices.* 5th ed. Belmont, CA: Wadsworth, 1997.

Halper, Donna L. *Full Service Radio: Programming for the Community.* Boston: Focal, 1991.

Howard, Herbert H., Michael S. Kievman, and Barbara A. Moore. *Radio, TV and Cable Programming.* Ames: Iowa State University Press, 1994.

Keith, Michael C. *Radio Programming: Consultancy and Formatics.* Boston: Focal, 1987.

MacFarland, David T. *Contemporary Radio Programming Strategies.* Hillsdale, NJ: Lawrence Erlbaum Associates, 1990.

Matelski, Marilyn J. *Broadcast Programming and Promotions Worktext.* Boston: Focal, 1989.

Matelski, Marilyn J. *Daytime Television Programming.* Boston: Focal, 1991.

Minow, Newton, and Craig L. LaMay. *Abandoned in the Wasteland: Children, Television, and the First Amendment.* New York: Hill, 1996.

Montgomery, Kathryn C. *Target, Prime Time: Advocacy Groups and the Struggle Over Entertainment Television.* New York: Oxford University Press, 1989.

Norberg, Eric G. *Radio Programming: Tactics and Strategy.* Boston: Focal, 1996.

Orlik, Peter B. *Electronic Media Criticism: Applied Perspectives.* Boston: Focal, 1994.

Owen, Bruce, and Steven S. Wildman. *Video Economics.* Cambridge, MA: Harvard University Press, 1992.

Peck, Janice. *The Gods of Televangelism.* Cresskill, NJ: Hampton, 1993.

Selnow, Gary W., and Richard R. Gilbert. *Society's Impact on Television: How the Viewing Public Shapes Television Programming.* Westport, CT: Praeger, 1993.

Vane, Edwin T., and Lynne S. Gross. *Programming for TV, Radio, and Cable.* Boston: Focal, 1993.

Warren, Steve. *Radio: The Book: A Fun Practical Programming Manual and Idea Book for Program Directors and Operations Managers.* Long Island: M.O.R., 1992.

# 8

# ELECTRONIC MASS MEDIA NEWS

If someone were to ask "Did you see the news yesterday?" you would probably assume the question refers to television news and you would probably be right. The wording of the question and your reaction illustrate an ever-increasing fact of life—many people rely on television news reporting so much that they think of it as the news. As far back as 1963, biennial national polls began to show that people mentioned television more than any other medium as one of their main sources of news (Fig. 8.1).

Polls still show people choosing television over newspapers, magazines, and radio as the most important and believable (Fig. 8.2) news medium, and television viewing continues to increase.[1]

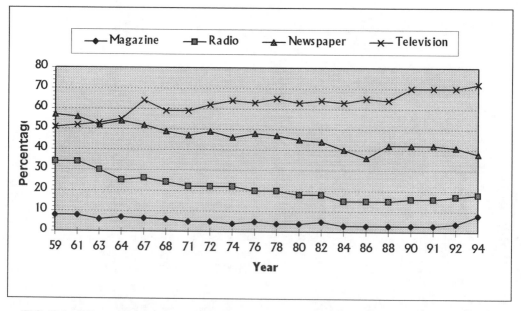

FIG. 8.1. **Where most people get news.** About every 2 years, from 1959 through 1994, the Roper Organization (now Roper Starch) conducted nationwide surveys of people 18 and older to determine where they get their news. Television has led all other media as a source of most news—a full 30 percentage points higher than the next most frequently mentioned source, newspapers. (Survey respondents could name more than one medium.) (*Source*: Roper Starch Worldwide, Inc. and National Association of Broadcasters. Used by permission.)

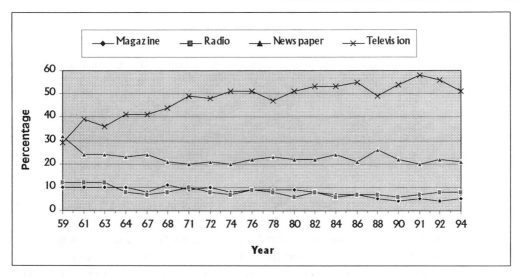

**FIG. 8.2. What news medium people believe most.** In the biennial surveys, television has led as the most believable mass medium since 1961. (*Source*: Roper Starch Worldwide Inc. and National Association of Broadcasters.)

There is certainly more television news available to viewers than ever before. As we approach the year 2000, local television stations are investing more and more resources in news, and some stations offer as many as 7 hours of local news programming in a single day. Stations also team with local cable systems to provide newscasts or news inserts on cable channels. The network news organizations are also faring well. The news divisions of ABC, CBS, and NBC actually show profits despite having news budgets approaching $400 million each. Of course, some broadcast networks, CNN, and other cable services offer news programming around the clock.

Radio has remained an important source of news. In fact, news-talk programming was among the fastest growing formats during the mid-1990s. Many listen to music, talk, and news on the radio as they get ready for work or school in the morning, travel in automobiles, and work in their homes or businesses. Research has shown that even when listening to stations featuring music programming, people want to hear news on the radio.[2]

Audiences consider radio important for immediate, ongoing coverage of local news. They turn to radio for information about road conditions and power outages during emergencies such as earthquakes, ice and snowstorms, tornadoes, and hurricanes. However, cable television news services—such as CNN, with its ability and reputation for providing live coverage of breaking stories, and The Weather Channel—have reduced radio's dominance of this kind of news coverage.

In this chapter, our subject is electronic news. We first explore the meaning of "news." Next, we examine radio newscasts, television and cable newscasts, and television and cable news services. Finally, we look at other forms of news programming—documentaries, on-the-spot coverage, and interviews.

## 8.1 NATURE OF NEWS

Broadly defined, we can say that news is the **reporting of recent, significant events.** But more specifically, we are interested primarily in **processed news**—news that has been gathered to a central point, put into a form suitable for public distribution and presentation, and disseminated to a mass audience.

### 8.1.1 What Are the Origins of News?

The modern concept of news can be traced back to a single technological development: the **printing press.** New developments—such as computers, remote editors, cellular phones, satellite communications, and tapeless recording—continue to have a profound impact on the collection and dissemination of news. However, before we can examine radio and television news operations of today it is important to understand the manner in which printed news developed.

***8.1.1.1 Newspapers Evolve.***   According to tradition, Johann Gutenberg of Mainz, Germany, introduced movable metal type in Europe about 1450. Just over 50 years later, newspapers appeared in Germany and Holland aimed at merchants and other persons in business. These first newspapers contained mainly news of shipping and commerce. England's first regularly published newspaper began in 1621; its first daily newspaper, in 1702.

Juan Pablos brought printing to the New World in 1539 when he set up a press in Mexico City. Stephan Day came to Massachusetts Bay in 1638 and helped to start a printing establishment. In 1690, Benjamin Harris published *Publick Occurrences,* considered to be the first North American news sheet. Authorities closed it down after only one issue.

The *Boston News-Letter,* America's first continuously published newspaper, began in 1704, and by 1715 it had some 300 subscribers. By 1750, the American colonies had 12 weekly newspapers; 25 years later the number had multiplied fourfold. The first daily appeared in 1783.

Most news published by the first newspapers was sent to their offices by interested parties or copied from other newspapers. It was not until the 19th century that newspapers started hiring reporters to gather news.

***8.1.1.2 Birth of Mass Communication.***   Before the 1830s, newspapers were written primarily for the privileged classes. Prices were high and circulations were low. However, as wage earners—including many foreign immigrants—moved to the cities, received the right to vote, and learned to read in free, tax-supported schools, publishers saw opportunities for large-circulation newspapers. By 1833 the new steam presses could produce thousands of copies per hour. Publishers filled papers with light, entertaining, and largely trivial content that most people found easy to read. They published sensationalized stories that urban audiences found interesting. They even lowered the price of the newspaper to 1 cent per copy, which earned them the name **penny press.** Circulations grew so large that revenue from advertising financed the publications. **Benjamin H. Day** started the first penny newspaper, the *New York Sun,* in 1833, and by 1836, the *Sun* had a circulation of over 30,000. Newspapers had become a mass medium, dependent on mass circulation and large advertising revenues.

*8.1.1.3 News Wire Services.*   Samuel Morse's invention of the telegraph in 1844 dramatically increased the speed with which news could be disseminated. This paved the way for another significant milestone in the evolution of the news business— the development of the news wire services (also called press associations and news agencies). By 1849 the first news wire service was organized. Six New York newspapers agreed to share costs to send boats into New York harbor to gather news. Later the service telegraphed national news from Washington, DC and international news from Boston. The wire service would eventually be called the Associated Press (AP) of New York. Despite the existence of a common news wire service, individual editors still wanted their newspapers to reflect particular party, cause, or political orientations, and a variety of editorial policies. So, AP decided to adopt an objective, no slant policy—to report only facts. Each AP-affiliated newspaper would then be free to rewrite wire service stories to fit its editorial slant. Some did, but many printed stories as they were written by AP. Eventually, this became the practice at most newspapers. Thus, objective reporting was born.

A competing wire service, the United Press, was organized in 1882, but went bankrupt in 1897. In 1907, E. W. Scripps founded the United Press Association (UP), and in 1909, William Randolph Hearst formed the International News Service (INS). In 1958, UP and INS merged to form what became the major domestic competition for AP, **United Press International** (UPI). By the 1980s UPI experienced financial difficulties and filed for bankruptcy in 1991. However, in 1992 UPI news services were maintained when the London-based Middle East Broadcasting Centre purchased the services for $3.95 million.

The Canadian counterpart to AP is **Canadian Press** of Toronto. Among the most significant overseas services today are **Reuters,** formed in London in 1851, and **Agence France Presse** (AFP) formed in 1944 as a successor to the French news service **Havas,** which was formed in 1835. **Tass** was founded in 1925 as the official news service of the Soviet Union. When the Soviet Union broke up **ITAR-Tass** became the major Russian service. **Kyodo News Agency** is the largest news wire service in Japan.

As much as 90% of the daily international news is provided by only five services—AP, UPI, Reuters, AGF, and Tass. This dominance can lead to a western bias in the news. For that reason **Third World news agencies** such as **Pacific News Service** (1970) have been formed to guarantee better coverage of news from developing countries.

Although still accepted and very widely used, the term *wire* is really misleading when referring to most of today's news services. **Satellite transmission** has replaced telegraph and telephone lines as the means by which news is distributed.

***8.1.1.4 Metamorphosis to Big Business.***    Excessive competition between two newspapers led to a period beginning in the 1880s we now refer to as **yellow journalism**. (The color *yellow* came from a cartoon published at the time in which the clothes of the central figure, the Yellow Kid, were printed in yellow.) Joseph Pulitzer's *New York World* and Hearst's *New York Morning Journal*— with circulation as high as 700,000 readers each—were characterized by overzealous competitive practices including **high levels of sensationalism, sloppy reporting, and outlandish stories.**[3] It is true that both newspapers, and especially the *World*, offered some quality journalism. The Pulitzer Prize for excellence in journalism is given in honor of the contributions and innovations of Joseph Pulitzer. Newspapers of this time are known for development of comics, editorial crusades against crime and corruption, and investigative reporting.

By 1910, the age of yellow journalism had ended, but sensational journalism returned in the 1920s. During this era of **jazz journalism, tabloid newspapers** appeared. New York provided three leading examples, the *Daily News,* the *Daily Graphic,* and the *Daily Mirror.* All played up sexual and sensational aspects of news, featured lots of photographs, and were printed on paper sheets smaller in size than other newspapers, which made them easy to read on crowded subways, trains, and buses. The term *tabloid* is now applied even to electronic journalism that emphasizes sensationalism as a means to attract audiences.

In the 1900s, Scripps put together the first chain of commonly owned newspapers. Hearst, Gannett, and others followed, buying newspapers in different cities and managing them from one central office. Gradually, chain and absentee ownership became the norm, and interests of owners shifted away from editorial influence to profits.

***8.1.1.5 Technological Innovations in News Media.***    By 1996, computer technology had allowed newspapers to offer a new type of service. **Electronic newspapers** now provide continuous updates of news and sports events for online subscribers. Anyone with a computer, a modem, and the necessary software can simply dial up the service from home and catch up on the day's events, weather information, updated sports scores, and classified ads. Many newspapers offer computerized news services for subscribers to online services. Newspapers also offer computerized **dial-up information services** that can be accessed without a computer. All you need is a touch-tone phone to dial up the latest news, sports, lottery numbers, and even developments on soap operas.

### 8.1.2 What Are News Outlets Like?

As we have seen, the pattern for mainstream, public news media was set in the late 19th century. These media evolved into what LeRoy and Sterling[4] called **mass news**—distributed by organized, large, imposing systems; attended by huge audiences; relied on by the public for reports of recent happenings.

***8.1.2.1 Ownership and Motivation in News.***     The main news outlets—organizations that package and present news to the public—are generally big businesses. Typically, they are **owned by publicly held corporations.** Corporate officers answer to stockholders and are **interested chiefly in profits,** not editorial policies. So, the manager of a particular newspaper is usually free to adopt any editorial stance as long as the paper earns a profit. With this freedom, editorial policies vary among commonly owned outlets, from conservative to liberal. Even liberal outlets, however, identify primarily with a middle-class, within-the-system approach to political and social issues.

Radio and television outlets seldom, if ever, adopt editorial stances. This means that television and radio news directors usually do not have the authority to slant newscasts to any particular political position, party, or candidate. In fact, to do so may place a broadcast station in violation of the equal opportunity law (*PRT,* 15.3.2) or political editorialization rules (*PRT,* 14.1.1.5). Radio and television outlets do, however, adopt various approaches to covering news. A television station may, for example, choose to feature sensationalized news stories or emphasize hard or soft news (*PRT,* 8.1.3.1).

***8.1.2.2 News Content.***     Although editorial policies of newspapers vary, the vast majority of news outlets report most news as objectively as they know how. (More subtle aspects of news reports, such as story placement, phrasing, and emphasis may contribute to the public's perception of bias.) Some observers attribute objective reporting to feelings of responsibility on the part of news outlet managers. Historically, **objectivity** also springs from at least two other sources—**reliance on wire services** and **need for large circulation.**

Radio and television stations, cable services, and newspapers are linked together by the news services. CNN, for example, offers stories and news packages to stations and other news outlets all over the world. AP and UPI, along with services provided by major newspapers including the *New York Times, Los Angeles Times,* and *Washington Post* provide a large percentage of the national and international news for hundreds of news outlets. Because these services are so pervasive, news **tends to be identical,** often verbatim, from outlet to outlet, city to city.

Keep in mind that news outlets are supported primarily by advertising revenues. To keep advertising rates up, outlets need the largest possible circulation or audience, including those persons who might disagree with any editorial stance taken. Therefore, mainstream news outlets—and here we do not mean tabloid news programs or supermarket tabloid-type publications—attempt to report the news straight and objectively and reserve opinion for clearly labeled editorials.

As part of the effort to increase and hold circulation and audience, news outlets produce much that is not, strictly speaking, news. Look carefully at the national cable news services and your local evening newscast; much of the time is taken up by commercials, sports, features, weather, and other nonnews content. Most daily newspaper space is devoted to advertising, syndicated features and columns, sports, family, and other specialized information.

### 8.1.3 What Is News?

This brings us to the problem of defining news. What exactly is this thing we have been calling *news?* Earlier we said that news is the reporting of recent happenings that have been gathered and prepared for dissemination to an audience. We have added to that definition by describing the development and present structure of news outlets and their motivations for turning out the type of product they do.

*8.1.3.1 News Value.* News is further defined by the way in which news outlet managers decide on a news story's **news value**—its ability to attract a large audience. A major factor in determining news value is whether a story is hard or soft. **Hard news** is the reporting of breaking news. Hard news stories are of interest because of their **timeliness** and **general significance** (e.g., election returns, passage of legislation, or natural disasters,) or their **violence** (e.g., murder and other crimes, or fatal accidents). Hard news stories decline rapidly in news value with passage of time.

**Soft news**, on the other hand, is reporting on news related to health, science, and other matters of human or community interest (e.g., proper care for pets, new methods of recycling, dangers of rollerblading) that lose news value relatively slowly. Sometimes it is difficult to distinguish between hard and soft news. Some stories, such as developments in recycling, could be categorized as both. Sometimes it is even difficult to distinguish between hard news, soft news, and sports. When baseball great Mickey Mantle received a liver transplant before his death in 1995, the story was carried by some stations as the hard news lead story and by others during sportscasts. Still others used the story to carry soft news features on advances in liver transplantation or the damage caused to the liver by excessive drinking of alcohol.

Although there are exceptions, lead stories on newscasts and front pages of newspapers tend to involve hard news. Soft news, including sports and other specialized news, is usually of secondary importance to hard news.

*8.1.3.2 Controls Over News.* There are other characteristics of news, characteristics that serve as means of control over, and thus limitations on, content. One classification system lists seven types of control[5]—**monopoly, source, government, internal, advertiser, self,** and **public.** The giant ownership conglomerates that control news media tend to reduce diversity of, and impose sameness on, content. Sources—people and institutions, private and government—control news about themselves through secrecy, news management, and manipulation and shaping of news before it reaches the media. Government influences news media through the court system, regulatory agencies, and policies. Internal control is exercised by media personnel. Publishers, managers, editors, producers, reporters, and camera crews all act as informational **gatekeepers,** allowing some news to flow through media pipelines (to mix metaphors) to the audience, stopping other news. Advertisers exercise control sometimes directly, but usually indirectly through media acceptance of establishment viewpoints and conceptions of reality.

Self-control through professional codes, standards of good practice, and adaptations to input from consultants and research firms also affect the flow of stories, especially in local television news. Input from the public provides some influence and some citizens' groups have profoundly affected broadcasting (*PRT,* 3.4.3).

### 8.1.4 What Is Radio–Television News?

So far we have discussed news in general terms. Now we examine radio and television news specifically. Broadcast stations transmit news, for the most part, at regularly scheduled times. A station occasionally interrupts other programming to present news **bulletins,** when a news report is so important it cannot wait for the regular newscast. On November 22, 1963, radio and television programming was interrupted all over the world to announce that President Kennedy had been shot. On rare occasions stations will even preempt programming to offer extensive coverage of a news story. Coverage of the Kennedy assassination lasted several days. More recently, stations and cable networks offered continuous coverage of the police "chase" of O. J. Simpson in his white Bronco and the Oklahoma City bombing. In fact, all of the top 15 rated cable shows for the week of April 17, 1995 were various segments of CNN's coverage of that bombing.

News radio stations and cable news services use news as their primary programming content; they run news and news-related material throughout the day. Major stories of interest receive continuous coverage and provide a boost to interests and ratings. Coverage of the O. J. Simpson murder trial doubled the ratings of many news-talk stations including large-market stations such as WMAQ in Chicago.

Not to be outdone by their newspaper counterparts, television news operations now offer **online news services.** KGTV, the ABC affiliate in San Diego, for example, has teamed up with ABC and *Business Week* magazine to offer the online news service *Newslink* on the Internet and World Wide Web. You can check it out at http://www.kgtv.com. The service provides considerably more detail than KGTV's newscasts and also offers news from ABC and *Business Week.*

### *8.1.4.1 Characteristics of Radio–Television News.*    Despite increased mobility of television news reporting and the versatility of cable news coverage, other media have yet to match radio for its ability to do live on-the-spot reporting. A radio reporter needs little equipment and can easily use a cellular telephone to report live coverage from the scene of a breaking news event. Television reporters are increasingly mobile, but camera operation usually requires at least one other person at the scene, plus some coordination and frequently online or postproduction editing either in a remote truck or at the studio. For example, video shot immediately after the bomb exploded near the federal building in Oklahoma City had to be edited because some images were too graphic for broadcast.

As shown by CNN's coverage of the outbreak of the Gulf War and the attack on the city of Baghdad, cable news services have been notably successful in presenting extended, live, on-the-spot coverage of protracted news events. Cable news services and radio stations, therefore, are more likely than television stations to report immediately and to carry ongoing, live reports from the scene of a news event. Broadcast television is limited—for the most part by choice—by a relatively rigid programming and commercial schedule that inhibits extending newscasts or breaking into sponsored programs with bulletins. Nevertheless, broadcast television will have a report on a late-breaking news item—often with videotape from the scene—long before the traditional newspaper is published. However, the newspaper account often includes detail and background information for which broadcast and cable have no time. The newspaper also contains a good many stories that the other media do not even report.

### 8.1.4.2 Local Radio–Television News Outlets.

Radio stations that carry news (other than those with all-news formats) may schedule it once an hour, at the same time each hour, or may vary this pattern. At radio stations with respectable news operations, major news items are rewritten and reported on each newscast, with updates and a few changes in details. Most newscasts are only 3½ minutes, which means, after commercials, really just over 2 minutes of actual news). One-minute newscasts are not uncommon, and many stations broadcast no news. Some stations do present extended or more frequent newscasts during morning and afternoon drive times.

All-news radio stations broadcast continuous news interspersed with features and commercials. News is repeated in cycles, 20 minutes or longer in length, so that a listener may tune in at any time and hear the full complement of news stories within a short period.

Television stations broadcast news less frequently but for longer periods than most radio stations. As a rule, network affiliates carry more local news than independents. There is usually an early morning and a noon newscast. Stations broadcast their **showcase** news program—longest, most elaborate, with the greatest number of recent or updated stories and videotape—in the early evening. Some stations air 90 minutes or more of early evening news. Affiliates of ABC, CBS, and NBC broadcast local news programs either before or after, or before and after, the network news. A final newscast airs at 10 p.m. or 11 p.m., usually 30 or 35 minutes in length. Some television stations also present short news summaries at sign-off and sign-on. During station breaks, many stations air **news capsules or headlines** that are primarily intended as promos for upcoming newscasts. Stations are also providing local news inserts on cable news channels such as CNN, CNN Headline News, and The Weather Channel. Cable operators also carry news segments, often produced by local television stations in the market.

### 8.1.4.3 Radio–Television Network News.

There are over 80 national and regional radio networks offering news, sports, and weather. Radio networks usually schedule news at least once an hour, increasing news feeds during morning and afternoon drive time. Larger radio networks, such as **ABC, CBS, CNN,** the

**Mutual Broadcasting System,** and **NBC Radio Network** may feed newscasts two or more times an hour along with features, commentary, and sports. **Associated Press** and **UPI** operate radio news networks in addition to their wire services.

Some networks offer expanded newscasts. CBS feeds its 15-minute *World News Roundup* during morning drive, and **NPR's** *Morning Edition* and *All Things Considered* air during morning and evening drive times, respectively. Business news is available through **CNBC Business Radio,** the **Wall Street Journal Radio Network,** and the **Dow Jones Radio Network.**

The three commercial broadcast television networks feed extended presentations in the early morning, the oldest being NBC's long-running *Today.* The television networks all air weekday showcase newscasts in the early evening. They have shorter feeds at other times, do 1-minute news summaries during prime time, and provide individual reports that affiliated stations can record and use on their own newscasts.

During the period between 1985 and 1987, the networks went on a staff-cutting binge; among those eliminated were hundreds of news employees, including respected and well-known veterans. The 1990s have seen somewhat of a turn-around, and by 1994 all three network news organizations were reporting a net profit.

The programming of the cable news services vary. CNN, for example, carries a number of extended newscasts interspersed with other informational programs. When important news breaks, CNN does not hesitate to suspend regular programming and provide extended live coverage. However, CNN Headline News prefers not to go live and instead offers tightly packaged summaries of major stories every 30 minutes. C-SPAN I and C-SPAN II (*PRT,* 7.4.2.4) provide unique, in-depth reporting on politics and public affairs, both foreign and domestic. CNBC specializes in business and financial news during the daytime, and The Weather Channel offers weather features as well as around-the-clock updates on national, international, regional, and local weather forecasts and conditions.

PBS's *The NewsHour with Jim Lehrer* differs from those of the other broadcast networks in that it has a full hour with no commercial breaks. The *News Hour* covers major news in summary fashion and also selects a few stories for treatment in depth.

***8.1.4.4 Other Radio–Television News Sources.*** During the 1980s, satellite relay capability spawned additional sources of television news. The birth of satellite news gathering (SNG), for example, gave rise to **SNG cooperatives.** A co-op consists of SNG-equipped television stations and a coordinating unit. The coordinator surveys the co-op's stations daily to assess what they will cover, identifies stories of general interest, and puts them on the satellite for other cooperating stations to use. It also helps arrange individual news exchanges—a co-op station in one city covers a story that is relayed to the requesting co-op station in another city. Co-ops have formed at national, regional, and state levels. Organizers included Conus Communications, Group W's Newsfeed, the three major broadcast networks, and local stations themselves. The Florida News Network is a co-op formed by stations in the largest television markets of that state.

Communications satellites spurred growth of firms that **syndicate video news, provide custom video coverage services,** and **create video public relations releases.** News syndicators put together news and information packages for distribution to stations and other clients. Their product ranges from soft news to hard, from individual stories to complete programs. A custom-service firm provides news coverage support in its market for out-of-town news outlets. A Jacksonville TV station, for example, wants to do a story in Washington, DC, and contracts for support with a Washington firm. The support varies with the client's need—a production crew, editing facilities, raw footage (unedited video), even a complete news package (a finished story). Some companies offer this same support for public relations purposes. Businesses and special-interest groups contract with these firms to create and disseminate video news releases and other promotional material to television news outlets and other destinations. By 1996, among companies that have provided one or more of these services were AP Express, Broadcast News Service, Independent News Network, Los Angeles News Service, Medialink, Mobile Video Services, Newslink, Potomac Communications, Professional Video Services, Sun World Satellite, Turner Broadcasting, TV Direct, and Washington Independent News.

### 8.1.5 Limitations and Problems of Radio–Television News

**Time** is the major limiting factor of television news. Reporters are typically limited to a maximum of about 2 minutes to cover stories. Stories read by newscasters are usually considerably shorter. But how many stories can really be reported in a 2-minute or less news summary? How many details can be given? In both cases, not many. A newscast may be on the air for 30 minutes, but the scripts and news packages actually account for a total of only 22 to 23 minutes. Commercials, credits, and a station break take up the rest of the time. A half-hour network news script, if set in type, would not even fill the front page of the *New York Times*.

The all-news radio stations and cable news services operate continuously and would seem to have all the time they need. On occasion, they do operate that way, particularly CNN and C-SPAN I and C-SPAN II. However, most of the time, all-news programmers package news in short, repeating cycles. Thus, television news, all-news radio, and cable news service editors must be extremely selective in the detail they include in each story.

Television's **visual** element presents a whole set of problems. First, which news story gets videotape or SNG coverage? Often it is an **event that is predictable,** where the assignment editor can schedule and set up the video equipment and personnel in advance. This means heavy coverage of public figures arriving and departing; of meetings; of ribbon cuttings, and grand openings. Good news operations try to air meaningful video and avoid the tendency to air **"talking** head" stories—those with tight shots of a news source being interviewed—just because the video is available. Still, **stories that have visual coverage**—videotape and SNG—are more likely to get on the air. Coverage of the opening of a new building with tape of the mayor cutting the ribbon may get as much newscast time as the less visual but more important story of the city auditor's report of a missing $3.5 million in city revenues. People do turn to television news to see things, and if the station does not use a lot of pictures—regardless of content—audience members may tune to a station that does.

Another problem involves those who **manipulate news coverage**—protesters who await the arrival of television cameras before beginning action; political thugs who plant bombs, hijack airplanes, take over embassies, and kidnap people in such manner as to make the 6 p.m. newscasts in the United States; major political parties that orchestrate national conventions to take advantage of television coverage; and public figures who plan announcements and news conferences for major visual impact.

Subtle pressures on news crews to **emphasize certain aspects** in covering stories—action, blood, and, above all, conflict—create another problem. These are visual news elements that get audiences. For example, during the "first television war" in Southeast Asia, network news film from Vietnam emphasized conflict and blood because reporters knew that was what the network wanted. The sight of wounded and dead U.S. military personnel brought war home to the public as never before, helping turn public opinion against the U.S. involvement. Yet subtle and equally important issues such as political aspects of the war went undercovered or unreported simply because they did not lend themselves to visual presentation.

**Questions of ethics** confront television reporters and technicians. Certainly, faking or fabricating a scene and coaching responses from subjects for the camera is unethical, and most television news organizations have established policies to prevent such practices. However, some situations are not easy to define as ethical or unethical. Suppose you were covering a demonstration against abortion rights, taping a group of persons praying in unison. You could hear the prayer clearly, but your microphone could not pick it up. What would you do? Ask the group to pray louder? Further, the very introduction of a television camera into a situation changes the nature of that situation. People behave differently when cameras are present. How would you correct for this? Would you tape them (in spite of their changed behavior) and use the tape anyway? Would that be ethical? Would you hide the camera?

A problem with video coverage derives from **commonly held conceptions of how video should be shot and edited.** Zoom lenses, camera angles, and skillful editing can alter reality. Warren Breed[6] once noted that novice newspaper reporters adopt news practices not from perceptions of audience needs but from what older newsroom hands do and say. It is the same in television news, including production of spot news reports and documentaries. News and documentary producers put together products that look good. In the process, they may use production and editing techniques that do not necessarily depict exactly the way the event happened. If they do, it is not to purposefully distort or alter reality but because of the way they had learned to produce news stories and documentaries. The results of such distortions can often come as a shock to those who appear in the news. The story appears on television, and individuals may see themselves seeming to say or emphasize things they had not intended, commenting on things they had never seen, and arguing with people they had never met.

Television's **ability to alter reality** had been noted as early as 1952.[7] However, it was not until 1967 that this ability assumed the proportions of a public issue. During the 1960s, American news media reported on the civil rights movement, riots, assassinations, and the war in Vietnam. Angered and frustrated by such reports, certain politicians and segments of the public began to look askance at the media carrying these reports, particularly television. In 1968, television provided pictorial coverage of demonstrations and events surrounding the Democratic National Convention in Chicago. Charges were leveled that coverage was biased and unfair and that news reports had been staged and distorted through editing. Subsequently, similar charges were made against a number of television documentary projects. As a result, most television news and documentary personnel have become sensitized to production techniques that they had previously taken for granted; the networks and many stations have instituted policies to eliminate deceptive techniques. Still the problem persists. In the 1990s, NBC admitted to rigging a truck's fuel tank to explode for the cameras.

A final problem involves the charge that television news is **more show business than news.** In the past, critics have made the case that television management, striving for high news ratings, has emphasized entertainment values at least as much as news values in news operations. Television business and news leaders have responded that theirs is a legitimate journalistic endeavor, albeit less comprehensive and limited in depth as compared to, say, a large-city daily newspaper.

In the early 1970s, competition for local news audiences became so keen that stations began hiring **news consultants** to boost ratings. Many in TV news believe consultants' suggestions emphasize cosmetic changes—use of youthful and attractive anchor reporters with little or no actual reporting experience; light and humorous banter ("happy talk") among anchor personnel; emphasis on stories with pictorial coverage, even when content might be inconsequential; and weather reporters with a weather quiz as well as a forecast. Station news personnel sometimes resent consultants, arguing that their impact has degraded the journalistic integrity of news.

In the mid-1990s, WCCO-TV in Minneapolis and other stations around the country began airing **family-sensitive newscasts.** These newscasts may cover breaking news but they **avoid details of violent crimes and sexually oriented stories** and do not show body bags or bloody victims. On the other end of the spectrum are stations that feature sensational crimes and sexually oriented content. WSVN in Miami, a Fox affiliate, has moved up significantly in news ratings since adopting a fast-paced style of newscast that emphasizes more sensational reporting techniques.

## 8.2 RADIO NEWS

Radio station news efforts vary greatly. At one extreme is the profitable service-oriented station with five or more full-time news and public affairs staffers and a number of daily newscasts. At the other extreme is the station that runs no news at all, in the belief that news does nothing to enhance profits and that radio deregulation in the 1980s lifted the requirement of even a minimal news operation. Just above this last example is the station whose sole news effort is its rock network's 1-minute newscast each hour—sometimes only during morning drive. In **rip 'n' read** operations, the disc jockey puts on a CD recording of a top hit, runs to the wire service machine, prints off the latest 5-minute news summary, runs back to the control room before the song ends, and then—without even looking over the copy—opens the microphone and reads the latest news "from the news room of KXZX" or wherever.

Most stations fall between these extremes. Consider a hypothetical small-market station with a full-time news staff of two. Although we call these staffers *reporters,* each actually fills additional roles as producer, editor, writer, and newscaster. A typical day starts around 5 a.m. The early-shift reporter arrives at the station to prepare for a series of newscasts—some less than 5 minutes, others as long as 15 minutes—starting at 6:30 and scheduled several times through wake-up and morning drive time. There may even be a **news block** of 30 minutes starting at 7 a.m.

First, the reporter **checks the wire** news and identifies the most recent hard news. Other material—sports, features, stock reports, commodities prices—is noted for later use. If the station is not a network affiliate, the reporter prepares local, state, national, and international news; if it is an affiliate of a news network, the network covers national and international news, and the reporter concentrates on state and local.

It would be unusual in a small market but in addition to AP and a national network, the station could also subscribe to a financial news service and affiliate with a state news network. AP, CNN, and CNBC as well as national and regional satellite news organizations offer extensive audio services that carry both regularly scheduled newscasts and feeds of **actualities—voices of people involved in a news event**—for use in local newscasts. Larger market stations may also have contracts with **computer accessed online news services** or data banks such as LEXIS–NEXIS. All good reporters also read the morning newspaper!

The reporter **checks all other available news sources.** There may be audiotape cartridges made the evening before that could be used on the morning newscast—local reports telephoned to the station, local news makers' statements, and special network **news feeds** (reports and actualities by network personnel sent as individual news stories to stations for use in local newscasts).

The reporter also makes "beat" telephone calls—police station, sheriff's office, hospital, National Weather Service, highway patrol, and any other institutions that might have had overnight activity that is newsworthy. Sometimes the reporter merely jots information down. Often however, the reporter records (with permission) the voice of the respondent for playback on the air. The taped statement (Fig. 8.3) that is played on the air during the story is called an **actuality** or a **sound bite**.

After gathering all pertinent news material, the reporter produces (assembles) the newscast. Some items are standard features every morning and are automatically included—the commodity report, the farm report, or the extended weather report. In dealing with hard news, however, decisions must be made as to which stories to include and how much time to devote to each one. The newscast is allotted an exact amount of time, and the reporter must select and prepare news, based on news value judgments, to fit precisely within that time.

News material must be **processed** for use. Processing includes **editing** (adding, subtracting, and changing words and sentences) a wire service story, **writing** a local story from scratch (Fig. 8.4), and preparing a sound bite for playback as part of the story.

**FIG. 8.3. Radio news reporter.** The radio reporter is cuing an audiotape of an interview with a newsmaker. Once the reporter selects the exact statement to be aired, it is dubbed onto a tape cartridge to be used during the newscast. The story is typed on the computer and printed for the newscaster.

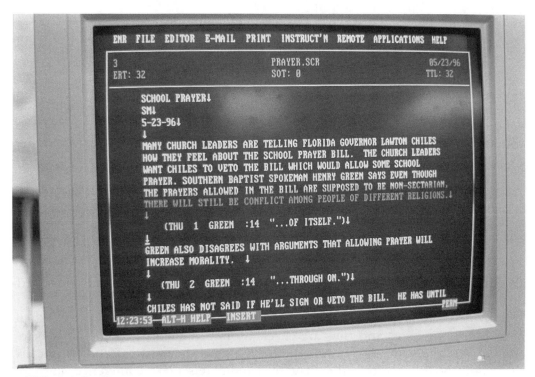

**FIG. 8.4. Radio news story.** Most radio news operations have tossed away typewriters in favor of the computer. Stories are typed, saved, printed for the newscaster, and stored for editing, updating, record keeping, and other archival purposes.

After the stories have been processed and the newscast is assembled, the reporter **confers with the audio technician** or disc jockey on duty. Both reporter and technician have **format sheets** that indicate when and how long each part of the newscast is to be—the weather, the news segments, the commercials, and so on. Both have done the routine many times, every weekday morning. Hence, the conference is less a matter of how to do the newscast than of what is unusual or different from the norm today. If the technician handles technical duties during the newscast, the reporter hands over **audio carts** containing the taped sound bites. Well-equipped stations, however, have a small studio set aside just for news, complete with an audio control board and cart machine for tape playback so that the reporter can engineer the newscast.

Between newscasts the reporter **updates** (rewrites to include new information) some stories, deletes some, and adds others. After the heavy early morning schedule of newscasts, the reporter may have only 2-minute hourly news summaries to prepare until the next extended newscast at noon.

A number of **sources and tools** are available as the reporter begins **gathering local news.** The handiest is the telephone, and the reporter makes liberal use of it. The newsroom may contain **radio receivers** or **scanners** that monitor police, fire, and other emergency frequency bands so the reporter will know when and where something happens as soon as it happens. Stories may be telephoned in by

**stringers**, people—often residents of outlying communities or regions—the station pays on a per-story basis to be part-time reporters. Listeners call in tips on news stories, often using cellular phones from the scene.

Individuals and organizations send or call in notices of meetings, elections, actions, stands taken, and press conferences. The publicity and public information offices of various government officials, institutions, and businesses will mail, bring, or call in material that they hope the station will use. The material may contain legitimate news but is often merely self-serving propaganda or advertising disguised as news.

Sometimes groups of commonly owned stations share exclusive news stories and coverage among themselves; a large station group may even maintain its own news bureaus in key cities. Stations also monitor the competition, checking other radio stations, television news, and newspapers for leads on major local stories.

Notice of a coming event is entered into a **future file**. Stations used to keep 31 folders, numbered consecutively for days of the month. Each day's folder was examined to see what news conferences, meetings, and special events are scheduled. Today, most stations keep future files on computers.

Usually, a radio reporter uses the telephone to cover most **beats** (places where news often originates and thus are checked on a frequent, periodic basis—e.g., city hall and the police station). Nonetheless, someone has to attend, physically, the school board meeting, the mayoral candidate's press conference, and the senator's address at the Rotary Club. With a second reporter going on duty at midmorning to cover outside events, the first reporter can stay at the station, run the newsroom, produce the newscasts, and receive and record telephone reports from various news sources and the second reporter. When the first reporter goes off duty, the operation may revert to a semi-rip 'n' read operation. If there is no second reporter, afternoon and evening newscasts are network-only or rip 'n' read.

## 8.3 TELEVISION NEWS

Addition of the visual element makes television news much more complex than radio. In radio news one or two people may do everything, but television news requires considerably more people who perform much more highly specialized tasks.

### 8.3.1 Local Broadcast Television News

We look at the news operation of a hypothetical, typical television station in a market of 150,000 to 300,000 homes. News operations for larger and smaller market stations will vary somewhat from the following description.

The head of the department is the **news director**, usually a television news specialist by training and experience. The news director sets policy and acts as overall supervisor for news activities and personnel. Many stations also have an **assistant news director** who more directly oversees the day-to-day operations of the newsroom and assembling of newscasts.

Perhaps the most critical person involved in the production of a newscast is the **producer.** Newscasts are put together—story by story—by producers (Box 8.1). They evaluate each story on the basis of standard news values, how it complies with station news policies, whether there is video or graphics, and how it might fit in the news program for maximum appeal. They decide which stories go on, how long they should be, and in what order, and often write the lead-ins and even entire scripts for some stories. However, producers must still answer to their supervisors—usually the news director and assistant news director. Some stations have an **executive producer** who serves as overall supervisor of producers. Most stations have news staff meetings during which the day's news stories are discussed and evaluated—some even designated for particular newscasts.

The **assignment editor** (Fig. 8.5) designates personnel to cover specific stories. As the day progresses, assignment editors serve a gatekeeping function as they monitor police radios and other sources for possible breaking stories. Assignment editors also use the futures file to keep track of upcoming events.

---

### BOX 8.1. NEWS PRODUCERS AT WORK

At WFLA-TV in Tampa, the newsroom centers around a "horseshoe" of six producer workstations, each complete with interconnecting computers. Producers of the various newscasts throughout the day can instantly call up versions of a story in progress or a version already broadcast without having to ask for scripts and exchanging hard copies of stories. (Photograph used by permission.)

**FIG. 8.5. Assignment editor.** The assignment editor, in consultation with news managers and producers, makes decisions about which stories will be covered and which news crews will be sent to which news locations. The various locations and crews are listed on the large board behind the assignment editor.

**Reporters** are the station's on-the-spot observers and explainers. They cover stories, interview people, write reports, work closely with camera crews, and appear in videotaped and live coverage. A **camera crew** usually consists of a reporter and a camera operator who is also called a **photographer, videographer,** or **shooter. Videotape editors** prepare, trim, and arrange visual images into a **story package.** At most stations the photographer works closely with or actually performs the duties of the video tape editor.

**Writers** take material from various news sources and rewrite or rework it into script form, to assigned length, and in the writing style preferred by the station. They write the script to include instructions on how and when live location shots, videotape, supers, graphics, and other pictorial materials are to be used.

**Graphics operators** prepare visual images that appear during the newscast—often over the shoulders of the newscasters but increasingly as visual elements of an actual story. Examples range from a simple image of a building on fire to a three-dimensional image of the space shuttle performing an intricate docking maneuver. Of course, the graphics operator works with the producer to make sure images reflect the content of the story. Some stations now purchase sophisticated graphics from national services such as *News in Motion* operated by Knight Ridder and Tribune. **Chyron operators** (named after the manufacturer of a computerized character generator used for many years) produce the characters that spell out names and locations during a newscast. The actual characters—letters or lines of text—appearing on the screen are called fonts or supers.

Once the producer has the stories in order and assigns running times, the news **lineup** (also frequently called a **rundown**) is prepared (Box 8.2). The duration of a television newscast is absolute. It is the producer's job to see that timing is precise. Using the lineup, producers and writers type the scripts into the computer, work with reporters and tape editors, and select other visual graphics materials. The lineup sheet contains terms that tell the newscasters, as well as the directors, tape operators, and graphics personnel, the type of each story to be aired and the

---

**BOX 8.2. UNDERSTANDING THE NEWS LINEUP
OR RUNDOWN SHEET**

The Channel 8 Noon lineup sheet shows the length and sequencing and identifies the source of video for each story. Terminology varies from station to station, but a working knowledge of the terms and abbreviations contained in the Channel 8 lineup will add to your understanding of the process of television news.

The **Page column** indicates page numbers for the stories. Each story has its own page number. Stories run before the first commercial break are prefaced with the letter "A." Page numbers after the first break follow the letter "B," and so on.

The **Slug column** contains the **slug**, or working name given to each story. Slugs preceded with a "T" indicate a tag or concluding remarks about the story usually made by one of the anchors. The double hyphen preceding a slug indicates that the slug is actually the name of a reporter. In this case the reporter is doing a live report or "live shot" from a remote location. The "P" means the tape segment of the story is a complete package, requiring only an intro by an anchor.

Entries in the **Video column** vary from station to station. At most stations **VO** stands for voice-over, which means the anchor reads copy over video—or while videotape about the story is shown on the screen. Channel 8 also designates the format of the video tape, so VO entries appear as M2/VO. The name of a reporter in the video column indicates a live shot from a remote location. This is usually preceded by video of an anchor introducing the upcoming story (INTRO RMT).

**SOT** stands for sound on tape and indicates that the tape to be aired includes sound and video. The TEACHER story contains a live shot of reporter LANCE W. and SOT video.

**M2/PKG** indicates a videotape package. This means the taped segment is a complete package. The anchor only introduces the story and the tape package tells the story. The tape may contain video of a news scene shown while a re-

**NOON LINEUP 6-1-95**
NOON
NEWS CHANNEL 8

| PAGE # | ANCHOR | SLUG | VIDEO | SHOT | TIME |
|---|---|---|---|---|---|
| A1 | R | HELLO | M2/VO | @ TOP | :18 |
|  | RG |  | TAG | 2 SHOT |  |
| A2 | G | POLK GENERAL—JENN SPEED | INTRO RMT JENN SPEED M2 / VO | S2 / SS DBLBX | 1:44 |
|  | G | T-POLK GENERAL | LIVE TAG | DBLBX |  |
| A3 | R | GAS LEAK | M2 / VO | SQ / SS | :27 |
| A4 | R | FIRE | M2 / VO | @ TOP | :19 |
| A5 | G | PROM ARREST | M2 / VO | 1 SHOT | :16 |
| A6 | G | TEACHER—LANCE W | INTRO RMT LANCE M2 / SOT | SQ / SS DBLBX | 1:21 |
|  |  | T-TEACHER | LIVE TAG | DBLBX |  |
| A7 | R | COKEBUST | M2 / VO TAG | 1 SHOT 1 SHOT | :23 |
| A8 | R | WATERS | M2 / VO | SQ / SS | :32 |
| A9 | G | SIMPSON P-SIMPSON | INTRO M2 / PKG | SQ / SS | :15 |
| A10 | G | ALLEN | READER | 1 SHOT | :15 |
| A11 | R | BOSNIA | M2 / VO | SQ / SS | :28 |
| A12 | R | TEXAS CRASH | M2 / VO | @ TOP | :19 |
| A13 | G | BUCS | M2 / VO-SOT | SQ / SS | 1:01 |
| A14 | G | MOSI—STEVE U. | INTRO RMT STEVE U. M2 / SOT | SQ / SS DBLBX | 1:46 |
|  | G | T-MOSI | LIVE TAG | DBLBX |  |
| A15 | G | HURRICANE | SS / FULL | 2 SHOT |  |
|  |  | BREAK - 1 |  |  | 2:09 |

CONTINUED

(Reprinted by permission of Kathy Green.)

porter is talking, shots of the reporter standing at or near a news scene, and even a sound bite of a news source. The anchor may or may not read a tag to the package.

A **reader** is a story read by an anchor. At some stations this means there are no videotape segments or graphics shown. Other stations may show graphics images over the shoulder of the newscaster during "readers."

The BUCS story video is designated as **M2/VO-SOT**. This means the anchor reads copy while videotape is shown until the instant that a sound bite appears on tape.

**SS/FULL** means still-shot full. This usually means a full-screen shot of a graphic image or slide is shown.

The **Shot column** reveals how graphics will be used and the types of camera shots for each story. The **@ TOP** indicates that the video tape is taken (or aired) from the top or very beginning of the story.

---

**BOX 8.2** (cont'd.)

SQ/SS stands for squeezed still store. These are graphics video images that most often appear over the shoulder of the anchors as they read. The term *squeeze* is used because the still image can be made as large or small as desired. **DBLBX** mean double box. This is a shot of two separate newscasters or scenes, framed within two boxes on the screen. In the POLK GENERAL story the anchor G and reporter JENN SPEED appear in the two boxes, exchanging comments.

The camera shots are simple. A 1 **shot** is a shot of one anchor, a 2 **shot** indicates both anchors.

---

source of sound and visual elements. The lineup also tells the running time for each story, and precisely how long into the newscast a particular story should begin and end. This allows the producer to adjust if the newscast is running short (**light**) or long (**heavy**).

As stories are completed, the producer calls each one up on the screen, prints it, and assembles the master script of the entire newscast. Each page contains the text of the story and information indicating whether there is video or a sound bite, which newscaster is to read the story (often indicated by the color of the paper for that page), and when to lead into or out of a commercial.

Newscasters or **anchors** narrate the newscast on the air, reading the story scripts that are projected directly into the lens of the camera by a prompting device—often called a TelePrompTer (trade name; Box 8.3). Newscasters have copies of the scripts so they can follow the producer's instructions and just in case the electronic prompter malfunctions. Newscasters also use the producer's lineup to know ahead of time the precise sequence of stories.

As newscast time nears (Fig. 8.6), a separate tape for each story containing a videotape segment is handed to a videotape operator to be loaded and called up on the newscast in sequential order. Graphics and other visual images are checked for proper sequencing. Script copies are printed and distributed to the producer, the newscasters, the director of the newscast program, and key members of the production crew. The newscasters rehearse the script. The director marks the script with standard directing cues (Box 8.4) and checks to ensure that all elements are in place and ready. Then the director starts the program. As with radio, the television news team and the production crew have used the same format for so long that actual production (Box 8.5) is second nature, a matter of plugging in each day's script to the routine.

It should be noted that separate staffs prepare sports and weather segments of the newscast, often with a meteorologist in charge of the latter. There are often additional news employees—clerical and research personnel, drivers, SNG operators, and even pilots of helicopters and light planes.

**BOX 8.3. WHY THEY DON'T OFTEN LOOK AT THE SCRIPT**

The news scripts appear in the camera lenses! A prompter is an electronic closed-circuit television system. It feeds a large-print version of the script to small video monitors attached to each of the cameras facing the newscasters. Newscasters can see it, but the words are not visible from the lens side of the glass. The script "scrolls" upward on the monitor as the newscaster reads, its speed controlled by an operator. Thus, the newscaster reads the news looking directly into the camera, glancing down at the desk copy of the script only for effect. (Reprinted with permission of Leonard Makinda.)

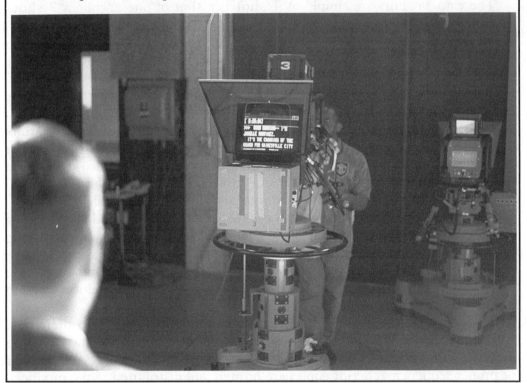

### 8.3.2 Television News Sources

News sources are basically the same as those for radio. Tips and leads come from the public and competitive media. Stories and visuals (graphics, tape, and satellite feeds) come from the station's own news staff, national and regional network and satellite feeds, news syndication services, stations in other towns, stringers, public relations offices of private and public institutions, and station group news bureaus. Organizations also provide VNRs that are prepared by the organization and delivered in the same format as most television news story packages. Although some outlets use no portion of VNRs during newscasts and others use only the video, some air the complete VNR as delivered. The ethics of using VNRs have been questioned because most audience members have no idea the story package

(a)

(b)

**FIG. 8.6. Noon newscast.** WFLA-TV in Tampa, Florida, gets ready for its weekday noon newscast. (a) News satellite operations. This is where WFLA receives feeds from various satellite sources. (b) Newscast story packages are edited by computer.

(c)

(d)

FIG. 8.6 (cont'd.) (c) The audio board operator waits for the signal to begin the newscast. (d) Anchor Gayle Guyardo watches as co-anchor Bill Ratliff tests the audio level just before airtime. (Photographs and other materials used by permission.)

---

### BOX 8.4. TV NEWS SCRIPT: DECIPHERING THE DIRECTOR'S COPY

Each news story is printed on a different page. The writer, Vihlen, has slugged the story in the upper left, indicating that it deals with the mayor and has videotape (V-T) as part of the story. The writer has also indicated that during the opening of the story, the newscaster should be seen in front of a picture of the city hall. The newscast producer has noted that the story contains 14 lines that at a reading speed of 2 seconds per line, add up to 28 seconds. The videotape lasts 31 seconds for a total of 59 seconds on the story. The big "3" in the upper left means that the story will be the third one reported on the newscast. Newscaster Ball will read the story, and (as noted at the bottom), Wekerle will read the next story. The director has marked the script, too. The story will open on camera 3 with camera 6 on the city hall graphic matted in behind. Videotape rolls on the term *four-year,* and the director dissolves to videotape on the word *finances.* During the tape, the director readies camera 2 with a close-up of Ball and, at the end of the tape, dissolves to 2. As Ball wraps up the story, the director readies camera 4 with a shot of Wekerle, who will read the next story and, on Ball's last word, takes (cuts to) camera 4.

## BOX 8.5. THOSE WEATHER GRAPHICS ARE REALLY *NOT* ON THAT BACK WALL

The weather reporter appears on-screen in front of a map on the wall, periodically turns to and looks at the map, and points out things we should notice about the weather. That map is replaced by other huge graphics—another map, satellite pictures of cloud cover, a summary of the 5-day weather forecast—and the reporter looks at and works with each of them in turn. How do they change the graphics so fast? Actually, as you see in the photograph, the wall behind the weather reporter is actually blank! Graphics are electronically generated, prepared in advance, stored, and then called up by the director according to cues in the script. The director uses an electronic effect called a **matte** to superimpose the camera image of the reporter over the electronic graphic. Although appearing to look toward the back wall, reporters are actually viewing an off-camera monitor showing the graphics. By watching that monitor, the reporter knows where to stand so as not to block the audience's view and where to point. The reporter uses a remote control to switch the graphics instantaneously. (Photograph used by permission.)

was not produced by the radio or television outlet or some other objective news service.

In addition to the broadcast wire services the outlet may have the AP newspaper wire, a computerized news service, special sports wires, a financial news service, photo transmission services, weather wires and city news services, and a number of other satellite delivered national and regional news services.

### 8.3.3 Network Television News

Broadcast network television news programs are put together much like those at local stations. Their emphasis, of course, is on national and international news. Network news operations often dispatch their own reporters (Box 8.6) and crews but rely heavily on affiliates and contractual arrangements with other news-gathering organizations to provide coverage of stories around the world. Pictorial coverage is transmitted by satellite to studios in New York. Evening showcase network news programs do not include sports and weather news on a regular basis.

Cable news services rely heavily on up-to-the-minute news and video, with live video feeds whenever possible. CNN operates an extensive system of domestic and foreign bureaus. CNN also picks up international material from video news services and stringers, and domestic material from television stations with which it has reciprocity agreements. CNN—as well as ABC, CBS, and NBC—has exchange arrangements with various news-gathering services around the world.

The two C-SPAN channels are noncommercial. They provide extensive coverage of Congress, which exemplifies a significant departure from the very concept of television news; whenever possible, C-SPAN covers an event in its entirety, from beginning to end, with no interruptions or cutaways.

CNN Headline News focuses primarily on hard news in capsule form, using as much video as possible. Informational programmers such as The Weather Channel and CNBC concentrate on a particular type of news. Some cable networks, such as MTV, which primarily emphasize entertainment programming, also feature news segments.

### 8.4 OTHER FORMS OF NEWS PROGRAMMING

Full-service news departments often produce other types of programs as well. These include interviews, news panel programs, remote (on-the-spot) coverage, news specials, editorial and commentary, and documentaries.

**Interviews** are programs in which a news maker or knowledgeable person is questioned at length. If two or more persons ask questions or answer them, the format is a **panel program.** NBC's long-running *Meet The Press* is an example of the former; PBS's *Wall Street Week,* the latter.

**Remote coverage** is live transmission from the scene of a news event. **News specials** are coverage or programs that deviate from the regular schedule. **Com-**

### BOX 8.6. SHARYL ATTKISSON, CBS NEWS CORRESPONDENT AND DISTINGUISHED PROFESSIONAL

Sharyl Attkisson began her news career as a broadcasting student at the University of Florida. While a student, she worked as a radio and television reporter and producer and anchor. After graduation, she moved from WTVX in West Palm Beach to CBS affiliates in Columbus, Ohio (WBNS) and Tampa, Florida (WTVT; Photograph used by permission).

In 1990, Attkisson was appointed anchor and reporter for CNN, covering the Gulf War, the Los Angeles riots, and the standoff and storming of the Branch Davidian compound in Waco, Texas. While at CNN, she interviewed major news makers such as Henry Kissinger, King Hussein, and Yasser Arafat, and coproduced special series including *The Gender Gap, Coming of Age,* and *Caring Choices.*

Attkisson became a Washington-based correspondent for CBS News in January 1995. Prior to that, she co-anchored the CBS News overnight broadcast *Up to the Minute.* She co-anchored live coverage of major events such as the election of Nelson Mandela and the signing of the Middle East peace agreement. She also anchored a special feature on NASA, which included interviews with Senator John Glenn and Edwin "Buzz" Aldrin.

**mentary** and **editorials** are expressions of opinion. Networks and cable news services label most expression of opinion as commentary. Some local news operations air true editorials, usually on local issues and delivered by the news director or the general manager. A **documentary** shows or analyzes an issue—for example, a news event or a social condition—in nonfictional but dramatic form. Television **minidocumentaries** often run daily as a regular feature in a station's early evening newscast. Each may deal with a separate subject, or one subject may be serialized over several evenings.

## NOTES

1. J. Driscoll, "Turnabout! New Study Finds People Learn More About the News from TV than from Print," *Bulletin* 744 (1992): 24–28; "Most Got More News on TV," *Gainesville Sun* 2 May 1991: A8; Hao Xiaoming, "Television Viewing Among American Adults in the 1990s," *Journal of Broadcasting and Electronic Media* 38 (1994): 353–360.

2. John W. Wright and Lawrence A. Hosman, "Listener Perceptions of Radio News," *Journalism Quarterly* 63 (1987): 802–808, 814.

3. Edwin Emery and Michael Emery, *The Press and America: An Interpretive History of the Mass Media,* 5th ed. (Englewood Cliffs, NJ: Prentice-Hall, 1984).

4. David J. LeRoy and Christopher H. Sterling, *Mass News: Practices, Controversies, Alternatives* (Englewood Cliffs, NJ: Prentice-Hall, 1972).

5. Peter M. Sandman, David M. Rubin, and David Sachsman, *Media: An Introductory Analysis of American Mass Communication* 3rd ed. (Englewood Cliffs, NJ: Prentice-Hall, 1982).

6. "Social Control in the News Room? A Functional Analysis," *Social Forces* 33 (1955): 326–335.

7. Kurt Lang and Gladys Engel Lang, "The Unique Perspective of Television and Its Effect: A Pilot Study," reprinted in *The Process and Effects of Mass Communication,* Ed. Wilbur Schramm and Donald F. Roberts (Urbana: University of Illinois Press, 1971).

## FURTHER READING

Barnouw, Erik. *Documentary: A History of Non-Fiction Film.* 2nd Rev. ed. New York: Oxford University Press, 1993.

Bliss, Edward. *Now the News: The Story of Broadcast Journalism.* New York: Columbia University Press, 1992.

Bliss, Edward and James L. Hoyt. *Writing for Broadcast News.* 3rd ed. New York: Columbia University Press, 1994.

Chantler, Paul and Sim Harris. *Local Radio Journalism.* 2nd ed. Boston: Focal, 1997.

Cohler, David K. *Broadcast Journalism: A Guide for the Presentation of Radio and Television News.* 2nd ed. Englewood Cliffs, NJ: Prentice-Hall, 1994.

Cremer, Charles F., Phillip O. Keirstead, and Richard D. Yoakam. *ENG: Television News.* New York: McGraw-Hill, 1996.

Garrison, Bruce, and Mark Sabljak. *Sports Reporting.* 2nd ed. Ames: Iowa State University Press, 1993.

Gunther, Marc. *The House That Roone Built: The Inside Story of ABC News.* Boston: Little Brown, 1994.

Hausman, Carl. *Crafting the News for Electronic Media: Writing, Reporting, and Producing.* Belmont, CA: Wadsworth, 1992.

Hesse, Jurgen. *The Radio Documentary Handbook: Producing and Selling for Broadcast.* Vancouver, Canada: International, 1987.

Houston, Brant. *Computer Assisted Reporting.* New York: St. Martin's, 1996.

Johnston, Carla B. *Winning the Global Television News Game.* Boston: Focal, 1995.

Kessler, Lauren, and Duncan McDonald. *The Search: Information Gathering for the Mass Media.* Belmont, CA: Wadsworth, 1992.

Killenberg, George M. *Public Affairs Reporting: Covering the News in the Information Age.* New York: St. Martin's, 1992.

Lindekugel, D. M. *Shooters: TV News Photographers and Their Work.* Westport, CT: Praeger, 1994.

MacDonald, R. H. *A Broadcast News Manual of Style.* 2nd ed. White Plains, NY: Longman, 1994.

Medoff, Norman J., and Tom Tanquary. *Portable Video: ENG and EFP.* 2nd ed. White Plains, NY: Knowledge, 1992.

Murray, Michael D. *The Political Performers: CBS Broadcasts in the Public Interest.* Westport, CT: Greenwood, 1994.

Reeves, Jimmie L. *Cracked Coverage: Television News, the Anti-Cocaine Crusade, and the Reagan Legacy.* Durham, NC: Duke University Press, 1994.

Shook, Frederick. *Television Newswriting: Captivating an Audience.* White Plains, NY: Longman, 1994.

Stephens, Mitchell. *Broadcast News.* 3rd ed. New York: Holt, 1993.

Stone, Vernon. *Careers in Broadcast News.* 6th ed. Washington, DC: Radio and Television News Directors Association, 1989.

Ullmann, John. *Investigative Reporting: Advanced Methods and Techniques.* New York: St. Martin's, 1995.

Weinberg, Steve. *The Reporter's Handbook: An Investigator's Guide to Documents and Techniques.* 3rd ed. New York: St. Martin's, 1996.

Whittemore, Hank. *CNN, The Inside Story.* Boston: Little Brown, 1990.

Wulfemeyer, K. Tim. *Radio-TV Newswriting: A Workbook.* Ames: Iowa State University Press, 1995.

Yorke, Ivor. *Television News.* 3rd ed. Boston: Focal, 1995.

# 9

## Commercials and Other Persuasive Announcements

Commercials. Everybody has something to say about them, mostly bad. But they work, and for those advertisers who pay for the programming you listen to and view, the fact that commercials work is very good, indeed. It is almost impossible to show direct cause–effect relations, that one buys a product because of a commercial. Still, the fact remains that increased sales follow effective use of radio and TV advertising.

*Commercial* and *ad* are shortened terms for **commercial announcement.** There are other kinds of announcements, so we use *announcement* to mean any unit of programming created to attract your attention in order to "sell"—a product, a service, a political candidate, a point of view, whatever—and for which the seller pays the electronic mass media outlet on which the unit is run. As with programmers, advertisers in the electronic mass media carefully design their announcements to reach targeted mass audiences.

In this chapter we examine commercial announcements by functional classification and by what makes them sell—strategies used in creating commercials, types of creative formats, appeals, approaches, and production. As with the rest of radio and TV, commercial announcements earn both criticism and praise, and we conclude the chapter with those views.

### 9.1 CLASSIFICATION OF ANNOUNCEMENTS

Announcements may be classified in several ways. Each classification defines announcements from a different point of view, and that helps us understand just what announcements are. Some common classifications include distribution medium, placement, length, purpose, marketing interest of advertisers, basis of payment, production medium, and method of production.

#### 9.1.1 Classified by Distribution Medium

**Advertising-supported electronic mass media,** by definition, carry advertising. This includes broadcasting, cable TV, DBS, wireless cable, many channels in

275

TVRO packages, and everything that carries commercials. Can we say that other forms of radio and TV do not carry advertising? What about public broadcast stations? Legally, those stations may not run advertising. But as discussed in *PRT,* 22.5, they do carry persuasive announcements, many of which bear a strong resemblance to commercials. In fact, there have been proposals to allow public stations to run commercials. Even religious networks run programs that sell religious articles and ask for donations.

Generally, subscription and pay-per-view services do not run advertising. After all, one of the major reasons that we pay for such premium services is the uncut, advertising-free programming. But is it really advertising-free? Look at premium service programming between movies and features. It consists of promotional announcements, advertising for upcoming programming and the service itself. This is the case, too, with most of the noncommercial basic services (*PRT,* 7.4.2.4); they promote upcoming programming and may actually advertise subscriptions to their own program guide or other service-connected items viewers can buy. True, it is self-advertising and runs between (rather than interrupting) program material; nonetheless, it is advertising.

### 9.1.2 Classified by Placement

Announcements may be classified by placement in six types. These types include advertising as programming, disguised as programming, within sponsored programs, within participation programs, within barter syndication programs, and at major programming breaks.

*9.1.2.1 Advertising as Programming.*    In some cases, **advertising is the programming.** An *advertising program* may sell one product or many different products. A program devoted to one product may, for example, take the form of a half-hour show that extols the virtues of a home exercise machine (Fig. 9.1). It could show up as a 5-minute infomercial on nutrition or cooking "brought to you by" a manufacturer of food products. For many years, radio and television did not run long-form advertising (*PRT,* 9.1.3) except for political and campaign messages.

One example of an advertising program that features a variety of brands or advertisers is the home shopping format (*PRT,* 7.4.2.3). Another is the local cable system advertising channel that often consists of one local ad message after another.

*9.1.2.2 Disguised as Programming.*    Let us set up a hypothetical situation to exemplify advertising disguised as programming. Several times a week a popular radio disc jockey mentions a particular restaurant over the air by name and in favorable terms. The restaurant does not pay the station for these plugs, but the disc jockey frequently eats there for free. Neither the audience nor the station knows anything about this arrangement. This is plugola, an illegal practice discussed in *PRT,* 9.1.6.7.

**FIG. 9.1. Advertising as programming: Infomercials.** This 30-minute commercial demonstrated the Perfect Abs exercise machine. The setting was a "fitness party," apparently at some beach. Between the demonstrations and sales pitches, this infomercial even cut away periodically to "commercials"—for Perfect Abs! (Used by permission of Perfect Abs.)

The **video news release** (VNR), another way to sneak promotion onto programming, grew rapidly during the early 1990s. Most VNRs, video descendants of the printed press release, tell one-sided stories designed to sell products, businesses, or political viewpoints. Some companies do their own VNRs, although most hire public relations firms to handle creation and distribution.

The VNR may be even more insidious than plugola, because it gets messages onto that supposed bastion of objectivity, the TV news program. VNR messages are constructed to look like news items. VNRs are usually distributed by satellite, and TV news departments are free to record and use them on the air in whole or in part. News producers routinely run VNRs as news with no counterbalancing material and with no attribution as to their source. Viewers believe they have seen an objective news story with all video and audio produced by news personnel instead of biased opinion from a public relations organization with a vested interest in selling its client's point of view.

**9.1.2.3 Within Sponsored Programs.**    Most programs clearly separate advertising from program content into **availabilities** (avails, places for announcements). In the sponsored program, all ads pertain to a single sponsoring entity (two, if the program is cosponsored). A sporting goods store may sponsor a 5-minute radio sports report weekday evenings. A car company may sponsor a network TV special to introduce its new models. In some cases, the sponsor provides not only the advertising messages but also the program itself. Detergent companies, for example, have produced soap operas aired by broadcast networks.

### 9.1.2.4 Within Participation Programming. In **participating advertising**, each avail may contain an announcement for a different advertiser. Advertisers usually prefer to spread announcements over different days and dayparts, so participating advertising is the dominant form on radio and television.

The mode of advertising time buying varies with the medium. An advertiser who buys 100 avails on TV or on network radio usually contracts for 100 **specific dates and times**. An advertiser who purchases 100 avails on a radio station usually buys **time periods**; the station decides exact times. For example, the radio advertising contract may specify that the purchased avails will all occur within 2 weeks and during a particular daypart (say, morning drive time) or scattered throughout the day—**ROS** (run of schedule), **BTA** (best times available), or **TAP** (total audience plan, also called maximum impact—a certain number to run in each of a number of different time periods).

Although not the norm, an advertiser can buy specific positions on a radio station, buy ROS on a radio network, or sponsor a program on a radio station or network. The advertiser can also buy **rotations** on a TV station. In rotations, an advertiser's commercial runs either at different positions in the same program every day (horizontal rotation) or in different programs during the same time period every day (vertical rotation).

At the local level, advertisers may "participate" on both syndicated and network programs. Programming from radio networks and ad-supported cable services contains **local windows** (avails) that affiliates may sell. Some broadcast TV network programs contain local avails, too. In prime time, however, affiliates have little to sell except at program breaks (*PRT,* 9.1.2.6).

### 9.1.2.5 Within Barter Syndication Programming. As explained in *PRT,* 7.3.2.1, **barter or cash-plus-barter programs** contain some advertising sold by the syndicator and some availabilities that the local programmer may sell. Therefore, an advertiser may deal with the syndicator or with the local outlet. The form is usually participating advertising.

### 9.1.2.6 At Programming Breaks. Programming breaks are formal interruptions for local advertising during network TV programming. They include station breaks and middle breaks. **Station breaks** are announcement positions between programs. **Middle breaks** are those within the temporary cut back to affiliates every 30 minutes during programs of 1 hour or longer. Advertisers pay hefty prices for program-break avails during prime time; viewing levels are high, and affiliates charge dearly. Ad-supported national cable services normally draw audiences much smaller than those of broadcast TV networks. Some cable systems, however,

do charge higher prices for programming-break avails during prime time on the more popular services.

### 9.1.3 Classified by Length

When classified by length, announcements may be divided into three categories. These consist of 60 seconds and less, longer, and program-length.

*9.1.3.1 60 Seconds and Less.*    At one time, the normal length for radio and TV announcements was **60 seconds.** The cost of TV advertising, however, rose drastically, and research seemed to show **30s** (30-second commercials) to be about as effective as 60s. A shift to the shorter length started during the late 1960s, and TV adopted the 30 as standard. There are still a few 60s, mostly on cable services and late at night on TV stations. These are often direct-response spots run as per inquiry ads (PIs; *PRT,* 9.1.6.5) or standing orders for unsold avails, bought at the lowest possible rate.

Television stations also offer a limited number of **10s** (10-second availabilities). Some are called **IDs** because they comprise the "extra" 10 seconds immediately before the station ID during a station break or middle break.

By 1990 another "standard" length emerged—the **15.** TV ad costs had continued to rise unabated. Some advertisers sought to save money by **piggybacking;** they would attempt to buy one availability and put in it short commercials for two different products. For example, if a 30 cost $100, the advertiser could run two 15-second commercials in a **split 30** for $100—the same price as two 10s. The NAB Television Code (*PRT,* 16.2.1) prohibited piggybacking availabilities of less than 60 seconds, unless the pitches for the two products were integrated and appeared to be a single commercial. In 1984 however, with the Code barely 1 year in its grave, the nonintegrated split 30 became a fact of life. Alberto-Culver, marketer of personal grooming products, had used various means (including an antitrust suit) to persuade the networks and several large station-group owners to drop bans on the split 30. By 1987 all networks sold **stand-alone 15s** (individual avails). By the end of the century the 15 was not yet the standard, but advertisers regarded it as an attractive alternative to the 30, and normally several 15s showed up in almost every network commercial pod, mixed in with the 30s and the occasional 60.

Most radio network commercials are 30s; most local and regional radio ads, 60s. Some stations restrict commercial length to the 30 for popular locally produced programs (e.g., sports talk). Also available in radio are **20s** and 10s.

*9.1.3.2 Announcements Longer Than 60 Seconds.*    Some announcements run longer than 1 minute. In the past some single-sponsor TV specials were of such a nature that the sponsor would forego the usual number of interruptions, opting instead to let commercial announcements run at natural breaks in content—between acts, or at the end of a long piece of music. In these cases, the sponsor used specially prepared commercials of **90 seconds or longer.**

During election years, candidates for elective political office sometimes use longer announcements. In presidential races networks edit down scheduled programs (generally in prime time) to make time available for **5-minute political announcements.**

### 9.1.3.3 Program-Length Announcements.

Until the 1980s responsible broadcasters did not air programlike commercials. Some advertisers attempted to disguise their extended pitches as programs. These **program-length commercials** would, as one FCC document described it, interweave "program content so closely with the commercial message that the entire program must be considered a commercial."[1] A group of garden supply dealers, for example, sponsors a program on home garden care, a program liberally sprinkled with mentions of the dealers' products. The FCC banned such commercials, and the NAB Code said they were "not acceptable."

These length restrictions, however, applied to broadcast television. Cable had none. The cable business touted its freedom to develop long-form commercials, to mix program and commercial content, as an advantage over broadcast TV. Cable TV provided advertisers with the opportunity to develop and refine the program-length commercial or advertising program. Infomercials, half-hour commercials, advertising channels, and the home-shopping format all were nurtured on cable.

Prohibitions against program-length broadcast commercials disappeared in the 1980s. The FCC, as part of its deregulation efforts (*PRT,* 3.5.1), lifted its ban in 1984. The Television Code had died the year before. Since then many TV stations have taken advantage of their "freedom" to broadcast program-length commercials; some, to adopt advertising-only formats.

## 9.1.4 Classified by Purpose

The purposes of announcements can be divided into four broad categories. These include straight advertising, institutional advertising, issue advertising, and corrective advertising.

### 9.1.4.1 Straight Advertising.

A **straight advertising announcement** tries to get you to do something that will supposedly benefit someone—you, someone else, or both. Many persuasive advertising announcements contain a direct call for action. These include commercials that try to get you to purchase some product or service, political advertising that urges you to vote a particular way, public service announcements (PSAs) that ask you to donate time or money, and promotional announcements (promos) that urge you to tune to the advertised programs.

Some announcements contain no direct call for action but instead attempt to create awareness, promote understanding, shape attitudes, or enhance recall. Ultimately, however, these announcements still try to get you to do something, and thus they may be included in our definition. For example, during the 1970s the Advertising Council (*PRT,* 9.4) developed TV PSAs showing an American Indian shedding a tear over litter and pollution. Their immediate purpose was to create awareness that we all play a role in environmental quality with the slogan, "People start pollution. People can stop it." Actually this PSA asked us to reduce our own environmental abuses—put trash in receptacles, commute by carpool or bicycle or public transportation, and so on.

### 9.1.4.2 Institutional Advertising.

**Institutional advertising** aims to enhance a company's image, that is, the general public's concept of the company. It attempts to make you feel a certain way toward the advertiser. As an example, in the wake of the 1973–1974 fuel shortage, prices for gasoline and other petroleum products rose drastically. At the same time major oil companies ran TV commercials not to sell gasoline, but to show what they were doing to alleviate the shortage—offshore drilling, construction of the Alaskan pipeline, and research into alternative forms of fuel. Several years later AT&T tried to dispel its image of a faceless, corporate bureaucracy. AT&T's "Hello America" TV commercials depicted the company as a group of smiling employees whose only concern was to make America's telephone system the best in the world. During the 1980s, Dow Chemical institutional commercials encouraged young people to "do great things." In 1996 several "official Olympics" firms ran institutional advertising to associate themselves with that year's Atlanta games. One Coca-Cola commercial, for example, featured what appeared to be a runner from a third-world country intercut with shots of his folks back home cheering him on.

### 9.1.4.3 Issue Advertising.

In **issue advertising,** the advertiser pays for broadcast time to expound one side of an issue. In the past, issue advertising sometimes resulted in Fairness Doctrine (*PRT,* 15.3.4) problems. For example, Esso (later renamed Exxon) paid for and NBC ran those Alaskan pipeline commercials just mentioned. Environmental groups filed a Fairness Doctrine complaint on the Esso spots. NBC said the commercials were institutional advertising, but the FCC ruled they presented one side of the controversial issue of the pipeline's ecological impact in Alaska and thus were subject to Fairness Doctrine obligations.[2]

### 9.1.4.4 Corrective Advertising.

If the Federal Trade Commision (FTC) finds advertising to be false or misleading, it may seek a consent order by which the advertiser promises to devote a certain percentage of its future ad expenditures for a certain period of time to "set the record straight." This is **corrective advertising.** The first such advertisers were ITT Continental Baking Company in 1971 and Ocean Spray Cranberries, Inc., in 1972. Both ran TV commercials as part of their corrective advertising. ITT Continental had allegedly touted its Profile bread as a dietary product; it agreed to advertise that Profile had about the same number of calories per ounce as other breads. Ocean Spray had said its cranberry juice cocktail had more "food energy" than other juices; its corrective advertising made clear that food energy was not protein and vitamins but calories.

The FTC won judicial sanction of corrective advertising in 1978. Three years earlier the FTC had ordered Warner-Lambert Co. to state in future advertising that its Listerine mouthwash would not help prevent colds or sore throats as previously advertised. Warner-Lambert appealed. A federal appeals court ruled in favor of the FTC and thereby upheld the FTC's authority to order corrective ads.[3] Listerine advertising, including broadcast commercials, had to contain the message, "Listerine will not help prevent colds or sore throats or lessen their severity," until the company had spent $10 million in advertising.

Critics questioned the effectiveness of corrective advertising. They pointed out that the initial advertising messages usually conveyed their incorrect impressions so effectively, so repeatedly, and for such long periods that it would be difficult to remove those impressions from consumer minds. The advertising and media businesses strongly opposed use of corrective ads, and so did the presidential administrations of Ronald Reagan and George Bush. As a result, the FTC largely discontinued corrective advertising after the 1970s.

At one time, the FTC attempted to create yet another announcement category—the **countercommercial**. The FTC proposed *counteradvertising* to the FCC as an extension of the Fairness Doctrine. Consumer groups would have the right of access to radio and TV to reveal negative aspects of advertising claims. In 1974 the FCC rejected the idea of countercommercials, and therefore they have never been run as such on TV and radio.

### 9.1.5 Classified by Advertiser

Announcements may be classified by marketing interest or scope of advertiser. These classifications include local, network, syndication, spot, and cooperative advertising.

**9.1.5.1 Local Advertising Announcements.**    **Local advertising** aims at persons living in the advertiser's community. The owner of a hardware store, hair dresser, restaurant, or auto dealership (Fig. 9.2) advertises in local media to reach local consumers.

**9.1.5.2 Network Advertising Announcements.**    Organizations that have products or services used by all types of persons and distributed nationwide would probably **place ads on national cable and broadcast networks.** Almost everyone brushes teeth, drinks beverages, and uses soap, so manufacturers of such products buy advertising on networks to reach large, nationwide audiences.

**9.1.5.3 Syndication Advertising Announcements.**    In **syndication advertising,** a company pays to have its commercials run on a barter program (*PRT,* 7.3.2.1). The syndicator tries to place the program in every market, so syndication advertising appeals to firms that offer widely used, nationally marketed products.

FIG. 9.2. **Local advertising.** The local Mazda dealer uses advertising on local television to reach its hometown audience. (Used by permission of Moore Mazda.)

***9.1.5.4 Spot Advertising Announcements.***    The same types of firms that use network and barter advertising also use **spot advertising**. In national spot advertising, the advertiser "spots" commercials around the country, choosing specific media outlets, programs, and dayparts that deliver the desired audience. Soap companies use, in addition to network ads, national spot advertising to get commercials on radio stations, TV stations' programs, and cable-system channels whose audiences have high percentages of homemakers.

National firms with specialized products and regional advertisers also use spot advertising. A tractor manufacturer, for example, places ads in markets where they reach lots of farmers. A brewery whose beer is available in just a three-state area advertises only within that area. Network advertising would be inefficient, reaching too many people; local advertising would reach too few.

Vertically programmed cable services (*PRT,* 7.4.2.1) could pose a threat to national spot business. Consider, for example, a cable network that specializes in health programming, aiming at persons concerned with health and fitness across the country. A vitamin marketer would pay less money and face less paperwork if it advertised on such a network rather than using national spot advertising. (Choice of advertising media, however, involves additional factors; the advertiser still might have to use national spot advertising.)

*9.1.5.5 Cooperative Advertising Announcements.* **Cooperative** (co-op) **advertising** combines spot and local advertising. In co-op, the local dealer buys advertising. The ad features the product of a national firm and ties it to the local dealer. The media outlet on which the ad runs sends the bill for the ad time to the dealer who, in turn sends a copy to the manufacturer. The manufacturer repays the dealer some portion of the cost.

### 9.1.6 Classified by Payment

Announcements are classified by payment to the medium. Categories are rate card, cut rate, sustaining, make-good, per inquiry, barter, plugola, promotional announcements, and payola.

*9.1.6.1 Announcements Paid at Rate Card Prices.* A **rate card** is a published list of a medium's charges for advertising time (*PRT*, 17.2). In most cases an advertiser pays **rate card prices** for advertising time.

*9.1.6.2 Announcements Paid at a Cut Rate.* Some media sell **off the card**—that is, below their published rates—an ethically questionable practice (*PRT*, 17.2.4). Here, the advertiser is said to pay a "cut rate." Many outlets, however, price their ad time using a grid system (*PRT*, 17.2.2) that recognizes and accounts for changes in value of individual avails. Use of the grid negates, to a large extent, the concept of selling off the card.

*9.1.6.3 Sustaining Announcements.* In electronic mass media, sustaining means that the medium itself bears the expense of a program or program element. A **sustaining announcement**, therefore, is one the medium runs for which it receives no payment. This category includes, for example, most PSAs.

*9.1.6.4 Make-Good Announcements.* A medium reschedules an ad that runs incorrectly—distorted, at the wrong time, not at all, or with some element missing. The medium does this to **make good** the problem. The advertiser does not pay extra for make-goods.

*9.1.6.5 Announcements Paid Per Inquiry.* In **per inquiry** (PI), the advertiser pays the medium based on the number of responses to the PI announcement. PIs include, for example, most 60-second commercials that give a toll-free number on which to order pots, knives, food steamers, exercise devices, or three-disc albums of the greatest hits in gospel or country or oldies rock or romantic music (Fig. 9.3). Each outlet airing such an announcement has a different telephone number and receives payment according to the number of viewers that order on its number.

*9.1.6.6 Announcements Paid by Barter.* In barter, the advertiser pays the medium in some form other than money. Barter includes several forms of exchange.

FIG. 9.3. Per inquiry. The how-to-order frame. (Used by permission of Westwood Promotions.)

In one, payment consists of goods or services. A cable system runs ads for an office supply firm in exchange for new furniture; a TV station runs commercials for a radio station in exchange for radio ads. At the local level, this is **tradeout**; at the national level, **barter**. In **time banking**, a national barter firm offers a radio or TV outlet opportunity to obtain goods-and-services payment before running any advertising; the outlet then owes availabilities to the firm. In another variation, payment consists of programming, as in **barter syndication** and **time banking syndication** (*PRT,* 7.3.2.1).

*9.1.6.7 Illegal Free Announcements: Plugola.*    In **plugola**, a program includes a **plug**—a free boost or advertisement for a product or service. The "advertiser" pays the individual who slipped in the plug, a performer, writer, director, or someone else affiliated with the program's creation. Neither audience nor medium is aware of the payment. Plugola is illegal.

*9.1.6.8 Promotional Announcements.*    A thin line divides a promotional announcement from plugola. With a **promotional announcement**, however, the medium receives payment and is aware of the announcement. TV game shows contain examples. Appearance and description of the prizes are plugs. Donation of prizes (and sometimes additional compensation to the programmer for using them) is payment. Phrases such as "Prizes courtesy of . . ." and "Promotional fees paid by . . ." identify the donors.

**FIG. 9.4. Animation.** Toucan Sam® and his family help sell Kellogg's® Froot Loops® cereal. (Kellogg's®, Froot Loops®, Toucan Sam® and character design are registered trademarks of Kellogg Company. Used with permission.)

***9.1.6.9 Illegal Promotion of Recordings: Payola.*** **Payola** is payment by a record company to a disc jockey for playing the company's records. Again, neither audience nor station is aware of the payment. Plugola and payola are both illegal and unethical (*PRT,* 2.3.3.3 and 3.3.1), but evidence of both surfaces from time to time.

### 9.1.7 Classified by Production Medium

Radio announcements may be **live** or on **tape.** Sometimes an announcement will **combine** elements—for example, a co-op commercial produced on tape by the national manufacturer's ad agency followed by a live tag giving the local dealer's name.

Television announcements may be on **videotape, film, slides, live,** or some combination. A co-op TV ad could consist of a manufacturer-supplied film commercial of the product followed by a frame displaying local dealer information with a booth announcer reading additional copy, all recorded on videotape.

### 9.1.8 Classified by Production Mode

In radio, a **straight announcement** features an announcer reading copy with no production frills. A **production announcement** mixes in sound effects, music, and multiple voices. On a **musical announcement** or jingle, people sing the ad message. Radio announcements often combine multiple production techniques.

In the TV **on-camera talent** technique, the performer speaks and is in view; in **voice-over,** the speaker does not appear on screen. Either technique may be used with realistic or nonrealistic action. **Realistic action** features real people. Nonrealistic action often takes the form of animation. **Animation** includes various kinds of animated art—cartoon characters (Fig. 9.4), products designed as cartoon characters reeling through space, flying letters and moving charts, two-dimensional models with moving parts. It may consist of "real" but normally inanimate objects moving in physically impossible ways—all of it fanciful animation recruited to sell us products on the screens of our TV sets.[4] Another production technique is to use a series of **still pictures.** Of course, one announcement may combine several production techniques; for example, realistic action combined with animation.

## 9.2 CREATIVITY IN ANNOUNCEMENTS

Although marketing may claim to be a science, much of advertising is still art. The effectiveness of an announcement depends largely on the creative elements that make it up—format, appeals, approach, and production skill.

### 9.2.1 Announcement Formats

The format of an announcement is the way the message is presented. Formats include description, demonstration, problem, dramatic, spokesperson, testimonial, endorsement, interview, program, cross-promotion, suggestion, symbolic, and abstract.

*9.2.1.1 Description Format.*   A **description format** announcement simply describes the product. It explains, for example, what the product can do for you, why your help is needed, what the product's properties are, and how it works.

*9.2.1.2 Demonstration Format.*   The **demonstration format** shows what the product is or does. It shows, for example, how the product coats the stomach, what a $1 donation will do, what a furniture company's 30-day delivery policy can mean, or how batteries in the Energizer bunny just keep going and going and going . . .

*9.2.1.3 Problem Format.*   The **problem announcement** poses a problem with which the audience can identify and shows how the product solves that problem. You are an adolescent, for example, who has problems with acne; the solution suggested by a TV commercial: Use Stridex Super Size Medicated Pads.

***9.2.1.4 Dramatic Format.***    The **dramatic format** (also called slice-of-life) is often based on a problem, too, but it sets up the problem within a miniature dramatic plot. In the mid-1990s we saw a series of dramatic commercials that simulated a developing, soap-opera-like boy-meets-girl situation to advertise Tasters Choice coffee. In a similar commercial series, we saw two people who almost did not meet finally get together with the help of MCI One cellular telephone service.

***9.2.1.5 Spokesperson Format.***    In some announcements a recognized **spokesperson extols the product.** Ed Reimers, Ed McMahon, and Arthur Godfrey were for years associated with Allstate Insurance, Budweiser, and Lipton Tea, respectively. During the 1980s the late John Houseman, a writer/director/actor with a distinctively authoritative voice, appeared in commercials for Smith Barney. More recently, Dr. Stanley Pearle has appeared on commercials for Pearle Vision, David Oreck has touted his Oreck Vacuum Cleaners, Tom Bodette promised to "leave the light on for ya'" at Motel 6, Candice Bergen promoted Sprint, and Whoopi Goldberg promoted MCI long-distance telephone services.

***9.2.1.6 Testimonial and Endorsement Formats.***    The **testimonial** format features individuals describing personal experiences with the product. The testimony may be given by a famous person, by an expert (such as Bob Vila who promoted Sears hand tools), or by a citizen unknown to most (such as "Dr. Christine Dresser, veterinarian and top breeder of champion pugs," who recommended Pedigree dog food). Closely related is the **endorsement** format. Endorsements usually involve celebrities, such as race car driver Alec Zanardi recommending Target Stores. Endorsements trumpet advantages of the advertised products, but the implicit pitch is that we should use them because the celebrity tells us to! As noted in *PRT,* 9.2.1.8, program-length commercials often utilize the celebrity endorsement format.

***9.2.1.7 Interview Format.***    In the **interview format** one person asks questions and another responds. Campbell's Soup used this format on radio commercials during the late 1970s: An announcer telephoned homemakers and got them to sing the Campbell's theme song. In two 1990s commercial series, off-camera interviewers convinced various people to try then comment on Sweet Rewards and Hamburger Helper (Fig. 9.5) from Betty Crocker.

***9.2.1.8 Program Format.***    With the rise in numbers of infomercials (Fig. 9.1) has come the rise of the **program format** for the program-length commercials. Some infomercials unabashedly copy program formats, often some variation of the talk show, complete with studio audience (whose members clap, laugh, cheer, and otherwise react on cue), host–guest setups, and often even celebrity "stars" as guests. Robert Vaughn, for example, has pitched for The Helsinki Formula hair renewer; Cher for Laurie Davis Hair Products; Pat Boone and Mike Ditka for

**FIG. 9.5. Interview format.** These two liked Hamburger Helper®. (Used by permission of General Mills, Inc., Brenda M. Davis, and DeWayne Ferris.)

MDR Fitness Tabs; Dennis Weaver for Autofom [*sic*] car wax; and Latoya Jackson for the Psychic Network.

***9.2.1.9 Cross-Promotion Format.*** An increasing number of announcements actually **advertise two or more different entities**. Many companies, for example, pay to link their names with the Olympic games. Every 4 years TV screens fill with commercials that, in effect, advertise both the wares of these firms and the Olympics. Advertisers tie in with high-profile motion pictures, especially those that offer marketing opportunities, such as many of the films from the Walt Disney Company.

***9.2.1.10 Suggestion Format.*** The **suggestion format** takes an oblique approach. Instead of emphasizing a product's merits, the commercial shows it being used in happy or desirable settings or associates it with a particular way of life. Back when cigarette commercials were legal (*PRT,* 3.1.4), tobacco firms often advertised this way. The Marlboro man and Salem's cool glades and icy springs sold many more packs than would any straightforward description of the actual benefits of drawing carcinogenic smoke from a burning weed into the lungs. Coca-Cola used suggestion cleverly and successfully (from the hippie/love/peace symbolism of its 1970s "I'd like to teach the world to sing . . ." commercials to the more recent image of an elephant swimming in the ocean) to sell its carbonated beverage. One 1990s commercial depicted a romantically inclined young man and woman in a beach setting to associate use of Finesse Shampoo with being beautiful and sexy; another used a montage of images showing young people doing various things and apparently having a good time to advertise jeans from J. C. Penney.

*9.2.1.11 Symbolic Format.*    The symbolic format uses analogy, representing traits of the product by featuring completely different objects. Animals have been particularly popular. In 1960s television commercials for the Dreyfus Fund, a lion strolled through New York's financial district and finally jumped onto and became part of the company's logo, representing the strength and solidity of that mutual fund. Cattle were popular in the 1980s; bulls, for example, appeared in ads for Schlitz malt liquor and Merrill Lynch. In a 1990s commercial General Motors used one of the great American symbols; the Statue of Liberty bent down to take a closer look at the Oldsmobile Aurora. Another spot depicted New York's financial district with water "streets" navigated by yachts, luxury ships, and a BMW.

*9.2.1.12 Abstract Format.*    A final production format is best described as **abstract.** Advertisers use unconventional editing, the synthesizer, digital effects, and computer animation to produce acoustically or graphically offbeat ads. They do so to appeal to young audiences, to portray the product as innovative, and to depict concepts and forces in abstract symbols. Exciting at first, repetitive use of this production style in countless music videos eventually made it almost a cliché.

### 9.2.2 Announcement Appeals

Appeals are implicit or explicit arguments used to get the attention of the audience. Most of us share certain psychological needs, and an announcement plays on these. An insurance company's TV commercial shows a family breadwinner ill or incapacitated and asks, "How well would your family be provided for if you were not able to work?" The commercial then urges that you ensure such provision by taking out a policy with the company. The commercial targets your desire for security.

There are many ways to categorize the various motivational needs and urges to which commercials appeal. Heighton and Cunningham[5] listed one set of categories: **security, threat, sex, love and sentimental, humorous, convenience, curiosity, ego, hero worship,** and **sensory.** Usually, an emotional appeal by itself does not persuade; facts and arguments must be presented to support and augment the appeal.

### 9.2.3 Announcement Approaches

The approach is the way the appeal and its supporting data are presented. Approaches include straightforward, hard sell, direct humor, self-ridicule and understatement, direct comparison, and suggestion.

*9.2.3.1 Straightforward Approach.*   The most effective approach is often the simplest, **straightforward** approach. This approach just presents persuasive arguments and data—no yelling, humor, or comparisons.

*9.2.3.2 Hard Sell Approach.*   Adherents of the **hard sell** contend it is particularly effective for brand name recall. The hard sell is a high-pressure, unrelenting pounding at the audience with persuasive data and repetition. In hard-sell ads the audio sounds even louder than most commercials, and there is a lot of copy read by the announcer. TV hard-sell ads often flash key words and phrases on the screen as the announcer says them, and they pound home the sales point with simplistic diagrams and demonstrations. Local automobile and mobile home dealers (Fig. 9.2) often use the hard sell for their commercials, some variation on "I'm ready to deal! *Deal!* Yes, I said DEAL!"

*9.2.3.3 Direct Humor Approach.*   Another approach is to use **direct humor.** Over the years, Alka Seltzer has been particularly successful at using direct humor in TV commercials. Alka Seltzer's "Stomachs," "Meatball Commercial" ("Mama mia, that's a spicy meatball!"), "I can't believe I ate that whole thing," and "Try it; you'll like it" all became classics of commercial humor. Humorous TV commercials for Wendy's Old-Fashioned Hamburgers, generated a national catch phrase—"Where's the beef?" Much later Bud Light commercials featuring a young man talking his way into a limousine (after first ensuring it was stocked with Bud Light) made "Yes . . . I am!" a national catch phrase. In a Bud Ice commercial, we saw a penguin get beer. In a Pepto Bismol commercial, we saw a man get nauseated after a nearly endless parade of birthday sweets. One of the most memorable series of humorous commercials was that for, again, the Energizer bunny, particularly those that looked like commercials for other products and were then interrupted by the rabbit.

*9.2.3.4 Self-Ridicule or Understatement Approach.*   Closely related to direct humor is **self-ridicule** or **understatement.** Benson and Hedges ran a TV ad series showing the disadvantages of smoking their long cigarettes—they bent or burned a hole when the smoker got too close to some object. This campaign continued in print long after cigarette advertising left the air in 1972.

*9.2.3.5 Direct Comparison Approach.*   Until the late 1960s commercials for a product never mentioned the name of a rival product. Advertisers assumed that if the audience saw or heard a competitor's name, that was free advertising for the competition. Comparisons were made between the advertiser's product and "Brand X" or "the other two leading manufacturers" or "greasy kid stuff" or "the high-priced spread." Most advertisers abandoned this simplistic view of consumer psychology, and commercials now do occasionally compare a product to its rival by name (Fig. 9.6). Two well-known comparative-commercial series were those by Schick for its Flexomatic electric shaver, challenged by competitors before an

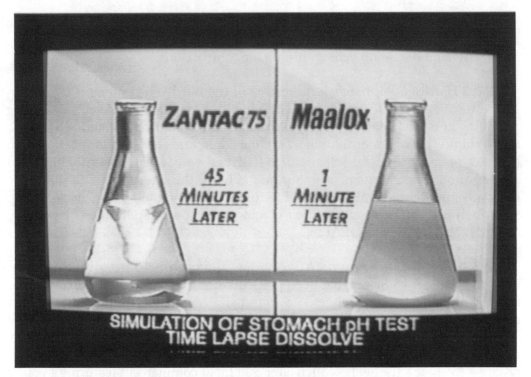

**FIG. 9.6. Direct comparison approach.** The antacid (Maalox) neutralizes acid in 1 minute, whereas the acid controller (Zantac 75) does not affect acid in 45 minutes. (Used by permission of Novartis Consumer Health, Inc.)

advertising self-regulatory group in 1973, and those by Coca-Cola and Pepsi Cola, comparing the two beverages by taste test, which led to a comparative ad battle in 1976. Twenty years later long-distance telephone carriers went head to head, using TV ads to explain why, for example, you could save money by switching from AT&T to MCI, or got better service by switching from MCI back to AT&T.

**9.2.3.6 Suggestion Approach.** The **suggestion approach** is part and parcel of the suggestion format (*PRT,* 9.2.1.10). Here, the announcement features something intangible, often not an intrinsic part of the product. It suggests (Fig. 9.7) without actually saying that use of the product leads to the good life, or sexual attractiveness, or power and domination over others.

### 9.3 CREATION AND PRODUCTION

The history of an announcement begins with the ad campaign of which the announcement is part. We illustrate with a national campaign, a complex situation compared to, say, the corner hardware store advertising a special on local radio.

The advertiser has secured the services of an ad agency (*PRT,* 17.1.5) and established a budget for the campaign. The agency analyzes the product that is to be advertised. The analysis asks and answers questions about the product: What

**FIG. 9.7. Suggestion approach.** One 1990s Nissan commercial series said nothing about handling, braking, acceleration, fuel efficiency, safety features, or any other aspect by which one might judge an automobile. Instead, these commercials showed a mysterious bespectacled man and a little dog, suggesting . . . ? (Copyright © Nissan, 1996. Nissan and the Nissan logo are registed trademarks of Nissan.)

is it? What does it do? How is it better than its competitors? At the same time, the agency also analyzes the product's buyers: Who are they? What is their lifestyle? When do they buy? Where? This study involves use of sophisticated and often expensive **marketing research,** both qualitative and quantitative (*PRT,* 27.1.1), and is carried on before, during, and after an advertising campaign.

After analysis of the research data on product and buyers, **advertising objectives** are formulated. These objectives do not aim toward goals such as increasing sales by 15% or share of the market by 5%. These are marketing goals. Advertising is certainly one way to work toward a marketing goal, but advertising objectives reach toward communication goals, such as introducing a new product, suggesting new uses for an old product, or publicizing a new feature of an existing product.

After objectives are defined, **strategies** are planned to meet those objectives. Campaign strategies include at least the following: devising content and form of messages, choosing the target audience at which to aim the messages, and selecting media to deliver messages to the audience. As a result of the first strategy, a **copy policy** (or **copy platform** or **campaign platform**) is developed. The copy policy guides the creation of advertising in all media; it states the theme or idea of the campaign, consumer appeals, and significant product characteristics.

The second strategy results in a **consumer profile,** a detailed analysis of the target audience by factors such as age, sex, lifestyle, buying habits, and education. The third strategy, the **media strategy,** builds a **media profile** to match the consumer profile. The media profile indicates media that will deliver the message to the target audience—this kind of direct mail; that type of magazine; newspapers and spot TV in these areas; spot radio on this format in those markets; participating ads during that daypart on network TV and cable; sponsorship of this special on network, cable, or barter syndication.

The agency prepares the **campaign plan** for presentation to the advertiser client. The plan includes general strategy and concepts and creative, media, and marketing recommendations. Storyboards, commercials, layouts, and copy are presented. If the plan is approved (usually with client-suggested changes), **media buying** begins. After careful study, the agency recommends specific media. In radio and TV this means specific stations, cable systems, cable interconnects, broadcast networks, national cable services, times, and programs. The agency prepares a schedule and, on client approval, negotiates contracts for purchase of ad time.

Agency writers develop commercials. They work from the copy platform, the advertising objectives, the campaign role assigned to radio and TV, and the product, its buyers, and other market data. Storyboards and sometimes even precommercials are prepared to help the client visualize how the TV commercial will look. Fact sheets may be created for certain radio stations. A **storyboard** represents each scene of the planned commercial with a small sketch, below which is typed dialogue, sound, and a description of action. A **precommercial,** an actual production of the commercial done by the agency on its own videotape equipment, is not broadcast quality and so is not used on the air. A **fact sheet** is not a complete script but contains only key facts on the product or service. Fact sheets are supplied to radio personalities who are effective at ad-libbing commercials.

### 9.3.1 Production of Radio Commercials

The entity that produces a radio commercial varies with the situation. In small markets and for small retailers, the **radio station** may produce local ads at no charge beyond that for broadcast time. The corner hardware store owner, for example, might deal directly with station sales personnel; no agency is involved. Station staff produces and broadcasts the ad. Sometimes the announcer will read a commercial live each time.

Most large advertisers have radio commercials professionally produced and sent to stations for use. In this case, the ad agency either puts the job out for bids to production houses or handles the production itself. A **production house** does all creative work. Often this even includes the script, based of course on the copy platform and subject to agency and advertiser approval. If done in-house, the script is written at the agency. A staff **producer/director** handles creative arrangements and talent—auditioning and hiring talent, contracting for original music, and securing musicians and a music director. Completed, taped, client-approved commercials are sent to radio stations.

### 9.3.2 Production of Television Commercials

Before a TV commercial begins production, the advertiser client must approve the storyboard. The ad agency production supervisor then writes a **spec** (specification) **sheet** describing the commercial and its production requirements and puts the project out for bids to selected **production houses.** The production houses submit **bids,** statements of how much money they would need to produce the commercial. The agency usually accepts the low bid, subject to negotiation over certain cost factors.

Once the client approves the agency's bid recommendation, representatives from the agency and production house meet to iron out preproduction details—set design, location, director, talent, and crew. An agency representative is designated producer. Agency producer and contract director work closely during production. The commercial is completed during postproduction then duplicated, and copies are sent to networks, stations, cable systems, and other selected outlets. Many firms use satellite to distribute finished ads to stations and cable systems.

At the local level, production may be handled by the **media outlet**—TV station, cable system, or whatever. Local outlets usually rent facilities at bargain prices (relative to costs of large-market production houses). A locally produced commercial rarely has the same high quality and slickness as one produced by a large production house. However, the savings for local advertisers may more than make up for the loss of slickness.

## 9.4 ADVERTISING COUNCIL

Established as the War Advertising Council in 1942, the Advertising Council reorganized under its present name after World War II. Its constituent and sponsoring organizations include major advertising and media trade groups. The Ad Council selects noncommercial organizations as clients, for which ad campaigns are prepared as a public service. Ad agencies donate services to the Ad Council, and each volunteer agency is assigned a client for which to plan and execute a campaign. The client pays only for materials—art work, engraving, printing, paper, tape, and slides. The media carry the campaign for free. Materials may cost up to several hundred thousand dollars yearly, but this out-of-pocket expenditure by a client yields millions of dollars worth of advertising and publicity. Ad Council campaigns have created memorable symbols and slogans—Smokey the Bear; Iron Eyes Cody, the Indian whose eyes brimmed with a single tear; and A Mind is a Terrible Thing to Waste. Some of radio and television's finest minutes have been Ad Council-produced PSAs (Fig. 9.8).

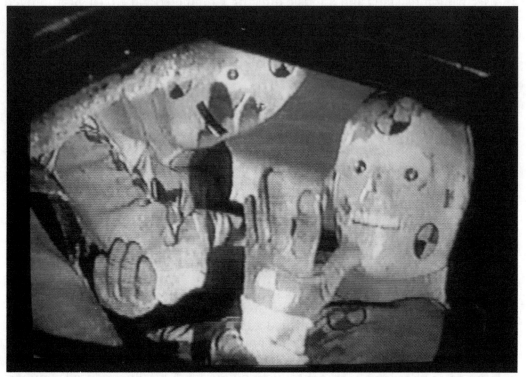

**FIG. 9.8. Ad Council PSAs.** These PSAs, promoting awareness of the automobile seat belt law, featured two crash test dummies who did not wear seat belts and suffered the consequences. They illustrated the theme, "Remember, you could learn a lot from a dummy. Buckle your safety belt." (Used by permission of The Advertising Council.)

Stations and cable systems also produce PSAs. They run these for local charities and other good causes.

### 9.5 CRITICISM

Commercials are the announcements most often criticized. This is understandable. On U.S. radio and TV, commercials are ubiquitous, frequent, interruptive, intense, repetitious, unavoidable, packed with highly persuasive elements, and often the product of what many see as large, profit-at-any-cost firms.

In print, the audience controls the situation. You choose whether and when to read newspaper or magazine ads. In radio and TV, the medium controls the situation. Without a remote control, you endure all advertising on the channel you view. You switch to another channel only to find more commercials. If you turn off the set or leave the room, you miss the program. Any feature that conspicuous and unavoidable on media as popular as radio and TV is bound to be criticized. A great deal of criticism is leveled at TV ads, particularly, because TV is the more popular and attention-getting medium.

Critics fault commercials for **lying,** for making claims that are not true. A commercial might, for example, misrepresent some feature of a product or service. It might falsely describe an advertiser's financial situation or ability to do business. It might feature bait-and-switch advertising.[6] Local and federal authorities, better business bureaus, and others bear down hard on false advertising, and there is relatively little outright lying on commercials.

**Puffery,** however, is another matter. Puffery is use of superlatives and general terms—*new, improved,* and *works wonders.* It is the half-lie, telling only good points about a product, making good points even better, and not mentioning negative aspects. The FTC allows advertisers latitude in claims on subjective aspects—feel, smell, taste, and appearance. At the same time the FTC requires advertisers to verify claims about performance, quality, safety, effectiveness, or comparative price. Advertisers who tout products as "number one in performance" or "more effective than the three leading competitors" must define terms and prove claims.

Somewhere between lying and puffery goes the **false demonstration.** Here, special techniques are used during production to show that a product has certain qualities, although in reality the product is not like or will not do exactly what the commercial purports to show. Two notorious false demonstrations took place on television commercials for Rapid Shave and Libbey-Owens-Ford autoglass (*PRT,* 14.2.2).

Critics complain that commercials assume and aim at insultingly **low intellectual levels.** Wording, repetition, arguments, and format—every element seems to patronize audiences.

Many object to the **salience** of commercials, their unavoidable conspicuousness. Salience embodies three elements—number of interruptions per program, clutter, and loudness. As for **number,** there actually is a high ratio of commercial minutes to program time. The now defunct NAB Television Code allowed stations to program over 25% of every hour during most of the day in commercials, promos, and other nonprogram content. The Radio Code allowed 30%, with provision for even more in special circumstances. The FCC adopted restrictions on commercial time similar to those of the NAB Codes. However the Codes are gone, and the Commission repealed its restrictions, so broadcasters no longer have even these liberal restrictions on total commercial time. Stations may now cram in as many minutes of commercials as they feel the audience will tolerate. The cable business, of course, never had a code that restricted commercial minutes.

As for complaints about the **number of interruptions,** again there does seem to be justification. The Television Code did place some restrictions on the number of interruptions and the number of commercials per interruption. Even then, advertisers and audience complained of **clutter,** too many different ads during each program interruption. Advertisers said that clutter caused their messages to get lost and forgotten among the sea of other commercials at each break. The audience just felt there were too many. With the codes gone, there is no businesswide limitation, and both the number of program interruptions and the number of announcements within each interruption have steadily increased.

Women's and minority groups have complained that commercials **reinforce negative stereotypes.** For years, ads showed women as dependent on men, concerned mainly with children and household, unable to cope with financial or mechanical complexities, valued primarily as ornaments or sex objects, and, when seen in roles other than housekeeper, employed as secretaries and teachers. Commercials rarely included racial and ethnic minorities except in highly stereotyped roles—servants, cooks, and peons who were lazy, shuffling, inscrutable, or wearing sombreros.

Since the early 1970s advertisers have attempted to rid commercials of objectionable depictions. They contend, however, that some stereotypes are needed to set up and resolve a situation in 15 or 30 seconds. So we still see a TV commercial world in which middle-class families buy hamburgers, fried chicken, and new automobiles; and women worry about clean clothes and shiny floors and succumb to men wearing after-shave lotions.

Consumer groups say commercials attempt to sell products to the wrong people or to sell the **wrong products** to all people. Critics have cited commercials for selling toys, junk food, and vitamins (fatal if swallowed in large doses) to children; for selling quack medicines, nostrums, useless gadgets, and religious charlatans to those least able to afford them (the old and poor and minority ethnic groups); and for selling large cars and leaded gasoline (which contribute to air pollution), cigarettes, and over-the-counter drugs to everybody.

Critics question **values** that commercials promulgate. Commercials teach, goes the argument, the values, philosophies, and behaviors they depict, values that may be dysfunctional; that is, work toward undesirable goals for both the individual and society. Commercials teach that it is good to be acquisitive, highly competitive, and conscious of status. They teach narcissism and that physical beauty is an end in itself. They teach us to take a pill when we feel bad, to see issues—no matter how complex—in simplistic terms, to think in slogans, to look no farther than the surface, and to aim for a Ken-and-Barbie doll existence of eternal, middle-class, plastic-wrapped youth.

Many persons criticize the **way commercials appeal to certain human motivations.** In the 1973 *CBS Reports: You and the Commercial,* Dr. Eric Fromm, the late well-known psychoanalyst, noted that commercials often use as motivation the fear of not being loved—attributable to body odor or split ends or baggy panty hose—that some product promises to alleviate. A second and related theme is the miracle; use this soap or that cooking oil and a miracle will happen. Commercials imply that love depends on a gadget: Use the advertised gadget, and attain the good life. Commercials promise that the product will turn us into beautiful, young people who never change. Fromm also said advertising molds us, makes us greedy, and makes us *want* more and more instead of trying to *be* more and more.

Commercials do not convince, Fromm said; they suggest. *Convincing* attempts to persuade through rational argument. *Suggesting* breaks down rationality to get audiences to believe the promises of commercials. Therefore, concluded Fromm, people know on a rational basis that claims for the products are nonsense, but at the same time they would like to hope there might be something to the claims. The result is a mixture of reality and fantasy that operates on the subconscious level.

Although most criticism is directed at commercials, PSAs have also come under fire. In 1976 public service groups and sympathizers in Congress petitioned the FCC to require that broadcasters air PSAs from a wider variety of sources. Over 70 disparate parties called for new rules, including Action for Children's Television, Sierra Club, National Gay Task Force, Public Media Center, and the United Church of Christ (UCC). The UCC commented that licensees had abdicated responsibility for PSAs to outside agencies, such as the Ad Council, which provide broadcasters with slick, noncontroversial PSAs. (See *PRT,* 22.5, for complaints about public broadcasting announcements.)

### 9.6 PRAISE

Not all words spoken about commercials are critical. For example, there is no doubt that, well done, electronic mass media advertising is effective. People who successfully use radio and TV ads are among the first to praise commercial announcements.

The skill and imagination of some commercials must be admired. Commercials are among the most carefully crafted radio–TV productions. Their original use of props, actors, animals, locations, special effects, computer-generated graphics and animation, and other elements to translate the fantasies of a copy writer into 30 seconds of sales pitch is legend. The Clio, cousin to the Oscar and the Emmy, is awarded annually to the winning commercial in each of several categories based on cleverness and artistry.

The skilled personnel and persuasive techniques honed on advertising are used to create public service messages designed to improve the common good. The success of Ad Council campaigns is due almost entirely to the selling skills of its agencies. Let us not forget, too, that advertising pays for programming on commercial channels. The music, the stars, and the news operations are all financed by advertising dollars. Even some programming on public broadcasting is funded by advertising or restricted forms of advertising (*PRT,* 22.5).

Finally, commercials, as integral parts of advertising, serve as key forces in the U.S. economy. Our economy is based in large part on mass production, mass distribution, and mass consumption. Commercials and the rest of advertising are vital to the maintenance of such an economic system.

### NOTES

1. FCC, Program Length Commercials, 26 R.R.2d 1023 (1973).
2. In re Wilderness Society and Friends of the Earth, 30 F.C.C.2d 643 (1971).

3. Warner-Lambert v. FTC, 562 F.2d 749, certiorari denied, 435 U.S. 950 (1978).

4. At one time, commercial producers used claymation and stop-motion (filming one frame at a time) techniques to achieve such effects—Pillsbury's Poppin' Fresh doughboy and various raisins, stomachs, and other commercial anthropomorphisms. Some still do, but most have embraced computer animation, and their settings and subjects exist only as digital signals on a hard drive.

5. Elizabeth J. Heighton and Don R. Cunningham, *Advertising in the Broadcast and Cable Media,* 2nd ed. (Belmont, CA: Wadsworth, 1984), 106–118.

6. The bait (often a bargain price advertised for a particular product) lures you into a store, whose personnel pull the switch (attempt to sell you a higher priced model once you are there).

## FURTHER READING

Book, Albert C. *The Radio and Television Commercial.* 3rd ed. Lincolnwood, IL: NTC Business Books, 1995.

Brady, Frank R., and J. Angel Vasquez. *Direct Response Television: The Authoritative Guide.* Lincolnwood, IL: NTC Business Books, 1995.

Dayan, Daniel. *Media Events: The Live Broadcasting of History.* Cambridge, MA: Harvard University Press, 1992.

Diamond, Edwin, and Stephen Bates. *The Spot: The Rise of Political Advertising on Television.* 3rd ed. Cambridge, MA: MIT Press, 1992.

Eicoff, Alvin. *Direct Marketing Through Broadcast Media: TV, Radio, Cable, Infomercials, Home Shopping & More.* Lincolnwood, IL: NTC Business Books, 1995.

Evans, Craig Robert. *Marketing Channels: Infomercials, and the Future of Televised Marketing.* Englewood Cliffs, NJ: Prentice-Hall, 1994.

Hagerman, William L. *Broadcast Advertising Copywriting.* Boston: Focal, 1990.

Hammelstein, Hal. *Television Myth and the American Mind.* 2nd ed. Westport, CT: Praeger, 1994.

Hampe, Barry. *Video Scriptwriting: How to Write for the $4 Billion Commercial Video Market.* New York: Plume, 1993.

Hughes, Elizabeth M. B. *The Logical Choice: How Political Commercials Use Logic to Win Votes.* Lanham, MD: University Press of America, 1994.

Kline, Stephen. *Out of the Garden: Toys, TV, and Children's Culture in the Age of Marketing.* New York: Verso, 1993.

Meeske, Milan D., and R. C. Noriss. *Copywriting for the Electronic Media: A Practical Guide.* 2nd ed. Belmont, CA: Wadsworth, 1992.

Orlik, Peter B. *Broadcast/Cable Copywriting.* 5th ed. Boston: Allyn & Bacon, 1994.

Rutherford, Paul. *The New Icons? The Art of Television Advertising.* Toronto: University of Toronto Press, 1994.

Savan, Leslie. *The Sponsored Life: Ads, TV, and American Culture.* Philadelphia: Temple University Press, 1994.

Schihl, Robert J. *Television Commercial Processes and Procedures.* Boston: Focal, 1992.

Schulberg, Peter. *Radio Advertising: The Authoritative Handbook.* Lincolnwood, IL: NTC Business Books, 1996.

Thompson, J. Walter Company. *A Look at 15-Second Commercials in the 90s.* New York: Author, 1990.

Weinbarger, Marc G., Leland Campbell, and Beth Brody. *Effective Radio Advertising.* New York: Lexington, 1994.

White, Barton. *The New Ad Media Reality: Electronic Over Print.* Westport, CT: Quorum, 1993.

White, Hooper. *How to Produce Effective TV Commercials.* 3rd ed. Lincolnwood, IL: NTC Business Books, 1994.

# III

## Physical Perspective

Broadcasting was the first nonmechanical mass medium. Printing, recording, and cinema each originated from different technological devices. All, however, were mechanical contrivances.

Broadcasting's bases—electronics and electromagnetic radiation—were radically different from those of older media, so different they even involved a different branch of physics. These physical bases have, in turn, affected all other aspects of broadcasting, from audience size to station licensing. The fact that broadcasting travels by electromagnetic energy, energy that has certain properties, has profoundly affected the history, regulation, and economics of radio and television, including cable and other nonbroadcast forms of radio and television. If you are going to understand radio and television, you must understand those physical properties.

We begin this section with a review of radio energy in chapter 10. We look at its nature and some of its propagation characteristics. In chapter 11, we survey the physical aspects of aural media—sound and audio, AM and FM, and other radio services. We conclude the section with chapter 12 by examining the workings of television and other electronic visual media, from light and the human eye through video and various video services.

# 10

# RADIO ENERGY

Programs from broadcast stations, multipoint distribution service (MDS), and direct broadcast satellites (DBS) are radiated from a transmitting antenna and sent to your receiver via radio energy. You cannot smell, feel, or see it, yet radio energy is the basis on which the entire structures of the electronic media are built. To a large extent, the peculiar characteristics of radio energy determine how these media are organized—the frequencies assigned to transmitters, the power they may use, their physical location, and their very licensed status. In this chapter, we examine the concept of radio energy waves and then the various characteristics of waves in different frequency bands. The term *radio* is used here in the generic sense to include television, microwave, and other such transmissions.

## 10.1 WAVES

Imagine that you hold one end of a long rope. Shake the rope rapidly up and down. Your arm's oscillation sets up a wave motion that travels the length of the rope. Hit a water glass with a spoon, and the glass vibrates, creating waves of sound that you can hear.

Radio waves, too, result from **oscillation.** Unlike the rope waves and the sound waves, however, radio waves require no material medium (such as a rope or molecules of air) for transmission. They can travel not only in the earth's atmosphere but also in the near vacuum of space.

A radio transmitter produces radio waves by feeding an oscillating form of electric current into a transmitting antenna. The current alternates direction of flow, first in one direction, then the other. Each change of direction is a half cycle. Two successive half cycles, one in each direction, make one complete oscillation or **cycle** (Fig. 10.1). Called **alternating current** (AC), this form of electricity includes normal household current that flows at a rate of 60 cycles per second. The rate for radio transmission, however is much higher, usually above 400,000 cycles per second.

In the transmitting antenna, the electric current creates coexistent **electrical** and **magnetic fields of force** around the antenna (Fig. 10.2). The direction in which the current flows determines the direction toward which these fields' lines

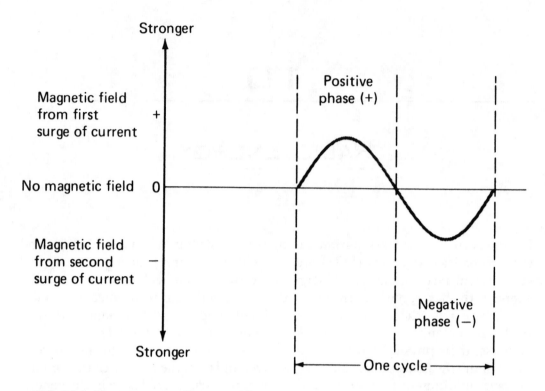

**FIG. 10.1. Sine wave as radio wave.** The sine wave is a graphic representation of a radio wave. (To further confuse things, the sine wave is also used to represent the radio-frequency current that generates the radio waves, the audio that modulates the radio frequency, the sound waves that cause audio, and the vibration of the sound source from which the sound waves originate.)

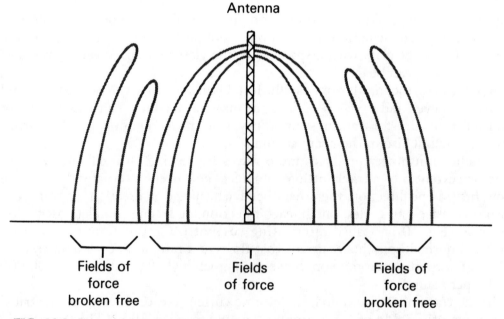

**FIG. 10.2. Lines of force radiating from antenna.** If the frequency of the AC is high enough, the fields of force break free and continue to travel as electromagnetic waves.

of force point; that is, their **polarity**. When the AC in the antenna reverses direction, it creates new electrical and magnetic fields around the antenna. These new fields, opposite in polarity, push the old fields away from the antenna. The AC again reverses direction, and the whole process starts over.

Because newly created fields push previous fields away from the antenna, they continually radiate outward. Two successive sets of electrical and magnetic fields of force—the **positive phase** and the **negative phase**, according to their respective polarity—constitute one radio wave.

The strength or **amplitude** (Fig. 10.3) of the AC in the transmitting antenna determines the strength of the radiated waves. The amplitude of the waves, in turn, determines the strength of the signal you get on your receiver.

At the receiving end, radio waves are "picked up" with yet another antenna. They **induce** (cause) in the receiving antenna a pattern of AC exactly like the oscillations in the transmitting antenna, although of much lower amplitude.

### 10.1.1 Attenuation

As they travel, radio waves **attenuate** (lose strength) for a number of reasons. This is illustrated in Fig. 10.4. A radio wave radiates outward from a transmitting antenna. As the wave travels, the circle becomes larger and the wave spreads itself ever more thinly, diminishing amplitude as it covers greater area. Eventually, the point is reached at which amplitude is so low that, for purposes of reception, there is no more wave. This is when the signal fades on your radio or television receiver.

Certain structures and electrical interference (particularly in cities) and terrain obstacles may create **dead spots** within a station's coverage area; that is, places where you should be able to receive the station but cannot. **Overlapping signals** or **interference** occur when the radio waves from one station collide with and distort or weaken those from another.

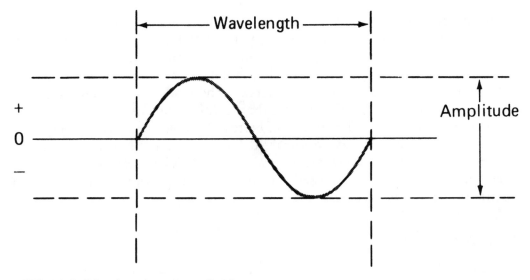

FIG. 10.3. Wavelength and amplitude.

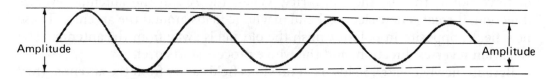

FIG. 10.4. Attenuation.

**Absorption** involves expenditure of energy by a wave as it travels. When radio waves travel through a vacuum, there is little absorption. But in anything denser, such as the earth's atmosphere, radio waves lose energy. The denser the medium, the more absorption occurs. In AM radio, for example, the earth conducts (i.e., allows to travel) the ground wave (*PRT*, 10.2.3.1), but it also absorbs much of the wave's energy. The ground waves of even the most powerful U.S. AM radio stations, operating with 50,000 watts of power and no interference, lose most of their punch after about 100 miles of travel. Sky waves, on the other hand, do not undergo much absorption. If the transmission is powerful and meets with minimal interference, its sky waves may bounce from the ionosphere to earth and back again to deliver powerful, clear signals thousands of miles away.

### 10.1.2 Velocity

Radio energy has a **velocity** of (i.e., it travels at) 300 million meters—186,000 miles—per second in a vacuum (it travels somewhat slower in the atmosphere). That figure should sound familiar; it is the speed of light. All electromagnetic energy (including radio waves and visible light) travels at that speed.

### 10.1.3 Frequency

Transmitters emit radio waves at a rate of thousands and millions per second, the exact rate varying according to service (AM or FM radio, TV broadcast, MDS, etc.). The number of waves a transmitter emits per second is, of course, determined by the number of cycles per second of alternating electrical current energy flowing to the transmitting antenna. The term **hertz** has been adopted as a name for cycles per second, honoring Heinrich Hertz, the scientist who first demonstrated the existence of radio waves. The number of hertz a station generates is its **frequency**. Because such large numbers are involved, prefixes are used as shortcuts; **kilo-** means times 1,000, and **mega-** means times 1,000,000. Thus 850 kilohertz (kHz) would be 850,000 cycles per second and 98.3 megahertz (MHz) would be 98,300,000 cycles per second.

### 10.1.4 Wavelength

Because radio energy velocity is constant, the only way to increase frequency (number of cycles/waves per second) is to shorten **wavelength** (Fig. 10.5). This

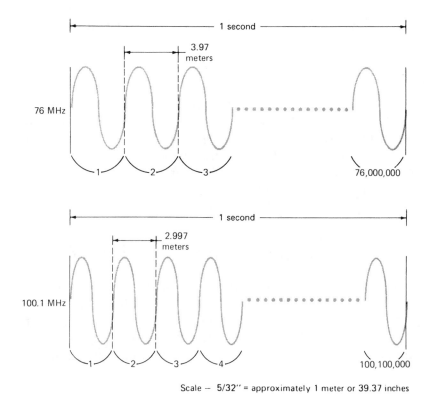

**FIG. 10.5. Frequency and wavelength.** Because velocity is constant, the only way to increase frequency (say from 7.6 MHz to 100.1 MHz) is to decrease wavelength (here, from 3.97 meters to 2.997 meters).

is easy to illustrate. Draw a horizontal line 3 inches long. Now use it as the middle line, and draw on it three sine waves (backwards Ss, lying on their sides) representing three radio waves, each of equal length, so that they take up the whole space. How long will each sine wave have to be? Obviously, 1 inch. Now draw another line 3 inches long, and put four sine waves on it. This time each will have to be ¾ inch long. You have to shorten wavelength to get more waves in the same 3-inch space.

Now, reread the previous sentence, substituting *time* for *3-inch space,* and the same principle applies—**speed being constant at all frequencies and wavelengths, you have to shorten the wavelength to get more waves** (i.e., to increase frequency) **in the same time period.** If you are confused at this point, just remember "longer and lower"—the longer the wave, the lower the frequency. The converse holds, too—the shorter the wave, the higher the frequency.

With radio energy velocity constant at about the speed of light, we should be able to figure frequency if given wavelength, and wavelength if given frequency. The formula is **frequency equals velocity divided by wavelength** or **wavelength equals velocity divided by frequency.** For example, an AM broadcast station operating at 1500 kHz is using a wavelength of 200 meters (300,000,000

÷ 1,500,000 = 200), that is, the length of each wave the station transmits is 200 meters long.

### 10.1.5 Review

Before going on, let us review. Alternating electrical current sets up thousands or millions of oscillations in the transmitting antenna. These oscillations produce radio waves, each with a positive phase and a negative phase, which travel outward from the source at close to the speed of light. When the waves contact a receiving antenna, they set up similar oscillations that the receiver amplifies and uses as the signal. The strength of a radio wave is its amplitude, which attenuates as the wave travels. Speed is constant, so that frequency and wavelength are inversely related.

## 10.2 FREQUENCY-RELATED CHARACTERISTICS

Because radio waves consist of electrical and magnetic fields, radio energy is a form of **electromagnetic energy**, as are X-rays, visible light, ultraviolet light, and other types of radiation. All radiate from a source and travel in waves at the speed of light. As mentioned in *PRT*, 10.1.1, electromagnetic energy needs no conduction medium; in fact, it travels most efficiently through a vacuum.

### 10.2.1 Electromagnetic Spectrum

If you arrange all forms of electromagnetic energy in order of frequency, from lowest to highest, you would have what is called the **electromagnetic spectrum.** At the highest frequencies (and shortest wavelengths) are cosmic rays. Below that, in descending order of frequency, come gamma rays, X-rays, ultraviolet rays, visible light, infrared rays, and, near the bottom, radio waves.

As shown in Fig. 10.6, the **radio portion** of the electromagnetic spectrum has been further divided. By international agreement, AM radio has been assigned to the medium frequency (MF) band; television channels 2 through 13 and FM radio are in the Very High Frequency (VHF) band; TV channels 14 through 70, the instructional television fixed service (ITFS), and the MDS are in the Ultra High Frequency (UHF) band; DBSs are in the super high frequency (SHF) band. Wavelengths in the ITFS, MDS, and DBS services are so short they are called **microwaves.**

### 10.2.2 Propagation

The manner in which radio waves travel—the paths they take—is called **propagation.** Propagation varies greatly with frequency.

*10.2.2.1 Ground Waves and Sky Waves.*   In the MF band, used by AM radio stations, ground waves and sky waves determine propagation. Ground waves follow the curvature of the earth (Fig. 10.7). Ground waves are relatively constant;

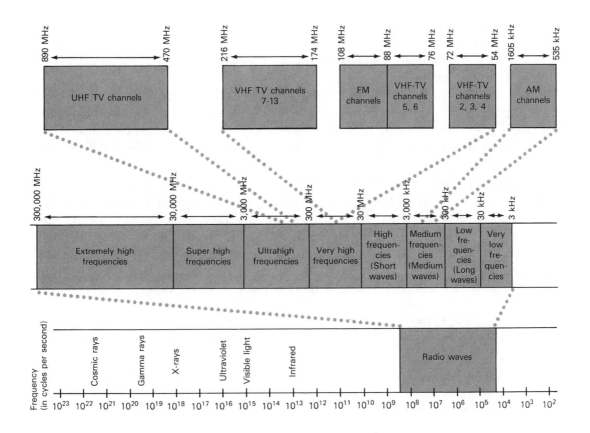

FIG. 10.6. Electromagnetic spectrum.

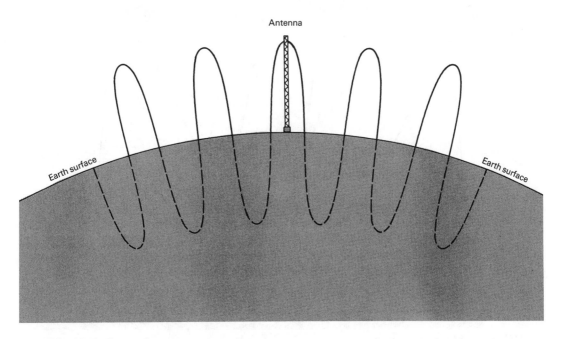

FIG. 10.7. Ground wave propagation.

at a given distance from the transmitter, they usually provide the same quality of reception most of the time.

Sky waves radiate away from the earth (Fig. 10.8). During the day, they travel unimpeded into space and serve no use to earthly propagation. At night, however, changes in the ionosphere, 30 to 200 miles above the earth's surface, cause many sky waves to bend and to return to the ground hundreds of miles from the transmitter.

During nighttime, then, sky waves expand a transmitter's reception area beyond that provided by ground waves. However, the quality of the signal in this expanded area varies more than in the ground-wave coverage area. As the ionosphere changes, the strength of the sky waves change, and listeners hear the signal "fade" in and out on their radio receivers. At times, freak ionospheric conditions make possible clear sky wave reception at distances of half a continent or more from the transmitter. Such reception is usually subject to severe fading.

***10.2.2.2 Direct Waves.*** Higher radio frequencies are closer to visible light in the electromagnetic spectrum and behave more like visible light rays. In VHF, UHF, and SHF, propagation is primarily by direct waves. Like light, direct waves travel in straight lines, may be blocked by physical objects, and may be reflected. This is illustrated in Box 10.1.

Like light, direct waves are also subject to **refraction** or bending. Perhaps you have had the experience of putting a straight pole into clear water and seeing the pole appear to bend. The pole seems to enter the water at one angle, then bend

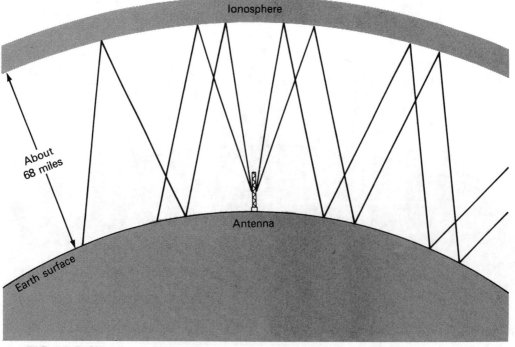

FIG. 10.8. **Sky wave propagation.**

## BOX 10.1. DIRECT WAVE PROPAGATION

Television and FM radio propagation have been described as **line of sight**, and to a large extent that is true. If you were to climb to the top of a television transmitter tower, for example, you could (on a clear day) literally see most of the station's primary coverage area—the area reached by its actual off-the-air, not delivered-by-cable signal. You see to the horizon but no farther; for all practical purposes, that is how far the television signal reaches. A series of hills looms up close on one side of you, blocking your view; they block the television signal, too, and people living on the other side of the hills cannot receive the station directly. Some neighborhoods are partially obscured from your view by tall buildings or other large structures; the people living in these areas pick up the television station with difficulty or not at all. Some tall buildings seem especially bright, reflecting quite a bit of light; they also reflect television signals. Residents living near these buildings receive one television signal directly from the station's transmitting antenna and another from the bounce off the reflective buildings. The result is ghosting (a double image) on the screen.

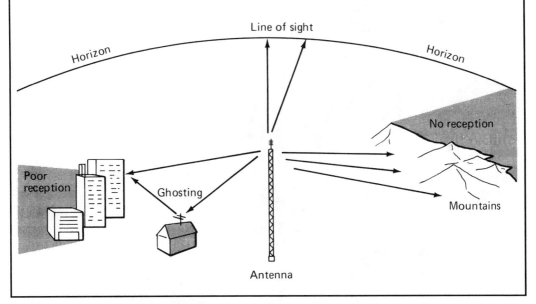

at the surface to another angle. The pole has not really bent, of course, but the light rays have. The light rays reflected from the submerged part of the pole travel through a relatively dense medium, water, then enter a less dense medium, air, and in the process they bend. This is called refraction, and it is why the straight pole looks bent. Similarly, VHF, UHF, and SHF waves can be bent as they pass through varying temperatures and weather conditions that affect density.

Attenuation, absorption, interference, reflection, and refraction all affect propagation at all frequencies to a certain extent. Some affect some frequencies more than others. Climate and weather play a large role in propagation. The next time a cold front, a warm front, a high pressure area, or a low pressure area is scheduled to move into your vicinity, note the changes in broadcast reception before, during, and after.

### 10.2.3 MF Coverage

**Coverage** refers to the physical area within which a radio wave may be received. MF coverage is affected by three factors—ground, frequency, and power.

*10.2.3.1 Ground.*   The term **ground** refers to electrical grounding. In MF transmission, part of the antenna is buried beneath the ground, and the whole antenna structure, ground and all, transmits. The object is to make maximum use of the ground waves, which requires a good electrical ground connection. Wet soil gives a better electrical ground than does dry, so that in MF transmission, the transmitting antenna is better off in a low swamp than on top of a dry, well-drained hill (Fig. 10.9).

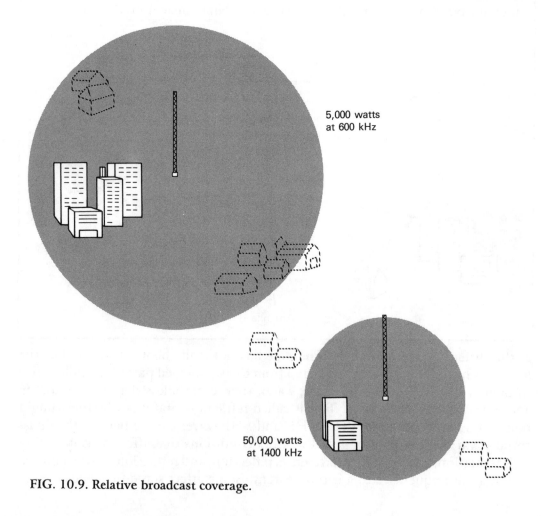

5,000 watts
at 600 kHz

50,000 watts
at 1400 kHz

FIG. 10.9. Relative broadcast coverage.

***10.2.3.2 Frequency.***    Frequency affects coverage in just the opposite from what you may think. In MF transmission, as in all transmission, the lower the frequency, the better the coverage (Fig. 10.10). This is because lower frequencies result from longer waves, and the longer the wave, the greater the distance one wavelength covers. For example, a station transmitting at 1600 kHz generates a wavelength of 187.5 meters, whereas a station at 540 kHz generates a wavelength of 555.6 meters. For every one wavelength the waves at 540 kHz travel, the waves at 1600 kHz must travel nearly three wavelengths, expending three times the energy in attenuation and absorption.

***10.2.3.3 Power.***    Power works just the way that seems most logical—the higher the power the transmitter pumps into the antenna, the farther the wave will travel, and the better the coverage. Because of ground wave propagation, radio transmission in the MF range is not as affected by hills and line-of-sight considerations as VHF and UHF transmission. Given enough power, ground waves surmount hills and range beyond the horizon.

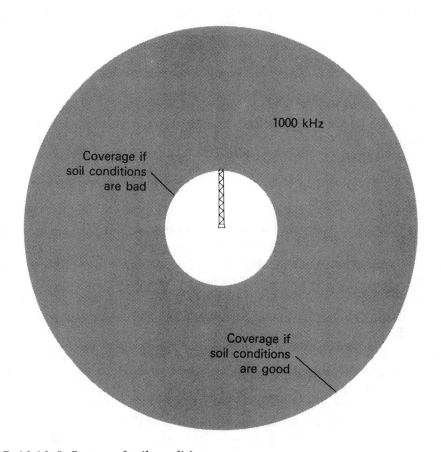

FIG. 10.10. Influence of soil condition.

## 10.2.4 VHF, UHF, and SHF Coverage

Coverage in the VHF, UHF, and SHF frequencies is affected by **antenna height, frequency,** and **power.** VHF and UHF propagation is by direct waves and is line of sight (although in reality, FM and TV station signals do spread beyond line of sight). Just as the higher you fly in an airplane, the more area you can see, so, too, the higher the antenna, the greater the coverage. Line of sight also means natural terrain features and human-built obstacles can block coverage, yielding dead spots and poor reception areas. ITFS and MMDS operate so high in the frequency bands that their coverage is literally line of sight; the transmitting antenna must be seen from the receiving antenna, and even leaves and foliage can block reception. In DBS, the receiving dish must have a clear "shot" at the satellite.

Frequency and power affect VHF, UHF, and SHF coverage as they do in all frequency ranges—lower frequencies and higher power yield greater coverage. Wavelengths in these frequency bands are so much shorter than in the MF band, that TV and FM broadcast stations operate with higher average power than do AM stations. DBSs, however, can operate at much lower power because the waves they transmit travel most of their journey through near-vacuum and low-density atmosphere.

## 10.3 DIGITAL BROADCASTING

Digital technologies are rapidly replacing the analog systems used for transmission and storage of sound and video. In this section we describe the differences between analog and digital communication, and the techniques and standards used to compress digital signals.

## 10.3.1 Analog Versus Digital

When Marconi first demonstrated wireless communication (*PRT,* 2.1.1), a vibrating metal sheet transmitted an electromagnetic signal corresponding to its movements; when the signal reached another sheet of metal, that sheet vibrated exactly as had the first. This "continuous wave" technique has been the standard for most of the history of telecommunication. A continuous wave carries continuous information about the characteristics of sound or picture to a receiver or storage medium. Analogous displays are reproduced at the receiving end.

In **digital** communication, the characteristics of the sound or picture or the respective analog signal are measured at fixed intervals. This periodic measurement is called **sampling.** The sampling occurs many times per second, a rate far beyond the range of human perception. Such characteristics as volume in audio or color saturation in video are expressed in numerical terms. More accurately, the technologies use binary coding. Binary digits are 0 and 1, or "off" and "on."

In audio, the sampling occurs at regular time intervals (Fig. 10.11). In video, the sampling occurs spatially. The characteristics of each picture element, or pixel

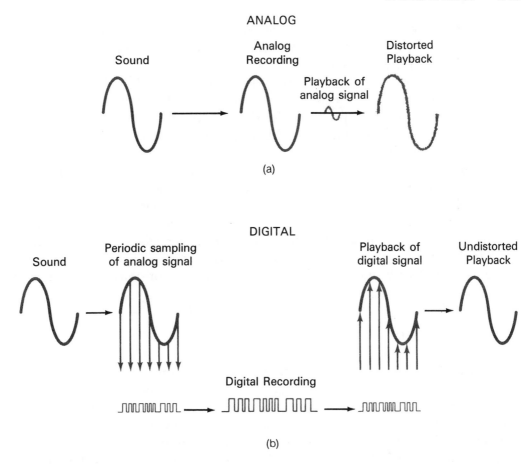

FIG. 10.11. Analog versus digital audio.

is sampled. The hue, chroma, and saturation of each of the red, green, and blue elements of the color picture (*PRT,* 12.1.2) are sampled separately, and expressed in the form of 8-bit numerical (i.e., **binary digit**) descriptions. An 8-bit character is called a **byte,** so each pixel would require 24 bits, or 3 bytes of information.

Most current technologies require that an analog signal be sampled and **encoded** into digital form, then transmitted (or stored in a medium such as a CD) and **decoded** into analog form. Newer technologies allow direct encoding. Of course, all digital representations require that the receiver decode the numerical information and convert it into a recognizable analog form; otherwise you would see a series of 0s and 1s marching across the television screen instead of your favorite program.

Digital technologies generally provide better sound and video reproduction than do analog. There are two reasons for this. First, interruptions in an analog signal, such as electrical interference or a scratch on a vinyl record, are more noticeable in analog systems. Second, each time an analog signal passes through an electronic processing device such as an amplifier or is duplicated or retransmitted, noise is added. Further, some signal information is lost. The more devices, the more noise and loss. In digital communication, the instructions for recreating the signal are transmitted, not the signal itself. So, each reproduction becomes an exact duplicate of the original.

Digital technology is particularly useful for postproduction processing (*PRT,* 6.2.5.2). Electronic digital devices allow an editor to delete, add, and rearrange sound or pictures, even to preview material with proposed edits—look or listen to what it will sound like with the edits in place—before the edit decisions are made final. Other digital devices stretch or compress recorded material without altering pitch; that is, speed it up or slow it down without making it sound like animated mice or sounds from beyond the grave. They can also change pitch without changing speed, add echo and delay, and otherwise alter or distort the quality of the material. Such gimmicks are used extensively in popular music recording and in creation of radio and television commercials. Video digital effects allow for special transitions between scenes, changing the colors of some or all elements in a picture, and even the inclusion of people or objects that were not present during shooting.

### 10.3.2. Compression

There is another significant advantage to digital communication, and that is the ability to **compress** the signal, or reduce the amount of channel capacity needed for transmission. Analog signals require a lot of channel capacity, or **bandwidth.** An analog television signal that creates sound and a moving picture at the NTSC standard of 30 frames per second and 525 scanning lines requires 6 MHz of channel space (*PRT,* 12.3). Stated in digital terms, the signal must be sent at a rate of about 140 megabytes of data per second (Mbps). Compression techniques can reduce that rate. In the late 1990s, broadcasters expected that by early in the next decade they would be transmitting a digital video signal on 1 MHz of spectrum.

In digital compression systems statistical probabilities are used by the decoder to fill in missing information that is not transmitted or stored. As a very simplified example, if Pixels 1, 2, 3, and 5 are each blue, there is a high probability that Pixel 4 would also be blue. Even if the pixel should really have been red, the small size of the element or the brief time it would be on the screen makes it unlikely the viewer will notice the error. In this scheme we eliminate 20% of the information that has to be transmitted or stored.

The scheme we have just described is called **intraframe** compression. Another approach is called **interframe** compression. Here, only the information that changes from frame to frame is transmitted. In NTSC scanning rates the picture changes 30 times each second, so relatively few changes actually occur from frame to frame.

Two characteristics are particularly important to the viewer of digital video. One is screen size and the other is **frame rate.**

*10.3.2.1 Screen Size.* We are used to seeing video on relatively large screens. However, some compression technologies will not provide suitable resolution on a normal-size screen. When the compressed image is displayed at too large a size it will appear "blocky." This is because one component of the standards is the number of pixels to be used. As the picture is expanded the pixels, too, grow larger. The result is a picture that has a mosaic appearance.

*10.3.2.2 Frame Rate.* NTSC scanning standards call for a frame rate of approximately 30 frames per second. This creates the illusion of movement out of a series of discrete images (*PRT*, 12.1.3). Because of the amount of computer memory required to decode and display the signal, some compression schemes do not allow for playback at 30 frames per second, or do so only if the picture remains below a certain size. Where the frame rate is below 30 frames per second, movement appears choppy or sporadic.

### 10.3.3 Compression Standards

To facilitate the development and use of digital compression, international standards have been agreed on by representatives of governments and industry. Although hardware and software developed by different companies will code and decode digital signals uniquely, each follows one of these basic standards.

The **Joint Photographic Experts Group (JPEG)** standard was established originally for compression of still images. **Motion JPEG** has been used in applications in which the frame rate (the number of frames per second) is low. In motion JPEG, picture re-creation occurs **progressively.** In other words, each frame is created in its entirety, then the next entire frame is created. As discussed in chapter 12, broadcast television uses an interlace scanning technique, in which the picture is created in two halves. Because of the physiology of the eye and brain, progressive scanning creates a moving picture that appears to flicker. The interlaced picture does not flicker.

The **Moving Picture Experts Group (MPEG)** has created a number of standards. **MPEG-1** has been widely used in such applications as video games and multimedia. Although MPEG-1 pictures can be re-created in frames of any size, the best quality occurs at a size of no more than $352 \times 240$ pixels. As with JPEG, the MPEG-1 picture is progressive, not interlaced. The digital information in an MPEG-1 system plays at about 1.5 megabytes per second, which produces a picture quality equivalent to a VHS videotape.

MPEG-1 quality is not sufficient for broadcast applications. **MPEG-2,** with a data rate of 1.5 to 15 Mbps meets those higher standards. Under the MPEG-2 standard the maximum picture quality is no more than $720 \times 483$ pixels. MPEG-2 digital coding allows interlace scanning.

The MPEG-2 standard is used in digital DBS services (*PRT*, 5.4.4), and by some cable companies. DirecTV and USSB use varying MPEG-2 data rates depending on the nature of the program. Programs with a great deal of motion, such as live sporting events, are transmitted at around 7.5 Mbps, whereas programs such as talk shows are sent at around 3 Mbps.

The MPEG-2 standard allows much of the compression and decompression to occur at the encoding stage. As a result, set-top decoders can be relatively simple and inexpensive.[1]

Proponents of HDTV (*PRT,* 12.5.2) originally developed the **MPEG-3** digital standard. However, researchers learned how to adapt the MPEG-2 standard for HDTV, and MPEG-3 is no longer used.

In 1993 researchers began developing an **MPEG-4** standard. Standards development is expected to continue until at least 1997, with November 1998 as the target for adoption. MPEG-4 is designed to be used for applications requiring relatively low data rates, such as interactive mobile multimedia, games, and electronic newspapers.[2]

## NOTES

1. Basil Halhed, "MPEG Video Compression," version of 19 December 1995, http://www.hei.ca/hei/mpeg2.html.
2. "MPEG-4," Web Site http://crs4.it.

## FURTHER READING

Benson, K. Blair, and Jerry Whitaker. *Television and Audio Handbook for Technicians and Engineers.* New York: McGraw-Hill, 1990

De Sonne, Marcia L. *Spectrum of New Broadcast/Media Technologies: Technological Developments Impacting Broadcasting Markets, Businesses, and Operations.* Washington, DC: National Association of Broadcasters, 1990.

Green, Derek Charles. *Radio Systems Technology.* New York: Wiley, 1990.

Watkinson, John. *Digital Compression in Video and Audio.* Newton, MA: Focal, 1995.

Watkinson, John. *An Introduction to Digital Audio.* Newton, MA: Focal, 1994.

Watkinson, John. *An Introduction to Digital Video.* Newton, MA: Focal, 1994.

# 11

## RADIO CHANNELS

How can more than 12,000 radio stations in the United States fit into just over 200 channels? How does sound become radio and vice versa? What is the difference between AM and FM?

These are some of the questions we answer in this chapter. In addition to the AM and FM bands, we look at other radio broadcasting channels, international service, and various forms of wired radio.

### 11.1 AM BROADCAST SERVICE

According to the FCC, an AM broadcast station is one **licensed for transmission of radiotelephone** (voice, music, etc.) **emissions** (radio waves) **primarily intended for reception by the general public and operated on a channel in the band** [that begins with] **535 kHz** (535,000 Hz).[1] This places AM radio in the medium frequency (MF) band.

For years, the AM broadcast band ended at 1605 kHz (1,605,000 Hz). In 1979 an international conference expanded the band to 1705 kHz (1,705,000 Hz). In the United States the expanded band was used to allow selected existing stations to "migrate" to more favorable frequencies. These stations were authorized to operate on higher power in their new frequencies, thus increasing coverage area and reducing interference on the previous channel.

In the broadcast services, a place for a station is a **channel.** An AM channel consists of its carrier frequency plus the upper and lower sidebands of the AM broadcast signal. (You will learn more about these terms in *PRT*, 11.3.3.1. For now, the *carrier* is the frequency at the center of the channel; *sidebands* are groups of frequencies generated by the broadcasting process and are located at frequencies directly above and below the carrier.) Each channel is **identified by its carrier frequency.** The carriers are **spaced at 10 kHz intervals,** with the first at 540 kHz. This works out to **117 channels** with the AM band at 535 to 1705 kHz. Most channels are used by more than one station, although a (relatively) small number of channels contain a large percentage of all stations.

### 11.1.1 AM Interference and Coverage

**Interference,** the mutual action of two sets of radio waves affecting each other, takes the form of **static** and **station interference** (Fig. 11.1). Static is electrical discharges and can be either **natural** or **induced.** Natural static results from atmospheric disturbances such as lightning. Induced static originates from electrical machines and devices—the faulty ignition system of an automobile, or a

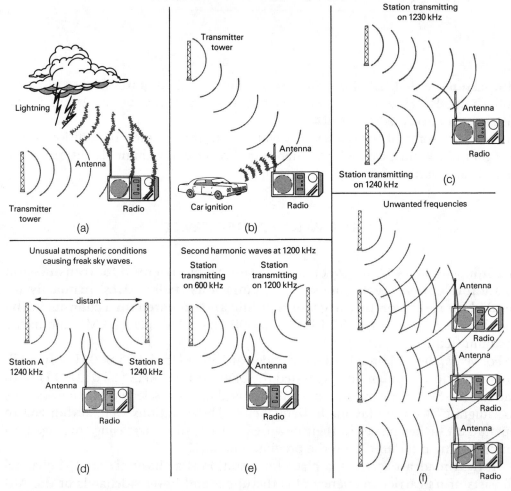

**FIG. 11.1. Types of interference in AM radio.** (a) Static—natural (lightning in this example). Radio simultaneously receives station signal and static. (b) Static—human-created. Radio simultaneously receives signal and static. (c) Station interference—adjacent channel. Radio tuned to 1230 simultaneously receives station on 1230 kHz and station transmitting on 1240 kHz. (d) Station interference—cochannel. Radio tuned to 1240 to receive Station A simultaneously receives signals from both Stations A and B. (e) Station interference—second harmonic. Radio tuned to distant station transmitting on 1200 kHz simultaneously receives nearby station transmitting on 600 kHz through its second harmonic frequency (1200 kHz). (f) Station interference—splatter. Station transmitting on one frequency overmodulates, and radios tuned to stations on other frequencies receive audio from the overmodulating station.

vacuum cleaner or mixer running in another room. These sources generate electromagnetic waves that mix and are received with incoming radio waves.

Station interference involves signals of two or more radio stations. You tune to one station but receive others on the same setting at the same time.

**Coverage** is the area within which a station's signal can be received. Because AM operates in the MF band, a radio station's coverage is dependent on **ground, power, and frequency** (*PRT*, 10.2.3). All else being equal, wetter soil, higher power, or lower frequency results in greater coverage. The FCC has defined two types of coverage areas—**primary and secondary**[2] (Fig. 11.2). Generally, a station's primary service area is that served by its ground wave; its secondary service area is that within which its sky wave is received with some degree of strength and consistency.

### 11.1.2 AM Channel and Station Classification

Early in the history of broadcasting, it became apparent that a system was needed to prevent massive interference among AM radio stations. Sky waves, particularly, caused problems; they were unpredictable and could skip long distances. The system that finally evolved included two related classifications—(a) **AM frequen-**

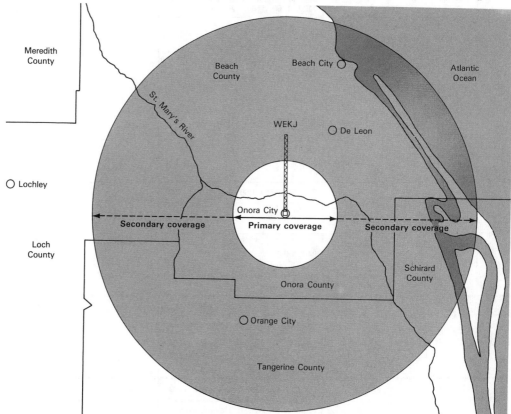

FIG. 11.2. Primary and secondary coverage area.

cies are classified as clear, regional, or local channels; (b) **stations, as I, II, III, or IV.** As you read the remainder of this section, refer to Fig. 11.3, which shows channel classification and its relationship to station classification.

*11.1.2.1 Clear Channels.* Clear channels are used by dominant stations and secondary stations. Of the 107 AM channels, 60 are designated clear channels.

**Dominant stations** provide primary and secondary service over relatively long distances. They operate with at least 10 kilowatts (kW; 1 kW = 1,000 watts) and no more than 50 kilowatts of power. On 25 of the 60 "clears," FCC allows one dominant station per channel, and it requires that one station to operate at 50 kW, the maximum allowed in the United States.

On another 22 clears, the Commission allows multiple dominant stations. These stations must operate so as to minimize cochannel interference. During the day, for example, two dominant stations on the same clear channel might use

| Channel classification | | | Frequencies (kHz) | Station classification | |
|---|---|---|---|---|---|
| | | | | Dominant | Secondary |
| Clear (60) | A (25) | | 640, 650, 660, 670, 700, 720, 750, 760, 770, 780, 820, 830, 840, 870, 880, 890, 1020, 1030, 1040, 1100, 1120, 1160, 1180, 1200, 1210 | I-A | II |
| | B (19) | U.S. Clears (11) | 680, 710, 810, 850, 1080, 1110, 1170, 1500, 1510, 1520, 1530 | I-B | II |
| | | Clears shared by U.S. and foreign countries (8) — with Canada (2) | 1070, 1130 | | |
| | | with Mexico (5) | 1000, 1060, 1090, 1140, 1190 | | |
| | | with Cuba (1) | 1560 | | |
| | Foreign clears (16) (No U.S. dominant stations) | Canada | 540, 690, 740, 860, 990, 1010, 1580 | None | II |
| | | Mexico (6) | 730, 800, 900, 1050, 1220, 1570 | | |
| | | Canada & Mexico (2) | 940, 1550 | | |
| | | Bahamas | 1540 | | |
| Regional (41) | | | 550, 560, 570, 580, 590, 600, 610, 620, 630, 790, 910, 920, 930, 950, 960, 970, 980, 1150, 1250, 1260, 1270, 1280, 1290, 1300, 1310, 1320, 1330, 1350, 1360, 1370, 1380, 1390, 1410, 1420, 1430, 1440, 1460, 1470, 1480, 1590, 1600 | III | |
| Local (6) | | | 1230, 1240, 1340, 1400, 1450, 1490 (These frequencies are classified as regional for Alaska, Hawaii, Puerto Rico and the Virgin Islands.) | IV | |

FIG. 11.3. AM channel and station classification.

nondirectional transmitting antennas (to radiate their ground waves equally in all directions) then at night switch to directional antenna arrays (to direct their sky wave transmissions away from each other).

Some of these latter 22 clear channels are shared; both the United States and another North American country operate dominant stations on them. The remainder of the 60 clears are foreign; the United States may operate no dominant station on any of these channels without prior agreement from the other country.

In addition to dominant stations, one or more **secondary stations** may transmit on a clear channel. Secondary stations are licensed to **protect** the signal of the dominant stations (i.e., not interfere with their primary service areas and much of their secondary service areas). They must use restrictive operational modes—transmit with relatively low power, reduce power at night, operate only in the daytime, use a directional antenna array, or employ some combination of these measures.

### 11.1.2.2 Regional Channels.
Forty-one frequencies are regional channels. A regional channel is one on which a number of stations may operate, each serving a population center and adjacent rural areas. None dominates; each operates to avoid interference with all others on the same channel, and some must use restrictive operational modes. The most powerful use 5 kW.

### 11.1.2.3 Local Channels.
The remaining six frequencies are local channels. A local channel is one on which many stations may operate, as many as 150 and more. These stations serve one city or town and the adjacent suburban and rural areas. Most operate with 1,000 watts day and night.

### 11.1.2.4 Station Classification.
The dominant stations on a clear channel are Class I stations. The secondary stations that operate on a clear channel are Class II stations.[3] Stations assigned to regional channels are Class III stations. Stations on local channels are Class IV stations.

### 11.1.2.5 New Stations.
Should you wish to construct a new AM radio station, you will find slim pickings. All Class I stations were taken years ago. If you want a clear channel dominant station, you will have to buy it.

In putting on a new AM station, the frequency you use determines the type of station you build. Therefore you must first find a frequency. You hire a consulting engineer who makes a **frequency search**; that is, studies existing AM radio assignments and measures the strength of their signals in the area where you wish to build. Again, pickings are slim. Most of the better frequencies have already been taken. In your application to the FCC, you must show that your proposed station would not interfere with existing stations.

### 11.1.2.6 Spectrum Management.
Most AM radio stations operate on regional and local channels. These 47 channels—44% of the total—represent 70% of the stations. Of the 60 clear channels, 14 have five or fewer stations operating on them.

Despite the apparent crowding of the AM dial, ways do exist at the policymaking level to add new stations. In the 1980s, for example, the FCC reduced the area in which the signals of Class I stations were protected. This made room for additional stations of other classes. Treaties between the United States and other North American countries permitted construction of new stations. On the other hand, given AM's diminishing audience shares, the need for so many new stations might legitimately be questioned.

Also during the 1980s, the FCC attempted to improve the lot of the 2,400 "daytimers." As explained earlier, a number of Class II and Class III stations have had to operate in the daytime only. This dawn-to-dusk operation can be extremely limiting. The winter sun rises late and sets early in the colder latitudes of the United States. During some months, a station restricting its programming to a sunrise-to-sunset schedule misses one or both of the two drive times, the most listened-to and potentially lucrative parts of the radio broadcast day.

The daytimers requested help, and the Commission responded along several fronts. Postsunset operations were authorized for some daytimers operating on domestic clear channels. The FCC worked with the State Department to negotiate agreements with Canada and Mexico to allow many daytimers on foreign clears to extend their broadcast day (including some that would be allowed 24-hour operation). The Commission promised daytimer licensees preferential treatment when they applied for new FM stations. The FCC proposed to permit about 1,600 daytimers operating on clear and regional channels to operate at night. Finally, the FCC stopped accepting applications for new AM daytimers.

## 11.2 FM BROADCAST SERVICE

The FM radio broadcasting band is 88 to 108 MHz, in the VHF portion of the radio frequencies, located just above television channel 6. There are 100 channels in the FM band, each 200 kHz wide (108 MHz – 88 MHz = 20 MHz ، 0.2 [which is 200 kHz] = 100). For convenience, the FCC customarily refers to FM channels by **channel number** as in television. The first FM channel is 201; the last, 300. Stations identify themselves to the public by **frequency**, similar to AM radio. The first FM channel frequency is 88.1 MHz (the center of a band of frequencies, 88–88.2 MHz), and the last is 107.9 MHz (107.8–108 MHz).

### 11.2.1 FM Interference and Coverage

Interference is rarely the problem in FM radio that it is in AM. As discussed in *PRT,* 10.2.2.2, propagation is primarily by direct waves and, therefore, is fairly predictable. Ground waves and sky waves do not figure into FM coverage. Additionally, the VHF band contains less static and other noise than the lower frequencies. Frequency, power, tower height, terrain, and human-constructed obstacles all affect coverage.

FM receiver design also helps station interference and static. In cochannel and adjacent channel interference situations, an FM receiver is better able to suppress the weaker signal than an AM receiver. Static signals attach themselves to positive and negative peaks of a radio wave, thus FM receivers eliminate static by **clipping** (removing) these peaks.

### 11.2.2 FM Station Classification

The FCC has adopted rules to provide for the orderly growth of the FM radio service, while minimizing signal interference. The Commission has divided the country into three zones, designated **I, I-A, and II**. Stations have been classified as **A, B1, B, C1, C2, C3, or C** according to power and antenna height. Figure 11.4 shows the zones and the classification system.

*11.2.2.1 Commercial FM.*    Commercial FM stations operate on the **80 channels** (221–300) in the nonreserved (i.e., commercial) portion of the FM band. In 1963, the FCC adopted a table assigning nonreserved channels to specific communities. Should you wish to build a new commercial FM station, you go to the FM **table of assignments,** look up your city, choose an unused channel assigned to that city, and apply for it. If there are no vacant channels, you either find a city that does have vacant FM channels or petition the FCC to amend the table of assignments to add a channel to your city.

In 1983, the FCC opened the FM band to additional stations. It adopted a new station classification system (the present one) and changed the required minimum distances between stations on the same and adjacent channels. The Commission estimated this action would allow room for up to 2,000 new FM stations.

*11.2.2.2 Noncommercial Educational FM.*    FM channels 201 to 220 are reserved for noncommercial educational stations. These 20 channels are not included in the FCC's table of assignments (except as noted later). Noncommercial FM stations are assigned on an individual application demand basis, much like AM.

Noncommercial FM stations are classified A, B, C, and D. Station classes A, B, and C parallel those in the commercial band. A station that operates with no more than 10 watts of transmitter power output is a Class D station. In 1978, the FCC stopped accepting applications for new Class D stations. Existing Class D stations were given four choices if they wished to continue to operate: (a) increase power to at least 100 watts ERP; (b) move to an unused commercial channel; (c) move to a new FM channel 200 (87.9 MHz); or (d) operate as a secondary station on a commercial or noncommercial channel.

### 11.3 SOUND AND AUDIO

We use the term **audio frequency** (AF, or simply "audio") to refer to a certain type of electronic signal. Audio is, in most cases, an analog of (i.e., resembles or is comparable to in certain respects) sound. In other words, audio is an **electric**

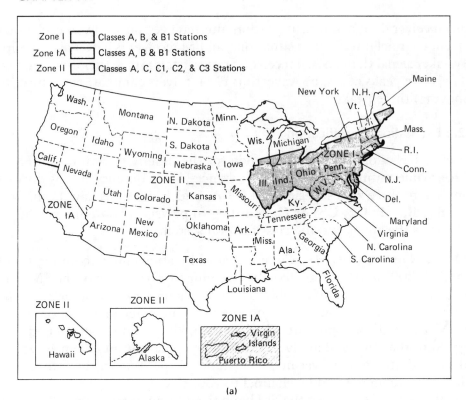

(a)

| Station Class | Effective Radiated Power (ERP in kilowatts—kW) | | Maximum Antenna Height Above Average Terrain (HAAT in meters (and feet)) | Zones to which allocated |
|---|---|---|---|---|
| | Minimum | Maximum | | |
| A* | .1 (100 watts) | 3/6 | 100 (328) | I, I-A, II |
| B1 | over 3 | 25 | 100 (328) | I, I-A |
| B | over 25 | 50 | 150 (492) | I, I-A |
| C3 | over 3 | 25 | 100 (328) | II |
| C2 | over 3 | 50 | 150 (492) | II |
| C1 | over 50 | 100 | 299 (981) | II |
| C | 100 | | 600 (1968) | II |

*Selected Class A FM stations may operate with 6 kw.

(b)

**FIG. 11.4. FCC's FM zones and station classification.** (a) Geographic boundaries of zones. (b) Station classification and assignment to zones.

**current that carries the pattern of sound in a form suitable for electronic manipulation.** Manipulation includes transmission. So we need to find out how sound originates and how it is converted to audio.

### 11.3.1 Sound

Sound originates with the **vibrating body** of a **sound source**—the human vocal folds in the larynx or the strings of a harp. A plucked harp string, for example, vibrates rapidly back and forth, compressing and rarefying adjacent air molecules. As the string moves in one direction, it pushes together molecules in front while creating a partial vacuum and rarefying (i.e., making less dense) the molecules behind. After it reaches the outermost point of movement in one direction, the string begins to swing back the other way, and the condensation–rarefaction process reverses sides.

*11.3.1.1 Sound Waves.*    As the string displaces the nearest air molecules, these molecules hit the next molecules, which then hit the next molecules, and so forth. This chain reaction creates repeating patterns of alternating condensation and rarefaction radiating outward from the vibrating body. If these patterns reach your ear, they set up vibrations in your eardrum similar to those of the harp string. The vibrating eardrum activates tiny mechanisms in your middle ear that transmit sensations to your auditory nerve, which, in turn, sends the information to your brain. Your brain interprets the result as sound. Figure 11.5 illustrates this process.

Each condensation–rarefaction combination is one wave. One set of back-and-forth movements of the vibrating body is one cycle.

*11.3.1.2 Frequency, Wavelength, Amplitude, and Pitch.*    The number of cycles per second—the frequency—determines the length of the sound waves. (We used these terms in *PRT,* 10.1.3 and 10.1.4, when discussing radio waves. But remember, this is sound energy, not electromagnetic energy.) Amplitude determines loudness. As the body vibrates harder, amplitude increases and grows louder. Frequency determines pitch. If the body vibrates at a frequency of 440 Hz, your brain hears the musical pitch A, sixth tone in the scale of C major. A frequency of 258 Hz is middle C; twice that number is C above middle C, and so on. Figure 11.6 shows relations among frequency, wavelength, and amplitude.

*11.3.1.3 Fundamentals and Overtones.*    Any given sound usually contains many different pitches. For example, let us say that you pluck the A string of a harp. You hear a note, A above middle C, the **fundamental** tone, the one to which the string is tuned. But at the same time that the whole string moves back and forth at a rate of 440 Hz, segments of the string also move back and forth independently and at faster rates. These vibrating segments also produce pitches called **overtones.** The shorter the segment, the faster it vibrates, and the higher the pitch it produces. Figure 11.7 illustrates overtone production. Overtones vary according to the type of vibrating body. When overtones are **consonant,** you perceive the sound as pleasing, even musical; when **dissonant,** as upsetting or jarring or as noise. Although overtone frequencies go higher, most of us cannot hear above 15,000 to 17,000 Hz. As we age or if we damage our hearing, the

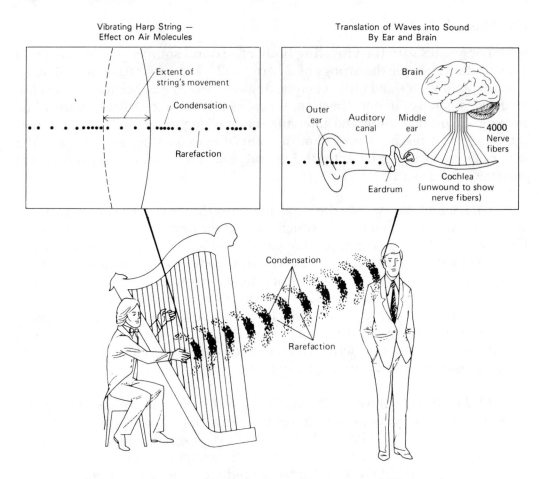

**FIG. 11.5. Origination, transmission, and reception of sound.** The condensation–rarefaction patterns (in the air molecules) radiate outward in all directions from the sound source. For clarity, the illustration shows the waves going only to the listener's ears, and the inserts show only one line of air molecules.

upper limit drops. However, most fundamentals are below 5,000 Hz, and most speech sounds go no higher than 3,000 Hz.

Structure and enclosure of the sound source also play a role in what you hear. The vibrating body and its sound waves cause other parts of the source to vibrate and amplify the sound. This is **resonance**, and as sound sources vary, so does resonance.

Vibrating body, overtones, and resonance are the factors that allow you to tell one sound source from another—a human voice from a harp from a trumpet from a clarinet—even though each produces the same fundamental tone. These factors also help you to tell one voice from another.

Most sound waves are highly complex. Overtones and resonance both complicate sound wave structure, as do factors such as two or more sound sources used in combination (orchestra, singing group, even one instrument on which two or

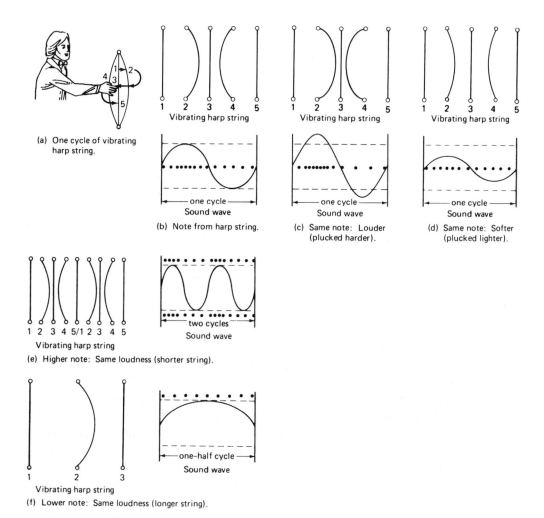

(a) One cycle of vibrating harp string.

(b) Note from harp string.

(c) Same note: Louder (plucked harder).

(d) Same note: Softer (plucked lighter).

(e) Higher note: Same loudness (shorter string).

(f) Lower note: Same loudness (longer string).

**FIG. 11.6. Sound waves: Frequency and amplitude.** In drawings (b) through (f), the numbered lines show what movements the harp string makes within a given time period [the same for each drawing, (b) through (f)], while the sine wave forms show what the resulting sound waves are like. Variations in the degree of string displacement [(c) and (d)] result in variations in amplitude. Variations in the number of cycles of string movement [(e) and (f)] result in variations in frequency and pitch.

more notes may be sounded simultaneously) and the acoustical properties (i.e., those qualities that determine how clearly sound can be heard) of the room in which sound is produced.

### 11.3.2 Audio

When sound energy is translated directly into electrical energy, the result is audio. To illustrate, let us use a 1,000-Hz tone, a pitch nearly two Cs above middle C.

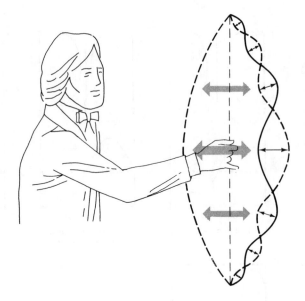

FIG. 11.7. **Creation of overtones.**

We shall make this a pure tone, that is a tone with no overtones, resonance, echoes, or what have you, such as might be produced by an electronic tone generator.

***11.3.2.1 Audio Sources.*** A microphone converts this sound into electrical energy. The sound waves cause a diaphragm in the microphone to vibrate, and its vibrations cause current to flow, the amount of current varying with the amount of sound pressure on the diaphragm. The result is a weak electrical current of 1,000 Hz (which is the same as 1 kHz). This electrical current is the audio, also called the audio signal and the audio frequency (AF). Figure 11.8 shows a microphone converting sound to audio.

The microphone is an audio source, that is, it originates an audio signal. Other sources include playback units for recordings and an electronic tone generator. A recording is simply a stored version of sound. An audio source—a CD player's optical sensor, a phonograph turntable stylus, a tape machine's playback head, or a film projector's photocell—translates the recording into audio. Typically, the heart of a tone generator is an oscillator. This oscillator produces an electrical signal that, when fed to a speaker, produces a tone. In other words, an electronic tone generator, such as a synthesizer, creates audio first, then converts it to sound.

The signal from one or more sources is fed to an **audio control board.** The board allows the audio technician to select the signal or combination of signals to be put **on the line,** that is, to be amplified and sent to the next point on the way to broadcast or cablecast (Fig. 11.9). From the audio board, the signal may be routed to either of two destinations. First, the signal may go live; that is, directly to the transmission point for immediate modulation and distribution to the public. At a radio broadcast station, that point is the transmitter; at a cable radio

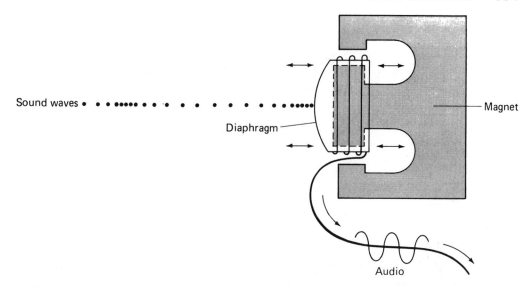

**FIG. 11.8. Microphone: Conversion of sound to audio.** In a dynamic microphone, a diaphragm and a voice coil are connected; when the diaphragm moves, the coil also moves. The voice coil is positioned between the poles of a magnet. Sound waves cause the diaphragm to move back and forth. Movement of the voice coil within the magnetic field sets up a weak current in the coil. Each back-and-forth movement results in one cycle of current. Sound waves cause the movement so that the current is an electrical reproduction of the sound waves. A wire connected to the voice coil carries off the current as audio.

station, the cable system's headend (*PRT,* 12.9.1); at a network, the network operations center.

***11.3.2.2 Audiotape.*** The second possible destination of the audio signal is a recording machine. In most cases, the recording medium is audiotape, usually thin plastic coated with magnetic oxide. In recording, the **audiotape machine** moves the tape past an electromagnetic record head; the record head impresses the audio on the tape in the form of magnetic patterns. To re-create the audio signal, the machine moves the recorded tape past a playback head, also electromagnetic; the playback head detects the patterns on the tape and translates them into electrical impulses. A recorded tape may be played back immediately, may be replayed repeatedly, may be edited, may be sweetened (have special effects added), may be duplicated (called a **dub**), may be erased, or may be used again for another recording.

Some audiotape machines are record-only units; some, playback-only; many do both. Two popular formats in professional audio are reel-to-reel and cartridge. The former is used primarily for recording and editing, particularly in critical situations (such as making master recordings for records and long-form radio programs); the latter for recording and playback in broadcast and cable outlets.

Most recorded music today is played back from digital media, such as the 5-inch CD. As discussed in *PRT,* 10.3, digitization begins with an analog signal that is then sampled. Usually, that analog signal is recorded first on audiotape.

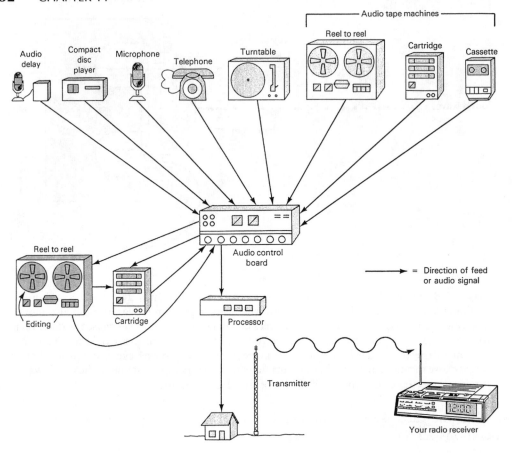

FIG. 11.9. Combining audio sources.

### 11.3.3 Modulation Process

**Modulation** occurs when one electrical signal causes another to change. The first signal usually consists of information—typically, audio or video. The second signal is a carrier frequency, product of a carrier current, a high-frequency alternating electrical current. Thus (before we get lost in detailed explanations) the carrier is changed so that it contains the information of the audio or video signal. That, basically, is modulation.

***11.3.3.1 Amplitude Modulation.*** To illustrate how modulation works, let us look at amplitude modulation. For our example, we use a carrier frequency of 1,000 kHz and the audio signal of 1 kHz (1,000 Hz) that we originated in *PRT,* 11.3.2.

In the AM radio transmitter, three main operations occur. The first two happen simultaneously—the oscillator generates the 1,000-kHz carrier frequency, and the incoming audio frequency signal is boosted and fed into the modulator. In the third operation, these two frequencies meet in the power amplifier, interact, and generate new frequencies. This is illustrated in Fig. 11.10.

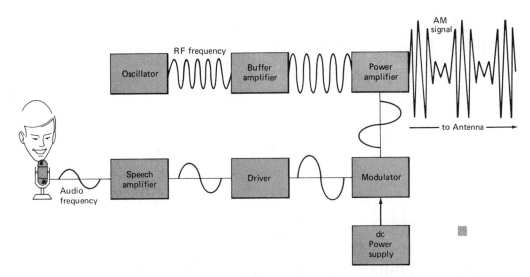

**FIG. 11.10. Block diagram of an AM broadcast transmission.** This diagram includes a few elements not mentioned in the narrative. The speech amplifier boosts the weak AF signal to feed the driver. The driver converts the AF signal into a large voltage and enough current to drive the modulator. The buffer amplifier boosts the radio frequency and prevents the modulated signal from reflecting back from the power amplifier. The DC power supply provides power to both the modulator and the power amplifier.

Two of these new frequencies are particularly significant— the **upper side frequency** (i.e., the higher end of the frequency range) and the **lower side frequency.** As a result of these new side frequencies, the amplitude or strength of the carrier is no longer constant. The carrier's amplitude now varies, rising and falling periodically. The rise and fall of the carrier amplitude forms a pattern that matches the audio signal. We have placed information about the sound wave on the carrier wave.

We now have a carrier of 1,000 kHz, whose amplitude is modulated so that it reproduces the pattern of the 1-kHz audio frequency; thus the term *amplitude modulation.* Because there are both upper and lower frequencies, the pattern is repeated so that the negative phase of the carrier now bears a mirror image of the pattern carried by the positive phase. This is illustrated in Fig. 11.11.

Side frequencies are generated on a sum-and-difference basis. The upper side frequency is equal to the sum of the carrier frequency plus the audio frequency. In our example, this sum would be 1,001 kHz (1,000 kHz [carrier frequency] + 1 kHz = 1,001 kHz). The lower side frequency is equal to the difference between the two frequencies, 999 kHz in our example (1,000 kHz – 1 kHz = 999 kHz).

So far we have dealt with a single audio frequency, one representing a pure tone. However, most sounds are complex. They result in a complex audio signal, containing a number of different frequencies—a **band** of frequencies, as shown in Fig. 11.12. When this complex audio signal modulates the carrier, it creates bands of side frequencies—an **upper sideband** and an identical **lower sideband.**

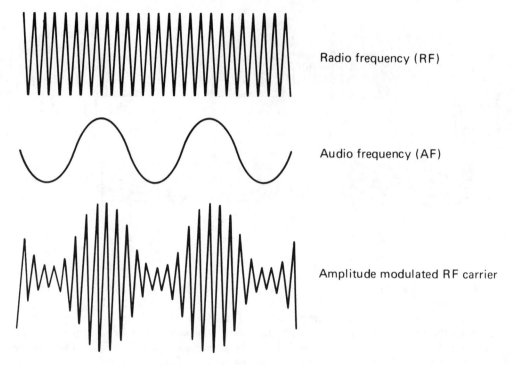

Radio frequency (RF)

Audio frequency (AF)

Amplitude modulated RF carrier

FIG. 11.11. Amplitude modulation.

***11.3.3.2 Frequency Modulation.*** In frequency modulation, amplitude remains constant, while frequency varies. Figure 11.13 shows this process. During the positive phase of one cycle of an audio signal, the modulated carrier increases frequency; during the negative phase, the modulated carrier decreases frequency. Audio frequency is reflected in the number of times the modulated carrier increases and decreases frequency each second. Audio amplitude is reflected in the number of carrier frequencies in each increase and decrease. For example, an audio signal of 440 Hz shows up in the modulated carrier as 440 increases and decreases of frequency per second. Low audio amplitude (say, a whisper) may increase and decrease frequency only 2 kHz; high audio amplitude (a shout) may increase and decrease carrier frequency by as much as 75 kHz.

## 11.4 RADIO TRANSMISSION AND RECEPTION

After the carrier is modulated, it is fed to the transmitting antenna. The presence of the modulated carrier in the antenna results in radiation of electromagnetic waves, as described in *PRT*, 10.1. The electronic pattern or structure of these waves corresponds to that of the modulated carrier, and thus the waves carry the encoded information.

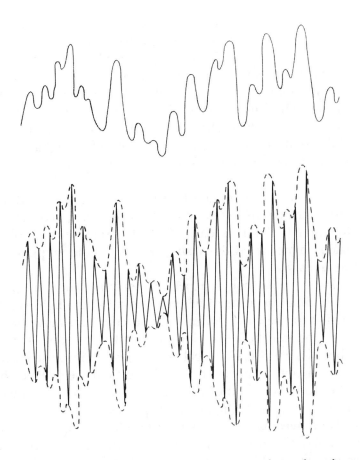

**FIG. 11.12. Complexity of signals.** Most sounds are complex and produce audio signals similar to the top drawing, above. Should this signal modulate a carrier in an AM transmitter, the result would be similar to the bottom drawing. Note the mirror image at top and bottom; these are the sidebands. On the drawing of the modulated carrier, the pattern of the audio signal is drawn in dashed lines to point out that the carrier's amplitude now reproduces the pattern. Technically, the audio signal itself is not part of the carrier; that is, the carrier does not carry the audio signal, only the pattern of that signal.

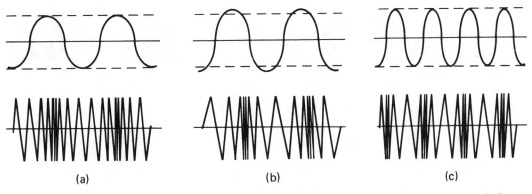

**FIG. 11.13. Frequency modulation of frequency and amplitude.** (a) Initial signal. (b) Increased amplitude. (c) Increased frequency.

When these waves reach a receiver, they go through several processes, so that you can hear the audio information as sound (Fig. 11.14). First, the waves come into contact with a receiving antenna. They induce a small electrical signal, a weak reproduction of the modulated carrier frequency. The signal moves into your receiver to the tuner. The tuner blocks all other frequencies except those of the frequency or channel to which you have tuned. The signal is then fed into a radio frequency amplifier that boosts the signal. The amplified signal next goes into a detector. Detection is the reverse process of modulation and recovers audio from the carrier.

In monaural radio, the recovered audio signal is fed to an AF amplifier for boosting, then to a speaker. In a stereophonic receiver, a stereo signal is split into component right and left channels, each of which is separately amplified and sent to separate speakers; a monaural signal simply goes to both amplifiers unchanged, exactly the same in each.

A speaker consists of voice coil, a paper or fiber cone, and a magnet. The voice coil consists of a number of turns of wire wound around a lightweight form that is, in turn, attached to the cone. Voice coil and cone can move back and forth. The voice coil is mounted between the poles of the magnet. The audio signal (which, remember, is a varying electrical current) is fed into the voice coil, which acts as an electromagnet. The varying magnetic field created by the voice coil interacts with the stationary field of the magnet on either side, causing the voice coil to move back and forth at the audio frequency rate. The cone, attached to the voice coil, also moves back and forth, alternately compressing and rarefying adjacent air molecules. If you are near the receiver when this happens, you identify the result as sound. Figure 11.15 illustrates the speaker process.

The sequence of events we have described represents analog transmission and reception. Digital transmission requires sampling the signal and sending a numeric representation of that signal. Once received, the numeric information is decoded into an analog representation of the original signal (*PRT,* 10.3).

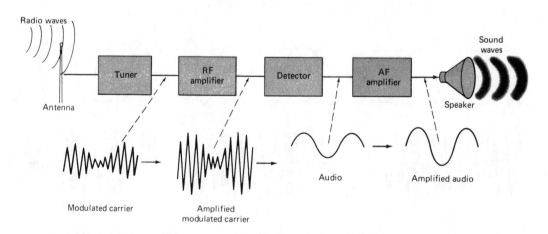

FIG. 11.14. Block diagram of an AM receiver.

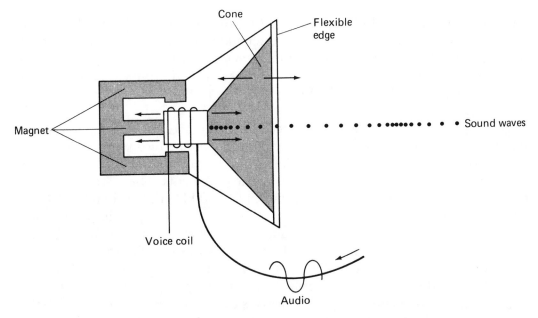

**FIG. 11.15. Speaker: Conversion of audio into sound.** Note the similarity in construction and operation to the dynamic microphone (Fig. 11.8).

## 11.5 AM CHANNELS

For years, FCC regulations allowed each AM radio station to occupy a 30 kHz bandwidth. Because the 30 kHz had to contain identical upper and lower sidebands, this meant an AM station could transmit a 15 kHz audio response bandwidth.

### 11.5.1 AM Frequency Response

In theory, 15 kHz was enough audio bandwidth to qualify as high fidelity. In practice, however, AM was a low-fidelity medium for a number of reasons. First, technical limitations in AM systems prevented transmission of the full 15 kHz.

Second, many radios were cheaply made. They had the simplest of circuits and tiny speakers. As a result, they reproduced a narrow audio frequency bandwidth. On such receivers, the sound of both AM and FM stations was little better than that of a telephone.

Third, AM was trapped in a cycle of degenerating fidelity for many years. Despite the 30 kHz occupied bandwidth (which equaled 15 kHz of audio bandwidth) allowed by the FCC, transmission of more than 20 kHz (10 kHz of audio) increased chances for interference from second adjacent channels. To mitigate interference, AM receiver manufacturers made sets that picked up less than the full 30 kHz. With reduced bandwidth capability, the receivers were not as liable to pick up interfering stations on second adjacent channels, but they would also not pick up the stations' high audio frequencies. As a result, the stations did not sound as good. To compensate, AM broadcasters used preemphasis; that is, they boosted the high frequencies of their audio signal. This caused even more interference, so the receiver manufacturers made AM radios that picked up an even narrower bandwidth. As a result of this cycle, the typical AM radio set reproduced an audio bandwidth of no more than 4 kHz compared to the 15 kHz response of FM.

Trade groups for broadcasters and receiver manufacturers formed a National Radio Systems Committee (NRSC) to study and make recommendations concerning this third problem. In 1987, the NRSC voted approval of new standards, and 2 years later, the FCC adopted them as requirements. These standards limit the bandwidth of audio a station can transmit to 10 kHz rather than the 15 kHz allowed by previous FCC rules. The standards call for a specific preemphasis curve—how much boosting of high frequencies the stations can do. Although AM stations appeared to give up 5 kHz of audio bandwidth under these standards, they would actually more than double their frequency response to a true 10 kHz, generally considered the low end of high fidelity. This would work out, however, only if manufacturers produced AM receivers that could reproduce a full 10-kHz audio bandwidth.

The advent of digital radio may allow AM stations to improve the quality of their signal. Some observers suggest that digital radio may eliminate the differences in the sound quality of AM and FM broadcasts (*PRT,* 11.8).

### 11.5.2 Stereophonic AM

When the FCC voted to allow AM stereophonic broadcasting in 1982, proponents of four different systems pushed aggressively for marketplace acceptance by receiver manufacturers and AM licensees. The FCC agreed, declining to select a single standard, unlike its practice in such decisions as color television. The four manufacturers were Magnavox, Motorola, Harris, and Kahn.

Each system was compatible with monaural AM, but none was compatible with the other stereo systems. A broadcaster who invested money to install one system was gambling. If that system became the standard—that is, if the majority of licensees and receiver manufacturers adopted it—then the broadcaster would be able to take advantage of audience listening trends to AM stereo. If another system became the standard, the broadcaster would have expended a considerable amount of money to transmit a stereo signal that few could receive. The audience would be able to pick up the station's nonstandard signal, but in monaural only for most. Several Japanese electronics manufacturers developed multisystem receivers, AM radios that would pick up and reproduce in stereo the signals from all four systems.

Magnavox and Harris eventually dropped out of the race. In 1987, the National Telecommunications and Information Administration (NTIA) announced the results of a study on AM stereo's progress. The NTIA said that stereo was vital to the future of AM broadcasting but concluded that the AM stereo marketplace had "stagnated." Today, a large proportion of AM stations have adopted nonmusical formats, eliminating much of the interest in stereo broadcasts.

### 11.5.3 Other Uses of AM Carriers

Under a 1982 rule, a utility company may lease the carrier of an AM station to transmit a subaudible (i.e., beneath the level of human hearing) signal. A utility company usually offers special rates to its customers who participate in this load management service. The utility installs a special receiver in the participating customer's home, business, or factory. During periods of peak load (i.e., whenever the most electricity or whatever is being used in the utility's service area), the utility transmits the subaudible tone via the AM station's signal. The special receivers pick up the signal and turn off the customers' appliances. When the peak load subsides, the utility transmits another subaudible tone that signals the receivers to turn the appliances back on.

In 1984, the FCC broadened its ruling. AM stations may now devote their carrier signals to any broadcast or nonbroadcast use that does not interfere with their main broadcast channel programming or the signals of other stations. This expanded ruling allows AM licensees to offer many of the same subsidiary services as FM.

### 11.6 FM CHANNELS

FM is said to be a **high-fidelity medium** because it is capable of reproducing most of the pitches that most of us can hear, from a low of 50 Hz to a high of 15,000 Hz. That wide range takes 15 kHz of each FM channel; sideband duplication accounts for another 15 kHz; and 25 kHz guard bands (frequencies not used for transmission) at either extreme of the channel use an additional 50 kHz. That leaves 120 kHz unused out of the 200 kHz FM channel. The FCC has authorized FM stations to use these frequencies to broadcast **stereophonically** and to transmit nonbroadcast channels in the **Subsidiary Communications Service** (SCS). Box 11.1 represents the upper sideband of an FM channel and shows some of these additional signals.

### 11.6.1 FM Multiplex

In developing a system of stereophonic broadcasting, there were three major requirements. First, one broadcast channel had to accommodate two audio channels. Second, some method had to be provided so that both stereophonic channels could be transmitted independently without interfering with each other (i.e., causing crosstalk). Third, stereophonic broadcasts had to be compatible with existing receivers.

## BOX 11.1. FM CHANNEL

We are looking at the upper sideband (100 kHz) of an FM channel. The channel's center frequency is at extreme left, where the solid horizontal line begins. The lower sideband (the other 100 kHz) of the channel) lies unpictured to the immediate left of the "Audio L + R" block. Numbers indicate the number of frequencies (in kHz) above the center frequency. The station using this channel broadcasts stereophonically and transmits one SCS. A monaural receiver utilizes only the "Audio L + R" signal and reproduces a monaural signal. A stereophonic receiver utilizes the subcarrier at 19 kHz above the center frequency to recover the "L – R" signal. The stereo receiver combines the L + R and L – R signals to produce separate left and right channels. Because this station transmits in stereo, the subcarrier for its SCS (and for any other SCSs it may wish to add) must operate between 53 and 99 kHz. This station's SCS subcarrier operates at 67 kHz and generates sidebands 7.5 kHz to either side (59.5–74.5 kHz). Only receivers equipped to utilize the SCS subcarrier can pick up the SCS signal. The guard band consists of frequencies left unused so as to avoid adjacent channel interference.

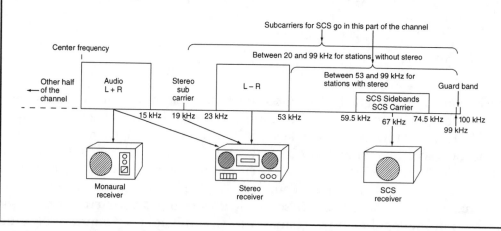

The **FM multiplex system** met all requirements. The word *multiplex* refers to the sending of two or more signals simultaneously over the same channel. FM stereophony uses **frequency multiplex**; that is, in addition to the main carrier frequency of a channel, subcarriers are generated and modulated to carry additional information. The right and left stereophonic channels are combined and transmitted on the main carrier, and certain accessory signals are transmitted on a subcarrier (Box 11.2). A stereophonic receiver has special circuitry that picks up the subcarrier and uses the accessory signals to separate the right and left stereophonic channels and to feed them to individual speakers. A monaural receiver can pick up the transmission but does not have the circuitry to utilize the subcarrier signals. A listener hears a monaural broadcast, the combined right and left stereophonic channels.

## BOX 11.2. MONAURAL AND STEREOPHONIC SOUND SYSTEMS

In monaural broadcasts (a), all sound sources are funneled down to one channel (here represented by one microphone picking up sound sources A, B, C, and D. When more than one microphone is used, audio signals from all microphones are simply blended together). The listener hears the sound as a blend (A+B+C+D) and perceives the source of the sound to be the speaker. In stereophonic broadcasts (b), all sound sources are funneled down to two channels—"right" and "left" (here represented by two microphones picking up A, B, C, and D; other microphones may be used, but their signals are blended into one of the two channels). The two signals are kept separate until transmission, at which time they are multiplexed together. A stereophonic receiver reseparates the right and left audio signals and feeds them to separate right and left speakers. The listener hears the sound binaurally, as though in the studio with the sound sources. When properly positioned, the listener perceives the sources of sound not to be the two speakers, but to be at various locations around the listening room, the same relative (to the microphones) locations of the sound sources in the studio.

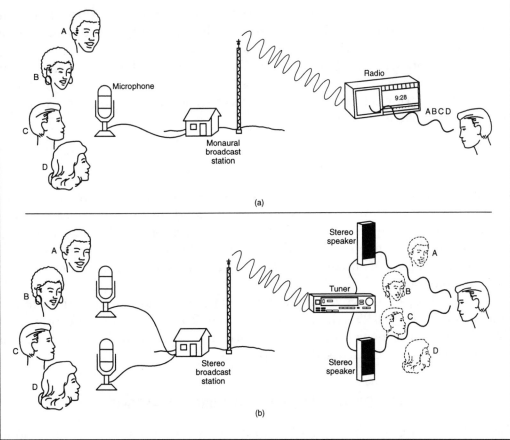

### 11.6.2 SCS and RBDS

Even with a stereophonic signal, there is still enough room left in an FM channel for still more subcarriers to transmit additional information. Some FM stations avail themselves of the FCC's liberal SCS rules and transmit nonbroadcast material. Users are equipped with special receivers tuned to the station's frequency. The receivers, in turn, have circuitry that allows them to pick up the SCS subcarrier. Home sets receive the station's normal broadcast programming, but most cannot receive the simultaneous SCS signal.

FM stations may use SCSs for any purpose, including point-to-point communication and common-carrierlike services, and may offer multiple SCS subcarriers in a single FM channel. In most cases, SCS provides a background music service. Some stations, however, provide specialized informational material for physicians, lawyers, or stockbrokers. Others offer radio paging (beeper) services, data transmission, and dispatch services. An SCS subcarrier can even transmit slow-scan video. Many noncommercial stations use their SCSs to provide reading services for the blind, but they may also use them to earn a profit (so long as the station continues to make a subcarrier available to the reading service on a nonprofit basis).

Broadcasters may also use a portion of their subcarrier for the **radio broadcast data system** (RBDS). Special receivers decode the data stream, which can contain such information as a station's call letters, special traffic information, or paging services. Acceptance of RBDS has been relatively slow in the United States, but in 1995 the Electronic Industries Association subsidized its adoption by large-market radio stations. The trade organization also began a promotional campaign to generate public interest in the service.

### 11.7 INTERNATIONAL BROADCAST SERVICE

By international agreement, certain groups of frequencies in the 6 to 25 MHz (high-frequency or **short-wave**) bands are allocated for broadcast between nations. Propagation characteristics change with the seasons, and a station usually wishes to broadcast programs simultaneously to different parts of the world, so that each international broadcasting station uses a number of different frequencies and multiple transmitters.

The FCC licenses nongovernmental international broadcasting stations in the United States. As of 1997 there were more than 20 such stations authorized by the FCC. Minimum power is 50 kW. Both private and governmental international broadcast stations are discussed in chapter 23.

### 11.8 DIGITAL AUDIO RADIO BROADCASTING

Radio stations are confronting a digital future. Whether that future will include new competitors, or will belong to existing broadcasters remains to be seen. The greatest advantage to digital radio is improved sound quality. Compression technologies would also allow six signals to be transmitted in the same spectrum space currently used for one radio station. However, digital radio has other capabilities. Suppose you are driving across country and want to listen to your favorite music format throughout the trip. Instead of searching the dial as you move out of range of a station, with digital broadcasting you might program your receiver before the trip. As you move out of range of one station the receiver searches for the next station playing your favorite format. Other uses might include specialized services, such as traffic or weather information or advertisements for hotels or restaurants ahead on the interstate.

Implementing digital radio will require regulatory and economic decisions. In the United States the most important decision involves approval of satellite-based services as possible competition to terrestrial broadcasting.

Most of the world's countries have accepted the idea of a satellite-based digital radio service. In 1992 the member nations of the International Telecommunications Union allocated the "L-band" (1452–1492 MHz) for digital radio. In the United States, however, those frequencies are used for aircraft telemetry, so 2310–2360 MHz was reserved for digital radio. In 1995 the FCC issued a Notice of Proposed Rule Making, asking for comments and suggestions about the creation of a satellite-based **digital audio radio service.**

In early 1997 the FCC authorized DARs believing it would reach underserved audiences in rural areas. Later in the year two companies won an auction for spectrum space. Satellite CD Radio and American Mobile Radio Corp each paid some $80 million for the right to offer DARs service. Receiving the 30 channels of CD-quality, commercial-free music would require a $200 receiver. Subscription charges would be about $10 per month. In approving DARs, the FCC said it would later consider imposing public service obligations on the operators.

Broadcasters in the United States oppose satellite-based digital radio. Satellite signals can cover the entire continent, eliminating the need for local broadcasts. To return to our example of the cross-country drive, a satellite service could provide a signal to your car, without you needing to switch channels. U.S. broadcasters advocate a terrestrial system using existing frequencies. They favor a system known as **in-band on-channel** (IBOC), in which broadcasters will use a portion of their allocated channel to transmit a digital signal. A similar proposal, with less support, is **in-band adjacent channel** (IBAC), which would allow stations to use vacant frequencies next to their own. Many observers doubt that these terrestrial technologies can overcome problems of channel capacity or interference problems that would not exist in satellite systems.

European and other countries favor a proposal known as **Eureka 147.** This satellite system uses a number of satellites in nongeosynchronous high earth orbit to provide signals on a continentwide basis. The Canadians, for example, have approved a system in which a satellite-based system in the L-band will join with terrestrial AM and FM broadcasters who will move from their current assignments to the new frequencies.

There are doubts about satellite-based services. Significant radio listening occurs outside the home, especially in automobiles. For such a system to succeed, cars will have to be equipped with satellite receivers. Without significant consumer demand, auto manufacturers are unlikely to offer the technology as anything but a very expensive option. If satellite-based services are authorized it is most likely that for a number of years drivers wanting access to digital radio will need to buy receivers from third-party suppliers.

## 11.9 WIRED RADIO

So far, we have discussed broadcast radio, that which goes "over the air" to reach your receiver. However, there are also radio services that use wire and other conductors for distribution.

One type of wired system is **cable audio service**. Many cable television systems charge a small extra fee to hook your FM receiver to the cable. You then use the FM tuner to select among the various services carried on the system. Most of these radio signals are from locally available stations. As with cable television, some cable systems import signals from stations outside their service area. Some cable systems offer special pay services that bring several channels of continuous music in a variety of formats. The music is usually uninterrupted by announcers or advertising.

Some colleges have **carrier current** stations. These feed a very low-power AM signal to the dormitory water pipes or power lines that, in turn, act as an antenna system. Radio receivers within the building are close enough to receive the station, but the signal does not carry beyond the walls. For this reason, such stations are also called "campus-limited" and "wired wireless." With their transmissions limited so as to prevent interference, the FCC does not require them to be licensed.

Finally, the FCC licenses stations in the **Travelers Information Service** (TIS). A TIS station uses a low-power roadside transmitter to feed conductors that parallel the highway. The conductors act as an antenna, and the transmission can be picked up on automobile radios in the immediate vicinity. A TIS station transmits information about hazards, directions to parking lots, food and lodging, and other such information. TIS stations operate at the extreme ends of the AM band, near or at busy air, train, and bus terminals, public parks, historical sites, interstate highway exchanges, bridges, and tunnels.

Internet-distributed audio services have also developed in recent years. Broadcast radio stations, networks, and program creators have used these systems to reach listeners outside their coverage area. The radio signal is digitized and may be stored for later retrieval by users, or may be available only at the same time as the original broadcast.

Audio signals can be retrieved and stored on a computer for later playback, or the signal can be retrieved as a "stream" from the host. "Streamable" signals are decoded and played back as they arrive, and the data are not stored by the computer. Streaming is particularly useful for lengthy programs such as sporting events or call-in programs.

## NOTES

1. 47 CFR § 73.1.
2. 47 CFR § 73.11.
3. The FCC makes further breakdowns of Class I and Class II stations.

## FURTHER READING

Benson, K. Blair, and Jerry Whitaker. *Television and Audio Handbook for Technicians and Engineers.* New York: McGraw-Hill, 1990.
Mazda, Fraidoon, Ed. *Principles of Radio Communication.* Newton, MA: Focal, 1996.
Roberts, Michael. *Sound Production: Technical Notes for the Non-technician.* Paris: Unesco, 1985.
Talbot-Smith, Mike. *Broadcast Sound Technology.* 2nd ed. Newton, MA: Focal, 1995.

# 12

## TELEVISION CHANNELS

The basic process of television transmission is the same as that of radio. The major difference, of course, is that television involves visual (picture) information. The visual signal is complex and requires wide bands of frequencies.

In this chapter, we start with visual perception—how our eyes and brains make use of light. Then we discuss the video signal—the conversion of light into an electronic analog. Next, we look at the television channel—the band of frequencies that carries the video signal and its various accessories. After that, we see how the television receiver makes use of that channel. Finally, we discuss the various modes of transmitting and receiving the TV channel—wireless and wired distribution—and the mechanics of some alternative video services.

### 12.1 VISUAL PERCEPTION

Television requires a lot of complex and expensive equipment, but the most complex part of the whole system is the device on which television depends for its very existence—your eyes. Television takes advantage of certain characteristics of the eye. If we want to know how television works, we must start with these characteristics.

### 12.1.1 Light

We see because our eyes are sensitive to light. All that we "see" is simply light—some direct, but most reflected. For example, you can see this page that you are now reading because light falls on the page, and the page reflects some of the light. Your eyes receive the light reflected from the page and, together with your brain, translate the particular pattern of light into a particular pattern of visual images. Your brain interprets this pattern as a page in a book.

Light is part of the electromagnetic spectrum (*PRT*, 10.2.1). Light—like radio signals—travels in waves and is measured by frequency and wavelength. Light, however, is far up the electromagnetic spectrum, and whereas radio waves are measured in meters, light waves are measured in millimicrons (mμ), each of which is one thousandth of a millionth of a meter.

346

## 12.1.2 Color

Our eyes are sensitive to light in different ways at different frequencies, and the different sensations that light produces are called *colors*. For example, we may perceive light in the range between 400 and 490 m$\mu$ as blue, between 500 and 560 m$\mu$ as green, and so on.

The sensation we call color may be described by three distinct psychological aspects—**hue**, the color itself (red, blue, green, yellow, etc.); **saturation** (also called **chroma**), the purity or strength of a color as pale, rich, washed out, and so on; and **brightness** (also **luminance** or **value**), whether the color is dark or light. These aspects are psychological because they are subjective, and each affects our perception of the others; if one changes, we see the result as a different color.

Keep in mind that we are discussing light, not pigment such as paint or crayons. Also remember that we are dealing with **physiological** color, not physical color. A physical color is pure, monochromatic, unmixed with other colors, and can be precisely described in terms of frequencies and wavelengths.

However, most light that reaches our eyes is not monochromatic, but a mixture of frequencies. White light, such as ordinary daylight (or the light reflected from this page), is a mixture; the various frequencies have, in a sense, canceled out each other so that we see no color. When one frequency in the mixture is stronger (highest intensity) than the others, we see color. If the highest intensity occurs in the yellow frequency region, we see yellow.

In some cases there is more than one strong frequency in the mixture. There could be, for example, one strong frequency in the red region and another in the green region. We would interpret the light hitting our eyes not as separate red and green, but (given the proper frequencies) as yellow. This is an example of physiological color and is apparently determined by the ratios of light picked up by the red-, blue-, and green-sensitive cones (color receptors) in our eyes. Given proper mixtures, we would see no difference between the pure, monochromatic yellow and the physiological yellow created from red and green.

These physiological colors are possible because of the **trichromatic nature of vision**; that is, over a wide range of brightness levels, our eyes can match almost any color by specific combinations of two other colors. Color television takes advantage of this to work its chromatic illusion. The camera breaks down light reflected from a televised scene into three colors—red, blue, and green (at wavelengths of 610 m$\mu$, 472 m$\mu$, and 534 m$\mu$, respectively)—called **primary colors**. When your home receiver screen reproduces the three colors in the same proportions, your eyes see all the various colors present in the original scene.

## 12.1.3 Persistence Of Vision

We watch an exciting chase scene unfold on our television screens, but the movement that we think we see is an illusion.

This illusion was first used for mass audiences in another medium, motion pictures. A movie camera actually photographs a scene as a series of still pictures (frames) taken one after another, 24 per second. The film is semitransparent so that light beamed through it projects an enlargement of the pictures.

When used in a movie projector, these separate still pictures are shown in such way as to create the illusion of motion. The projector places one frame in front of a light source, the light projects the picture twice very briefly, and the projector moves the first frame out and the next one in. This action is repeated 24 times per second.

The TV screen, similar to the movie projector, is capable only of reproducing a series of electronic still pictures or frames. In the case of our chase scene, each still picture is slightly different from the others.

At this point, we still have a series of still pictures, but a trick of the eye called **persistence of vision** translates still pictures into motion. When you look at an object and then glance away, the retina of your eye retains the image of the object for the briefest of instants; this is persistence of vision. As you watch a motion picture or a television program, your eye retains the image of each frame long enough so that by the time the next picture appears, your brain has connected the two, and you see an illusion of motion instead of a series of still pictures.

## 12.2 VIDEO SIGNAL

We are now ready to investigate the mechanics of video, to find out how light, the primary colors, and persistence of vision make pictures. We begin with the key device, the color camera, the origin of the video (picture) signal.

### 12.2.1 Color Cameras

Three main parts of the color television camera help create the video signal—the **lens**, the **internal optical system**, and the **video pickup**. The lens is external to the camera but attached to it. The lens gathers light reflected from the scene to be televised and focuses it onto the internal optical system inside the camera. The internal optical system, called a **beam splitter**, consists of combinations of prisms, mirrors, and color filters, the purpose of which is to break up the light from the scene into its red, blue, and green components. Each of these three components is focused onto a separate video pickup or **imager**.

### 12.2.2 Video Pickups

Video cameras have evolved over the years. Originally the pickup consisted of large vacuum tubes that required that subjects be brightly lit (and those lights generated an uncomfortable amount of heat). The vacuum tube gave way to solid-state tubes that were smaller, lighter, and required more comfortable amounts of light. Today, most video cameras use one of two overall types of pickup. One is the **charge coupled device** (CCD; Fig. 12.1). The other, **digital cameras,** became available in the second half of the 1990s. These devices record information digitally, rather than using the analog technology historically found in cameras. The digital information can then be transferred directly to a computer-based nonlinear editing system.

The CCD, a solid-state imager, makes possible the tubeless television camera (Fig. 12.1). This large-scale integrated circuit measures about an inch square and $\frac{1}{16}$ inch thick. The scene being televised is focused on the CCD's imaging surface or optic. The imaging surface consists of nearly 200,000 "photo site" capacitors—the picture elements, or **pixels**—arranged in columns and rows on an area with a 3 × 4 aspect ratio. The reception of light energy by a photo site liberates electrons proportionate to the intensity of light at that location. A potential well holds the light-generated charge. The charge then transfers, first to a vertical (digital) store register, and then to horizontal (analog) storage, a shift register from which it is clocked out as a continuous video signal. This transfer process passes the charge pattern from one capacitor to the next.

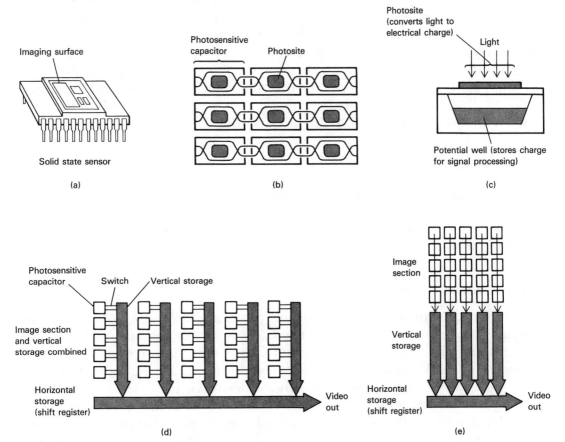

FIG. 12.1. **Charge-coupled device.** (a) The CCD itself. (b) Detail of a section of the imaging surface. (c) Side cutaway view of one photo site capacitor. The configuration of the vertical storage area defines two basic CCD technologies—(d) an *interline transfer* CCD integrates the storage area with the optic; (e) a *frame transfer* CCD uses a separate storage area.

### 12.2.3 Scanning Pattern

Signal readout from a CCD follows a pattern. There are **525 lines** or rows of photo site capacitors, and each capacitor includes a switch. All switches open in alternating rows, and the accumulated charges transfer to the first (vertical) frame store. Next, they transfer to the second (horizontal) frame store, from which they emerge to become the video signal. (Additionally, some CCD cameras include a mechanical shutter that completely shuts out light during transfers.) Each full electronic still picture is called a **frame** and the action occurs at a speed of **30 frames per second** (fps).

Thirty fps would seem to be enough to make us see an illusion of smooth motion, especially considering that silent film achieves the illusion at 16 fps. However, a film projector shows each frame twice, so silent film actually utilizes 32 frame projections per second. Also, as screen brightness increases, our eyes are not as easily tricked into blending together a sequence of pictures. The television screen is so much brighter than the motion picture screen that even at 30 fps we would still see **flicker**—a constant, regular variation in the overall brightness of the television screen. Therefore, to eliminate flicker, American television actually shows **60 half-pictures per second.** The electron beam scans **every other line** until it reaches the bottom of the target, then it jumps back to the top and starts over, scanning the lines it skipped the first time. This is called **interlace scanning** (Fig. 12.2). The beam scans 262½ lines on each pass, called a **field**, so there are **two fields per frame** and **60 fields per second.**

### 12.2.4 Signal Processing

Video signals from the video pickups combine in various ratios to form three intermediate signals—one for brightness, two for colors. These are added to produce the **composite video signal**, which consists of **luminance** and **chrominance** components.

### 12.2.5 Camera Configurations

A **camera control unit** (CCU) provides power and drive pulses (to direct the scanning pattern) for the camera. The CCU is usually located apart from the camera, and one person operates several CCUs at once. A **camera cable** connects camera and CCU, delivering drive pulses to, and composite video from, the camera. Camera, cable, and CCU are the **camera chain.**

The cameras discussed earlier are the type used for studio productions and for scheduled remotes (broadcasts of planned events that take place outside the studio; Fig. 12.3). Two other types of camera are the film chain and the minicamera. The **film chain** is basically a camera that has been mounted permanently in a stationary position. Adjacent film and slide projectors focus their beams into the lens of the camera. The whole works—camera, projectors, and associated

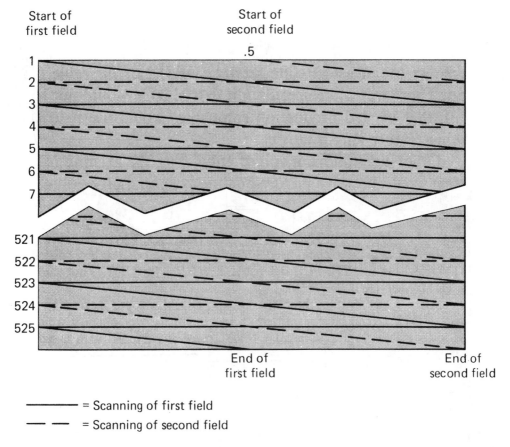

Start of
first field

Start of
second field

.5

1
2
3
4
5
6
7

521
522
523
524
525

End of
first field

End of
second field

——————— = Scanning of first field

—— —— = Scanning of second field

**FIG. 12.2. Interlaced scanning pattern.**

control equipment—is the **telecine unit**. For many years this was the means for integrating slides and films into a television program. Today telecines are most commonly used to transfer films to videotape. Feature film production also utilizes telecines to transfer film to videotape for postproduction work. The completed footage is then transferred back to film. The **minicamera** or **camcorder** often uses no cable; its video can be recorded or relayed short distances via radio waves.

### 12.2.6 Video Storage and Playback

Not all video signals originate from a camera. For example, a VTR may serve as a video source. Like an audiotape recorder, a VTR records the electronic signal in the form of magnetic patterns on tape. Like an audiotape recorder, the VTR can play back a recording immediately; no further processing or developing are necessary.

**Optical media** also might be used. These might be a video disc, CD-ROM, or DVD. In these technologies a video signal is converted to digital form, and the digital code is embedded as pits into the surface of the disc by a laser. When played

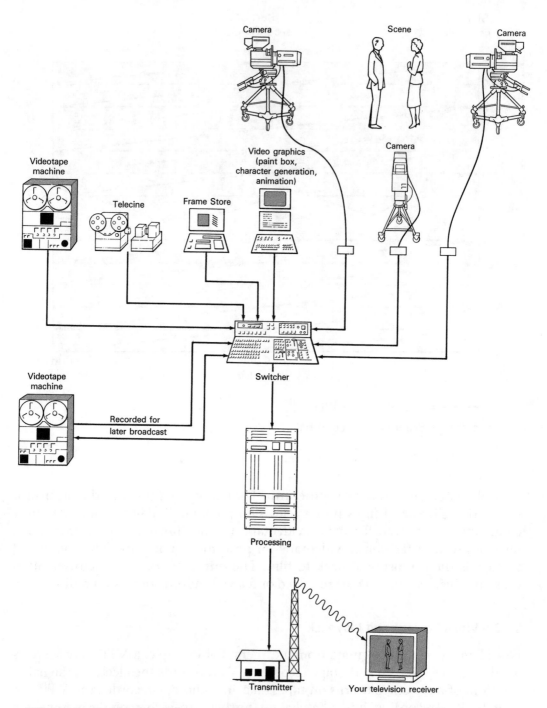

**FIG. 12.3. Combining video sources.** Video sources include the playback head of a videotape machine, the pickup tube of the film chain in the telecine unit (for film transfer), frame (still) store, video graphics generator, and live studio and remote cameras. These feed to the switcher for mixing and special effects. From there, a number of things may happen to the video signal—it may be recorded for later broadcast; it may be sent to the transmitter for immediate transmission; or it may be both recorded and transmitted at the same time.

back, a laser reads the patterns of pits as digital information, which can then be converted to analog form.

### 12.2.7 Other Video Sources

Several devices utilize computer technology to produce "pure" (not originated by a camera) video signals. These include the frame store, character generator, paint system, and 3-D graphics and animation systems.

The **frame store** (electronic still store) performs a task similar to that of slide projectors in a telecine unit. An electronic camera scans a live scene or artwork, and the electronic image (the frame) is stored in digital form in a memory unit along with dozens of other frames. A frame may be recalled instantly for broadcast, production, or alteration.

A **character generator,** sometimes called a **font machine** or **font,** contains a repertoire of shapes that can be placed on the screen. Its circuitry creates letters and numerals in several different fonts, styles, and sizes. It may also produce a limited number of other figures. Material produced by a character generator can be stored and then called up when needed. Most often, such material takes the form either of captions and identifying titles placed on another picture or of full frame messages (as, e.g., the screen that tells you how to use your bank card and the toll-free telephone number to order a product at the end of a TV commercial).

A **paint system** consists of computer and software, electronic stylus, digitizing tablet, and color video monitor. It may also include a character generator and a frame store. When the system is used to create video graphics, the video signal is held in a buffer for modification and display. The artist may create a completely new image "from scratch" or may alter an existing video image—perhaps to change an advertiser's logo slightly or to add artwork to a frame from a videotape shot on location. The more elaborate systems provide so many control functions that the artist creating video graphics actually has greater flexibility than one who uses traditional paints and brushes.

The video graphics artist can create the illusions of three dimensions (3-D) and animation with a **3-D animation system.** With this system, an object may be drawn in one position and then rotated to show it in other positions. The system has built-in logic circuits and large-scale frame storage that assist in creating the many individual "slightly different" frames needed for animation. Once an initial drawing is completed, the human input required to animate it is minimal. Once created, an animated sequence is stored for recall and use in production.

### 12.2.8 Combining Video Signals

Most television programs use video signals from a number of sources. Any source or combination of sources may be **put on the line,** that is, selected to send the video on to the next point in the production process (Fig. 12.3). The selection of the video signal or combination of video signals to go on the line is **mixing,** also called **switching.**

The mixing controls are known collectively as the **switcher**. Additionally, there is usually an **effects generator** associated with the switcher, and between the two devices, various visual effects may be achieved, ranging from a simple **cut** (instantaneous replacement of one picture by another) to exotic **mattes** and **keys** (part of one picture is inserted into another).

## 12.3 TELEVISION CHANNELS

The 6-MHz-wide television channel accommodates two carrier frequencies. The first is at 1.25 MHz (from the channel's lowest frequency) and is modulated by the composite video signal; the second, at 5.75 MHz, is modulated by the audio signal.

### 12.3.1 Video Modulation

As shown in Fig. 12.4, the upper and lower sidebands of the video signal are not mirror images of each other. The former extends 4.5 MHz above the carrier; the latter, only 1.25 MHz below, a result of **vestigial sideband** modulation. This is normal amplitude modulation with one sideband partially suppressed. The color component is in the sidebands of the **color subcarrier**.

Figure 12.5 shows that the luminance and chrominance sidebands overlap. The technique by which these two different signals share the same frequency space is called **frequency interlace** or **interleaving**—placing the clusters of color energy between the clusters of video energy.

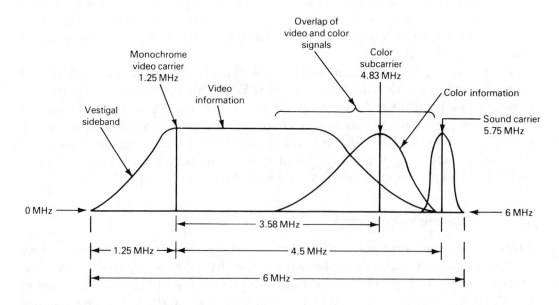

FIG. 12.4. Broadcast television channel.

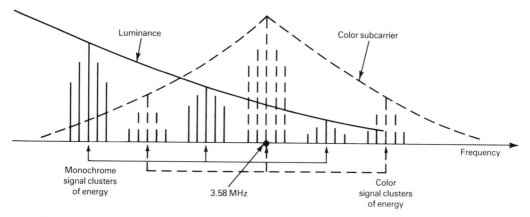

FIG. 12.5. Interleaving of color information.

As mentioned at the beginning of this section, the luminance signal modulates the amplitude of the video carrier. The saturation part of the chrominance signal modulates the amplitude of the color subcarrier. The hue part of the chrominance signal modulates the phase of the color subcarrier, varying the angle of the wave slightly for each hue. Thus the **video signal is amplitude modulated** (AM) and the **color signal is both AM and phase modulated.**

### 12.3.2 Accessory Signals

In order for the home color receiver to recover the phase modulated hue information, a special signal is sent as part of the composite video signal. This is the **color burst** (Fig. 12.6), and its purpose is to ensure that the electronic circuits in your home color receiver are exactly in phase with the original subcarrier frequency. The color burst is an accessory signal—a nonpicture signal sent as part of the video signal—that accompanies color transmissions.

Two other accessory signals are part of all television transmissions, both color and monochrome. These are **sync pulses** and **blanking pulses.** Sync pulses keep your receiver's scanning beam synchronized with the camera's scanning. Blanking pulses cut off the electron beam when it moves from the end of one line or field to the beginning of the next. This between-lines movement is called **retrace**, and the blanking pulse prevents retrace lines from showing on the screen.

The video signal is **negatively modulated.** This means that as darker areas of the scene are scanned, the video signal increases in amplitude. The amplitude of the signal can be boosted to a point beyond the darkest shade a TV set can reproduce. Sync, blanking, and color burst pulses are inserted between each line of scansion, all at this **blacker than black level** of amplitude (Fig. 12.7). The same technique is used to send signals for closed captioning and teletext (*PRT,* 5.5.2 and 5.5.3) in the vertical blanking interval; that is, during the period when the scanning beam returns from the end of one field back up to the top of the frame to begin scanning another field.

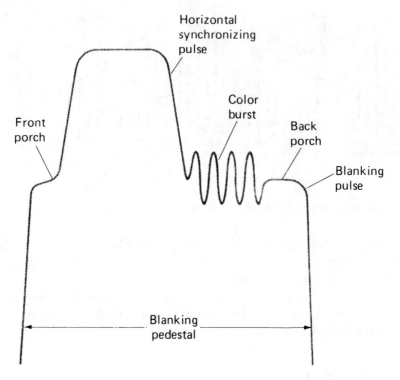

FIG. 12.6. Accessory signals: Color burst, sync, blanking.

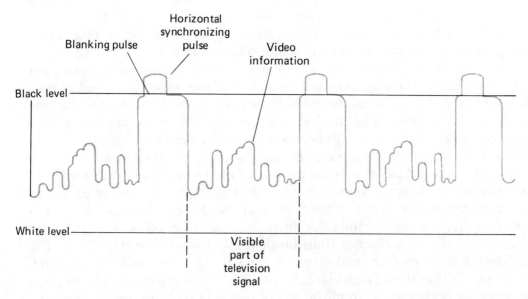

FIG. 12.7. **Video and accessory signals.** This diagram shows three horizontal lines of video signal with accessory signals.

### 12.3.3 Television Audio

Whereas the video signal is AM, the **audio signal is frequency modulated** (FM). The audio signal sidebands extend 25 KHz to either side of its carrier.

FCC rules allow broadcasters to use any system for **multichannel television sound** (MTS). However, on recommendation of an industrywide Broadcast Television System Committee (BTSC), the FCC specified that all systems had to "protect" (i.e., not interfere with) the workings of an MTS system developed by Zenith and dbx, Inc. The FCC thus set a standard but at the same time encouraged marketplace advances in technology.

BTSC MTS allows both stereophonic and second-audio-program (SAP) transmission. The TV stereo sound system is similar to that of FM radio in that it consists of a main channel (which combines both left and right channels) and a stereo subcarrier. The SAP is transmitted by means of yet another subcarrier. An example of use of the SAP might be a television station whose service area includes a large number of Hispanics and transmits a Spanish translation of program audio on the second channel.

## 12.4 TELEVISION RECEIVERS

The existing color television system is **compatible**—you may watch the same color telecast on either a color receiver or on a monochrome receiver (in black and white, of course). Compatibility is possible because both the color receiver and the monochrome receiver utilize the video signal ("the picture" without color). Color receivers have special circuitry that detects and makes use of the color signal (which colors "the picture"), so when you watch a color telecast on a color receiver, you see color pictures. A monochrome receiver lacks this circuitry, but because it receives the video signal, you see color telecasts in black and white.

Your television receiver must reconstruct the various picture components from the composite signal. Using the color burst and the chrominance component, it retrieves the green, red, and blue signals. Other circuits detect and make use of sync and blanking pulses.

The **color picture tube** (Fig. 12.8) is the device that creates the picture. The three separate color signals feed into the base of the picture tube where there is an **electron gun** assembly. The inside of the face of the tube—that is, the other side of the glass screen that you watch—is coated with many thousands of tiny separate **color phosphors**—red, blue, and green. Just in back of the phosphor screen is a **mask**.

The gun assembly fires at the screen three separate electron beams, the intensity of each controlled by its respective red, blue, or green signal voltage. (Remember, electrons themselves have no color; they only carry information about color.) The beams scan the screen, and their scanning matches that of the video pickup—30 fps (60 interlaced fields). The mask helps to direct and sharpen the three electron beams so that they hit the proper color phosphors. The beams strike the

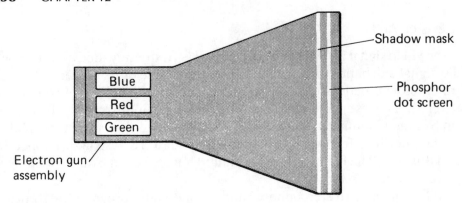

**FIG. 12.8. Color receiver picture tube.**

phosphors, making them glow briefly at intensities that vary with those of the beams (Fig. 12.9). However, the beams scan so quickly that we cannot see those brief instances when phosphors are not glowing.

This means that the only colors actually on the screen are red, blue, and green (in varying proportions, of course). At normal viewing distances, characteristics of our eyes are such that we do not see the individual phosphors. As discussed in *PRT,* 12.1.2, we blend together these three physical primary colors so that we see a full range of physiological colors.

**Sound** reproduction is less complicated. After being split from the video signal, the audio signal goes through its own circuitry. The process is similar to that for radio (*PRT,* 11.4). The result is that sound is reproduced by the television speaker.

Monochrome receivers pick up only the luminance signal from a color telecast. The single video signal feeds into the base of the monochrome picture tube. The gun assembly fires a single beam at the rear surface of the screen. Because there is only one beam, there is no mask. The phosphors all glow white.

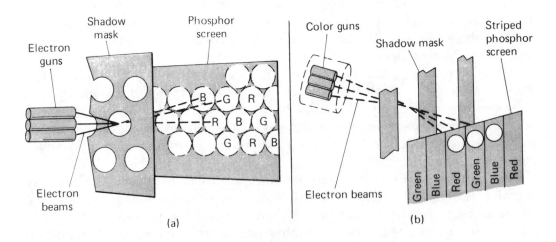

**FIG. 12.9. Two types of color television tubes.** (a) Shadow mask. (b) Aperture grill.

## 12.5 ADVANCED TELEVISION SYSTEMS

The television system just described gave many years of service, since proposed by NTSC in 1941 and 1953 (*PRT,* 3.1.1). However, as time passed and technology progressed, complaints developed. Critics compared NTSC picture quality unfavorably to the newer, higher resolution systems found in some foreign countries. Engineers pointed out the difficulty of achieving color consistency when switching from one video source to another—even from one camera to another in the same studio.

One major source of NTSC color problems was the composite nature of the signal, the fact that the luminance and chrominance components were frequency multiplexed (*PRT,* 12.3.1). Further, the very process of production and distribution made the problem worse. At every point between camera pickup and the home screen where something had to be done to video, the NTSC signal had to be first taken apart (decoded) then reassembled (encoded) afterward. Each manipulation further degraded the signal.

In the early 1980s the Japanese network, NHK, demonstrated a new technology, dubbed **high-definition television** (HDTV). This approach increased the number of scanning lines to 1,125, and changed the picture's shape to 16:9 from the NTSC's 4:3 ratio. The picture would be created at 60 fields per second. Thus, HDTV promised a more sharply defined picture that showed more area in a shape better suited to the physiology of human eyesight. The two significant technical drawbacks to the HDTV proposal were that existing production equipment and home receivers would have to be replaced, and that the analog HDTV transmission required as much as six times the spectrum space as the existing system.

### 12.5.1 HDTV

The Japanese demonstration of HDTV and developments by European manufacturers raised concern that the United States would lose control of this new technology as it previously had with the VCR and CD.[1] U.S. electronics manufacturers would lose world markets to the Japanese and Europeans. Further, the military saw high-definition video technology as a potentially important component of fighter aircraft targeting and display systems. Therefore, the Department of Defense also worried about the technology being outside of U.S. control.

Because of these political and economic concerns, the U.S. government encouraged development of a domestic system. The FCC had plenty of help in its continuing inquiry into HDTV standards. An Advanced Television Systems Committee (ATSC) consisting of representatives from the various trades and companies that would be affected by changes in consumer television technology was formed in 1983. The FCC itself had formed an Advanced Television Services (ATV) advisory committee. The networks and the major broadcast trade associations sponsored an Advanced Television Test Center (ATTC). ATTC would provide facilities for ATSC and ATS to test the various advanced systems. Major cable operators formed Cable Television Laboratories, Inc.

The HDTV problem was to set a U.S. standard—one single system that everyone could agree on, use, and market. The standard-setting problem actually encompassed two issues. One involved a search for a **production standard**—a system for making HDTV images. The other had to do with a **transmission standard**—a system for **broadcasting** HDTV images. In practice, the two could be considered separately; any HDTV transmission standard could broadcast images made with any HDTV production standard. The idea, however, was to have just one of each.

*12.5.1.1 Compatibility.*    Regardless of the standard to be adopted an important issue was how to introduce HDTV. If people did not buy receivers capable of displaying HDTV there would be no incentive for broadcasters to transmit the signals. And why would the consumer spend the estimated $1,000 or more for a receiver if there were no signals? The problem was similar to that faced with the introduction of color television. Based on that experience, broadcasters and others supported adoption of a standard that would be compatible with existing NTSC transmissions. When it became obvious that solution would not be possible, the FCC declared a "simulcast" solution. The FCC said that for a period of time broadcasters would transmit an NTSC signal on one channel and an HDTV transmission on a second channel assigned to the licensee.

*12.5.1.2 Digital Solution.*    The ATV committee was charged with testing the various proposals for HDTV systems. All approaches, including those developed by the Japanese and the Europeans were based on analog technologies. Then, in 1990, shortly before the ATV committee was to begin its evaluative tests, one of the applicants (General Instruments) proposed a digital standard for HDTV. Soon, four of the other applicants adopted digital approaches. In tests the digital systems demonstrated their superiority over the remaining analog proposal by NHK.

*12.5.1.3 Grand Alliance.*    Each of the remaining proposals had strengths, but also important weaknesses. Led by its chairman, former FCC Chairman Richard Wiley, the ATV committee encouraged the remaining applicants to propose a "best of the best" standard combining elements of all of the proposals. After months of negotiation, a "grand alliance" was announced, composed of American and European entities: AT&T, the David Sarnoff Research Center, General Instrument, MIT, North American Philips (a subsidiary of the Dutch company N.V. Philips), Thomson Consumer Electronics (a French company that later purchased RCA's consumer electronics operations), and Zenith.

As the grand alliance developed the digital HDTV technology, two important developments occurred. In early 1995 the FCC encouraged the committee to consider scanning formats for standard definition television (SDTV) that would also be available in the proposed digital standard. In other words, a digital signal could be transmitted, creating a picture with less resolution than high definition.

The ATV committee included the SDTV standard in its recommendation to the FCC, but some observers worried that broadcasters would choose to continue transmitting programs in the existing format rather than spending money on new transmitters, production, and playback equipment needed for HDTV.

Another development may have significantly more important consequences for the electronic media industries. In 1994 the grand alliance reported that its system could carry multiple data streams. In effect, a broadcaster might have as many as six "channels" to offer (later tests were to push that to 24 channels in a 6 MHz digital stream).

### 12.5.2 ATV Proposed Standard

As expected, the advisory committee recommended in 1995 that the FCC adopt the advanced television system proposed by the Grand Alliance. The proposal includes five subsystems: scanning, video and audio compression, transport, and transmission.

Scanning would include two possible HDTV schemes. They would vary according to the number of lines and pixels, and frame rates. An SDTV approach includes two possible formats: 480 lines × 704 pixels in 4:3 or 16:9 aspect ratio, or, 480 lines × 640 pixels per line in 4:3 aspect ratio. Both SDTV formats would be either interlace or progressive scanning.

The proposed system would use a Dolby five-channel audio system and MPEG-2 compression (*PRT,* 10.3.3). Most important, the system would allow for interoperability. In other words, digital schemes could be used by cable television and satellite technologies, as well as terrestrial broadcasting.

The scanning issue—interlace versus progressive—was the subject of significant debate. Progressive scanning is used by computer systems, and the computer industry believed that adoption of that system would be to its competitive advantage. Motion picture technicians also supported the progressive scanning standard because it is used in computer animation and special effects systems. The broadcast and cable industries argued in favor of interlace scanning. Finally, the industries and the FCC agreed that there would be no federal standard. The market would decide between the computer standard and the broadcast.

Ultimately, successful implementation of a broadcast advanced television system would rely on the availability of receivers. Clearly, no broadcaster could stop broadcasting in NTSC if viewers could not receive ATV signals. Consistent with its earlier statement that a simulcast solution be used, the FCC proposed that broadcasters be given a second channel for ATV transmission. For a period of time the station would simulcast—NTSC on one of its channels, and ATV on the other. After a transition period, during which manufacturers would stop making NTSC receivers, the first channel would be returned to the public for reallocation through the government. The Telecommunications Act of 1996 institutionalized the idea. Congress instructed the FCC to allocate a second channel to broadcasters. Two political issues quickly arose. First, as broadcasters discussed how they might use the extra spectrum they would be assigned, some members of Congress raised the issue of spectrum fees. They suggested that broadcasters should pay for the additional channel. Broadcasters opposed the spectrum fee idea and argued further that they should not have to return the second channel. Instead, they said the second channel would allow them to compete with other multichannel providers, such as cable.

To spur the introduction of ATV the FCC required affiliates of the four major commercial networks in markets 1 to 10 to begin digital broadcasts by May, 1999. Affiliates in markets 11–30 must begin ATV service by November, 1999. These start dates were selected with an eye on the sale of ATV sets to consumers during the 1998 and 1999 winter holidays.

The ATV idea does not necessarily require that broadcasters transmit HDTV. Many ask if consumers really desire the improved picture quality. Further, broadcasters will have to offer dual services for some time, and will require new and expensive transmitters. Although film is already "high definition," video is not. Existing file footage would have to be converted, but pictures in a 4:3 aspect ratio cannot be changed to a 16:9 aspect ratio without distorting the existing picture. Broadcasters may find it more logical to use the ATV technology and additional channel to transmit additional SDTV programs, data, or other signals. Congress and the FCC issued statements reemphasizing their expectation that broadcasters would transmit HDTV programs.

Competition could spur broadcasters to transmit in high definition. Cable operators and digital satellite services have channel capacity that would allow them to transmit in high definition without additional transmission expenses, although they might have to eliminate some existing channels to free up bandwidth for both NTSC and HDTV transmissions during the transition period. Program services that rely heavily on motion pictures would be able to convert to a high-definition format relatively quickly. If consumers consider the HDTV picture to be an incentive for watching one channel over another, broadcasters would have little choice but to convert to HDTV.

In Fall 1996, WRC in Washington, DC became the first fully equipped HDTV station. The NBC owned and operated station would test equipment and programming for 3 years, using the standards agreed to by the Grand Alliance. The project was funded by equipment manufacturers and broadcasters. The broadcasts used a second, UHF, channel assigned to WRC, and included data transmissions and interactive services in addition to the HDTV programming.

## 12.6 TELEVISION BROADCAST SERVICE

The television broadcast service operates on **68 channels** spread across two different frequency bands. Television channels are identified by numbers, 2 through 69.[2] Each channel is **6 MHz wide,** so wide that all 100 FM radio channels could fit in the space of 3½ television channels, and the entire AM radio band could be repeated nearly six times within the space of one television channel.

### 12.6.1 Television Transmission Band and Allocations

Television channels 2 through 13 lie in the VHF band. Channels 2, 3, and 4 encompass the frequencies 54 to 72 MHz; 5 and 6, 76 to 88 MHz; and 7 through 13, 174 to 216 MHz. The FM radio band lies just above channel 6 (which is why you can often pick up television channel 6 sound on the lower end of your FM radio dial), and frequencies between channels 4 and 5 and between the FM band and channel 7 are used for other purposes.

Channels 14 through 69 are in the UHF band, encompassing a continuous band of frequencies from 470 to 806 MHZ. Thus there is a big gap of 254 MHz (used for other purposes) between channels 13 and 14.

When the FCC first opened UHF for television broadcasting in 1952 (*PRT,* 3.1.5), it created 70 new channels—the UHF television band extended all the way up to 890 MHz, and the highest channel number was 83. However, in 1970, the FCC reallocated channels 70 through 83 in the UHF broadcast band to land mobile radio services.[3] Next, the Commission reallocated certain unused UHF assignments involving channels 14 through 20 in the 25 largest markets to the land mobile services. Channel 37 was reallocated to radio astronomy use.

Like FM radio, television signal propagation is primarily by direct waves. Coverage is determined largely by antenna height, frequency, power, and terrain. With careful planning, cochannel and adjacent-channel interference are rarely problems.

Also like FM radio, the FCC table of assignments allocates specific television channels to specific communities. However, unlike FM, the television table assigns educational noncommercial channels to specific communities; the TV table reserves about 20% of the specific allocations for noncommercial use.

### 12.6.2 New Television Stations

Should you wish to build a new full-service television station, you must do one of three things. First, you look for a vacant channel allocated to the community in which you want to build the station. If there is such a channel, you apply for it. However, you will probably find all local channels taken.

Second, you look for a vacant channel assigned to a nearby smaller market. Using that channel, perhaps you can locate the station so that it puts a signal over the desired community; there is a limited amount of freedom in locating a station. Again, most of those channels have been taken.

Third, you petition the FCC to amend the table of allocations, probably to have a vacant channel moved from another location to the desired community. The petition would have to demonstrate that the move would meet all relevant mileage separation requirements as spelled out in the FCC rules to prevent interference. Then, if the FCC were to grant the petition, you could apply for permission to build a television station. But the channel is open for other applicants, too; convincing the FCC to amend the TV table of allocations does not mean that you automatically get the channel.

Theoretically, you would have a much easier time applying for a low-power television station (LPTV). LPTVs are not included in the table of allocations. Instead, you apply for an LPTV on a demand basis, somewhat similar to the situation in AM radio. When the FCC opened the LPTV service in 1982, however, thousands applied to construct stations. For each of the choicest channels and locations, there were usually a number of different applications.

### 12.6.3 Television Transmission and Reception

A television broadcast transmitter actually consists of two transmitters—one each for the video and audio signals (Fig. 12.10). The output of both the video transmitter and the audio transmitter are combined, and the combined signals power the antenna to generate transmission waves.

Just as in radio, the transmitted waves induce a weak electrical signal in the television receiving antenna. This signal feeds to a tuner, which blocks all frequencies except those for the channel to which you are tuned. The signal is boosted, and video, audio, and accessory signals are recovered from the carrier and used as described earlier.

## 12.7 COMMUNICATION SATELLITES

Communication satellites are essentially relay stations in the sky. Because of their altitude, a line-of-sight signal to satellites and back can cover as much as one third of the earth's surface. Modern communication satellites are placed in either fixed, geostationary orbits around the equator (Fig. 12.11), or in nongeostationary polar

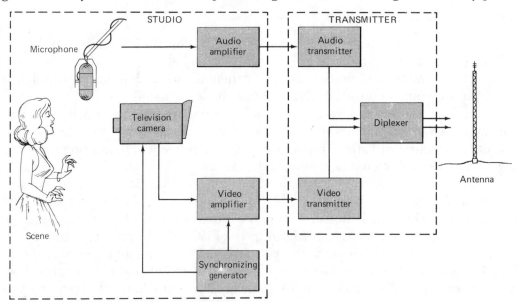

FIG. 12.10. Block diagram of television station and transmitter.

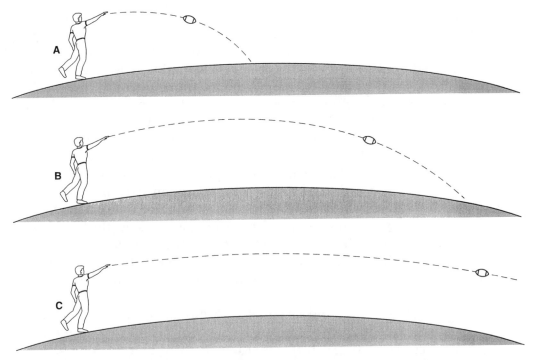

**FIG. 12.11. How a satellite orbits.** Some people believe orbiting satellites "fly" in space like an airplane. In fact, the satellite is actually in "free fall." Imagine a football player passing a ball with a small amount of effort (a). After a few yards the ball settles to earth. With more effort (b) the ball goes higher and farther before returning to earth. Now, imagine the ball being thrown so high and hard that it literally goes over the horizon (c). At sufficient height and speed an object goes beyond the atmosphere, into space. As it falls back to earth, gravity catches the satellite, and "whips" it around before it can drop completely to earth. Eventually the object will lose sufficient forward motion, and will drop to earth, just like our football example.

orbits in which the satellite's position changes in relation to the earth. They receive signals from the earth, process the signals, and transmit them back to earth. On the ground, receiving dishes capture and process the signal.

### 12.7.1 Satellite Orbits

The laws of physics dictate that an object placed in orbit approximately 22,300 miles above the equator will match the rotational speed of the earth. In other words, as seen from the earth the satellite will appear to be in a fixed location. This geostationary (or geosynchronous) orbit is very useful for communications (the orbital belt is called the Clarke Belt; see *PRT*, 5.3.2). Transmission facilities can be permanently aimed at a specific satellite, and receiving dishes can either be fixed or can be moved to predetermined locations to find a specific satellite.

The greatest problem with the use of the geostationary orbital belt is that there is a fixed number of satellites that can be placed in orbit. To prevent signal interference, communication satellites must be placed 2° apart in the orbital arc (approximately 900 miles apart). Thus, no more than 180 satellites can fit into the entire belt. Of course, only a portion of the arc is useful to any country. For example, a satellite placed in orbit over the Indian Ocean cannot reach North America.

Most industrialized nations have the technical ability to launch communication satellites. Further, many other countries, and groups of countries (such as the Arab states of the Middle East) have simply paid private companies and foreign governments to construct and launch their communication satellites.

International agreements reached through the International Telecommunications Union have designated orbital slots for specific countries. As the Clarke belt has become filled, disputes have arisen between countries claiming orbital slots that would preclude the orbital claims of others. Over the years some countries along the equator have also argued that they should be compensated for allowing others to use their "airspace."

Launching a satellite the size and weight of a city bus into an orbit 22,300 miles over the equator is expensive. Satellites are launched first into a parking orbit a few hundred miles above the earth. Then, using on-board maneuvering rockets, the satellite is moved into its final orbit. In recent years the space shuttle has carried satellites into parking orbits.

Because of the expense of launching satellites into a geostationary orbit, and the limited space of the Clarke belt, many satellites are placed in **low earth orbits** (LEOs; Fig. 12.12). These satellites typically orbit from north to south, passing over the polar regions, and may be anywhere from a few hundred to a few thousand miles high. As they follow a polar route, the earth moves west to east below them. The satellite, therefore is over a particular spot for only a short time. The ground station must move along with the satellite in order to keep it in range. Eventually, it will move beyond the horizon, out of the range of the ground station.

The solution is to place multiple satellites in orbit. Thus, one satellite moves in range as another moves out. This system can require a large number of satellites to provide continuous service. For example, the proposed **Iridium Project** for worldwide personal communications will require almost 70 satellites in low earth orbit.

Another orbital technique is use of **high elliptical orbits** (HEOs). Here the satellite's **apogee** (highest point of the orbit) may be tens of thousands of miles high, and its lowest point, or **perigee,** might be only a few hundred miles above the earth. The satellite is at or near apogee for much of its orbit, and at that height its signal may reach as much as one third of the earth's surface. Thus, three or four satellites can serve a continent. As one satellite moves out of the coverage area, another replaces it. The European proposal for digital audio broadcasting (DAB) will use an HEO orbital system (*PRT,* 11.8).

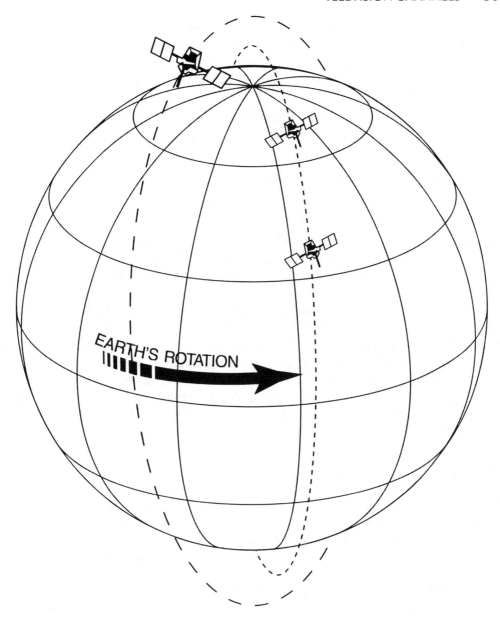

**FIG. 12.12. Low earth orbits.** In the low earth orbit the satellite is in free fall from pole to pole (polar orbit). As it moves from north to south, the earth rotates below, so that from the ground the satellite appears to be moving across the sky.

### 12.7.2 Satellite Uplinks

Transmissions to a satellite are called **uplinks.** The same term is applied to the equipment used to make the transmission. Uplink facilities can be portable, such as an SNG truck, or located in a permanent location. The uplink includes transmitters and equipment to locate the satellite. In permanent locations, such as those used by a broadcast network, the uplink would be aimed continually at one satellite. In the case of **ad hoc** (i.e., occasional) transmissions, such as might be used by a network transmitting a feed from a football game, the operators of the uplink facility contact the company leasing the transponder. Once permission is given to begin a transmission, a video signal and audio tone are transmitted to test the link. Transponders are leased for a specific time period, and once the time is over the transponder control center will instruct the uplink to end its transmission to allow another uplink to access the transponder.

### 12.7.3 Satellite Downlinks and Receivers

Satellite receivers are relatively uncomplicated technologies. The **dish** essentially acts as a mirror that captures the relatively weak signals transmitted from the satellite. There is a direct relation between dish size and the power of the satellite signals: The weaker the power, the larger must be the dish. Satellite dishes have traditionally been circular parabolas, but new technologies allow the use of flat dishes.

The satellite dish receives the signals and reflects them to the **feedhorn,** the first element in the **outdoor electronics**. From the feedhorn, the signal goes through the **low noise amplifier** (LNA), then through coaxial cables to the **indoor electronics** (Fig. 12.13). The **block downconverter** changes the gigahertz range satellite frequencies to the megahertz range usable by television sets. After downconversion, the signal may be **descrambled** if necessary. The indoor electronics may also include equipment to move the dish to locate satellites in various orbital slots.

### 12.7.4 Satellite Transponders

The heart of the communications satellite is the **transponder**. This piece of equipment receives the signal from earth, changes the frequency, amplifies the signal, and transmits the signal back to earth. Why must the transponder change the signal's frequency? Because otherwise there would be cochannel interference between the signal going to and from the satellite!

Transponders are assigned specific frequencies. All Transponder 1s use the same frequency, all Transponder 2s use the same frequency, and so on. A transponder will have its frequency fixed before launch, although a communications satellite might have a mix of C- and Ku-band transponders (*PRT,* 12.7.6). Typically, the broadcast networks and other program services have used C-band, although some are shifting to Ku-band. Many occasional users, such as business television programs, may need to transmit both C-band and Ku-band because of the receiving capabilities of their participants.

Many of the communication satellites currently in orbit have 12 transponders, although new satellites can carry 40 or more transponders. Each transponder is able to transmit two full-motion analog video channels. The two channels are **polarized** vertically or horizontally to allow two transmissions on the same

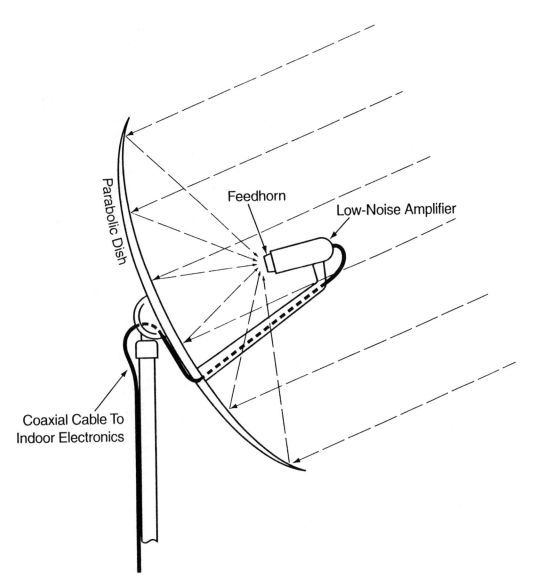

**FIG. 12.13. Satellite receiving dish.** The transmissions from the satellite are reflected from the dish, which focuses them into the feedhorn. From the feedhorn the signal goes to the low noise amplifier and then by coaxial cable into the indoor electronics system.

channel. Digital compression techniques increase the number of signals that can be transmitted.

The broadcast networks and other full-time satellite users usually own or lease multiple transponders on a satellite. One transponder is used for program feeds to the eastern time zone and a second feeds the western time zone. At least one transponder is used for closed-circuit feeds to affiliates—program previews, news feeds, and the like. At least one transponder is kept in reserve as a backup.

The coverage area of a satellite transmission is called its **footprint**. The size of the footprint might be the entire continental United States, or a **spot beam** might send the signal to only the eastern half of the country (Fig. 12.14). A transponder's footprint is set before launch and cannot be changed once the satellite is in space.

Transmissions intended to reach more than one part of the globe require multiple hops between earth and satellites. For example, a transmission from Europe to the United States is sent to a satellite over that continent, then down to earth at an **Intelsat** (*PRT,* 23.4.4) receiving station, then back to an Intelsat satellite over the Atlantic. From there it is sent to a receiving station in the United States. Of course, all of this is happening at 186,000 miles per second, but a transmission from one part of the globe to another may require a second or more to be completed; thus, a delay sometimes occurs during live news feeds between a network anchor and a correspondent in the field.

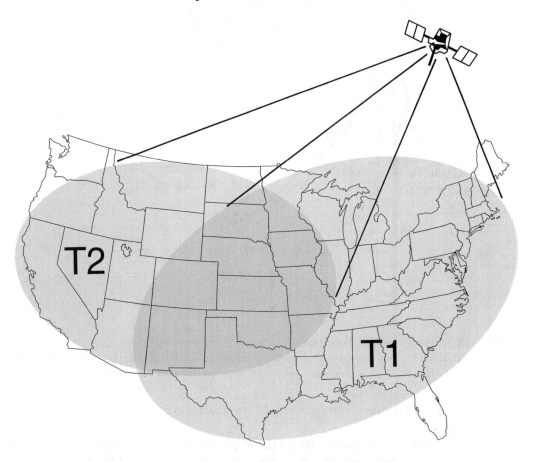

**FIG. 12.14. Satellite footprints.** The signal of each satellite transponder is set before launch so that it will cover a specific geographic area. Here, the footprint of Transponder 1 covers most of the continental United States west of the Rockies. Transponder 2 covers the midwest and mountain area.

Why not simply transmit the signal from one satellite to another, without coming back to earth? One problem is that it would be very difficult to locate a bus-sized satellite, 900 miles away, moving at 18,000 miles an hour. Second, for the signal to travel from one side of the globe to another, it would have to pass through multiple satellites, each of which would have to dedicate a transponder to that task.

### 12.7.5 Satellite Power Supplies and Guidance

Building and launching a communications satellite costs hundreds of millions of dollars. Placed into the Clarke belt, a satellite will remain for decades before its orbit degrades to the point where it falls back into the atmosphere. However, the useful life of a communications satellite is less than its orbital life.

Batteries are a key element in determining the satellite's life. When the satellite is facing the sun, solar batteries are used (the large panels deployed when the satellite is in orbit are solar arrays). However during the half of the day when the earth is between the sun and the satellite, batteries must be used. Current storage batteries used in communication satellites have a life of about 10 years.

Batteries add to the weight of the satellite, increasing the launching costs. The development of lighter batteries has allowed satellite engineers to increase the power and number of transponders.

Finally, the satellite contains **telemetry and guidance** equipment, including small maneuvering rockets. Although the satellite remains in more or less a fixed orbit, it does, in fact drift somewhat in space, creating the possibility that an uplink may miss the satellite and go off into space, or that the satellite might interfere with others in orbit. So, signals from the ground periodically fire the small rockets to keep the satellite in a stable orbit.

### 12.7.6 Satellite Transmission Spectrum

Satellite services are assigned to a number of different parts of the spectrum. Two frequency bands used by the U.S. electronic media are the **C-band** (usually described as being in the 4–6 GHz band) and the **Ku-band** (12–14 GHz). C-band uplinks use the 6 GHz band and downlinks use the 4 GHz band. Ku-band uplinks use the 14 GHz band; downlinks, the 12 GHz band.

Networks first used C-band to distribute programming to cable systems and TV stations. Because of power limitations, the signals are relatively weak, so receiving dishes must be large, typically 10 feet across. A significant problem with C-band is that it shares spectrum space with the terrestrial microwave system, heavily used for telephone communication.

This limits flexibility in using C-band for uplinking signals from remote sites. Before a transmission can be made, a spectrum search is required to demonstrate to the FCC that there will be no interference with local microwave traffic.

The Ku-band is dedicated to satellite traffic. Therefore, higher power can be used, allowing for relatively small dishes, 3 feet or less in diameter. Ku-band can also be used on an ad hoc basis for such purposes as SNG. Ku-band uplinks do suffer from interference caused by heavy rain.

There are other frequency bands assigned to such services as maritime communication and personal communication services. As previously mentioned, the **L-band** (1452–1492 MHz) has been proposed as the location of DAB by most countries except the United States.

## 12.8 ITFS, MDS, AND OFS

The **instructional television fixed service** (ITFS), the **multipoint distribution service** (MDS), and the **operational fixed service** (OFS) consist of 20, 10, and 3 channels respectively in the 2 GHz (2000–3000 MHz) band. The waves at these frequencies are so short they are called **microwaves.** When radiated omnidirectionally at 100 watts of power, as in ITFS, MDS, and OFS, these waves have a range of 30 miles. Any obstruction in the path between transmitting and receiving antennas will block the signal. This includes foliage, as well as more solid objects. ITFS, MDS, and OFS are separate services, but in 1983, the FCC adopted rules that allowed programmers to mix channels from the three services and offer the subscription service that became known as wireless cable (multichannel TV; *PRT,* 5.2).

In an ITFS or MDS system, video and audio signals originate just as they do in broadcast or cable TV. They are then combined and used to modulate the carrier frequency for transmission. The ITFS or MDS transmitting antenna radiates the signal. Receiving antennas, built especially to pick up these high frequencies, capture the signal. A converter demodulates the video and audio signals down, then feeds them to a descrambler (when necessary) and onto an unused channel on your television set.

Tests have been made of **local multipoint distribution service** (LMDS). This service would operate in the 28 GHz band and have a coverage area of only a few miles. However, in major cities such a signal would still enable the LMDS operator to reach a significant population.

## 12.9 CABLE TELEVISION TECHNOLOGY

Coaxial cable is a **broadband** medium; that is, it conducts a wide range of frequencies. A coaxial cable (Fig. 12.15) acts as a "pipe," down which an electromagnetic wave may be propagated. The wave resembles those transmitted by broadcast stations. It neither suffers nor causes external (to the cable) interference and, through modulation (Box 12.1), can carry as many as 80 or 90

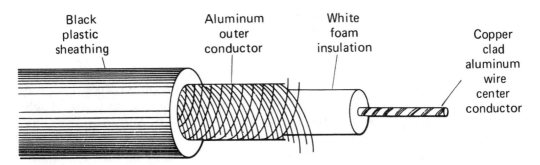

FIG. 12.15. Coaxial cable.

6-MHz television signals, depending on the quality of the cable and the amplifiers used in the system.

The typical cable system uses 450 MHz amplifiers, enabling them to transmit between 50 and 60 channels. To carry such additional services as data or telephone amplifiers of at least 550 MHz are considered minimum (Fig. 12.16). Many cable systems facing competition from telephone companies and refranchising pressures have begun building systems with 750 MHz amplifiers.

In many cable systems, portions of the coaxial cable links are being replaced by optical fiber. This technology uses laser beams to transmit digital pulses down very thin glass fibers. There is no interference from other electromagnetic waves, and virtually unlimited numbers of signals can be transmitted. Tests in the mid-1990s demonstrated that a single fiber could simultaneously carry as many as 64,000 television channels a distance of more than 300 miles before needing further amplification.[4] Many cable systems are using fiber in trunk lines, with copper coaxial feeder and drop cable. These combined coaxial cable and optical fiber cable systems are said to be **hybrid fiber-coax** (HFC).

### 12.9.1 Headend and Signal Origins

A tall tower usually sits close to the building housing the headend. This tower contains various antennas to pick up nearby television stations, any local radio stations the system carries, and microwaves that relay signals from distant TV stations. Nearby will be at least one large satellite receiving dish to bring in cable networks. Additional signals may go to the headend from studios, videotape machines, telecine units, and other sources; from electronic text sources; and from home security services and other two-way and ancillary sources.

The headend contains distribution amplifiers, interference filters, multiplex equipment, switching gear, and other devices that process incoming signals. Therefore, all signals—direct off-the-air, microwave-relay, satellite, local origination—go to the headend for processing and from there to subscribers.

## BOX 12.1. MODULATION AND "STACKING" OF COMMUNICATIONS

A relatively simple example will help explain how modulation lets us use a single communications channel to carry multiple messages simultaneously. Imagine that you run a telephone company that serves two neighboring towns. Each town has one telephone, and the telephone subscriber in one town calls the telephone subscriber in the other town quite often. All of a sudden, business in both towns booms, and another person in each town applies for telephone service. You know that there will be times when both telephones will be in use in both towns, interurban acquaintances using their telephones to talk to each other. Your long-distance telephone channel capacity between cities will have to increase 100%. You find that construction of another line between towns would be prohibitively expensive.

You decide to use modulation. How does it work? What happens when two conversations travel over the same line? Why don't they interfere with each other? The frequency response range of a telephone is roughly 400 to 2,800 Hz. One conversation can go over the long-distance line at this "voice frequencies" range, just as it used to. The second conversation goes from the subscriber's phone in one city to a modulator in that same city. Your modulator uses a carrier frequency of 6,000 Hz. Through the voice frequencies interacting with the carrier frequency on a sum-and-difference basis, the frequency range for the second call is 3,200 to 6,280 Hz. Notice that this frequency band is so high that even the lowest frequencies are higher than the highest frequencies of the first conversation. The second conversation can now be sent over the same long-distance line simultaneously with the first conversation. At the other end of the line, a demodulator recovers the voice frequencies (gets them back down to the range of 400–2,800 Hz) of the second conversation and sends them on (and here you do need a second line) to the subscriber. Obviously, you need a modulator and a demodulator in both towns, but you get the idea. This form of modulation, carrier current telephony, allows a single conducting medium to carry as many as 1,860 messages simultaneously. Use of coaxial cable increases this tremendously; optical fiber, even more.

Pulse code modulation (PCM) also allows multiple simultaneous telephone conversations. This is the way it works. Samples are taken of the amplitude of the waves made by the voices. When sampled often—thousands of times per second—enough information is obtained to make a listener hear what sounds like the full conversation. Because only samples are taken, there can be spaces between the samples of one conversation into which samples from other conversations can be inserted. As long as the timing is correct for insertion and recovery, one line can carry several dozen conversations at the same time. The samples of conversations are encoded and transmitted digitally, and many

**BOX 12.1** (cont'd.)

foresee this **digital compression** as a way to squeeze broadband communications (such as television channels) into narrow-band channels (such as normal telephone lines).

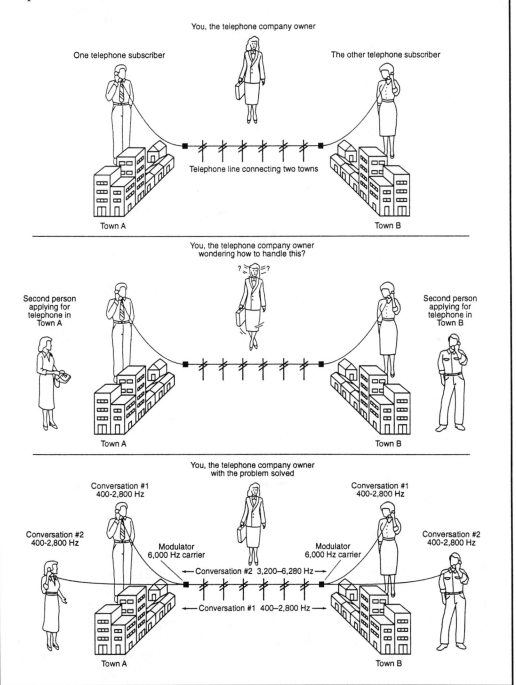

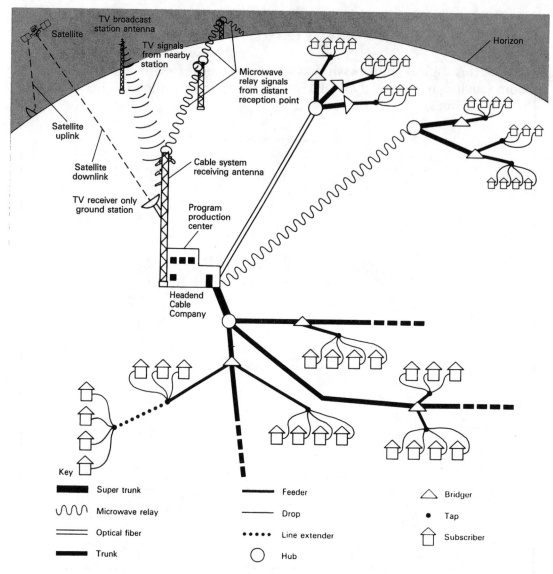

**FIG. 12.16. Cable system layout.** This system uses a combination of direct off-air reception, microwave relay (to bring in signals of stations too distant for direct off-air reception), and satellite reception.

## 12.9.2 Cable Channels

Cable systems carry a television signal with the same AM format as used in broadcast television. A cable system need only "translate" an incoming signal onto the frequency of the proper cable channel. Cable channels 2 through 13 operate with the same carrier frequencies as broadcast channels 2 through 13. A set of midband channels fills most of the gap between channels 6 and 7, and superband and hyperband appear above channel 13. The 5 to 30 MHz bandwidth is dedicated to upstream (return) transmission, although few systems have installed the necessary equipment to offer two-way service.

### 12.9.3 Cable Television Signal Distribution

A cable system that serves a large area or population will establish a number of distribution hubs. A **hub** serves a smaller area and may contain a headend. Hub systems overcome the noise and attenuation caused by the amplifier **cascade**. Processed signals from the headend proceed to the hubs by way of a coaxial **supertrunk, microwave,** or **optical fiber.** Three or four **trunk lines** branch from each hub. A **bridger** branches a trunk into four or more **feeder lines.** A **tap** on the feeder carries signals into homes through **drop lines.** In-line amplifiers keep the signals boosted throughout the length of the system. This type of cable system architecture, called a **star configuration,** can also allow the system to provide different programs or advertising to different parts of its franchise area (Fig. 12.17). Star architecture also seems to be the most efficient method of providing interactive services, such as video on demand. The idea is to deliver requested signals to the hub on the high-capacity trunks, and locate the digital-to-analog conversion technologies at the hub. Coaxial feeder cable then delivers signals to the subscriber. Cable system architectures typically use fiber to deliver signals to neighborhood **nodes,** with coaxial feeds serving 500 to 2,000 homes.

### 12.9.4 Cable Television Subscriber Hookups

If the cable system offers 12 or fewer channels in its basic service, it puts all signals on the 12 VHF channels on the cable. In this case (and if the system offers no pay channel) the drop line can be attached directly to the receiver's antenna terminal. A cable system may place a VHF broadcast signal on a different cable channel to avoid ghosting. When a cable system carries a nearby VHF television station's signal "on channel" (broadcast channel 4 on cable channel 4), the station's signal may be so strong that it gets onto the cable wiring (and into your receiver) directly. In such a case, you would see a double image on channel 4—the stronger one by way of the headend; the weaker, from the direct pickup.

If the cable system offers more than 12 channels, additional channels are used—midband, superband, and hyperband, according to the capacity of the system. If you, the subscriber, have a **cable-ready receiver,** you will probably be able to pick up most or all of these additional channels by selecting channels numbered higher than 13. If your receiver is not cable-ready, you will have to use a **converter.** The drop line connects to the converter, which sits on or near your receiver, and a short cable connects the converter to the receiver. A **block converter** moves all cable channels to either the VHF band or to the UHF band; you use your receiver's channel selector. A **general converter** feeds all signals into one channel (say, channel 3) on your receiver, so you leave the receiver set on that channel; you use a channel selector on the converter to change channels.

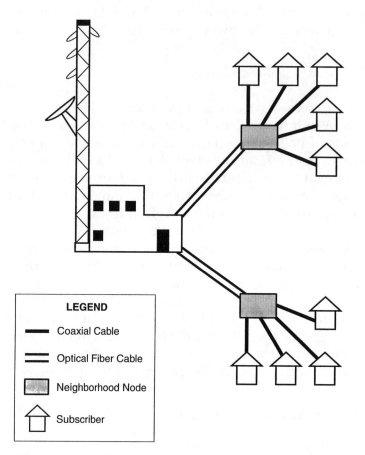

**FIG. 12.17. Star configuration cable architecture.** Many cable systems are changing from the traditional tree-and-branch system of cable signal distribution, shown in Fig. 12.16, to a star configuration to make use of fiber optic technologies. In this configuration, fiber is used to deliver a digital signal to neighborhood receivers, called nodes. At the node, the signal is converted to analog, and transmitted by coaxial cable to the individual subscriber. This configuration allows the cable system to use fiber for digital transmission along most of the path from the headend, without having to face the significant expense of converters at each subscriber's set.

A cable system utilizes converters for pay channels, even when total service is 12 channels or less. In this case, the converter unscrambles the pay signal. A less sophisticated approach is to place traps at each drop. Traps are simply filters that allow or prevent certain frequencies to pass through to the subscribers. If a subscriber elects a pay service the cable system can send a technician to remove a trap without having to enter the customer's premises.

A more sophisticated approach is the use of **interdiction** technologies. These filters and decoders typically serve a group of subscribers. The system can service the equipment without entering the subscriber's home, but these devices are more difficult for signal thieves to overcome than traps.

A satellite master antenna (SMATV) system operates much like a cable system. However, it distributes only to the multiple-dwelling unit with which it has a contract. The array of programming signal inputs may not be as extensive.

### 12.9.5 Cable System Addressability and PPV

Many cable systems have installed technology that permits **signal addressability.** This refers to the capability to send over the system a signal that applies only to one specific point and to nowhere else. In **one-way addressability,** the cable operator's computer sends a signal directly to cable system equipment located in or near a subscriber's home. This equipment could be an electronic "gate" at the tap or a converter on top of the subscriber's television receiver. The signal directs the equipment to turn on or off basic cable service, premium channels, or other services, according to what the customer has ordered. In **two-way addressability,** the subscriber can send a signal directly to the cable operator's computer.

Most cable PPV systems make use of addressability. In a system that has one-way addressability, the subscriber must request unscrambling (and willingness to pay for) a PPV offering through other technology, usually the telephone. The request is programmed into the computer. The computer then generates and transmits through the cable the code that turns on the converter's unscrambling electronics. A two-way addressable system would permit the subscriber to send the request simply by pressing a button on the PPV converter.

### 12.9.6 Cable Modems

Growth of the Internet, especially the World Wide Web, opened business opportunities for cable TV systems. Their high-capacity coaxial cable and fiber optics were ideal for handling computer traffic in addition to video signals. There were two problems to overcome. First, communication had to be two way, not downstream only as with video. These systems could be asynchronous, however. In other words, there would be more traffic in one direction—from the cable system—than in the other—from the subscriber.

In some cases, a cable system can retrieve and store data within its computers. Subscribers would access the data over local pathways. In more complex systems, data can be stored at a variety of locations. To allow subscribers to access data in this configuration, cable systems would have to be interconnected in a manner similar to telephone carriers (*PRT,* 12.10)

The second and more complicated issue requires that the computer signals have to be converted to signals that could be processed by television sets. The solution was the use of **cable modems.** Although similar in function to the traditional modem attached to many home computers, cable modems are more complex. In addition to modulating and demodulating signals, the device might also incorporate a tuner, encryption and decryption technology, signal routing capability, and more. The cable industry began testing these devices in selected systems in the mid-1990s. A computer graphic that would take 6 to 8 minutes to download with a typical 28.8-baud computer modem would take 1 second in a cable system. The downside was the cost. The price for a cable modem was several hundred dollars, a significant cost for either the cable system or the subscriber.

## 12.10 TELEPHONE-BASED VIDEO SERVICE

Communication technologies merge and converge. The Telecommunications Act of 1996 removed line-of-business restrictions, allowing cable and telephone companies to enter each other's territories and businesses. To fully understand the similarities and differences between the competitors, an examination of telephone technologies is in order.

### 12.10.1 Basic Telephone Technology

One of the most common uses of technology by most Americans is to place or receive a telephone call. With little or no thought about what is involved we press a few buttons or pick up a receiver and in moments are talking with someone across town, across the country, or on another continent. Transmitting signals from one point to another, such as in a traditional cable television system, is relatively simple. Adding the capacity for any single point on the system to respond to the signal adds significant complexity. Allowing any point to enter into two-way communication with any other point on the network makes for a system of astonishing complexity.

Telephone service was once so mundane that it was known in the industry as **POTS—Plain Old Telephone Service**. Today it has evolved into a complex world of services and technologies.

To make your phone call you dial a number. Each phone in the world has a unique combination of numbers. Your signal enters the **Public Switched Telephone Network** (PSTN) where it goes to the **central office** for routing, or **switching.** If you are calling someone in your town, the call may go directly from the central office to the other phone. If the call is to someone served by a different central office, the call will go from one central office to the next, and then be routed to its destination (Fig. 12.18). Traffic from the telephone to the central office or the central office to a telephone has traditionally used copper wire trunk lines, but increasingly occurs through optical fiber or wireless transmission (such as cellular telephones). Traffic between central offices might occur by any combination of microwave relay, satellite, coaxial copper wire, or optical fiber.

If your phone call was sent to someone in your town or a nearby town, chances are the call was made using a **local exchange carrier** (LEC), the local telephone company. Historically the LEC was a Bell operating company (BOC), or one of the independent telephone companies such as GTE or United Telephone. Today it might be the cable television company or another provider.

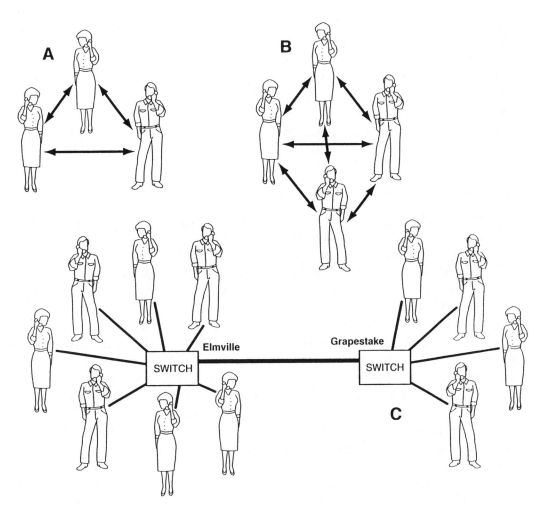

**FIG. 12.18. Telephone switching**. A key component of a telephone system is the switch, which allows calls to be routed efficiently. In (a) three subscribers can maintain contact among themselves with three lines. As we see in (b) simply adding a fourth party makes the connections significantly greater. Imagine trying to link all of the telephone users in your city with dedicated lines! In (c) we see how a switch can be used to route calls among a number of subscribers, each of whom needs only one line between their phone and the switch. Further, a single line from the Elmville switch to the Grapestake switch can allow the users to communicate with each other.

Companies that provide telephone service operate within a **local access and transport area** (LATA), the geographic area within which it may offer service. If you wish to call from one LATA to another you use the services of a **long-distance carrier.**

Until the 1996 Telecommunications Act each of these companies was likely to be a separate entity. Before the 1984 breakup of AT&T the LEC and long-distance carrier were probably both "Ma Bell" subsidiaries. All of the equipment required to make the call also was probably manufactured by an AT&T subsidiary. Now any of these services might be offered by the "telephone company," your local cable system, or another entity.

Traditional voice telephony was delivered over low bandwidth copper wires. Each telephone circuit consisted of two wires, and to eliminate interference the wires are twisted around each other. Thus, the simple telephone technology is called **twisted-pair**. Although twisted-pair POTS remains adequate for voice traffic, the addition of fiber optics, coaxial cables, and the development of digital technologies allows carriage of data and video signals as well as voice.

## 12.10.2 Digital Services

In 1948 Bell Labs engineer Claude Shannon published a scientific paper in which he looked at communication as a process of information transmission. Shannon's "Mathematical Theory of Communication" opened the way for the development of digital technologies in the telephone industry. In the decades since, a number of hardware and software solutions have been applied to the problem of increasing the speed and capacity of these transmissions.

**Integrated services digital networks (ISDN)** transmit voice and data over the same line, with bandwidth allocated depending on the specific need. The customer pays for the service based on the combination of time and amount of bandwidth used. ISDN can use existing twisted-pair wires, with digital interfaces added on the customer premises and, of course, at the telephone central office. In this way the entire process is performed digitally; in the analog POTS system signals must be converted to or from analog form at the premises and at the central office. As a result, overall quality is reduced.

Some radio stations use ISDN connections between their studios and transmitters. The higher capacity digital lines deliver a better quality audio signal to be broadcast. Full-motion digital video can be transmitted with ISDN as long as sender and receiver have the necessary **codecs**, or coders and decoders, to change the signal to or from analog form.

A newer technology, **broadband ISDN** (B-ISDN), can transmit greater data rates. For example, users can transmit video at 15 fps, suitable for videoconferencing or some educational applications. In B-ISDN, six channels can be combined to transmit a 30-fps full-motion video signal. Before B-ISDN can be fully employed, however, significant rebuilding of the telephone system will be required. Replacing the existing network with the fiber optics, switches, and other technologies needed for B-ISDN may take a decade or more. In the meantime, other technologies with greater capabilities may become available.

## 12.10.3 Switching Technology

You may have seen an old movie in which a character tells a telephone operator, "Connect me with the police." The scene cuts to the operator who pulls up a thick wire and plugs it into one of a number of sockets in front of her. The operator is switching the call; that is, routing it from one point to the next. The manual switches portrayed in old movies have long since disappeared from the telephone system. Digital communication and the demand for higher capacity have led to the development of a myriad of switching technologies.

Traditionally, switching was based on allocating space to messages. This is accomplished by allocating each message its own circuit. This solution carries with it a serious problem of capacity: Imagine how much infrastructure would have to exist to meet the telecommunication needs of even a small city.

One approach was to allocate channel space to each message, analogous to placing broadcast stations on different frequencies. In **frequency division multiplexing** (FDM), each analog voice signal is transmitted on a carrier wave, each of which has a different frequency.

The use of digital signals opened new possibilities for increasing switching capacities. **Time division multiplexing** (TDM) has been used since the mid-1970s. Recall that in converting an analog signal to a digital signal it is sampled at different points in time (*PRT,* 10.3.1). In TDM switches, a portion of one signal is sampled and transmitted, then a portion of a second signal, and then a third. The next portion of the first signal is then sampled, and so on. At the final switch the message is reassembled, based on the time it was transmitted (i.e., message A might consist of segments transmitted at Time 1, Time 4, Time 7, etc.).

**Packet switching** has become a common technique in digital communication. The digital signal is broken into small segments, or packets, and information is added regarding the destination and the location in the message in which the packet belongs. The packets can then be routed independently, taking whatever path is available at the time it is sent. When the packets reach their destination they are reassembled. Packet switching is often used in conjunction with **store and forward** applications such as e-mail. Here, the packets are assembled and transmitted when a path is available.

The growth of ISDN, especially broadband services, has created the need for further developments in switching. **Asynchronous transfer mode** (ATM) is similar to packet switching in that the data are broken into small groups or cells (although the cells are larger in ATM). The user selects a class of service based on the amount of data to be sent and the desired quality of the transmission. A "virtual" channel is then created, and the cells are transmitted, usually in sequence, for reassembly at the other end. Because the cells arrive sequentially, ATM can be used to transmit full-motion video and similar applications.

## NOTES

1. This section relies heavily on the Federal Communications Commission Advisory Committee on Advanced Television Service "Advisory Committee Final Report and Recommendation," 28 November 1995, http://atsc.org/finalrpt.html.

2. In North America the frequencies that would be occupied by Channel 1 are used for nonbroadcast communication service. In many countries Channel 1 is used for television services.

3. Two-way radio for public safety.

4. "Super Fiber," *Tele.Com* June 1996, http://www.teledotcom.com/0696/tdc0696headend_fiber.html.

## FURTHER READING

Baldwin, Thomas F., Steven McVoy, and Charles Steinfield. *Convergence: Integrating Media, Information and Communication.* Thousand Oaks, CA: Sage, 1996.

Benson, K. Blain, and Jerry Whitaker. *Television and Audio Handbook for Technicians and Engineers.* New York: McGraw-Hill, 1990.

Goff, David R. *Fiber Optic Reference Guide.* Newton, MA: Focal, 1996.

Grant, August. *Communication Technology Update.* 5th ed. Newton, MA: Focal, 1996.

Hartwig, Robert L. *Basic TV Technology.* 2nd ed. Newton, MA: Focal, 1995.

Heath, Steve. *Multimedia and Communications Technology.* Newton, MA: Focal, 1996.

Hopkins, Gerald L. *The ISDN Literacy Book.* Reading, MA: Addison-Wesley, 1995.

Inglis, Andrew F. *Satellite Technology: An Introduction.* Newton, MA: Focal, 1991.

Lindberg, Bertil C. *Digital Broadband Networks & Services.* New York: McGraw-Hill, 1995.

Maral, Gerard. *VSAT Networks.* Chichester, UK: Wiley, 1995.

Minoli, Daniel. *Telecommunications Technology Handbook.* Boston: Artech, 1991.

Mirabito, Michael M. A., and Barbara Morgenstern. *The New Communication Technologies.* 3rd ed. Newton, MA: Focal, 1997.

Nmungwun, Aaron Foisi. *Video Recording Technology: Its Impact on Media and Home Entertainment.* Hillsdale, NJ: Lawrence Erlbaum Associates, 1989.

Smith, C. Cecil. *Mastering Television Technology: A Cure for the Common Video.* Belmont, CA: Wadsworth, 1988.

Ulloth, Dana R. *Communication Technology: A Survey.* Lanham, MD: University Press of America, 1991.

Van Tassel, Joan. *Advanced Television Systems.* Newton, MA: Focal, 1996.

Watkinson, John. *Television Fundamentals.* Newton, MA: Focal, 1996.

Weiss, S. Merrill. *Issues in Advanced Television Technology.* Newton, MA: Focal, 1996.

West, Don, and Chris McConnell. "The Brave New, Brand-New World of Television: Interview with Joseph A. Flaherty." *Broadcasting & Cable* 15 April 1996: 32–38.

Wood, James. *Satellite Communications and DBS Systems.* Newton, MA: Focal, 1992.

Zettl, Herbert. *Video Basics.* Belmont, CA: Wadsworth, 1995.

# IV

## LEGAL AND ETHICAL PERSPECTIVE

Each of us has a stake in this next section. Most regulation aims at ensuring that mass-media operation does not harm individuals—such as children—and in some cases, that it actually furthers the common good. At the same time, governmental regulation should allow operators to earn a profit. Theoretically then, as citizens and consumers, we play at least some role in the regulation of radio and television. Also theoretically, the more effectively the media voluntarily operate with our good in mind, the less the government needs to regulate. Over the years, Congress and the FCC have demonstrated considerable difficulty in determining precisely how much regulation is necessary.

We divide our investigation of regulation into four chapters. In chapter 13, we focus on the Communications Act of 1934 and its various amendments; in chapter 14, governmental regulation; in chapter 15, First Amendment issues; and in chapter 16, media ethics.

Like the business to which they apply, law and regulation of radio and television constantly change. New issues arise and old ones evolve. Arguments, court cases, hearings, and investigations continually explore and define the uses of electronic mass communication.

# 1 3

## ELECTRONIC MASS COMMUNICATION LAW

The basic law regulating radio, television, and cable is the **Communications Act of 1934.** This law provides for use of the radio frequencies. It also singles out broadcasting as being special and different from all other uses. It provides for both the existence of broadcast stations and for their regulation. It also establishes policies for cable television regarding rates and program distribution, and for the regulation of telephone companies. In this chapter, we trace the origins and authority for government regulation, survey the overall nature and status of broadcasting and cable under the 1934 law, and review sweeping changes to the law passed by Congress in 1996.

### 13.1 ORIGINS AND AUTHORITY

Article I, Section 8, of the constitution of the United States contains the **commerce clause,** giving Congress **power to regulate interstate commerce.** The United States is, of course, a representative democracy. Congress, therefore, acts as the people's representative in all national regulation. Radio, television, cable television, telephone, and satellite communications are considered interstate commerce. Early on, the U.S. Supreme Court ruled that Congress' power extends to all kinds of commercial dealings involving more than one state and to the formulation of rules to regulate those dealings.[1] Later, the Court ruled that the term *commerce* includes interstate electrical communication.[2] Still later, the Court held that all radio communication is, by nature, interstate.[3] These decisions established the right of Congress to regulate broadcasting (and other uses of the radio frequencies). A 1968 Supreme Court decision affirmed federal regulation of cable television.[4]

Congress wrote the basic law of radio, but it also created an independent agency and gave it authority to make specific rules and regulations. A federal court ruled in 1929 that Congress had the power to establish such an agency.[5] Five years later Congress passed the Communications Act of 1934,[6] which created the present agency, the Federal Communications Commission. Although amended many times—substantially in 1996—over 60 years later this act is still the primary law regulating civilian electronic media and telephone communications. Congress—through the **commerce committees** of its two houses—still has ultimate control over the electronic media and monitors the functioning and adequacy of the Communications Act, including FCC regulation.

## 13.2 RADIO–TELEVISION LAW

The Communications Act of 1934 serves as the basis for regulation of cable television, telephone companies, telegraph communications, and such services as citizen band radios, police, shipping, and aviation communications via radio.[7] The act applies

> to all interstate and foreign communication by wire or radio and all interstate and foreign transmission of energy by radio which originates and/or is received within the United States, and to all persons engaged within the United States in such communications or such transmission of energy by radio and to the licensing and regulating of all radio stations.[8]

Keep in mind that when the Communications Act was passed in 1934 there was no such thing as television, satellite distribution of programming, or World Wide Web. Later on Congress stipulated that the term *radio* would apply to television as well.

### 13.2.1 Structure of the Communications Act

The Government Printing Office publishes federal laws in the **United States Code** (U.S.C.). **Title 47** of the U.S.C. contains the Communications Act of 1934 as amended. The act consists of major divisions called **titles**. Each title contains numbered paragraphs called **sections**, the contents of which are outlined in Box 13.1.

The Communications Act originally had six titles. In 1984 Congress passed cable legislation that it placed in Title VI. The former content of Title VI became a newly created Title VII. Cable legislation has twice been significantly revised since 1984 but is still contained in Title VI. Title VII deals with unauthorized reception of communication and the president's war emergency powers.

### 13.2.2 Characteristics of the Communications Act

From the perspective of radio and television, three aspects of the 1934 act stand out—its **comprehensiveness**, its **flexibility**, and its **establishment of the FCC**. Profiting from the lesson of the Radio Act of 1912 (*PRT*, 2.1.7), Congress wrote the Radio Act of 1927 to be comprehensive enough to cover all types of radio

---

**BOX 13.1. SECTIONS OF THE
COMMUNICATIONS ACT OF 1934
48 Stat. 1064 (1934) 47 U.S.C.A. § 151 et seq.**

Congress Asserts Regulatory Control Over Radio,
Television, Cable, Satellite Communications,
Telephone

| | |
|---|---|
| Title I: | Defines the purposes of the act and specifies terms, organization, duties, and general powers of the Federal Communications Commission. |
| Title II: | Regulation of common carriers, including telephone and telegraph. |
| Title III: | Title III is divided into four parts. Parts II and III apply to uses of radio on ships and boats. Parts I and IV apply directly to broadcasting as follows: (I) radio and TV licensing, programming restrictions, and other regulations that deal specifically with broadcasting; and (IV) special provisions pertaining to noncommercial educational broadcasting. |
| Title IV: | Spells out procedural and administrative provisions such as hearings and appeals of FCC decisions. |
| Title V: | Prescribes penalties, including fines, for violators of laws or FCC regulation. |
| Title VI: | Regulation of cable television. |
| Title VII: | War emergency powers of the president and other general provisions. |

---

communication—maritime, broadcasting, amateur, and common carrier. The Communications Act of 1934 contains most provisions of the 1927 law. This means that some principles first written into law in 1927 still cover interstate communications. They allow for regulation of technology and developments that were brand new, still in the laboratory, or not yet even dreamed of in 1927—TV, FM radio, microwave relay, subcarrier uses, ultrahigh frequencies, and satellites.

Congress also wrote the Communications Act to be flexible. The law set forth basic principles and created the FCC to carry out the intent of those principles. It established a general legal framework and provided the FCC with **discretionary powers** to make specific rules and regulations. This gives the FCC broad powers to set up criteria for licensing, to grant or refuse licenses, to attach conditions to licenses, to revoke licenses, to specify how and where stations are to operate, to place limits on cable ownership, and to change regulations to keep up with changing conditions and technology.[9]

FCC rules and regulations have the same force of law as legislation passed by Congress. However, the Communications Act is given additional flexibility because radio and television stations, cable operators, telephone companies, citizens groups, and others have **the right to challenge FCC decisions and regulations in the federal courts.**[10]

Finally, the Communications Act **established the FCC.** The Commission carries out the specific functions prescribed by the act, makes rules and regulations, checks to see they are being followed,[11] and takes corrective or punitive action where they are not.[12] In other words, the FCC regulates.

## 13.3 STATUS OF BROADCASTING UNDER LAW

In writing the Communications Act, Congress defined the legal status of broadcasting. Under this law, **broadcasting** is (a) a unique form of electrical communication, unlike any other, (b) a function of the private sector, not of the government, and a form of expression (c) that is distributed via radio frequencies, a scarce natural resource in the public domain (d) to which the government may limit access, and (e) that has limited protection under the First Amendment.

### 13.3.1 Unique Form of Electrical Communication

First, the Communications Act of 1934 recognized broadcasting as a unique form of radio communication. Section 153(b) defines radio communication as any transmission by radio of intelligence. Section 153(o) then defines **broadcasting** as **radio communication intended for reception by the general public,** clearly distinguishing broadcasting from other forms of radio communication.

Two important distinctions are worth noting. First, most regulations affecting broadcasting are not written in the 1934 act. They are contained in rules, regulations, policies, and decisions handed down by the FCC. Second, note that the law's definition of broadcasting emphasizes **reception** of radio communication by the public. Such emphasis has traditionally distinguished broadcasting from common carriers. Section 303(b) defines a **common carrier** as **radio or interstate wire communication facilities for hire,** a definition that emphasizes the **sender** of the message. Telephone and telegraph are both examples of common carriers. Common carriers provide what the government considers **essential communication services,** and Congress wrote Title II of the act to ensure reliability and continuity of these services. The notion of essential service dates back to the regulation of the railroad industry. Trains were heavily regulated because they were considered essential to transport the nation's goods. Government, therefore, had vested interest in assuring development and maintenance of an efficient, nationwide, interconnected railroad system.

Revisions to the Communications Act in 1996, court decisions, and FCC policy changes have blurred what was once a clear distinction between common carriers and broadcasters. Still, there are differences. Common carriers are **more closely regulated,** including the **rates** they may charge and the **services** they may provide. For example, although telephone companies now face competition, you still probably have only one local telephone company in your town. It provides your local phone service but does not supply the messages to be sent over your telephone lines; you do.

The FCC regulates the companies that provide phone service and the network of **interstate** long-distance communications to which your phone company is attached. Additionally, most states have public utilities commissions that regulate local telephone and **intrastate** long-distance communications.

A broadcast licensee, on the other hand, faces **more direct competition** and has the **freedom to determine rates and services.** The licensee also provides, or at least is responsible for, the **programming** broadcast over the radio or television station. True, a broadcast station must be licensed and is subject to some regulation, but the licensee is basically an entrepreneur in competition with other broadcast licensees and may charge whatever advertising rates and (to a large extent) may provide whatever programming services the market will bear.

Keep in mind that the differences between common carriers and broadcasters have diminished significantly over the past few years. Telephone companies face increasing levels of competition. You can already choose among several alternatives for long-distance service, and **cable companies can now offer local telephone service.** The Telecommunications Act of 1996 requires phone companies to allow cable systems to **interconnect with the telephone infrastructure on reasonable terms.**

The presence of competition usually means a reduction in government regulation. Florida, for example, passed a state law in 1995 that phases out state regulatory commission price controls on local phone service if competition emerges. Soon after this law was passed, Time Warner, the nation's second largest cable operator even before the Turner Broadcasting merger (*PRT,* 20.4.3.1), announced plans to offer telephone service in the Tampa Bay area in direct competition with GTE.

As cable companies venture into the telephone business, **telephone companies are gearing up to provide video services** in direct competition with cable television. This means telephone companies will be supplying the messages, or content, just as broadcasters and cable operators do. These changes have forced us to throw away traditional distinctions and adopt new terminology. For example, because both provide services previously monopolized by the other, cable and telephone companies are more accurately called **telecommunication companies.**

Note, also, that the law's definition of broadcasting does not limit it to the traditional services—AM and FM radio and TV channels 2 through 69. Thus, law and regulation of broadcasting affects any wireless medium the FCC may authorize, including cable television, so long as it is intended for the general public.

### 13.3.2 Function of the Private Sector

Second, the Communications Act of 1934 affirms that private entities—people or corporations—may use the radio frequencies.[13] By the time Congress passed the Radio Act of 1927, the pattern for broadcasting in the United States was set. Radio broadcasting had become a commercial advertising medium operated to earn a profit. Congress accepted the status quo. Contrary to the arrangement in many other countries—in which broadcasting was some combination of monopoly, noncommercial, and government-operated or government-chartered service—the U.S. Congress specified **private operation** as one of the basic assumptions of its first comprehensive radio law. The FCC has reserved channels for noncommercial FM and television stations. Congress has set up and funded the national and noncommercial Corporation for Public Broadcasting. However, by and large broadcasting in the United States is still privately operated and commercial.

### 13.3.3 Distributed Through Radio Frequencies

Government retains ultimate control of the radio frequencies and requires all broadcast licensees to meet certain responsibilities and operate within certain limitations. Congress wrote this into the law because broadcasting is considered to be a form of expression distributed through use of a scarce natural resource in the public domain. Public domain simply means owned by the government. The natural resource is the electromagnetic spectrum (*PRT,* 10.2.1). It is **scarce** because only a limited number of stations can operate in any given geographical area, and the people desiring broadcast licenses far outnumber the available frequencies. This **scarcity rationale** provides the basis for the **public interest doctrine.** Under this doctrine the FCC may limit the time individuals are allowed to **use the frequencies**[14] and require that individuals use the frequencies to **serve the public interest, convenience, and necessity.**[15] This means the FCC has the authority to regulate programming content and take away the licenses of stations that ignore or violate policies.

Some argue that FCC regulation under the public interest doctrine—especially regulation of programming content—is a violation of broadcasters' First Amendment rights of free speech. In the 1943 case **NBC v. United States,** the Supreme Court ruled otherwise, holding that the right of free speech does not include the right to operate a broadcast station.[16] The Court supported the scarcity rationale by holding that regulation is necessary because the airwaves are limited. Over 25 years later in the **Red Lion** case the Supreme Court again upheld the scarcity rationale and FCC regulation of programming content (*PRT,* 15.3.4.2).[17]

### 13.3.4 Government May Limit Access

The fourth legal characteristic of broadcasting is a logical extension of the previous two—the government may restrict access to the radio frequencies. Section 301 of the Communications Act **restricts use** of the radio frequencies **to those so licensed.** However, not everyone who wants full-time use of a channel in the broadcast frequencies can have it. The FCC chooses who does and who does not get a license. Some of the criteria an applicant must meet are spelled out in Sections 308(b), 310, and 313.

Even if the applicant meets all criteria and the FCC grants a license, Sections 304 and 309(h)(1) make clear that the licensee **does not own the frequencies**. Further, the licensee must operate the station within all applicable conditions, rules, and regulations or, as prescribed in Sections 307(d) and 312(a), **lose the license**.

### 13.3.5 Limited First Amendment Protection

Finally, the Communications Act applies the constitutional guarantee of free speech to broadcasting. **Section 326** states that the FCC does not have the power of censorship and may make no regulation that would interfere with the right of free speech by means of radio. The fact is, however, that broadcast licensees **do not have the same degree of First Amendment protection enjoyed by the print media**. Certain types of broadcast content that are protected by the First Amendment—such as programming that is indecent—may be restricted. Other types—such as response time for opponents of political candidates who are endorsed by broadcasters—may be required when it would be in the public interest to do so[18] or when it would enhance the public's First Amendment right to hear all points of view.[19] No such regulations or restrictions apply to print.

In chapter 15 we discuss in detail the complicated relations involved in broadcasting and the First Amendment. For now, let it suffice to say that the broadcast licensee does have protection of freedom of speech under the First Amendment. However, that protection is limited by requirements to operate in the public interest—the result of utilizing a scarce, natural resource in the public domain.

## 13.4 DISSATISFACTION

The Communications Act is flexible, and it has served well over the years. Congress has amended the Act almost continuously, but most amendments have supplemented the basic thrust of the Act.

### 13.4.1 Congressional Rewrite Attempts

From 1981 to 1995 a number of bills were introduced to dramatically revise or replace the Communications Act. None made the transition to law. One problem was that proposed changes always involve so many different and powerful interest groups. The law affects all interstate wire and wireless communication. So, a bill that made common carriers happy would make cable operators unhappy. A bill that made cable operators happy would make common carriers and broadcasters unhappy.

Another problem stemmed from interest groups that perceived change as a threat. One bill that proposed to levy fees on users of the spectrum drew opposition from broadcasters. The same bill would have eliminated many require-ments and restrictions on broadcasters and deleted the concept of the public interest. This drew opposition from citizen and public interest groups.

### 13.4.2 Marketplace Regulation

Mark Fowler, President Ronald Reagan's first FCC chair, accelerated the push for revision in the early 1980s. Fowler echoed Reagan's commitment to eliminate what the administration saw as unnecessary regulation of business. He considered the concept of scarcity,[20] on which much program regulation was based, to be erroneous and no longer valid. He cited the expanding number of channels available from broadcasting, cable, and other sources. He urged that channel operators be allowed to program with few or no FCC requirements or restrictions, arguing that audiences would tune to those channels, broadcast or otherwise, that best catered to their wants and needs. Those would be the channels to survive; therefore marketplace forces would regulate to serve the public interest. The FCC would regulate only when necessary to protect the public and maintain efficient functioning of the marketplace.

Fowler and his supporters also called for elimination of a basic assumption underlying the Communications Act—the public nature of the radio frequencies. The frequencies would no longer be in the public domain, licensed to broadcasters obligated to operate in the public interest, convenience, and necessity. Broadcast-ers would own them. They could buy, sell, and program their frequencies for whatever the market would bear without FCC permission and without having to make promises or commitments concerning programming.

Neither Congress nor the FCC fully adopted Fowler's marketplace approach. However, significant deregulation has occurred, and the Communications Act of 1996 reflects Fowler's philosophy. The public interest doctrine has been retained, but Congress liberalized or eliminated many regulations. Some changes were justified on the basis that competition and marketplace forces would provide adequate controls.

### 13.5 TELECOMMUNICATIONS ACT OF 1996

The 1996 Act significantly revised regulation of the telecommunication industry. From a deregulatory perspective, the Act accomplished each of the following:

1. Significantly relaxed radio, television, and cable ownership limitations (*PRT,* 19.1.1.1). In fact, national radio ownership limits were completely elimi-nated.
2. Extended broadcast licensing terms to 8 years for radio and television stations (*PRT,* 19.1).

3. Simplified the license renewal process and provided broadcasters with an expectation of renewal unless serious policy violations are noted and barred the FCC from even considering a competing application unless a station's license renewal has already been denied (*PRT,* 19.1.1.7).
4. Deregulated nonbasic cable rates (*PRT,* 19.2.3.5).
5. Allowed telephone companies to enter the cable television business or provide video programming, even in areas where they provide local telephone service.
6. Preempted any local and state restrictions on cable companies that want to provide local telephone service (*PRT,* 13.6).

The 1996 Act was not entirely deregulatory. Congress required manufacturers to place V-chip technology in all new television receivers so that viewers could block out objectionable programming. The Act also required the television industry to develop a ratings system to warn viewers of programs with sexual or violent content. Fines for cable and broadcast obscenity were increased from $10,000 to $100,000 and cable operators were required to scramble any programming a customer determined to be unsuitable for children. For the first time, the 1996 Act gave cable operators the authority to refuse to accept programs which they considered to be indecent or obscene for public and leased-access channels.

### 13.6 CABLE REGULATORY AMENDMENTS

In 1984, Congress enacted an extensive communications amendment called the Cable Communications Policy Act. For the first time, cable was regulated under direct law, rather than by inference from legislation intended for broadcasting and other forms of interstate communication. The 1984 Cable Act established national policy concerning cable communications, but essentially deregulated the industry by reducing the regulatory power of both the franchising authorities (the cities) and the FCC.

The 1984 Cable Act caused immediate controversy. As cable operators increased subscriber fees during the 1980s, cities regretted having given up regulatory power. They joined broadcasters to lobby Congress in demanding new legislation.

That legislation appeared in the form of the Cable Television Consumer Protection and Competition Act of 1992. This Act reregulated rates and other aspects of cable operations. The 1992 Act also forced vertically integrated cable companies to make their programming available to competing technologies (such as wireless cable) on "fair terms" and banned cable systems from serving more than 25% of subscribers across the nation.

The Telecommunications Act of 1996, however, was distinctly deregulatory. The act gave small cable operators immediate exemption from rate regulation for the cable programming service tier (e.g. MTV, CNN, USA, etc.). Rates for other

systems would be deregulated **whenever the system faced "effective competition."** The law also made it more difficult for customers to petition the FCC to
challenge a system's rate system. In addition to relaxing cable ownership restrictions, the 1996 Act **paved the way for telephone companies to enter the cable
television business** by preempting any state and local restrictions. At the same
time, the Act **opened the door for cable operators to provide local telephone
service** by requiring phone companies to negotiate with cable operators regarding
interconnection with the telephone system.

Ownership restrictions were relaxed to the extent that network–cable cross-
ownership was permitted. However, the Act forbids telephone companies from
purchasing cable systems except in rural areas with a population less than 35,000.

## 13.7 OTHER CHANGES TO THE COMMUNICATIONS ACT

Even before the 1996 Act, Congress had frequently amended Title 47 of the
U.S.C. Amendments include all-channel television receiver legislation passed in
1962, the Communications Satellite Act of 1962 (*PRT,* 5.3.2), the Educational
Television (ETV) Facilities Act of 1962 (*PRT,* 22.1.2), and the Public Broadcasting
Act of 1967 (*PRT,* 22.1.3).

In 1973, Congress amended Title 47 to deal with television coverage of
professional sports. Prior to 1973, professional football teams routinely blocked
local television coverage of home games. In response to complaints, Congress
amended the Communications Act to bar such professional sports "blackouts" if
all tickets were sold 72 hours before game time. The statute expired in 1975. An
attempt at a permanent law failed in 1976, but the National Football League has
continued to follow the expired sports blackout rule.

Congress approved a number of amendments during the 1980s. They relaxed
ownership limits and abolished the fairness doctrine. They also allowed the FCC
to use a lottery to award frequencies and channels in services such as LPTV, cellular
radio, and the MMDS. Now, when two or more parties applied for the same
facility, the Commission could choose the licensee by drawing lots, a system much
quicker and less complicated than the comparative hearing process it replaced.

The 1981 amendments also changed the nature of the Commission. Previously,
the FCC had been a permanent agency. Now, it was put on a short-term basis;
Congress had to reauthorize it every 2 years, otherwise it would cease to exist. In
1982, Congress reduced the size of the FCC. After comprising seven commissioners since 1934, the FCC became the five-member commission it is today.

A court case involving licenses of stations owned by RKO resulted in another
amendment.[21] Section 331 of the Communications Act required the FCC to
renew the license of any VHF television station that agreed to move to any state
that had no commercial stations. In order to keep WOR-TV in New York City,
RKO moved the station across the river into New Jersey.

## NOTES

1. Gibbon v. Ogden, 9 Wheat 1 (1824).
2. Pensacola Telegraph Co. v. Western Union Telegraph Co., 96 U.S. 1 (1878).
3. Federal Radio Commission v. Nelson Bothers Bond & Mortgage Co., 53 Sup. Ct. 627, 633–634 (1933).
4. United States v. Southwestern Cable Co., 392 U.S. 157 (1968).
5. General Electric Co. v. Federal Radio Commission, 31 F. 2d 630.
6. 48 Stat. 1064, 19 June 1934.
7. 47 U.S.C. § 151.
8. 47 U.S.C. § 152.
9. 47 U.S.C. §§ 154(i), 303, 307, 309.
10. 47 U.S.C. § 402.
11. 47 U.S.C. §§ 303(n), 403.
12. 47 U.S.C. §§ 307(d), 312, 501-503.
13. 47 U.S.C. § 307(a).
14. 47 U.S.C. § 301.
15. 47 U.S.C. §§ 307(a), 307(d), 309(a), 311(b), 303(f).
16. NBC v. United States, 319 U.S. 190 (1943).
17. Red Lion Broadcasting Co. v. FCC, 395 U.S. 367 (1969).
18. National Broadcasting Co. v. United States, 319 U.S. 190, 227 (1943).
19. Red Lion Broadcasting Co. v. Federal Communications Commission, 395 U.S. 367, 390 (1969).
20. The scarcity factor derives from physical limitations on the number of stations that can operate in an area (*PRT,* 11.1.1 and 13.3.3). Program regulation was based on the premise that, because not everyone can broadcast, those who do must be regulated so they use their stations for the benefit of all.
21. Multi-state Communications, Inc. v. FCC, 728 F.2d 1519 (1984).

## FURTHER READING

Carter, T. Barton, Marc A. Franklin, and Jay B. Wright. *The First Amendment and the Fifth Estate: Regulation of Electronic Mass Media* (4th ed.). Westbury, NY: Foundation, 1996.

Holt, Darrel. "The Origin of 'Public Interest' in Broadcasting." *Educational Broadcasting Review* 1 (1967): 15.

Kahn, Frank J., Ed. *Documents of American Broadcasting.* 4th ed. Englewood Cliffs, NJ: Prentice-Hall, 1984.

Krattenmaker, Thomas G., and Lucas A. Powe, Jr. *Regulating Broadcast Programming.* Cambridge, MA: MIT Press, 1995.

National Association of Broadcasters. *Legal Guide to Broadcast Law and Regulation.* Washington, DC: Author, 1996.

Smith, F. Leslie, Milan Meeske, and John W. Wright, II. *Electronic Media and Government.* White Plains, NY: Longman, 1995.

Whitley, Jack W., and Gregg P. Skall. *The Broadcaster's Survival Guide: A Handbook of FCC Rules and Regulations for Radio and TV Stations.* New York: Scripps, 1988.

# 14

## REGULATION OF ELECTRONIC
## MASS MEDIA

**Regulation** means **control or direction by government agency according to rule, principle, or law.** Primary responsibility for regulation of electronic mass media belongs to the FCC. However, because so many of the electronic mass media advertise themselves and run the advertising of others, they are also subject to regulation by the Federal Trade Commission (FTC). Each of the three branches of the federal government influences regulation. Even state and local governments can affect radio and television, especially cable TV.

### 14.1 FEDERAL COMMUNICATIONS COMMISSION

The FCC consists of **five commissioners** who set policy and a **federal agency** that carries it out (Fig. 14.1). The President of the United States appoints the commissioners with the advice and consent of the Senate. Commissioners must be citizens and have no financial interest in any industry the Commission regulates. No more than three may belong to the same political party. Each commissioner chooses a small personal staff that can include various combinations of secretaries, lawyers, engineers, and economists.

The terms of the commissioners are 5 years and terms are fixed. This means that if one individual leaves the commission 3 years into a term, the replacement is appointed for the remaining 2 years. When the term expires, the replacement commissioner may be reappointed to a full 5-year term.

The president designates one of the five commissioners to **chair** the Commission. This individual presides at meetings of the commissioners, serves as chief executive, and represents the Commission before Congress and other agencies and groups. The Commission conducts its business in meetings and must meet at least once each month at its Washington, DC, headquarters.

The agency consists of **bureaus** and **staff offices**. The staff offices supply support services, but it is the bureaus that have responsibility for the main areas of FCC concern. In an effort to keep up with changes in the businesses it regulates,

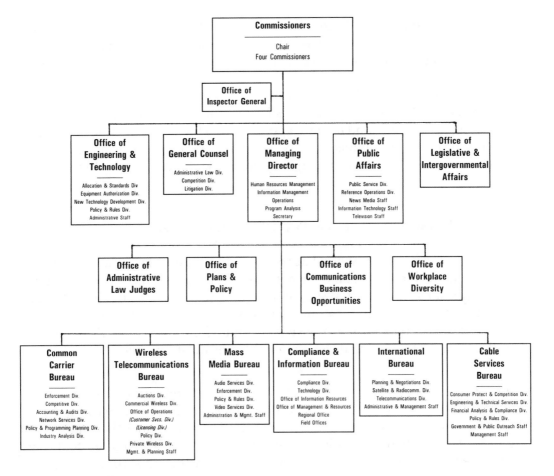

FIG. 14.1. FCC organization.

the FCC has, from time to time, altered the number and names of its bureaus. By the late 1990s the bureaus numbered six, and their primary areas of concern were the following:

1. **Mass Media Bureau**: Broadcasting.
2. **Cable Services Bureau**: Cable television systems.
3. **Wireless Telecommunications Bureau**: Point-to-point communications such as cellular telephone, paging, and amateur radio.
4. **Common Carrier Bureau**: Interstate wireline "common carrier" services such as telephone and telegraph companies.
5. **International Bureau**: Shortwave broadcasting, satellites and earth stations, and international treaties and agreements.
6. **Compliance and Information Bureau**: Operating FCC field offices, monitoring, investigation, technical inspection, resolution of interference problems, and response to questions from the public and regulated businesses.

The FCC has **executive, legislative, and judicial** functions. It performs the duties specified in the Communications Act, it makes rules and regulations, and it holds hearings, weighs evidence, and renders decisions on certain disputed matters.

The Commission has **delegated authority** to the bureaus to act on most routine business. For example, the Mass Media Bureau takes final action on most broadcast station license and renewal applications. However, all rule formulations, all license revocations, all major policy decisions, and many decisions on actions appealed from lower levels of the agency are made directly by the five commissioners.

### 14.1.1 Statutory Requirements and Regulatory Implementation

The Communications Act says what to do, and FCC rules say how to do it. The how is often much longer than the what. A single phrase—one or two lines in the Communications Act—is often supplemented by pages of specifics in FCC rules. In addition to the Communications Act, other laws affect broadcasting as well, such as the U.S. Criminal Code, the Federal Trade Commission Act, the Copyright Act, the Civil Rights Act, and the National Labor Relations Act.

***14.1.1.1 FCC General Powers.*** Section 303 of the Communications Act spells out the general powers of the FCC. Several of these powers center on traffic duties; that is, ensuring that broadcast stations operate in such manner that they do not interfere with each other. This section also gives the FCC power to license operators, to inspect stations, to regulate network-affiliated stations, to require that stations keep certain records and paint and illuminate transmission towers, to assign and require stations to use call letters, and to require that new television receivers be equipped to receive certain signals.

Two provisions in Section 303 are particularly important. One directs the Commission to study new uses and encourage more effective use of the radio frequencies in the public interest. The other directs the FCC to make rules and regulations necessary to carry out the intent of both domestic laws and all international agreements to which the United States is a party. These international agreements deal with traffic problems—who uses what frequencies—and are made at both regional (neighboring countries) and worldwide levels. The world organization is the International Telecommunications Union (ITU).

One ITU responsibility is to assign first letters for call letters in each country. ITU assigned to the United States the letters K, N, W, and part of the As. The FCC, in turn, has assigned to stations call letters beginning with W east of the Mississippi River and K west of the Mississippi. Some pioneer broadcast stations, however, received call letters before the government set up the present rules. WBAP, for example, is in Fort Worth, Texas, and KDKA is in Pittsburgh, Pennsylvania.

*14.1.1.2 Licensing.*    Sections 307 through 311 and 319 of the Communications Act give the FCC **discretionary power to license and to set up criteria** for licensing. No station may operate without a license, and thus licensing is one of the FCC's most important powers. Congress' 1996 amendments to the Communications Act increased the license terms for both radio and television broadcast stations to 8 years (from 7 years for radio, 5 for TV). FCC rules stagger these 8-year terms by state so that a manageable percentage of the total number of licenses come due at any given time. The licensing process for broadcast stations is discussed in *PRT,* 19.1.1.2.

*14.1.1.3 Sponsorship Identification.*    Section 317 of the Communications Act requires identification of sponsors and advertisers. If parties other than the station licensee pay for or furnish a program or program element, the station must so announce and identify the sponsor or donor. This requirement pertains even if the station is noncommercial. It also applies to a cable system's local origination programming (*PRT,* 7.4.1.1). With respect to commercials, mention of the advertiser's trade name or product meets the requirement. Section 317 applies to the licensee or cable operator, and Section 508 prohibits plugola and payola (*PRT,* 9.1.6.7 and 9.1.6.9) by applying the sponsorship identification requirement to employees, program production and creative personnel, and program distributors.

The sponsorship identification requirement does provide for exceptions. It excludes material furnished to the station for free or at a nominal charge when the material comes "with no strings attached." For example, many radio stations normally get recordings free from distributors. The distributors hope the stations will play them over the air and thus stimulate retail sales of the recordings. However, the stations may use the recordings or not as they prefer, so the Commission requires no sponsorship identification announcement when they are broadcast.

The FCC may also waive the requirement. The Commission has provided such waivers for certain types of "want ad" (listener swap shop) programs and for films produced originally for theatrical release. Many films contain plugs that are not disclosed as such; without the waiver they would have to be substantially altered for television use.

*14.1.1.4 Political Programming.*    Section 315 of the Communications Act contains the **equal opportunities** requirement. If a licensee allows a candidate for elective public office to use a broadcast station, the licensee must then allow all other candidates for that office the chance to use the station for the same length of time and for the same cost. You may hear this called the "equal time" requirement. Section 315, however, requires equal opportunity, not equal time. The licensee does not, for example, have to *give* an impecunious candidate matching time to reply to an opponent who bought time.

Section 315 excludes certain news and public affairs programs from the requirement. It specifies that a station **may not censor** political candidate broadcasts. It stipulates that a station may charge candidates no more than its **lowest unit rate** during a period of 60 days prior to a general election, 45 days prior to a primary. Quantity discounts and other rate advantages the station gives its most favored advertiser must also be given to a political candidate, no matter how little time the candidate buys. This rule applies only to availabilities (avails; places for commercials) of the same class or type. A station does not, for example, have to sell a candidate prime-time avails at the same price it charges for much less expensive overnight avails, nor must it figure in barter (*PRT,* 9.1.6.6) and per-inquiry (*PRT,* 9.1.6.5) spots when calculating lowest unit rate.

Section 312(a)(7) of the Communications Act contains the **candidate-access requirement.** A station must make available (by gift or by sale) reasonable amounts of time to candidates for federal elective office. Whereas Section 315 covers both broadcast stations and operator-produced locally originated programming on cable systems, Section 312(a)(7) applies only to stations.

The **Zapple Doctrine** applies a "quasi-equal opportunities" rule to supporters of and persons who represent a candidate. When a licensee allows such persons to use a station's facilities during an election campaign to urge their candidate's election, to discuss campaign issues, or to criticize an opponent, the licensee must afford "comparable time" to supporters of other candidates for the same office.[1]

***14.1.1.5 Support of Political Candidates and Editorializing by Noncommercial Licensees.***    The Public Broadcasting Act of 1967 (*PRT,* 22.1.3) added Section 399 to the Communications Act. Section 399 prohibits noncommercial stations from supporting or opposing political candidates. Originally, this section also banned public stations from editorializing. Congress subsequently changed the wording to prohibit editorializing only by public stations that received funds from the tax-supported Corporation for Public Broadcasting. Nonetheless, in 1984 the U.S. Supreme Court ruled that the prohibition on editorials was too broadly written and, therefore, unconstitutional.[2]

***14.1.1.6 Equitable Distribution.***    The Communications Act's Section 307(b) provides for the "fair, efficient, and equitable distribution of radio service to each" state and community. This seems to say that each city and state should have the same number of stations, but there are far fewer broadcasters who want to serve the beautiful, relatively unpopulated reaches of Wyoming than who wish to serve the wall-to-wall people (and potentially far greater return on investment) of Los Angeles.

The FCC has made efforts to see that all persons benefit from local broadcast service. For example, the Commission constructed the table of assignments in both television (*PRT,* 12.6.1) and FM (*PRT,* 11.2.2.1) in an attempt to serve the intent of 307(b). In dealing with competing applications (*PRT,* 19.1.1.3), the FCC gave a slight advantage (a "preference") to applicants who proposed to serve communities with few or no local stations. Docket 80-90 FM channels (*PRT,* 2.5) went primarily to communities that lacked full-time radio stations. In 1983, on the other hand, the FCC eliminated policies designed to ensure that a station serves its community of license rather than nearby large markets.[3]

***14.1.1.7 Other Regulatory Requirements.***    Section 325 of the Communications Act prohibits willful transmission of false distress signals. It requires a station planning to rebroadcast the signal of another station to get permission first from that other station. Section 326 **forbids censorship** by the FCC.

For years, the final word on broadcast of lottery information was Section 1304 of the Criminal Code. That statute placed a flat ban on the broadcast of lotteries or information about lotteries. During the 1970s Congress passed a measure that allowed stations to broadcast information about official state lotteries in states that had them. In 1988 Congress loosened the prohibition further to **permit announcements promoting all legal lotteries.**[4] As a result, broadcasters can now advertise lotteries conducted by any of the following:

1. Nonprofit organizations.
2. Governmental organizations.
3. Commercial entities, as long as the lottery is occasional and not the primary purpose of the organization.

Congress did, however, leave authority over lotteries to the states. Some states continue to ban lotteries and lottery advertising, so despite liberalization of federal laws, licensees in those states may still not broadcast lotteries.

Section 1464 of the Criminal Code **prohibits transmission of obscene, indecent, or profane language.** Section 1343 of the Criminal Code **prohibits fraud** by wire, radio, or television. Sections 312 and 503 of the Communications Act authorize the Commission to remove the licenses of those who violate Section 1304, 1464, or 1343 of the Criminal Code.

In 1996 Congress amended Section 303 of the Communications Act to require a TV program rating system. The ratings were to warn parents of material they might wish to prevent young children from viewing. Congress also directed the FCC to require that new TVs sold in the United States with 13-inch or larger screens have a blocking capability, the so-called **V-chip** (V for violence). Viewers could set their receivers to detect ratings and to block offensive (to them) programming. The rating system was to be voluntary; that is, programmers did not have to televise the signals used by the V-chip. On the other hand, if networks or producers actually rate a program, then that rating would have to be transmitted. The television business developed and introduced their ratings scheme in late 1996 (*PRT,* 16.2.2).

That same 1996 law **required that video programming be closed captioned** (*PRT,* 5.5.2). It directed the FCC to conduct an inquiry and report to Congress on the extent to which captioning was already being done. Then the Commission was to adopt rules to ensure that all future programming would be captioned, although the law did provide for exemptions. The FCC was also to report to

Congress on ways to implement a **video description service.** This service would provide audio descriptions of on-screen events for visually impaired TV viewers. These laws apparently applied to all video programming regardless of medium.

FCC rules require stations to establish a continuing program to afford equal employment opportunities to all persons (*PRT,* 19.1.1.6). The FCC has also enacted rules to implement the National Environmental Policy Act. These rules are designed to minimize negative impact on the environment by construction of communications facilities. Similar restrictions and requirements apply to cable. Local origination programming is subject to lottery and obscenity restrictions, and cable systems must establish equal employment opportunity programs. Both cable systems and broadcast stations must participate in the **Emergency Alert System** (EAS).

EAS, based on FCC-specified equipment and procedures, is designed to deliver emergency information quickly to the public. In the event of war or other large-scale disasters, EAS may be activated at the local, state, or national level. The previous system, the 40-year-old Emergency Broadcast System (EBS), could no longer accommodate advances in communications, so in 1994 the FCC replaced it with EAS. EAS, based on digital technology, provides much more flexibility and reliability than did EBS. It minimizes risk of failure or confusion due to human error, common under EBS. EBS delivered warnings only through radio and TV sets. EAS delivers warnings not only through broadcast receivers but also through specially equipped pagers, CD players, and other devices—even when they are shut off.

### 14.1.1.8 Additional Requirements for Cable and Other Media.

Sections 611 and 612 of the Communications Act deal with cable access channels. Section 611 permits the franchising authority to require that the cable system provide channel capacity for public, educational, and governmental use. Section 612 requires that some channels be designated for commercial use on systems of 36 or more channels. Persons not connected with the cable operator may use these channels on a leased-access basis (*PRT,* 7.4.1.3). The operator sets the rates for use and may run other types of programming on these channels when they are not needed for access use.

The operator may refuse to transmit leased-access programs that contain obscenity, indecency, or nudity. Otherwise the operator may exercise no editorial control over access programming.[5] Furthermore, except for obscene material, Section 638 relieves the cable operator of criminal and civil liability for access programming.

Section 641 requires that all multichannel video suppliers (e.g., cable systems, wireless cable systems, DBSs) scramble sexually explicit adult programming.[6] Section 639 provides fines and prison terms for transmission on a cable system of material that is "obscene or otherwise unprotected by the Constitution." Section 640 directs that a cable system, when a subscriber so requests, must scramble or fully block such programming.

Section 613 permits the government—a state or a franchising authority—to own a cable system. The government-owner must set up an entity separate from the franchising authority to carry out the actual operation of the cable system. The government may, however, directly control programming on the system's educational and government access channels.

In 1996 Congress amended Section 223 of the Communications Act to outlaw transmission over computer networks of several categories of material. The prohibited content included messages and postings that annoys or harasses the recipient, or discusses abortion devices and procedures. The legislation also prohibited computer network content that aimed sexually explicit material at persons under age 18, but the U.S. Supreme Court ruled this part of the Communications Decency Act to be unconstitutional.[7]

***14.1.1.9 Cable and OVS Carriage Rules.***    Five cable rules impact the broadcast-station signals that a cable system carries. Four aim to protect broadcast stations. These include the retransmission consent, must-carry, syndicated exclusivity, and network nonduplication rules. The fifth, the sports blackout rule, protects attendance at sports events. In 1996 Congress also applied most of these rules to telephone companies that operate open video systems (OVS; *PRT,* 5.13.2.2).

**Must-carry** originated as an FCC rule. It required a cable system to carry the signals of local television stations. Excluded were the signals of LPTV stations and broadcast teletext. Court decisions invalidated different versions in 1985 and 1987.[8] Congress, however, wrote must-carry into law in 1992,[9] and the U.S. Supreme Court validated it in 1997.[10] The 1992 law tied must-carry to a new option for commercial TV stations, **retransmission consent.** A broadcaster who opted for retransmission consent announced, in effect, "No one may carry my signal and sell it to subscribers without getting my permission to do so." This requirement for permission applied not just to cable systems and open video systems but also to any other multichannel video programming distributors, such as wireless cable systems, DBS, and TVRO program packagers.

Under that 1992 law, all full-power TV stations qualified as either must-carry or retransmission consent.[11] A noncommercial educational TV station had no choice; it automatically qualified as must-carry, and local cable systems had to carry it. A commercial TV broadcast licensee, on the other hand, got to choose every 3 years between must-carry and retransmission consent status. In most cases, of course, a broadcaster's motivation to opt for retransmission consent was to negotiate with MVSs for payment in return for permission to carry the station's signal.

Under **syndicated exclusivity** (syndex), a TV station could force local cable systems to delete syndicated programming that duplicated that of the station. **Network nonduplication** required a cable system to blank out imported broadcast network programming when it duplicated that of local affiliates. The FCC eliminated the syndex rule in 1980. Over the next decade, however, cable experienced enormous audience and revenue growth. The Commission believed that the lack of syndicated exclusivity was harming television stations and might restrict the supply of syndicated programs. In response, it put new syndex rules into effect and expanded the network exclusivity rules in 1990.[12]

In programming, **exclusivity** is the right to be the only outlet in a market to show a syndicated program. The resurrected syndex rule permitted a station to enforce its exclusivity against local cable and OVSs that carried distant stations (whose signals are imported from other markets) that showed the same program. A syndicator could enforce exclusivity for a program in all markets for the first year after the program was first sold to a TV station. A station could negotiate for national exclusivity; thus, a superstation with national rights to a syndicated program would be the only station to show it.

The old network nonduplication rule covered only simultaneously aired duplicative network programming. The revision allowed an affiliate to demand protection against all duplicative network programming, even when aired at another time.

The final rule in this set is **sports blackout.** This rule applies to cable and OVSs that serve communities within which a sports event takes place. An example will show how it works. Let us say a sports production and syndication firm has the rights to televise a football game. All tickets are not yet sold, and so although TV stations in other communities carry the game, no local station carries it. It would be tempting for a local cable system or OVS operator to pick up the signal of one of the distant stations that carries the game and put it on the system for local subscribers. However, under the sports blackout rule, the syndicator, as broadcast rights holder for the game, can tell these local systems not to carry the game live.[13]

*14.1.1.10 FCC Rule-making Procedure.*    As mentioned in *PRT,* 14.1, the Communications Act authorizes the FCC to make "rules and regulations."[14] The process begins with a suggestion to make, amend, or delete a rule (Fig. 14.2). The suggestion can come from almost any source—in or out of the Commission, in or out of the government. All suggestions go to the appropriate FCC bureau or office for evaluation. A suggestion that survives staff screening goes to the full Commission.

In some cases, the proposal involves only editorial changes to an existing rule. Here, the commission may issue a *Report and Order* adopting the change with no further action necessary. Some rule proposals take the form of a formal petition. If the FCC does not believe such a proposal has value, it issues a *Memorandum Opinion and Order* (MO&O) that denies the petition.

The process gets more complicated when the FCC likes a proposal that calls for substantive change. Here, the FCC issues a **Notice of Proposed Rulemaking** (NPRM), a **Notice of Inquiry** (NOI), or a combination of the two. NPRMs call for comment on a specific proposal to change the rules. NOIs ask for information or suggestions on a certain topic. When the Commission issues an NOI, it must eventually follow up with either an NPRM that proposes a specific rule or an MO&O that concludes the inquiry.

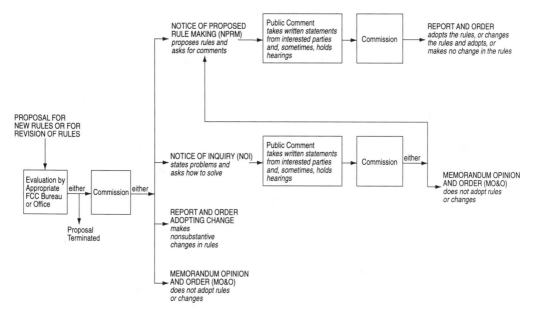

FIG. 14.2. FCC rule-making process.

Interested parties or any member of the public can file comments. Later they can also file responses to the comments. Occasionally the Commission may decide to hold oral arguments or hearings on the matter. Hearings or not, after everyone has had a chance to comment and the record is closed, the FCC considers all comments and either changes the proposal, adopts it in its original form, or decides not to adopt it. The Commission then issues a **Report and Order** announcing its action.

A rule goes into effect 30 days after publication in the *Federal Register.* During that time, any interested party may petition for reconsideration. Failing that, the rule may be challenged in court. If no one successfully challenges it, the rule stands as an enforceable regulation until the FCC changes or repeals it or Congress overrides it with new legislation.

The FCC may also utilize a less formal **policymaking** procedure. The Commission examines a particular area of concern, reviews previous decisions in the area, and establishes guidelines or expectations. The Government Printing Office publishes regulations, including policy formulations, from all agencies in the *Code of Federal Regulations.*

***14.1.1.11 Hearings and Appeals.***   The Communications Act requires that the FCC hold hearings on certain matters. The purpose is to ensure that all parties involved **have a chance to make their views known** so that the FCC may take them into account in reaching a final decision. The Communications Act requires hearings in two situations: (a) during certain rule-making proceedings, and (b) in cases that require adjudication. **Adjudication** means the formal giving, pronouncing, or recording of an opinion, so an adjudicatory hearing would be a hearing for the purpose of rendering an adjudication.

For the sake of discussion, let us imagine a particular situation that requires an adjudicatory hearing. Our hearing involves an application to renew a broadcast license. The Mass Media Bureau has found that the applicant's station had serious, recurring problems during the licensing period now concluding. These problems involved, among other things, an improperly lighted transmission tower, improper station identification, transmission at power levels greater than those authorized, and failure to have the transmitter operating within specifications. The station's signal has interfered with those of other stations in the area, and those broadcasters have complained to the FCC. The station had been cited and fined several times because of these problems but had apparently done little or nothing about them. Such practices seem to cast doubt on the applicant's ability to operate a station, so the matter of the renewal application is set for hearing.

The first step in the hearing process is for the commission to **issue an order for the hearing.** The Commission's order contains, among other things, the time, place, and nature of the hearing; a statement as to the reasons for the Commission's action; a statement as to the matters of fact and law involved; a statement as to the issues involved; and a statement of legal authority and jurisdiction under which the hearing is to be held.

The most important part of the order is the **designation of issues.** An issue is a single point in dispute; in the final decision, disposal of the issues determines the fate of the applicant. The parties to the proceeding petition to enlarge, change, or delete issues. The issues in our case deal with the problems themselves, whether the applicant knew of them, and why nothing was done to correct them. The last issue asks whether, in the light of evidence received on the other issues, the public interest would be served by renewing the applicant's license.

The order goes by mail to parties to the proceeding and is published in the *Federal Register.* These parties (which, in our case, include the neighboring stations that complained) have 20 days to respond in writing that they will appear. If the applicant does not respond, the Commission dismisses the license renewal application "with prejudice"; that is, the applicant loses all rights and cannot make another application. Other parties to the proceeding who fail to respond forfeit their right to be heard in the matter.

In our case, action on the part of the FCC's Mass Media Bureau has led to the hearing. The Mass Media Bureau thus becomes the applicant's adversary in the hearing and gives testimony and introduces evidence to oppose the applicant. This is common in broadcast matters, because part of the Bureau's job is to examine applications and the applicants.

The hearing itself resembles a trial. An **administrative law judge** (ALJ) presides, as is the case in most adjudicatory hearings. ALJs are Commission employees. They have authority to issue subpoenas, administer oaths, examine witnesses, and rule on admission of evidence. An ALJ must render an impartial or independent opinion. This means the ALJ may not ask other employees and officers of the FCC for definitions, interpretations, and opinions on an informal basis. All such questions must be "on the record."

After conclusion of the hearing, the ALJ issues an **initial decision**. Unless reviewed, the initial decision eventually becomes final and effective. **Review** results from appeal by one of the parties involved (e.g., the applicant or the Mass Media Bureau) or by direction of the commissioners. Most initial decisions go to the **Review Board**, a permanent body of three or more senior Commission employees. The Board issues a final decision, which, in turn, is subject to review by the five commissioners, that is, the **full Commission**. Some initial decisions, however, go directly to the five commissioners.

Section 405 of the Communications Act allows people who are "aggrieved or whose interests are adversely affected" by a Commission decision to **petition for rehearing**. FCC decisions may also be appealed directly to the **federal courts**, and many are.

The applicant in our imaginary case has lost all the way up the ladder. The ALJ's initial decision found the violations were so serious and repeated so often that the license should not be renewed. The applicant appealed first to the Review Board and then to the full Commission, but the decision was the same. The applicant (whom we shall call "Applicant Broadcasting, Inc.") appeals the FCC decision to the federal court. Because the decision is to deny renewal of a license, Applicant Broadcasting must make its appeal to a specific appeals court, the U.S. Court of Appeals for the District of Columbia. The case thus becomes *Applicant Broadcasting, Inc. v. FCC.*

In its decision, the appeals court can either **affirm** or **reverse** the Commission decision. If it is the latter, it **remands** (i.e, sends back) the case to the FCC to carry out the judgment. The party that loses the case may petition the U.S. Supreme Court to review the decision of the appeals court.

In our case, the appeals court affirmed the FCC's decision, so Applicant petitions the **U.S. Supreme Court** for review. The case remains *Applicant Broadcasting, Inc. v. FCC.* (If the FCC had lost at the appellate level and petitioned for review, the case would have become *FCC v. Applicant Broadcasting, Inc.*) The Supreme Court may or may not grant certiorari (in effect, review the decision), depending on the principles involved. If it does not, the decision of the lower court stands.

***14.1.1.12 Declaratory Ruling.*** The FCC may issue a declaratory ruling, a legal device to terminate a controversy or remove an uncertainty, and the Commission has done so on occasion. For example, in the *Pacifica* "dirty words" case (*PRT,* 15.3.5.1), the FCC issued a declaratory ruling in which it attempted to clarify its definition of the term *indecent.*

***14.1.1.13 Enforcement.*** The Communications Act gives the FCC six methods to deal with a licensee that violates the act, FCC rules, or terms of the license. Sections 401, 501, and 502 authorize the Commission to call on any U.S. district attorney to **prosecute violators in court.** Section 503(b) allows the Commission to levy a **forfeiture** (fine). Section 312(b) authorizes the FCC to issue a **cease and desist order.**

Section 307(c) allows the FCC to grant **short-term renewals,** that is, to renew a transmitter license for a period of less than its full license term. The Commission can use the short-term renewal when it wishes to review, for example, a broadcast station's performance sooner than the normal 8-year interval.

Section 307(d) also gives the commission the option to **deny renewal,** and Section 312(a) allows it to **revoke** the license, to take it away before renewal time. Denial of renewal and revocation of license are both serious sanctions—the broadcasting business refers to them as "the death penalty" for a station—and the FCC rarely uses them; nor does the Commission often use court prosecution or cease and desist orders, because other sanctions are easier to apply.

In addition to the sanctions granted by the Communications Act, the Commission uses three other methods of enforcement. In one, the FCC simply writes a **letter** to the licensee. The letter describes the matter under question and asks, in effect, "What about this? Please explain," or "What do you plan to do about this?" Some call this the **"raised eyebrow"** technique.

A second nonstatutory enforcement method involves a **consent order.** Here, the alleged violator signs an agreement to comply with specified laws, rules, or policies. This does not, however, constitute admission to the alleged violations.

In the third nonstatutory enforcement method, the FCC grants a **conditional renewal** of a license. The FCC may condition license renewal on specific licensee behavior—for example, serving the community of license better, or improving hiring practices to bring in more women and minority staff members.

The FCC does not license cable systems, so it cannot use license-affecting enforcement methods on erring cable operators, but it can use all the rest. And in 1994 it developed yet another, the **social contract** between customers and operators,[15] aimed specifically at cable rate cases. The first social contract was in 1995 with MSO Continental Cablevision.[16] The 6-year contract settled 370 complaints against the MSO and, in return for regulatory flexibility, called for Continental to refund $9.5 million to consumers through "in-kind" payments such as free installation or premium channels. Time Warner, Cox Communications, Times Mirror Cable Television, and other MSOs soon took advantage of this method to solve rate-complaint problems.

### 14.1.2 FCC Public Interest Considerations

The Communications Act gives the FCC little specific control over programming. Yet it directs the Commission to grant broadcast licenses and renewals only if the **public interest, convenience, and necessity** will be served thereby. Over the years the FCC took the position that one primary means by which stations serve the public interest was their programming; therefore, of necessity, the FCC had to examine broadcast programming. The federal courts consistently supported this view. Congress has not seen fit to amend the Act to preclude FCC regulation of broadcast programming and, in committee hearings of past years, has even scolded the Commission for not paying enough attention to programming.

Throughout its history, the FCC has trod a thin line between censorship and program regulation. The Commission would not tell a broadcast station that it could or could not air a particular program, but it did hold that the station had a responsibility to provide programming that **met the varied needs of its home community** and adopted policy statements, rules, and procedures to ensure that the station met that responsibility. The station decided how it would meet the needs of the community. The station designed its own programming. And then, when the station's license came up for renewal, the FCC had the authority and duty to review overall programming, to compare the station's performance during the preceding license period to promises it made on the last renewal application, and to determine whether it operated in the public interest.

This routine, although nice in theory, rarely worked in practice. The Commission granted most broadcast license renewals if the applications were filled out properly. Normally, the FCC questioned a station's renewal only if there were problems with its application form or if the station's file contained serious and frequent complaints from third parties, such as the public or other stations. So, in fact, very little was lost in 1981 when the FCC adopted a postcard sized renewal form that required no information on programming and dropped formal ascertainment requirements (*PRT,* 15.3.3.5) for commercial radio and television.

Nonetheless, there are still mechanisms for ensuring that a station serves the public interest. Each quarter, every station must put in its public file (*PRT,* 15.3.3.6) a list of its programs that dealt with community issues during the preceding 3 months. Citizens can make their views known to the station and, if necessary, to the Commission. Serious and frequent complaints may lead the Commission to order a hearing; quite often, one of the questions the hearing seeks to answer concerns whether renewal of the station's license would serve the public interest.

The anti-"public interest" rhetoric of the 1980s (*PRT,* 13.4.2) left its mark in at least one respect. Congress did not use the words *public interest* even once in writing the Cable Communications Policy Act of 1984. That phase eventually passed; the Telecommunications Act of 1996, for example, deregulatory though it was, contained 46 uses of the term *public interest.*

### 14.1.3 Network Regulation

The Communications Act **does not require that networks be licensed.** However, the FCC does license network-owned stations, and Section 303(i) gives the Commission authority to make special regulations for network-affiliated stations. When the FCC adopted its **Chain Broadcasting Regulations** in 1941 (*PRT,* 2.2.5.5), the rules applied through affiliated stations. Most began "No license shall be granted to a . . . broadcast station . . ." and then went on to spell out what the FCC prohibited.

### 14.1.3.1 Chain Broadcasting Regulations Eliminated for Radio.

The Chain Broadcasting Regulations were designed to end network control of affiliated stations, to shift control from networks back to licensees, those legally responsible for the stations. They worked, but over the years conditions changed, and need for the regulations ended. By 1977 the FCC had repealed all Chain Broadcasting Regulations as they applied to radio.

### 14.1.3.2 Fin-Syn, PTAR, and Other TV Network Rules.

All Chain Broadcasting Regulations were retained for television. In 1996, however, Congress directed the FCC to relax its dual network prohibition. Under the change a company that already owns a broadcast TV network could start another, but it could not acquire an already existing network.

Five additional rules applied only to television networks. One said that a network **may not act as national sales representative for nonnetwork time on affiliated stations** (except for those it owns). In 1995, however, the FCC proposed repealing or eliminating this ban against "repping" nonowned stations. A second TV-only rule **gave independent TV stations first choice to air network programs not broadcast by a regular affiliate** in some specific situations.[17] A third, the **network financial interest rule**, prohibited a network from owning in whole or in part any of its programs that it did not produce itself, and the fourth, the **network syndication rule**, prohibited a network from syndicating programming in the United States; trade press headline writers dubbed these the **fin-syn** rules. The fifth, the **prime-time access rule** (PTAR), prohibited network affiliates in the 50 largest markets (in effect, all markets) from airing over 3 hours of network programming (including off-net programming) during the four hours of prime time. In adopting the network syndication and financial interest rules, the FCC broke precedent and, rather than applying them through affiliated stations, applied the rules directly to the networks—"[N]o television network shall. . . ."

The fin-syn rule and PTAR rule aimed at fostering competition and diversity in the programming marketplace. During the 1950s and 1960s the TV broadcast networks had established dominance in the program syndication field. Independent production houses that wished to produce TV programs had, realistically, only ABC, CBS, and NBC as customers. Additionally, the networks demanded some equity (share of ownership) and syndication rights to programs they carried. Because the best programming had been produced for the networks, and the networks now held syndication rights to that programming, TV stations that wished to lease and air syndicated programs had, realistically, only the syndication arms of ABC, CBS, and NBC as suppliers and only the off-net programs they offered as product. In response, the FCC adopted PTAR and fin-syn in 1970.

Over the years, PTAR changed in detail, but the principles remained intact. The ban included both current network and off-net programming. It created the access hour. The only stations who could program off-network (and "on-network," were it available) programs in the access hour were affiliates in markets below the top 50, independent stations, and affiliates of new networks whose prime-time programming totaled less than 15 hours a week.

As a result of these three rules, original programming developed for the syndication market that might otherwise have never seen the light of day—programming for access (such as *Entertainment Tonight*) and for other dayparts (such as *The Oprah Winfrey Show* and the various *Star Trek* series). PTAR also yielded unexpected benefits. First, it strengthened independent stations. Through competitive programming, the independents significantly improved their ratings. Second, affiliates made money. Their access programming typically generated lower ratings than network programming would have. Still, the affiliates made much more from their own time sales for the access slot than they would have received in compensation if the networks had programmed the slot.

Production houses, syndicators, independent TV stations, even many affiliates all profited by and wanted to retain, in whole or in part, fin-syn and PTAR. ABC, CBS, and NBC opposed the rules and continually argued for their elimination.[18] This resulted in years of tinkering with the rules, court challenges, and other legal bickering. At the same time, however, the television business itself was changing with the result that, by the mid-1990s, the big three TV networks no longer dominated the programming market. That being the case, concluded the FCC, fin-syn and PTAR were now superfluous, and in 1995 the Commission eliminated all three rules.[19]

### 14.1.4 Advertising and Commercial Limitations

During the 1980s the FCC eliminated most of its restrictions on advertising. These included regulations or policies on commercial minutes per hour; program-length commercials; false, misleading, or deceptive advertising;[20] alcohol advertising;[21] and advertising aimed at children.

### 14.1.5 Children's Programming and Advertising

Over the years individuals and citizen groups have argued that children have special requirements as a radio–TV audience. Children need protection, for example, from accidentally tuning in certain types of sexually oriented material. The FCC reacted by channeling such material to late night.

In a 1974 Children's Television Report and Policy Statement, the FCC urged licensees to increase programming on both weekends and weekdays that would educate as well as entertain children. Further, the FCC said children's programming efforts by a licensee would be reviewed at license renewal time.[22]

Things went downhill from there for children's programming advocates. The FCC revisited the issue in 1979, found little improvement, and asked for comment on several rule-making options.[23] These ranged from setting children's programming quotas to rescinding the 1974 policy statement. In 1983 the Commission—well into its deregulatory phase (*PRT,* 3.5.1)—chose the latter.[24] The amount and variety of children's programming already being televised, said the FCC, was substantial and diverse; mandated quotas were not needed. At license renewal time, a station would have to show that programming needs of children in its community had been met. However, in making that showing, the station could count children's programming by other media in the market, such as cable and public television.[25]

The Commission's record in the area of advertising aimed at children is equally spotty. The 1974 policy statement had placed limitations on advertising during children's programming. It called for a clear separation between programming and advertising, prohibited program hosts or characters from selling products, and limited ad time to 9½ minutes an hour on weekends and 12 minutes on weekdays. In 1986 the FCC said that those 1974 limitations had been eliminated as part of the general deregulation of television 2 years earlier.[26]

Other commercialization issues came up, and the Commission refused to deal with them. In 1983 the National Association for Better Broadcasting (NABB), a citizens group, complained that children's series produced by a toy company and based on the company's toys (Fig. 14.3) were really program-length commercials. In barter syndication[27] of such programs, said the NABB, Section 317 of the Communications Act required that the broadcaster make known to the audience that the manufacturer had provided the program. In another proceeding, Action for Children's Television (ACT), another citizen group, asserted that toy companies' offers to share profits with stations airing their shows might lead to program choices based on profit rather than the public interest. The FCC rejected both complaints[28] in 1985.

Then along came interactive children's shows. Several companies announced plans for this product tie-in scheme. The programs would transmit inaudible signals causing specially designed toys to react. ACT filed a petition asking that the FCC declare the toys against the public interest.

Efforts of children's programming advocates began to pay off in 1987. ACT had appealed the FCC's 1984 decision to abolish its 1974 children's commercial guidelines, and the court remanded the case, saying the FCC had not adequately justified elimination of those limitations.[29] NABB had appealed the FCC's program-length commercial decision, and the court overruled that Commission action.[30] In response, the FCC opened a rule-making procedure, requesting comments on commercial guidelines for children's shows, the nature of commercial matter, and interactive toys.[31]

ACT and others had also lobbied Congress for legislation on children's programming and advertising. Congress wrote legislation, but President Ronald Reagan vetoed it in 1988. Congress tried again, and 2 years later the **Children's Television Act of 1990** (CTA) became law. The CTA limits advertising aimed at children to 12 minutes per hour on weekdays and 10½ minutes per hour on weekends. The commercial limits apply to cable operators as well as television broadcasters, and pertain to programs aimed at children ages 12 and under. The FCC developed guidelines based on the 1990 act to help licensees determine the

(a)

(b)

FIG. 14.3. **Toys as television.** (a) Teenage Mutant Ninja Turtles™, the children's animated TV series. (b) Teenage Mutant Ninja Turtles™, the toys. (Teenage Mutant Ninja Turtles™ is a trademark owned and licensed by Mirage Studios. Used by permission.)

educational and informational needs of their communities. One study, however, showed that the rules were so broad that licensees, in reporting programs they had broadcast to fulfill FCC requirements, cited series from *Leave It to Beaver* to *Bucky O'Hare and the Toad Wars*. The FCC launched an inquiry to determine more precisely what broadcasters must do to comply with the CTA.[32] In 1996 President Bill Clinton met with leaders of the TV broadcasting business and convinced them to support airing at least 3 hours of educational shows for children each week.

### 14.1.6 Regulatory Weaknesses

We have described what should be an ideal mechanism for regulation. Feed in a problem—an erring licensee, competing applications, need for corrective action or new policy; spin it through regulatory and decision-making machinery, powered by the desire to ensure service in the public interest; and out should come the perfect solution—the sanction, the choice of best applicant, the proper action or cure-all policy. Unfortunately, it does not work that way. Anyone who has ever dealt with government agencies knows that even the best are not too efficient and are prone to making mistakes. Historically the FCC has not been one of the best; some critics have even said it was one of the worst. Critics have generally listed the following as the FCC's major weaknesses over the years.[33]

**14.1.6.1 Politically Motivated Appointments to the Commission.**     Commissioners often have not been the types of people needed to guide the nation's civilian communications policy. Individuals are appointed to the Commission not based on their ability to regulate in the public interest but as political favors and, during the 1980s, to mold the Commission to conform to an ideological bent.

**14.1.6.2 Decisions Made without Citizen Involvement.**     For years the Commission did not encourage citizen participation in licensing matters, rule-making procedures, and hearings. During the 1970s the FCC reversed that policy and attempted to encourage such public participation.

**14.1.6.3 Decisions Made Under Pressure from Business Lobbyists.**     The Commission, bombarded by myriad lobbying efforts, loses sight of the public interest. Commissioners find it hard not to adopt the view of the regulated companies—that is, let the business run itself, but regulate all competitors to the hilt. Broadcasters, large cable operators, the huge interstate common-carrier firms, and their lobbyists and lawyers are in constant touch with the commissioners. They are always ready to provide information, help, and advice. They are the milieu within which the commissioners work and theirs is the viewpoint most often heard. Some commissioners and staffers, after leaving the FCC, have taken high-paying jobs in the regulated businesses.

Commissioners who bucked the trend and tried to force the issue of public interest from the public's point of view have been branded as mavericks and troublemakers. These commissioners were not playing according to the "rules of the business" and were vilified and harassed by broadcasters and the trade press.

### 14.1.6.4 Decisions Made with Inadequate or Biased Information.    The FCC agency is a bureaucracy. It consists of a hierarchy of chiefs and a staff of civil servants, many of whom are more interested in keeping pensions intact than in problem solving, innovation, and clearing up backlogs. The commissioners must deal with matters and base decisions on information these middle-level staff personnel put before them. These staffers often choose matters for FCC consideration based not so much on what will serve the public as on what will serve their own private interest. In addition, as communications become more technically complex, commissioners have difficulty educating themselves adequately in order to make competent technical judgments.

### 14.1.6.5 Unreasonable Delays in Resolving Matters.    Efficiency is strangled in red tape. Huge backlogs of work build up, causing unreasonable delays. The Commission can take months, even years, to resolve individual matters.

### 14.1.6.6 Decisions Made Without Consideration of Precedent.    In reaching a decision on a matter, commissioners may simply ignore past FCC decisions. As a result, decisions are inconsistent; that is, the Commission applies different principles in different ways in similar cases.

### 14.1.6.7 Sanctions Not Used; Policies Not Followed.    The Commission does not follow its own guidelines or use the sanctions available to it. As a result, licenses are renewed routinely, irrespective of how well the stations met the public interest standard. Rarely are licenses revoked, even for the most serious violations of law and regulation. Even before the FCC and Congress loosened ownership limitations, during the decades when the stated policy of the Commission was to diversify ownership of broadcasting, the Commission granted license transfers that concentrated station control into fewer and larger corporate structures and created more and more absentee owners.

### 14.1.6.8 Inability to Make Long-Range Policy.    Critics contend that the FCC does not seem to be able to formulate long-range policy. The heavy press of ongoing, everyday matters is so burdensome that little time is left for long-range planning. When the Commission does attempt to make policy, it is buffeted from all sides—the executive, the legislative branch, and the regulated businesses. As a result, the FCC is reactive, taking matters as they come and allowing electronic interstate communication to develop willy-nilly with no plan or purpose. It has not been able to delineate an effective and coordinated long-range policy within which communication technologies can develop, evolve, and be regulated.

## 14.2 FEDERAL TRADE COMMISSION

Like the FCC, the Federal Trade Commission (FTC) is an independent federal regulatory agency created by Congress under its constitutional power to regulate interstate commerce. Congress passed the **Federal Trade Commission Act** in 1914,[34] establishing the FTC and banning "unfair methods of competition." Twenty-four years later, Congress amended the act by passing the Wheeler–Lea Act.[35] The Wheeler–Lea Act prohibits "unfair and deceptive acts or practices in commerce" and thus allows the FTC to protect the consumer from deceptive advertising.

The overall purpose of the FTC is to enforce a number of federal antitrust and consumer protection laws. Under these laws, the FTC focuses on the nation's markets, the economic arenas in which goods are bought and sold. It aims to ensure that the markets function competitively, smoothly, and free of unnecessary restriction. Toward those ends, the FTC takes action to eliminate unfair or deceptive trade practices, to stop acts that threaten consumers' opportunities to exercise informed choice. Among such acts are deceptive advertising in any medium. So in matters involving unfair or deceptive advertising in the electronic media of mass communication, it is the FTC that exercises jurisdiction. The FTC also deals with allegations of deception and misuse in audience rating surveys.

### 14.2.1 Organization and Operation

The FTC's structure resembles that of the FCC. Both have five commissioners, working bureaus, field offices, and administrative law judges.

An FTC investigation of deceptive advertising begins with a complaint or an allegation of wrongdoing. This can originate from almost any source—a letter from a consumer or business, a Congressional inquiry, a newspaper or magazine article, other federal agencies, the Better Business Bureau, or the FTC's own monitoring activities. The FTC may conduct public investigations, but most are nonpublic. This, maintains the FTC, protects both the investigation (so that a guilty party may not "cover its tracks") and the advertiser or subject being investigated (so that, if innocent, the advertiser's reputation is not damaged). If the investigation leads the FTC to believe that the advertiser has broken the law, the Commission may seek voluntary compliance through a **consent order.** In signing the order, the advertiser legally binds itself to stop the disputed practice but does not admit guilt. Failing that, the FTC may issue an **administrative complaint**, and the matter goes to an ALJ for **hearing.** If evidence sustains the complaint, the ALJ (or the FTC on appeal or review) issues an initial decision that requires the advertiser to **cease and desist** the deceptive advertising. The advertiser may appeal the cease and desist order to the full Commission.

The **federal courts** figure in FTC operation in three ways. First, cease and desist orders may be **appealed.** Second, the government may **sue violators** of cease and desist orders. Third, in some cases, the FTC may seek a court **injunction** to halt advertising even before a hearing. The injunction remains in effect until final FTC or court disposition of the case. Violators of cease and desist orders or the FTC act are subject to **fines** and **imprisonment**. The FTC also uses **publicity** for enforcement, publicizing complaints and cease and desist orders.

In 1971 the FTC introduced another regulatory option—**corrective advertising.** The Profile Bread, Ocean Spray, and Listerine television commercials discussed in *PRT,* 9.1.4.4, are examples of corrective advertising. Also in 1971 the FTC began its **advertising substantiation program.** The FTC selects certain advertisers and asks them to prove advertising claims they make for their products. Responses are made public.

The FTC also plays a positive role in prevention of deceptive practices. Its **trade regulation rules** target specific businesses (e.g., the used car business) and apply to all outlets within that business (e.g., all used car dealers). Trade regulation rules, like FCC rules, have the force of law.

### 14.2.2 False Advertising

Section 15 of the Wheeler–Lea Act defines a "false advertisement" as one that is "misleading" in a material respect. **Misleading** refers not only to what an advertisement says, but also what it does not say. In other words, the FTC looks for both **direct falsehoods** and **failure to reveal material facts**—for example, facts concerning consequences from use of a product, or facts concerning a product's value in treating illness or pain.

Three of the most famous cases of deceptive broadcast advertising come from the 1960s—the **sandpaper case,** the **Libby-Owens-Ford** (L-O-F) **Glass case,** and the **Geritol case.** In fall 1959 three new commercials ran on TV to advertise Rapid Shave. They supposedly demonstrated how the aerosol shaving cream was "super-moisturized" to shave "a beard as tough as sandpaper." Rapid Shave was spread on sandpaper, and a razor shaved a swatch clean of grit. What the commercials did not say was that the "sandpaper" was really a piece of Plexiglas covered with sand. The FTC found that to actually shave off the grit, sandpaper had to soak in the lather for about 80 minutes. The FTC issued a cease and desist order. The U.S. Supreme Court upheld the decision, ruling that undisclosed use of Plexiglas constituted a "material deceptive practice."[36]

In the L-O-F Glass case, a TV commercial invited the audience to compare views through the glass of two different automobiles. One showed distortion in ordinary auto glass; the other, the minimum distortion in L-O-F safety glass. The audience was not told that scenes purported to be filmed through L-O-F safety glass were actually shot through an open window! The FTC issued a cease and desist order, which a federal court upheld.[37]

J. B. Williams Company advertised its patent medicine, Geritol, heavily on TV. The ads touted the product as a remedy for tiredness, loss of strength, nervousness, or irritability due to iron-deficiency anemia. They failed to explain that, of the people who suffered from those symptoms, only a relative few actually had iron-deficiency anemia, and therefore Geritol would not help most of these people. The FTC issued a cease and desist order in 1964. It also required Williams to make an **affirmative disclosure** in its advertising that, in the great majority of people, iron and vitamin deficiency do not cause such symptoms.[38]

## 14.3 EXECUTIVE, LEGISLATIVE, AND JUDICIAL BRANCHES

Congress created the FCC, the FTC, and other such agencies to carry out its intent as embedded in various laws. However, these agencies are not part of Congress, nor do they answer to the president or the federal courts. They are **independent regulatory agencies**, created to operate outside regular departments of government. However, the three regular branches of government—executive, legislative, and judicial—also impact regulation. How they do so is reviewed in the following sections.

### 14.3.1 Executive Branch

A number of departments in the executive branch deal with radio and television. Some of the more important include the Executive Office of the President, the National Telecommunications and Information Agency (NTIA), the Department of State, and the Department of Justice.

*14.3.1.1 Executive Office of the President.*   Section 606 of the Communications Act gives the president authority to assume certain powers during war and other national emergencies. Under these powers the president may regulate, operate, and even appropriate civilian stations.

Section 305 gives the president responsibility to allocate radio frequencies used by the federal government. Such allocations are coordinated through the Interdepartmental Radio Advisory Committee (IRAC) and NTIA. IRAC includes representatives of major frequency users among governmental agencies. NTIA advises, chairs, and facilitates IRAC. The FCC represents Congress and nongovernment frequency users at IRAC meetings.

The Office of Management and Budget (OMB) coordinates agency budget requests and draws up the administration's budget for submission to Congress. It evaluates and suggests changes in agency structure and functioning. An agency that wishes to adopt a new application or form or change an old one must first secure OMB approval. All of these directly affect the FCC, the FTC, and other agencies involved in regulation of radio and television.

The president has at least four ways to influence ongoing civilian communication policy and regulation. First, the president can **recommend legislation.** For example, the Communications Act of 1934 resulted in large part from a recommendation by President Franklin D. Roosevelt. President Bill Clinton played a major role in the inclusion of the so-called V-chip in the Telecommunications Act of 1996.

Second, the president can use the **appointive power**. With careful appointments, the FCC's ideology can be molded to reflect that of the president. Third, the president can use **departments and offices in the executive branch**. For example, all agencies funded by the government must submit annual budget requests to OMB. Because OMB is a unit of the Executive Office of the President, the potential exists for the president to exert economic pressure. Fourth, the president can use **informal means** such as prestige of office and speeches.

*14.3.1.2 NTIA.*    The NTIA is a division of the Commerce Department. In addition to performing the duties already mentioned, NTIA advises the secretary of commerce and the president on overall communication policies, international treaties and agreements, federal research and development activities, and spectrum management. NTIA also makes public broadcasting facilities grants. The head of the NTIA is titled administrator and has the governmental rank of assistant secretary of commerce for communications and information.

*14.3.1.3 Department of State.*    The Department of State makes arrangements for treaties and agreements involving international communications and prepares delegations for regional and world conferences on radio. To prepare for and staff delegations for such activities, the State Department draws on the personnel and expertise of the FCC, other agencies, and even business organizations involved in communications.

The FCC, the NTIA, and the State Department all have international communications responsibilities. A key person in this increasingly important area is the State Department's coordinator for international communication and information policy. As the title implies, this person attempts to coordinate the work of, and makes suggestions to, all federal agencies involved in international communications matters, including interagency task forces and committees. The coordinator is a deputy assistant secretary of state and heads the department's International Communications and Information Policy staff.

*14.3.1.4 Department of Justice.*    The FCC and the FTC may call on the Justice Department and its federal district attorneys to prosecute enforcement and punishment proceedings in the federal courts. The Justice Department's Antitrust Division may prosecute violations of the antitrust and preservation-of-competition sections (313, 314) of the Communications Act. The Criminal Division prosecutes those whose programming includes illegal lottery information, fraud, obscene or indecent language, or false advertising (Sections 1304, 1342, and 1464 of the U.S. Criminal Code and 14 of the FTC Act). The Department's Solicitor General office represents the agencies in decisions that have been appealed to the federal courts.

The network programming consent decrees illustrate how the U.S. Department of Justice can impact regulation of electronic mass media. As discussed in *PRT,* 14.1.3.2, by 1970 the TV broadcast networks had established dominance in the program syndication field. The Justice Department filed antitrust suits in federal court against ABC, CBS, and NBC, charging that the practices by which they achieved this dominance were monopolistic. Eventually the networks signed consent decrees—NBC in 1977,[39] ABC and CBS in 1980[40]—and the court accepted the decrees as resolution to the suits. These decrees had much the same effect as the FCC's fin-syn rules (*PRT*, 14.1.3.2): The networks could neither syndicate nor acquire financial interest in programs produced by others. Eventually the networks convinced the Justice Department that changes in the television business rendered these prohibitions moot, and the Justice Department notified the court that it supported lifting the decrees. In 1993 the federal court removed the decrees,[41] and in 1995 the FCC eliminated the fin-syn rules. These barriers out of the way, ABC, CBS, and NBC could now invest in and syndicate shows produced "out of house."

### 14.3.2 Congress

Congress shapes regulation directly through **legislation** and indirectly through **appropriation** and the Senate's **confirmation** power over presidential appointees. Both chambers rely heavily on recommendations of the appropriate committees. Congressional **appropriations committees** hold the purse strings for the regulatory commissions and the CPB. **Special committees** may be appointed, whose activities affect regulation of radio and TV.

The House and Senate **commerce committees**[42]—specifically, their **communications subcommittees**—review proposed and existing legislation that deals with radio and television. They investigate regulation, regulators, and regulated to determine if additional legislation is needed. The Senate commerce committee examines appointees to the FCC, FTC, and CPB board and recommends for or against the appointees' confirmation by the Senate. Presidential appointments may also be held up in committee. In 1988, for example, the FCC operated with only three commissioners because the Senate commerce committee did just that.

Like the president, Congress also uses informal means to influence regulation. Especially effective is the **hearing.** When the FCC takes some action that congressional leaders do not like, they hold a committee hearing and demand the commissioners' presence for testimony and chastisement. **Individual senators and representatives** also influence regulation. If the FCC makes a decision that licensees or cable operators do not like, they complain to contacts in the state's congressional delegation. The senators and representatives, in turn, pressure the FCC.

### 14.3.3 Federal Courts

Violators of law or of regulatory commission rules, decisions, or orders may be tried in federal courts. The courts may issue **writs** (formal legal documents ordering or prohibiting some action), impose **fines, sentence to jail,** and even

**revoke broadcast licenses.** The courts also hear and rule on appeals from Commission decisions. Over the years, court decisions have played a major role in shaping radio and television regulation. See, for example, accounts of the Brinkley, Shuler, and WLBT cases in *PRT,* 15.3.3.1 and 15.3.3.3 and the *Red Lion* case in *PRT,* 15.3.4.2.

## 14.4 STATE AND LOCAL GOVERNMENTS

All broadcasting is interstate in nature and therefore subject to primary regulation by Congress and the FCC. Congress has established federal regulation over cable television, too. However, state and local governments may also affect broadcast stations and other media. For example, several states have forbidden the advertising of alcoholic beverages; such a ban includes beer and wine commercials. Ownership of most media outlets takes the form of a corporation; each state has its own statutory requirements for **incorporation**, and a licensee or operator must meet those requirements and file for approval with the state. States and municipalities **tax** and **regulate** businesses. State legislatures have enacted laws that pertain to **noncommercial broadcasting**—to establish state agencies; to fund stations, agencies, and programming projects; or to specify procedures and operations. City **zoning and safety ordinances** affect location of studios, headends, and towers.

Cable, dependent as it is on a local franchise, is especially subject to city, county, and state regulation. A local governmental authority issues the franchise and adopts the ordinance that will govern cable TV within its boundaries. Absent the presence of effective competition, cable operators must apply to local franchising authorities to raise rates on the basic service tier. Some states have enacted cable legislation, and a few have established cable television commissions or councils to assure uniform franchising and regional planning.

## NOTES

1. Letter to Nicholas Zapple, 23 F.C.C.2d 707 (1970) (*reaff'd in re*: Complaint of Committee for the Fair Broadcasting of Controversial Issues, 25 F.C.C.2d 283 (1970)); and First Fairness Report, 36 F.C.C.2d 40 (1972). Zapple actually derived from the Fairness Doctrine, discussed in *PRT,* 15.3.4.1.

2. FCC v. League of Women Voters of California, 468 U.S. 364.

3. Suburban Community Policy, 53 Rad. Reg. 2d (P & F) 681.

4. Charity Games Advertising Clarification Act, Pub. L. No. 100-625, 100 Stat 3205 (1988), codified at 18 U.S.C. § 1307.

5. Denver Area Educational Telecommunications Consortium Inc. v. FCC, 116 S. Ct. 2374 (1996).

6. Playboy Entertainment Group, Inc. v. United States, 945 F. Supp. 772 (1996); aff'md 117 S. Ct. 1309 (1997).

7. Reno v. American Civil Liberties Union, 117 S. Ct. 2329 (1996).

8. Quincy Cable TV, Inc. v. FCC, 768 F.2d 1434; certiorari denied, National Association of Broadcasters v. Quincy Cable TV, Inc., 106 S.Ct. 2889 (1986); and Century Communications Corp. v. FCC, 835 F.2d 292.

9. Cable Television Consumer Protection Act of 1992, Pub. L. No. 102-385, 106 Stat. 1460.

10. Turner Broadcasting Sys. v. FCC, 117 S. Ct. 1174.

11. Under that same law, some LPTV stations qualified for must-carry in some specific situations. Most, however, did not. 47 U.S.C. § 534(c).

12. Amendment of Parts 73 and 76 of the Commission's Rules Relating to Program Exclusivity in the Cable and Broadcast Industries, 3 F.C.C.R. 5299 (1988); *on reh'g,* 4 F.C.C.R. 1711 (1989).

13. 47 C.F.R. § 76.67. Both the syndex and the sports blackout rules exclude systems with less than 1,000 subscribers.

14. 17 U.S.C. § 303(r).

15. Implementation of Sections of the Cable Television Consumer Protection and Competition Act of 1992: Rate Regulation and Adoption of a Uniform Accounting System for Provision of Regulated Cable Service, 9 F.C.C.R. 4527 (1994).

16. 10 F.C.C.R. 12651 (1995).

17. Basically, this rule applies in a three-station market where only two of the stations are affiliates. 47 C.F.R. § 73.658(k)(2)–(4). There are other specifics that determine when this rule applies, but they are beyond the scope of this discussion.

18. As a result of various legal maneuvers, the rules never applied to Fox Broadcasting, even after its weekly prime-time programming surpassed the 15-hour limit.

Ironically, despite their opposition, the rules may actually have strengthened the position of one of the big three. *Broadcasting & Cable* editor Don West wrote, the "government pushed ABC into being a true third network by passing the Prime Time Access Rule, which reduced the number of time slots in which all the networks had to compete against each other and—by reducing spot inventory—increased the value of everyone's time" "DeSales Street," 13 April 1992: 16.

19. Evaluation of the Syndication and Financial Interest Rules, 8 F.C.C.R. 3282 (1993); Review of the Prime Time Access Rule, 78 Rad. Reg. 2d (P & F) 1076 (1995); Review of the Syndication and Financial Interest Rules, 10 F.C.C.R. 12165 (1995). In 1993, a federal court also lifted a consent agreement that mirrored the fin-syn rules (*PRT,* 14.3.1.4).

20. Unnecessary Broadcast Regulations, 57 Rad. Reg. 2d (P & F) 913 (1985).

21. In the Matter of Elimination of Unnecessary Broadcast Regulation and Inquiry into Subscription Agreements Between Radio Broadcast Stations and Music Format Service Companies, 54 Rad. Reg. 2d (P & F) 1043, 1049 (1983).

22. Children's Television Report and Policy Statement, 50 F.C.C.2d 1; affirmed on reconsideration, 55 F.C.C.2d 691 (1975).

23. Children's Television Programming and Advertising Practices, 75 F.C.C.2d 138 (1979).

24. Children's Television Programming and Advertising Practices, 96 F.C.C.2d 634.

25. In Action for Children's Television v. FCC (756 F.2d 899 (1985)) the federal court of appeals agreed that a station could count other media but did not feel the FCC had eliminated the obligation for licensees to present programs for children. In Washington Association for Television and Children v. FCC (712 F.2d 677 (1983)) the court ruled that the FCC's policy on children's programming did not require regularly scheduled children's programming.

26. Revision of Programming and Commercialization Policies, 98 F.C.C.2d 1076 (1984), *reconsideration denied,* 100 F.C.C.2d 358 (1986).

27. In barter syndication, a syndicator provides a station with a program or series in exchange for some inventory (commercial positions) within the program.

28. Action for Children's Television, 58 Rad. Reg. 2d (P & F) 61; and Children's Programming (Profit-Sharing Arrangements), 58 Rad. Reg. 2d (P & F) 90.

29. Action for Children's Television v. FCC 821 F.2d 741 (1987).

30. National Association for Better Broadcasting v. FCC, 830 F. 2d 270 (1987). The FCC subsequently readdressed the issue and determined that a TV station, in a barter syndication deal, does not get the program or series for free, that the commercial inventory it gives up in exchange for the program often has considerable value. Section 317, therefore, did not apply; stations do not have to identify toy companies involved in barter syndication. The court bought this argument. Complaint of National Ass'n for Better Broadcasting against TV Station KCOP(TV), 4 F.C.C.R. 4988, *aff'd*, 902 F.2d 1009 (1990).

31. Revision of Programming and Commercialization Policies, Ascertainment Requirements, and Program Log Requirements for Commercial Television Station, 53 Rad. Reg. 2d (P & F) 365 (1987).

32. Policies and Rules Concerning Children's Television Programming: Revision of Programming Policies for Television Broadcast Stations, 8 F.C.C.R. 1841 (1993).

33. Critiques of the Commission that have often been quoted in the past include the following: Barry Cole and Mal Oettinger, *Reluctant Regulators: The FCC and the Broadcast Audience* (Reading, MA: Addison-Wesley, 1978); Nicholas Johnson and John Dystel, "A Day in the Life: The Federal Communications Commission," 82 *Yale L. J.* 1575 (1973); and Erwin G. Krasnow, Lawrence D. Longley, and Herbert A. Terry, *The Politics of Broadcast Regulation,* 3rd ed. (New York: St. Martin's, 1982).

34. 38 Stat. 717 (1914).

35. 52 Stat. 111 (1938).

36. FTC v. Colgate-Palmolive Co., 380 U.S. 374, 390 (1965).

37. Libby-Owens-Ford Glass Co. v. FTC, 352 F.2d 415(1965).

38. J. B. Williams Co v. FTC, 381 F.2d 884 (1967).

39. United States v. National Broadcasting Co., 449 F. Supp. 1127 (1978).

40. United States v. CBS, 45 Fed. Reg. 34,463 (1980); and United States v. ABC, 45 Fed. Reg. 58,441 (1980).

41. United States v. NBC, 842 F. Supp. 402 (1993).

42. In the House of Representatives it is the Committee on Commerce; in the Senate, the Committee on Commerce, Science, and Transportation.

## FURTHER READING

Bensman, Marvin R. *Broadcast/Cable Regulation.* Lanham, MD: University Press of America, 1990.

Bittner, John R. *Law and Regulation of Electronic Media.* 2nd ed. Englewood Cliffs, NJ: Prentice-Hall, 1994.

Braun, Mark Jerome. *AM Stereo and the FCC: Case Study of a Marketplace Shibboleth.* Norwood, NJ: Ablex, 1994.

Caristi, Dom. *Expanding Free Expression in the Marketplace: Broadcasting and the Public Forum.* New York: Quorum, 1992.

Carter, T. Barton, Marc A. Franklin, and Jay B. Wright. *The First Amendment and the Fifth Estate: Regulation of Electronic Mass Media.* 3rd ed. Westbury, NY: Foundation, 1993.

Drake, William J., Ed. *The New Information Infrastructure: Strategies for U.S. Policy.* New York: Twentieth Century, 1995.

Emeritz, Robert, Ed. *Pike & Fischer's Desk Guide to Communications Law Research.* 1993–94 ed. Bethesda, MD: Pike & Fischer, 1993.

Federal Communications Commission. *Information Seekers Guide: How to Find Information at the FCC.* Washington, DC: Author, 1994.

Ferris, Charles. *Cable Television Law: A Video Communications Guide.* 3 vols. New York: Bender, 1983 (twice-a-year updates).

Flannery, Gerald, Ed. *Commissioners of the FCC, 1927–1994.* Lanham, MD: University Press of America, 1995.

Ginsburg, Douglas H., Michael Botein, and Mark D. Director. *Regulation of the Electronic Mass Media: Law and Policy for Radio, Television, Cable, and the New Video Technologies.* 2nd ed. St. Paul, MN: West, 1991.

Godek, Stephen. *Determinants of Public Interest: Cable Communications Policies.* Lanham, MD: University Press of America, 1996.

Johnson, Leland L. *Toward Competition in Cable Television.* Cambridge, MA: MIT Press, 1994.

Krattenmaker, Thomas G., and Lucas A. Powe, Jr. *Regulating Broadcast Programming.* Cambridge. MA: MIT Press, 1994.

National Association of Broadcasters. *Legal Guide to Broadcast Law and Regulation.* 4th ed. Washington, DC: Author, 1994.

Ray, William B. *The Ups and Downs of Radio–TV Regulation.* Ames: Iowa State University Press, 1990.

Richards, Jef I. *Deceptive Advertising: Behavioral Study of a Legal Concept.* Hillsdale, NJ: Lawrence Erlbaum Associates, 1990.

Smith, F. Leslie, Milan Meeske, and John Wright II. *Electronic Media and Government: The Regulation of Wired and Wireless Mass Communication in the United States.* White Plains, NY: Longman, 1995.

# 15

## ELECTRONIC MASS MEDIA AND THE FIRST AMENDMENT

Earlier we said broadcasting enjoys limited protection under the First Amendment to the Constitution of the United States (*PRT*, 13.3.5). In this chapter, we look at how that protection is limited and why. We also look at types of communication that are exceptions to the First Amendment including defamation, violations of personal privacy, copyright infringements, and obscenity.

### 15.1 ORIGINS AND PURPOSES OF THE FIRST AMENDMENT

The intellectual and philosophical climate of the 17th and 18th centuries provided ideal conditions for growth of faith in natural rights. The individual was thought to be a rational being, one who could listen to all arguments, weigh the merits, and, through the power of reason, make an intelligent choice. Given the power to reason, people could govern themselves. However, to govern themselves well, they needed **access to the greatest possible flow of information and opinion**—to an uninhibited **free marketplace of ideas.**

In 1644, poet John Milton wrote a famous essay called **"Areopagitica"** in which he urged that authority should open up the closed philosophical arena for debate. **Only through the free flow of ideas,** wrote Milton, **would society be able to attain truth.** Seventeenth-century philosopher John Locke argued that each individual has a "natural right" to life, liberty, and property. Liberty included freedom to speak and to publish, rights considered indispensable to self-government.

Yet, as the U.S. Constitution emerged from the Federal Convention in 1787, it contained no declaration of natural rights. Democratic leaders, farmers, and the mercantile class all demanded the new national charter guarantee their hard-won rights. The result was a series of 10 amendments—the **Bill of Rights**, the first of which states in part, "Congress shall make no law . . . abridging the freedom of speech, or of the press. . . ."

## 15.2 EXCEPTIONS TO FREEDOM OF PRESS

Most legal scholars agree that freedom of speech does not allow somebody to shout "Fire" in a crowded theater (unless of course there is actually a fire). However, some believe strongly that rights guaranteed by the First Amendment are **absolute**. They agree with the late Supreme Court Justice Hugo Black who said, "[The First Amendment] says 'no law,' and that is what I believe it means."[1] The majority of courts and legislatures, however, do not share Justice Black's absolute interpretation. They recognize situations in which a person or a mass medium **loses First Amendment protection** and **may be punished** for something said or published. Exceptions to an absolute freedom of speech and press include defamation law, right of privacy, material protected by copyright, some court proceedings, prior restraint, lack of access, lack of reporter's privilege, and prohibitions against obscenity.

Are radio and television part of *the press* as the term is used in the First Amendment? For purposes of this section, the answer is yes. Radio and television must endure all limitations imposed on print media. These limitations apply equally to all media—broadcast and cable networks; programmers who produce and originate their own material in cable systems, the MDS, and DBS; electronic text and database services; producers of materials for videodiscs and videocassettes; and all the rest. Remember from *PRT*, 14.1, that additional limitations have been placed on broadcasters. We discuss these limitations later.

### 15.2.1 Defamation

Defamation is **communication that harms a person's reputation or damages a person's standing in the community.** In a defamation case, the defamed person (the **plaintiff**) brings a **civil suit** against the defamed (the **defendant**) for **damages** (monetary compensation for suffering caused by the defamation) in a **court** of law. Media defendants who lose defamation suits often must pay large damage awards. Settlements are also very expensive, and even when the media win, attorney fees can amount to several hundred thousand dollars.

Defamation consists of two categories, **libel** and **slander.** Historically, **spoken** defamation was slander; **written or printed** defamation was libel. Libel is considered more serious because written messages possess a **permanence of form,** meaning they can be passed along from reader to reader. Written messages are also considered to be **more intentional.** Therefore, courts award higher damages in libel cases.

Although a defamation by radio or television most resembles slander, it is **treated by the courts as libel.** This is because the effect is considered as severe as that of print media. A slanderous comment on a popular network television program reaches tens of millions of persons! Most radio and television programming is recorded or exists as a script, and usually both. So, the defamation could be rebroadcast or repeated and possess the same permanence of form as print messages. Courts have also reasoned that many defamatory comments uttered on taped programs **could have been deleted** before transmission.

When a defamation occurs on a broadcast station, the **licensee is liable** (legally responsible) for damages, no matter when it occurs, who said it, or who supplied it (including commercials produced by others). In the 1959 **WDAY case,**[2] the U.S. Supreme Court provided one exception. Section 315 of the Communications Act forbids a licensee to censor material aired by political candidates. Therefore if a candidate, using a station's facilities (broadcasting) under Section 315, utters a defamation, the licensee pays no damages. This kind of blanket immunity is called **absolute privilege.**

For some time, Congress has provided similar immunity for cable operators. When a PEG or leased-access channel carries access programming (*PRT,* 14.1.1.8), the cable operator may exercise no editorial control except to censor obscene and (since 1996) indecent material. Therefore, Congress protects operators from liability for defamation in access programming.

Common carriers, because they do not control the content of messages, are not liable for defamatory messages. However, in 1995 a New York court ruled that Prodigy, a computer online service provider, could be sued for libelous statements its customers post on the Internet. An unknown Prodigy user had posted a message charging that an investment banking firm was a "cult of brokers who either lie for a living or get fired." The court reasoned that Prodigy was more like a publisher than a telephone company because it controlled and sometimes screened the messages.[3] A different New York court ruled that a similar company—CompuServe—was not responsible because the company did not screen messages.[4]

To win a defamation suit, the plea of **truth** is the oldest and was, for years, the news media's most used defense (Box 15.1). If the medium can prove the defamation to be true, the plaintiff, in most cases, cannot recover libel damages. But truth is often hard to prove. In 1964, the U.S. Supreme Court gave media defendants a much better defense. In its decision in *New York Times* v. *Sullivan,* the court wrote that fear of libel judgments might keep quiet some who had legitimate criticisms of government. If so, libel law would defeat the purpose of the First Amendment. Therefore **public officials** who wished to recover damages must prove the defamatory statement "was made with 'actual malice'—that is with knowledge that it was false or with reckless disregard of whether it was false or not."[5]

At first, this only applied to public officials, defined by the courts to mean **any persons elected to public office.** Since the *Times*–Sullivan case, courts have expanded the definition to include **any government employee.**

Ten years later, the Court expanded the actual malice requirement to include **public figures.**[6] Public figures include **persons of widespread fame or notoriety** (recording artists, local news celebrities, movie stars) and, to some extent, **people, even on the local or neighborhood level, who had injected themselves into the debate of a controversial** public issue for the purpose of affecting the outcome.

---

### BOX 15.1. DEFENSES AGAINST LIBEL SUITS

At least five defenses are used against libel suits:
1. **Statute of Limitations**: 1 to 2 years in most states.
2. **Truth**: Not used as often as you might expect because truth is difficult to prove, there are usually more effective defenses available, and libel suits are usually not filed when the statements are true.
3. **Absolute Privilege**: Some defamatory statements are fully protected, including statements of public officials acting in their official capacity and false and defamatory statements made by political candidates. Remember, when statements are not covered by absolute privilege, public officials and public persons still have to prove actual malice to win a libel suit.
4. **Qualified Privilege**: Media can cover official proceedings, such as city council meetings, and report any comments made during the meeting. However, they must be fair and accurate and in most cases must name their sources.
5. **Neutral Reportage**: Allows news reporters to air statements made by reliable sources that could be defamatory—even when the reporter doubts the accuracy of the statements.
6. **Opinion and Fair Comment**: Allows media to make statements that are clearly identifiable as opinion.

---

The actual malice requirement gave media significant protection against libel suits. Suppose a radio news operation defames a public official by making a false statement. The official cannot recover damages without proving (a) the news operation knew the statement was false or had serious doubts about it, but aired it anyway; or (b) the operation aired it without first taking normal precautions to check its validity. Both are hard to prove. Keep in mind that public officials must prove actual malice only for comments about their official conduct—not statements about their private lives!

The Court has given additional protection to news media. Any person, public or private, suing for libel must prove some form of **fault or media error**. Most states require that private persons prove **negligence** (often the failure to check information adequately or to use the right kind of sources) or a **lack of reasonable care** on the part of the media. In 1986,[7] the Supreme Court ruled that **even private persons involved in matters of public concern** must prove a defamation is false to win a libel suit.

You may wonder whether a **retraction** will reduce the severity of libel damages. Court decisions suggest otherwise. In cases where newscasters name the wrong person in crime stories, the person defamed does not even have to be identified by the media as having committed the crime. In 1993 a Buffalo television station broadcast a strongly worded retraction after incorrectly naming and identifying a restaurant owner as the victim of a beating by members of organized crime. Despite the retraction, the owner sued for libel and won over $15 million in damages.

Talk radio presents libel problems for radio licensees. Use of a delay system helps, but some courts have held that stations are fully responsible for preventing callers' slanderous remarks.

### 15.2.2 Right of Privacy

Since the *New York Times* and Gertz decisions made it more difficult to win libel suits against the media, there has been an increase in suits claiming invasion of privacy. When radio or television airs material that invades someone's privacy, courts in most states allow that individual to recover damages. A medium invades privacy and opens itself to a civil suit if it does any of the following to or concerning someone without permission:

- **Releases intimate, private facts** that are *not newsworthy* and can be considered offensive to a reasonable person.
- **Intrudes into private property.**
- **Creates a false public impression** (usually referred to as a **false light**).
- **Appropriates for commercial purposes elements of personality or identity.**

This pertains to all programming, including advertising.

Technological advances increase the potential for invasion of privacy. The very technology of cable television is intrusive. After all, if a wire carries information into a home, that wire could also carry information out of the home—without the residents even being aware! Congress has recognized this technological fact of life and built privacy protection for the cable subscriber into legislation.

A cable operator may collect data used in the aggregate—so long as it does not identify individual subscribers. On the other hand, the law restricts collection and use of information about personal viewing habits and, if those restrictions are violated, allows the subscriber to sue for invasion of privacy.

Technology also makes it easy for electronic news gatherers to invade privacy. The courts have ruled that **whenever technology is used to gain access to what would otherwise be private, invasion of privacy has occurred.** Technological devices include telephoto lenses, powerful, highly directional microphones, and even a stepladder, if used to peer over a fence into private property. On the other hand, **the act of showing an event on television does not make it private—if it occurred in public.** A prominent citizen who publicly stumbles through a civic event in a drunken stupor cannot claim invasion of privacy just because the behavior was recorded and shown on television.

**Homes are almost always private property.** Media may enter private property under certain (newsworthy) conditions, but should leave when asked to by the owner. CBS had to pay settlements when news crews entered a private home and took photographs of a victim of spousal abuse and in a case where news crews followed federal agents into a home during a raid. NBC lost a privacy suit when camera crews followed paramedics into the home of a heart attack victim.

To avoid creating false public impressions, news producers should be cautious when using file footage. A Washington, DC television station found this out when airing a feature on the disease herpes. As the newscaster said, "For the 20 million Americans who have herpes," the video showed a close-up of a woman who just happened to be walking down a Washington street. The courts allowed the woman to pursue her false light suit, agreeing that anyone watching the broadcast could have assumed that she had herpes.[8]

Professionals involved in production of dramatic programming must be wary of a second form of false light called **fictionalization**. This occurs when a documentary or even a docudrama **embellishes or changes the facts of a story** in a manner that portrays actual persons involved in the story in a false light. NBC lost a fictionalization suit when it incorrectly portrayed an airline crash victim—a naval officer—as being out of uniform, smoking cigarettes, and directing prayer groups.[9]

News personnel can also run into fictionalization problems. A *Cleveland Plain Dealer* reporter "embellished" a story about the family of a man killed when a bridge across the Ohio River collapsed. The reporter exaggerated the effects of the accident, including remarks that the children now lived in poverty and the widow refused even to talk about the accident. The Supreme Court ruled that the reporter portrayed the family in a false light.

Because appropriation involves the unauthorized use of a person's name, picture, or likeness for commercial gain, it is not surprising that many appropriation invasion of privacy suits involve advertising. *Wheel of Fortune*'s Vanna White was able to stop Samsung Electronics from using a robot designed in her image in an advertisement. The robot, decked out in a gown, wig, and jewelry, was shown standing next to a quiz game wheel.[10] Jacqueline Onassis obtained an injunction to prevent a "look-alike" from appearing in a Christian Dior ad.[11] Bette Midler won $400,000 because an ad agency hired a Midler "sound-alike" to sing one of her hit records on a Ford commercial.[12]

### 15.2.3 Copyright

As a general rule, a programmer must get permission to air material created by another person. To do otherwise is to risk suit for infringement of copyright. Copyright is the **right to control or profit from a creative work.** Copyright provisions are spelled out in **Title 17 of the United States Code.** Copyright covers the following works: literary; musical (including words); dramatic (including any accompanying music); pantomimes and choreographic; pictorial, graphic, and sculptural; motion pictures and other audiovisual works; and sound recordings. Literary works include books, newspapers, magazines, corporate house organs, newsletters, and annual reports. A copyright holder's exclusive rights **last for the life of the work's creator plus 50 years.** Exclusive rights for a company-held copyright **last 100 years or 75 years from the date of publication, whichever is shorter.**

Among the rights included in copyright law are those to perform or display the work publicly and to authorize someone else to perform or display it publicly. Presentation on radio or television is a public performance. Thus when a medium leases a motion picture, program, or series, it pays for more than just the tape or film. It also pays for the permission from the copyright holder to air the work.

Copyright law spells out **exceptions.** Noncommercial broadcasters get special breaks on certain copyrighted material. Clearance and payment are not necessary to use U.S. Government works and works in the **public domain** (those not copyrighted or those on which the copyright has expired).

### 15.2.3.1 Radio–TV Music and Copyright.    Most commercial radio stations depend on music for programming. Almost all music is copyrighted. Two organizations represent most music copyright holders in the United States, the **American Society of Composers, Authors, and Publishers** (ASCAP) and **Broadcast Music, Inc.** (BMI).

An all-industry committee, representing station licensees, negotiates individually with ASCAP and BMI. They agree on an all-industry contract. Under terms of the contract a licensee agrees to pay a certain percentage of gross revenues (minus specified deductions) to the music copyright organization. In return, the station may use any composition in the organization's catalog. A licensee may wish to negotiate individually or may elect to use no copyrighted music. Most, however, accept the all-industry contract (or **blanket license,** as it is often called) for both ASCAP and BMI. Both organizations also offer a **per-program license**; stations pay a percentage of advertising revenue derived from a program in return for use of ASCAP or BMI music on that program.

Those who wish access to literally all music also contract with the **Society of European Stage Authors and Composers** (SESAC). ASCAP, BMI, and SESAC distribute money collected from stations to the copyright holders.

In some situations, those who receive broadcast music should pay royalties. This does not apply to a small restaurant or bar where a radio or TV plays for the enjoyment of customers, as long as the video or sound system is not too sophisticated. It does apply in larger stores, where sound systems more elaborate than that found in homes are used. In 1981, the courts ruled that Gap clothing stores violated music copyright by playing broadcast signals throughout their stores.[13] The court reasoned that copyright law does apply when over-the-air broadcasts are played to a large number of people for commercial purposes.[14] Many stores now purchase rights to music services.

Television stations have never liked the blanket license. Much of their programming comes to them already packaged—programs from networks and syndicators and commercials from advertisers and agencies—and the content, including music, was beyond their control. They objected to paying revenue-based fees that gave them access to over 4 million BMI and ASCAP compositions for which they had little use. They argued for **source licensing,** whereby the producers of syndicated programming would acquire the music performance rights. The stations would need licenses only for music used in the few programs and commercials they produced themselves, perhaps even obtaining them directly from the copyright holders. Because BMI and ASCAP refused to grant such an option, the stations sued, portraying the blanket license as an unreasonable restraint of trade. They lost on appeal.[15]

### 15.2.3.2 Cable Television and Copyright.

With respect to copyright responsibility, we can divide cable system video content into two broad categories, nonbroadcast programming and the signals of broadcast stations. Nonbroadcast programming consists of satellite-delivered services (except for superstations), PEG (*PRT,* 7.4.1.2) and leased-channel programming (*PRT,* 7.4.1.3), and local origination (*PRT,* 7.4.1.1). The satellite-delivered services generally contract for nationwide performance rights, so local cable operators do not pay royalties to the copyright holder. The operator has no editorial control over access programming so does not pay royalties for copyrighted material used therein. The operator bears full copyright responsibility for programming the system acquires itself or produces itself, including both standard television and locally created nonstandard material such as electronic text channels.

The copyright law of 1976 grants a cable operator a compulsory license[16] to carry distant nonnetwork broadcast signals. This includes satellite-delivered superstations as well as any nonnetwork distant signals the system imports on its own (say, through microwave relay). Every 6 months the operator pays a royalty based on a percentage of subscriber revenue to a **copyright arbitration royalty panel** convened by the librarian of Congress. The arbitration panels replaced the much-criticized Copyright Royalty Tribunal (CRT) that was abolished in 1993.

**Local broadcasters can choose** whether to (a) require a cable system to carry their signal, or (b) require the cable system to pay a fee to carry their signal. If the second option is selected, the cable company can refuse to pay the fee and refuse to carry the station. The law was drafted this way because local signals would still be available to viewers without cable. In reality, most television stations choose the must-carry option.

### 15.2.3.3 TVRO and Copyright.

In 1988, Congress passed a bill that created a compulsory license for satellite distribution of broadcast signals to backyard satellite dish owners (TVRO, *PRT,* 5.4.2). TVRO packagers (*PRT,* 7.4.4) such as Satellite Broadcast Networks and Netlink (*PRT,* 20.7) that deliver station signals to rural dish owners also received a compulsory license. The license does not allow satellite operators to transmit network programs to homes already covered by over-the-air broadcasters.

The 1988 bill also attempted to deal with TVRO piracy. It established stiffer penalties for piracy of satellite signals and made the manufacture, assembly, and modification of unauthorized descramblers a felony punishable by a stiff fine and imprisonment up to 5 years.

***15.2.3.4 Home Recording and Copyright.*** The development and marketing of the home VCR opened a whole new area of problems with copyright. The television production houses did not even want the typical viewer to be allowed to record programs and movies shown on television. In 1976, Universal City Studios and Walt Disney Productions brought suit against Sony, which produced the Betamax recorder, for copyright violation. In 1984, the Supreme Court ruled[17] that use of a home VCR to tape broadcast programming for later viewing ("time shifting") was exempt from copyright law. The court said that time shifting was fair use (Box 15.2) of copyrighted works.

A video store can buy videotapes and rent them to the public under what is called the **first-sale doctrine.** The copyright statute does not specifically mention it, but court decisions have interpreted the act as allowing such.[18] Under this doctrine, a copyright owner who sells a copy of a copyrighted work receives a royalty from the sale but does not receive further royalties as long as the copy is rented or resold for private use. The copyright owner retains all other rights. The first-sale doctrine does not apply to phonograph records. Congress specifically amended Section 109(b)(1) of the copyright act to exclude the rental of phono-

---

### BOX 15.2. "PRETTY WOMAN" AND FAIR USE OF COPYRIGHTED WORKS

The Copyright Act of 1976 allows fair use of copyrighted works in certain situations and sets forth measures to determine whether a particular use is a fair use:

1. Purpose and character of the use, including whether such use is commercial or nonprofit and educational.
2. Nature of the copyrighted work.
3. Amount and substantiality of the portion used in relation to the work as a whole.
4. **Effect on potential market value** of the copyrighted work.

One example of fair use is *parody,* a satirical or comical imitation of another work. In *Campbell* v. *Acuff-Rose Music* (114 S. Ct. 1164 [1994]), the Supreme Court ruled that a 2 Live Crew parody of Roy Orbison's song "Pretty Woman" did not violate copyright of the original even though the parody used the same music, was intended for commercial purposes, and copied the "heart" of the original. Because the new work was parody, reasoned the court, it did not violate copyright because it altered the original with "new expression, meaning, or message." The new lyrics "departed markedly" from the original and could even be interpreted as social commentary on the simplicity of the old lyrics. The court said copyright was not violated even if the parody version destroyed the market value of the original. The court did express concern about how often the opening musical phrase of the original was copied.

graph records (or CDs) without permission of the copyright holders, except by nonprofit libraries or educational institutions. Congress believed that about the only reason you would rent a CD would be to copy it. (See also *PRT,* 5.8 for a discussion of the copyright worries that devolved from the digital audiotape recorder.)

### 15.2.4 Free Press Versus Fair Trial

These two constitutional rights often conflict. One result is that reporting of federal and some state court proceedings is restricted. The Sixth Amendment guarantees individuals the right to a fair trial. The First Amendment guarantees freedom of speech and press, which, presumably, includes the right to report public trials. But does media coverage destroy the rights of a defendant before the trial can even start? Media publicity, according to many, prejudices people so much that it is impossible to select an impartial jury and to get a fair trial. The criminal cases and televised trials of boxer Mike Tyson, William Kennedy Smith, and O. J. Simpson clearly illustrate the extreme levels of media publicity before and during a high-profile trial. Reporters and editors maintain that media reporting protects the right to a fair trial, and that the First Amendment takes preference over the Sixth.

*15.2.4.1 Trend Toward Open Trials.*    During the 1980s, the U.S. Supreme Court strengthened the First Amendment right of the public and the press to attend judicial proceedings. The court said that a judge may close a trial only after demonstrating a compelling need to protect the rights of the defendant.[19] Grand jury and juvenile proceedings are still ordinarily closed.

Some judges have issued **gag orders.** Here, the judge tells reporters what they can and cannot report and how they are to report it. Violations are prosecuted as contempt of court, which can result in fines and jail sentences.

U.S. Supreme Court decisions indicate disapproval of most such prior restraints on publication. Its 1976 decision in *Nebraska Press Association* v. *Stuart*[20] strictly limited gag orders. Judges have been successful in restraining persons involved in a case from talking to the press, but most attempts to punish the media for violation of restraint orders after publication do not meet constitutional muster.[21]

*15.2.4.2 Cameras in the Courtroom.*    For years, judicial proceedings could not be covered by electronic and photographic means. The belief was that electronic media distracted participants and witnesses.

In the 1965 *Estes* v. *Texas* decision[22] the Supreme Court reversed Billy Sol Estes' conviction because his trial had been televised. Read the court's decision and you would think cameras would have never been allowed in courtrooms again. The cameras, according to the court, created an uncertain impact on jurors, negatively impacted the quality of witness testimony, caused mental and physical harassment of defendants, and placed additional burdens on the judge. Actually, the television camera crews in the Estes case were disruptive, and four jurors had watched the pretrial hearings on television. The court's decision reinforced reluctance to open trials to cameras.

A few years later, however, some state court systems moved toward allowing cameras and microphones in the courtroom. During a 1-year experiment in Florida in 1979, few distractions were noted. Florida state courts adopted rules that allowed near restriction-free courtroom coverage by radio and television. Two years later, the Supreme Court upheld the rules. In *Chandler* v. *Florida,*[23] the court said that states could develop such rules so long as they did not violate the defendant's right to a fair trial. In order to make a successful Sixth Amendment appeal, the defendant would have to demonstrate such an impairment—that radio–TV coverage had adversely affected witnesses or jurors or the ability of the jury to decide the case fairly.

Following the *Chandler* decision, the American Bar Association permitted judges to allow coverage (a) if authorized by supervising appellate courts or other authorities, and (b) if consistent with fair trial rights—being unobtrusive, not distracting, and not interfering with administration of justice. Other states began experiments, and by 1995 most allowed some form of camera coverage of courtroom proceedings.

Federal courts may also be opening up to cameras. In 1996 the judicial conference voted to allow the 13 Circuit Courts of Appeal to decide for themselves about camera coverage of civil and perhaps even criminal cases. The U.S. Supreme Court and for the most part federal district (trial) courts continue to ban camera coverage of all proceedings.

### 15.2.5 Prior Restraint

**Prior restraint** refers to the government preventing publication. Normally, the First Amendment forbids such prevention. In the 1931 *Near* decision,[24] Chief Justice Hughes said that the main purpose of the constitutional guarantee of freedom of expression is to prevent prior restraint. Hughes did, however, list instances in which the government could legitimately prevent publication.

In 1971, federal courts issued injunctions to prevent publication of what came to be known as the **Pentagon Papers**. The injunctions lasted 15 days. The Pentagon Papers were a massive top-secret Defense Department study about U.S. involvement in Vietnam. The *New York Times* and *Washington Post* obtained copies and began to publish articles on the study. Government injunctions halted publication, so the newspapers appealed. The U.S. Supreme Court lifted the injunctions, but not before it, too, had voted 5–4 to halt publication until the case could be heard. Additionally, the Court's decision seemed to allow the government to exercise prior restraint if it could meet the "heavy burden of showing justification."[25]

In 1990, the U.S. government invoked a prior restraint against CNN. CNN had obtained recordings of telephone conversations between Panamanian dictator

Manuel Noriega and his attorney. The calls were made while Noriega was in a Miami jail after his arrest following the U.S. invasion of Panama. Defense attorneys moved to stop CNN from using the tapes. The courts issued a restraining order, but CNN, claiming First Amendment protection, used some of the tapes anyway. As a result, CNN was convicted of criminal contempt and forced to either pay a stiff fine or announce that ignoring the restraining order was an error. CNN choose the latter.[26]

### 15.2.6 Access and Reporter's Privilege

Two exceptions to freedom of press involve a reporter's sources of information. One has to do with access; the other with reporter's privilege.

*15.2.6.1 Access.*   Access here refers to **the ability to get to sources** of information. The idea of necessity of access grows from the same philosophical soil as the First Amendment. The government of the United States is based on the presumption of an informed citizenry. That being the case, news media have an obligation to enhance the media's ability to report. The government should allow reporters access to information on its own performance and operation, except where national security or public welfare would be compromised. However, such is not always the case.

Denial of access takes several forms—**classification** (as top secret, secret, or confidential), supposedly to protect against unauthorized disclosure in the interests of national defense; **agency-created barriers and dodges** (also called "the run-around") to avoid releasing information; and **executive sessions** or **secret meetings** of decision-making bodies. Many states and the federal government[27] have enacted **government-in-the-sunshine** (open meetings) and **open records laws** designed to tear down barriers to access. Such laws help, but a determined official can still sometimes delay or even deny access. Sometimes the mere fact that government records are contained in computer files makes them more difficult to obtain.

*15.2.6.2 Reporter's Privilege.*   News reporter's privilege refers to **the ability to protect a confidential source from identification** in legal and legislative proceedings. The news media contend that if a source provides information to a reporter with the provision that the source's identity remain secret, the First Amendment protects that reporter from having to reveal the source or to yield notes, tape, film, and other unpublished information about the source. The media maintain that confidential communications between reporter and source are privileged (do not have to be revealed) in a manner similar to those between lawyer and client or priest and penitent. Besides, conclude the media, if the courts force reporters to reveal confidential sources, informants will stop talking. This affects the public's right to know and violates the First Amendment.

A number of states have adopted **shield laws** to ensure that reporters do have some form of privilege. There is no national shield law, however. And, in its 1972 *Branzburg* v. *Hayes* decision,[28] the U.S. Supreme Court refused to recognize any sweeping reporter's privilege. The court suggested that in all cases except grand jury proceedings, the reporter's wish to protect a confidential source must be balanced against the government's need to know to determine which should prevail Since 1972, lower courts have relied on the concurring and dissenting opinions in *Branzburg* to create a limited First Amendment privilege from testifying. Further, reporters seldom have to testify when criminal defendants or litigants in civil suits (except those to which the medium is a party) seek information. Still, reporters from both print and electronic media have spent time in jail, not because they were criminals, but because they wished to preserve the confidentiality of their sources.

Newsroom searches, however, are a different matter. Congress provided a measure of relief against newsroom searches by law enforcement authorities in 1980. In its 1978 ruling in the *Stanford Daily* case,[29] the U.S. Supreme Court had interpreted the Fourth Amendment to the Constitution to mean that police need only have a warrant to search a newsroom. Police took advantage of this ruling and made a number of searches in 1980. Congress responded by passing the **Privacy Protection Act of 1980,**[30] also called the **Newsroom Search Law.** Under this act, law enforcement officials must get a subpoena before searching a newsroom in most situations. The subpoena must specify what is sought, and is generally more difficult to obtain than a warrant. Some state legislatures have passed similar laws.

### 15.2.7 Obscenity

Most of us agree that obscenity deserves no First Amendment protection. Disagreement comes in defining obscenity. After all, something you consider pornography might be considered art to someone else, and vice versa. Legislatures and courts have long attempted to define *obscene,* and most definitions have centered on sexual matters.

The U.S. Supreme Court provided a widely accepted definition in its 1973 *Miller* decision.[31] The Court, borrowing from previous decisions, ruled that material must meet each of the following criteria to be regarded as obscene:

1. The **average person, applying contemporary community standards** (local standards, not national), **finds the work, taken as a whole, appeals to prurient** (meaning sexual in a lewd or lustful manner) **interest.**
2. The work **depicts or describes, in a patently offensive manner, sexual conduct specifically defined by state law.**
3. The work **lacks serious literary, artistic, political, or scientific value.**

Material that meets all three criteria is obscene and merits no First Amendment protection.

Broadcasters are held to much stricter standards (*PRT,* 15.3.5), but cable television and satellite programmers have been targeted in a number of obscenity cases. Those using the Internet to send obscene material are sought after and prosecuted, especially when children are in any way involved. Perhaps the most controversial aspect of the Telecommunications Act of 1996 was the provision that made it a crime to transmit sexually oriented and other "indecent" materials to minors under 18 over computer networks. The Communications Decency Act (CDA), as it was called, did not require that the material in question meet the criteria of the Miller test or be judged obscene. This was the first time government attempted to apply the indecency standard to any medium other than radio and television. In 1997 the Supreme Court struck down the CDA. The Court ruled that the CDA violated the First Amendment rights of Internet users, and reasoned that the Internet was hardly a scarce commodity and could not be compared to the broadcast spectrum.[32]

## 15.3 ADDITIONAL EXCEPTIONS TO FREEDOM OF RADIO AND TELEVISION

Even with all the exceptions previously described, the United States still enjoys one of the greatest latitudes for freedom of expression of any country. Radio and television, however, have an additional set of restrictions.

### 15.3.1 Exceptions by Law and Regulation

The **Communications Act and FCC rules** impose on broadcast licensees considerable programming requirements—things they must or must not do. As examples, consider the following: broadcast stations must operate a minimum number of hours each day; certain types of recorded material must be identified as such;[33] broadcast stations must identify themselves to listeners at certain times and in a certain manner;[34] and cigarette advertising is prohibited on radio and television.[35] Additional restrictions are discussed in the following and in *PRT,* 14.1.1 through 14.1.5.

### 15.3.2 Section 315 and Candidate Debates

One of the most important programming requirements—a major fact of regulatory life for broadcasting and cable—is **Section 315** of the Communications Act. Congress wrote the **equal opportunities** provision (*PRT,* 14.1.1.4) into Section 315 to ensure that broadcasters treat all candidates for the same political office equally. Equal opportunities means a relatively equal **amount of time** during relatively equal **time periods** and at the **same cost** to all.

The legislators reasoned that the public interest and the free marketplace of ideas are better served when the audience can hear all candidates equally, rather than only those favored by the licensee. However, some broadcast licensees say they find the mechanisms of Section 315 so intricate and so burdensome that they allow no state and local candidates to advertise.[36] In these cases the provision defeats its own purpose; it silences the very political debate the Congress intended to promote.

Special legislation suspended Section 315 rules for the presidential and vice-presidential races in 1960.[37] The networks jointly arranged and broadcast four 1-hour question-and-answer sessions featuring Senator John F. Kennedy and Vice-President Richard M. Nixon. Kennedy, much less known than Nixon before these so-called **Great Debates,** went on to win the election by a slim margin.

The FCC made possible candidate debates on a continuing basis with its 1975 adoption of the **Aspen rule.**[38] Under this rule, candidate news conferences and debates both qualified as "on-the-spot coverage of a bona fide news event" and, as provided in Section 315(a)(4), were **exempt from equal opportunities requirements.** The spot-news exemption was extended in 1983 to permit coverage of debates arranged by broadcasters[39] and in 1987 to permit coverage of debates arranged by political candidates themselves.[40] In 1996, ABC, CBS, Fox, and NBC, along with PBS, agreed to provide free time to presidential candidates.

### 15.3.3 FCC Concern with Programming

As discussed in *PRT,* 14.1.2, the FCC traditionally examined programming as one means to determine whether the public interest would be served by granting or renewing a broadcast license. Broadcasters claim that FCC review of programming violates both the First Amendment and Section 326 of the Communications Act (which forbids FCC censorship). Yet, the courts have consistently upheld the FCC.

***15.3.3.1 Judicial Affirmation.***    The first ruling came in the 1931 **Brinkley case,** *KFKB* v. *FRC.*[41] The Federal Radio Commission (FRC), forerunner of the FCC, had denied John Brinkley's application for renewal of KFKB's license based on his use of the station to peddle patent medicines. Brinkley appealed on the grounds that the Commission's actions amounted to censorship. In its decision, the court equated censorship with "prior scrutiny," ruling that FRC review of **past conduct** to determine whether a license renewal would serve the public interest does not constitute censorship.

The next ruling came in the 1932 **Shuler case,** *Trinity* v. *FRC.*[42] The FRC had denied Reverend Bob Shuler's application for renewal of KGEF's license because he allegedly used the station for defamatory and other objectionable utterances. Shuler appealed on both First and Fifth Amendment grounds. An appeals court ruled that the FRC had not denied Shuler's freedom of speech. Shuler could continue to say whatever he wished; he just could not do so on the radio. As for the Fifth Amendment, the court ruled that because KGEF's frequency was not Shuler's property, the government had the right to withdraw it without compensation.[43]

*15.3.3.2 FCC Statements.* But what was programming in the public interest? What did it consist of? What should a station program to avoid trouble at renewal time? The Commission hesitated to set forth specific programming guidelines. After all, the law forbade censorship, and guidelines smacked heavily of prior restraint. Once the Brinkleys and Shulers were cleared off the air, the FCC rarely used its program review power. The Commission routinely approved renewal applications, based entirely on engineering reports, without examining past programming.

During the late 1930s and early 1940s the FCC received a number of complaints on programming. Investigations found widespread programming abuses. The Commission decided to act. The result was the 1946 **Blue Book** (*PRT,* 2.2.5.6), which attempted to provide guidelines for renewal. The Commission never actually revoked or denied renewal of a single license based on Blue Book criteria.

The FCC's **1960 Programming Policy Statement** contained two new guidelines. First, the broadcaster should **ascertain the tastes, needs, and desires of the community** to which the station was licensed. Second, the broadcaster should **decide what specific programs and program types** would meet these needs. The policy statement offered some programming suggestions but proposed to rely primarily on the broadcaster's own judgment. In the 1962 **Suburban case,**[44] the courts affirmed the FCC's right to require ascertainment of local needs.

*15.3.3.3 Public Participation in the Licensing Process.* Until 1966, the broadcast audience had almost no say in the licensing process.[45] The **WLBT case** changed that.

In 1964, the Office of Communications of the United Church of Christ (UCC) petitioned the FCC on behalf of Black citizens of Jackson, Mississippi. UCC asked to present evidence and arguments opposing the license renewal of television station WLBT in Jackson. The church alleged racial discrimination in programming. The FCC responded that UCC had no standing and granted WLBT a short-term renewal. When UCC appealed, the appeals court ruled that the public **could intervene in renewal proceedings.**

Ultimately, the court agreed with UCC and ordered that WLBT's license not be renewed. As a result of the WLBT case, the public gained a mechanism to affect programming of a broadcast station. Subsequently, many licensees not only opened their doors to citizen and audience groups, but also listened and negotiated. Such negotiations were usually most effective when carried on by an organized group representing the interests of a particular segment of the community, for example, Blacks, Hispanics, or classical music lovers.

The Telecommunications Act of 1996 may adversely affect public participation in the renewal process. The FCC is still interested in public complaints about a station. However, the 1996 act allows broadcasters to assume their license will be renewed if there is no serious pattern of problems. Also, the FCC can no longer consider competing applications until it decides against renewing the existing license.

***15.3.3.4 Entertainment Formats.***   During the 1970s, public interest groups formed all over the country, encouraged not only by the WLBT cases, but also by the WHDH decision (WHDH and *RKO* cases). Audience activist groups even attempted to affect entertainment programming, including radio station formats. One such attempt involved WEFM, a Chicago station that had programmed classical music since it signed on in 1940.[46] WEFM's licensee, contending it was losing money, contracted to sell the station in 1972. The prospective new owner proposed to program rock music. A citizens' group filed a petition with the FCC to deny transfer of license or, barring that, to conduct a hearing. After initially accepting the petition, the FCC issued a policy statement on the matter in 1976.[47] The Commission said it would no longer get involved in format disputes; selection of a format was up to the licensee, and its success or failure should be determined by the marketplace.

In 1981, the Supreme Court upheld the FCC policy of licensee discretion in entertainment formats.[48] As a result, the Commission has been successful in staying out of the format business, although an appeals court did rule that misrepresentation of programming intentions by a licensee warrants FCC attention.[49]

***15.3.3.5 Ascertainment.***   For 20 years, the requirement initiated in 1960 that a station licensee ascertain community needs grew in importance. The trend was reversed when the Commission eliminated formal ascertainment requirements as part of its 1980s general deregulation.[50] These cuts did away with prescribed formal interviews with community leaders and the public. Each quarter, however, stations must put in their public files a list of programs that provided significant treatment of community issues during the preceding 3-month period.[51]

***15.3.3.6 1973 License Renewal Rules.***   In 1973, the Commission revised license renewal procedures in an effort to encourage dialogue between the public and the broadcast stations. The actions included adoption of an annual programming report, a revised television renewal application form, and rules requiring stations to maintain a public file and to broadcast periodically certain public notices. The programming report, based on an annual composite week, called for information on news, public affairs, and other programming. The renewal form required information concerning specific programming areas, for example, public service announcements and children's programming.

The rules required the **public file** be kept at the station or other accessible place for members of the public to request and examine during regular business hours. The file was to contain (among other things) the following: copies of applications and reports the station had filed with the FCC, the station's equal opportunity model program, a copy of the FCC publication, *The Public and Broadcasting—A*

*Procedural Manual,* letters received from the public, requests for time by political candidates, documentation of ascertainment procedures, and a list of the station's programs that had addressed community needs.

The rules also required that stations broadcast **public notices** of their license renewal. Announcements would allow the public to examine a copy of the renewal application, and comment on it and whether the station met public interest requirements.

The Telecommunications Act of 1996 requires television stations to maintain a file of "comments and suggestions" from the public regarding violent programming. The station's license renewal application must contain a summary of the file.

### 15.3.3.7 Deregulation.

Deregulation (*PRT,* 3.5.1) has eliminated a number of the requirements of the 1973 renewal rules. At the same time, deregulation seemed to repudiate the rationale for program regulation, a rationale that had been spelled out over a period of 50-plus years by the FRC and the FCC, the federal court system, and the Congress of the United States.

The deregulation of commercial radio began in 1981; commercial television and noncommercial broadcasting, in 1984.[52] In these two actions, the Commission eliminated programming-related requirements in three key areas. First, the FCC discarded guidelines used in processing license applications. These guidelines had limited commercial minutes per hour and required at least some news, public affairs, and other nonentertainment local programming. Elimination of the commercial guidelines also lifted a prohibition against program-length commercials (*PRT,* 9.1.3.3). Second, the Commission abolished a requirement that stations use program logs and retain and allow the public to examine them. Third, the FCC dumped formal ascertainment requirements, described earlier.

In 1981, the Commission adopted a short-form renewal application. The short form replaced a complicated, multipage application that required detailed submissions and attachments to explain various aspects of station operation, including programming. The short form consisted of five questions (four of which were to be answered *yes* or *no*) and a statement whereby the person who signed certified that all information on the form was true. Adoption of the short form automatically eliminated any composite week reporting, programming promises for the upcoming licensing period, reports on ascertainment procedures, and information on programming areas of special concern, such as public affairs. The Commission also eliminated the annual programming report and a requirement for broadcast of a twice-monthly announcement of licensee obligation. In 1996, Congress further streamlined the renewal process by abolishing comparative renewal proceedings (*PRT,* 19.1.1.7).

Congress and the FCC rationalized the changes with a marketplace argument, which asserted that electronic media outlets should survive or fail because of public preferences. If the public wanted news, public affairs, special programming for children, controls on advertising, or local programming, then the public would support by tuning in the electronic media outlets that provided such things. Those media outlets would thrive; others would either change or not do as well, perhaps even go out of business. If the public did not want these things, the media would change to reflect what they did want. Government should not mandate programming requirements or restrictions. The media and the public would determine survival, and government should not interfere with the process.[53]

### 15.3.4 Fairness Doctrine

Another victim of deregulation (*PRT,* 3.5.1) was a nearly four-decades-old public-issue programming requirement. The FCC articulated the requirement in a 1949 statement[54] that reversed the Mayflower decision (*PRT,* 2.2.5.4) and announced that broadcast licensees could editorialize. The FCC noted that, in the U.S. system of broadcasting, the right of the public to be informed took precedence over the right of a station to air the licensee's private opinion and exclude all others. That being the case, the Fairness Doctrine required broadcast licensees to (a) **provide some programming that deals with controversial public issues,** and (b) **afford reasonable opportunity for discussion of contrasting points of view on controversial issues of public importance.** The policy became known as the Fairness Doctrine because the licensee was required to provide **overall balance in treating controversial issues.**

*15.3.4.1 Fairness and Implementation.*    Basically, it worked like this. If a broadcaster aired a particular view on a controversial issue of public importance, that broadcaster had the duty to afford reasonable (not necessarily equal) opportunity for presentation of contrasting views at some time (not necessarily on the same program).

In 1967, the FCC converted two aspects of Fairness into formal rules—the **Personal Attack and Political Editorial** rules.[55] These rules required a station to notify and give reasonable opportunity for reply to (a) an individual who had been attacked during a broadcast discussion of controversial public issues, (b) a political candidate against whom the station had editorialized, and (c) all candidates running against a candidate who had been editorially endorsed by the station. The Commission also developed the **Zapple Doctrine** (*PRT,* 14.1.1.4) in 1970.

*15.3.4.2 Fairness and Red Lion.*    The U.S. Supreme Court upheld the constitutionality of Fairness in the Red Lion case. In 1964, WGCB, in Red Lion, Pennsylvania, aired a program in which Reverend Billy James Hargis discussed a book critical of the Republican presidential candidate, Senator Barry Goldwater. Hargis attacked the book's author, Fred J. Cook. Cook asked to reply and the station refused, so Cook complained to the FCC. Citing the Fairness Doctrine, the Commission ordered WGCB to give Cook reply time. The station appealed on grounds that the Fairness Doctrine was unconstitutional. The appeals court in Washington, DC, ruled against WGCB, and the station appealed.

Meanwhile, the FCC had adopted the Personal Attack and Political Editorial rules. The Radio–Television News Directors Association challenged those rules in another court. An appeals court in Chicago declared the rules and Fairness unconstitutional. The FCC appealed, and the Supreme Court consolidated both cases as *Red Lion* v. *FCC*.[56]

In its 1969 decision, the Supreme Court ruled that the Fairness Doctrine was constitutional. The court based its decision on the scarcity rationale—the notion that the airwaves were a scarce resource. Government, therefore, could restrict broadcasters' First Amendment rights.

### 15.3.4.3 Fairness and Reevaluation.

In a 1974 policy statement, the FCC had said that adherence to the Fairness Doctrine was the most important criterion of evaluation at license renewal time.[57] Then, in an about-face in its **1985 Fairness Report**,[58] the FCC said things had changed since the Supreme Court's Red Lion decision. The marketplace had evolved, and "compelling documentation" showed that Fairness had a "chilling effect," which actually caused broadcasters not to air controversial-issue programming. The FCC even concluded that Fairness violated the First Amendment!

The courts also expressed a new posture toward Fairness. In 1984 the Supreme Court indicated a willingness to reassess the scarcity factor[59] (*PRT,* 13.4.2 and 13.3.3), a major basis for Red Lion. A 1986 appeals court ruling held that 1959 amendments to Section 315 of the Communications Act had not written the Fairness Doctrine into law,[60] and a 1987 decision noted that, in the light of the 1985 Fairness Report's findings, the FCC's failure to start procedures to eliminate or modify Fairness was subject to court review.[61]

Finally, in the 1987 **Meredith** decision, a federal appeals court required the FCC to consider the constitutionality of the Fairness Doctrine. Meredith's Syracuse station, WTVH-TV, had run ads that promoted construction of a nuclear power plant. The Syracuse Peace Council opposed the plant and complained to the Commission. The FCC, apparently hoping to force the courts to settle the issue, ruled that WTVH had violated the Fairness Doctrine and ordered it to air opposing views. Meredith appealed, and the court ruled against the FCC. After all, the Commission itself had concluded the Fairness Doctrine was unconstitutional. The court demanded that the FCC reconsider.

### 15.3.4.4 Fairness and Recantation.

In its 1987 **Syracuse Peace Council**[62] decision, the **FCC abolished the Fairness Doctrine**, concluding that its enforcement was no longer in the public interest.[63] The FCC said Fairness had a "chilling effect" that caused broadcasters not to air controversial-issue programming, that it inhibited expression of unorthodox opinions, and that it caused unwarranted government intrusion into program content. The amount and type of information sources had increased so much since 1969 and Red Lion that Fairness was no longer necessary. Constitutional protection should cover broadcasting and print equally, focusing on similarities between the two media, not differences. The appeals court affirmed the FCC on the basis of Fairness not serving the public interest but never ruled on the constitutional issue.[64] The FCC's action eliminated the basic requirements of Fairness **but left in place the Personal Attack and Political Editorial rules and the Zapple Doctrine.**

### 15.3.5 Indecency

Section 1464 of the Criminal Code provides fines and prison penalties for anyone who uses "obscene, indecent, or profane language" on the radio waves. The courts defined *obscene* in the Miller case (*PRT*, 15.2.7). They also defined *profane*—language that invokes Divine condemnation or contains blasphemous statements,[65] such as "Damn you" or irreverent use of "By God" (although the FCC no longer penalizes for an occasional "damn" or "By God"). However, they did not define *indecent.*

Most broadcast language that offends through sexual connotation does not meet all three Miller tests and thus is not legally obscene. Yet, radio and television programs—unlike adult books, magazines, and the more hard-core motion pictures—are obtained directly in the home, requiring no more audience initiative than the turn of a switch. They occupy large percentages of time for many persons. They easily reach children, as well as those adults who take offense at sexually oriented material. Most years, the FCC receives more complaints about objectionable language than anything else. Therefore, the FCC felt that the public interest required establishment of a standard for radio and television that was stricter than Miller. This standard defined indecent material, and it received judicial sanction in the WBAI case.

*15.3.5.1 WBAI Case.*    This case began with a complaint from a man who, with his son, happened to hear Pacifica-owned WBAI-FM in New York broadcast a cut from a record album by George Carlin, a comedian. The cut contained several common sexual and scatological slang terms. The FCC ruled the broadcast "indecent" and took the occasion to issue a declaratory ruling[66] to indicate what the term meant.

The Commission said indecent refers to **words that describe sexual or excretory activities and organs in a patently offensive manner.** The indecency standard did not include the dominant appeal to prurient interest criterion from Miller. Only if a program containing indecent material (a) were run late at night when least likely that children would be in the audience, and (b) the programmer had made a solid effort to warn adults in advance that the program contained such material[67]—only then would literary, artistic, political, or scientific value redeem it (make it worthwhile). In 1978, the U.S. Supreme Court affirmed the FCC's indecency standard.[68]

*15.3.5.2 New Enforcement Standards.*    The FCC dealt with succeeding cases as though the indecent standard referred only to those specific words at issue in the WBAI case. Further, the Commission defined "late at night" as after 10 p.m. The precise time, window, or "safe harbor" during which indecent material could be broadcast would become a subject of enduring controversy. But during the mid-1980s, citizens' groups put considerable pressure on the Commission to do more about enforcing Section 1464 of the Criminal Code.

In 1987, the FCC responded by announcing[69] its intention to use the judicially sanctioned definition of *indecency* from the WBAI case. Future enforcement would extend beyond the "seven dirty words" of the WBAI case to a broader range of patently offensive programming. Further, even at 10 p.m., the audience might contain significant numbers of children. Broadcasters, therefore, should not assume that indecent programming could safely air after 10 p.m.

The FCC took action against three radio stations about which it received complaints. KPFK-FM in Los Angeles had broadcast excerpts from *Jerker*, a play that included explicit descriptions of homosexual fantasies. WYSP-FM in Philadelphia had aired objectionable language in what the FCC considered a pandering and titillating fashion during Howard Stern's morning drive-time program. (Stern would later become a primary target of FCC indecency action.) KCSB-FM in Santa Barbara, California, had broadcast a recording that contained explicit sexual language, "Making Bacon," by the Pork Dukes.

A 1988 appeals court decision[70] upheld the WYSP-FM action but vacated those on KPFK-FM and KCSB-FM; their programming had aired after the Commission's previous "safe harbor" began at 10 p.m. Further, the court said the FCC had not adequately justified changing the safe harbor to midnight.

Congress then entered the scene by passing a law instructing the Commission to enforce the ban on indecency 24 hours a day. Few, however, gave this new law much chance to survive a court challenge. Sure enough, in 1992 the Supreme Court let stand a lower court's ruling that the 24-hour ban was too broad a limitation on freedom of expression.[71]

To show how confusing things became for broadcasters, KZKC-TV in Kansas City ran afoul of the new indecency enforcement in 1987. The station had aired the movie *Private Lessons* at 8 p.m. The film contained, among other sexually oriented material, scenes of a nude female attempting to seduce a young boy. The FCC levied a $2,000 fine. However, after the court ruled against the ban, the FCC rescinded the fine.

In 1992, Congress passed new legislation moving the safe harbor back to midnight to 6 a.m. for all stations except public broadcasting stations that left the air before midnight. The FCC adopted the same guidelines in 1993. The issue seemed somewhat settled until, once again, the court struck down the new guidelines in 1995, mostly because the law provided different time constraints for public and commercial broadcasters. The court ordered the FCC to establish the safe harbor from 10 p.m. to 6 a.m.

By the mid-1990s, the FCC had stepped up enforcement of indecency standards. In 1995 Infinity Broadcasting Corporation agreed to settle indecency actions against the *Howard Stern Show* by paying $1.7 million. Under terms of the agreement, the FCC dismissed pending complaints against all Infinity stations.

Broadcasters continued to challenge the FCC, but their hopes of gaining relief from indecency regulation were dealt two swift blows early in 1996. First, the Supreme Court let stand a lower court decision that **upheld the 10 p.m. to 6 a.m. safe harbor.**[72] The appeals court had ruled that the safe harbor was necessary to protect children.

One week later the Supreme Court **upheld the FCC's authority to fine stations who violate indecency policies.**[73] Broadcasters had unsuccessfully argued that the fines were unconstitutional because there was no chance for a quick court review when fines are handed down and the threat of fines directly affected programming decisions. At the time the court handed down these decisions the FCC was reviewing over 150 new indecency complaints. The stations face fines up to $25,000 per violation.

### 15.3.6 First Amendment and Cable Television

In passing the first major cable legislation, the Cable Communications Act of 1984, Congress attempted to sort out program control of cable systems. Most of the provisions remained in effect when Congress passed new cable legislation in 1992 and 1996. Franchising authorities still have the power to regulate cable systems, but only within the parameters of federal law and FCC regulation (*PRT,* 15.3.6.2).

Most cable operators must provide leased channels (*PRT,* 14.1.1.8). The franchising authority can require public, educational, and governmental channels (*PRT,* 14.1.1.8). The franchising authority can take an active hand in programming educational and governmental channels but otherwise cannot control programming content.

The FCC does not regulate cable programming as closely as broadcasting. Only when cable systems **originate programming** are they required to comply with the Section 315 "equal opportunities," political editorialization, and personal attack rules. Of course, cable operators can be prosecuted for transmitting obscene programming (*PRT,* 15.3.6.1).

In the landmark 1994 decision *Turner Broadcasting System v. FCC,* the U.S. Supreme Court ruled that **cable programming is protected by the First Amendment.** Whether the must-carry rules—a major issue in the case—were constitutional was not established, but the Court ruled that **cable operators had greater First Amendment protection than broadcasters.** The court repeated the Red Lion scarcity rationale (*PRT,* 15.3.4.2), concluding that cable systems were not restricted by the limits of the broadcast spectrum. The court also reasoned that only one licensee could broadcast on a frequency at a time, but technological advances allow cable operators to program a large number of channels.[74] The court stopped short of affording cable the same high level of First Amendment protection given the print media. A newspaper, the court reasoned, cannot control what other newspapers citizens may read, but a cable system has some control over which programming services are available to the viewing public.

*15.3.6.1 Obscene and Indecent Cable Programming.* Cable operators that carry obscene programming face a fine or imprisonment. The state of Utah attempted to go even further, passing legislation that defined and totally prohibited indecent cable programming. This state law authorized fines for cable operators whose systems carried programmed depictions or descriptions of naked human buttocks and genitals and female breasts. A 1987 U.S. Supreme Court decision[75] affirmed lower court rulings that the Utah statute violated the First Amendment.

The Telecommunications Act of 1996 significantly changed one related aspect of cable program regulation. For the first time, system operators were allowed to **censor obscene or indecent programming** on PEG or leased-access channels. The Supreme Court quickly struck down the provision as it applied to access channels but let stand the lease channels provision. The court also ruled that Congress cannot force cable operators to segregate and place on one lease channel all programs deemed indecent.

The 1996 act also required cable operators to **scramble any program that a subscriber might think is unsuitable for children.** As a result, the FCC hastily passed a rule requiring cable operators to scramble or otherwise block any indecent programs during hours when children are likely to be watching. The FCC stipulated those hours to be the same (6 a.m.–10 p.m.) as for broadcasters.

*15.3.6.2 First Amendment and Cable Franchising.* Just 2 years after Congress passed the 1984 cable act, court decisions questioned its constitutionality. They opened the franchising process to examination in the light of the First Amendment. One such proceeding reached the Supreme Court—the **Preferred case.**[76]

Preferred Communications, Inc., applied for a cable franchise in Los Angeles. The city refused because Preferred had not participated in the auction for the single franchise in the area. Preferred contended the refusal violated the company's First Amendment rights; the area contained sufficient space on public utility structures and public demand would support more than one cable system. The question of whether the First Amendment was a legitimate consideration in the franchise process was argued all the way to the Supreme Court. The court said that attempts to secure a cable franchise "plainly implicate First Amendment interest." However, the court refused to settle the First Amendment question. The practical issue was settled when the 1992 Cable Act **required cities to grant franchises to competing cable companies.** An appeals court, perhaps relying on the Supreme Court's direction, later ruled that Los Angeles, by denying access to competing cable operators, exacted "too heavy a toll on the First Amendment interests at stake here."[77]

### 15.3.7 First Amendment and Other Media

Generally, newer FCC-regulated media have fewer content restrictions and requirements than broadcasting. In adopting rules for these media, the Commission attempted to use the print model; the media were given, as much as possible, freedom from government regulation of editorial decisions similar to that enjoyed by newspaper, magazine, and book publishers. Most of these media may not transmit obscenity, tobacco advertising, information on illegal lotteries, and similar statutorily forbidden material. On the other hand, the less they resemble broadcasting—service intended for reception by the general public—the more they tend to be free of *broadcast-type regulation.*

The LPTV service is broadcasting, but even LPTV stations have fewer programming rules than their full-service competitors. LPTVs do not even have minimum schedule requirements (*PRT,* 3.5.2.3). Broadcast-type regulation applies on a sliding scale based on the station's ability to originate programming. For example, LPTV stations that have no local origination facilities, that simply rebroadcast full-service stations or satellite programming, have no political programming or access obligations. Must-carry rules (*PRT,* 14.1.1.9) do not include LPTV.

Regulation of other wireless media operators varies with the type of service. If other parties originate programming over which the transmitting licensee exercises no editorial control, the licensee is a **common carrier** and is so regulated.

The programmer, however, whether the licensee or simply a common-carrier customer, is regulated according to the intent of the programming service.[78] If the programmer intends transmissions for reception by the public at large, it is **broadcasting,** and broadcast-type regulation applies.

If the programmer intends to limit access to the transmissions—as in subscription programming—the process is not broadcasting. Instead, it is **point-to-multipoint communication,** according to the FCC, and therefore not subject to broadcast-type regulation. Here, the programmer uses transmission techniques to prevent the reception of programming by nonsubscribers. The signals cannot be received without special antenna converters or decoding equipment supplied by the programmer.

Common carrier, broadcasting, and point-to-multipoint—these regulatory categories cover DBS, subscription television stations, and, to some extent, wireless cable (multichannel TV; *PRT,* 5.4 and 12.8). A multichannel medium may even be regulated by channel according to the use of that channel. In a six-channel DBS or a four-channel multipoint distribution service (MDS; *PRT,* 5.2) facility, for example, two channels could operate (and be regulated) as broadcast services and the others as subscription services. MDS was originally strictly a common-carrier service; in 1987, however, the FCC gave MDS licensees the option to operate as noncommon carriers, freeing them to program their own channels.

The FCC does not apply broadcast-type regulation to subsidiary communications services (SCS; *PRT,* 11.6.2) offered by radio stations. A radio licensee may lease out an SCS channel for programming by others but must retain control over material transmitted. A 1986 court decision ruled that the FCC may not preempt state public utilities commission regulation when regulated intrastate carrier services are offered by SCS.[79]

Broadcast teletext is not subject to broadcast-type regulation[80] with the exception of equal opportunities for political candidates.[81] The FCC applies common-carrier regulation when a station leases its vertical blanking interval for data transmission. Cable legislation has excluded satellite master antenna television systems (SMATV) from federal requirements for cable systems, and, of course, local franchise requirements do not apply to SMATVs, either.

## NOTES

1. "Justice Black and First Amendment 'Absolutes': A Public Interview," *New York University Law Review, 37* (1962): 548.

2. Farmers Educational and Cooperative Union v. WDAY, 360 U.S. 525.

3. Stratton Oakmont, Inc. v. Prodigy, 23 Media L. Rep. 1794 (1995).

4. Cubby, Inc. v. CompuServe, Inc., 776 F.Supp. 135 (S.D.N.Y.) 1991.

5. 376 U.S. 254, 279–280 (1964). Boldface added.

6. Gertz v. Robert Welch, Inc., 418 U.S. 323 (1974).

7. Philadelphia Newspapers v. Hepps, 475 U.S. 767 (1986).

8. Duncan v. WJLA-TV, Inc., 106 F.R.D. 4, 10 Media L. Rep. 1395 (D.D.C. 1984).

9. Strickler v. NBC, 167 F. Supp. 68 (1958).

10. White v. Samsung Electronics America, Inc., 971 F.2d 1395 (1992).

11. Onassis v. Christian Dior-New York, Inc., 472 N.Y.S.2d 254 (1984).

12. Midler v. Young and Rubicom, 944 F.2d 909 (1991); Midler v. Ford Motor Co. 849 F.2d 460 (1988).

13. Solar Music v. Gap Stores, 668 F.2d 84 (1981).

14. Solar Music v. Gap Stores, 516 F. Supp 923 (1981), affirmed 688 F.2d 84 (1981); Broadcast Music, Inc. v. United States Shoe Corp., 678 F.2d 816 (1982).

15. Buffalo Broadcasting Company v. American Society of Composers, Authors, and Publishers, 744 F.2d 917, certiorari denied 469 U.S. 1211 (1985).

16. 17 U.S.C. § 111.

17. Sony Corporation of America v. Universal Studios, 464 U.S. 417.

18. United States v. Atherton, 561 F.2d 747 (1977).

19. Richmond Newspapers v. Virginia, 448 U.S. 555 (1980); Globe Newspaper Co. v. Superior Court, 457 U.S. 596 (1982); Press-Enterprise v. Superior Court (I), 464 U.S. 501 (1984).; and Press-Enterprise v. Superior Court (II), 478 U.S. 1 (1986).

20. 427 U.S. 539.

21. Landmark Communications v. Virginia, 435 U.S. 829 (1978); and Smith v. Daily Mail, 443 U.S. 97 (1979).

22. 381 U.S. 532.

23. 449 U.S. 560 (1981).

24. Near v. Minnesota, 283 U.S. 697.

25. New York Times v. U.S. and U.S. v. Washington Post, 403 U.S. 713, 714 (1971).

26. Cable News Network, Inc. v. Noriega, 498 U.S. 976 (1990).

27. 5 U.S.C. § 522.

28. Branzburg v. Hayes, In the Matter of Paul Pappas, and U.S. v. Caldwell, 408 U.S. 665.

29. Zurcher v. Stanford Daily, 436 U.S. 547.

30. 42 U.S.C § 2000aa.

31. Miller v. California, 413 U.S. 15.

32. Reno v. American Civil Liberties Unoin, 117 S. Ct. 2329.

33. 7 CFR § 73.1208.

34. 47 CFR § 73.1201.

35. 15 U.S.C. § 1335 (1969).

36. Except as required under Section 312(a)(7).

37. Public Law 86-677, 74 Stat. 554 (1960).

38. Petitions of Aspen Institute and CBS, 55 F.C.C.2d 697 (1975). A federal appeals court upheld the Commission's interpretation in Chisholm v. FCC and Democratic National Committee v. FCC, 588 F.2d 349 (1976); certiorari denied, 429 U.S. 890 (1976).

39. Petitions of Henry Geller, 95 F.C.C.2d 1236.

40. Request for Declaratory Ruling by WCVB-TV, 63 R.R.2d 665.

41. 47 F.2d 670.

42. 62 F.2d 850.

43. 288 U.S. 599 (1933).

44. Henry v. FCC, 302 F.2d 191; certiorari denied, 371 U.S. 821 (1962).

45. NBC v. FCC, 132 F.2d 545 (1942), affirmed, 319 U.S. 239; and FCC v. Sanders Bros., 309 U.S. 470 (1940).

46. Citizens Committee to Save WEFM v. FCC, 506 F.2d 246 (1974).

47. Development of Policy re: Changes in the Entertainment Formats of Broadcast Stations, 60 F.C.C.2d 858.

48. FCC v. WNCN Listeners Guild, 450 U.S. 582.

49. Citizens for Jazz on WRVR, Inc. v. FCC, 775 F.2d 392 (1985).

50. Deregulation of Radio, 84 F.C.C.2d 968 (1981); Deregulation of Commercial Television, 98 F.C.C.2d 1076 (1984).

51. Deregulation of Radio, 104 F.C.C.2d 505 (1986); Programming and Commercialization Policies (Reconsideration), 104 F.C.C.2d 526 (1986).

52. See note 41.

53. The marketplace argument also assumed that the scarcity factor was no longer valid. This aspect is discussed in PRT 13.4.2.

54. Editorializing by Broadcast Licensees, 13 F.C.C. 1246.

55. CFR §§ 73.123, 73.300, 73.598, 73.679.

56. 395 U.S. 367 (1969).

57. 48 F.C.C.2d 1.

58. General Fairness Doctrine Obligations of Broadcast Licensees, 58 R.R.2d 1137.

59. FCC v. League of Women Voters of California, 468 U.S. 364, 376 n. 11.

60. Telecommunications Research and Action Center v. FCC, 801 F.2d 501, rehearing denied, 806 F.2d 1115, certiorari denied, 107 S.Ct. 3197 (1987).

61. Radio–Television News Directors Association v. FCC, 809 F.2d 860.

62. 63 R.R.2d 541.

63. The public interest obligation itself, however, continued.

64. Syracuse Peace Council v. FCC, 867 F.2d 654 (1989).

65. Duncan v. U.S. 48 F.2d 128 (1931). Subsequent rulings interpreting the constitutional guarantee of freedom of religion have all but negated profane language as an offense.

66. Pacifica Foundation, 56 F.C.C.2d 94 (1975).

67. In the Matter of a "Petition for Clarification or Reconsideration" of a Citizen's Complaint against Pacifica Foundation, 59 F.C.C.2d 892 (1976).

68. Pacifica v. FCC, 438 U.S. 726 (1978).

69. New Indecency Enforcement Standards to Be Applied to All Broadcast and Amateur Radio Licensees, 62 R.R.2d 1218.

70. Action for Children's Television v. FCC, 852 F.2d 1332.

71. Action for Children's Television v. FCC 932 F.2d 1504 (1991); certiorari denied, 112 S.Ct. 1281 (1992).

72. Action for Children's Television v. FCC 58 F.3d 654 (1995); certiorari denied, 116 S.Ct. 701 (1996).

73. Action for Children's Television v. FCC, 59 F.3d 1249 (1995); certiorari denied, 116 S.Ct. 773 (1996).

74. Turner Broadcasting System, Inc. v. FCC, 114 S.Ct. 2445 (1994).

75. Wilkinson v. Jones, 480 U.S. 926.

76. 476 U.S. 488 (1986).

77. Preferred Communications, Inc. v. Los Angeles, 13 F.3d 1327 (1994).

78. Subscription Video, 2 F.C.C.Rcd. 1001 (1987); affirmed, National Association of Better Broadcasting v. FCC, 849 F.2d 665 (1988).

79. California v. FCC, 798 F.2d 1515.

80. Amendment to the Commission's Rules to Authorize the Transmission of Teletext by TV Stations 53 R.R.2d 1309 (1983); affirmed on reconsideration, 101 F.C.C.2d 827 (1985).

81. Telecommunications Research and Action Center v. FCC, 801 F.2d 501 (1986).

## FURTHER READING

Carter, T. Barton, Juliet Lushbough Dee, Martin J. Gaynes, and Harvey L. Zuckman. *Mass Communication Law in a Nutshell.* 4th ed. St. Paul, MN: West, 1994.

Carter, T. Barton, Marc A. Franklin, and Jay B. Wright. *The First Amendment and the Fourth Estate: The Law of Mass Media.* 6th ed. Mineola, NY: Foundation, 1994.

Holsinger, Ralph L., and Jon P. Dits. *Media Law.* 4th ed. New York: McGraw-Hill, 1997.

Lipschultz, Jeremy H. *Broadcast Indecency: F.C.C. Regulation and the First Amendment.* Newton, MA: Focal, 1996.

Middleton, Kent R., and Bill F. Chamberlin. *The Law of Public Communication.* 4th ed. White Plains, NY: Longman, 1997.

Overbeck, Wayne, and Rick D. Pullen. *Major Principles of Media Law, Annual Edition.* Fort Worth, TX: Harcourt Brace, 1996.

Pember, Don R. *Mass Media Law.* 9th ed. Boston: McGraw-Hill, 1997.

Read, William H., and Walter Sapronov, Eds. *Telecommunication Law, Regulation, and Policy.* Norwood, NJ: Ablex, 1996.

Smith, F. Leslie, Milan Meeske, and John W. Wright, III. *Electronic Media and Government: The Regulation of Wired and Wireless Mass Communication in the United States.* White Plains, NY: Longman, 1995.

Zelezny, John D. *Communications Law: Liberties, Restraints, and the Modern Media.* 2nd ed. Belmont, CA: Wadsworth, 1997.

# 16

# ETHICS AND SELF-REGULATION
# IN ELECTRONIC MASS MEDIA

Radio and television are highly competitive businesses. They can also be very lucrative. Therefore, why not bend the rules just a little and get the jump on the competition? Or go ahead and run that questionable advertising for an extra few hundred dollars? Some managers do, but many do not. Why not? Certainly they fear the wrath of the federal government. But there are also two other factors—factors that both deter misconduct and stimulate performance above the required legal minimum standards. These factors are ethics and self-regulation. In radio and television, *ethics* refers to a personal sense of what is right and what is wrong on the part of individuals who make major policy decisions for the operation—persons such as licensees, members of the board of directors, corporate officers, general and system managers (for convenience sake, we use the term *managers* to refer to these policymakers). *Self-regulation* is the translation of those personal ethics into systematic rules of conduct.

## 16.1 ETHICAL CONSIDERATIONS

Contrary to implications of some critics, there is nothing wrong with running an electronic medium to make money. Given a capitalistic system such as that of the United States, earning a profit is a desirable goal. However, some of the means employed to the end of making money could be considered inherently wrong, means that seem to violate certain obligations and responsibilities. We call such means unethical. Means that do meet these obligations and responsibilities are ethical.

What do we mean by *ethical means, ethical operation,* and *ethical practices?* The nouns in these terms are easier to define than their common adjective. For illustrative purposes, let us use the example of a broadcast licensee who runs a commercial radio or television station. *Means* are ways to earn a profit. A commercial broadcast licensee operates a station to earn a profit, therefore *operation* of the station is the licensee's means. *Practices* refers to things a licensee does in operating a station. All three terms are closely related, and they apply to almost any kind of radio and television entity—a cable system, a broadcast network, or whatever. We use these terms interchangeably to refer to **the things managers do in operating a radio and television entity so as to earn a profit.**

As for ethical, it would seem logical to employ our definition of ethics—the individual manager's personal sense of what is right and what is wrong, but **right and wrong are relative concepts.** For example, in 1973, Reverend Carl McIntire announced plans to open a pirate radio station on board a ship just outside the U.S. territorial limit off Cape May, New Jersey. Doubtless, this was an act of pure conscience on the part of the minister; the FCC had not renewed the license of his seminary's radio stations, and Reverend McIntire told reporters he was ready to risk going to jail to broadcast "the message God wants me to preach." Yet, whereas Reverend McIntire may have believed his plan to be the right thing to do (given the circumstances in which he found himself), it is conceivable that the federal government and the licensees with whose station signals the pirate transmitter would interfere would have viewed the pirate station as wrong. Therefore, our first definition of ethics is not adequate for our present discussion of ethical.

The dictionary defines ethical as "conforming to professional standards of conduct." There are at least two problems with this definition. First, it seems to imply existence of a profession. Radio and television, however, **do not fit many of the characteristics attributed to a profession.** A profession often requires advanced academic training, as in medicine and law. A profession stresses service. We have already discovered that commercial radio and television stations operate to earn a profit, but service is both a function of individual manager decisions and mandated by legal documents, such as laws and franchises. Second, our dictionary definition does not tell us to what or whose standards to conform, beyond that of the vague and probably invalid term *professional.*

### 16.1.1 Moral Obligations

Somehow, then, our definition of "ethical" should include the concepts of (a) effects on other persons, and (b) specificity—that is, kinds of acts or things that are ethical. Perhaps we can combine these two concepts by speaking in terms of obligations, duties radio and television managers are bound to perform as a result of moral responsibility. There would seem to be at least three sets of such obligations: (a) those of any business, (b) those of a medium of mass communication, and (c) those of an entity who uses means of delivery held in trust for the common good.

*16.1.1.1 Obligations of a Business.*    There are laws to protect the individual consumer. There are laws to preserve competition and prevent restraint of trade. But over and above legal requirements, there are also moral responsibilities. These responsibilities are based on the idea of the common good. Businesses are expected to produce good products and services at fair prices. They are expected to pay and deal with their employees on a fair and equitable basis. They are expected to contribute toward the betterment of the community in which they do business. They are expected to follow the Golden Rule in dealing with customers and competitors. Just as in any other business, managers are expected to accept this responsibility and run a radio or television entity so as **to produce a good product, to treat employees fairly, to contribute to the community, and to be an honest competitor and a good neighbor.**

### 16.1.1.2 Obligations of a Medium of Mass Communication.

Like newspaper publishers, radio or television managers are subject to laws and judicial decisions involving defamation, invasion of privacy, pornographic material, and false and misleading advertising. But also like publishers, radio and television managers operate instruments of tremendous potential for contribution to the public well-being. As such, publishers and managers have certain obligations to society, corollaries of the **social responsibility theory of mass communication.**

According to this theory, the press, which includes all media for reporting news, is guaranteed freedom by the Constitution and so is obliged to perform certain essential functions of mass communications in society. In 1948, the Commission on Freedom of the Press, a University of Chicago project funded by private enterprise and staffed by scholars, suggested five such functions. The media should

1. Present a truthful account of the day's news in such way as to give it meaning.
2. Serve as a forum for the exchange of ideas.
3. Present a representative picture of the various groups that make up society.
4. Present and clarify goals and values of society.
5. Provide full access to the day's intelligence.

National surveys show the public increasingly relies on television for news. It is important, therefore, for television licensees to meet the second set of obligations and carry out the five functions the Commission outlined.

### 16.1.1.3 Obligations From Use of Resources Held in Trust.

Unlike other businesses, many radio and television outlets do not own means of distribution. Broadcast stations, wireless cable systems, DBS, and other wireless media use radio frequencies, natural resources in the public domain. Cable operators use the right-of-way in their service areas, areas held and controlled by local governmental authorities on behalf of residents.

The Communications Act of 1934 requires the FCC to determine whether the public interest would be served before granting any license for use of the radio frequencies. It also allows the Commission to place certain requirements on licensees consistent with the public interest. Franchise agreements require cable systems to be responsive to the community and provide the public with a wide diversity of information sources and services.

These are minimum requirements. The manager should regard them as such. The manager has a positive obligation to use the outlet to serve the good of the overall public.

Justice Byron R. White, in writing the Supreme Court's Red Lion decision, alluded to this obligation with respect to broadcasting. He noted that only a few persons in each community can be licensed to operate a broadcast station. However, those who do receive licenses could be required to operate as proxies or fiduciaries. The same reasoning applies to extralegal, moral obligations—**the outlet has been authorized to employ resources held in trust for the common good and should use them for the common good.**

### 16.1.2 Ethics of Fulfilling Requirements

The term *ethical* also seems to imply the concept of **voluntary.** No one requires managers to operate a radio and television entity in an ethical manner; managers should do so voluntarily. The FCC has fewer than 2,000 employees to regulate all interstate common carriers and millions of radio transmitters in the various services, to say nothing of over 11,000 cable systems, 12,000 radio stations, and 3,000 television stations in all 50 states, the District of Columbia, Guam, Puerto Rico, and the Virgin Islands. With this workload, it is impossible to check the performance of every outlet. A careful but unethical manager could bend or break a few rules, and no one would ever know. The Telecommunications Act of 1996, with its streamlined license renewal process and extended license terms, further decreases the chance the FCC will discover unethical behavior.

There are also **degrees** of ethicality. Regulatory requirements can be fulfilled to the best of the manager's ability, or they can be fulfilled grudgingly, with the least amount of effort possible.

### 16.1.3 "Ethical" Defined

Having looked at some of the implications of the term *ethical,* let us now attempt to define ethical practices as they apply to radio and television. Ethical practices are the things a manager does to operate a commercial radio and television entity for profit in such way as to fulfill certain obligations it has as a business, as a medium of mass communication, and as an entity authorized to use resources held in trust for the common good. The licensee operates this way voluntarily and in response to a personal sense of what should be done, of what is right and what is wrong.

### 16.1.4 Ethical Managers

It is possible to be both ethical and unethical. For example, a radio station might program well for the community, yet engage in all manner of unfair business practices. Generally, however, **a radio or television entity is mostly ethical or mostly unethical,** especially at the local level.

**Size has little to do with ethicality.** You might think that a large, successful group-owned outlet could afford to be more ethical than a mom-and-pop operation. You could also argue that the locally owned small outlet has to operate ethically because it is so close to and so dependent on its public and its advertisers. However, there are examples of large and small outlets that do as little as they can for as much as they can get.

An ethical manager does not have to be a hero, but it does take **compassion**—empathy and the milk of human kindness. It also requires **strength**—when the chips, the ratings, the subscribers, the rates, and the gross are down; when the profit-and-loss statement (*PRT,* 19.1.2.1) is full of red ink, or when the competition is hot, it takes a strong will to resist certain unethical practices.

Specifically, what are the types of things that an ethical manager might do that makes the operation ethical? As we said earlier, simply doing what is required could be considered ethical, but some managers have taken a more positive approach. Some examples from small-market radio stations include the following: airing the weekly high school speech and drama class program at a decent time rather than 10 a.m. Sunday morning; employing a full-time news reporter and stringers when, as the only radio station in town, a rip 'n' read operation would do; lending space or equipment to a competitor whose station has been destroyed; mounting an appeal for clothing, shelter, and food for a destitute family; scheduling a hard-hitting investigative documentary in spite of opposition from several advertisers; running an editorial favoring the side that seems best for the community in a heated local controversy; establishing paid internships to help young people get started in broadcasting; hiring and training handicapped persons; and hiring and training poor youngsters of all ethnic backgrounds.

### 16.1.5 Unethical Managers

Motivations for unethical conduct in radio and television are the same as in any other field—drive for power and desire for prestige. However, in most cases the immediate stimulus is much simpler—**money.** A radio and television outlet has the potential to be very lucrative. When an outlet loses money, the manager often continues to operate in the hopes it will begin to pay off. Because the manager's job may be at stake, it is easy to see how ethics may be sacrificed to cut costs enough to stay in business.

At the other end of the spectrum is the already successful outlet whose management feels it must squeeze maximum profit from the business. The owner in this case is often a corporation whose owners are hundreds or thousands of stockholders. When profits, subscribers, sales, or ratings drop, so do stock prices; the stockholders suffer, and managers get fired. Thus managers run the outlet as a profit machine, reacting to financial results instead of good taste and sense of responsibility.

At least three factors support the assertion that radio and television seem particularly vulnerable to the lure of money and are often unfavorably compared to the daily press. First, **time is limited.** If a newspaper wishes to make more money, it adds more pages and sells more advertising to fill them. A broadcast station or a cable channel, however, cannot add more time. To earn more money it must either add commercials or attract a greater audience so that it can raise advertising rates. A radio and television outlet attracts greater audiences by airing more popular programs that because of audience tastes, usually mean programs with less serious or community-oriented content.

Second, **advertising-supported radio and television does not maintain strict separation of content and advertising considerations.** In preparing a daily newspaper, all space not taken by advertising belongs to the editor, and the editor is relatively free to select news, information, and entertainment to fill this "news hole." In radio and TV, most content is selected specifically for the purpose of attracting an audience for the ads. This content–advertising relation is rooted in the very origins of commercial broadcasting (*PRT,* 2.1.5 and 2.1.8).

Finally, **policymakers in radio and television have traditionally come largely from the areas of sales and marketing.** In newspapers, the editor makes content decisions, and editors have come up through the content ranks—copy, rewrite, and reporter. In broadcast stations, the manager makes the content decisions, and many station managers have come up through the ranks of sales. They see their medium as a sales vehicle and do whatever is necessary to make their outlet attractive to advertisers. In cable, the route to the policymaking level often originates in marketing; policymakers view their selection of channels as a "package" to be "marketed" to the maximum number of homes, to generate additional revenue with subscribers "upgrading" to ancillary services and multiple pay-cable channels. With these three factors—limited time, a strong content–advertising relation, and sales and marketing orientation of managers—it would be surprising if radio and television were not more vulnerable to the lure of the dollar than the daily press.

### 16.1.6 Unethical Business Practices

For our purposes, unethical practices show up in two main areas of radio and television operation—**business and programming.** Unethical business practices include rate cutting, double billing, ratings distortion, clipping, and blacklisting. In **rate cutting** or **selling off the card,** an outlet retains its existing rate card. However, if sales personnel cannot sell time at rate card prices, they are allowed to make special deals with clients at lower prices. This practice can set off rate-cutting wars involving all outlets in a market, benefiting no one.

**Double billing** is tied to cooperative advertising (*PRT,* 9.1.5.5). In double billing, the outlet issues two bills to the local advertiser. One reflects the amount the advertiser actually paid, for example, "50 one-minute spots in class AAA time @ $5.00 = $250." The other shows a higher amount, for example, "50 one-minute spots in class AAA time @ $10.00 = $500." The local advertiser sends the higher bill to the manufacturer and, according to the amount involved and the terms of the co-op deal, recovers most or all of the expenditure or even makes a little money. In the case of double billing, both the radio or television outlet and the local business act unethically.

**Ratings distortion**—a broadcast outlet's attempt to inflate ratings—has been condemned by the trade itself (*PRT,* 18.2.3.3). Station advertising rates are based on ratings, so the station or cable operation that distorts the ratings process sets itself up to charge advertisers for audience it does not have. At the same time, it gets an unfair, unearned competitive advantage over other stations in the market.

A broadcast station that deletes network programming or superimposes local material over it is **clipping.** The affiliate may clip off the opening or closing of a program—often during closing credits—to gain a few seconds of time to sell. Clipping is unethical because the station deletes material it has promised to air in its affiliation contract with the network. Clipping may even pose legal problems. If the station clips programs but certifies to the network (for affiliate compensation) that it carried the programming in full, the clipping may be illegal.

A **blacklist** is a scheme that causes persons to be refused employment. Blacklists did not end with the close of the 1950s (*PRT,* 2.3.3.1). They still exist in various forms. One is the "you'll never work again" ploy. Here, management passes word that a former employee is alcoholic or undependable or has some other characteristic that makes for a poor job candidate. If untrue, the individual spreading such stories may become a defendant in a libel suit. A second common blacklist type might be called "don't hire my employees." When, for example, an outlet operates in the red, employees may fear financial collapse will abolish their jobs, so they apply at other outlets in the market. To prevent personnel from leaving, management asks the other outlets not to hire them.

### 16.1.7 Program Practices Under Question

Unethical practices seem to show up most blatantly with respect to commercials. One such practice is **deception in production,** often a false demonstration. Two famous false demonstration cases were the sandpaper and the Libby-Owens-Ford auto-glass cases (*PRT,* 14.2.2). More recently, Volvo apologized for reinforcing the roofs of vehicles used in a commercial.

Some radio and television outlets accept advertising for **borderline products.** These products may not be illegal, but an outlet exhibits questionable ethics in advertising them. Borderline products include quack medicines; services of palm readers, fortune tellers, and faith healers; shady real estate promotions; and get-rich-quick schemes.

Unethical outlets may accept **questionable advertising.** Examples include deceptive advertising (such as bait-and-switch) and program-length commercials (*PRT,* 9.1.3.3). The latter increased in number markedly during the 1980s.

Closely related are **phony products** and **shady advertisers.** The commercial describes the phony product in glowing terms, says that it is not sold in stores, cautions that supplies are limited, and urges you to write or call ("Operators are standing by!"). Then (a) you get the product and either it does not come anywhere near the commercial's description or you find the stores flooded with them at half the price 2 months later; or (b) you send in money and receive nothing; subsequent inquiries are returned to you marked "Moved; left no forwarding address." Other shady advertisers include the discount merchant who uses bait-and-switch advertising, the used car dealer who sells primarily to persons of low income for low down payments and usurer's interest rates, and almost any business that promises much more than it can deliver without some catch.

So far our discussion has centered on advertising, but unethical practices show up in other types of programming as well. For example, in *PRT,* 3.3.3, we discussed rigging of big-money quiz shows in the 1950s. The rigging supposedly enhanced "entertainment values," which, interpreted, meant ratings. In *PRT,* 8.1.5, we discussed ethical problems in news, most of which grew out of the drive for high ratings. These included emphasis on stories that feature conflict, that are particularly visual, or are attractive just because videotape is available, and the staging of news scenes and deceptive editing of videotape.

There is also the question of news bias. Each of us perceives the same thing in different ways, a result of differential learning (*PRT,* 25.2.2.1). As long as human beings report the news, there will be this kind of bias. Far different is the manager who orders news slanted, often for commercial reasons. If a local newscast features a 2½-minute story on the arrival of new pickup trucks at the local Chevrolet dealer, you can bet the car dealer is or soon will be one of the outlet's major advertising clients. Such practices hardly present a truthful account of the news, serve as a forum for the exchange of ideas, or fulfill any kind of public interest obligations.

Sometimes news reporters have pictures or information that present ethical dilemmas. How much footage should be shown of a badly injured car crash victim? Many stations would show none at all. What about pictures and names of crime victims? Courts have ruled that the news media cannot be prevented from disclosing the names of rape victims. Most radio and television stations, however, have strict policies against such disclosure even when the information is in a police report or other public record.

Bad journalistic decisions sometimes involve more than questionable ethics. An Orlando, Florida, television station reached an out-of-court settlement after being sued for showing a close-up of the skull of a murdered 6-year-old child. The family, after attending memorial services for the girl who had been abducted 3 years earlier, watched the news broadcast in shock.

## 16.2 SELF-REGULATION

When ethics are translated into policy, the result is self-regulation. Because managers' ethics are reflected in an outlet's operation, each outlet has some sort of self-regulation. Many outlets have no formal written policies; new employees must learn policy by osmosis—posted memos, the grapevine, and the like. Some outlets have policy books that each new employee must read. These range in size from a couple of double-spaced typewritten pages to large and detailed volumes that attempt to cover every department and every eventuality.

### 16.2.1 NAB Codes

For years, many broadcast stations relied on the Codes of the National Association of Broadcasters (NAB). The codes formed the basis for station policies, either formally, as subscribers, or informally, through general influence on the trade. The codes were the best known products of broadcasting self-regulation.

There were two—the Radio Code and the Television Code—and they represented the collective average ethics of the subscribing stations, a set of rules that the licensees agreed should serve as minimum ethical standards. The first Radio Code was written in 1929; the first Television Code in 1951. Both were revised many times. As a result of pressure from the FCC and Congress, the NAB (with the support of some network initiatives) amended the program standards of its Television Code in 1975 to include a **family viewing standard.** The standard was aimed at reducing sex and violence in content and said, "[E]ntertainment programming inappropriate for viewing by a general family audience should not be broadcast during the first hour of network entertainment programming in prime time and in the immediately preceding hour. . . ." Guilds representing television writers, producers, directors, and actors challenged the family viewing standard in court. In 1976, a federal judge ruled that the standard was unconstitutional. An appeals court threw out the ruling in 1979,[1] and the Supreme Court denied a petition for review in 1980, allowing the appeals court decision to stand. Actually, the NAB had suspended enforcement of the program standards 4 years before (at the time of the first ruling).

Meanwhile, the advertising standards came under attack. In 1979, the government filed an antitrust suit against the NAB. The Justice Department charged that the TV Code's **limitations on advertising** restricted the amount of television advertising time available and, therefore, kept TV commercial rates artificially high. In 1982, an initial court ruling went against the NAB. After negotiations, the association deleted the advertising standards and the Justice Department dropped the suit.

At this point, the codes were empty shells. Both programming and advertising standards—the primary content of the codes—were suspended. The NAB closed down the Code Authority, released its staff, and shut its offices. Early in 1983, the NAB officially dissolved the codes.

There is more than a little irony in this episode. The government—in the form of the Justice Department—dealt a blow to the codes. Yet, the case could be made that one main purpose of the codes' very existence was to appease the government. Repeatedly over the years, Congress, the FCC, or the FTC would perceive some problem with broadcasting and propose a law or rule; the NAB, in turn, would amend the codes to take care of the problem, to demonstrate that government action was not needed, that the trade could regulate itself. One can only wonder whether the code might have eliminated the need for the V-chip or the ratings system mandated by Congress in the Telecommunications Act of 1996. Indeed, according to the court decision in the family viewing standard case, the NAB adopted that standard as a result of pressure on the trade by Commissioner Richard Wiley when he chaired the FCC.

As for the advertising standards, the FCC's Blue Book (*PRT,* 2.2.5.6) had criticized stations for airing too many commercials; the NAB subsequently tightened standards. At one point, the Commission had instructed its staff to question any license renewal application in which a station proposed to exceed NAB code guidelines on number of commercial minutes per hour. Here was a case in which the government actually (but unofficially) adopted code standards as its own. All government restrictions on length and number of commercials have since been eliminated.

The codes were by no means perfect. Critics contended they were picky and overly specific, an open invitation to work around them and to observe the letter but not the spirit of the standards. They criticized the codes for their voluntary nature, which meant that at any given time a large number of stations were nonsubscribers. They noted that the public did not know what the codes and the seals were or did; few in the audience knew or cared whether a station subscribed to the code, or even whether it had violated the code and lost the right to display the seal. They criticized the codes for being defensive and reactive, that changes came only after the threat of government action. Within the trade, there were those who said the codes were not tough enough. There were also those who said that there should be no codes at all, that they did not do what they were supposed to do, and that true self-regulation had to occur at the level of the individual station licensee.

Defenders argued that the codes were industry standards against which all stations could be measured. If there was a movement toward growth of a professional spirit in broadcasting, it was best reflected in the codes. The codes acted as a shield against intrusion by government; according to strict libertarian interpretation of First Amendment theory, the less government interference, the better off we are. Despite their voluntary nature, the codes did have an overall effect on programming and advertising standards. For example, code bans on the advertising of whiskey and depictions of people drinking alcohol in commercials were so effective and so well known, many believed they were federal law or regulation (which they were not).

### 16.2.2 Program Ratings

As a result of requirements of the Telecommunications Act of 1996 programmers had to develop a **ratings system**. The ratings would alert viewers concerning violent and indecent material in upcoming programming. The ratings were to work in conjunction with the so-called V-chip so that viewers could block programming they found objectionable. Jack Valenti, president of the Motion Picture Association of America (MPAA; whose members include major providers of TV programming) headed the committee that drafted the original TV rating system, and it turned out to look much like that of the MPAA. The TV rating system, based primarily on appropriateness of programming for certain age groups, was introduced in late 1996 and it sparked immediate criticism. Opponents decried the system because it did not indicate the reason a program had received a certain rating. As a result the sytem was revised in 1997 to include the letters *V, FV, S, L,* and *D* so viewers would be able to tell why a program had been judged to be not appropriate—violence (fantasy or real), sex, language, or dialogue (Box 16.1). The broadcast and cable TV networks began using the system in October 1997.

The TV business calls the rating system *Parental Guidelines,* and it is largely self-administered and self-policed. Networks and producers of each show determine the rating for that show. A program's rating appears in the upper corner of the TV screen for 15 seconds at the start of each show. The TV business also asked *TV Guide,* daily newspaper TV logs, and other such listings to include the ratings.

An Oversight Monitoring Board, comprised of people drawn from the television business, attempts to ensure uniformity and consistency in applying the Parental

---

**BOX 16.1. TELEVISION RATING SYSTEM**

The television ratings system is based on the following combination of six categories of aged-based ratings and 5 letters that provide content warnings:

- **TV-Y All Children**: Appropriate for all children. Whether animated or live action, the program is not expected to frighten younger children.
- **TV-Y7 Directed to Older Children**: For children age 7 and older. Material may be more appropriate for children able to distinguish between make-believe and reality. May include mild physical comedic violence, or may frighten children under the age of 7. If the program contains intense or combative fantasy violence the designation will be **TV-Y7-FV.**
- **TV-G General Audience**: Suitable for all ages. Contains little or no violence, no strong language, and little or no sexual dialogue or situations.
- **TV-PG Parental Guidance Suggested**: Parental guidance is suggested. Program may contain infrequent coarse language (L), limited violence (V), some suggestive sexual situations (S) or sexually suggestive dialogue (D).
- **TV-14 Parents Strongly Cautioned**: May be unsuitable for children younger than 14. Program may contain strong coarse language (L), intense sexual situations (S) or intensely suggestive dialogue (D), or intense violence (V).
- **TV-MA Mature Audience Only**: Designed to be viewed by adults and therefore may be unsuitable for children under 17. Program may contain crude language (L), explicit sexual activity (S), or graphic violence (V).

Guidelines. The Board examines programs whose Guidelines may have been inappropriate and reviews publicly criticized programs.

### 16.2.3 Other Vehicles for Self-Regulation

For years, each of the three national commercial television networks had its own **broadcast standards department.** Staff editors would review thousands of commercials and programs annually to ensure that they met network standards. If they found problems—taste, deception, or whatever—they suggested deletions or changes, requested substantiation, or referred to outside experts for an opinion. They could check at all stages of production, from script to release print, and request changes at any or all points along the way. Even outside organizations checked with network standards departments in advance. Advertising agencies, for example, asked for review of commercials that would run on the network, starting with storyboard or script. During the later 1980s, however, the networks **substantially reduced their standards departments.** At least four factors contributed to this action: **general personnel and expense trimming, lessening of regulatory pressures, the "need" to compete with less restricted programming on cable, and a marketplace-driven perception that the moral climate had changed.**

The **National Advertising Review Board** (NARB) acts on complaints concerning advertising. Although NARB is concerned with national advertising in all media, a substantial number of cases have involved television commercials. The NARB was formed in 1971 through the efforts of various trade groups in the advertising community. Representatives from advertisers, agencies, and the general public sit on the Board. Complaints about a firm's advertising go to the National Advertising Division of the Council of Better Business Bureaus. If the matter is not resolved at that level, it goes before the NARB. The final decision of the NARB is sent to the advertiser and made public. If the decision goes against the firm, the firm is expected to modify or withdraw the advertising in question. Otherwise the NARB informs the appropriate government agency.

NARB is corrective (after the fact) as opposed to trade association codes and network standards departments, which are preventive. The NARB was formed primarily to forestall government regulation as well as expensive and publicly damaging lawsuits against advertisers by the public and even by other, competing advertisers.

For 11 years, a somewhat parallel group operated for news, the **National News Council** (NNC). A task force published a report in 1972 that urged establishment of an independent and private national news council. NNC was organized and opened for business in 1973. Funds came from a variety of private, research, media, and industrial foundations. Complaints about accuracy and fairness of news reports went to the NNC, which made public its actions and decisions.

The NNC was not really self-regulation. Like the NARB, the NNC was a corrective, nongovernmental regulatory body, set up to forestall government involvement. But unlike the NARB, the NNC was not set up by practitioners to police itself. In fact, some news personnel tended to resent any kind of watchdog agency, contending that the agency infringed on the very First Amendment it sought to protect. The three original TV broadcast networks cooperated, as did the wire services and many other news organizations. Nonetheless, its adversaries were powerful and influential, including (among others) the *New York Times* and the American Society of Newspaper Publishers. After fighting an uphill battle for acceptance over more than a decade, the NNC voted itself out of existence in 1984.

Some other self-regulation efforts that affect broadcasting include those of **major advertising and trade groups** and of **organizations of individuals** who work in broadcasting. For example, various trade groups in the advertising community have adopted The Advertising Code of American Business. The Council of Better Business Bureaus has a Fair Practice Code for Advertising and Selling. The Proprietary Association, trade organization of over-the-counter drug manufacturers, has its own code that covers advertising. Financial institutions have a code of ethics and specific guidelines for advertising. The Radio-Television News Directors Association, an individual membership organization for broadcast news personnel, has a Code of Broadcast News Ethics that describes, in positive terms, what broadcasters should be and do. Many broadcast news people belong to the Society of Professional Journalists and Sigma Delta Chi, a group that has its own code of ethics.

## NOTE

1. Writers Guild of America v. FCC, 423 F.Supp. 1064.

## FURTHER READING

Black, Jay, Bob Steele, and Ralph A. Barney. *Doing Ethics in Journalism: A Handbook with Case Studies.* 3rd ed. Greencastle, MA: Sigma Delta Chi Foundation/Society of Professional Journalists, 1997.

Bugeja, Michael. *Living Ethics: Developing Values in Mass Communication.* Boston: Allyn-Bacon, 1996.

Christians, Clifford, G., John P. Ferre, and P. Mark Fackler. *Good News: Social Ethics of the Press.* New York: Oxford University Press, 1993.

Christians, Clifford G., Kim B. Rotzoll, and Mark Fackler. *Media Ethics: Cases and Moral Reasoning.* 4th ed. White Plains, NY: Longman, 1995.

Commission on Freedom of the Press. *A Free and Responsible Press.* Chicago: University of Chicago Press, 1947.

Day, Louis A. *Ethics in Media Communications: Cases and Controversies.* 2nd ed. Belmont, CA: Wadsworth, 1997.

Dennis, Everette E., and John C. Merrill. *Media Debates: Issues in Mass Communication.* 2nd ed. White Plains, NY: Longman, 1996.

Fink, Conrad C. *Media Ethics: In the Newsroom and Beyond.* Hightstown: McGraw-Hill, 1988.

Fink, Conrad C. *Media Ethics: The Daily Realities.* Needham Heights, MA: Allyn-Bacon, 1995.

Goodwin, H. Eugene, and Ron F. Smith. *Groping for Ethics in Journalism*. 3rd ed. Ames: Iowa State University Press, 1994.

Gordon, David, John M. Kittross, and Carol Reuss. *Controversies in Media Ethics*. White Plains, NY: Longman, 1996.

Gross, Larry P., John S. Katz, and Jay Ruby, Eds. *Image Ethics: The Moral Rights of Subjects in Photographs, Film, and Television*. New York: Oxford University Press, 1988.

Hulteng, John L. *The Messenger's Motives: Ethical Problems of the News Media*. 2nd ed. Englewood Cliffs, NJ: Prentice-Hall, 1985.

Kowet, Don. *A Matter of Honor*. New York: Macmillan, 1984.

Lambeth, Edmund B. *Committed Journalism: An Ethic for the Profession*. 2nd ed. Bloomington: Indiana University Press, 1992.

Lester, Paul M., Ed. *Images That Injure: Pictorial Stereotypes in the Media*. Westport, CT: Praeger, 1996.

Limburg, Val E. *Electronic Media Ethics*. Boston: Focal, 1994.

Matelski, Marilyn J. *TV News Ethics*. Boston: Focal, 1991.

Moore, Roy L. *Mass Communication Law and Ethics*. Hillsdale, NJ: Lawrence Erlbaum Associates, 1994.

Powell, Jon T., and Wally Gair, Eds. *Public Interest and the Business of Broadcasting: The Broadcast Industry Looks at Itself*. New York: Quorum Books, 1988.

Schramm, Wilbur, and William L. Rivers. *Responsibility in Mass Communication*. 3rd ed. New York: Harper, 1980.

# V

## ECONOMIC PERSPECTIVE

The desire for profit drives the dominant form of radio and television in the United States. People invest in and operate local and national outlets to make money. Here we examine electronic mass media as businesses. Successful businesses generate enough revenue to cover expenses and to yield a profit. We divide our survey of the economics of radio and television as follows: techniques and institutions involved in the sale of time, chapter 17; syndicated audience research, chapter 18; structure and operation of local outlets, chapter 19; and structure and operation of networks, chapter 20.

People also invest time, experience, talent, and skill in radio–TV as employees. These individuals, too, hope to earn enough in salary and commissions to meet personal expenses as well as long-range savings goals. Many also enjoy the work, which is why they have chosen a career in radio–TV instead of brain surgery, corporate accounting, nuclear physics, or some other less demanding field. We look at careers in the electronic mass media in chapter 21.

# 17

## SALES AND ADVERTISING

In commercial radio and television, advertising revenues are vital. As discussed in chapter 9, advertising underwrites programming and supports operations. It also generates profit. For owners, profit is the whole point of running a commercial radio or television outlet. It is no coincidence that promotions to manager often go to those on the sales staff.

We begin this chapter by discussing advertising in general. Next we look at advertisers and advertising agencies. Then we focus on radio and television as advertising media—rate cards, time sales, advertising representatives, and network time sales.

### 17.1 NATURE OF ADVERTISING

The dictionary defines *advertising* as "the business of preparing and issuing public notices or announcements, usually paid for, as of things for sale, needs, etc." Most of us encounter so much advertising so often that we almost accept it as an inevitable part of the environment. However, look at the nature of the basic transaction involved: It is indirect.

Consider, for example, radio–TV advertising. A conventional ad-supported radio or TV outlet must appeal to an audience. It uses programming to attract the audience, but that costs money. The medium must earn revenue from a third party, an advertiser who wishes to expose the medium's audience to commercial messages. After the medium airs the message, the advertiser can receive estimates of the audience for the message and may even experience a change in sales. However, there is no direct measure of the message's effectiveness, no way to tell if Commercial A led Audience Member B to purchase Product C.

Two major types of commercial advertising are institutional and product. **Institutional advertising** attempts to have the public think of the advertiser in a certain positive way. **Product advertising** attempts to sell a specific commodity by creating a new market or by winning a bigger share or increasing size of an existing market.

## 17.1.1 Advertising Media

The advertising business—firms that pay for and produce advertisements—consists of advertisers, advertising agencies, sales representatives, specialty firms (e.g., research companies and media buying services), and media. Major advertising media include newspapers, broadcast TV, cable TV, radio, magazines, direct mail, and outdoor (billboards and rental signs). Minor media include car cards, matchbooks, subway posters, giveaways, and merchandising tie-ins (e.g., shirts imprinted with a product's name, toy trucks with a real company's name on the trailer, toys and other items based on characters or incidents in movies or TV).

Advertising pays part of the cost of many media outlets in the United States (Table 17.1). Ads take about 60% of the space in newspapers and magazines yet generate over 75% of their revenues. Advertising supports commercial broadcasting almost entirely. It helps support many national and regional program services distributed primarily by cable. Cable systems derive most revenue from subscribers but also sell advertising.

Some media get almost total financial support directly from the audience. These include recordings, books, movies, and subscription and pay-per-view services on cable and other multichannel video media. Look carefully, however, and you see that advertising has come to these media. As noted in *PRT*, 9.1.1, some premium channels do, indeed, carry ads. Recordings, books, and movies carry ads in the form of promotion for their own products. Although you pay $5 and up for a ticket, you still may have to sit through commercials in a movie theater.

**TABLE 17.1**
Total U.S. Advertising Expenditures (in Millions)

| Medium | Amount |
| --- | --- |
| Newspapers | $11,744.6 |
| Consumer magazines | 8,463.0 |
| National newspapers | 1,092.1 |
| Sunday magazines | 999.9 |
| Outdoor | 909.8 |
| Broadcast television | 24,612.0 |
|   Network | 11,893.2 |
|   Spot | 12,718.8 |
| Cable TV networks | 2,970.2 |
| Radio | 1,872.1 |
|   Network | 599.8 |
|   Spot | 1,272.3 |
| Total | 55,022.0 |

*Note.* National advertisers spent over $55 billion in measured media in 1994. *Measured* means that something—such as viewers of programs or copies of magazines—was counted by someone—such as an audience rating company. (*Source: Advertising Age*)

### 17.1.2 Advertising Trade Groups

Advertisers, agencies, and media have formed trade organizations. Some of the important organizations include the American Advertising Federation, the American Association of Advertising Agencies, the Association of National Advertisers, the National Association of Broadcasters, and the National Cable Television Association.

The **American Advertising Federation** (AAF) represents all segments of the advertising business—advertisers, media, agencies, advertising service companies, various media and advertising associations, and local and college advertising clubs. AAF sponsors the annual American Advertising Awards, whose national trophy is the ADDY. When a single voice must speak for advertising—to Congress, the Federal Trade Commission or whatever—the AAF usually provides that voice.

The **Association of National Advertisers** (ANA) includes more than 300 major corporations comprising over 2,000 companies that advertise products and services on a national basis. ANA provides informational, educational, and representational services for its members. It also works with other trade groups and the actors' unions to negotiate union contracts for talent in electronic mass media commercial production.

The **American Association of Advertising Agencies** (AAAA), **National Association of Broadcasters**, and **National Cable Television Association** are the trade associations of advertising agencies, commercial broadcasting, and cable systems, respectively. Additionally, the **Radio Advertising Bureau** and **Television Bureau of Advertising** promote the broadcast media as advertising vehicles, and the **Cabletelevision Advertising Bureau** does the same for cable.

The ANA, the AAAA, the AAF, and the Council of Better Business Bureaus all helped organize and support the National Advertising Review Board (*PRT,* 16.2.3). The AAAA and the ANA founded the Advertising Research Foundation (ARF) in 1936 to encourage research in advertising. ARF's membership has grown to include more than 350 advertisers, advertising agencies, media companies, research firms, educational institutions, and international organizations.

### 17.1.3 Advertising Pros and Cons

In *PRT,* 9.5, we reviewed criticisms of radio and TV commercials. Critics also complain about advertising in general. Concerning content, they charge that advertising induces us to buy things we cannot afford and do not need, appeals primarily to emotions rather than to intellect, is biased, makes conflicting claims about competitive products (Have you ever seen a product advertised as second best?), is repetitious, annoying, and forced on people. Some economists condemn advertising as wasteful and unnecessary for adding to the cost of advertised products.

Social critics charge that advertising manipulates our lives, molds us, and makes us believe that consumption is a major goal of life, irrespective of social consequences. They say advertising emphasizes private and political interests at the expense of human and social interests.

Critics contend advertising monopolizes consumer information, depriving the public of the diversity of opinion needed for informed choices. Many persons believe that advertisers, agencies, and media have no ethics; that the advertising business uses any means, no matter how unscrupulous, and tells any story, no matter how untrue, to get us to buy products, no matter how shoddy, dangerous, or unnecessary. Electronic mass media advertising, particularly broadcast and cable television, receive special attention from critics for loudness, frequency, intrusiveness, clutter, and other complaints discussed in *PRT,* 9.5.

In reply, defenders say that advertising does not coerce. They remind us that, unlike some propaganda that is hidden, advertising is out in the open and that, as consumers, we must exercise judgment in the marketplace. They explain that advertising appeals to emotions because we are motivated largely by emotional drives, and repetition is needed to reach those not reached previously.

Advertising, assert its defenders, really serves a desirable social purpose. Our economy is based on fast turnover of merchandise. Advertising, according to one text,

> provides selective buying information, assures us of uniform quality, saves us time in shopping, helps to lower prices through mass production and mass selling techniques, improves our standard of living by educating us about new products, serves cultural and intellectual ends, as well as those of a purely material nature, and enables us to enjoy the mass media at small expense.[1]

The advertising business contends that all advertisers should not share the blame for the few who use poor taste and unethical practices. The business points to rising standards and self-regulation efforts.

### 17.1.4 Marketing Scope of Advertisers

We can classify advertisers into three categories based on marketing interest or scope—local, regional, and national. A **local advertiser** serves one community and aims advertising messages at the citizens of that community. For example, an automobile dealer's business comes primarily from the town in which the dealership is located; the dealer advertises in local media to reach local people only.

A **regional advertiser** sells goods and services in more than one community, but not on a national basis. A regional brewery, for example, advertises beer only in the three states in which it is available. In radio–TV, regional advertisers use state and regional networks and regional spot advertising.

A **national advertiser** distributes products nationally and advertises all over the country—for example, automobile manufacturers and nationally distributed beer. In radio–TV, national advertisers use network, syndication, or spot advertising, or some combination thereof. National advertisers often spend huge sums on advertising (Fig. 17.1). During the mid-1990s, Procter & Gamble spent so much that their yearly billings in cable and broadcast TV alone totaled $1.24 billion.

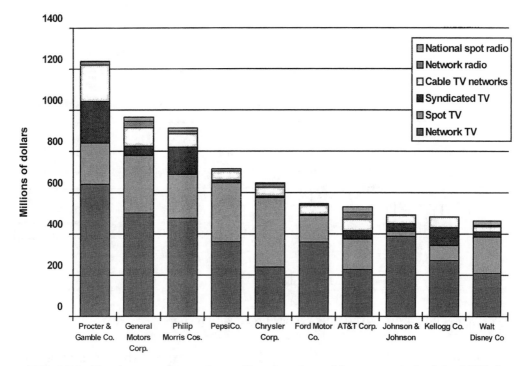

**FIG. 17.1. Ten largest electronic media advertisers.** Huge sums, indeed. In 1995, for example, these 10 companies alone spent nearly $7 billion in electronic media advertising. Their total advertising expenditure was even more; this figure does not reflect spending for newspapers, magazines, direct mail, and other nonelectronic advertising. (*Source: Advertising Age.*)

Many advertisers, particularly local advertisers, deal directly with the media. Sometimes the medium prepares some or all advertising, as with the hardware store and the radio station in *PRT,* 9.3.1. Sometimes, the local advertiser is large enough to have in-house advertising specialists as is the case with many department stores.

### 17.1.5 Advertising Agencies

Most large advertisers hire advertising agencies (Fig. 17.2), firms that specialize in the creation and placement of advertising. Actually, any size advertiser may use an agency, including our locally owned corner hardware store. Just as there are local, regional, and national advertisers, so there are **local, regional, and national advertising agencies.**

The main products of an advertising agency are its services, evident from our look at agency operation in *PRT,* 9.3. A **full-service agency** provides **creativity** (ideas around which a campaign is built), **research and planning** (ways to get those ideas across in specific media), **supervision** (of production of materials and their use by media), and **media selection and buying.**

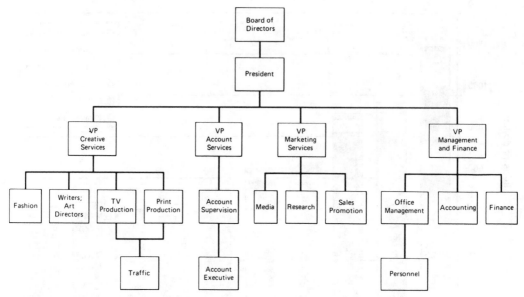

FIG. 17.2. Full-service advertising agency organization chart.

In effect, the media pay for these basic services. In the normal agency compensation arrangement:

1. The agency places advertising for the client.
2. The client pays the agency for space and time based on the media's full rate card (*PRT,* 17.2) prices.
3. The agency, in turn, pays the media full rate card prices minus a **15% commission.**

For example, a station charges $1,000 for radio advertising; the agency collects $1,000 from the advertiser, pays the station $850, and keeps $150 as its commission. However over the years full-service agencies' earnings from media commissions have declined to about 50% of their income. Clients pay the other 50% in direct charges and for materials and services used to prepare advertising—typography, production, printing, artwork, and photography. Some agencies have dropped the commission system and operate entirely on a fee basis.

In addition to independent, full-service agencies, there are house and boutique agencies and media buying services. An advertiser may establish its own agency, a house agency, to save the 15% commission or to get better, more efficient advertising. A boutique agency (or modular agency) sells each service separately. The client buys the specific service needed and usually pays on a fee basis. A media buying service specializes in purchasing advertising time and space and attempts to get better prices for its clients than do agency media buyers.

### 17.1.6 Target Audiences for Advertisers

Most advertisers do not wish to reach all people. Instead, they want to reach only those who might be interested in buying their goods and services. These people are the target audience. One job of advertising research is to **identify and suggest methods to reach the target audience**—describe its characteristics, specify media that will best reach it, and suggest approaches to persuade it to buy.

Crucial to identifying and reaching the target audience are the concepts of market, demographics, cost per thousand, and efficiency. **Market** refers to specific cities and surrounding areas in which a product is sold. That regional brewery in *PRT,* 17.1.4, for example, wishes to reach only the 10 markets within the three states where its beer is sold.

Market also means prospective buyers for the product—who and where they are. This is where **demographics** and psychographics come in. *Demography,* the statistical study of populations, provides quantitative information—how many persons there are in various age brackets, of each sex, who earn annual incomes of stated amounts, who have completed specific amounts of schooling, and so on. Analyses of population by age, sex, income, education, and other characteristics are demographic breakdowns or simply demographics. Market researchers also divide populations based on leisure activities, personality traits, personal interests, attitudes, opinions, values, and needs. Such qualitative breakdowns are **psychographics** or **lifestyle research**. Advertising researchers study the demographics and psychographics of media usage to determine which media reach people with characteristics to whom the product should appeal. Those are the media in which the product will be advertised most heavily.

### 17.1.7 Comparing Advertising Costs: CPM

Advertisers compare costs of media outlets by computing how much they would pay to reach 1,000 people or homes or whatever the target audience. This is **CPM**, cost per thousand (M stands for *mille,* Latin for thousand). For example, a radio station may use a contemporary music format to gain top ratings and charge $27.50 to air a 1-minute commercial. Another station may program country music and charge only $18. The country station seems less expensive, but the contemporary station reaches 5,000 persons, whereas the country station reaches only 3,000. The contemporary station's CPM is $5.50 ($27.50 ÷ 5 = $5.50); the country station's, $6.00 ($18 ÷ 3 = $6.00). Therefore, the contemporary station is really less expensive.

The lowest CPM is not always best, however. If a farm implement dealer were to advertise on the contemporary station, the audience might contain a high percentage of **waste circulation**, people with no interest in buying cultivators and harrows. The country station's audience, on the other hand, might be packed with potential buyers of farm implements. Here, the dealer would find the country station more efficient—less waste circulation and a lower CPM (based on target audience).

CPM is difficult to use across media. The M represents different things in different media. In radio it usually means thousands of persons reached; in broadcast TV, thousands of persons or households, and in newspapers and magazines, number of copies sold (but two or more persons often read one copy, so the M is no indication of the number exposed to an advertisement).

## 17.2 ELECTRONIC MASS MEDIA RATE CARDS

A medium states the prices it charges for advertising under various conditions on a **rate card.** Conditions include factors such as length or size, frequency, and placement of the ad. The salesperson uses the card to calculate for a potential client exactly what the advertisement cost would be in any situation.

### 17.2.1 Radio Station Rate Cards

A radio station's **base rate** is usually what the station charges to broadcast a 1-minute commercial one time, often in a specific daypart. Most advertisers qualify for discounts of one kind or another, and so few really pay the base rate. The base rate, then, is just that—a base from which to figure various discounts for which an advertiser may be eligible.

The radio station's rate discounts are **variables,** and the station's card will usually list these variables (Fig. 17.3). The rate may vary, for example, by **lengths of time** the advertiser buys. A 30-second avail (Box 17.1) costs 80% to 90% of the 1-minute rate; a 10-second avail, 50% to 65%; and sponsorship of a 5-minute feature or news program costs one and a fraction times the 1-minute rate.

Rates may also vary by **time of day.** In most cases the radio station chooses the exact time commercials run, but the advertiser may specify the daypart. Stations charge the highest rate for dayparts with the largest audience, usually morning and afternoon when most people drive to or from work. Rate cards list these as "AAA" time or something similar. Smaller stations may combine all nonpeak time under one rate; others divide remaining hours by audience levels and price them accordingly. Stations in the smallest markets often do not differentiate among dayparts and charge a single rate. Some stations in large markets use a grid card, similar to the TV cards described in the next section.

Radio stations also sell avails scattered through different time periods (ROS, BTA, or TAP; *PRT,* 9.1.2.4). They usually charge more for specific positions—for example, 4:45 p.m. every weekday, or immediately after the 6:00 p.m. sports report.

Small- and medium-market stations may issue two cards—one each for **local** and **spot** (*PRT,* 17.4) rates. A station receives national and regional spot sales revenue with 15% deducted by ad agencies and with another 15% due out for the station's sales rep firm. So the station raises rates for spot advertising over those

| ROCK104 - WRUF-FM - Advertising Rates effective January, 1996 | | | | | |
|---|---|---|---|---|---|
| Inventory Demand Level: | ONE | TWO | THREE | FOUR | FIVE |
| First Class - your choice of time | $75 | $70 | $65 | $60 | $55 |
| 6am-8pm - limited days | $55 | $50 | $45 | $40 | $35 |
| 6am-8pm - four to five days | $50 | $45 | $40 | $35 | $30 |
| 6am-8pm - full week rotation | $45 | $40 | $35 | $30 | $25 |
| Saturday 10a-5p | $60 | $55 | $50 | $45 | $40 |
| Evenings 8p-12mid | $35 | $25 | $20 | $15 | $10 |
| Weekends 6a-12mid | $40 | $30 | $25 | $20 | $15 |
| Monday-Sunday 6am-mid | $40 | $35 | $30 | $25 | $20 |
| Radio Dominator Plan<br>50 commercials<br>Mon-Sun 6am-Midnight | $1,995 | $1,795 | $1,595 | $1,395 | $1,195 |
| 24 Hour Standby plan | $30 | $25 | $20 | $15 | $10 |

<u>Special 15% bonus plan:</u> **Double the number of commercials in your weekly schedule and pay only 15% of the earned rate. Additional commercials will run Monday-Sunday best time available and are pre-emptible without notice. Make goods will be scheduled only if there is available time in the week.**

Two-Three-Four part and Saturation Plans provide for even distribution of commercials by time period. Demand grid three (3) commercials are pre-emptible with advanced notice. Demand grids four (4), five (5) and all BTA (Best Time Available commercials) are pre-emptible without any notice. Make-goods will be scheduled without notice and only if inventory permits.

FIG. 17.3. Radio station rate card. (*Source*: WRUF.)

for local advertising. This higher rate structure is the **spot rate card.** Many stations, however, use one card and charge the same rate for both local and spot sales.

---

### BOX 17.1. SPACE AND TIME

First, some definitions: In radio–TV sales, an **availability** (or avail) is a place for a commercial. **Inventory** is the total number of such places in a program, or a daypart, or a week, or some other time period. Second, a lesson in the basic physics of advertising media: **space** is expandable; **time** is not. When a print medium—a newspaper, for example—wishes to sell more advertising, it expands space by adding more pages. For most electronic mass media, however, there is no equivalent to adding more pages. An electronic medium, say a TV station, cannot add more time. Its inventory is therefore finite and, once depleted, there is nothing more to sell. Most outlets set their **sell-out rate**, the point at which they consider their inventory depleted, at about 85% of total avails sold. They use the other 15% for purposes such as promotion of their own programming, make-goods (*PRT*, 9.1.6.4), and public service announcements.

---

## 17.2.2 Television Station Rate Cards

Compared with radio, TV stations charge more for avails and tend to price more by time of day. This results from TV's higher audience levels and the greater fluctuation of those levels from program to program. TV rate cards typically list specific commercial slots—dayparts and programs—each with its own price for avails. They have no ROS rate but may offer rotations (*PRT*, 9.1.2.4). Most stations use one card for both local and spot sales.

The 30-second avail is standard in broadcast TV. A 60-second avail often costs double the 30-second rate; an ID (10-second avail) costs 50%. Advertisers can buy program positions (e.g., a half-hour block) at vastly discounted rates.

Television rate cards list prices in a **grid** pattern. The list of commercial slots forms one axis of the grid; grid positions form the other axis. Dollar amounts fill the grid field, and the number of grid positions determines the number of prices for each commercial slot. With this arrangement, each slot often has five or six prices, in decreasing amounts down the grid.

TV stations usually let their rates "float" according to supply and demand. As inventory for a time period is sold, rates go up; the more positions sold, the higher the price for those remaining. Some stations use the grid to adjust rates. For any given quarter,[2] the sales manager designates a grid position for each commercial slot as the price for avails in that slot. As advertisers place orders for avails in an upcoming quarter, the sales manager periodically designates higher grid positions for that quarter. Avails in high-demand slots cost most and get the greatest number of upward grid adjustments. Avails in low-demand slots cost the least; their cost rarely moves up.

Larger, more successful stations may opt for the ultimate in rate flexibility and choose not to issue a printed rate card. Instead, they keep a "virtual" rate card on a computer program. As rates change, they issue printouts to their sales staff.

### 17.2.3 Cable System Rate Cards

As discussed in *PRT,* 17.3.2, cable systems often sell on the basis of "TV advertising at radio prices." The cable system rate card (Fig. 17.4) may even undercut some radio stations. In cable the 30-second avail is standard, and price variables may include ROS, BTA, TAP, and fixed position.

A cable system's card typically resembles a radio grid card. The card lays out prices in rows and columns—rows correspond to grid positions, columns to dayparts. Neighboring cable systems often affiliate with an **interconnect,** a cooperative venture that allows an advertiser to place messages on multiple systems with one transaction. An interconnect's rate card may list differential pricing for the interconnect and for various combinations of systems on the interconnect.

Cable sales dayparts may not parallel those of broadcasters. One scheme, for example, divides cable avails into four overlapping dayparts (in ascending order of cost): 6:00 a.m. to noon, noon to midnight, 3:00 p.m. to midnight, and 6:00 p.m. to midnight.

Unlike broadcast TV and radio, cable sales staffers deal in multiple channels. These include ad-supported local origination channels, automated channels, classified-ad channels, and local windows on national cable networks. Clients can buy avails in one or any combination, but grid position may vary by channel.

### 17.2.4 Off The Card

Advertising agency and independent media buyers routinely attempt to buy time at prices below those on the rate card. Some stations may, indeed, sell **off the card,** below their published rates. The stimulus may come from several factors—how much the station needs the business, how much management wants that particular account, or how much total money is involved. Sometimes station personnel suggest the lower price. If a station salesperson cannot sell a prospect at rate card prices and the station needs the money, the salesperson may offer the prospect a cut rate.

The simplest way to sell below published prices is to cut rates without publishing a new card. Other ways include plugola (*PRT,* 9.1.6.7) and payola (*PRT,* 9.1.6.9). Per-inquiry advertising (*PRT,* 9.1.6.5) and tradeout (*PRT,* 9.1.6.6) are potentially rate-cutting transactions. In chapter 16, we looked at other practices, the result of which is to cut rates, for example, airing commercial promotions as news.

### 17.2.5 Network Rate Cards

TV broadcast networks usually make public just their program rates. They reveal prices for avails within network programs only on request from bona fide media buyers. Radio networks list charges for 1-minute and 30-second avails and, where applicable, time-of-day and quantity discounts.

C A B L E
I N T E R C O N N E C T
*Gainesville/Ocala*

# ADVERTISING INFORMATION

**Cable Rep Advertising**

## SUBSCRIBERS

| | |
|---|---|
| Interconnect | 73,500 |
| Zone 1 (Gainesville) | 46,500 |
| Zone 2 (Ocala) | 27,000 |

## HOMES PAST PENETRATION

| | |
|---|---|
| Interconnect | 77% |
| Zone 1 (Gainesville) | 76% |
| Zone 2 (Ocala) | 79% |

## Commercial :30
## Interconnect Rate Card #10

| GRID | 6a - 12a | 12p - 12a | 3p - 12a | 6p - 12a |
|---|---|---|---|---|
| I | 40 | 50 | 62 | 93 |
| II | 34 | 42 | 53 | 79 |
| III | 29 | 36 | 45 | 67 |
| IV | 24 | 30 | 38 | 57 |
| V | 20 | 26 | 32 | 48 |
| VI | 17 | 22 | 27 | 41 |

- :60's at 1.75 x :30 rate
- All daypart placement in best times available
- Agency discount to licensed agencies
- Lower grids preemptable
- Grids may vary by network
- Fixed programing available

Zone 1 Only (Gainesville) 65% Of Interconnect Rate
Zone 2 Only (Ocala) 45% Of Interconnect Rate

## NETWORKS AVAILABLE

FIG. 17.4. **Cable system rate card.** (Courtesy of Cable Rep Advertising. Used by permission.)

### 17.3 LOCAL TIME SALES IN ELECTRONIC MASS MEDIA

At the local level, stations and cable systems must sell themselves to merchants, businesses, and advertising agencies in their communities. This is the job of the sales staff.

Broadcast sales staff are usually an integral part of their stations. Some cable systems, however, contract with other firms that specialize in selling local cable advertising. In the following section, the discussion focuses on in-house sales staffs, although most points also apply to contract sales units.

#### 17.3.1 Sales Staff

The **sales manager** is a key figure in radio and TV. The sales manager answers directly to the general manager, supervises the local sales staff, and maintains liaison with the rep firm, the station's national sales representative. The sales manager may also oversee the traffic department. In larger operations a general sales manager may head the department, supervising a local sales manager (in charge of local sales people), a national sales manager (keeps in contact with the rep), a sales support staff (assembles information to augment sales efforts), and the traffic department.

Media outlet sales personnel, called **account executives,** attempt to convince business people in the community to buy advertising time. Before they buy, advertisers are **prospects**; afterward, **clients.** Account executives usually sell avails, but occasionally they sell sponsorships of a program.

The sales manager holds a staff meeting at least once a week, often daily. In these meetings the sales manager points out new prospects, listens to problems and suggests solutions, explains policy and procedures, discusses competitive position, and encourages sales effort. The sales manager also works with individual account executives, even accompanying them on sales calls when more experience and ability to bargain is needed.

The station pays the sales manager a salary plus a percentage of total sales. Compensation arrangements for account executives vary: straight **commission** (percentage of individual sales), salary-plus-commission, and draw-plus-commission. In the latter arrangement, the account executive receives a regular salary called a **draw** but must sell a minimum dollar amount of advertising; any sales above that minimum earn a commission.

The sales manager assigns each account executive a **quota**. This quota is the minimum revenue the account executive must bring in. New account executives are assigned a client list but are expected to expand the list, adding new clients or persuading old ones to buy more advertising.

#### 17.3.2 Tools For Selling

A good account executive makes maximum use of available tools and resources. One tool is the **rate card.** The account executive must know the rates forward and backward and be ready to suggest a schedule that meets client needs and budget.

A second tool is **audience ratings.** The account executive has to understand ratings thoroughly. Only one outlet in town can have the largest audience, but others may have the largest audience at certain key times, or the largest number of women 18 to 34 years old, or the largest African American audience, or some other salable feature. The account executive must know this information to show the prospect how the outlet is a must-buy for reaching potential customers or a more efficient buy than competing outlets.

Where ratings are concerned, cable system account executives usually operate at a disadvantage. Broadcast-style rating methodologies do not work well for cable. Cable account executives can sometimes finesse the lack of audience data by offering prospects the chance to advertise on television at radio prices. They also emphasize the opportunity to target audiences precisely. A client's advertising circulates only to the franchise area, whereas local broadcast advertisers pay for waste circulation because station signals spill over to other towns. The client can also advertise in complementary programming contexts; a sporting goods store, for example, can buy local availabilities on the Outdoor Life Channel and ESPN.

A third tool is **knowledge of the outlet and the market.** The account executive must know information such as potential audience (signal coverage or cable penetration); production capabilities; who buys what, and where they shop for it; and strengths and weaknesses of rival media.

A fourth tool consists of internal **support resources.** The traffic department, for example, schedules client advertising. The outlet may provide personal computers with special software—from programs that suggest advertising schedules to online research services that provide custom-tailored analyses of audience lifestyle and purchasing patterns. In larger outlets, sales-support staffers draw on computer sources, brochures about the outlet, and other promotional material to prepare information packets customized for individual prospects. Account executives use these packets in their sales presentations.

A fifth tool is the help of **advertising media trade organizations**—Cabletelevision Advertising Bureau, Radio Advertising Bureau, and Television Bureau of Advertising. They supply member outlets with direct sales aids—sales ideas, case histories, examples of effective commercials, and statistics on the dimensions of their respective media. They conduct seminars to improve skills of local sales personnel. They work with major advertisers and agencies, selling them on their respective media.

### 17.3.3 Art of Local Sales

One of the most creative jobs in radio and television is sales. It is an art. An account executive whose concept of sales is to wander into a prospect's business and ask, "Wanna buy some time today?" is rarely successful. A good account executive sells not time but (a) **radio or television advertising** (b) on **a particular outlet.**

The account executive must match the outlet's capabilities and resources to the prospect's advertising needs, then demonstrate that match to the prospect.

### 17.3.3.1 Local Sales as an Educational Process.

The account executive often has to start from scratch, educating the retailer on the value—perhaps even the existence—of local radio or TV advertising. If the retailer has advertised at all, it has probably been in the newspaper. Newspaper advertising is tangible. The retailer can admire the proofs or tear sheets and post copies all over the establishment. Radio and TV advertising is ephemeral. It has nothing the retailer can hold. The account executive must expand the retailer's view of advertising and **educate the retailer away from any print-only, tangible-copy orientation.**

Even the best sales job rarely persuades a prospect to increase the ad budget to include radio or TV. More often, the successful account executive convinces the retailer to **divert part of the advertising budget from some other medium**—usually newspaper—and put it into the station or cable system.

The educational process must often include **how to use broadcast advertising.** For example, Thursday newspapers usually contain supermarket advertising. Each ad lists dozens of items and prices. A reader can browse the newspaper to see which store has the best prices. Some supermarket managers expect radio and TV advertising to do the same thing as newspapers. These managers want direct conversion of their newspaper ads to electronic media—lists of products and prices. Consumers cannot browse commercials, and so such "list" commercials are largely ineffective. The account executive has to convince the manager to use commercials to advertise a few items or some distinctive feature—a special sale, the freshness of the store's produce or the fine quality of its meat, or the convenience of shopping at the store.

### 17.3.3.2 Local Sales Presentation.

The account executive's formal proposal to a prospect is the **presentation.** Considerable preparation goes into this presentation. Before beginning to assemble the presentation, the account executive visits and gets to know the prospect. Account executive and prospect discuss marketing and advertising aims and problems, but no attempt is made to sell time. The account executive researches the prospect's business—notes best-selling lines and features, observes customer types, and tracks sales and advertising patterns. Using this research and the various selling tools, the account executive puts together a package of plans and materials to show how advertising on the station or cable system would help achieve goals and reach consumers. This is the presentation.

The presentation often takes the form of a booklet. It may contain suggestions of how and when to advertise on the outlet, recommendations on how to tie that advertising with other advertising (even suggesting additional advertising on other radio or TV outlets or in other media), cost breakdowns, sample scripts, success stories of similar businesses that have used the outlet, and standard promotional material adapted to fit the particular prospect (e.g., coverage maps and ratings data showing how the outlet reaches the prospect's customers). The account executive talks through the booklet with the prospect. Accompanying materials may include a tape or a storyboard of a commercial done on **spec** (speculation, hoping to get the sale).

*17.3.3.3 Local Sales And Local Service.*    The sale will probably not be closed at this point. The account executive may have to return several times, revise the plan, bring the sales manager along on a call, even bring the prospect to the studio for a tour and red-carpet treatment. Nor does the sales job end when the contract is signed. The account executive oversees the medium's in-house handling of the client's advertising and periodically checks back with the client to improve the schedule and ensure satisfaction. This sale plus follow through is **servicing the account.** A radio or television account executive sells a service; clients who get that service tend to remain clients.

### 17.3.4 Tradeout and Barter as Local Sales

If based on rate card and retail prices, tradeout and barter (*PRT,* 9.1.6.6) are perfectly ethical. Some firms specialize in barter on a national basis; they offer anything—automobiles, furniture, vacations—in return for which they put the outlet's availabilities into their time bank (*PRT,* 7.3.2.1). Too much barter and tradeout cause cash flow problems, and employees and creditors prefer to receive payment in legal tender rather than movie tickets, car washes, and McDonald's coupons.

### 17.3.5 Impact of Barter Syndication on Local Sales

Barter syndicators make money from ad sales. They give programming to local outlets; they may even pay large-market outlets to carry their programs. Barter programming sounds like a good deal, but there are drawbacks. It **reduces salable inventory.** Also, both barter syndication and time banking contracts may specify that the **outlet owes the full amount of commercial time, whether or not the programming is used.** Cancellation of a barter series could result in many "free" spots. Additionally, TV licensees and their reps have expressed concern over the **effect of barter syndication on national spot advertising revenue.** As a national ad vehicle, barter yields the same result as network and national spot—national ads run on local stations. So when a national advertiser invests in barter, where does the money come from? Barter syndicators say it comes from money that would otherwise go to the networks. Reps and some station executives contend that barter takes money away from spot advertising budgets.

### 17.3.6 Per Inquiry Advertising as Local Sales

Per inquiry (PI; *PRT,* 9.1.6.5) can be an excellent revenue producer. Some PI advertisers, for example, give a TV station or a cable channel standing orders for all unsold inventory. The station or channel then runs the ad for record albums or kitchen goods or whatever in any availability not otherwise purchased. The revenue earned by the station may even exceed the comparable rate-card cost for the time.

### 17.3.7 Time Brokering and Leased Access as Local Sales

In **time brokering,** the outlet sells large blocks of time to a third party, the broker, at discounted rates. The broker then sells segments of the time to advertisers at higher rates and pockets the difference. The outlet runs the ads. The broker is usually an independent contractor, not a station staffer. A radio broker may even program the brokered time. A broadcast licensee, however, is responsible for everything transmitted and so should monitor and maintain control of the programming.

Many of the TV local marketing agreements of the early 1990s (*PRT,* 3.6.1) involved time brokering. Pittsburgh's WPGH-TV, for example, contracted to program another Pittsburgh station, WPTT-TV, 13 hours a day and sell all the commercial positions. WPGH-TV's control extended even to design of WPTT-TV's logo.[3]

Federal law actually mandates that cable systems be open to a form of time brokering. As discussed in *PRT,* 14.1.1.8, most cable systems must provide leased access, channel capacity that others may lease. The lessee then may program the channel, sell time on it, or whatever.

### 17.4 NATIONAL AND REGIONAL TIME SALES IN ELECTRONIC MASS MEDIA OUTLETS

In spot advertising, the advertiser "spots" ads on specific markets, media outlets, programs, and time periods that deliver the desired audience. National and regional spot advertising account for more than 20% of all radio station revenue and more than 50% of all TV station revenue.

### 17.4.1 Advertising Representatives

This brings up the question of how a local outlet gets spot business. Ideally the outlet would hire someone just to sell time to advertisers and agencies. That would be impossible. First, spot advertisers would be inundated with thousands of account executives, each working for a different outlet. Second, spot advertisers and their agencies are spread among nearly every large city in the country. A radio or TV outlet would have to keep a full-time account executive in New York, another in Los Angeles, a third in Chicago, and so on. This would be fiscally absurd for all but the largest group-owned stations and cable MSOs. Instead, outlets contract with a type of firm already mentioned several times in this chapter, the **advertising representative—the "rep"** for short.

Reps are independent firms that attempt to persuade spot advertisers to buy time on client outlets (Fig. 17.5). Reps must be able to provide advertisers with immediate and current information on rates and availabilities. Each rep has branch offices in various major advertising centers and represents many outlets. National reps have offices in at least three of the largest markets; regional reps, fewer. The national trade organization for broadcast reps is the **Station Representatives Association.**

Reps work on a commission basis. Reps for radio and most cable systems receive 15% of the advertising revenues they generate. Television station reps receive anywhere from 8% or 9% to 15%, the percentage decreasing as station market size increases. Some reps supply additional services to client stations, providing advice, research, and materials on everything from sales and promotion to management and programming.

In *PRT,* 17.3.1, we mentioned that the station maintains contact with the rep. The sales manager or national sales manager communicates continually with the

FIG. 17.5. National and regional electronic mass media rep firms.

rep, advising on avails, sending copies of station promotional material, notifying of changes in rates and programming, and ensuring that the rep is representing the outlet to national and regional advertisers.

### 17.4.2 Trends in Representation

Three developments in broadcast station representation should be noted. One is the **house rep** or **self-representation**. Here, a group licensee sets up a national sales department at the corporate level to represent stations in the group. A second development involves the **rep network**. The rep network is an unwired network (discussed in *PRT,* 17.4.3) organized by an advertising representative.

The third development involves **multistation representation**. Originally, broadcast reps handled only one station in any given market to avoid representing direct competitors. During the 1970s the number of stations per market increased dramatically. There was no commensurate increase in the number of reps; several rep companies restricted the number of stations on their client lists, merged, or went out of business. As a result, many radio stations found it difficult to get good representation. Radio reps eased the problem by representing several noncompeting (appealing to different target audiences) stations in one market. TV reps did somewhat the same. Typically, a TV rep formed two competing divisions, one that would represent network affiliates; the other, independent stations.

### 17.4.3 Unwired Networks as Regional and National Sales Vehicles

The **unwired network**, also called an **advertising network** or **spot network**, is not interconnected and carries no common programming. Instead, it consists of stations in various markets grouped together to attract regional or national advertising. In buying time on an unwired network, an advertiser can—with just one buy transaction—have commercials run in every market served by the network. The network takes a commission off the top of all revenue and pays the rest out to its stations.

Some unwired networks are run by firms that were organized specifically to go into the unwired network business. Some unwireds, however, were put together by rep firms. If organized by a rep, the unwired network may consist solely of the rep's client stations. Or, the rep may add nonclient stations, particularly in important markets where the rep has no clients.

The unwired network may be regional or national in scope. Some spot networks feature flexibility; spot radio networks organized on a state-by-state basis, for example, allow a regional advertiser to reach, say, just the Kansas agriculture market. Spot networks may cost less; when TV network and barter ad time gets scarce and expensive, some national advertisers try to negotiate with unwired TV networks for better prices.

Just as reps do not like barter syndication, they do not like most unwired networks for about the same reason: They figure that ad dollars invested in unwired networks would otherwise have gone to spot advertising on individual stations. Reps do like, however, the unwired networks they organize themselves, the so-called **rep networks.**

### 17.4.4 Cable Interconnects

An interconnect ties together cable systems in contiguous or nearby franchise areas into a single advertising buy for regional and national advertisers. A cable rep handles sales for the interconnect on a commission basis. A **hard interconnect** links systems by microwave, coaxial cable, or optical fiber. The interconnect downlinks advertiser-supported cable networks, inserts its commercials in the **local windows** (availabilities within network programming for use by affiliated systems), and distributes them to the interconnected systems. The systems receive compensation, free network-produced programming, a division of the interconnect's profits, or some combination thereof. A **soft interconnect** parallels an unwired network in broadcasting. There is no electronic interconnection. Instead, a cable sales office or rep has the power to sell availabilities on the whole group of systems or any one system.

## 17.5 SELLING NETWORK TIME

Network sales is more than simply local outlet sales writ large—much more. A major complication for networks involves their relation with their local affiliates. First, both networks and affiliates go after the national advertising dollar. This means that networks compete with their own affiliates. Second, networks need affiliates. A network without affiliates could reach no audience, could make no money, and would be no network. A local outlet can exist—even thrive—without network affiliation. Many broadcast stations do just that. Even cable systems, given the franchise monopoly most enjoyed in the past, could probably survive without advertising-supported networks.

Satellite or optical fiber technology can alter this relation. Networks could send programs directly to viewer homes (in which case they would no longer be networks). At this writing, however, the traditional network–affiliate relation is in place and still a major element in network sales.

### 17.5.1 Television Broadcast Network Sales

In TV broadcast network time sales, stakes are high and competition is fierce. Programming, overhead, and everything in TV networking is expensive. Returns can more than justify the investment, so each broadcast network attempts to sell as close as possible to its sell-out rate.

Some advertisers still invest in sponsorship, usually sponsoring specials. Most broadcast network advertising, however, is done on a participation basis—the network provides the programs, and advertisers buy availabilities within those programs. Formal rate cards are rare. Prices are based roughly on ratings, season of the year, and time of day.

Network inventory is sold in two ways—up front and scatter. Each spring the networks announce their program schedules for the following fall. Heavy network advertisers wish to reserve the best availabilities, so right away their ad agencies bargain with network sales staff. This is **up-front** buying. The agency buys specific commercial positions in specific weekly program series.

The **scatter** market begins when up-front buying ends. Here the buyer purchases any combination of avails from remaining network inventory—perhaps a continuing position in a weekly series for several months, or a number of positions scattered over the entire schedule for a week or two. As air dates draw closer, the networks drop prices of unsold positions, and agency buyers can often pick up good positions at bargain prices.

### 17.5.2 Radio Broadcast Network Sales

The purchase of radio network time is less frantic, less expensive, and more flexible than that of television. There are no "new seasons" in radio networks. Nonetheless, broadcast radio networks usually introduce major programming changes in the fall, and advertising purchasing patterns do somewhat parallel those of network TV, complete with an up-front buying season.

In radio, most availabilities are in news, sports, features, commentary, or, in some newer networks, music. The buyer can buy sponsorship or participation advertising, fixed position, or run of schedule. Prices vary by time of day, number of affiliates, size and type of audience, and other factors. Broadcast network radio is difficult to sell to new clients; most agency buyers prefer to invest in television broadcast networks to reach large numbers of persons and in spot radio to reach specific audiences.

### 17.5.3 Sales in Satellite-Delivered Advertising-Supported Program Services

Often called cable networks or basic services, the satellite-delivered advertising-supported services provide programming for cable systems and other multichannel competitors of broadcast TV. These services make major programming changes in the fall. As multichannel media have garnered increasing shares of audience and available advertising revenue, they have relied less on shows recycled from the broadcast networks and more on original programming. These changes fostered time-buying patterns that parallel those of the broadcast networks. This has been especially true of services that schedule broad-appeal programming and compete head-on with the broadcast networks for audience, such as USA Network, Lifetime, TNT, and Family Channel. However, even narrow-appeal services follow these buying patterns. Ad agency media buyers buy them in an up-front purchasing season, and these services have adjusted their sales and programming to accommodate.

### 17.5.4 Compensation: Sharing Network Sales Revenues

Broadcast stations expect to be paid when they **give up time to network programming that contains advertising**. After all, they earn their money from the sale of time. Broadcast networks, therefore, share advertising revenue with affiliated stations. An affiliate's share is **compensation,** the amount based on the affiliate's network hourly rate. That rate, determined by negotiation between station and network, is based on factors such as size of the station's market and the affiliate's competitive position within the market. The station gets a percentage of the rate (say, 30%–32% for the 6 p.m.–11:00 p.m. period), the percentage varying by daypart. The affiliation contract specifies both rate and percentages. An affiliate sends to the network a monthly listing of each network program and commercial carried; the network pays the affiliate based on this report. During the late 1980s, ABC, CBS, and NBC tried to reduce compensation payments as a means to cut network expenses. Fox pays compensation. When UPN and the WB launched in 1995, the former operated primarily on a barter arrangement; affiliates of the latter actually paid to carry network programs.[4]

Radio compensation involves much less money than television. Broadcast radio networks pay monetary compensation to large- and medium-market affiliates. In smaller markets, the **compensation may be the programming itself and local windows** in which the station may sell advertising—in other words, barter.

Most satellite-delivered advertising-supported program services charge their affiliates. A cable operator, for example, typically pays 15 to 25 cents a subscriber a month to carry one of these services. This might seem unfair, but keep in mind that cable systems earn most money from subscriber fees. The operator touts to prospective subscribers the number and variety of channels on the system. Thus, advertising-supported cable networks do not deprive a cable operator of revenue-producing time; instead they **contribute to the revenue-producing value of the system**. Additionally, the cable networks carry local-window availabilities that affiliates may sell to advertisers.

The pattern does vary. Some religious services come free to the operator. Home shopping channels pay a percentage of all sales made in the operator's franchise area. A few ad-supported networks pay their affiliates—for example, a one-time incentive stipend to a system when it first signs on. Cable networks that make affiliate payments often avoid the term *compensation*, instead using *support package, incentive*, or *bonus package* and tying it to promotional and satellite reception expenses.

### NOTES

1. Edwin Emery, Phillip H. Ault, and Warren K. Agee, *Introduction to Mass Communications* (New York: Dodd, 1965) 163–164.

2. In business, a quarter is a 3-month period used for fiscal planning, accounting, and reporting purposes: first quarter = January–March; second quarter = April–June; third quarter = July–September; fourth quarter = October–December.

3. Geoffrey Foisie, "Independents Network for Survival," *Broadcasting & Cable* 1 March 1993: 11.

4. Joe Flint, "WB Backs off after Paramount Successes," *Broadcasting & Cable* 15 November 1993: 10; David Tobenkin, "New Players Get Ready to Roll, *Broadcasting & Cable* 2 January 1995: 33.

## FURTHER READING

Bovée, Courtland L., and William F. Arens. *Contemporary Advertising.* 4th ed. Homewood, IL: Irwin, 1992.

Bovée, Courtland L., et al. *Advertising Excellence.* New York: McGraw-Hill, 1995.

Eastman, Susan Tyler, and Robert A. Klein, Eds. *Promotion and Marketing for Broadcasting and Cable.* 2nd ed. Prospect Heights, IL: Waveland, 1991.

Eicoff, Alvin. *Direct Marketing Through Broadcast Media: TV, Radio, Cable, Infomercial, Home Shopping, and More.* Lincolnwood, IL: NTC Business Books, 1995.

Ford, Bianca, and James Ford. *Television and Sponsorship.* Boston: Butterworth, 1993.

Keith, Michael C. *Selling Radio Direct.* Newton, MA: Focal, 1992.

Kern-Foxworth, Marilyn. *Aunt Jemima, Uncle Ben, and Rastus: Blacks in Advertising, Yesterday, Today, and Tomorrow.* Westport, CT: Greenwood, 1994.

Warner, Charles, and Joseph Buchman. *Broadcast and Cable Selling.* Updated 2nd ed. Belmont, CA: Wadsworth, 1993.

White, Barton. *The New Ad Media Reality: Electronic Over Print.* Westport, CT: Quorum, 1993.

Zeigler, Sherilyn K., and Herbert H. Howard. *Broadcast Advertising: A Comprehensive Working Textbook.* 3rd ed. Ames: Iowa State University Press, 1991.

# 18

## AUDIENCE RESEARCH
## AND RATINGS

You may have heard someone say, "They're canceling my favorite television program! How can they do that? Everybody I know likes it!" Or, "My favorite radio station changed its music format! Why?"

More than likely, in both cases, the answer has something to do with ratings. A rating is an estimate of audience size—the approximate number who saw or heard a particular program segment. Ratings data are used to decide which programs or time segments are most popular and to determine how much clients will pay for advertising. Ratings numbers are also used in formulas, such as that used to calculate cost per thousand or CPM (PRT 17.1.7), which allow broadcasters and advertisers to compare one station's audience size and cost of commercials with another.

In this chapter we discuss both audience research and ratings. We first look at ratings terms, methods, and companies. Then we examine basic formulas that show how ratings data are actually used by stations, cable operators, and advertisers.

### 18.1 AUDIENCE RATINGS

Media managers need to know how many individuals are in the audience and who they are in order to make programming decisions, set commercial rates, and sell commercial time to advertisers. Advertisers need the same information to determine first, which outlet, network, or program has the audience they want, and later, whether they reach the size of audience for which they pay. Ratings data provide estimates of specific audiences. A programmer or advertiser can tell, for example, how many women, age 18 to 34 listened to each radio station in a market for each time segment of the day. Such information is provided by independent organizations—not connected with any radio or television medium, advertiser, or advertising agency. The two most prominent are Arbitron, specializing in radio ratings, and A. C. Nielsen, which provides television and cable ratings data.

### 18.1.1 Basic Concepts of Audience Survey Research

Audience research firms do not count the entire audience of a program or station. Such a count would be prohibitively time consuming and expensive, would not allow repeats of the count (so broadcasters and advertisers could see trends and changes), and is not even necessary to meet accepted standards of accuracy. Instead they use **statistical surveys**. In a statistical survey, the firm selects a relatively small group (or sample) of individuals and collects data on the group's **tuning activity** (listening or viewing). The firm then **projects** the results from the sample to the entire market population, reporting the group activity as an **estimate** of tuning for the entire audience.

One important task in the survey is to define **audience**. The audience is a collection of individuals, but individual whats? Whatever the answer, that is the **elementary unit,** the basic unit about which a statistical survey gathers information. In audience research, the elementary unit is often the **household.** All households within the survey area make up the **population.** Out of the population, the research firm randomly selects a **sample,** the households about whose members it hopes to collect audience tuning data. A. C. Nielsen and Arbitron samples, for the most part, include only those households with telephones. Once a household is selected and agrees to participate, listening and viewing data are collected from each member of the household.

### 18.1.2 Audience Survey Samples

Most people doubt whether a sample can represent the entire population of a city, region, or country, but it can. The sample, of course, must meet stringent requirements. The audience research firm must select the sample using a detailed procedure spelled out in advance and published along with the results. The sample must be a **probability sample,** also called a **random sample** because it is based on **random selection** procedures. In a random selection, each unit of the population must have an equal chance of being selected for the sample, and each unit in the sample must be selected strictly by chance. This means that when an audience research firm surveys your area, your home has as much chance of being selected for the sample as any other. Random samples are better than those selected nonrandomly for two reasons. First, they are more likely to be representative of the entire population and second, we are able to actually calculate an estimate of sampling error.

The size of the sample determines the accuracy of the survey; as sample size increases, so does accuracy. However, a law of diminishing returns governs sample size. As more units go into the sample, each addition contributes less accuracy. Eventually, an increase in accuracy of just one tenth of 1% requires the addition of hundreds of units. Research firms select a sample size that yields acceptably accurate results without being too large and prohibitively expensive. Sample size may range from several hundred for small markets to 3,000 to 4,000 or more for large markets.

The research firm reports tuning activity of household members by categories. They categorize primarily by sex and age and sometimes by race. As the sample is subdivided into categories, the number of sample persons in each category gets smaller. Smaller numbers reduce accuracy (*PRT,* 18.1.5).

With the sample intact, however, surprisingly few units are needed. For example, Nielsen uses a national metered sample of just 4,000 households to gauge the number of viewers nationwide that watch network television programs. You might think that the TV-owning household population of the entire United States would require a much larger sample, but it does not work that way. The size of a sample needed to achieve a certain statistical precision is about as adequate for a nation of more than 90 million households as for a city of 90,000 (Box 18.1).

One caution about the sample—no one person represents you. Many people object to ratings methodology because of the imagined effect of some little old man in Peoria who turns on the television set in his living room so *Matlock* and *Barnaby Jones* reruns can amuse the cat as he naps. This is a needless worry. This man's home, if selected for the Nielsen Television Index national sample, would be one of 4,000. It is the viewing activity of the sample as a whole that approximates the viewing activity of the population as a whole. On the other hand, the viewing activity of all persons in the sample who are male and 55 years or older does reflect to a high degree the viewing activity of all persons in the population who are male and 55 years or older. However, our little old man by himself does not represent all persons in Peoria or all persons 55 and older.

### 18.1.3 Audience Survey Markets

There are two distinct levels of broadcast and cable audience research surveys—national and local. A **national** survey yields data on audiences for network and syndicated programs. The population is all units in the continental United States, and the sample is drawn randomly from that population.

A survey in a **local market** yields data on audiences for local outlets and programs. Usually, a local market consists of an area's largest city and those surrounding counties in which that city's stations are most often heard and watched. The survey report, however, lists not only those in the market, but all stations or cable programs to which people listen or view. The population is all units within the market, and the sample is drawn accordingly.

The research firm's local report includes breakdowns for the entire market and the central urban area. Each research firm has different terminology and different concepts regarding what area makes up the market of any given locale (Box 18.2). However, most reports refer to the urban area that is the heart of the market as the **metro area.**

The metro area is normally the same as the metropolitan statistical area as defined by the U.S. Department of Commerce. For the more inclusive geographic concept—metro area plus surrounding counties—Nielsen has developed the concept of the **designated market area (DMA).** Any market whose stations

---

### BOX 18.1. HOW CAN A SAMPLE OF 1,000 REPRESENT A POPULATION?

Try this interesting experiment—hypothetically (unless you happen to have 100,000 beads handy). Imagine 100,000 beads in a washtub; 30,000 are red and 70,000 white. Mix thoroughly, then scoop out a sample of 1,000.

Even before counting, you know that all beads in your sample are not red, nor would you expect your sample to divide exactly at 300 red and 700 white. As a matter of fact, the mathematical odds are about 20 to 1 that the count of red beads will be between 270 and 330—or 27% and 33% of the sample. In short, you have now produced a "rating" of 30, plus or minus 3, with a 20-to-1 assurance of statistical reliability.

These basic sampling laws would not change even if you drew your sample of 1,000 from 95 million beads instead of 100,000—assuming that the 95 million beads had the same ratio of red to white. This is a simple demonstration of why a sample of 1,000 is about as adequate for a nation of 95 million households as for a city of 100,000. (*Source*: Nielsen Media Research. Used by permission.)

---

achieve the largest total percentage of the TV audience in a county is considered the home market for that county; Nielsen then assigns the county to that market's DMA. Nielsen assigns every county to one DMA; there is no overlap. DMAs were originally designed to delineate television markets, but advertisers and agencies now use them in dealing with other media. The parallel Arbitron delineation for DMA is the **area of dominant influence**.

---

## BOX 18.2. TERMINOLOGY FOR AUDIENCE SURVEY AREAS OF MEASUREMENT

### ARBITRON

- **Metro rating area**: The smallest area, based on standard Metropolitan Statistical Area (MSA) data provided by the federal government.
- **Area of dominant influence** (ADI): Includes counties where home stations receive a preponderance of viewing. *Preponderance* really means that home stations are the "most" watched in those counties. ADIs are mutually exclusive. Up to 3 adjacent ADIs are assigned to a market.
- **Total survey area**: The geographic area containing all counties necessary to account for 98% of the audience of home stations. TSAs overlap.

### NIELSEN

- **Metro area**: Same as Arbitron metro rating area.
- **Central area**: Same as the metro area, but assigned in unincorporated areas where no MSA data are available.
- **Designated market area** (DMA): Corresponds to Arbitron's ADI; is defined as all counties in which home stations receive substantial viewing. Like preponderance, *substantial* means the largest percentage of viewing is to home stations.
- **Nielsen Station Index** (NSI area): Corresponds to Arbitron's TSA except that the NSI accounts for 95% of the audience.
- **Station total area**: Measured during sweeps, accounts for 100% of home station's audience.

---

Nielsen utilizes meters to constantly survey the 30 largest markets. However, during the months of February, May, July, and November, they conduct diary surveys in all markets, small and large, during the same time period. This is called a **sweep.** Results from the sweeps not only tell individual stations in a market how they are doing, they also allow a network to gauge its own general effectiveness and that of its affiliates. Arbitron also conducts winter, spring, summer, and fall surveys for radio markets. Smaller markets may be surveyed only once a year, but many large to midsized markets are surveyed almost continually.

### 18.1.4 Ratings and Shares

A research firm reports the results of its audience survey as ratings and shares. For illustration purposes, assume that a firm conducts a television audience survey in a market of **100,000 households, using a random sample of 1,000 house-**

**holds.** The research firm uses the household as the elementary unit and reports results as the number of households tuned to the market's stations. As you follow this illustration, refer to Fig. 18.1.

***18.1.4.1 Program Ratings.*** Let us look at a specific time—say, 8:30 to 9:00 p.m. one Wednesday during the survey. The firm's analysis of the data shows the following:

- 198 sample homes tuned to WAAA, channel 2.
- 213 to WBBB, channel 5.
- 227 to WCCC, channel 8.
- 154 to WDDD, channel 37.
- 108 to all other channels.

The **rating** for each station is the **percentage of sample households tuned to the station.** Remember, there are 1,000 households in our imaginary sample. Therefore, for WAAA, the rating is calculated as follows: 198 ÷ 1,000 = 0.198. This tells us that WAAA has a rating of 19.8. If we want to project the rating to the entire population, we calculate 19.8% of 100,000. Because 100,000 × .198 = 19,800 we estimate that there were 19,800 households tuned to WAAA from 8:30 to 9:00 p.m. Calculations show the rating for WBBB is 21.3; WCCC, 22.7; and WDDD, 15.4.

***18.1.4.2 HUT and Share.*** Note that television receivers were operating in a total of **900 sample homes** (198 + 213 + 227 + 154 + 108 = 900) in our imaginary survey.[1] In the other 100, the residents were not at home or not watching. These 900 homes, expressed as a percentage of the total sample, make

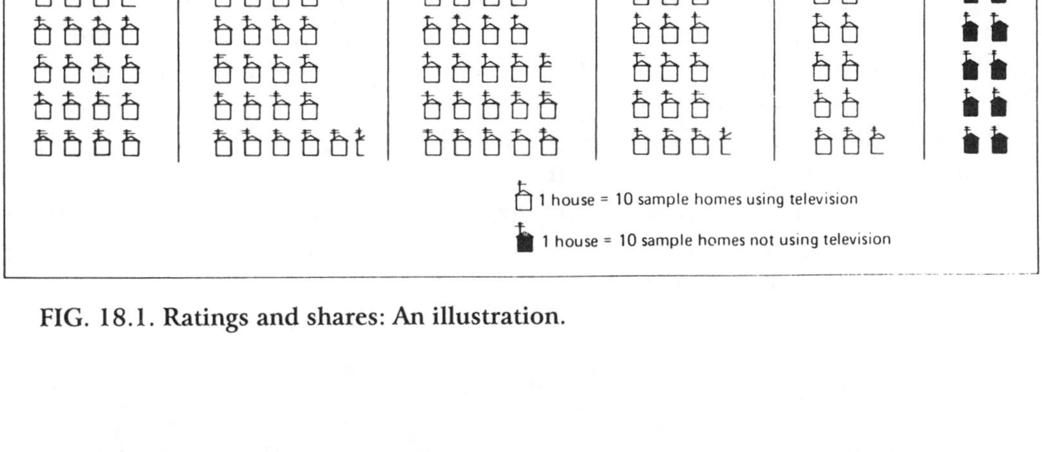

| Random sample – 1000 Homes – Basis for rating | | | | | |
|---|---|---|---|---|---|
| 1000 ÷ 900 = 90 HUT<br>Homes Using Television (HUT) – 900 Homes – Basis for audience share | | | | | Not using television or not at home – 100 Homes |
| 198÷900 = 22 Share<br>198÷1000 = 19.8<br>Rating<br><br>WAAA – 198 Homes | 213 ÷ 900 = 23.7 Share<br>213 ÷ 1000 = 21.3 Rating<br><br>WBBB – 213 Homes | 227 ÷ 900 = 25.2 Share<br>227 ÷ 1000 = 22.7 Rating<br><br>WCCC – 227 Homes | 154 ÷ 900 = 17.1 Share<br>154 ÷ 1000 = 15.4<br>Rating<br>WDDD – 154 Homes | All others –<br>108 Homes | |

1 house = 10 sample homes using television

1 house = 10 sample homes not using television

FIG. 18.1. Ratings and shares: An illustration.

up **households using television (HUT).** In our example, HUT is calculated as $900 \div 1,000 = 0.90$. This gives us a 90 HUT rating.

A station's **share** (or share of the audience) is **the percentage of the audience (all households in the sample actually using television) tuned to that station.** WAAA's share would be $198 \div 900 = 0.22$—a 22 share.

It is important to understand the relation between ratings and shares. It would be extremely unlikely, but a station could actually have a rating of 1 and a share of 100, if the 1% watching that station were the only ones with their sets turned on. In this case the HUT would also be 1. You should see that **a station's share will always be higher than its rating.** This is true because a station's percentage of the viewing audience will always be more than its percentage of the total population. If, theoretically speaking, there was a time period when all households turned on their televisions so that HUT = 100, **all stations' ratings would be equal to their shares.**

### 18.1.4.3 Types of Ratings.

The WAAA example yielded **program ratings.** A research firm also reports longer range audience estimates—for example, 1 week of a radio station's morning drive time, or a television station's 6 p.m. newscast across a 4-week period.

We must determine what qualifies as listening or viewing (Box 18.3). By way of explanation, suppose a research firm includes you in its sample. The firm will count you in the audience of a station or program only if you "tune in" (listen to or view) that station or program for a minimum length of time. Traditionally, firms have specified at least 5 minutes in a 15-minute period. Even shorter time periods are now being used for television, especially for measurement of national audiences.

In determining a station's average rating, the firm counts you every time you are in the audience. In cumulative ratings, you are counted just once. Consider a radio station's morning drive time. Arbitron often breaks down calculations into 15-minute segments or quarter-hours. For an entire week, the morning drive daypart consists of 60 quarter-hours (3 hours = 12 quarter-hours × 5 weekdays = 60). For each of those 60 quarter-hours, the firm counts the total number of persons tuned to the station. Then it adds all those totals and divides by 60. The quotient (the result of the division) is, of course, an average. In this example, it is the station's **average quarter-hour rating** for morning drive time. How were you counted more than once? If you listened to the station every morning, Monday through Friday, 6:15 to 7:00 a.m., you were part of that station's audience for 3 quarter-hours all five mornings; therefore, you were counted 15 times.

The **cumulative rating** or **cume,** on the other hand, is not an average. **Cume is the total unduplicated audience.** In our example, to obtain the cume audience the research firm would count you once, because you were listening from 6:15 to 7:00, but would never count you again, even though you were tuned in for two additional quarter-hours each morning.

---

### BOX 18.3. QUICK GUIDE TO RATINGS TERMS

- **Rating**: Percentage of all households tuned to your program (or) percentage of all potential listeners tuned to your station.
- **Homes using TV** (HUT): Percentage of households with sets turned on.
- **Persons using radio** (PUR): Percentage of persons with radios on.
- **Share**: Of TV households with sets on, the percentage tuned to your station.
- **Average quarter-hour persons** or **average persons (AQH)**: The average number of persons listening during a specified quarter-hour.
- **Cume**: The number of different persons listening during a time period. Also called circulation, reach, and unduplicated audience.
- **Exclusive cume (Exclusives)**: Number of different people who listened only to your station.
- **Average quarter-hour rating (AQHR)**: Percentage of all persons listening during a specified period. AQHR is usually broken down into demographic groups.
- **Cume rating**: Percentage of total population or demographic subgroup that listened during a specified time period.
- **Gross impressions**: Total number of persons, but not different persons, who were listening during a particular client's spot schedule.
- **Gross ratings points**: The total number of ratings points achieved during a particular client's spot schedule.
- **Cost per thousand (CPM)**: How much it will cost a client (advertiser) to reach 1,000 persons (but not different persons) on your station in a given time period.
- **Reverse cost per thousand**: How much a competing station in your market would have to charge to reach 1,000 persons as cost effectively as your station. Or, how much you would have to charge to be as cost effective as your competitors.
- **Cost per rating point**: How much it cost an advertiser to reach 1% of all potential listeners in your market on your station.
- **Target audience efficiency (TAE)**: The percentage of your total audience composed of your target audience.
- **Turnover**: A quantitative indication of the extent to which people tune in and out of your station.
- **Horizontal maintenance**: The ability of your station to hold an audience; shows percentage of people listening during the week who also listen in a particular daypart.
- **Frequency**: The average number of times a typical listener to your station will hear a client's commercial message.

---

Advertising sales personnel often refer to reach and circulation. By **reach,** they mean the cumulative audience for a program series, whereas **circulation** is the cume of a station or a network. Both reach and circulation show the number of households or individuals estimated to be in the audience at least once over a length of time.

### 18.1.5 Projection and Sampling Error

Although based on a sample, ratings purport to describe viewing behavior of the population. The ratings data, therefore, are **statistical estimates,** not exact percentages. If we were to conduct an actual **census** and measure viewing behavior of every household in the population, our data would differ somewhat from that of a sample of the population. This difference is called **sampling error,** a problem that is inherent in the process of sampling.

An audience research firm that uses a random sampling method and follows correct procedures in planning and executing a survey can calculate an estimate of the sampling error. This estimate is reported in the confidence level. The **confidence level** expresses the degree of probability that the sampling error falls within a certain range. For example, in our survey with a sample of 1,000 we may say that the probability is 95% (or 19 chances out of 20) that WAAA's 19.8 rating is in error by no more than ±2.6 (plus or minus 2.6%). Or stated another way, odds are 20 to 1 that the actual percentage of the TV household population watching WAAA at 8:30 to 9:00 Thursday evening is somewhere in the range of 17.2 to 22.4 (19.8 − 2.6 = 17.2; 19.8 + 2.6 = 22.4). To be 95% certain is very good. Unfortunately, because we are measuring viewing behavior utilizing a sample, we are never totally sure that our findings accurately represent the population. Even if we are 95% certain, there is a 5% possibility that the ratings obtained were completely wrong due to sampling error or chance.

These same limitations apply when projecting the rating into numbers of units. As we saw in *PRT,* 18.1.4.1, when we multiply our imaginary rating times the population (0.198 × 100,000) we obtain an estimated audience of 19,800 households. We can say there is a 95% probability that 19,800—give or take as much as 2,600—of the market's TV households tuned to WAAA.

When social scientists conduct survey research, they often use the 95% figure. **Ratings firms generally calculate to a lesser confidence level,** say 68%. This lowers the stated sampling error but because we are only 68% certain, the chance that actual error exceeds the stated error is greater.

The range of possible error also varies with the size of both the audience (the rating) and the sample. Because ratings reports break the sample down into demographic categories, **the range of error for ratings in each category is greater than that for the entire sample.** If, for example, working women 18 years and older represent only 200 persons out of a sample of 1,000, those 200 persons, in effect, become a separate sample. The ratings report shows what percentage of those 200 working women tuned to each station. Because 200 is a significantly smaller sample than 1,000, ratings for working women contain a greater margin of error than those for the entire sample.

A careful look at a Nielsen ratings report reveals that for each demographic category, Nielsen reports the **minimum rating needed to achieve a 25% or a**

**50% error range.** The range of error is much larger—most likely 50%—for a program that receives a rating of 2 than for one receiving a 22. This is because such a small number of households in the sample—only 2%—reported viewing this program. Fifty percent may seem terribly high, but consider that an error range of 50% on a rating of 2 means that the real rating is probably between 1 and 3. However, a 50% error range on a rating of 22 would create a range so large (11–33) that it would render the rating estimate virtually meaningless.

### 18.1.6 Data Gathering

Research companies use several methods to gather tuning activity data from the sample. Some of the primary methods include the personal interview, the telephone interview, the diary, the tuning meter, and the people meter.

#### 18.1.6.1 Personal Interview.
In the personal interview, an interviewer goes to the sample home and questions individuals on listening or viewing within the past 24 hours. This is the **recall method,** and the interviewer often uses a **roster** (list) of outlets and programs to help respondents' memory. Personal interviews can yield detailed information, including data on out-of-home viewing and listening and opinions on programming. On the other hand, respondents may not remember accurately, or they may inadvertently report listening or viewing for the past several days as though it occurred the preceding day. The roster may bias the data in favor of listed outlets. A small percentage of audience behavior is measured through personal interviews.

#### 18.1.6.2 Telephone Interview.
Telephone surveys usually take one of two forms, recall or coincidental. In **telephone recall** the interviewer asks what listening or viewing the respondent has done within a specified previous time period, often that day plus the previous evening. In a **telephone coincidental** survey the interviewer asks what the respondent is viewing or listening to at the time of (coincidental with) the telephone call. The interviewer might also ask how many persons are listening or viewing. The coincidental method can be quite reliable because the respondent does not have to remember which station was viewed or listened to during a given time period.

Telephone surveys are fast and—compared to personal interviews—inexpensive. Most research firms now use **computer-assisted telephone interviewing,** usually called **CATI.** The interviewer reads questions off a monitor and enters data directly into a computer, thus eliminating the need for paper questionnaires for every respondent and greatly reducing the burden of coding responses.

A telephone interview can yield detailed information, including likes and dislikes. The ratings firms use procedures to make sure that unlisted numbers and new listings not yet published are included in the sample. Still, telephone research presents a number of problems. For one thing, any telephone sample by definition excludes nontelephone homes, and many people with phones refuse to cooperate, suspicious that the interview is a sales pitch or even a prelude to crime. Telephone research also requires the use of a number of different interviewers who must be extensively trained and, of course, paid for their work.

Telephone recall is subject to the same memory problems as personal interview recall. Because telephone coincidental surveys measure only a given instant, they provide no basis for calculating the cumulative audience. Research firms must also restrict the hours of coincidental surveys because respondents might resent late-night and early-morning calls.

### 18.1.6.3 Household and Personal Diaries.

The diary method relies on self-administration by the respondent. Both Arbitron and Nielsen use the diary method extensively. Nielsen uses diaries to measure local television viewing in over 200 markets. Ratings diaries consist of an easy-to-fill-out log of viewing or listening activities. The research firm calls households selected for the sample and asks if household members would consent to participate. In television surveys, the firm sends one diary for each television receiver in the household. Instructions tell family members to write in the log when the receiver is turned on, to what channel and program it is tuned, and the sex and age of each person watching, including visitors.

In radio, the firm sends one diary for each person 12 years and older in the sample household. Individuals take the pocket-sized diaries (Fig. 18.2) with them and record time of listening, call letters or dial setting of the station, and whether they listen at home or elsewhere. They fill out age, sex, and address in the back of the diary.

The diaries usually request a record of 1 week's listening or viewing activities. The instructions ask that respondents, at week's end, put the prestamped and addressed diaries in the mail. Often the firm provides some small payment to encourage completion and return.

As with other methods, the diary has both advantages and disadvantages. It picks up data at all hours, provides information on audience composition, samples both urban and rural audiences, and is fast and economical. On the other hand, diary families may become self-conscious of tuning activity, listen or view more or less than normally, or choose programs they ordinarily would not select. Additionally, if respondents do not keep up the diaries as requested, they may end up recording a whole week's listening or viewing on the last day, resulting in omissions and errors.

### 18.1.6.4 Tuning Meter.

Nielsen uses tuning meters to collect television set tuning information automatically (Fig. 18.3). The tuning meter, which Nielsen calls a **Micro-Processor Home Unit,** monitors whether the receiver is on and, if so, to which channel it is tuned.

# You count in the radio ratings!

**No matter how much or how little you listen, you're important!**

You're one of the few people picked in your area to have the chance to tell radio stations what you listen to.

This is *your* ratings diary. Please make sure you fill it out yourself.

**Here's what we mean by "listening":**

"Listening" is any time you can hear a radio – whether you choose the station or not.

When you hear a radio between Thursday, February 16, and Wednesday, February 22, write it down – whether you're at home, in a car, at work or someplace else.

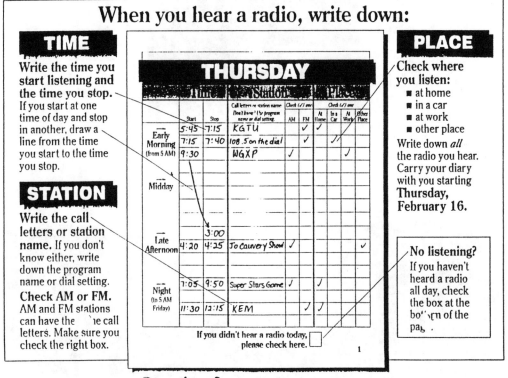

## When you hear a radio, write down:

**TIME**

Write the time you start listening and the time you stop.

If you start at one time of day and stop in another, draw a line from the time you start to the time you stop.

**STATION**

Write the call letters or station name. If you don't know either, write down the program name or dial setting.

**Check AM or FM.** AM and FM stations can have the ̄ ̄e call letters. Make sure you check the right box.

**PLACE**

Check where you listen:
- at home
- in a car
- at work
- other place

Write down *all* the radio you hear. Carry your diary with you starting **Thursday, February 16.**

**No listening?** If you haven't heard a radio all day, check the box at the bo'' ̄ ̄n of the pa ̄ ̄.

### THURSDAY

| | Time | | Station | Place | | | | | |
|---|---|---|---|---|---|---|---|---|---|
| | | | Call letters or station name<br>Don't know? Use program<br>name or dial setting | Check (✓) one | | Check (✓) one | | | |
| | Start | Stop | | AM | FM | At Home | In a Car | At Work | Other Place |
| Early Morning (from 5 AM) | 5:45 | 7:15 | KGTU | | ✓ | ✓ | | | |
| | 7:15 | 7:40 | 108.5 on the dial | ✓ | | ✓ | ✓ | | |
| | 9:30 | | WGXP | ✓ | | | | ✓ | |
| Midday | | | | | | | | | |
| Late Afternoon | | 3:00 | | | | | | | |
| | 4:20 | 4:25 | Jo Cauvery Show | ✓ | | | | | ✓ |
| Night (to 5 AM Friday) | 7:05 | 9:50 | Super Stars Game | ✓ | | ✓ | | | |
| | 11:30 | 12:15 | KEM | | ✓ | ✓ | | | |

If you didn't hear a radio today, please check here. ☐

1

**Questions?** Call us toll-free at 1-800-638-7091.

**FIG. 18.2. Sample diary page.** (Courtesy of The Arbitron Ratings Co. Used by permission.)

As with diary methodology, the audience research firm first contacts each household selected for the sample and asks for participation. If the household agrees, the firm sends personnel to install the meter. Metered samples consist of 300 to 500 households in each market. The tuning meter is connected to receivers, cable boxes, VCRs, and satellite dishes in the sample household and continuously monitors tuning. The data are easily downloaded into Nielsen's computers because each meter in the sample has its own telephone line.

For years, the standard time period for measurement has been 5 minutes. Audience members tuned to a program for fewer than 5 minutes were not counted in that program's ratings. Because remote controls have significantly increased

(a)

(b)

FIG. 18.3. Nielsen meters. The pictures show a 1949 example of (a) a Nielsen audimeter and more current versions of (b) Nielsen's tuning meter and (c) people meter. (Photographs courtesy of A. C. Nielsen Media Research. Used by permission.)

(c)

FIG. 18.3 (cont'd.)

the amount of channel switching (or surfing), Nielsen now collects meter measurements once every minute. Ratings numbers are reported as an average per minute. Therefore, a 30-minute program receiving an overnight metered rating of 18 actually had an **average rating of 18 for each of 30 minutes**.

Meter methodology yields quick results; subscribers may receive household ratings and shares as early as the morning after the program has run. These reports are **overnights**. Currently, over 30 markets are equipped with sufficient meters to provide overnight ratings.

The tuning meter method eliminates human error and forgetfulness. It is valuable in making analyses and tabulations of results. Because of the low expense, the meter remains in and collects data from a sample household longer than other methods; this reduces effects of hypoing (*PRT,* 7.7) and self-consciousness. The meter also has major limitations. It cannot collect demographic data, so it does not tell who was in the audience. Worse yet, it does not really know whether anyone was even watching the television.

***18.1.6.5 People Meter.*** Unlike the tuning meter, the Nielsen People Meter does collect demographic data and is designed to be operated only when someone is viewing. The people meter attempts to combine the best features of the diary and the tuning meter. It records who-watched information, feeds data by telephone lines, and allows overnight reporting. The meter accepts age, sex, and viewing information on individual household members and visitors. Viewers press buttons on a remote-control device to identify themselves and "log on" and "log off." The people meter has flashing lights to remind household members to activate and deactivate the meter. The meter stores the information, then transmits it when called by the research firm's computer.

During the mid-1980s, AGB Television Research, the U.S. subsidiary of a British firm, played a major role in forcing adoption of people meter technology. The concept was not new. Nielsen was interested as early as 1957 and began testing in 1978. Nonetheless, AGB caused a stir by announcing a large-scale field test of its people meter in Boston. AGB's ultimate goal was to develop a full-fledged national audience measurement service. Shortly after, both Arbitron and Nielsen also announced people meter field tests. All three companies launched regular people meter service in 1987.

Also in 1987, R. D. Percy & Co. started local people meter service in New York. The major advantage of Percy's system was that it was **passive**, meaning it did not require people to punch buttons or actively do anything. An infrared device counted the number of persons in the television room. AGB's service lasted only 1 year, and of the three major broadcast networks, only CBS had signed on. AGB's deficits mounted. Percy had cash flow problems. In 1988, AGB suspended its national rating service about the same time Percy gave up as well. Both left legacies, however—use of the people meter in audience research and exploration of "passive" people-counting devices.

People meters represented a major change in survey technology. They also triggered heated debate and criticism. Nielsen's national people meter sample, it seems, did not deal kindly with broadcast television. Compared to Nielsen's diary-based ratings and local market ratings, people meter reports showed lower HUT figures and lower broadcast network ratings. Network prime-time rating levels dropped 10%. The networks argued that flaws in the service caused at least part of the decline—the sample overrepresented pay-cable households, some demographic groups tended to use the meter more conscientiously than others, and many children did not use the meter properly.

The basic criticism seemed to be that some people were not pressing the buttons. On the other hand, the trade had for years accepted diary measurements, a system at least as flawed as people meters. In some diary households, for example, members conscientiously log their viewing on the first day, then forget about it until it is time to return the diary, when one person would try to remember what everyone had watched the rest of the week and write in best guesses. These diary flaws favored the networks. Ironically, then, people meters may have been criticized—at least in part—not because they were more flawed than diaries, but because they were less flawed or flawed in a different manner. Meanwhile, development proceeds on people meter technology. Efforts continue to develop a passive system that would identify specific TV viewers in Nielsen homes without requiring any action on the part of those viewers.

## 18.2 AUDIENCE RATINGS ORGANIZATIONS

Audience research companies syndicate services. A subscriber pays a fee and receives copies of pertinent research reports and permission to use them. Subscribers consist primarily of stations, cable and broadcast networks, and ad agencies. The media bear the largest cost of audience research, but agencies specify information included in the reports. After all, sellers (radio, TV, and cable outlets) must package products (advertising time) to appeal to their customers (agencies).

Only subscribers may use a rating report. The report includes ratings of nonsubscribing outlets, but a nonsubscriber may not promote ratings to public or advertisers, even if it has the highest rating in the market. A number of firms syndicate audience research. The best-known include Statistical Research, Inc., Arbitron Ratings Company, and Nielsen Media Research.

### 18.2.1 Statistical Research, Inc.

Statistical Research, Inc. conducts **RADAR—Radio's All-Dimension Audience Research—the only network radio measurement service**. RADAR uses telephone recall to collect data. A computer generates random telephone numbers to select a nationwide probability sample of individuals. The respondents, about 250 each week, constitute a panel, and RADAR calls and interviews each one every day for 1 week about the previous day's listening. RADAR interviews year-round. It issues two reports annually, generally in February and July, each of which deals with the most recent year's listening. RADAR measures national radio usage and network radio only.

*18.2.2 Arbitron Ratings Company*   Arbitron, in business since 1948, measures radio audiences in local markets. Arbitron uses diaries to survey more than 261 radio markets that include 98% of all persons 12 years and older in the United States. Markets are measured at least once each spring (May–June). Many markets are measured four times a year. Because each survey period lasts 12 weeks, stations in many markets receive almost continuous (48 weeks a year) ratings data (Box 18.4 and Fig. 18.4). Arbitron draws a new sample for each of the 12 weeks, and each respondent keeps a diary of listening for only 1 week.

Arbitron electronically scans, checks for errors, and edits the diaries. Because each diary's contents are electronically entered into a computer, Arbitron subscribers can call up and examine the actual diaries supplying the data for ratings. The entire radio report is available to stations on software, which allows sales personnel to generate client proposals based on ratings, geography, and demographics.

Arbitron's major television service was discontinued in 1994. Arbitron had introduced its **ScanAmerica** people meter service in 1987 in Denver as a comprehensive television viewing and consumer local service. In addition to viewing behavior, the ScanAmerica service asked sample households to provide

---

### BOX 18.4. MAJOR SECTIONS OF AN ARBITRON RADIO BOOK

- **Metro audience trends**: Lists share, average-quarter-hour persons (AQH), and cume rating for each station for the last four measurement periods.
- **Target audience**: Lists AQH, cume, rating, and share for each station. Listing provided for metro and total survey area (TSA).
- **Specific audience**: Lists, by gender and age breakdown, AQH, rating, share, cume, cume rating for the metro area; also AQH and cume for the total survey area.
- **Audience composition**: Lists metro AQH for each station as a percentage of the total listening audience.
- **Hour-by-hour**: Lists metro AQH and rating for each station for each hour of the day.
- **Listening location**: Lists each station's percentage of metro listening occuring at home, in a car, and "other" locations.
- **Exclusive audience**: Lists, for the metro area, total number and percentage of each demographic group that listened exclusively to each station.
- **ADI target audience**: Lists AQH, rating, and cume for each demographic category for each station in the ADI.
- **Overnight listening**: Lists AQH and cume for the midnight to 6 a.m. audience for the metro and total survey area. Also contains 24-hour/7-day cume totals.

---

purchasing information by running a scanner wand over the Universal Product Code symbol on every item purchased. Arbitron's computer picked up both viewing and purchasing data. The rating trade refers to the **simultaneous tracking of two streams of information**—in this case television viewing and purchasing behavior—as **single source**. The information sought is appealing to both media and advertisers, but the ScanAmerica service was time-consuming and cumbersome for sample household members and was not successful.

In 1995 Arbitron and VNU Business Information Services, Inc. joined forces to produce and market a another single source service called the Scarborough Report. The **Scarborough Report** had previously provided the largest 58 markets with extensive consumer behavior information, including banking practices, beverages consumed, computer usage, drug and grocery store patronage, health care, household shopping, and lifestyle information. When combined with Arbitron ratings data, the report will allow radio stations to **determine the consumer and lifestyle behavior of its listeners**, such as the kind of cars they purchase and drive, the extent to which they eat at fast-food restaurants, where they live, and where they shop.

Another Arbitron service provides radio stations in 11 large markets with radio, television, and cable audience measures, as well as information on newspaper readership and consumer behavior. The radio ratings are pulled from Arbitron's syndicated radio market service, and television (including cable) data are collected

## Metro Audience Trends[*]
### PERSONS 12+

| | MONDAY-SUNDAY 6AM-MID | | | | | MONDAY-FRIDAY 6AM-10AM | | | | |
|---|---|---|---|---|---|---|---|---|---|---|
| | SPRING 87 | SUMMER 87 | FALL 87 | WINTER 88 | SPRING 88 | SPRING 87 | SUMMER 87 | FALL 87 | WINTER 88 | SPRING 88 |
| **WAMA** | | | | | | | | | | |
| SHARE | ** | ** | ** | ** | .7 | ** | ** | ** | ** | .5 |
| AQH(00) | ** | ** | ** | ** | 20 | ** | ** | ** | ** | 22 |
| CUME RTG | ** | ** | ** | ** | .8 | ** | ** | ** | ** | .6 |
| **WDAE** | | | | | | | | | | |
| SHARE | 3.8 | 3.7 | 2.2 | 2.9 | 2.1 | 3.2 | 3.9 | 2.6 | 2.9 | 2.3 |
| AQH(00) | 114 | 108 | 67 | 88 | 62 | 133 | 148 | 107 | 125 | 93 |
| CUME RTG | 7.4 | 7.0 | 4.6 | 5.0 | 4.6 | 4.2 | 3.8 | 2.8 | 2.9 | 2.3 |
| **WFLA** | | | | | | | | | | |
| SHARE | 3.8 | 3.7 | 5.1 | 4.4 | 5.9 | 4.5 | 4.4 | 6.3 | 3.8 | 7.0 |
| AQH(00) | 114 | 108 | 154 | 137 | 174 | 183 | 169 | 262 | 162 | 289 |
| CUME RTG | 10.0 | 9.6 | 11.9 | 9.9 | 10.0 | 5.3 | 5.8 | 7.0 | 5.8 | 6.8 |
| **+WFLZ** | | | | | | | | | | |
| SHARE | 3.5 | 3.9 | 4.1 | 4.7 | 4.6 | 3.2 | 3.9 | 3.5 | 4.4 | 4.3 |
| AQH(00) | 104 | 112 | 125 | 145 | 135 | 132 | 149 | 144 | 189 | 176 |
| CUME RTG | 7.8 | 7.9 | 9.4 | 9.8 | 11.7 | 5.0 | 4.9 | 5.8 | 5.6 | 5.8 |
| **WGUL** | | | | | | | | | | |
| SHARE | 1.3 | .5 | .7 | .5 | .6 | 1.3 | .3 | .9 | .3 | .7 |
| AQH(00) | 39 | 15 | 22 | 14 | 17 | 54 | 12 | 38 | 14 | 29 |
| CUME RTG | 2.2 | 2.2 | 2.4 | 1.9 | 1.9 | 1.2 | .9 | 1.5 | .9 | .8 |
| **WGUL-FM** | | | | | | | | | | |
| SHARE | 3.2 | 2.9 | 4.5 | 2.7 | 2.7 | 2.5 | 2.6 | 4.5 | 2.5 | 3.0 |
| AQH(00) | 95 | 84 | 136 | 83 | 81 | 101 | 98 | 186 | 106 | 124 |
| CUME RTG | 4.8 | 4.7 | 5.9 | 4.7 | 5.3 | 3.0 | 2.9 | 4.1 | 2.8 | 3.0 |
| **WHBO** | | | | | | | | | | |
| SHARE | 2.0 | 2.1 | .9 | 1.3 | 1.0 | 1.5 | 1.2 | .7 | 1.2 | 1.0 |
| AQH(00) | 59 | 62 | 27 | 41 | 30 | 61 | 45 | 30 | 52 | 42 |
| CUME RTG | 3.0 | 3.0 | 2.5 | 2.6 | 2.1 | 1.2 | 1.6 | 1.0 | 1.2 | .9 |
| **WKRL** | | | | | | | | | | |
| SHARE | 3.4 | 4.8 | 3.2 | 3.8 | 4.0 | 2.6 | 4.6 | 2.7 | 2.9 | 3.5 |
| AQH(00) | 101 | 138 | 97 | 116 | 117 | 106 | 174 | 111 | 126 | 143 |
| CUME RTG | 8.3 | 10.0 | 8.9 | 7.6 | 8.7 | 4.6 | 5.7 | 4.6 | 3.7 | 5.2 |
| **WLFF** | | | | | | | | | | |
| SHARE | 1.1 | .6 | .6 | .5 | .4 | 1.1 | .4 | .5 | .5 | .3 |
| AQH(00) | 34 | 17 | 19 | 15 | 13 | 46 | 17 | 19 | 22 | 14 |
| CUME RTG | 2.1 | 1.6 | 1.3 | 1.6 | 1.4 | 1.3 | .7 | .7 | .7 | .7 |
| **WLVU-FM** | | | | | | | | | | |
| SHARE | ** | ** | .5 | ** | .4 | ** | ** | .3 | ** | .3 |
| AQH(00) | ** | ** | 14 | ** | 13 | ** | ** | 13 | ** | 13 |
| CUME RTG | ** | ** | 1.4 | ** | 1.9 | ** | ** | .3 | ** | .7 |
| **WNLT** | | | | | | | | | | |
| SHARE | 5.1 | 3.9 | 4.0 | 5.2 | 4.0 | 5.1 | 4.3 | 4.3 | 4.9 | 4.0 |
| AQH(00) | 150 | 113 | 121 | 159 | 118 | 211 | 166 | 178 | 210 | 164 |
| CUME RTG | 9.9 | 9.9 | 11.0 | 10.0 | 11.1 | 5.8 | 5.8 | 6.2 | 6.2 | 6.3 |
| **WPSO** | | | | | | | | | | |
| SHARE | .4 | .6 | .6 | ** | .3 | .2 | .3 | .4 | ** | .1 |
| AQH(00) | 12 | 17 | 18 | ** | 9 | 10 | 13 | 18 | ** | 4 |
| CUME RTG | .9 | .6 | 1.4 | ** | .9 | .4 | .3 | .5 | ** | .4 |
| **WQYK** | | | | | | | | | | |
| **WCBF** | | | | | | | | | | |
| SHARE | ** | ** | ** | ** | .3 | ** | ** | ** | ** | .2 |
| AQH(00) | ** | ** | ** | ** | 9 | ** | ** | ** | ** | 7 |
| CUME RTG | ** | ** | ** | ** | 1.1 | ** | ** | ** | ** | .2 |
| **WQYK-FM** | | | | | | | | | | |
| SHARE | 6.4 | 5.3 | 8.0 | 8.7 | 7.9 | 6.3 | 5.8 | 7.4 | 9.7 | 7.7 |
| AQH(00) | 190 | 155 | 242 | 267 | 233 | 258 | 223 | 308 | 419 | 317 |
| CUME RTG | 12.3 | 11.3 | 14.2 | 14.6 | 13.2 | 6.9 | 6.0 | 8.4 | 9.1 | 8.7 |
| **WRBQ** | | | | | | | | | | |
| SHARE | 1.0 | 1.1 | 1.1 | .8 | .4 | 1.3 | 1.5 | 1.2 | 1.0 | .7 |
| AQH(00) | 29 | 33 | 32 | 24 | 11 | 54 | 56 | 49 | 44 | 28 |
| CUME RTG | 3.8 | 3.9 | 5.5 | 3.2 | 1.8 | 2.2 | 1.8 | 1.8 | 1.7 | 1.0 |
| **WRBQ-FM** | | | | | | | | | | |
| SHARE | 17.8 | 16.9 | 14.5 | 16.6 | 16.7 | 19.6 | 19.6 | 17.5 | 20.5 | 18.7 |
| AQH(00) | 528 | 492 | 437 | 513 | 494 | 805 | 748 | 727 | 883 | 770 |
| CUME RTG | 30.3 | 30.0 | 30.1 | 30.3 | 30.0 | 21.3 | 20.6 | 20.5 | 22.3 | 20.6 |
| **WRXB** | | | | | | | | | | |
| SHARE | 2.0 | 2.1 | .8 | .7 | 1.4 | 2.0 | 2.4 | 1.0 | .8 | 1.8 |
| AQH(00) | 58 | 60 | 23 | 22 | 42 | 81 | 92 | 41 | 34 | 75 |
| CUME RTG | 3.0 | 2.7 | 2.1 | 1.9 | 2.4 | 1.7 | 2.0 | 1.4 | 1.0 | 1.6 |
| **WSUN** | | | | | | | | | | |
| SHARE | 3.6 | 3.3 | 2.7 | 3.4 | 3.7 | 4.7 | 3.8 | 3.5 | 4.2 | 4.6 |
| AQH(00) | 107 | 96 | 80 | 105 | 108 | 191 | 146 | 147 | 183 | 190 |
| CUME RTG | 7.7 | 7.5 | 7.5 | 8.2 | 7.3 | 5.0 | 4.2 | 4.5 | 4.7 | 4.4 |
| **+WTKN** | | | | | | | | | | |
| **WPLP** | | | | | | | | | | |
| SHARE | 3.3 | 3.4 | 3.7 | 2.6 | 1.1 | 3.9 | 3.8 | 4.7 | 3.4 | 1.1 |
| AQH(00) | 98 | 100 | 111 | 79 | 32 | 158 | 146 | 196 | 145 | 45 |
| CUME RTG | 7.0 | 7.3 | 7.9 | 6.2 | 4.2 | 3.5 | 4.6 | 5.3 | 4.4 | 1.8 |
| **WTMP** | | | | | | | | | | |
| SHARE | 2.1 | 2.0 | 1.7 | 1.8 | 2.3 | 2.5 | 2.0 | 1.6 | 1.5 | 2.1 |
| AQH(00) | 62 | 57 | 52 | 56 | 68 | 104 | 77 | 66 | 65 | 87 |
| CUME RTG | 4.4 | 5.1 | 4.4 | 4.2 | 2.8 | 2.3 | 2.5 | 2.3 | 1.9 | 1.9 |
| **WUSA** | | | | | | | | | | |
| SHARE | 5.0 | 5.0 | 4.8 | 5.2 | 6.0 | 5.2 | 4.8 | 4.5 | 5.2 | 5.3 |
| AQH(00) | 149 | 144 | 145 | 162 | 176 | 212 | 182 | 187 | 225 | 217 |
| CUME RTG | 11.3 | 11.6 | 12.3 | 10.7 | 12.8 | 5.8 | 6.3 | 5.7 | 6.2 | 7.6 |

Footnote Symbols: * * Station(s) not reported this survey.   + Station(s) reported with different call letters in prior surveys - see Page 5B.

**ARBITRON RATINGS**

TAMPA-ST. PETERSBURG-CLEARWATER            6
* See page Iv Restrictions On Use Of Report for restrictions on the use of Trends data.

FIG. 18.4. Example of "Metro Audience Trends," report from an Arbitron radio book. (Courtesy of The Arbitron Ratings Co. Used by permission.)

through diaries. Consumer information is obtained through a follow-up telephone interview and a questionnaire on the television diary. Arbitron delivers the data on computer software.

Arbitron's corporate parent, Control Data Corporation, also owns **Broadcast Advertisers Reports (BAR).** BAR monitors commercials that appear on broadcast and cable television networks, television stations, and radio networks. Stations, advertisers, and advertising agencies use BAR's syndicated reports. These reports provide a variety of information on the monitored commercials, such as time, origin (station or network), length, product, brand, advertiser, agency, and average value.

### 18.2.3 Nielsen Media Research

A. C. Nielsen is the only major research firm that measures television audiences at both the local and national levels. Nielsen, a subsidiary of Dun & Bradstreet, began in 1934 as a marketing research firm. Several years later the firm bought rights to the first meter, a mechanical recorder, and by 1940 Nielsen was in the radio audience measurement business. Nielsen adapted its recorder and added television research in the late 1940s, then discontinued radio measurement in 1964.

*18.2.3.1 Local Television Market Reports.*    Nielsen measures some 220 local markets during the sweeps weeks in November, February, May, and July each year. Viewing data are collected for 4 weeks during each sweep period but each sample household completes a diary for only 1 week of viewing. Sample size depends on the market size. In the Tampa–St. Petersburg, Florida, market, for example, data are collected from around 1,200 households.

The diary methods provide local ratings data. Nielsen distributes local ratings in a printed report called *Viewers in Profile* (Fig. 18.5 and Box 18.5) and by computer either online or on floppy diskette.

As mentioned previously, Nielsen also uses tuning meters in the top 30 markets. The tuning meters provide overnight national ratings, but are also used in conjunction with diaries to provide more reliable data for the *Viewers in Profile* local reports.

*18.2.3.2 Network Television Ratings.*    **Nielsen Television Index (NTI)** reports broadcast television network ratings. NTI uses a national sample of 4,000 or more households equipped with **Nielsen People Meters.** For years, Nielsen offered the only regularly scheduled network rating service. During the 1980s, others entered the business, but programmers and advertisers continued to regard NTI as the standard.

In 1988, Nielsen began the **ScanTrack Plus Service,** its version of single source data. Aimed at advertisers more than broadcasters, Scantrack Plus does not utilize Nielsen's People Meter. The service provides extensive consumer behavior infor-

# JACKSONVILLE, FL

WK1 2/02-2/08 WK2 2/09-2/15 WK3 2/16-2/22 WK4 2/23-3/01

WEDNESDAY 9:00PM - 11:00PM

| METRO HH RTG | METRO HH SHR | STATION | PROGRAM | DMA HH RATINGS WEEKS 1 | 2 | 3 | 4 | MULTI-WEEK AVG RTG | MULTI-WEEK AVG SHR | SHARE TREND NOV '94 | MAY '94 | FEB '94 | DMA RATINGS PERSONS 2+ | 18+ | 12-24 | 12-34 | 18-34 | 18-49 | 21-49 | 25-54 | 35+ | 35-64 | 50+ | WOMEN 18+ | 12-24 | 18-34 | 18-49 | 25-49 | 25-54 | WKG | MEN 18+ | 18-34 | 18-49 | 21-49 | 25-49 | 25-54 | TNS 12-17 | CHILD 2-11 | 6-11 |
|---|---|---|---|---|---|---|---|---|---|---|---|---|---|---|---|---|---|---|---|---|---|---|---|---|---|---|---|---|---|---|---|---|---|---|---|---|---|---|---|
| 1 | 2 | | | 3 | 4 | 5 | 6 | 7 | 8 | 11 | 12 | 13 | 15 | 16 | 17 | 18 | 19 | 20 | 21 | 22 | 23 | 24 | 25 | 26 | 27 | 28 | 29 | 31 | 32 | 34 | 35 | 36 | 37 | 38 | 39 | 40 | 41 | 42 | 43 |
| 4 | | | R.S.E. THRESHOLDS 25+% | 9 | 9 | 9 | 9 | 3 | | | | | 2 | 2 | 10 | 5 | 5 | 4 | 4 | 3 | 3 | 4 | 3 | 3 | 13 | 9 | 5 | 5 | 4 | 5 | 3 | 11 | 5 | 5 | 5 | 5 | 16 | 10 | 13 |
| 1 | | | (1 S.E.) 4 WK AVG 50+% | 3 | 3 | 3 | 3 | 1 | | | | | 1 | 1 | 3 | 1 | 1 | 1 | 1 | 1 | 1 | 1 | 1 | 1 | 4 | 2 | 1 | 1 | 1 | 1 | 1 | 3 | 1 | 1 | 1 | 1 | 5 | 3 | 4 |
| | | 9:00PM | | | | | | | | | | | | | | | | | | | | | | | | | | | | | | | | | | | | | |
| 7 | 10 | WAWS | AVG. ALL WKS | 3 | 8 | 7 | 6 | 6 | 9 | 12 | 24 | 14 | 4 | 4 | 7 | 7 | 7 | 6 | 6 | 4 | 3 | 3 | 1 | 4 | 7 | 6 | 6 | 6 | 5 | 5 | 4 | 8 | 6 | 5 | 4 | 3 | 6 | 3 | 3 |
| 3 | 5 | | CELEB 1ST LOVE | 3 | | | | 3 | 4 | | | | 1 | 1 | | 1 | 2 | 1 | 1 | 1 | | | | 1 | | 1 | 1 | 1 | 1 | | 1 | 3 | 2 | 2 | 2 | 2 | | | |
| 8 | 12 | | PARTY OF 5-FOX | | 8 | 7 | 6 | 7 | 11 | | | | 5 | 5 | 10 | 9 | 9 | 7 | 7 | 5 | 3 | 4 | 2 | 6 | 9 | 8 | 7 | 8 | 7 | 7 | 5 | 10 | 7 | 6 | 5 | 4 | 8 | 4 | 4 |
| 2 | 4 | WJCT | AVG. ALL WKS | 1 | 2 | 2 | 2 | 2 | 3 | 3 | 3 | 1 | 1 | 1 | | | | 1 | 1 | 1 | 1 | 1 | 1 | 1 | | | 1 | 1 | 1 | 1 | 1 | | | | 1 | | | | |
| 1 | 2 | | INSIDE THE FBI | 1 | | | | 1 | 2 | | | | | | | | | | | | 1 | | 1 | 1 | | | | | | | | | | | | | | | |
| 3 | 5 | | AMERCN EXPRNCE | | 2 | | | 2 | 4 | | | | 1 | 1 | | | | 1 | 1 | 1 | 1 | 1 | 1 | 2 | | | 2 | 2 | 2 | 3 | | | | | | | | 2 | |
| 2 | 3 | | MYSTERY-SENSES | | | 2 | | 2 | 3 | | | | 1 | 2 | | 1 | 1 | 2 | 2 | 2 | 2 | 2 | 2 | 2 | | 1 | 2 | 2 | 2 | 1 | 2 | 1 | 2 | 2 | 2 | 2 | | | |
| 3 | 4 | | LIVE-LNCLN CTR | | | | 2 | 2 | 3 | | | | 1 | 1 | | | | 1 | 1 | 1 | 2 | 1 | 2 | 2 | | | 2 | 2 | 2 | 2 | | | | | | | | | |
| 8 | 13 | WJKS | ROSEANNE-WED | 8 | 8 | 9 | 4 | 7 | 12 | 14X | 20 | 20 | 5 | 5 | 7 | 8 | 9 | 7 | 7 | 7 | 4 | 4 | 2 | 7 | 11 | 12 | 10 | 9 | 9 | 7 | 4 | 6 | 5 | 5 | 5 | 5 | 6 | 3 | 1 |
| 10 | 16 | WJXT | AVG. ALL WKS | 7 | 9 | 10 | 12 | 10 | 16 | 22 | 17 | 36 | 6 | 7 | 1 | 2 | 3 | 6 | 6 | 7 | 9 | 9 | 9 | 8 | 2 | 3 | 6 | 7 | 7 | 5 | 6 | 3 | 5 | 6 | 6 | 6 | | 2 | 2 |
| 6 | 10 | | CBS SP MOV-WED | 7 | | | | 7 | 13 | | | | 4 | 5 | | 1 | 1 | 3 | 3 | 4 | 7 | 7 | 9 | 6 | | | 3 | 4 | 5 | 3 | 4 | 2 | 2 | 2 | 3 | 3 | | | |
| 10 | 14 | | NANNY-WED | | 9 | | | 9 | 14 | | | | 6 | 6 | 3 | 2 | 3 | 5 | 4 | 6 | 8 | 9 | 8 | 8 | 6 | 5 | 8 | 7 | 7 | 5 | 3 | | 3 | 3 | 3 | 4 | | 6 | |
| 11 | 16 | | CBS SPC MV-WED | | | 10 | | 10 | 15 | | | | 5 | 7 | | 2 | 3 | 5 | 5 | 6 | 9 | 7 | 10 | 6 | | 1 | 4 | 5 | 4 | 3 | 8 | 5 | 6 | 7 | 8 | 7 | | | |
| 15 | 24 | | GRAMMY AWARDS | | | | 12 | 12 | 20 | | | | 8 | 10 | | 4 | 6 | 10 | 11 | 12 | 12 | 13 | 9 | 11 | | 5 | 11 | 13 | 13 | 10 | 10 | 6 | 10 | 11 | 12 | 11 | | 2 | |
| 7 | 11 | WNFT | AVG. ALL WKS | 7 | 3 | 5 | 8 | 6 | 9 | 3 | 1 | 3 | 4 | 5 | 1 | 4 | 5 | 5 | 5 | 6 | 5 | 6 | 5 | 4 | 1 | 5 | 4 | 5 | 5 | 4 | 6 | 5 | 6 | 6 | 7 | 7 | 1 | | |
| 8 | 13 | | POINTMAN | 7 | | 5 | 8 | 6 | 11 | | | | 4 | 6 | 1 | 4 | 5 | 5 | 6 | 7 | 6 | 7 | 6 | 5 | | 4 | 4 | 5 | 6 | 5 | 7 | 5 | 7 | 7 | 7 | 8 | 1 | | 1 |
| 4 | 6 | | MAGIC BKBL | | 3 | | | 3 | 5 | | | | 2 | 3 | 1 | 4 | 5 | 3 | 4 | 4 | 2 | 2 | 2 | 3 | 3 | 7 | 3 | 3 | 3 | 4 | 3 | 3 | 3 | 4 | 4 | 4 | | | |
| 14 | 22 | WTLV | AVG. ALL WKS | 11 | 13 | 15 | 10 | 12 | 20 | 14 | 14 | 14 | 7 | 9 | 4 | 4 | 4 | 7 | 8 | 8 | 11 | 10 | 12 | 10 | 4 | 5 | 9 | 9 | 10 | 8 | 7 | 3 | 5 | 6 | 6 | 6 | 4 | 1 | |
| 13 | 22 | | DATELINE-WED | 11 | 13 | | | 12 | 20 | | | | 6 | 8 | 4 | 5 | 5 | 7 | 7 | 7 | 9 | 8 | 11 | 9 | 3 | 6 | 8 | 8 | 9 | 8 | 7 | 5 | 5 | 6 | 6 | 5 | 4 | | |
| 16 | 25 | | NBC MOV-WK-WED | | | 15 | | 15 | 22 | | | | 9 | 11 | 5 | 3 | 3 | 8 | 9 | 9 | 15 | 13 | 16 | 14 | 7 | 3 | 11 | 11 | 12 | 12 | 7 | 2 | 5 | 6 | 7 | 6 | 5 | | |
| 11 | 17 | | HUNT-AMZ TRSRS | | | | 10 | 10 | 17 | | | | 7 | 8 | 4 | 3 | 3 | 7 | 7 | 8 | 11 | 11 | 11 | 9 | 2 | 5 | 8 | 9 | 9 | 3 | 8 | | 5 | 6 | 7 | 8 | 5 | 3 | |
| 63 | | | HUT/PUT/TOTALS* | 57 | 66 | 66 | 60 | 62 | | 62 | 68 | 72 | 41 | 48 | 28 | 36 | 41 | 44 | 46 | 48 | 52 | 51 | 56 | 53 | 32 | 46 | 50 | 54 | 54 | 46 | 43 | 35 | 38 | 39 | 41 | 41 | 24 | 18 | 17 |
| | | 9:30PM | | | | | | | | | | | | | | | | | | | | | | | | | | | | | | | | | | | | | |
| 6 | 11 | WAWS | AVG. ALL WKS | 2 | 8 | 7 | 6 | 6 | 10 | 12 | 24 | 14 | 4 | 4 | 7 | 7 | 7 | 5 | 6 | 4 | 2 | 3 | 1 | 4 | 7 | 6 | 5 | 5 | 5 | 5 | 4 | 8 | 5 | 5 | 4 | 3 | 5 | 3 | 3 |
| 2 | 4 | | CELEB 1ST LOVE | 2 | | | | 2 | 4 | | | | | 1 | | 1 | 1 | 1 | 1 | 1 | | | | | | | | | | | 1 | 3 | 2 | 2 | 2 | 2 | | | |
| 8 | 12 | | PARTY OF 5-FOX | | 8 | 7 | 6 | 7 | 11 | | | | 5 | 5 | 10 | 8 | 9 | 7 | 7 | 5 | 3 | 4 | 2 | 5 | 9 | 8 | 7 | 7 | 7 | 7 | 5 | 10 | 7 | 6 | 4 | 4 | 7 | 4 | 4 |
| 2 | 4 | WJCT | AVG. ALL WKS | 1 | 2 | 2 | 2 | 2 | 3 | 3 | 3 | 1 | 1 | 1 | | 1 | 1 | 1 | 1 | 1 | 1 | 1 | 1 | 1 | | 1 | 1 | 2 | 1 | 1 | 1 | 1 | 1 | 1 | 1 | 1 | | | |
| 1 | 2 | | INSIDE THE FBI | 1 | | | | 1 | 2 | | | | | | | | | | | | 1 | | 1 | 1 | | | | | | | | | | | | | | | |
| 2 | 4 | | AMERCN EXPRNCE | | 2 | | | 2 | 3 | | | | | 1 | | | | 1 | 1 | 1 | 1 | 1 | 1 | 1 | | | 1 | 1 | 1 | 2 | | | | | | | | | |
| 3 | 4 | | MYSTERY-SENSES | | | 2 | | 2 | 4 | | | | 2 | 2 | | 2 | 3 | 2 | 3 | 3 | 2 | 2 | 2 | 2 | | 2 | 2 | 3 | 2 | 1 | 2 | 3 | 3 | 3 | 3 | 3 | | | |
| 3 | 4 | | LIVE-LNCLN CTR | | | | 2 | 2 | 4 | | | | 1 | 1 | | | | 1 | 1 | 1 | 2 | 1 | 2 | 2 | | 1 | 2 | 2 | 2 | 2 | | | | | | | | | |
| 8 | 13 | WJKS | ELLEN-ABC-WED | 7 | 9 | 7 | 4 | 7 | 12 | 13X | 18 | 17 | 5 | 5 | 5 | 7 | 8 | 7 | 7 | 7 | 4 | 4 | 2 | 7 | 9 | 12 | 9 | 9 | 8 | 7 | 4 | 4 | 5 | 5 | 6 | 5 | 5 | 2 | 1 |
| 10 | 16 | WJXT | AVG. ALL WKS | 7 | 7 | 10 | 12 | 9 | 15 | 24 | 17 | 36 | 5 | 7 | 1 | 3 | 3 | 6 | 6 | 7 | 8 | 8 | 9 | 7 | 2 | 3 | 6 | 7 | 7 | 5 | 6 | 4 | 5 | 5 | 6 | 6 | 1 | 1 | |
| 6 | 11 | | CBS SP MOV-WED | 7 | | | | 7 | 13 | | | | 4 | 5 | | 1 | 1 | 2 | 3 | 4 | 7 | 6 | 9 | 6 | | | 3 | 4 | 5 | 3 | 3 | 2 | 2 | 2 | 2 | 3 | | | |
| 7 | 11 | | DAVES WRLD-WED | | 7 | | | 7 | 12 | | | | 4 | 4 | 3 | 2 | 3 | 4 | 3 | 4 | 5 | 6 | 5 | 6 | 6 | 5 | 6 | 5 | 5 | 4 | 2 | . | 1 | 1 | 2 | 3 | | 2 | |
| 11 | 16 | | CBS SPC MV-WED | | | 10 | | 10 | 15 | | | | 5 | 7 | 1 | 3 | 3 | 5 | 5 | 6 | 9 | 7 | 10 | 6 | | 1 | 4 | 5 | 4 | 3 | 8 | 5 | 6 | 7 | 8 | 7 | 2 | | |
| 15 | 24 | | GRAMMY AWARDS | | | | 12 | 12 | 22 | | | | 8 | 11 | | 5 | 6 | 11 | 12 | 13 | 13 | 14 | 10 | 11 | | 5 | 12 | 14 | 14 | 11 | 10 | 7 | 10 | 11 | 13 | 11 | | 1 | |
| 7 | 11 | WNFT | AVG. ALL WKS | 7 | 3 | 5 | 7 | 6 | 9 | 3 | 1 | 4 | 4 | 5 | 1 | 4 | 5 | 5 | 5 | 6 | 5 | 5 | 5 | 4 | 1 | 5 | 4 | 5 | 5 | 4 | 6 | 5 | 6 | 6 | 7 | 7 | 1 | | |
| 8 | 13 | | POINTMAN | 7 | | 5 | 7 | 7 | 11 | | | | 4 | 6 | 1 | 4 | 5 | 6 | 6 | 7 | 6 | 7 | 6 | 5 | | 5 | 5 | 6 | 6 | 5 | 7 | 5 | 7 | 7 | 7 | 8 | 1 | | 1 |
| 4 | 6 | | MAGIC BKBL | | 3 | | | 3 | 5 | | | | 2 | 3 | 1 | 4 | 5 | 3 | 4 | 3 | 1 | 1 | 1 | 3 | 3 | 7 | 3 | 3 | 3 | 4 | 3 | 3 | 3 | 3 | 4 | 3 | | | |
| 14 | 23 | WTLV | AVG. ALL WKS | 12 | 13 | 15 | 9 | 12 | 21 | 14 | 15 | 14 | 7 | 9 | 4 | 5 | 5 | 7 | 8 | 8 | 11 | 10 | 12 | 10 | 4 | 6 | 9 | 9 | 10 | 8 | 7 | 4 | 5 | 6 | 6 | 6 | 4 | 1 | |
| 13 | 23 | | DATELINE-WED | 12 | 13 | | | 12 | 21 | | | | 6 | 8 | 4 | 6 | 6 | 7 | 7 | 7 | 9 | 8 | 11 | 9 | 3 | 7 | 8 | 9 | 9 | 9 | 7 | 6 | 5 | 6 | 6 | 6 | 3 | | |
| 17 | 26 | | NBC MOV-WK-WED | | | 15 | | 15 | 24 | | | | 9 | 11 | 5 | 4 | 4 | 9 | 9 | 10 | 15 | 13 | 16 | 15 | 7 | 5 | 12 | 12 | 13 | 13 | 7 | 2 | 5 | 6 | 7 | 6 | 5 | | |
| 12 | 19 | | HUNT-AMZ TRSRS | | | | 9 | 9 | 17 | | | | 7 | 8 | 4 | 3 | 3 | 6 | 7 | 8 | 11 | 11 | 11 | 8 | 2 | 5 | 7 | 8 | 8 | 2 | 8 | | 5 | 6 | 7 | 8 | 5 | 3 | |
| 62 | | | HUT/PUT/TOTALS* | 55 | 64 | 65 | 57 | 60 | | 61 | 66 | 72 | 39 | 47 | 26 | 36 | 40 | 43 | 45 | 47 | 50 | 49 | 54 | 52 | 30 | 47 | 49 | 53 | 53 | 45 | 41 | 33 | 37 | 38 | 40 | 40 | 23 | 13 | 12 |
| | | 10:00PM | | | | | | | | | | | | | | | | | | | | | | | | | | | | | | | | | | | | | |
| 5 | 10 | WAWS | FOX 30 NEWS-10 | 5 | 7 | 4 | 2 | 4 | 8 | 11X | 11 | 9 | 2 | 3 | 2 | 2 | 3 | 3 | 3 | 3 | 3 | 3 | 2 | 3 | 2 | 3 | 4 | 3 | 4 | 3 | 3 | 3 | 3 | 3 | 3 | 3 | 1 | | 1 |
| 1 | 2 | WJCT | AVG. ALL WKS | 1 | 1 | << | 1 | 1 | 1 | 2 | 2 | | | | | | | | | | 1 | | 1 | 1 | | | | | 1 | 1 | | | | | | | | | |
| 1 | 2 | | INSIDE THE FBI | 1 | | | | 1 | 1 | | | | | 1 | | | | | | | 1 | 1 | 2 | | | | | | 1 | 1 | 1 | | | | | | | | |
| 2 | 3 | | AMERCN EXPRNCE | | 1 | | | 1 | 2 | | | | | 1 | | | | 1 | 1 | 1 | 1 | 1 | 1 | 1 | | | 1 | 1 | 1 | 2 | | | | | | | | | |
| << | | | AGNST THE ODDS | | | << | | << | | | | | | | | | | | | | | | | | | | | | | | | | | | | | | | |
| 1 | 2 | | PLACIDO DOMNGO | | | | 1 | 1 | 2 | | | | | | | | | | | | 1 | | 1 | 1 | | 1 | | | | | | | | | | | | | |
| 10 | 18 | WJKS | PRMTM LIVE-WED | 8 | 7 | 9 | 11 | 8 | 16 | 9 | 17 | 10 | 4 | 5 | 1 | 3 | 4 | 5 | 6 | 6 | 6 | 6 | 6 | 6 | 1 | 6 | 6 | 7 | 7 | 6 | 5 | 3 | 5 | 5 | 6 | 5 | 1 | | |
| 11 | 21 | WJXT | AVG. ALL WKS | 10 | 8 | 10 | 11 | 10 | 19 | 27 | 21 | 46 | 6 | 7 | 2 | 3 | 4 | 6 | 7 | 7 | 9 | 9 | 9 | 8 | 2 | 3 | 7 | 8 | 8 | 7 | 7 | 5 | 6 | 6 | 6 | 6 | | | |
| 10 | 19 | | NRTHRN EXP-WED | 10 | 8 | | | 9 | 17 | | | | 5 | 7 | 3 | 3 | 4 | 6 | 7 | 7 | 8 | 9 | 8 | 8 | 2 | 3 | 7 | 8 | 9 | 7 | 5 | 5 | 5 | 5 | 4 | 4 | | 1 | |
| 11 | 19 | | CBS SPC MV-WED | | | 10 | | 10 | 18 | | | | 5 | 7 | 1 | 3 | 3 | 5 | 5 | 5 | 9 | 7 | 11 | 5 | 2 | 2 | 3 | 3 | 3 | 1 | 8 | 5 | 6 | 7 | 8 | 7 | | | |
| 14 | 29 | | GRAMMY AWARDS | | | | 11 | 11 | 24 | | | | 7 | 9 | | 3 | 4 | 9 | 10 | 10 | 12 | 13 | 9 | 10 | | 4 | 11 | 13 | 12 | 11 | 8 | 5 | 7 | 8 | 9 | 8 | | | |
| 2 | 4 | WNFT | AVG. ALL WKS | 3 | 2 | 1 | 1 | 2 | 3 | | 6 | 5 | 2 | 1 | 3 | 3 | 2 | 2 | 2 | 2 | 1 | 1 | | 1 | 3 | 3 | 2 | 1 | 1 | 1 | 2 | 2 | 2 | 2 | 2 | 2 | 3 | 1 | 1 |
| 2 | 3 | | RICHARD BEY SH | 3 | 2 | 1 | 1 | 2 | 3 | | | | 2 | 1 | 3 | 3 | 2 | 2 | 2 | 2 | 1 | 1 | | 1 | 3 | 3 | 2 | 1 | 1 | 1 | 2 | 2 | 2 | 2 | 2 | 2 | 4 | 1 | 1 |
| 3 | 5 | | MAGIC BKBL | | 2 | | | 2 | 4 | | | | 1 | 1 | 1 | 2 | 3 | 2 | 2 | 2 | 1 | 1 | 1 | 1 | 3 | 2 | 1 | | 1 | 1 | 2 | 3 | 3 | 3 | 3 | 3 | | | |
| 12 | 23 | WTLV | AVG. ALL WKS | 10 | 11 | 15 | 8 | 11 | 21 | 19 | 18 | 12 | 7 | 8 | 4 | 5 | 6 | 7 | 7 | 8 | 10 | 9 | 11 | 10 | 5 | 6 | 9 | 9 | 9 | 7 | 6 | 5 | 5 | 6 | 5 | 6 | 3 | 1 | 2 |
| 12 | 22 | | LAW&ORDER-NBC | 10 | 11 | | | 11 | 20 | | | | 7 | 8 | 5 | 7 | 8 | 7 | 8 | 8 | 8 | 8 | 10 | 9 | 3 | 8 | 8 | 9 | 10 | 5 | 7 | 8 | 7 | 7 | 6 | 6 | 3 | 2 | 3 |
| 18 | 30 | | NBC MOV-WK-WED | | | 15 | | 15 | 27 | | | | 8 | 10 | 4 | 3 | 3 | 8 | 9 | 9 | 14 | 13 | 15 | 15 | 7 | 6 | 12 | 13 | 13 | 13 | 6 | | 4 | 5 | 5 | 5 | 4 | | |
| 9 | 18 | | HUNT-AMZ TRSRS | | | | 8 | 8 | 17 | | | | 5 | 6 | 3 | 2 | 3 | 4 | 4 | 5 | 9 | 9 | 11 | 7 | 6 | 4 | 6 | 5 | 4 | 3 | 6 | 1 | 3 | 3 | 4 | 5 | | | |
| 54 | | | HUT/PUT/TOTALS* | 52 | 55 | 57 | 46 | 52 | | 50 | 55 | 61 | 32 | 40 | 17 | 24 | 28 | 35 | 37 | 39 | 46 | 44 | 49 | 43 | 19 | 32 | 39 | 41 | 43 | 34 | 36 | 24 | 31 | 32 | 35 | 34 | 11 | 6 | 6 |
| | | 10:30PM | | | | | | | | | | | | | | | | | | | | | | | | | | | | | | | | | | | | | |
| 3 | 5 | WAWS | EXTRA | 2 | 4 | 2 | 1 | 2 | 5 | 4X | 5 | 6 | 1 | 1 | 2 | 1 | 1 | 1 | 1 | 1 | 1 | 1 | 2 | 2 | 2 | 2 | 1 | 1 | 1 | 1 | 1 | 1 | 1 | 1 | 1 | 1 | 1 | | |
| << | | WJCT | AVG. ALL WKS | 1 | << | << | << | << | | 1 | 1 | | | | | | | | | | | | 1 | | | | | | | | | | | | | | | | |
| 1 | 2 | | INSIDE THE FBI | 1 | | | | 1 | 1 | | | | | 1 | | | | | | | 1 | 1 | 2 | | | | | | 1 | 1 | 1 | | | | | | | | |
| 1 | 1 | | GANGS | | << | | | << | | | | | | | | | | | | | | | 1 | | | | | | | | | | | | | | | | |
| << | | | AGNST THE ODDS | | | << | | << | | | | | | | | | | | | | | | | | | | | | | | | | | | | | | | |
| << | | | PLACIDO DOMNGO | | | | << | << | | | | | | | | | | | | | | | | | | 1 | | | | | | | | | | | | | |
| 10 | 20 | WJKS | PRMTM LIVE-WED | 7 | 7 | 8 | 10 | 8 | 17 | 11 | 18 | 9 | 4 | 6 | 1 | 3 | 4 | 5 | 6 | 7 | 7 | 7 | 6 | 7 | 1 | 6 | 6 | 7 | 8 | 7 | 5 | 3 | 5 | 5 | 6 | 5 | 1 | | |
| 11 | 22 | WJXT | AVG. ALL WKS | 10 | 8 | 9 | 11 | 9 | 20 | 30 | 23 | 48 | 6 | 7 | 1 | 3 | 4 | 7 | 7 | 7 | 9 | 9 | 9 | 8 | 1 | 3 | 7 | 8 | 9 | 7 | 7 | 5 | 6 | 7 | 7 | 6 | | | |
| 10 | 20 | | NRTHRN EXP-WED | 10 | 8 | | | 9 | 18 | | | | 5 | 7 | 3 | 4 | 6 | 7 | 7 | 8 | 8 | 9 | 7 | 8 | 2 | 4 | 8 | 8 | 10 | 8 | 6 | 7 | 6 | 7 | 6 | 5 | | 1 | |
| 10 | 18 | | CBS SPC MV-WED | | | 9 | | 9 | 17 | | | | 5 | 6 | | 1 | 2 | 4 | 4 | 4 | 9 | 7 | 11 | 5 | | | 3 | 3 | 3 | 1 | 8 | 3 | 5 | 6 | 6 | 6 | | | |
| 14 | 29 | | GRAMMY AWARDS | | | | 11 | 11 | 25 | | | | 7 | 9 | | 3 | 4 | 9 | 10 | 10 | 12 | 13 | 9 | 10 | | 4 | 11 | 13 | 12 | 11 | 8 | 5 | 7 | 8 | 9 | 8 | | | |
| 2 | 4 | WNFT | RICHARD BEY SH | 2 | 2 | 1 | 1 | 1 | 3 | | 7 | 5 | 1 | 1 | 3 | 2 | 2 | 2 | 2 | 1 | 1 | 1 | | 1 | 3 | 2 | 2 | 1 | 1 | 1 | 1 | 2 | 2 | 2 | 2 | 2 | 3 | 1 | 1 |
| 12 | 25 | WTLV | AVG. ALL WKS | 10 | 11 | 16 | 8 | 11 | 23 | 22 | 19 | 14 | 7 | 8 | 4 | 5 | 5 | 7 | 7 | 8 | 10 | 9 | 11 | 10 | 4 | 6 | 9 | 9 | 9 | 7 | 6 | 5 | 5 | 6 | 5 | 6 | 3 | 1 | 2 |
| 11 | 23 | | LAW&ORDER-NBC | 10 | 11 | | | 11 | 21 | | | | 7 | 8 | 5 | 7 | 8 | 8 | 8 | 8 | 8 | 7 | 9 | 9 | 3 | 8 | 8 | 9 | 10 | 5 | 7 | 8 | 7 | 7 | 6 | 6 | 3 | 2 | 3 |
| 18 | 33 | | NBC MOV-WK-WED | | | 16 | | 16 | 30 | | | | 8 | 11 | 4 | 3 | 3 | 8 | 9 | 9 | 15 | 13 | 15 | 15 | 7 | 6 | 12 | 13 | 13 | 13 | 6 | | 4 | 5 | 5 | 5 | 4 | | |
| 9 | 19 | | HUNT-AMZ TRSRS | | | | 8 | 8 | 18 | | | | 5 | 6 | 2 | 2 | 2 | 4 | 4 | 5 | 9 | 9 | 11 | 6 | 4 | 3 | 5 | 5 | 4 | 3 | 6 | 1 | 3 | 3 | 4 | 5 | | | |
| 50 | | | HUT/PUT/TOTALS* | 49 | 49 | 53 | 44 | 49 | | 44 | 51 | 58 | 30 | 37 | 15 | 23 | 27 | 33 | 35 | 36 | 43 | 42 | 46 | 41 | 18 | 32 | 37 | 39 | 41 | 32 | 33 | 22 | 29 | 30 | 32 | 32 | 9 | 5 | 5 |
| 1 | 2 | WEDNESDAY 9:00PM - 11:00PM | | 3 | 4 | 5 | 6 | 7 | 8 | 11 | 12 | 13 | 15 | 16 | 17 | 18 | 19 | 20 | 21 | 22 | 23 | 24 | 25 | 26 | 27 | 28 | 29 | 31 | 32 | 34 | 35 | 36 | 37 | 38 | 39 | 40 | 41 | 42 | 43 |

TIME PERIOD

*Nielsen has been advised that a station(s) conducted a special promotional activity. See page 3.*

FEBRUARY 1995 74

FIG. 18.5. Example of a "Daypart Summary," report from a Nielsen television book. (Courtesy of A. C. Nielsen Media Research. Used by permission.)

---

**BOX 18.5. MAJOR SECTIONS OF A NIELSEN LOCAL
TV MARKET REPORT**

Listings are provided for various time periods and for several demographic categories.

- **Daypart summary section**—Lists the following: metro ratings and shares, DMA ratings and shares, and share trends for each station over the last four ratings books; percentage distribution of audience in the metro and DMA; ratings of each station in the three most significant adjacent DMAs; average weekly cume totals; and total audience numbers.
- **Program averages section**—Breaks down by program, lists metro ratings and shares, DMA household ratings and shares, and DMA total audience numbers.
- **Time period section**—Breaks down by time period, beginning with every half-hour of the day, lists metro ratings and shares, DMA household ratings and shares, and DMA total audience numbers.
- **Persons share section**—Breaks down into every measured age and gender category, lists DMA ratings, shares, and share trends for various time periods.
- **TV households and persons trend section**—Breaks down by various time slots and lists the following DMA averages for the past 5 years: HUT, rating, and share for households and for various age and gender categories. Separate listings are provided for the November, February, May, and July ratings books for each year.
- **Program index section**—Alphabetical listing of every program aired during the measurement period. Lists current share and share trends over the past four ratings books.

---

mation in addition to ratings data. ScanTrack specializes in coverage of the nation's grocery industry. The data can show, for example, on a Super Bowl Sunday, the percentage of Super Bowl television viewers who purchased beer or soda along with hot dogs. The home device consists of a wand to record product purchases coupled with a Microprocessor Home Unit.

*18.2.3.3 Cable Ratings.*    Nielsen established **Nielsen Home Video Index (NHI)** as its commitment to measuring new video forms—cable television, pay cable, satellite networks, local cable systems, pay-TV services, and program suppliers. Nielsen measures popular advertising-supported and subscription cable networks, as well as providing services to cable operators in local markets. Local cable ratings are made available in Nielsen's *Cable Activity Report.* People meter data are used to compile national cable ratings that are issued in the *Cable National Audience Demographics Report.* Companies can also commission Nielsen to do special studies on cable. Nielsen claims its cable database is the largest and most complete in the world. Clients number in the thousands for services such as Cable On Line Data Exchange, Cable Audience Profile, and cable coincidentals.

Reports specializing in cable are necessary because cable programming services are not included in Nielsen's local television audience **reports unless they achieve a DMA cume rating of at least 19.5%.** In other words, to even be listed in the television book, a cable service must be viewed by at least 19.5% of the market's households during the survey period.

Premium channels such as HBO and Showtime are particularly difficult to measure because of the high amount of time-shifting that occurs as audience members record movies and other programs for later viewing. Baldwin and McVoy[2] suggested five reasons why broadcast-style audience measurement is not appropriate for cable. First, the large number of signals available on a cable system fragment the audience much more than the four or five TV stations in a market, so a larger sample is needed. Second, people find it much harder to identify one of the 30 cable channels than one of the four or five local TV stations. Third, certain advertiser-supported pay channels supposedly attract an audience that is higher than average on the socioeconomic scale—the type of person least likely to cooperate with an audience survey. Fourth, the four or five TV stations in a market share the high cost of syndicated audience research, whereas the one cable franchise would have to bear the entire cost. Fifth, cable should be measured in cumes only—for example, the number of different persons who viewed a particular cable channel at least once during a week.

Some cable executives have suggested yet a sixth reason that broadcast-style ratings should not be used for cable. They contend that because a cable channel audience may be small but upscale, the measurement of that audience should yield qualitative data (how much the audience liked the program; how closely they paid attention), as well as quantitative data.

### 18.2.3.4 Syndicated and Other Program Ratings Services.

Syndicated programs air at different times on stations across the country, so measurement techniques for national audiences differ from those used for networks. Nielsen provides a market-by-market analysis of over 300 syndicated programs in its *Report on Syndicated Programs.* Nielsen also provides separate reports for Public Broadcasting System and religious programming. Nielsen's **Cassandra,** a computer software system, reports national ratings and other information on syndicated, network, and local programs. Cassandra provides information on lead-ins and lead-outs as well as competition for programs.

Nielsen's **AMOL** system (automated monitoring of lineups) tracks TV programs showing on stations and cable systems all across the country. Under this system, a **coded ID number is embedded in the top edge of the picture and transmitted in the vertical blanking intervals of TV programs.** The codes, not visible on screen, identify program and episode and are downloaded into Nielsen's computer system. Without AMOL, Nielsen could not provide national data on syndicated programs or commercials. Nielsen uses similar technology in its **Monitor-Plus** system, which monitors and provides data on commercials telecast across the nation.

## 18.3 POLICING AND PROBLEMS

In the early 1960s broadcasters began to rely heavily on ratings in evaluating and making decisions on broadcast programming. Questions emerged regarding the methodology used by the research firms and the accuracy of their results. A congressional committee investigation in 1963 and 1964 confirmed weaknesses and shortcomings in audience measurement.

### 18.3.1 Electronic Media Rating Council

The National Association of Broadcasters (NAB) led efforts to form a body to ensure that rating services met certain standards. NAB joined with ABC, CBS, NBC, the Radio Advertising Bureau, Station Representatives Association, and Television Bureau of Advertising to form the Broadcast Rating Council in January 1964. In 1982, the organization changed its name to the **Electronic Media Rating Council (EMRC)**. Various media groups, including broadcast and cable, sit on EMRC's board of directors.

EMRC's main objective is **to maintain and improve the quality and credibility of electronic media audience measurement.**

### 18.3.2 Distortion of Radio Ratings

Despite the efforts of EMRC and the research firms, problems arise. For example, station employees and their families are not supposed to be selected for the sample, but occasionally someone will slip through. Stations occasionally use blatant attempts to influence ratings. Some radio stations, for example, have aired announcements such as "If you're keeping a rating service diary, remember you're listening to WAAA" and "If you have a friend filling out a little book, tell him or her about the new Y-100."

### 18.3.3 Distortion of Television Ratings

Several incidents during the May 1987 sweeps highlighted problems with television ratings. A Los Angeles station chose sweeps time to broadcast nightly features on Nielsen families during its 11 p.m. news. "What better way to boost news ratings," asked *Broadcasting* rhetorically, "than do an eight-part series on Nielsen families in the middle of the May sweeps, promote it heavily and have [the Nielsen families] tune in to find out about themselves?"[3] At the same time, stations in Minneapolis, Orlando, and Atlanta hired a firm to conduct a "survey." The firm sent out thousands of "questionnaires" at the beginning of sweeps, asking recipients to watch the sponsoring station "as often as possible, then offer your reactions."[4]

Of course, stations customarily engage in contest *hypoing* (*PRT,* 7.7) during sweeps, and ratings books will mention such efforts in footnotes. The line, then, between acceptable hypoing and unacceptable distortion is, at best, thin.

EMRC responded to these problems with new guidelines. The council said that hypoing consists of **contests, advertising, special programs, and other promotional efforts.** Such activity often cancels itself out because most stations do it. Distortion, said the council, encompasses activities aimed directly at the sample that could influence sample respondents to view or report viewing differently than they would have normally. EMRC listed examples of distortion that had occurred during the May 1987 sweeps. It also included contests run only during sweeps that award prizes more valuable than those usually awarded.

The council recommended that research firms take one or more of the following measures to deal with distortion—add a footnote that describes the distorting activity—now a common practice, delete the time period during which the distortion occurred, print ratings both with and without the affected programming, and delist (omit the ratings of) the station for the entire period.

### 18.3.4 Other Ratings Problems

Some problems arise from the very nature of survey research and ratings. For example, reports from two firms sometimes show different ratings for the same time period. The firms try to explain the disparities, citing differences in sampling procedures, statistical treatment of data, and definition of market. A survey researcher may see a 23,000-person difference in HUT as the logical result of different approaches of two different firms. But a station manager—who must devise a rate card and deal with ratings-conscious media buyers—may see it another way.

Another problem with ratings is more subtle, widespread, and long range—their misuse by radio and television programmers. As ratings go up, so do advertising rates. Therefore programmers carefully tune their product to attract maximum audiences. The result is a predominance of inoffensive, middle-of-the-road programming and near total absence of minority taste programming—for example, documentaries; serious music, drama, and dance; and minority racial and ethnic programming.

### 18.4 USING AUDIENCE RATINGS

Ratings are used for much more than simply compiling average quarter-hour audiences, shares, and cume. The data do provide gross measures that indicate how many listeners are exposed to a client's commercials. However, ratings numbers also provide the basis for understanding how a station's audience turnover rate compares with competitors, how much a station must charge for its commercials to reach an audience as cost effectively as other stations, and to what extent listeners in one daypart tune in during other dayparts.

## NOTES

1. We are assuming that all receivers in multiset households tune to the same station. If a household contains two or more sets and all tune to the same program, the household counts in that program's audience only once. However, if the various sets tune to different programs, then the household counts in the audience of each of those stations.

2. Thomas F. Baldwin and D. Stevens McVoy, *Cable Communications* (Englewood Cliffs, NJ: Prentice-Hall, 1983): 285–286.

3. "KABC-TV series on Nielsen draws fire," 8 June 1987: 38.

4. Quoted in "Lines blur between hype and distortion in local sweeps," *Broadcasting* 29 June 1987: 40.

## FURTHER READING

Balon, Robert E. *Rules of the Ratings Game.* Washington, DC: National Association of Broadcasters, 1988.

Beville, Hugh Malcolm, Jr. *Audience Ratings: Radio, Television, Cable.* Rev. ed. Hillsdale, NJ: Lawrence Erlbaum Associates, 1988.

Buzzard, Karen. *Electronic Media Ratings: Turning Audiences into Dollars and Sense.* Boston: Focal, 1992.

Dominick, Joseph, and James Fletcher, Eds. *Broadcasting Research Methods.* Boston: Allyn-Bacon, 1985.

Ettema, James S., and D. Charles Whitney, Eds. *Audience Making: How the Media Create the Audience.* Thousand Oaks, CA: Sage, 1994.

Fletcher, James E., Ed. *Handbook of Radio and TV Broadcasting: Research Procedures in Audience, Program and Revenues.* New York: Van Nostrand, 1981.

National Association of Broadcasters. *NAB Research Definitions.* Washington, DC: Author, 1987.

Warner, Charles. *Broadcast and Cable Selling.* 2nd ed. Belmont, CA: Wadsworth, 1993.

Webster, James G., and Lawrence W. Lichty. *Ratings Analysis: Theory and Practice.* Hillsdale, NJ: Lawrence Erlbaum Associates, 1991.

Wimmer, Roger D., and Joseph R. Dominick. *Mass Media Research: An Introduction.* 4th ed. Belmont, CA: Wadsworth, 1994.

# 19

## LOCAL OUTLETS

The basic unit in U.S. radio and television is the local outlet. Thousands of relatively small radio and television outlets, owned by hundreds of licensees and operators, provide programming for millions of Americans. Despite DBS and other direct-to-home media, it is the local outlet that provides you with local information. Further, broadcast and cable networks are useless without local stations and cable systems. No matter how elaborate and exciting a network's programming, your community cannot receive it unless a station, cable system, or other local outlet elects to carry it.

Let us consider broadcasting as an example. Other countries started with more efficient systems—a small number of high-powered transmitters that covered the entire country. A few sources or even a single agency handled all programming. By comparison, the United States' local stations seem redundant and expensive. Yet, the U.S. system can serve local needs, a capability long absent from some other nations' systems. The station functions as a member of the community, providing entertainment, information, and opinion. It is an employer, hiring, firing, and training personnel. It is a mixture of show business and marketing, a meeting ground for commerce and art. Most important to the commercial station owner, the station is a business, an investment from which to expect a profitable return.

In this chapter we concentrate on the local commercial radio or television outlet. We look at station licensees—types of owners, limits on ownership, and the difficult task of getting, keeping, and transferring a license. We examine station income and expenses. We see what a station is like inside and who works there. We review the organization of a cable system and local outlets in other forms of TV. Then we discuss unions in radio and TV. Finally, we look at some of the major trade associations pledged to protect the interests of radio and television.

### 19.1 BROADCAST STATIONS AS LOCAL OUTLETS

A **licensee** is the person or corporate entity entrusted with operation of a broadcast station by the FCC. Although the licensee can own the physical plant—land, building, equipment, transmitter—the frequencies on which the station operates are borrowed, terms of the loan being operation in the public interest. A licensee must sign a waiver disclaiming ownership of frequencies. The license itself is temporary, and the licensee must reapply every 8 years. However, if the actual distinction between the two words is understood, *owner* can be used synonymously with *licensee*.

### 19.1.1 Broadcast Station Ownership and Licensing

The owner of a broadcast station may be one person, a partnership, or a group of persons. If more than one person, shares of ownership may be equal or varied. The use of creative financing (*PRT,* 3.5.3.2) brought new concepts of ownership to broadcasting, such as the **limited partnership** (Box 19.1).

Often the official owner is a corporate entity. Even if one individual is sole owner, that owner may incorporate for tax or other purposes. An owner whose sole or main business is one broadcast station is a **single owner.** A **group owner** has two or more stations in different cities. An owner with an AM and an FM radio station in the same city is a **single owner with an AM–FM combination,** even when the stations program independently. An owner with two stations in the same service (AM, FM, or TV) whose signals overlap (i.e., are in the same city) is a **duopoly owner.** Owners may enter into a **local marketing agreement**: One station contracts with a second station in the same city to provide that second station with certain services.

Some licensees also own other media—for example, newspapers, cable systems, or magazines. Broadcasting mixed with other media in the same locale is **cross-media ownership.** Broadcasting mixed with other media in different locations is **media conglomerate ownership,** particularly when the media holdings are large and extensive. Broadcasting mixed with other types of businesses—say, a trucking line, an airline, a kitchen appliance firm, and a tire company—is **conglomerate ownership.**

#### 19.1.1.1 Limitations On Broadcast Station Ownership.

The Communications Act of 1934 and the FCC set up two general types of restrictions on ownership of broadcast stations. One concerns who qualifies for a license; the other, how many licenses an individual (or group or corporate entity) may hold.

---

**BOX 19.1. LIMITED PARTNERSHIP**

A limited partnership consists of two type of partners:

1. A **general partner,** who puts up relatively little money, assumes all liability, and runs the business.
2. **Limited partners,** who invest heavily, assume no liability, take no part in directing or setting policy for the business, and reap tax, profit, resale, and other benefits.

---

*Licensee Qualifications.*    The Communications Act specifies qualifications that must be met before a broadcast license is granted. The applicant must be a citizen of the United States or, if a corporation, must be owned mostly by citizens; must never have had a previous license revoked by a court for violating antitrust laws; and must have filed a written application. Additionally, the act directs the FCC to grant a broadcast license only after determining the grant would serve the public interest, convenience, and necessity.

The FCC asks for information about an applicant's **citizenship, character, financial, technical, and "other" qualifications.** The Commission frowns on applicants whose records include any of the following: violations of FCC rules and policies or the Communications Act; misrepresentations (lies) or lack of candor before the FCC; fraudulent programming; and certain types of fraud, antitrust, and felony as they bear on the applicant's ability to comply with broadcasting regulation. Every applicant must certify possession of sufficient financial resources; some applicants may be asked for additional financial information. The applicant does not have to be qualified personally as a technician but does have to show plans for equipment and staff that reflect adequate technical preparation.

*Licensee Limitations.*    For years, the FCC had rules limiting the number of stations in which one commercial licensee could hold financial interest. The aim of these rules was diversification—to prevent broadcast stations from being owned or controlled by relatively few individuals and corporations. The Commission reasoned that such monopoly would reduce the number of outlets for different views and ideas, while raising the number of absentee owners unfamiliar with the needs and interests of the communities in which their stations were located. During the late 1970s and the 1980s, however, the FCC questioned many of its previous assumptions and relaxed rules that derived from those assumptions.[1] In the Telecommunications Act of 1996, Congress directed the FCC to relax several rules even further. It also instructed the Commission to review all ownership rules every 2 years and repeal or modify those that increasing competition had made no longer necessary.

As a result, by the late 1990s, limitations on station ownership had been watered down as follows:

• **Duopoly** (common ownership of multiple stations in the same service whose signals otherwise overlap; once completely forbidden): One licensee can own eight radio stations in one market, as many as five of which could be in the same service. The 1996 legislation required the FCC to consider changing the TV duopoly rules for broadcast television. Those local ownership rules are summarized in Table 19.1.

• **One-to-a-market** (1970 rule that prohibited a new licensee from acquiring both radio and television stations in the same city): FCC amended this rule in 1989 to make certain stations eligible for waivers to the rule. The Telecommunications Act of 1996 directed the Commission to extend its waiver policy to the 50 largest markets.

**TABLE 19.1**
Local Limits on Broadcast Station Ownership

| Radio | | | |
|---|---|---|---|
| *Number of Stations in the Market* | *Number of Stations Permitted Under Common Ownership* | | *Other Limitations* |
| | *Total* | *In one service (i.e., AM or FM)* | |
| 14 or fewer | 5 | 3 | May own no more than half the commercial stations in the market. |
| 15–19 | 6 | 4 | None. |
| 30–44 | 7 | 4 | None. |
| 45 or more | 8 | 5 | None. |
| Television | | | |

FCC must consider changing the duopoly rule for television. If changed, "grandfathers" existing LMAs that comply with FCC rules, and permits future LMAs to be formed, consistent with FCC rules.

• **National multiple ownership** (originated 1940; for years allowed one party to own up to seven stations nationwide in each service—TV, AM, and FM—for a total of 21): Relaxed by the FCC several times until one party could own 52 radio and TV stations nationally,[2] and the signals of that party's TV stations could cover as much as 25% of the nation's households.[3] In 1996 Congress told the FCC to delete all numerical caps for radio and TV station ownership and to increase the national audience reach cap to 35%.

• **Newspaper–broadcast cross-ownership** (adopted in 1975): Forbids broadcast stations to be co-owned with newspapers in the same market.

• **TV–cable cross ownership** (adopted in 1970): Forbids a party from owning both a TV station and a cable system in the same market. Congress wrote this into law in 1984 and repealed the law in 1996 but left the FCC's original rule in place.

*19.1.1.2 Broadcast Station Licensing Process.*   The process to get a license for a new broadcast station is long and complicated. Many things can go wrong and further complicate the process.

In this section, we trace the steps to license a new broadcast station. We assume that the applicant has done the necessary preliminary work—found a channel, incorporated or otherwise organized, and raised money. That being done, the applicant **files a written application for a construction permit** (CP)[4] on a specific form with the FCC. The application requires technical information and data on the applicant's citizenship, character, and financial qualifications. The applicant must also run a notice about the proposed station in the newspaper.

At the FCC, the staff **receives the application and checks it.** If substantially complete, the application is accepted, and the applicant is notified to supply any missing information. If not substantially complete, the application is returned.

At this point, at least four problems could occur. Any one could delay grant of the CP and generate additional expense for the applicant. Those four problems are as follows:

1. Someone could **petition to deny the application.** The petition must meet several tests for the FCC to accept it; if accepted, the FCC examines and either denies the petition or designates the matter for hearing.
2. Others could apply for the same channel. This means the FCC now has **competing applications** and must dispose of them as outlined later (*PRT,* 19.1.1.3).
3. Someone may file an **informal objection** to the grant of the construction permit. This is neither as serious nor as formal as the petition to deny or as competing applications, but it could lead to the next problem.
4. The FCC may, on its own volition, hold a hearing anytime it has reason to believe that the public interest might not be served by the grant of the CP. This is a **hearing on motion by the Commission.**

Let us suppose that the application runs into none of these problems. If the FCC determines that construction of the station would serve the public interest, then the **CP is granted.** The Commission actually has the power, if it finds that the public interest would be served thereby, to waive the requirement for a CP. This is rare, and for all practical purposes, a would-be licensee must have a CP before beginning construction.

Once the CP is granted, the applicant is a permittee and may build the station. The time limit is **24 (for TV) or 18 (for all others) months to complete construction,** although the FCC may grant extensions. On completion, the station **runs equipment and program tests.** The permittee then **applies for and receives the station license,** changing status from permittee to licensee.

### 19.1.1.3 Choosing Among Competing Applications for Broadcast Channels: Comparative Criteria, Lotteries, and Auctions.

For years competing applications for AM, FM, and full-power TV stations had to go through a cumbersome, time-consuming process that involved hearings before an FCC administrative law judge (ALJ). Considering evidence presented at the hearings, the ALJ evaluated each applicant using **comparative criteria,** which had been adopted by the FCC and reflected various stated policy goals of the Commission in licensing. Then, in the initial decision, the ALJ awarded the license to the applicant that showed superiority in these criteria.

Applicants learned to respond to the comparative criteria. They promised whatever it took in the areas of programming and ownership to win a license. Once on the air, their long-range operation and management structure bore little resemblance to their promises. And because most applicants aimed submissions at the FCC's criteria, most applications looked good, making the FCC's job of choosing the best applicant almost impossible. The ALJ would have to base the initial decision on points of difference that laypeople saw as esoteric at best. Other applicants often appealed the decision all the way to the federal courts. By the time side issues had been cleared and all appeals exhausted, years could pass, costing both applicants and taxpayers a great deal of money.

A 1982 amendment to the Communications Act authorized the FCC to use a **lottery system to select from among mutually exclusive applications** (two or more applicants apply for one channel). The FCC said that it would use a lottery only as a tie-breaker in comparative proceedings. If the ALJ found two or more applicants equally qualified, then the award of the license would be determined using random selection procedures, that is, by lot. But a 1988 court decision[5] ruled the FCC's procedures invalid because they did not comply with requirements spelled out in the law. Two years later the FCC decided it would not use lotteries at all but would instead work to improve the efficiency and integrity of the traditional comparative hearing process.[6]

In 1994, however, the FCC announced that it was putting a freeze on comparative proceedings. A federal court had clouded the legality of the criteria in its *Bechtel* v. *FCC* (1993)[7] decision. So the Commission said it would process no more comparative proceedings until it decided what to do next. Meanwhile, in 1993, Congress had passed legislation authorizing the auction of certain frequencies. This was a first, and although the law said nothing about the regular broadcast frequencies, some viewed it as a precedent that could eventually affect the manner in which broadcast licensees are selected.

The FCC did, however, take advantage of the lottery option for low-power television, wireless cable, the instructional television fixed service (*PRT,* 5.2), and cellular telephone. Just as applicants had learned to use the comparative criteria, so, too, did they quickly learn to use the lotteries. This was most evident in lotteries for cellular telephone frequencies. No one doubted that cellular licensees would make a lot of money. This encouraged speculation. Groups that had neither resources nor intention of providing cellular telephone service submitted applications, the idea being that they would sell frequencies they won to actual telephone service providers for a huge profit. They circumvented FCC attempts to ferret out speculators, and disputes concerning applications held up the award of many licenses. The winners did, indeed, make big bucks, often by means of a private auction at which they sold their newly won frequencies to service providers for the highest bid.

Meanwhile, political rhetoric had thrust the issue of the national debt into the spotlight. The amount owed by the United States had become so large that interest payments alone reached almost unimaginable proportions. Noting the lucrative success of FCC lottery winners in auctioning frequencies, Congress decided to remove the middle level from the auction process so the government could make money.

In the Omnibus Budget Reconciliation Act of 1993,[8] Congress authorized **auctions of frequencies for nonbroadcast services.** The FCC used competitive bidding to award frequencies for several telephone and interactive services. By

1996 FCC auctions had generated over $9 billion for the U.S. Treasury. With auctions of nonbroadcast frequencies successful at generating revenues, some voices in government argued for competitive bidding for broadcast channels. The FCC demonstrated the efficacy of such an idea in 1995 and 1996 when it auctioned frequencies for two broadcastlike services, MMDS (for wireless cable) and DBS. Some legislators called for the analog-to-digital conversion plans for over-the-air TV (*PRT*, 12.5.2) to include a channel auction. Broadcasters did not like that idea.

***19.1.1.4 Change in Broadcast Station Facilities, Ownership, and Control.*** A licensee may wish to change facilities. Typically, the change might be to raise power, to expand allotted operating time, to move to a different channel or location, to modify antenna array, or to install improved transmitting equipment. To do so, the licensee must apply for a CP.

The Communications Act stipulates that any change in ownership or control of a broadcast station must be considered by the FCC before that change takes place. If a licensee wishes to sell a station, that licensee must first apply to the FCC. On receipt of the application, the Commission considers whether the public interest would be served by the transfer. The FCC is prohibited from inviting and considering competing applications, limiting its choice to approval or disapproval of the transfer.

Some applicants apply for a station not to operate it but to sell it at a profit. This is **trafficking** in station licenses, a practice that was rife after the 1952 end of the freeze on TV licensing (*PRT*, 3.1.2–3.1.3). Trafficking negates the concept of licensing a station to serve the public interest. For years the FCC barred a licensee from selling a station within 3 years of acquiring it. The Commission repealed its antitrafficking rule in 1982, saying that market conditions no longer warranted retention. Two years later, the Commission raised limits on station ownership, and the 1980s buy–sell frenzy began in earnest (*PRT*, 3.5.3.2).

The FCC is interested in other forms of change of control. Trading in major blocks of stock in a corporate licensee, for example, could alter control of that licensee. The licensee would still own the station, but a new party would control the corporation. A similar situation could occur in a partnership. Such changes require prior written permission of the FCC.

***19.1.1.5 Renewal of Broadcast Station Licenses.*** There are two exceptions to the 8-year renewal period for broadcast licenses. One is the short-term renewal (*PRT*, 14.1.1.13). The other occurs when a new station gets its first license between renewal periods for its state. The station must renew early to get "in phase" with the state's other stations.

A station files for renewal no later than 4 months before expiration of its current license. A filing fee must accompany the application. In completing the renewal application, a TV applicant must respond to, among other things, requirements of the Children's Television Act of 1990. The form asks whether the licensee has conformed to limits the act places on advertising, and it calls for an attachment showing compliance with the act's programming requirements. TV stations must also include a summary of any "comments and suggestions" they have received from the public concerning violent programming. Other renewal duties include broadcast of public notices of renewal and insertion of certain material into the station's public file. This material includes statements that the public notices were broadcast and a copy of the completed renewal application.

### *19.1.1.6 Other Broadcast Station Regulatory Requirements.*    Copies of certain documents—generally, agreements or contracts that affect station management or programming—must be (according to the type of document) either filed with the Commission or retained at the station for possible FCC inspection. Each year, the licensee must either file an FCC Ownership Report or certify the accuracy of the current report on file with the commission. Broadcasters and other media regulated by the FCC must pay a yearly regulatory fee, a legislatively mandated payment intended to reimburse the government for the cost of regulation. The licensee must air programming that deals with community issues and note such programming in the station's public file. A broadcast station must maintain a public file and each TV station must keep written comments and suggestions from the public on violent programming.

Under federal law, every station must establish a program to afford minorities and women equal opportunity in employment. This program aims to include women and minorities in both the general station staff and in the upper level staff—officials, managers, professionals, technicians, and sales personnel. A station applying for license renewal submits a Broadcast Equal Employment Opportunity Program Report plan with its renewal form. Stations with five or more employees complete the program report in detail and also submit an Annual Employment Report.

### *19.1.1.7 Loss of Broadcast License.*    In *PRT,* 14.1.1.13, we said that two FCC sanctions involve loss of license—denial of renewal and revocation. Three studies[9] of FCC action during the period between 1934 and 1988 found that only 147 licenses had been removed, and that 30 different types of violations were cited in those removals. The seven most frequently cited are listed in Table 19.2. The greatest number of violations were misrepresentation—that is, lying to the Commission. The second and third most frequent violations were engineering-type problems; the fourth, licensee character qualifications. The fifth resulted from licensees ceasing to broadcast without notifying the FCC; the sixth, from not programming as promised in the renewal application; the last, from failure to submit required FCC reports in correct form.

Occasionally someone will file with the FCC a **petition to deny renewal** of a station's license. The charge is that the licensee has not done well in serving the public. If the FCC finds the petition to have merit, it may designate the matter for hearing. This rarely happens. It has happened enough, however, that the

**TABLE 19.2**
Violations Resulting in License Removals: 1934–1988

| | |
|---|---|
| Misrepresentation | 60 |
| Control violations | 47 |
| Technical | 37 |
| Character qualifications | 17 |
| Abandonment | 13 |
| Promise versus performance | 13 |
| Report violations | 11 |

*Note.* Based on Hallock 92.

licensee may attempt to negotiate with the petitioning party rather than risk going through the expense and time of an FCC hearing. If the negotiation is successful and the petitioner agrees to withdraw, they seek FCC approval of the settlement.

Conditions of a petition-to-deny settlement have often required the licensee to pay the petitioner. This gave rise to charges by licensees that most such petitions amount to blackmail. In 1989 the FCC revised its rules to curb such practices, labeling them "abuses" of the renewal process.

In the past, licensees also complained about vulnerability to **strike applications.** It worked like this. A station's license to operate on, say, TV broadcast channel 6 would come up for renewal. The incumbent would apply to renew the license, but another party would also file to operate on channel 6. If the matter went to hearing, the challenger seemed to have an unfair advantage. After all, no matter how good the incumbent's record in serving the public interest, the challenger could promise more. And the challenger's application would certainly be structured to look better than the incumbent's record in any weighing of comparative criteria (*PRT,* 19.1.1.3). The incumbent licensee, wishing to avoid the expensive and time-consuming hearing process, often elected to pay the challenger in return for withdrawing the competing application—which, according to many broadcasters, was probably why the challenger had filed the strike application in the first place.

The FCC attempted to tilt the process back toward the incumbent licensee with policy and rule changes during the 1980s. Congress, however, closed the door on comparative renewal proceedings in 1996. It amended the law so that the **FCC may not even consider a competing application unless it first decides to deny renewal of the incumbent's license.** Barring violations of rule or law that are serious or that constitute a pattern of abuse, an incumbent whose station has served the public interest will have its license renewed.

*19.1.1.8 Distress Sales and Minority Preferences.*    One FCC concern over diversity of ownership and control focused on the lack of minority ownership in the electronic media. Without such ownership, reasoned the FCC, viewpoints of African Americans, Hispanics, and other racial or ethnic minorities would not be well represented in the electronic segment of the marketplace of ideas. So the

Commission adopted procedures to encourage the sale of broadcast stations to minorities. One was the **distress sale policy.** Here the FCC gives a break both to licensees faced with renewal or revocation hearings and to minorities who wish to get into broadcast ownership. A licensee faced with such a hearing can sell the station to an applicant with significant minority interest at a "distress sale" price, 75% of the station's market value, before the hearing begins.[10]

### 19.1.2 Financial Management of Broadcast Stations

The primary purpose of any business is to earn a profit. Expenses are deducted from revenues, and the result—the **bottom line**—determines whether the business has been successful. Because a commercial broadcast station is a business, the owner considers its bottom line to be crucial. Profits make everyone happy; owners get return on investment, employees may get raises, capital improvements may be made to the station, programming and other services to the community may be expanded, and new employees may be hired. Losses can mean layoffs, continued use of poor equipment, and cutbacks in programming. Continued losses can lead to sale of the station or surrender of its license.

#### *19.1.2.1 Financial Statements: Balance Sheet and Income Statement.*
Broadcasters and all other businesses use certain procedures to track revenues and expenses. These procedures constitute the **accounting process.** Accounting yields a set of **financial statements**, documents that provide useful information about the financial standing of the station—information such as whether it has made a profit or lost money.

One financial statement, the **balance sheet** (Table 19.3), reflects the general economic condition of the station as a business. The balance sheet is so called because it sets forth the value of the station's assets, liabilities, and equity balanced in this way:

$$\text{Assets} + \text{Liabilities} = \text{Equity}$$

(Liabilities is a negative value; adding it to assets results in subtraction.) In other words, if the station assets were sold off at face value and all creditors paid from the proceeds, the remainder would go to the licensee. (The total station, however, is generally worth more than the sum of its liquidated assets.)

Another financial statement, the **income statement,** shows licensee economic activity through time. Also called a **profit and loss statement,** the income statement sets forth revenue, subtracts from it expenses incurred in earning that revenue, and derives income after taxes, the bottom line mentioned earlier. A commercial broadcast station receives most of its **revenue** from ad sales. Other sources include network compensation, talent fees, charges for use of facilities, syndication or sale of programs, merchandising, and return on investment. Money the station pays out constitutes **expense,** and expenses are frequently categorized into four areas—programming, technical, selling, and general and administrative.

**TABLE 19.3**
Broadcast Station Balance Sheet

| (*Date*) | | |
|---|---|---|
| | *This Year* | *Last Year* |
| *Assets* | | |
| Current assets | $ | $ |
| Cash | | |
| Temporary investments | | |
| Receivables, less reserves | | |
| Inventories | | |
| Broadcasting rights | | |
| Prepaid expenses | ___ | ___ |
| Total current assets | | |
| Fixed assets, less depreciation | | |
| Deferred charges | | |
| Broadcasting rights, noncurrent | | |
| Other assets | | |
| Intangibles | ___ | ___ |
| Total assets | $___ | $___ |
| *Liabilities and Capital* | | |
| Current liabilities | | |
| Accounts and notes payable | | |
| Taxes and amounts withheld from employees | | |
| Accrued expenses | $___ | $___ |
| Total current liabilities | | |
| Deferred income taxes | | |
| Deferred credits | | |
| Long-term debt | | |
| Other liabilities | ___ | ___ |
| | ___ | ___ |
| Capital stock | | |
| Additional paid-in capital | | |
| Retained earnings | | |
| Treasury stock | | |
| Common | ( ) | ( ) |
| Preferred | (___) | (___) |
| | ___ | ___ |
| Total capital | | |
| Total liabilities and capital | $___ | $___ |

*Note.* Used by permission of Broadcast Financial Management Association.

Salaries, wages, and commissions usually make up the greatest expenditure in each area. Typically, TV stations spend most on programming; radio stations, on general and administrative, with programming as the second largest expense.

*19.1.2.2 Factors in Broadcast Station Profitability.*   As outlined in Box 19.2, station revenue levels vary by station type. Most stations of all types, however, experience periods during which, for one reason or another, profits drop or losses occur. When that happens, some managers panic. They cut ad rates, program cheaply, accept questionable advertising, fire experienced talent, and drop trade association memberships. Such action may trim losses in the short run but lead to more serious problems in the long run as audiences notice that quality has dropped.

A good manager builds in reserves that may be cut temporarily to reduce losses. If a station has good programming and acceptable audience levels, the first items cut are waste and inefficiency. Some managers actually raise ad rates when profits fall or losses are incurred. Assured they have quality programming that attracts target audiences, they know advertisers will continue to buy time, even if prices are higher. Some managers spend even more, pumping money into promotion, sales, and programming, sustaining greater losses over a short period to regain the competitive edge that pays off in the long run.

*19.1.2.3 Factors in Broadcast Station Valuation.*   Buyers and sellers of broadcast properties use various factors to determine market value of a station. In addition to those measures set forth in Box 19.3, one important factor is station revenue. **Cash flow,** for example, reflects the money left after meeting necessary expenses—that is, the money available to make payments on long-term financial obligations. Because most buyers borrow heavily to buy stations, they figure the worth of a station by the cash it generates to service the buyer's debt. They evaluate a station using cash-flow multiples—for example, 6.5 times cash flow. **Leverage** refers to money borrowed on the business itself (rather than on the value of its hard assets), on the business's ability to generate payback cash; a station purchased largely on such a basis is said to be **highly leveraged.**

---

**BOX 19.2. RELATIVE ABILITY OF BROADCAST STATIONS
TO GENERATE REVENUES AND PROFITS**

On the average,

- Full-service TV stations make more than radio stations.
- VHF television stations make more than UHF stations.
- Large-market TV stations make more than small-market stations.
- TV network affiliates make more than independents.
- Network-owned television stations—all large-market VHF affiliates—are much more profitable than other stations.

In radio, the factors vary somewhat. The edge in earnings and profitability tend to go to stations in the FM band, in large markets, with high power. Network affiliation does not have the same value as in television. Keep in mind that we are dealing with averages; you can most certainly find exceptions.

---

### BOX 19.3. BROADCAST STATIONS PRICING CRITERIA

Among the factors that buyers and sellers of broadcast stations consider in pricing a broadcast station are the following:

- Station itself—management, programming, program inventory, financial obligations, and technical facilities (quality, power, antenna and physical plant, and whether they can be upgraded).
- Competition—number of stations, types of other stations (AM, FM, VHF, UHF), and technical facilities.
- Market—cost of programming (how much do stations pay in the market?), availability of programming (have the other stations already bought up the best product?), advertising revenue, economic health, and business trends.
- State of the national economy (especially interest rates) and pending legislation (that might affect ability to profit or worth of the station).

---

### 19.1.3 Broadcast Station Organization

One common classification breaks station operation into six major areas—management, business, sales, programming, news, promotion, and engineering (Figs. 19.1 and 19.2). Each of these may contain subdepartments, for example, production as part of programming. Larger stations may have more major departments; an increasing number of TV stations, for example, have the research director report directly to the general manager. Smaller stations may have fewer major departments; for example, some news personnel report to program directors, and some station managers head both business and sales areas.

### 19.1.4 Small Stations and Large Stations

There are broadcast stations, primarily radio, best described by the term **mom-and-pop**. The typical mom-and-pop radio station is relatively low powered, licensed to a community with a population under 40,000, and run by a family. The husband and wife divide duties—one may act as both general manager and sales manager; the other may keep books, make out payroll, pay bills, and send out invoices. One may take an active hand in programming, doing a daily special interest show or auditioning records. Children pull air shifts or work as office help. The few other employees include two or three air personnel who double in news, sales, or engineering; a full-time account executive or two; a secretary-receptionist who types logs; an engineer; a program director who works an air shift; and a news reporter who also works a short DJ shift. Licensee and employees know the town, and the town knows them. Often the station uses tradeout (*PRT,* 9.1.6.6) to get a new car, office furniture, or whatever the station needs.

At the other extreme is the large-market TV station. Here the licensee is usually corporate and absentee. A personnel department hires, fires, retires, and keeps

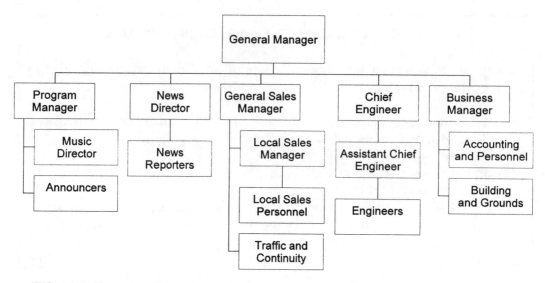

FIG. 19.1. Typical radio station organization chart.

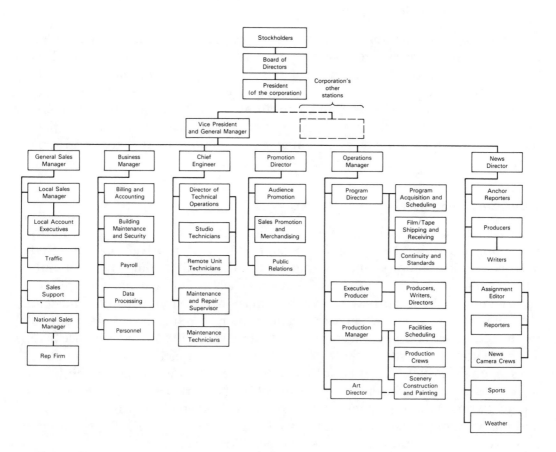

FIG. 19.2. Typical television station organization chart.

track of 100 or more employees. Workers may form unions, believing that they stand a better chance as a group than as individuals to get raises, added employee benefits, and improved working conditions.

## 19.2 CABLE SYSTEM ORGANIZATION

A cable TV system is not licensed by the FCC. Instead, it is franchised by the government of the area it serves. A cable system builds, uses, and maintains a physical communication distribution network to deliver its signal. It derives most revenue from subscriber fees. For these reasons, cable system organization differs somewhat from that of a broadcast station.

### 19.2.1 Cable System Operator

The franchise holder is called the **cable system operator.** Individual franchisees operate some systems, primarily in small towns and rural areas. A few local governments operate their own cable systems (although the cable business opposes municipal ownership). Some schools, colleges, and other institutions operate cable systems. For the most part, however, the typical cable system operator is **private and corporate** and is a **multiple system operator** (MSO; operates more than one system).

During the period of cable's greatest growth, the 1970s and 1980s, three restrictions limited system ownership. Under those restrictions, a party owning a cable system was prohibited from also owning (a) a TV network or, in the same area as the cable system, (b) a TV station or (c) a telephone system.[11] Congress added a fourth limitation in 1992: One party could not own a cable system and, in the same community, build or buy a wireless cable or satellite master antenna television (SMATV) system.

In 1996, however, Congress **repealed the first three limitations and modified the fourth.** The modification allowed common ownership in the same community of a cable system and wireless cable or SMATV system so long as the cable system faced effective competition (Box 19.4). The 1996 act also eliminated a requirement that an operator, on building or buying a cable system, keep that system at least 3 years before selling it. With the 1996 change, operators were free to buy cable systems in the morning and sell them that afternoon.

These 1996 changes reflected a fundamental shift in regulatory philosophy. Government had once restricted the regulated communications businesses in order to protect them from each other and to keep the level of service up and consumer cost down. Now it lowered barriers specifically so that each could get into the other's activity and compete. Those companies that gave the best service at the lowest price would survive; others would have to change or go out of business. Competition, not government rule, would keep service up and cost down. Under this philosophy, cable operators were allowed to offer telephone service in their cable service areas. Customers, of course, would have to find telephone service as convenient to use from one company as from another, so established local telephone companies had to allow newcomer competitors (such as cable-system-based telephone services) to tie into their equipment. But the local telcos, in turn, were allowed into two activities they had long sought: long-distance telephone carriage and, in their own service areas, video programming and delivery. The first would compete with established long-distance telephone carriers; the second with cable systems, especially big MSOs.

That same 1996 legislation eased regulation on other aspects of cable operation and are noted in the following paragraphs. One of the most interesting deregulatory provisions allowed cable operators to change the status of their systems. In writing the 1996 law, Congress created the concept of the **open video system** (OVS). Most discussion of OVS centered on its probable usefulness to telephone companies that wish to get into the cable business, and OVS is defined and explained later (*PRT,* 19.3.2) within that context. Little noted, however, was a provision of the act that, depending on the results of an FCC inquiry, could allow cable operators to change their operations from cable systems to OVSs and thereby avoid many of the local and federal requirements on cable systems.

### 19.2.2 Cable Ownership Patterns

Even before 1996, cable had fewer ownership restrictions than broadcasting. As a result, the cable business established ownership patterns long barred in broadcasting. There was, for example, no citizenship requirement, and Canadian firms invested heavily in U.S. cable systems. There was no rule barring common ownership of a daily newspaper and a cable system that served the same area, nor was there a cable duopoly rule. A cable operator could own systems in adjacent communities, which would allow economic advantages from sharing certain facilities among the separate systems. During the late 1990s, large MSOs took advantage of this freedom to pursue a strategy of **clustering,** to buy, sell, and trade among themselves to acquire contiguous groups of cable systems that served a single, large-market area. Clustering, they felt, would prepare them to offer new services, such as local telephone service, and to compete more efficiently against telcos, DBS providers, and wireless cable operators. Clustering would also allow the MSOs to claim wider franchise areas, most or all of big markets, which would make their systems much more attractive for regional and national advertisers.

### 19.2.3 Cable System Franchising Process

A cable TV franchise grants permission to operate in a particular area. Specifically, the franchise allows the operator to lay cable in rights-of-way controlled by the franchising authority. A large city may divide into several areas, each separately franchised. FCC rules establish minimum standards for franchising, but a local government awards the franchise.

***19.2.3.1 Cable Television Ordinance.***   Typically, a **city council** draws up and adopts a **cable television ordinance** (a municipal statute). The ordinance takes into account FCC requirements and spells out terms of the franchise—what a cable system operator may and must do, length of franchise period, time allowed to build the system, franchise fee (percentage of gross revenues the cable operator pays the city), and complaint procedure. The ordinance also creates a cable television advisory committee to provide aid and information to the city council on cable matters.

***19.2.3.2 Federal Cable System Franchise Restrictions.***   Federal law places limitations and requirements on the franchising authority and the franchising process. The authority may require channel capacity for public, educational, and governmental (PEG) use.[12] The authority may make requirements for facilities, equipment, and broad categories of video programming or other services but may not require specific video programming or services (other than PEG channels). The authority and the cable operator may, however, put an agreement in the franchise to limit or prohibit obscene cable services.[13]

The franchise fee may not exceed 5% of the operator's gross revenues from basic service each year.[14] The authority may not regulate the cable system as a common carrier or utility.[15] In awarding a franchise, the authority must ensure that all neighborhoods and groups have cable service, irrespective of income.[16] (Some operators may be tempted to **cream skim**—wire only affluent neighborhoods because they have the potential of high subscribership and low vandalism rates.)

***19.2.3.3 Award of the Cable System Franchise.***   The city advertises a **request for proposal (RFP),** which invites prospective franchisees to submit applications. These applications describe the system the applicant would build—number and types of channels, tiers, and services; subscriber fees; programming; facilities; ownership; and financial support. The city compares applications; it may pay a consultant to help, analyzing each proposal to determine which offers the best combination of services and the most realistic financial projection. In a public proceeding, the city council chooses the best proposal and awards the franchise. After the award, there may be negotiation on specific terms of the franchise.

***19.2.3.4 Cable System Construction and Operation.***   The franchisee must then build the system, adhering to promises made in the application, to the requirements of the franchise, and to FCC rules and statutory requirements. Federal law does provide means, however, for the operator to request changes in requirements for facilities, equipment, or PEG channels.[17] To obtain modification of the franchise agreement, the operator must make either of two cases to the franchising authority:

1. Demonstrate that the requirement is commercially impractical and, therefore, inappropriate.
2. Show that the modification would not change the service required by the franchise.

On completion of the system, the operator files with the FCC a registration statement. This statement requires identification, location, and signals carried. At that point, the system begins operation.

The operator wishes to ensure that all who receive local cable service pay for it. Federal law helps by prohibiting cable signal piracy. Persons who pirate signals or who manufacture and sell piracy equipment are subject to fines and jail terms.[18]

### 19.2.3.5 Cable System Subscriber Rates and Competition.

A cable system is free to set rates without first getting approval in any of the following situations:

1. The local franchising authority chooses not to regulate cable service.
2. The cable system faces effective competition (Box 19.4).
3. The cable system is operated by a small company.

If the local franchising authority does choose to regulate and the cable system does not face effective competition, **cable rates are regulated by the franchising authority or directly by the FCC** itself. A franchising authority must be certified by the FCC to regulate rates. The law spells out procedures for certification, disapproval of certification, FCC review of authority-set rates, and revocation of jurisdiction. In the event of disapproval or revocation, the FCC regulates system rates directly until the franchising authority is certified.

The regulated rates are **those subscribers pay for the basic service tier** (*PRT,* 7.5.1), **installation, and monthly equipment rates.** In regulating basic service tier rates, the franchising authority or the FCC uses guidelines developed by the Commission.

The 1992 cable act provided for regulation of the subscriber rates for cable programming services; that is, extended basic tiers (*PRT,* 7.5.1). Under law only the FCC could regulate such rates, and it could do so only if requested by subscribers or by state or local authorities. The 1996 cable act, however, declared that **all regulation of subscriber rates on extended basic tiers would cease in 1999.** Further, it **ended immediately all rate regulation for small cable systems.**

For years, most cable systems operated as monopolies. They had no multichannel video competition and no rate regulation. The cable business opposed the idea of another system competing with the original franchisee. They referred to such a challenger as an **overbuild**, a term semantically loaded to imply that the additional system was unneeded and extraneous. As discussed in *PRT,* 19.2.1, the 1996 cable act encouraged establishment of alternate multichannel video systems to compete with existing cable systems. However, Congress "sweetened" this bitter pill by writing the law so that cable operators could enter and compete with telephone companies and other communications businesses.

### 19.2.3.6 Cable System Franchise Renewal.

Toward the end of the franchise period, the operator submits a proposal to the franchising authority for renewal.

---

### BOX 19.4. EFFECTIVE COMPETITION FOR CABLE SYSTEMS

Section 623(l)(1) of the Communications Act (47 U.S.C. § 543[l][1]) says **effective competition** exists when the cable system operates in one or more of the following three contexts:

1. Serves less than 30% of the households in the franchise area.
2. Competes with at least one other multichannel provider that is both
   a. Available to at least 50% of the area's households *and*
   b. Subscribed to by over 15%.
3. Competes with at least one local-exchange-carrier-based service that offers video programming directly to subscribers by any means (except DBS), so long as the service's programming is comparable to that of the cable system.
- A **multichannel provider** is a business that makes multiple channels of video programming available to subscribers or customers, for example, another cable system, a wireless cable system, a DBS service, or a TV receive-only satellite program distributor.
- A **local exchange carrier** is a telephone company.
- **By any means** translates as just that: telephone-company-based-video service qualifies as effective competition no matter what the actual means of delivery, and there are no minimum percentages as with non-telephone-company multichannel providers.

  For example, any of the following scenarios would qualify as effective competition to an existing cable system:

- A telephone company forms a subsidiary that builds and programs a cable system to which 13% of area households subscribe.
- A telephone company builds and programs a wireless cable system that covers 37% of the area's households.
- An independent firm, not owned by a telephone company, programs a video service, pays a telephone company for use of telephone lines to deliver the service to subscribers, and has 7% of total area households as subscribers.

---

Hearings may be held. If no problems appear, the franchising authority renews the franchise. If, on the other hand, the authority wishes to deny renewal, the denial must "be based on one or more adverse findings"[19] concerning the operator's record with the system.

### 19.3 TELEPHONE COMPANY ORGANIZATION FOR VIDEO SERVICE

AT&T and its affiliated regional Bell operating companies (RBOCs) had, for years, wanted to expand beyond telephone service into other areas of the communication business. One area they targeted was cable TV. After all, with technological advances in optical fiber and digital compression, they could deliver video channels over the same standard twisted-pair copper wire through which they provided telephone service. They could not, however, go into the cable business because they were, by law, information carriers, not information providers. The 1984 breakup of the Bell system led to the newly independent companies being allowed to offer new products and services. Within their respective service areas, however, the RBOCs still could not operate cable-system-like services. They could acquire and operate cable systems outside their service areas, and some did.

### 19.3.1 Three Choices for Telephone Company Video Service

In writing the 1996 telecommunications act, Congress eliminated the ban against telephone companies providing video programming in their own service areas. Under this law, a telephone company may operate a video service in one of three modes: **as a cable system, as a common carrier, or as an open video system.** A telephone company that chooses to operate its video service under the first or second option is regulated accordingly. For example, if a telephone company operates a cable system, it must obtain a franchise, provide access channels, and abide by federal requirements such as must-carry. If it operates its video service as a common carrier, it provides facilities for others to program but no programming of its own.

### 19.3.2 Requirements for OVS

Congress created the OVS option as a compromise. An OVS may program its own channels, but it must also lease channels, on request, to other programmers, companies not connected through ownership or management ties with the OVS, on a nondiscriminatory basis. Should demand for channel capacity exceed supply, the OVS may program no more than one third the capacity itself; the remainder must be dedicated to lease out.

For the most part, OVSs are free from cable regulation. An OVS does not have to comply with legal requirements for leased access, franchising and franchise regulations, rate regulation, equipment compatibility, consumer protection, and customer service. It does have to comply, however, with rules on network nonduplication, syndicated exclusivity, must-carry, and retransmission consent. Although an OVS does not need a franchise to operate, the franchising authority may require the system to provide for PEG access channels; the franchising authority may even impose fees on the OVS's gross revenues.

As noted in *PRT,* 19.2.1, the 1996 act allows cable operators as well as telephone companies to qualify for OVS regulation. Although the law allows common ownership of telephone companies and cable systems in the same market, it bars a telephone company from buying a cable system, and it bars a cable system from buying a telephone company. There are exceptions; such a buyout would be legal, for example, if the telephone company and the cable system were in a rural area with fewer than 35,000 people. But the purpose of the 1996 law in eliminating ownership restrictions was to encourage competition—a telephone company starts a video service to compete with the existing cable system, or a cable system develops telephone service to compete with the existing telephone company—not to encourage one potential competitor to merge with or buy out another.

## 19.4 ORGANIZATION OF OTHER ELECTRONIC MASS MEDIA OUTLETS

A wireless cable (multichannel TV; *PRT,* 5.2) system requires the marketing, installation, and customer service functions of a cable system. SMATV systems (*PRT,* 4.4) have captive customers and need little in the way of marketing and customer support. Wireless cable and SMATV systems rarely do local production, so they need no studios or creative staff. However, licensees of many instructional television fixed service systems do have active local production capabilities. Technical needs of wireless cable and ITFS systems are unique.

Physical and personnel needs of an LPTV station vary with the purpose of the station. If it operates as a translator, an automated repeater of another TV station, it needs space only for its antenna, a small structure to house the electronics, and no full-time staff. An LPTV station that functions like a full-service station needs proportionately more space and staff. The typical LPTV station that does local programming has a staff of 10 to 15 persons, each of whom does several different jobs. LPTVs that operate as part of a wireless cable system simply supply channels for the multichannel service, and the relevant space and personnel needs are those of the system as a whole.

Personnel and facilities requirements of national media also vary with purpose. A DBS programmer, for example, might lease transponder and ground station facilities, in which case it would need studios, control rooms, business offices, operational staff, and administrative personnel. If the DBS service operated on advertising support, it would need a sales staff similar to that of a network. A packager that retails satellite networks to dish owners would need no studios or ad sales operations, but it would need staff and facilities for national marketing, subscriber recruiting, sign-up, and billing. A DBS service that operated on a subscription basis would have these same national needs.

## 19.5 UNIONS IN ELECTRONIC MEDIA

Primary unions in radio and TV for engineers and technicians (often including camera operators and floor personnel) are the **International Brotherhood of Electrical Workers** (IBEW), **National Association of Broadcast Employees and Technicians** (NABET), and **International Alliance of Theatrical Stage**

**Employees and Moving Picture Machine Operators of the United States and Canada** (IATSE; originally a film industry technical union). For directors, the primary union is **Directors Guild of America**; for writers it is the **Writers Guild of America**. NABET also has some nontechnical employees, particularly in the news area.

For performers, the primary unions are the **American Federation of Television and Radio Artists** (AFTRA) and the **Screen Actors Guild** (SAG). SAG, a film industry performers' union, has jurisdiction in film television; AFTRA, in live and tape-recorded radio and television. However, with the convergence of technologies, the differences between film and electronic technologies in radio and television, from the performer's point of view, became all but moot, and SAG and AFTRA considered merging.

Cable television's growth during the 1970s and 1980s attracted both IBEW and the **Communication Workers of America** (CWA). CWA, a telephone workers' union, pushed hard to organize cable employees. Among other unions active in electronic media are the American Guild of Variety Artists, International Brotherhood of Teamsters, and many specialized locals, such as Motion Picture and Videotape Editors Guild Local 776 (IATSE).

Unionization includes few advantages for radio and TV outlets. Most managers prefer not to have unions in their shops. For the employee, unions have advantages and disadvantages. Unionization brings the power of collective bargaining, a help to obtain better wages and benefits. Even the existence of unions—perhaps at other outlets in the market—can yield better pay and hours at a nonunion outlet, as management attempts to keep employees happy and the union out. In a union situation an employee with a complaint can go to the union's shop steward, generally more sympathetic than the licensee's personnel manager.

On the other hand, many employees regard radio and TV as creative media, the studio and the control room equipment as creative tools. Many disc jockeys want to run the audio console, spin records, operate cartridge machines, and announce; they "play" the equipment as integral parts of their show. Many TV reporters like to shoot, edit, and write intros for their own news tapes. In both cases, unionization makes integration of functions difficult. A disc jockey in a unionized shop works with a technician who runs the console and associated equipment; a reporter has a camera operator shoot and an editor put together the tape. The unions argue, however, that such division of labor allows the disc jockey and reporter to concentrate on the essence of their jobs—being an air personality and gathering news—without having to worry about the mechanics of equipment operation.

During the 1980s and 1990s, electronic media unions, like unions in other fields, lost membership and influence, victims of automation and corporate downsizing. NABET, for example, in a 1987 settlement with NBC, agreed to the elimination of some 200 union jobs. The settlement followed a 17-week strike by 2,800 technicians and others. NBC immediately disposed of 35 slots by wiping out two low-level news job categories and let go about 20 news writers. Several weeks later, the network offered 10 shares of GE stock to each of the 5,000 network employees who had continued to work during the strike. A month after that, NBC announced its conversion to robotics, which cut the need for production crew members and operators.

## 19.6 TRADE ASSOCIATIONS

As do owners of businesses in other fields, owners of radio and television outlets band together into trade associations. Of all radio–television media, broadcasting is the oldest and has the greatest number of local outlets, so it has the greatest number of trade associations.

### 19.6.1 Broadcasting Trade Associations

Broadcasting trade associations represent stations in specific geographical areas (e.g., state associations in nearly every state) and with special interests (e.g., Association of Independent Television Stations, Association for Maximum Service Television [TV stations operating at maximum effective radiated power], Television Operators Caucus [large-market group owners]). Trade associations protect and enhance the ability of members to do business. The **National Association of Broadcasters** (NAB) is the largest and most comprehensive.

***19.6.1.1 NAB.*** Since its formation in 1922, the NAB has grown, broadened in scope, absorbed several other organizations, and sponsored formation of still others. Following are just some of the major tasks of NAB:

- Keep constant watch on and lobby FCC, Congress, and other government agencies.
- Provide members with literature, conferences, and workshops on matters ranging from bookkeeping to dealing with the FCC.
- Formulate engineering standards.
- Fund research.

NAB's annual convention brings together all business leaders of broadcasting and includes speeches, seminars, luncheons, receptions, and a giant trade fair of radio–TV equipment.

Station licensees join NAB. A group owner takes a separate membership for each station. Annual dues are based on station income. Licensees elect members to the board of directors, NAB's governing body. The board has two divisions, the radio board and the television board, each with a chair and places for network representatives. The chairperson of the joint board is elected, a working broadcaster; the NAB president is an appointed, salaried, full-time staff member. Both work closely with the executive committee, a small steering group based on the board.

NAB headquarters are in Washington, DC. NAB operates through staff divisions and standing member committees and member task forces. Staff divisions deal with concerns common to all broadcasters and with organizational and internal housekeeping matters. They range from member services (such as professional publications, promotional items, good rates on insurance and car rentals) to government relations (lobbying). Member committees, on the other hand, are more specialized and deal with matters of current and continuing concern to broadcasting and to specific groups of broadcasters. They vary from the Research Subcommittee on Local TV Audience Measurement and the Digital Audio and Satellite Sound Broadcasting Task Force to groups with concerns as broad as copyright and the future of broadcasting. NAB also maintains the Television and Radio Political Action Committee, which contributes money toward reelection of representatives and senators favorable to NAB's point of view.

In addition to worries from external sources—a sometimes-hostile Congress, an occasionally truculent FCC, some activist citizen groups, threat of new electronic entertainment technologies—NAB has had internal problems. Many spring from its varied constituency. NAB attempts to represent (a) two media (radio broadcasting and television broadcasting) that consist of (b) local outlets in a variety of settings and situations.

For example, what in the world does a large-market, group-owned, network-affiliated VHF TV station have in common with a small-market, mom-and-pop Class II AM radio station? Not much. Each has its own set of problems. The ideal solution to those problems often works to the detriment of some other group of licensees, in which case the comprehensive trade association finds itself between a rock and a hard place. If it works on behalf of one class of licensees, it antagonizes another. From time to time, licensees form trade associations that represent their particular situation, groups such as the Clear Channel Broadcasting Service, the National Committee for UHF Television, and the Association of Independent Television Stations. A major drawback of separate organizations, however, is that none have the economic and political clout of the comprehensive NAB.

### 19.6.1.2 Special Licensee Organizations.
Some associations look out for the interests of minority and other special types of licensees. Black licensees may be eligible for membership in the National Association of Black Owned Broadcasters and Hispanic licensees can be members in American Hispanic Owned Radio Association. National Religious Broadcasters, an organization of religious (primarily Christian) licensees, has become increasingly important over the years. The Country Radio Broadcasters and the Concert Music Broadcasters Association represent interests of licensees that program in those particular areas.

### 19.6.1.3 Individual Member Organizations.
Whereas NAB is an association of station licensees, there are organizations for individuals who work in or with stations. Some of these include the Academy of Television Arts and Sciences

(sponsor of Emmy awards for prime-time and local Hollywood programs), American Women in Radio and Television, Broadcast Cable Financial Management Association (accounting and financial personnel), Federal Communications Bar Association (lawyers who practice before the FCC), International Radio and Television Society, Broadcast Designers Association (art direction), National Academy of Television Arts and Sciences (sponsor of Emmy awards for all other national and local categories), National Association of Television Program Executives International (television station programmers; sponsors a convention every year that has become a major factor in marketing programming to stations), Promax International (promotion directors), Radio Television News Directors Association, Society of Broadcast Engineers, and Society of Motion Picture and Television Engineers.

### 19.6.2 Cable Trade Associations

As the cable business grew, so did the number of cable trade associations. Cable operators have formed trade associations at the state level to defend their interests in the various legislatures. They have also formed some regional organizations, such as the Southern Cable Television Association.

At the national level, the best known organization is the National Cable Television Association (NCTA). NCTA serves much the same role for cable operators that NAB does for broadcasters. Comparison is almost inevitable; NCTA is the younger organization, with a smaller membership, financial base, and staff. Nonetheless, NCTA has been extremely effective, particularly in dealing with Congress, the FCC, and other organizations. It has proved its effectiveness repeatedly, carefully choosing targets for action. In negotiations over rules and laws that affect cable, NCTA has achieved compromises that allowed its members to grow and thrive. NCTA has headquarters and full-time staff in Washington, DC; members elect the board of directors that sets policy. In addition to lobbying, NCTA offers membership services, sponsors an annual convention, and maintains its own political action committee. In 1986, NCTA established the National Academy of Cable Programming to take charge of its annual CableACE awards.

The **Community Antenna Television Association** (CATA) is a second national trade association for cable systems. However CATA specializes in protecting the interests of small systems.

Cable also has organizations for individuals. One of these is the Cable Television Administration and Marketing Society (CTAM). CTAM emphasizes the importance of a profitable system, an integral part of which is marketing the cable service to the public. CTAM helped to set up Cabletelevision Advertising Bureau. Some other cable organizations include the following: National Federation of Local Cable Programmers, Society of Cable Television Engineers, and Women in Cable and Telecommunications.

## 19.6.3 Other Electronic Mass Media Trade Associations

When a new medium opens, or when an old medium is put to a new use, the first entrepreneur to make use of the "new" has a monopoly. When the second enters, competition begins—and the two form a trade association. Some other electronic mass media trade associations include the Community Broadcasters Association (LPTV licensees), National Translator Association (LPTV stations that pick up the signal of a full-power TV station that cannot be received well locally and rebroadcast it on a different channel), NIMA International (advertisers using, and programmers of, infomercials, TV shopping, interactive shopping, and per inquiry), Satellite Broadcasting and Communications Association (television receive-only and DBS), and Wireless Cable Association.

The **International Television Association** (ITVA) deserves special attention. This organization serves corporate television—business, industry, and government users of video. Corporate television emphasizes internal use of video, so the public rarely sees the product of ITVA members. Nonetheless, from the point of view of production and innovative use of television, ITVA members do some of the most interesting and creative things in the field. There are ITVA chapters in most areas that have a high concentration of corporate headquarters and major facilities. Some colleges have ITVA student chapters.

## NOTES

1. In 1979 and 1984, for example, the Commission did away with certain types of ownership restrictions that applied to large markets and to regional concentrations of stations.

2. Under both the 1985 12-12-12 rule and the 1992 12-20-20 rule, one party could actually hold ownership (but not controlling) interest in more than the respective 36- and 52-station limits. Under the latter rule, for example, one party could hold attributable ownership (i.e., ownership that "counted" toward the FCC limits) in (a) an additional three AM and three FM stations (for a total of 23 stations in each radio service), as long as the additional stations were controlled (more than half owned) by small businesses or racial minorities; and (b) an additional two TV stations (total of 14) as long as the additional stations were controlled by racial minorities. Further, one party could own TV stations that covered no more than 25% of the nation's households, even if the number of stations owned was less than 12. F. Leslie Smith, Milan Meeske, and John W. Wright, II, *Electronic Media and Government: Regulation of Wireless and Wired Mass Communication in the United States* (White Plains, NY: Longman, 1995) 174.

3. Again, there were provisions for ownership interest to exceed these audience-coverage limitations. Nationwide, one party could hold interest in minority-controlled TV stations whose collective signals reached as much as 30% of the nation's households. In computing the audience percentage limits, UHF television stations were credited with only half the homes in their market areas.

4. Do not confuse the construction permit with a building permit. The former is issued by the FCC, a federal independent regulatory agency, and it allows a would-be licensee to assemble and test transmitting and associated technical equipment in preparing to operate a broadcast station. The latter is issued by a local government, a city or county, and it allows an individual to erect or modify a building, ensuring that construction complies with local codes and ordinances. You, for example, could get a building permit and erect a structure that would some

day be, you hope, a broadcast station, and you could do so without having a construction permit, but you could not hook up and run tests on a transmitter without grant of a CP from the FCC.

5. Telecommunications Research and Action Ctr. v. FCC, 836 F.2d 1349.

6. Random Selection of Broadcast Applicants, 5 F.C.C.R. 4002.

7. 10 F.3d 875. The Bechtel appeal aimed specifically at the FCC policy of awarding comparative credit to an applicant who, if granted a license, would participate in the day-to-day management of the station. The court ruled that the integration of ownership in management criterion was arbitrary and capricious and therefore unlawful. The FCC's freeze is reported in "Washington Watch," *Broadcasting & Cable,* 3 January 1994: 53. The FCC had already made changes to streamline procedures, speed up appeals, and encourage settlements among competing applicants. Comparative Hearing Process, 6 F.C.C.R. 157 (1990); and Comparative Hearing Process (Reconsideration), 6 F.C.C.R. 3403 (1991). It also opened a review of the criteria themselves. Reexamination of the Policy Statement on Comparative Broadcast Hearings, 7 F.C.C.R. 2664 (1992), and 8 F.C.C.R. 5475 (1993).

8. Pub. L. No. 103-66, 107 Stat. 312 (1993).

9. John D. Abel, Charles Clift, III, and Fredric A. Weiss, "Station License Revocations and Denials of Renewal, 1934–1969," *Journal of Broadcasting* 14 (1970): 411; Fredric A. Weiss, David Ostroff, and Charles E. Clift, III, "Station License Revocations and Denial of Renewal, 1970–1978," *Journal of Broadcasting* 24 (1980): 69; and Clay D. Hallock, "Station License Revocations and Denials of Renewal," 1981–1988: FCC Regulatory Sanctions and Philosophy in Perspective," thesis, University of Florida, 1989.

10. As part of its 1980s deregulatory efforts the FCC attempted to abolish minority preferences and questioned their constitutionality. In 1987 Congress forbade the FCC to repeal the policy. Pub. L. No. 100-202, 101 Stat. 1329 (1987). In 1990 the U.S. Supreme Court ruled minority preferences constitutional. Metro Broadcasting, Inc. v. FCC, 497 U.S. 547.

Another FCC effort to increase minority ownership was the **tax certificate program.** The Commission would issue a certificate to any party who sold a station or cable system to a minority. The certificate permitted the seller to defer paying taxes on capital gains (i.e., profit made on the increase in the station's or system's value when sold) on the sale so long as proceeds from the transaction were reinvested in media properties within 2 years. Large media businesses, however, found ways to use tax certificates primarily to avoid paying taxes. This came to a head in 1995 with the proposed sale of cable systems from Viacom, the media programming giant, to Tele-Communications, Inc., the country's largest cable multiple system owner. The sale was structured so that Viacom would get a tax break worth up to $600 million. Congress quickly passed a bill that killed the program. See Self-Employed Health Insurance Act of 1995, at 2, Pub. L. No. 104-7, 109 Stat. 93 (1995). Despite criticisms, the minority ownership tax certificate program had actually worked. One study by *Broadcasting* magazine of stations that had been purchased over the previous 15 years using the tax certificate showed that the "overwhelming majority" were still controlled by minorities. "Minority Tax Certificates: Doing the Job," *Broadcasting* 8 April 1991: 68.

11. Under this rule, a telephone company could operate a cable system where it did not provide telephone service. It could petition the FCC for permission to provide both telephone and cable television service in areas so sparsely populated that a cable-only operator could not survive financially. Congress wrote the FCC's telco-cable rule into law in 1984.

12. Communications Act, Section 611 (47 U.S.C. § 531).

13. Communications Act, Section 624 (47 U.S.C. § 544).

14. Communications Act, Section 622(b) (47 U.S.C. § 542[b]).

15. Communications Act, Section 621(c) (47 U.S.C. § 541[c]).

16. Communications Act, Section 621(a)(3) (47 U.S.C. § 541[a][3]).

17. Communications Act, Section 625 (47 U.S.C. § 545).

18. Communications Act, Section 633 (47 U.S.C. § 553).
19. Communications Act, Section 626(d) (47 U.S.C. § 546[d]).

## FURTHER READING

Albarran, Alan B. *Management of Electronic Media.* Belmont, CA: Wadsworth, 1997.

Baldwin, Thomas F., and D. Stevens McVoy. *Cable Communication.* 2nd ed. Englewood Cliffs, NJ: Prentice-Hall, 1988.

Czech-Beckerman, Elizabeth Shimer. *Managing Electronic Media.* Boston: Focal, 1991.

Ditingo, Vincent M. *The Remaking of Radio.* Boston: Focal, 1995.

Hilliard, Robert L. *Television Station Operations and Management.* Boston: Focal, 1989.

Johnson, Leland L. *Toward Competition in Cable Television.* Cambridge, MA: MIT Press, 1994.

Johnson, Leland L., and Deborah R. Castleman. *Direct Broadcast Satellites: A Competitive Alternative to Cable Television?* Santa Monica, CA: Rand, 1991.

Keith, Michael C., and Joseph M. Krause. *The Radio Station.* 3rd ed. Boston: Focal, 1993.

Krasnow, Erwin G., J. Geoffrey Bentley, and Robin B. Martin. *Buying or Building a Broadcast Station: Everything You Want—and Need—to Know But Didn't Know Who to Ask.* 2nd ed. Washington, DC: National Association of Broadcasters, 1988.

Lange, Mark R. *Radio Station Operations.* Vincennes, IN: Original, 1992.

Lavine, John M., and Daniel B. Wackman. *Managing Media Organizations: Effective Leadership of the Media.* New York: Longman, 1988.

Marcus, Norman. *Broadcast and Cable Management.* Englewood Cliffs, NJ: Prentice-Hall, 1986.

Martin, Robin B., and Erwin G. Krasnow. *Radio Financing: A Guide for Lenders and Investors.* Washington, DC: National Association of Broadcasters, 1990.

O'Donnell, Lewis B., Carl Hausman, and Philip Benoit. *Radio Station Operations: Management and Employee Perspectives.* Belmont, CA: Wadsworth, 1989.

Pringle, Peter K., Michael F. Starr, and William E. McCavitt. *Electronic Media Management.* 3rd ed. Boston: Focal, 1995.

Quinlan, Sterling. *The Hundred Million Dollar Lunch.* Chicago: O'Hara, 1974.

Roberts, Ted E. F. *Practical Radio Promotions.* Boston: Focal, 1992.

Sherman, Barry L. *Telecommunications Management: Broadcasting/Cable and the New Technologies.* New York: McGraw-Hill, 1995.

# 20

# ELECTRONIC MASS MEDIA
# NETWORKS

Only a few years ago, people using the term *networks* were almost always referring to the so-called Big Three—ABC, CBS, and NBC. The commercial networks as they were called—home of the stars, bright lights, glamour, fame and publicity, big money, large audiences, the big time, the ultimate.

Today, the networks are still associated with all of this. The difference is that there are many more television networks. Since 1980, audiences for new broadcast and cable networks such as ESPN, MTV, CNN, Fox, and Nickelodeon, just to name a few, have increased dramatically. You may be just as likely to watch a college basketball game on ESPN or a situation comedy on Fox as any competing program offered on ABC, CBS, or NBC. As a result, audience shares for the original Big Three are much smaller than they were before the 1980s.

Still, whether broadcast or cable, television networks are big business. But what are networks? How and why do they operate? And who are the networks?

In this chapter we seek to answer those questions. We examine the nature of networks, the financial aspects of networks, and the ever evolving network organizations. Finally, we review criticisms of the network system.

## 20.1 NETWORK CONCEPT

All radio, television, and cable networks share several characteristics. Each has two or more interconnected outlets such as the local network affiliate broadcast station in your home market. All outlets receive the same network programming simultaneously. The term *network* also refers to organizations feeding the programs. To most of us, "the networks," usually means the program distributors, not their affiliated outlets.

### 20.1.1 Functions and Purposes of Networks

People form networks to make money. On advertising-supported networks, they hope to sell commercial time to regional and national advertisers. The network system has certain advantages for both advertisers and affiliates.

Commercial networks offer advertisers **convenience, economy,** and **quality.** A firm that buys network time has actually bought time on a group of outlets with one purchase and one bill. The firm pays less for network advertising than for comparable spot advertising on the same outlets. The firm's commercials appear within the context of slick, well-produced programming, and they appear **simultaneously** on outlets across the nation.

Commercial networks offer programming to affiliates. An affiliated station or cable system receives contemporary, highly promoted programming that it could not afford to produce on its own. A broadcast television network can fill almost two thirds of a station's schedule. Network programming increases a TV station's generalized audience-pulling power. An affiliated station, therefore, can usually charge more for advertising than an independent. Advertising-supported cable networks offer cable-system affiliates local advertising windows (*PRT,* 17.4.4) and an increased variety of programming to attract subscribers.

Pay networks are also designed to make money but work somewhat differently. Here, the economic relation of audience to network is direct. The audience pays to watch uninterrupted, uncut programming. Pay networks offer cable and satellite master antenna systems additional subscriber revenues. They also increase the marketing attractiveness of the systems because some households subscribe just to get the pay channels.

### 20.1.2 Network–Affiliate Relations

Most permanent, full-time, full-service broadcast network organizations have a somewhat stable lineup of affiliated stations. Most cable franchise areas still have only one cable system, so each network tries to get one of a limited number of channels on that system.

An **affiliate contract** ties together the network organization and its outlets. Contract terms vary with individual affiliates. Most broadcast network contracts say that the network will provide to the affiliate (a) programming, (b) delivery of the programming, and (c) compensation, a share of the advertising revenues from the programming (*PRT,* 17.4.4).

This sounds like a one-sided good deal for the affiliate. Remember, however, that a television affiliate gives hours of airtime to the network for little cash return. The amount of network compensation varies, but averages only about 5% of station revenues. If the station had sold those hours, it could possibly have earned much more money. TV broadcast networks pay out less than 10% of gross advertising revenues for compensation. The networks' more than 90% pays for high-cost overhead, such as the programming, program development, promotion, and time sales expense.

The network economic pinch of the late 1980s (*PRT,* 3.5.3.4) led ABC, CBS, and NBC to reexamine the very concept of compensation. Network executives renegotiated with affiliates, and in the case of a few stations, compensation was eliminated entirely. Although compensation slightly increased again in the mid-

1990s, some experts predict that the days of compensation to affiliates in all but the largest markets are numbered.

Advertising-supported cable networks usually charge cable system affiliates on a per-subscriber/per-month basis. *PRT,* 17.5.4, describes some exceptions. A pay-cable network (premium service) contract requires the affiliated system to pay a fee for each subscriber to that particular premium service.

Ordinarily, a broadcast station affiliates with just one national network. Many stations, however, particularly radio stations, affiliate with a national network and regional or special networks. In markets with only one or two commercial television stations, one station may affiliate with more than one national network. The station may have **primary** affiliation with CBS and carry most of its programs, and an additional **secondary** affiliation with Fox. The station airs Fox network programs as convenience and scheduling allow.

Affiliates may refuse to carry a network program. The network, in turn, may offer the program to another station in the market. In a three-station market, a broadcast TV network with no primary affiliate must give first-call rights on certain programming to any unaffiliated station in the market. The rule applies to the first 15 hours of prime-time and weekend programs and sports programs.

Broadcast affiliates usually transmit network programming as they receive it. Sometimes, however, they **delay broadcast** (DB)—tape a program as it comes over the line and transmit it at a later time. They may DB network programs that conflict with valuable local programming or that management feels should air at later hour. In the central time zone many stations air syndicated programming after the 10 p.m. local news. This means that late-night broadcast network programs, such as those hosted by Jay Leno, David Letterman, and Ted Koppel, are not seen for up to an hour after the local news. Affiliates receive advance information on content and mechanics of handling programming through network telex and closed-circuit conference calls.

## 20.1.3 Distribution of Network Programming

Distribution provides the means for interconnection. It gets programs from network organizations to affiliates. Typically, the network arranges and pays for distribution costs. Most networks use satellite relay to distribute programming.

***20.1.3.1 AT&T.*** For over half a century, before the development of microwave relay and changes in telecommunications law, AT&T had a near monopoly on network distribution. AT&T owned the long-distance lines that tied the nation together, including the high-quality coaxial cable needed for broadcast. National networks and many state and regional networks had to pay AT&T for distribution.

***20.1.3.2 Microwave Relay.*** The development of microwave relay changed that somewhat. In microwave relay, a modulator converts the network signal to microwave frequencies for long-distance transmission. A transmission reflector focuses the microwave signal to a beam aimed at the next tower some 30 miles distant. The reflector at the distant tower picks up the beam, and a transmitter beams the signal to the next tower. The process repeats until the signal reaches its destination. AT&T replaced long-distance telephone lines with microwave and other companies eventually built microwave relay systems.

***20.1.3.3 FM Sideband.*** Some state radio networks have used FM sideband for distribution. The network fed a signal to high-power FM stations. The stations transmitted network programming on subcarriers (*PRT,* 11.6.2). Affiliated stations used special receivers to pick up the signal for broadcast.

***20.1.3.4 Satellite Relay.*** Development of satellite relay broke AT&T's monopoly on network distribution (*PRT,* 5.3). By the late 1970s, cable and public broadcasting networks found that satellite relay delivered a better quality signal that was more reliable and flexible than any other method of distribution. Some also found it less expensive than AT&T.

***20.1.3.5 Optical Fiber.*** Promoters of fiber optics would like to bring network distribution back to earth. Optical fiber offers a broader transmission band than coaxial cable. It also offers secure transmission without scrambling, requires fewer amplifiers, and transmits video signals virtually without interference. Cable companies such as MCI have major investments in fiber optics. The greatest drawback to further development and network use of fiber optics is cost. The question seems to be which among the various methods of interconnection will prove to be most cost effective?

***20.1.3.6 Rebroadcast.*** Occasionally stations—mostly radio—interconnect by rebroadcast. One station first gets permission to rebroadcast the signal of another. The rebroadcasting station then tunes a regular receiver to, picks up, and retransmits the signal of the originating station. Quality suffers, and interference can be a problem, but it is quick and cheap. A few small-market radio stations have used rebroadcast to get network programming.

### 20.1.4 Network Variations and Parallels

Our definition of network requires interconnection and simultaneity of reception. This excludes **tape networks** that send programs to outlets on videotape. Sometimes, outlets send programs to each other after use. The last outlet returns the program to the originating organization. This is a **bicycle network.** Other nonnetworks include broadcasting spot networks (*PRT,* 17.4.3) and cable soft interconnects (*PRT,* 17.4.4).

By our definition, a DBS does not qualify as a network, nor does a TVRO program packager (*PRT,* 7.4.4). TV superstations do qualify. Satellite relay distributes superstation programming to cable system affiliates beyond the reach of their broadcast signals.

A **temporary network** exists to distribute a one-time event or a finite series of programs. The network often starts when a nonnetwork organization gets radio or TV rights to sports events. The organization arranges for a group of outlets to carry its coverage. Temporary networks based on big-league and major university sports may change affiliate lineups every season.

An **ad hoc network** is a temporary network set up to carry just one program. An advertiser may bypass the broadcast networks and create a network to distribute a one-time entertainment program. A few pay-per-view events distribute on an ad hoc network of cable systems and sometimes in theaters.

## 20.2 PROFIT AND LOSS IN NATIONAL NETWORKING

For years, the three largest broadcast network organizations (ABC, CBS, and NBC) have found the national network business to be extremely profitable. By the 1990s, however, competition from cable and new broadcast networks as well as other sources of programming significantly reduced audiences and potential advertising revenues for the original big three.[1]

Broadcast and cable network operations generate most revenue through sale of time for advertising (Table 20.1). Out of broadcast networks' gross revenues come affiliate compensation, commissions (advertising agencies, representatives, and others), and any discounts the networks grant for cash payment. As with stations, salaries rank among the highest expense items for both radio and television broadcast networks.

Programming is the most costly single expense category. For radio networks, most of their programming consists of news, so most of their programming budget goes for news and public affairs. Television broadcast network programming is so costly that it accounts for about half of all network expenses.

Much of the competition for broadcast television networks comes from cable networks (*PRT*, 3.5.2.1). As cable penetration climbed during the 1980s, cable networks gained audience and advertising, often at the expense of the broadcast networks. This allowed cable networks during the 1980s to move toward stability and improvement and an increasing number began earning profits (*PRT*, 4.3.2).

**TABLE 20.1**
TV Network Revenues and Profits for 1996 (in millions)

| TV Network | Revenue | % Change From 1995 | Profit | % Change From 1995 |
|---|---|---|---|---|
| Capital Cities/ABC | $3,125 | –2 | $410 | 9 |
| CBS | $2,581 | 2 | $25 | — |
| NBC | $4,000 | 33.8 | $380 | 15.2 |
| Fox | $1,700 | 24 | $90 | 20 |

*Note.* From Steve McClellan, "Big Year for the Big Four," *Broadcasting & Cable* 3 March 1997: 4.

## 20.3 DEREGULATION OF NETWORKING

In 1995 the FCC eliminated the last major restriction on broadcast networks programming—the **Prime Time Access Rule.** The rule prohibited networks from providing more than 3 hours of prime-time programming to affiliates on weekdays (*PRT,* 14.1.3.2). The FCC also abolished the **financial interest rules** that had prohibited ABC, CBS, and NBC stations in the 50 largest markets from purchasing off-network programs that had previously aired on those networks. The FCC has also abolished restrictions that prevented the broadcast networks from participating fully in the domestic syndication market.

Broadcast network deregulation has continued. In 1996, the FCC eliminated the dual network rule, meaning **that one corporation could now own more than one broadcast network.** The FCC was also set to eliminate (a) the territorial-exclusivity rule that said a broadcast network and its affiliates could not block another station in the affiliate's market from airing network programming originally rejected by the affiliate; (b) the exclusive affiliation rule that allowed broadcast networks to prevent affiliates from airing programming from another network; and (c) the time-option rule that prevented broadcast networks from placing a "hold" on an affiliate's airtime without specifying whether or how the time would be used. These rule changes reflected the FCC's belief that ABC, CBS, and NBC could no longer dominate the television industry.

## 20.4 SCOPE OF NETWORKING

Until the mid-1990s when you heard someone say "the three major broadcast networks," the description was intended to differentiate the original Big Three from "fourth networks" and cable networks. This changed by 1995, with the astounding growth of the Fox network, the addition of the WB (Warner Brothers) and United Paramount Network (UPN), and the realization that PBS was indeed a significant broadcast network. Now, use of the term *broadcast networks* refers to all noncable network programming services. The number of regional and state networks has also increased dramatically.

### 20.4.1 Major Commercial Broadcast Networks

ABC and CBS have seen significant ownership changes in the 1990s (*PRT,* 3.6.2). In a deal finalized in 1996, Walt Disney Company purchased Capital Cities/ABC, Inc. (CC/ABC) for $18.5 billion to form a huge entertainment conglomerate. In 1995, Westinghouse purchased CBS, Inc. (radio and television) for $5.4 billion, creating the largest broadcast station chain in television and radio. In 1986, General Electric purchased NBC's parent company RCA for just over $6 billion, placing the network under new ownership. GE later sold off the radio network interests to Westwood One for $50 million. The trend continues as large conglomerates purchase and lay plans to purchase large chains of radio and television stations.

### *20.4.1.1 Disney/Capital Cities/ABC, Inc.*

The Walt Disney Company owns vast theme parks in Los Angeles, Orlando, France, and Japan. Disney also owns Touchstone Films, a highly profitable motion picture company, and broadcast stations in major markets. Capital Cities/ABC already owned the ABC network, broadcast stations, publishing activities, and cable programming. Both companies owned magazines and newspapers when they merged in 1985. Through its publishing group, CC/ABC put out trade and consumer periodicals that range from *Iron Age/Metal Producers* to *High Fidelity*. It owns daily and weekly newspapers, shopping guides, specialized database services, and a religious communications firm. Some of its publication units also put out books, visuals, and newsletters; conduct meetings and seminars; provide syndication, marketing, and research services; and sell insurance products. Through its broadcast group, CC/ABC participates in ownership of three cable networks. It holds ownership interest in Arts & Entertainment and Lifetime and controlling interest in ESPN.

### *20.4.1.2 CBS, Inc.*

When Westinghouse purchased CBS, it became the owner of the second largest network in the world. Once a diversified entertainment conglomerate, CBS had sold off most holdings not directly related to broadcasting, including its magazine, book publishing, music publishing, and record divisions. This left the corporation with its network, broadcast stations, other real estate, half interest in CBS/Fox, a home video partnership with Twentieth Century Fox, and a great deal of cash. So, in addition to the CBS network facilities and other CBS holdings, Westinghouse owns an increasing number of television and radio stations.

### *20.4.1.3 General Electric.*

GE divides its diverse activities into four categories. **Technology** businesses include aerospace, defense, aircraft engine, factory automation, medical systems, and plastics. **Core manufacturing** businesses include construction equipment, lighting, major appliances, motors, power systems, and transportation systems. **Support operations** consist of corporate trading, petroleum, semiconductors, and international operations. **Services** businesses include NBC, financial services, and communications and services. Communications and services, in turn, encompasses communications satellites, computer rental and maintenance, business teleprocessing network, design and development of information systems, and assorted communications services for business and the military.

### *20.4.1.4 Broadcasting Activities.*

ABC, CBS, and NBC all have headquarters and production facilities in New York City and executive offices and production studios in Los Angeles. Each network includes owned and operated television stations (O & Os), O & O spot sales organizations, and the networks' programming activities—news, sports, and TV entertainment. They also have departments of engineering and operations, standards, business affairs, marketing, sales, affiliate relations, and public relations.

ABC and CBS both have radio divisions. The radio division oversees the firm's radio O & Os, radio networks, and associated activities. NBC sold its radio businesses in the late 1980s.

ABC and NBC have active cable programming interests. ABC's parent company owns cable networks. ABC and NBC share ownership of Arts & Entertainment. NBC also has half-interest in and programs the cable network CNBC, and through its investment in Rainbow Program Enterprises, other national and regional cable programmers (*PRT*, 3.5.2.1 and 3.6.4). NBC Productions does programs and series for cable networks. All three networks distribute programming overseas, and because the remaining restrictions on financial interest and syndication have been lifted, the networks are now involved in first-run and other domestic program distribution.

### 20.4.2 Fourth Networks

The trade has traditionally used the term *fourth network* to mean another ABC/CBS/NBC-style commercial operation. During the three decades following DuMont's demise (*PRT*, 3.1.4), the three major networks operated unchallenged.

The development of satellite relay significantly improved the survival odds for networking (*PRT*, 5.3). Organizations took advantage of this new distribution technology to start national broadcast television networks.

*20.4.2.1 Fox, Inc.* The most successful fourth network began operation in 1987. Fox now has affiliates in all of the nation's major markets and consistently places programs among the top 10 in weekly Nielsen audience ratings. The parent company, Fox, Inc., encompasses a motion picture studio, a television station group, and the Fox network.

Fox also produces programming—some even for ABC, CBS, and NBC—and distributes programming through first-run and international syndication, pay cable, and home video. Fox includes Twentieth Century Fox Film Corp., Fox Television Stations, and Fox Broadcasting Co. Australian K. Rupert Murdoch put together the whole group (*PRT*, 3.5.2.7) as part of News America Publishing, Inc. Murdoch owns newspapers in several major U.S. cities. The Murdoch empire contains over 250 incorporated subsidiaries worldwide including newspapers in England and Australia and Sky Channel, Europe's dominant satellite cable network.

*20.4.2.2 UPN and The WB.* In 1995, two new broadcast networks—both affiliated with large studios that produced television programming—began operation two nights each week. UPN was a joint venture of the Paramount Television Group/Viacom and BHC Communications, Inc., a subsidiary of Chris-Craft

Industries. The network's strategy for success was to use its own large-market stations along with UHF and LPTV affiliates to reach viewers. By 1996, UPN claimed 152 affiliates and reached 93% of the nation's households.

The launching of WB was a joint effort by Warner Brothers and The Tribune Company, which owns six stations including New York's WPIX and KTLA in Los Angeles. In barely 1 year, WB's Saturday morning children's programming achieved critical acclaim and substantial ratings success. By 1996 WB reached 83% of the nation's households.

### 20.4.2.3 Univision.

Univision-Spanish International Network feeds a 24-hour schedule of Spanish-language programs. By the 1990s, Univision's affiliates included more than 30 stations. Univision programs a full range of programs including news and information. Most programming originates in the United States, but Protele, an affiliate of Mexico's Televisa network, has a long-term contract to supply programs for Univision. As a rep (*PRT,* 17.3.1), Univision specializes in spot TV sales for Spanish-language stations. Cable systems also carry Univision.

The origins of Univision date from the early 1960s. Formerly Spanish International Network, a 1986 corporate realignment gave the network its present name. In 1988, a division of Hallmark Cards purchased Univision.

### 20.4.2.4 Home Shopping Network.

The advent of HSN changed the concept of a network. It also changed the conventional medium–advertiser–audience relation (*PRT,* 17.1). First, HSN attracts an audience with continuous advertising, uninterrupted by entertainment or informational programming (*PRT,* 7.4.2.3 and *PRT,* 9.1.3.3). Second, it generates revenue directly from the audience. Third, sales result solely from network messages, a direct measure of advertising effectiveness. Fourth, the network is the advertiser and so does not deal with a third party to generate revenue. Affiliate compensation is based on sales.

HSN dates back to 1977 when a Clearwater, Florida, radio station carried a shopping service that urged listeners to call and order discounted merchandise. Renamed the Home Shopping Channel, the service moved to several Tampa cable systems in 1982. Three years later, the service changed its name to Home Shopping Network and launched national satellite distribution to cable systems. In 1986, HSN started a second channel, bought television stations, and announced formation of a broadcast network. HSN's owned stations would, of course, carry HSN programming; so, contrary to normal practice, when HSN bought a station, it did not buy rights to syndicated programming for which the station had previously contracted, and this meant the syndicators did not get their money.

### 20.4.2.5 Telemundo Group, Inc.

In 1987, Telemundo Group, Inc., combined its TV stations with a growing network operation. The network targeted the Hispanic population. Initial offerings included drama, music and variety, movies, and news. Telemundo's Spanish-language television stations formed one of the country's largest TV station groups.

### 20.4.3 National Satellite and Cable Networks

Satellite or cable networks proliferated rapidly in the 1980s. Individuals and organizations saw the continued growth of cable. They looked at the success the major broadcast networks had enjoyed and wanted to get in on the ground floor of this new video distribution medium (*PRT,* 4.2.7).

At first, new cable networks encountered serious problems. Most took the form of "how-to-gets": how to get sustained financing until the operation could turn the corner and generate a profit, how to get advertisers, how to get a continuing supply of programming, or how to get on the right satellite, one that most cable systems could receive.

One important how-to-get involved shelf space. **Shelf space** meant channels on cable systems. Especially in the 1980s, cable systems simply did not have enough channel capacity to include every new network that went on the satellite. They already carried signals of local TV stations, premium channels, popular satellite basic services, electronic text, and access programming. Cable operators tried to avoid duplication, too. After all, a subscriber could watch only one direct-response marketing service at a time (*PRT,* 7.4.2.3): Why carry more?

Operator ownership seemed to answer some of the how-to-gets. Multiple system operators (MSOs) wished to encourage development of cable programming. They wanted their systems to carry as much programming as possible that was not originating from the signals of broadcast TV stations. This would make cable subscription more appealing to consumers. It also negated broadcasters' argument that cable competed with TV stations using the station's own signals.

Programmers found MSOs willing to invest in satellite network operations. MSO investment provided startup and operating funds for the networks. It also meant the MSOs now had ownership interest in the networks. Given a selection of new networks, a cable system would tend to choose for carriage those in which its operator had invested.

Other satellite network investors include broadcasters, broadcast networks, and owners of other media. During the 1980s, the broad-based media giants Time Warner, Inc. and Viacom emerged as the largest, most aggressive satellite network operators. They also launched what became some of the most successful cable networks on television.

***20.4.3.1 Time Warner, Inc.*** Time began in 1923 as a magazine publisher. Fifty years later, its media holdings included cable systems (through its subsidiary, American Television and Communications, one of the country's largest MSOs, and through its half interest in another MSO, Paragon Communications), book publishers (Time-Life Books; Scott, Foresman & Co.; Book-of-the-Month Club; and Little Brown and Co., among others), and equity in Turner Broadcasting, as well as magazines (*Time, Sports Illustrated, People, Fortune, Money,* and *Life,* among others, plus ownership interest in *McCall's, Parenting, Working Woman,* Whittle Communications, and others). Time's programming activities included **HBO, Cinemax, and HBO Video.**

Time also made financial news in 1989 by merging with Warner Communications. This created the giant Time Warner media conglomerate (*PRT,* 4.3.4). The merger married the dominant pay-cable service with a major production studio. Warner also operated a large number of cable systems (Time, of course, already owned extensive cable system operations) and significant music and recording businesses. Other Warner interests included TV stations, music and book publishing firms, and *Mad Magazine.*

In 1995, Time Warner purchased the entire Turner Broadcasting System for $7 billion to $8 billion in stock. The merger meant that Time Warner would become the largest media company in the world. Time Warner now controlled CNN and CNN Headline News, as well as TNT and all of Ted Turner's other cable interests and massive film libraries.

***20.4.3.2 Viacom International, Inc.***    Viacom originated when the FCC's now defunct prime-time access and financial interest and syndication rules temporarily put the major broadcast TV networks out of the syndication business. CBS was forced to spin off its domestic syndication arm to CBS stockholders, forming the basis for Viacom. In 1987, National Amusements, owner of a large chain of movie theaters, bought out Viacom. Viacom had continued to handle program syndication (*The Cosby Show, All in the Family,* and others) but had also expanded to production of movies, prime-time network TV series, and miniseries; programming and cable ventures overseas; cable systems; and TV and radio broadcast stations. Its satellite cable networks consisted of Showtime, The Movie Channel, MTV, VH-1, Nickelodeon, Nick at Nite, and Viewer's Choice, a pay-per-view service.

In 1994, Viacom purchased both Paramount Communications and the Blockbuster Entertainment Group. Some analysts suggest that these purchases set off the acquisition fury that has resulted in deals involving Disney and ABC, CBS and Westinghouse, and Time Warner and Turner Broadcasting.

***20.4.3.3 Other Cable Networks.***    The list of cable television networks reaching 10 million households or more continues to grow. As cable systems add shelf space and competition intensifies from DBS and even telephone companies, the number of cable networks seems likely to increase.

## 20.4.4 Broadcasting and Satellite and Cable

Broadcast and cable do not readily divide into neat, separate cubbyholes. A few examples illustrate. HSN operates both cable and broadcast networks. It also owns television stations. Univision and Telemundo are broadcast networks. They also feed cable systems in areas where they have no station affiliates. CBN runs a cable network. It also operates a radio network and owns broadcast stations. Some CBN Family Channel programs run on television stations. So do the programs of several other cable religious networks.

The Turner Broadcasting operation really blurs the lines between cable and broadcast. Turner's holdings, now controlled by Time Warner, include cable networks and WTBS, a television station that programs as a cable network. Time Warner has proposed to transform WTBS into more of pure network operation. CNN makes its news available to TV stations. The Turner holdings also include a cartoon channel, a radio network, and a satellite news gathering co-op for television stations.

### 20.4.5 Television News Networks and Services

Several news services could be classified as networks. For example, Independent Network News (INN), a New York-based service of the Tribune Co., uses satellite interconnection to feed complete nightly and weekly newscasts. Some program syndicators fit in this category. Paramount's *Entertainment Tonight* uses journalistic techniques to assemble a daily satellite feed of soft and show-business news.

### 20.4.6 Special Television Networks

Some firms get TV rights to an event and pay one of these firms to set up a network and handle production and distribution. Two firms that offer such network services are Bonneville and IDB Communications' Hughes Television Network. Wold Communications, a pioneer in the field, merged with Bonneville in 1988. All arrange for production, satellite uplink, and transponder facilities. In addition, syndicators used Wold to distribute program series to stations on a continuing basis.

### 20.4.7 LPTV Networks

By 1990, several national networks fed programs to LPTV stations. These included The Learning Channel, Country Music Television, Telemundo, ACTS, FamilyNet, Capitol TV Network, Channel America, RFD TV, Video Marketing Network, and most of the religious cable networks. The Fox Network took on its first LPTV affiliates in 1988. Since then, Warner Brothers and UPN have used LPTV stations to get into markets where an affiliation was otherwise unavailable. LPTV stations became more attractive to networks in the 1990s when the FCC allowed them to identify themselves by traditional four-letter call signals.

### 20.4.8 Radio Network Organizations

Radio networks provide quality programming to stations. They furnish programming content that affiliates might find difficult to produce on their own. They provide a programming product that sounds polished and slick. Yet, they do not dominate an affiliate's schedule and dictate its format, as do TV networks. Instead, they blend with and improve a station's programming. Most radio networks provide programming for the cost of a few availabilities. Some even pay monetary compensation to affiliates (*PRT,* 17.5.4).

The major national radio network firms include ABC, CBS, Westwood One, and American Urban Network. The organization of a radio network usually parallels its major functions, with departments of sales, programming, promotion, engineering, and affiliate relations. All use satellite relay for distribution.

Some programming and news services resemble networks. Major services include Satellite Music Network, Associated Press, Turner Broadcasting, and Dow Jones. These firms, too, use satellite distribution.

### 20.4.8.1 ABC and CBS Radio Networks.    ABC Radio Networks includes six full-service radio networks, two talk services, weekly entertainment shows, and concert tour sponsorship. CBS Radio Networks consists of two networks and a program syndication unit. Both firms own radio stations and both firms' networks target different audiences (*PRT,* 2.5.3), continuing the concept of format-specific networks that ABC pioneered. All, however, feature primarily news, information, and sports. ABC also carries one of network radio's most popular individual programs, the commentaries of Paul Harvey. In 1989, ABC purchased Satellite Music Network, a satellite-delivered music programming service.

### 20.4.8.2 Westwood One.    During the mid-1980s, Westwood One, Inc., bought its way into the first rank of radio network firms (*PRT,* 2.6). Westwood One began as a program distributor. The purchase of Mutual Broadcasting System gave the firm its first 24-hour, full-service network organization. Its NBC purchase brought in the NBC Radio Network, The Source, and Talknet. Westwood One integrated various functions of NBC and Mutual, including their respective news organizations. In the process, management cut out duplication and overlap in the two networks.

Norman J. Pattiz, a former TV station account executive, started Westwood One in 1975 with an initial investment of $10,000. Just 13 years later, Westwood One had grown into the second largest network radio company in annual billings. By the early 1990s, difficult financial times had forced Westwood One to sell off all of its radio stations. In 1993, Infinity Broadcasting purchased control of Westwood One in a three-way deal in which Westwood One first purchased Unistar from Infinity. Infinity then used the proceeds to purchase 25% ownership of Westwood One. Infinity had previously (in 1989) merged with Transtar, a 24-hour satellite-delivered music network.

### 20.4.8.3 American Urban Network.    In 1992 National Black Network and Sheridan Broadcasting Network merged to form the American Urban Network (AUN). AUN provides Black and urban contemporary stations with news, features, and daily sports reports.

***20.4.8.4 News Services.***   The two major news wire services operate Associated Press Network News and UPI Radio Network. Both operate 24 hours a day, 7 days a week, and feed a full schedule of news, sports, features, business and financial news, farm reports, consumer information, and other material. These are **services**; stations subscribe to them. Programs come to a station with no advertising but include slots into which the station may insert commercials. AP also cooperates with WSM in Nashville, Tennessee, to offer the long-form Country Music Overnight on a barter basis and UPI operates Spanish Radio Network.

Turner Broadcasting's CNN Radio provides long-form news programming. Dow Jones distributes *The Wall Street Report* designed for AM and *The Dow Jones Report* for FM stations.

## 20.5 REGIONAL NETWORKS

Television stations group together into so-called regional networks to sell national or regional spot advertising time; such networks do little or no interconnected programming. Many of the more than 100 regional radio networks are also really sales groupings with no common programming. But there are exceptions. The Intermountain Network, for example, feeds over 130 stations in 10 western states.

Cable has set up regional networks. These include so-called interconnects (*PRT,* 17.4.4), some of which actually interconnect nearby systems and regional cable sports networks.

## 20.6 STATE NETWORKS

A state network feeds radio stations within a single state. State networks have enjoyed success over the last decade. They have their own trade association, the National Association of State Radio Networks.

Most state networks feed hourly newscasts, sports, and features of state interest. Many also feed farm and commodity news. Network–affiliate arrangements often take the form of barter rather than compensation (*PRT,* 17.3.5). Sometimes, the network actually takes the form of a news service for which the affiliate must pay. Increasingly, state networks use satellite relay instead of more traditional forms of distribution.

The North Carolina News Network (NCNN) exemplifies the setup of a state radio network firm. Formerly, NCNN used telephone lines to distribute programming. Back in 1983, the network completed a transition to satellite relay.

NCNN feeds scheduled daily programming to over 90 affiliates in North Carolina; each uses an earth receive station provided by the network. NCNN programming originates at WRAL-FM in Raleigh. Programming consists of hourly newscasts that emphasize North Carolina news, several daily sportscasts, and eight weather summaries. Other programming consists of Sunday public affairs material and daily special interest topics.

Later, NCNN acquired the rights to broadcast football and basketball play-by-play for Duke University and North Carolina State University. Capitol Broadcast Co., which owns NCNN, used these sports rights as the nucleus for creation of the Capitol Sports Network, which operates in tandem with NCNN. Capitol, a group station owner, also operates the Virginia News Network and the University of Virginia Sports Network.

Other regional and state networks include those of college and professional team sports. Sometimes networks organize to broadcast a particular event—a gubernatorial inauguration or state capitol reports during a legislative session.

### 20.7 TVRO AND DBS FIRMS

In *PRT,* 20.1, we exempted TVRO programmers and DBS from our definition of a network. Nonetheless both allow instantaneous distribution of programming over a wide area. Also, activity in these media involve networks. Therefore, this is a good place to discuss TVRO and DBS firms. A more detailed discussion is presented in *PRT,* 5.4.

Some individual programmers allow the home TVRO audience to pick them up at no cost. Others set up services specifically for the TVRO audience. Among the former are the Public Broadcasting System and some of the direct-response marketing and religious networks. TVRO programmers include K-SAT Broadcasting, a talk and call-in radio show run by home-TVRO advocate V. C. Dawson, and Stardust Theater, owned by former NBC programmer Paul Klein, proprietor of the now defunct adult Tuxxedo Network. SelecTV, a pay programmer that feeds subscription TV stations, SMATV systems, and LPTV stations, also has TVRO subscribers.

Four of the leading TVRO programming packagers include the National Rural Telecommunications Cooperative (NRTC), Satellite Broadcast Networks (SBN), Satellite Direct, Inc., Tempo, and Netlink. NRTC represents more than 300 rural electric and telephone cooperatives. It got into the TVRO packaging business as a service to co-op members who own backyard dishes.

SBN originated the idea of network-affiliate superstations. Formed by former Group W Cable executives, SBN operated under the trade name Primetime 24. SBN picked up one affiliate each of ABC, CBS, and NBC, scrambled the signals, and put them on the satellite. They retailed the package to the TVRO market. Subsequently, NBC sued SBN for violation of copyright. However, in 1988 Congress gave copyright clearance for SBN and similar firms to engage in satellite delivery of network affiliates' signals.

Viacom's Showtime/The Movie Channel created Satellite Direct, Inc. (SDI), in 1986. SDI retails its packages through, among other outlets, home TVRO dish dealers. It even works with an advisory board from the home TVRO trade.

TCI, the nation's largest cable MSO, controls both Tempo and Netlink. These two firms offer packages directly through a toll-free telephone number and cable operators. Cooperating cable operators receive a commission. The two TCI firms handle back-office support for authorization (of TVRO reception), billing, and collection.

Netlink reached carriage agreements with the major broadcast TV networks. Its package includes signals from affiliates, as well as superstations and basic and pay-cable services. Netlink limits distribution of affiliate signals, however, to those dish owners who cannot receive a broadcast network signal off the air or from the local cable system. Despite this limitation, broadcast TV affiliates view the Netlink-network agreement with trepidation. They worry this might be the first step to **bypass** stations and deliver network programming directly to viewers.

During the mid-1980s, U.S. business interest in high-power Ku-band DBS declined. The 1985 demise of the United Satellite Communications venture (*PRT,* 5.4.1) had dampened investor enthusiasm for any kind of DBS. Subsequent Japanese and European activity, however, resulted in fully functioning DBS companies.

Two U.S. firms had been in on the DBS concept almost since the beginning. United States Satellite Broadcasting Co. (USSB) and Dominion Video Satellite had filed in the initial 1982 round of applications (*PRT,* 5.4.1). Hubbard Broadcasting, group station owner and developer of the SNG cooperative (*PRT,* 5.4.4), created USSB specifically to establish a foothold in DBS. Hubbard's USSB now offers 25 channels of programming including HBO and Showtime.

The original plans of Dominion, the other pioneer, included religious and family programming. Dominion tried several schemes over the years to secure financing, but the FCC had given the firm only until December 1992 to build and launch its DBS system. When Dominion failed to meet the deadline, the FCC revoked permission. After an auction, the Commission reassigned the channel in 1996 to MCI on the basis of a $682-million bid.

Hughes DirecTV offers about 150 channels, mostly sports oriented. Hughes was boosted by an investment of more than $100 million from AT&T that gave the telephone giant 25% ownership of DirecTV.

## 20.8 CRITICISMS OF THE NETWORK SYSTEM

Despite all the changes, when most persons speak of "the networks," they still refer not to CNN, HBO, or Hughes Television Network, but to the original three television networks—ABC, CBS, and NBC, and perhaps Fox. Many of the faults attributed to networks are faults of the rest of the trade as well, but focusing on the rest of the trade is difficult, consisting, as it does, of scores of networks and programmers and thousands of stations and cable systems in all states and territories. So critics aim for the most obvious targets, "the networks."

Most criticism centers around programming and can be traced to what critics see as the networks' insatiable drive for ever-higher profits. Fred Friendly, a former CBS news executive, explained that corporate officers run the networks as "profit machines," keeping stock prices high by keeping profits high. Higher ratings translate into higher profits. Therefore ratings determine the worth of a program, not its intrinsic value as entertainment or information. As a result, say critics, light entertainment—and not even very interesting light entertainment—fills network channels. The desire for ratings forces out most thought-provoking programming.

Public interest groups played a role in passage of content provisions of the Telecommunications Act of 1996. Groups most often complain that network programs teach values that hinder effective functioning of the individual and society. The programs present untrue pictures of society. Constant complaints that the networks show too much sex and violence reached Congress, resulting in passage of the V-chip provision and the requirement to institute a program content ratings system.

Complaints also focus on depictions of women and various racial and ethnic minorities that are seen as unfair, untrue, or unbalanced. They say that commercials (and all advertising) condition us to buy for the sake of acquisition and that programming reinforces such conditioning. Critics especially decry programs children watch, particularly violent content and programs that amount to glorified commercials for products shown in the programs.

In the past, Congress has investigated the networks for everything from quiz show scandals to bias in news and documentaries. The FCC has investigated and adopted rules to prevent network control of affiliates. The FCC and some production houses said that networks dominated program production, all but curtailing first-run programming. The FCC responded by passing rules to correct that situation. The U.S. Department of Justice even filed suit against the networks, charging them with monopoly over prime-time programming.

In the past, creative people have complained of the prudishness of network standards departments. Advertisers and advertising agencies criticize networks for the high prices of advertising time, for commercial clutter (*PRT,* 9.5), and even for violence in programming.

Affiliates have criticized the networks. Strong affiliate opposition led the networks to cancel plans to expand early evening newscasts to 1 hour. Affiliates objected to the network-Netlink home TVRO packaging agreement.

The frequency and intensity of criticism increased over the years as television (and thus the networks) came to occupy more of our time and attention. Even as criticism increased, viewing levels rose. However, as we move toward the turn of the century, change is apparent. The success of the Fox Network and cable networks may have redirected the focus of criticism. With the increase in cable penetration of U.S. television homes, more persons have gained access to cable networks. As the number of cable networks increased, viewers found they had genuine alternatives in popular programming. Broadcast network audience shares dropped, and interest groups began targeting cable programmers. By 1996, the FCC had abolished the long-standing restraints on networks including the PTAR and restrictions on networks regarding syndication and financial interests in programs. Consent decree agreements reached with the courts regarding the antitrust suits have been lifted. Why? Because times have changed. Congress has already forced its V-chip and program ratings system on the networks. The networks now face considerably more competition than ever before. True, the huge media conglomerates created by acquisitions of NBC, ABC, and CBS raise new concerns, but complaints are turning, in part, to the competitors, especially cable.

Criticism of cable will likely increase. Communities are taking legal action to ban adult programming from local systems. Religious and citizen groups marshal forces to fight adult channels and sexually explicit material on other channels. Critics denounced the level of violence and treatment of women in music video programming. National Coalition on Television Violence (NCTV) measurements showed that HBO and Showtime/The Movie Channel were twice as violent as broadcast networks. NCTV even found high levels of violence in programming segments on The Disney Channel and CBN. Critics charged that cable operators wielded too much power over programmers. They noted that MSOs had forced the scrambling of signals then began buying into the networks. As we approach the turn of the century, the nature of networks appears as volatile as any aspect of the radio and television industry.

## NOTE

1. "Season Opener is a Net Loss," *Broadcasting* 30 October 1995: 6.

## FURTHER READING

Bagdikian, Ben H. *The Media Monopoly*. 5th ed. Boston: Beacon, 1997.

Barnouw, Erik. *Tube of Plenty: The Evolution of American Television*. 2nd Rev. ed. New York: Oxford University Press, 1990.

Block, Alex B. *Outfoxed: Marvin Davis, Barry Diller, Rupert Murdoch, Joan Rivers, and the Inside Story of America's Fourth Television Network*. New York: St Martin's, 1990.

Friendly, Fred W. *Due to Circumstances Beyond Our Control*. New York: Vintage, 1968.

Goldberg, Robert, and Gerald J. Goldberg. *Citizen Turner: The Wild Rise of an American Tycoon*. New York: Harcourt, 1995.

Goldenson, Leonard H., and Marvin J. Wolf. *Beating the Odds: The Untold Story Behind the Rise of ABC*. New York: Simon and Schuster, 1991.

Halberstam, David. *The Powers That Be*. New York: Knopf, 1979.

Litman, Barry Russell. *The Vertical Structure of the Television Broadcasting Industry: The Coalescence of Power*. East Lansing: Michigan State University Press, 1979.

Kellner, C. A. "The Rise and Fall of the Overmyer Network," *Journal of Broadcasting* 13 (1969): 125.

Mazzocco, Dennis. *Networks of Power: Corporate TV's Threat to Democracy*. Boston: South End, 1994.

Paper, Lewis J. *Empire: William S. Paley and the Making of CBS News.* New York: St. Martin's, 1987.

Weaver, Pat. *The Best Seat in the House: The Golden Years of Radio and Television.* New York: Knopf, 1994.

Whittemore, Hank. *CNN, The Inside Story.* Boston: Little, Brown, 1990.

# 21

## CAREERS IN ELECTRONIC
## MASS MEDIA

Now it is time to talk about you. You are reading this book. That means you have at least some interest in radio and television. Chances are good that you may even want to work in the field. That is the subject of this chapter—working, earning a living, and making a career in radio and television. We first survey career opportunities—types and availability of jobs, pay, and advancement. Next, we look at what you can expect if you stay in the trade and how your career will develop. Then, we suggest some ways to prepare for a career in radio and television. Finally, we discuss your first job—how to get it and how to keep it.

### 21.1 CAREER OPPORTUNITIES

First things first. Yes, you can get a job and make a career in radio and television. The profession and industry have changed. Self-employed *freelancers* have become more common. There are more broadcast stations, more cable networks, satellite services, and more corporate and home video. In sum, there are more opportunities. Several assumptions, however, underlie that statement and all that follows. First, you start at the **career entry level**—the place where jobs are (a) available (b) for beginners. That place is not the networks, not a major Hollywood program producer, not a big market, and not a big station.

Second, you should be likable, clean, and do not smell bad. You should work hard and have a reasonable amount of intelligence and creativity. You should enjoy meeting new people, have confidence in yourself, and respect the feelings of others. You should avoid illegal drugs and drink moderately, if at all. You do not have to be a prodigy or a star to get in and stay in the trade. Jerks, drunks, and louts find it almost impossible.

#### 21.1.1 Types of Jobs

By *jobs* we mean a salaried, commission, or contract position at a radio or television facility. Facility includes such organizations as broadcast stations, cable systems, corporate video departments, or production companies.

Some production and news personnel are hired on a contract or freelance basis, with pay being based on an hourly, daily, or per-project fee. These, too, are jobs in radio and television.

Many people enjoy the freedom and variety freelancing provides. Freelancers are often paid a higher wage than staff employees, but are responsible for their own health and life insurance, social security, and other benefits. Freelance videographers and other crafts people often provide their own equipment. Freelancing can be difficult at first, until you have established a reputation and professional contacts. Freelancers must market themselves constantly, staying in continual contact with professional employers.

Most people think of the industry in terms of the visible positions. Disc jockeys, anchors, and television directors are important to the industry, but there are many more jobs than those in radio and television.

We exclude engineering. Engineering is a highly specialized area. It requires that you understand technical aspects of radio and television. It involves installation, maintenance, and repair of equipment, and often it requires design of circuitry and wiring. If you plan to go into radio–TV engineering, you must have an affinity for it.

We exclude administration. This encompasses jobs found in any business office—secretarial, filing, typing, and billing. It also includes highly specialized skills that require a degree or experience, such as accounting and bookkeeping. Clerical positions, customer service representatives, or other entry-level administrative positions can provide a foot in the door to other positions in a radio or television facility, but we do not approach these as career paths.

Most people considering radio–TV careers do not mean engineering or administration. They look for jobs in writing, performance, news, production, sales, or promotion. We assume that you have similar interests and focus the remainder of the chapter on jobs in those areas.

## 21.1.2 Special Note on Sales

The term *sales* encompasses two areas. In one, the outlet sells time to advertisers. In the other, the outlet sells some programming service to the public, as in cable television.

Often, young persons ignore sales as a radio–TV career area. They fall in love with programming areas, such as production, news, or performance. They see those aspects as the ends of business. Sales—if they think about it at all—is some necessary evil. They compare it to hustling encyclopedias door to door or peddling used cars—vaguely dishonest, definitely boring, and noncreative.

Wrong on all counts. This is a good a place to clear up a few misconceptions.

First, most managers and owners view sales as a major thrust of the business. They recognize the importance of programming areas as means to the end of sales. The sales area provides the lifeblood of the facility. It generates the money that allows the other areas to exist, without sales there is no facility.

Second, sales personnel sell a valid, needed service. Businesses must advertise, and radio and television advertising is effective. As for subscriber sales, few other forms of entertainment offer so much for so little. Even a subscription fee as high as $45 a month breaks down to just $1.50 a day. Figuring in tickets, refreshments, gasoline, and sitter fees, one couple could barely go to the movies twice for $45.

Third, sales has the greatest potential for creativity of any area in the outlet. For example, refer to the advertising sales process described in *PRT,* 17.3.3. Preparing an effective sales presentation takes more inventiveness than playing records, pushing a camera, or even directing the evening news.

Fourth, sales personnel often have the best chance to get to managerial positions. Look at it from the owner's point of view: Programming areas generate expenses and the sales department earns revenues. Naturally, the owner selects someone who makes money to manage the outlet. Broadcast station managers often come from the area of advertising sales. Cable system managers often come from the marketing area, for which subscriber sales is the entry-level position.

Other sales areas that can provide a satisfying career include selling syndicated programming to stations, representing production companies to potential clients, and representing networks seeking channel space on cable television systems. Other elements of the industry, such as the ratings companies also rely on their sales force.

### 21.1.3 Other Electronic Mass Media Employment Areas

We leave out performance areas such as music, dance, graphic art, and design. They have their own career paths. People who do these things in radio–TV settings usually consider themselves in music, dance, or art, not radio or television.

On the other hand, people sometimes overlook certain areas. **Public broadcasting** is one. Public stations often do more local production than commercial stations. This means more opportunity to exercise production skills.

Cable and broadcast television have both fostered the growth of **promotion.** Promotion forms an essential part of a cable system's marketing plan. It serves a TV station as ammunition in the ratings battle. For a large-market station, one additional rating point can yield thousands of dollars. Effective promotion can make the difference.

**Corporate television** (*PRT,* 24) offers excellent career opportunities, particularly for a person interested in production and writing. Corporate television often features starting pay, benefits, and advancement opportunities better than those of broadcast or cable. Governments at all levels are producers of radio and video, and the military can provide an entry point both for civilians and recruits.

All cable systems need subscriber marketing staffers. Many need advertising sales executives. A system that does local origination may also need personnel with skills in news, writing, production, and performance.

**Advertising and public relations firms** need people with radio–TV skills. They create, write, supervise, and produce. Some ad agencies have their own production facilities.

### 21.1.4 Why Radio–TV?

The only reason to go into radio and television is because you **want to work** in radio and television. You probably will not make much money in your first job—a living, maybe. Count on no more than the federal minimum wage. Be pleasantly surprised if offered more.

Use this test to determine if you really want to work in radio and television.

- Do you enjoy just being inside a radio or television facility—any facility, no matter where it is?
- Do you enjoy doing something in radio–TV—no matter what?
- Do you enjoy working in radio or television so much that getting paid—no matter how little—would be frosting on the cake, would be almost secondary in importance?

If you answered "yes" to each question, go to it. Good luck in your radio–TV career. If you answered "no" to any question, choose another field. For your first job, is it important that you live in a large city; "work near home"; make a lot of money; direct, or report sports, or play DJ at an AOR station? Do not go into radio–TV. In first radio–TV jobs, the work is too long, too hard, too low-paid, and too often in the boondocks not to enjoy it for itself.

### 21.1.5 Attitudes—Theirs and Yours

We have set forth two views on the purpose of a radio–TV outlet. Owners and managers consider the outlet a business, and its purpose is to earn a profit (*PRT,* 19, introduction; *PRT,* 19.1.2). On the other hand, many people go into their first radio–TV jobs with the idea that the outlet is a creative medium, that its purpose is to provide them a chance to create and experiment. Obviously, these two views clash.

Radio–TV does permit creative development, but a beginning employee should keep four points in mind. First, the outlet is a business—an advertising or subscription sales medium. Second, the owner considers all staffers—particularly those who appear before microphone or camera—as salespersons, even though they may not directly service accounts. Third, the owner pays the salaries. Fourth, individual creative development comes within the employment concept developed in the first three points.

### 21.1.6 Availability of Jobs

If you are a beginner, you begin where beginners begin. **Beginner** refers to a person who has never held a salaried job in radio or television. Where beginners begin means small outlets in small markets. Small market managers would like to hire experienced people. Often, however, they cannot pay enough to attract them. Instead, they must hire and train beginners. After a few years, the employees, no longer beginners, move on to the glamour and higher pay of larger markets. This means that many small-market outlets suffer a continual personnel turnover. It also means small markets are the best places for a beginner to look for a job.

Persons who wish to work in some areas may be able to start in slightly bigger markets. For example, medium-market stations and cable systems may take on beginning salespeople. Corporate television facilities tend to be in large cities.

The corporate changes of the 1980s and 1990s (*PRT*, 3.5.3.2) had an impact on radio–TV employment. Large businesses went through a period of "slimming down." In the process, they got rid of many jobs and the people who had filled them. Radio–TV firms were no exception (*PRT*, 3.6.1). This affected few beginner-type jobs directly. However, the decrease in large-market positions could have slowed advancement along the normal career pattern. In other words, people in radio–TV may not have as much opportunity to move to larger markets and better pay; they may have to stay in one job longer. In that respect, the layoffs certainly had the potential to make beginner-type jobs more scarce.

The slimming down affected corporate video. Some large businesses decided they could save money by closing down internal video departments. When the firms needed video production, they would contract for it. In many cases they hired their own former employees, but as independent contractors who would be responsible for their own benefits.

This was just one factor that increased work for production companies. Another was the plan by cable networks to buy more original programming (*PRT*, 7.4.2.1 and 7.4.3.1). The increase in work, however, would not necessarily translate into an increase in full-time positions at the production companies themselves. Most production companies are small. They contract for crews, facilities, and studios on an as-needed, or freelance basis. Larger firms with studios and a permanent staff have their pick of veteran production personnel when they hire for full-time or contract positions. Turnover is slow and newcomers find the program production field difficult to enter.

### 21.1.7 Pay and Advancement

If you go into an area other than sales, you will not receive much pay as a beginner (sales personnel frequently earn more than others in first jobs). By your second or third job, however, you will have that important commodity, experience. You should be able to move to a decent salary. Whether you ever make one of those $100,000-plus big-market salaries is up to you.

There are a small number of high-profile, highly paid professionals in the electronic media professions. The top network anchors are compensated with seven-figure salaries, and network executives and famous disc jockeys are similarly well paid. These are the people at the top of the profession. They have unusual talents, have usually worked their way up after a number of years of lower salaries, and often have tenuous holds on their jobs. As in any business, you rise as fast and as far as your capabilities and your desire allow. The intelligent, hard-working, creative individual can advance—to larger outlets, to larger markets, to more responsible positions. At the same time, as jobs get better, competition gets keener.

We hope that all of you reach these heights in your careers, but do not make the mistake of thinking that your starting salary will be as high as a 20-year network veteran.

One 1995 survey of people holding jobs in video production at independent and corporate facilities found the median salary (the point at which half make more and half make less) to be $37,500. Remember, this includes people with many years of experience. The starting salaries in production are more likely to be less than $20,000.[1]

A survey by the Radio Television News Directors Association found the average salary for a reporter at a television station in markets ranging between 100 and 150 was $18,112, whereas those in markets below 150 averaged $16,968. Anchors at stations in these smaller markets, where most professionals begin their careers, had average salaries of $27,030. The average radio station news anchor, regardless of market, earned $23,072, whereas the average radio reporter earned a salary of $16,387.[2] Remember, these are average salaries, not beginning salaries.

## 21.2 CAREER PATTERNS

The usual career pattern in broadcasting and cable starts in a small outlet in a small market and moves to progressively larger markets (Fig. 21.1). A typical radio broadcasting career might begin in a station serving a city with a population of 25,000 or less. After 2 or 3 years, the individual moves to a medium market of, say, 100,000. After 3 to 5 years, the next step may be a large market—500,000 to 1.5 million. From there—with luck, talent, and perseverance—one goes to Los Angeles or New York.

Most persons, of course, do not go all the way to the super-large markets. This does not necessarily mean their careers have stagnated. Some enjoy life in a particular locale and decide to stay. Some work up to larger outlets but not necessarily larger markets. Some advance within an outlet or an ownership firm—a station group or cable MSO. Some go into other work—advertising, public relations, or freelance production.

At any rate, you will probably have to change jobs to advance your career. On the other hand, avoid a spotty employment record. Six months at one job, a year at another, 4 months at a third—this type of record does not reassure a manager that you are dependable and steady. Two years is a good minimum at which to aim for any one job. The longer you are at one place of employment, the better your resumé looks to the prospective employer.

This career pattern helps to explain why beginners have difficulty getting jobs in large markets. The people with whom they compete have paid their dues, as it is called. They started in smaller markets and have years of experience. Naturally, managers hire the experienced people.

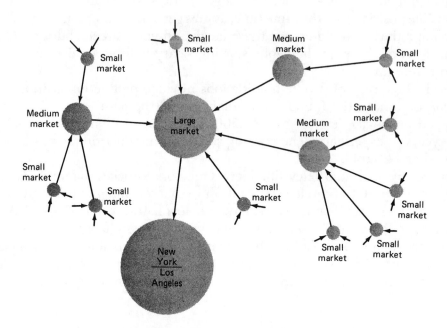

FIG. 21.1. Career pattern in radio–TV.

You will have difficulty breaking into big-time television without experience. News reporters come from local outlets, from wire services, or from newspapers. Sports announcers have worked at local outlets or have previously made names for themselves in other fields. Directors start as script clerks or assistant directors on television commercials, begin at local outlets, or come from other media.

Writers must have agents. Production firms usually look at an unsolicited script only when presented by a recognized agent. A fledgling writer must attempt to find an agent who will take on new talent. (Agents often will not represent writers who have no previous credits.)

Performers may have an even harder time breaking into the big time. Actors have usually performed in stage productions before they get their first part in a television commercial or bit part in a dramatic program.

Some persons can skip a few dues-paying years. These include the exceptionally talented, those who managers hire because of public pressure or government requirements (*PRT*, 19.1.1.6), or persons who have personal ties with management. If you fit one of these categories, take advantage of it. However, as a beginner in a big-market outlet you may find yourself at a disadvantage. The small-market outlet serves as a training ground, a learning vehicle, an educational process, and a place to make mistakes. The big-market outlet does not. You will have to learn in an organization not prepared to deal with beginners.

## 21.3 CAREER PREPARATION

You may wish to prepare for your career in radio–TV through a formal educational program. Three popular options include trade school, a bachelor's degree program, and an associate degree program. You may also wish to consider workplace training.

### 21.3.1 Trade Schools

Trade schools offer training in radio and television skills. Many first became known for their radio–TV electronics courses, but trade schools also teach courses in production areas, such as camera operation, commercial copy writing, and disc jockey work.

Manufacturers such as Sony and Avid also conduct courses in operating their equipment. Although most people who attend these schools are sent by their employers, those with little experience might also pay the tuition to take advantage of the opportunities.

Trade school courses run 8 weeks to a year. The exact length varies with subject and school. Every requirement in their curriculum focuses directly on radio–TV. They award no academic degrees but grant certificates of completion. Many advertise effective placement services to help graduates get a first job. Most operate for profit.

The best trade schools do an unbeatable job of preparing people for first jobs in a short time at low cost. The worst are scams. If you wish to work in an operational job such as a disc jockey shift, you should consider a trade school. Before you enroll, check the school's placement record, look at its facilities, and ask for an opinion from three or four graduates and the Better Business Bureau.

### 21.3.2 Baccalaureate Degree Programs

Many colleges offer the opportunity to learn about radio–TV. The required program of study typically takes 4 years. When a student successfully completes all requirements, the school awards an academic degree, generally a bachelor of arts or bachelor of science.

The college radio–TV program has a split personality. It must provide a liberal arts education. It must also teach vocationally oriented subjects such as radio–TV writing, production, and law. Many schools add yet a third dimension to their curricula. In these programs, students also study radio and television as informational and cultural forces in society.

You may feel that your career preparation should include a radio–TV degree program. After all, a college degree still commands respect. Many employers require a degree, particularly for promotion to upper level, decision-making positions. You must, however, bear in mind what the degree program is and what it is not. Its primary purpose is to provide a **broad education**. By definition, a broad education includes elements of English composition, humanities, life sciences, physical sciences, social sciences, and mathematics. Many of the best radio–TV academic programs actually require their students to take at least 75% of course work from areas completely outside mass communication. The radio–TV degree program is not occupational training.

Hundreds of colleges provide degree study in radio–TV. The department that offers radio–TV major courses varies from school to school. Its name typically includes one or more of these words: broadcasting, communication, journalism, speech, mass communication, radio and television, and telecommunication.

A radio–television department may apply for accreditation. Accreditation certifies the department has been measured against and met a national standard. In its investigation of a department, the accrediting agency evaluates elements such as budget, curriculum, facilities, faculty, and library holdings. The Accrediting Council on Education in Journalism and Mass Communications (ACEJMC) accredits in the area of radio–TV. You can attend an ACEJMC-accredited program with some certainty of getting an excellent education in radio–TV. On the other hand, many fine, respected departments never apply for accreditation.

Do not get a graduate degree before your first job. A master's degree does not substitute for experience. It does not make you more attractive to potential employers and it can even be a hindrance. Managers may consider you overeducated for entry-level jobs. Rarely do you need a master's degree to work in radio or television. Primary reasons to get a master's degree include desire for advanced, usually theoretical academic work; preparation for employment in quantitative research, such as with an audience-rating firm; qualification for the few jobs in public broadcasting and at community colleges that require one; and as prelude to doctoral study. Persons headed toward management may find the master of business administration degree helpful. You will benefit from at least 3 to 5 years of experience before starting master's study.

The doctorate is a research degree. Doctoral study consists of research and theory, not creative or production courses. Most universities require faculty to have or be well on their way toward completion of a doctorate.

### 21.3.3 Associate Degree Programs

Some community colleges have radio–TV programs. They provide a heavy concentration of skills courses. They also require liberal arts courses such as English, government, and history. They grant an associate in arts degree. Faculty members normally have at least a master's degree and some experience in the trade. Most of these schools have good facilities, maintain a student-operated station or cable channel, and emphasize good teaching. If you want an academic degree, skills course, a minimum of other requirements, and a collegiate setting, look into a community college radio–TV program.

### 21.3.4 Workplace Training

You can also learn about radio–TV by working in a radio–TV outlet. This is workplace training, and its advantages as career preparation are obvious. It puts you directly in the trade. You get experience and learn while doing what you want to do.

These are also its chief disadvantages. In workplace training, you learn "how it is done" at a particular outlet, and that is not necessarily how it is done at most of the outlets in the trade. Further, you often learn how to do just one particular job. You do not get the global view of radio–TV and career opportunities that even a trade school course can give.

Nonetheless, workplace training gives you hands-on experience. Take advantage of it, particularly in combination with one of the formal educational programs described earlier. You are looking for training, experience, eventually a good recommendation, and, in some cases, a chance at employment. Some workplace training situations are really paid jobs. You are, however, still a beginner. Paid or not, the workplace is doing you a favor by taking you on. Remember that, and treat the training situation as a job that you need and like. Be reliable, responsible, responsive, on time, thorough, and courteous. Keep at it and do not quit after a month or two. Often, you will draw the menial assignments; do them well and cheerfully, without complaint.

Some of the more popular forms of workplace training include volunteer work, campus outlet positions, internships, and outright employment, part time and full time. Each of these include elements of on-the-job training.

*21.3.4.1 Volunteer Work.* A few local outlets use unpaid volunteer personnel to augment professional staff. Check, for example, community-licensed public broadcast stations and the access-channel coordinators for cable systems.

*21.3.4.2 Campus Outlet Positions.* Some colleges and trade schools operate their own outlets. These range from campus-limited radio stations (*PRT,* 11.9) and cable channels to full-service television stations. These facilities, often run by students, offer opportunity for on-air experience. Some institutions also operate closed-circuit facilities (*PRT,* 22.9) to produce video instructional materials. They often use students in the crew positions. When students receive pay for working in an on-campus position, they often have the title **student assistants.** If your school has such positions, make maximum use of them. Get involved early.

Many broadcast managers do not consider college radio to be sufficient experience for potential employees. Unlike professional outlets, many college stations are loosely managed. Disc jockeys are often given little or no direction, and often do not follow a play list. Although this environment may be a great deal of fun, professional disc jockeys usually follow very tightly planned program formats, and have relatively little freedom in what they play or in what they say (*PRT,* 7.2.1).

Another criticism of college stations is that most are noncommercial. As we have discussed, commercial broadcasting is a profit-seeking business. College disc jockeys often do not learn about the importance of ratings, or that what they say or do can affect the willingness of advertisers to buy time.

***21.3.4.3 Internships.*** In an internship, students work at a radio or TV outlet off-campus for academic credit. Some internships are part time and others are full time. The student interns at the installation to learn something new. The installation may or may not pay the intern but the learning aspect should dominate. When a student gets an internship primarily for a paycheck, the nature of the position alters and moves closer to that of a job. Federal wage and hour laws and, in some conditions, union contracts, insurance liability, and other legal constraints require that interns must receive some form of compensation, either pay or credit.

Try for an internship. It can give valuable experience. Sometimes, it leads directly to a job offer.

***21.3.4.4 Employment.*** Here, the individual works at a radio or TV outlet for pay. In most cases, 40 hours a week constitutes **full-time** employment. Most outlets insist that job applicants have some demonstrated competence to qualify for a full-time job, even if it is only experience in a related field or a college degree in something. Some of the smallest outlets do have to hire and train rank beginners, people with no qualifications other than glimmerings of talent and a willingness to learn.

The typical **part-time** job requires 10 to 20 hours per week. Often, these consist of off-time periods—weekends and overnight. Outlets often hire beginners and train them for these positions.

A part-time job allows you to earn and learn in radio–TV while doing something else full time. That something else might consist of a 40-hour-a-week job that keeps food on the table while you work at the outlet for peanuts and the chance to learn a radio–TV skill. It might be a full academic schedule, 15 or more semester hours, so you can finish school while earning money and getting experience. In such situations, you must be willing to give up chunks of leisure time and, often, sleep. The part-time job, however, provides an excellent opportunity to gain genuine resumé-building experience.

***21.3.4.5 On-the-Job Training.*** Nothing beats experience—not trade school, not a college degree. No matter what your academic preparation, your first job will probably be at the entry level—a small outlet in a small market. As suggested in the previous section, you really need no specific career preparation in some entry-level jobs. Your supervisor and coworkers teach you what you need to know. This is **on-the-job training** (OJT).

Why bother with academic training? For one thing, it gives a slight competitive edge for that entry-level job. Having gone through a radio–TV curriculum, the graduate at least knows concepts, nomenclature, and station operation and may have even worked on the school FM station. He or she will be familiar with FCC rules and regulations. Later in a career, when the individual is ready to move into a position of increased responsibility, a bachelor's degree may give a competitive edge. Increasingly, the trade requires a college degree for promotion into management.

## 21.4 FIRST JOBS

Your first job may be the most important of your career. That is where you get experience. The trick is to get that first job and then keep it.

### 21.4.1 Finding Them

You may hear talk that colleges allow too many students to study radio–TV and that graduates do not find jobs. Indeed, many cannot find jobs—because they do not know how and where to look. Here, the colleges sometimes inadvertently contribute to the problem. Big-market outlets set standards for the trade, so instructors often use them as examples in class. Rarely do students hear about entry-level positions, the advantages of starting in a small market, or the necessity of experience as a prerequisite for big-market employment. Naturally, when students graduate, they go to big markets to look for a job. Just as naturally, the big-market outlets, who have their pick of experienced people, do not hire these beginner graduates. The graduates then say there are no jobs available and the big-market managers complain that the colleges graduate too many people in radio–TV. Meanwhile, entry-level jobs go begging.

Additionally, some persons restrict the geographical area in which they will work. In doing so, they also restrict their chances of getting a first job. If you insist on working "near home," then you may have a long wait. If you live in a large city, you may wait even longer. Even though you live there, to the stations you are still a beginner. Meanwhile, jobs are open in other parts of the country—in towns that could even be nicer than your own, in areas about which you have only heard, full of people who could become your closest friends.

You must apply in person. Unlike many industries, radio and television facilities rarely recruit on college campuses. Those facilities who hire at the entry level seldom have the time or other resources needed for elaborate recruiting programs. The larger stations, networks, and production facilities hire working professionals, not beginners. So those entering the field must be aggressive in seeking out opportunities.

Most managers have file drawers full of resumés, but when they have openings, they hire someone who walks through the door and applies. Resumés, tapes, letters of reference, and sample copy support, but do not take the place of, a personal visit. Letters and telephone calls rarely yield job offers. Mass mailings of resumés benefit no one but printers and the U.S. Postal Service.

If you are seeking a job in production or news, employers will want to know what you are able to do. A paper resumé does not allow a news director or production manager to judge your abilities and talents. A **resumé tape** (also called a **demo tape** or **demo reel**) will be necessary.

A resumé tape will contain 5 to 10 minutes of your best work. If you are a reporter, provide examples of different types of stories you have covered. If seeking a production job, include excerpts of programs you worked on. Normally, production resumé tapes will not contain entire programs (a commercial or PSA might be the exception). A disc jockey will want to demonstrate abilities at reading advertising copy, introducing records, and facility with handling production elements.

You will want to include a brief explanation of the content. A paper document containing the information should accompany the tape. Many professionals include a brief introduction of each segment with a slate, or even a stand-up or voice-over.

Most productions, especially in video, are collaborative efforts. No employer expects you to have done everything in the production. Provide clear identification of your role (e.g., audio, camera operator), and, of course, provide clips that will show off your abilities.

Do not exaggerate. Your shortcomings will become quickly apparent if you are hired under false pretenses. And do not presume that no one will know that you really were the production assistant, not the videographer: You never know who else might be applying for a job or who is looking at the resumé tape.

Today most resumé videotapes are submitted in VHS format. Audiotapes are usually cassettes. Be sure to include a stamped, self-addressed envelope with your tape. If you are sending your tape "blind," even that tactic might not get your tape back to you. Your resumé tape is an investment in your career. It should be of the highest professional quality. Expect to invest some money, and spend more for postage.

Plan your visits. Use *Broadcasting & Cable Yearbook*, road maps, and other reference material. Call to set up appointments about a week before your visits, and be on time.

Check other sources of job leads. These include trade-press classified ads, state trade association job bulletins, and school placement center listings. Follow up such a lead immediately, otherwise the job will be gone.

You may have difficulty finding corporate TV facilities. Most of the usual reference sources do not list them. One long-range job-hunting strategy involves attending meetings of the nearest chapter of International Television Association. Take advantage of the lower rate and join as a student member, if eligible. Volunteer to run registration tables, straighten chairs, or hand out name tags. This gives you a chance to get to know and impress the members. If you have anything on the ball, they will remember you when they have openings.

The cliche "It's not what you know, but who you know" is true. Join organizations that will enable you to network with professionals.

## 21.4.2 Keeping Them

Attitude has a lot to do with keeping a first job. Here are a few hints on attitude. First, remember the owner pays your salary. Do what management says, in the way management says to do it. Above all, be dependable!

Second, consider your job a continuation of your education. Even if you have been graduated from a top urban university and work with a bunch of high school dropouts in a coffee-pot radio station at a wide spot in the road, you can learn from them. Those station people have worked in the trade longer than you and they know more than you. Learn from them. Here, you begin to develop what "marketable skills" you really have to offer.

Third, be friendly and courteous. Avoid office politics, stay away from the malcontents, do your part, and be responsible.

Finally, expect the worst shifts, the longest hours, the weekend assignments, and the dog client list. You are the new employee. But those things should really not matter. After all, you are working in radio or television. That is what counts.

### NOTES

1. "Annual Salary Survey," *Video Systems,* August 1995.
2. Bob Papper and Andrew Sharma, "Salaries Going Up," *RTNDA Communicator,* May 1995.

### FURTHER READING

Alexander, James P. *Internships in Communications.* Ames: Iowa State University Press, 1995.

Becker, Lee B., Jeffery W. Fruit, Susan L. Caudill with Sharon L. Dunwoody, and Leonard P. Tipton. *The Training and Hiring of Journalists.* Norwood, NJ: Ablex, 1987.

Ciofalo, Andrew, Ed. *Internships: Perspectives on Experiential Learning.* Melbourne, Australia: Krieger, 1992.

daSilva, Raul. *Making Money in Film and Video: A Freelancer's Handbook.* 2nd ed. Newton, MA: Focal, 1992.

Farris, Linda Gudess. *Television Careers: A Guide to Breaking and Entering.* Fairfax, CA: Buy The Book, 1995.

Jacobs, Bob. *How to Be an Independent Video Producer.* White Plains, NY: Knowledge, 1986.

Jurek, Ken. *Careers in Video: Getting Ahead in Professional Television.* White Plains, NY: Knowledge, 1988.

# VI

## COMPARATIVE PERSPECTIVE

So far, we have concentrated on profit-seeking electronic mass media in the United States. Now, we examine alternative forms of radio and television—noncommercial in chapter 22, foreign systems in chapter 23, and corporate video in chapter 24. These alternatives provide us with bases for comparison and, as such, help us to understand better the American mass commercial system. We shall also learn that, in some cases, these alternatives have taken on characteristics of the commercial system.

# 22

## NONCOMMERCIAL RADIO
## AND TELEVISION

Public broadcasting, educational broadcasting, and noncommercial broadcasting are all names of an idea that has been only partially realized in the United States. Unlike some other industrialized countries of the world, the commercial system dominates radio and television in the United States. Nonetheless, the United States does today have a noncommercial system that offers the public alternative programming, something it lacked for years. Despite setbacks and problems, that system gains audience and adherents as it matures. New technologies and regulatory changes of the 1980s and 1990s created new challenges for public broadcasting, and brought new concepts for financing and organizing the system.

In this chapter we focus on public broadcasting, but we also look at other forms of noncommercial radio and television.

### 22.1 HISTORY OF NONCOMMERCIAL RADIO AND TV

Some of the very first AM broadcast stations were started by educational institutions, often the physical sciences departments of colleges and universities. Soon, however, the technical novelty of broadcasting wore off, and the financial reality of operating expenses set in. Some educational licensees began selling advertising and many more gave up their licenses.

#### 22.1.1 Struggle for Reserved Channels

At times, it seemed as though the government connived with commercial interests to wrest frequencies from educational licensees. Educational licensees would find their frequencies changed, their power reduced, and their status changed from full-time to share-time operations.

***22.1.1.1 NAEB.*** In 1925, educational licensees organized to fight such treatment and to urge that radio channels be reserved for education. They called their organization the Association of College and University Broadcasting Stations.

Nine years later, it reorganized as the **National Association of Educational Broadcasters** (NAEB).

### 22.1.1.2 Noncommercial Radio Channels.

During the period between 1921 and 1936, 202 licenses were issued to educational institutions. Out of this total, only 38 stations were on the air at the beginning of 1937, and some of these operated on a commercial basis. Educators tried to have some AM channels reserved for education when Congress was about to pass the Communications Act of 1934. However, commercial broadcasters convinced Congress and the FCC that their stations were already carrying educational material, and Congress made no educational reservations. Shortly thereafter, the commercial broadcasters' educational programs began to disappear.

Through efforts of the NAEB and other organizations, the FCC realized that channel reservations were needed if education was to have a broadcast voice. In 1940, when the FCC established the first FM band at 42 to 50 MHz (*PRT*, 2.4), it set aside 5 of the 40 channels for noncommercial educational use. Five years later, the Commission moved FM to its present position and **reserved the first 20 channels** for noncommercial educational stations.

In 1948, the FCC authorized **low-power** operation for stations in the reserved band. This way, an educational institution could go on the air with a 10-watt transmitter for little initial investment, gain experience and expertise, and later improve facilities and power.

### 22.1.1.3 Noncommercial Television Channels.

By this time, television had begun to grow, and the FCC imposed a freeze (*PRT*, 3.1.2). The Commission had reserved no channels for education in its 1941 authorization of television. Now, during this period of reconsideration, commercial broadcasters argued against the idea of educational reservation, but this time, educational broadcasters responded. The NAEB played a key role as coordinating and rallying point for their efforts. They found a sympathetic audience in **Frieda Hennock**, first female member of the FCC. Hennock worked hard to persuade her colleagues to the idea of educational reservations.

In 1950, the NAEB and several other elements of the educational community formed the **Joint Committee on Educational Television** (JCET). JCET successfully coordinated the effort to convince the FCC of the need for reserved channels.

The FCC's 1952 *Sixth Report and Order* (*PRT*, 3.1.2) provided for educational television. Among other things, it established an expanded table of assignments, reserved nearly 12% of those assignments for noncommercial educational television (ETV) stations, and opened the UHF band. Many of the new ETV reservations were on UHF channels.

## 22.1.2 Federal Funding: Noncommercial Educational Facilities

Now the educational community had its own television channels, but the problem of where to get money to build and operate stations remained. By the end of 1953,

Houston's KUHT and Los Angeles' KTHE were the only educational stations on the air, and KTHE signed off the following September. The **Ford Foundation,** through its **Fund for Adult Education** (FAE), subsidized the initiation and operation of a number of stations. But the stations' minuscule budgets came mostly from the institutions to which they were licensed—communities, state universities, school systems, and state educational television authorities.

Congress passed the **Educational Television Facilities Act of 1962** to provide federal matching funds for construction of noncommercial television stations. The ETV Facilities Act directed the Secretary of Health, Education, and Welfare to work with state agencies to award funds for construction, purchase, and improvement of the physical facilities of ETV stations. (Congress later moved responsibility for facilities funding to the National Telecommunications and Information Agency.)

The 1962 act helped put new stations on the air and expand the facilities of others. The year before its enactment, there were 60 ETV stations on the air. By the end of 1966, the number reached 121. Many of the new stations operated on UHF channels, having received additional encouragement when Congress adopted all-channel receiver legislation in 1962 (*PRT,* 3.1.5). Now it was time to upgrade programming.

### 22.1.3 Federal Funding: Noncommercial Educational Programming

The NAEB had been active in program exchange among educational radio stations as early as 1935. In 1949, the NAEB started a bicycle network (*PRT,* 20.1.4)—taped program series, circulated by mail among radio stations.

The Ford Foundation financed and encouraged the most ambitious television program exchange of the early years. Ford's FAE organized the Educational Television and Radio Center in 1952. The next year, the Center found a home in Ann Arbor, Michigan. In 1956, the Ford Foundation assumed direct financial responsibility for the Center. In 1959, the Center moved its administrative offices to New York City and added "National" to its name. Later, the name was shortened to **National Educational Television** (NET). Using a bicycle network to ship its films and tapes to stations, NET was educational television's first and primary source of national programming—its network—until 1970.

Despite NET and other programming efforts, educational broadcasting failed to achieve the critical mass needed to fund and distribute high-quality programming. However, a local versus national resentment had begun. A number of ETV station managers carped about perceived high-handed programming decisions made by NET in New York.

A 1964 conference of ETV station personnel recommended formation of a commission to suggest national policy on ETV. In 1965, the Carnegie Corporation provided the funds, members were appointed, and a staff was hired. Endorsed by President Lyndon Johnson, this blue-ribbon panel was the **Carnegie Commission on Educational Television.** In its February, 1967 report,[1] the commission urged creation of a Corporation for Public Television to receive and disburse government and private funds and improve programming. President Johnson presented legislation for a congressionally chartered nonprofit **Corporation for Public Broadcasting** (CPB) to encompass both radio and television. Congress passed the **Public Broadcasting Act of 1967**, extended the ETV Facilities Act for 3 more years, and authorized funds.

The Act changed the name of the noncommercial service from *educational* to *public* broadcasting. It aimed to strengthen programming by providing for increased funding. However, national programming did not begin on a regular basis right away. The Ford Foundation funded a weekly *Public Broadcasting Laboratory,* distributed by live interconnection. However, most programming was locally produced or came to stations on tape or film from NET.

The Public Broadcasting Act prohibited CPB from owning or operating network service, so in 1969, the Corporation created the **Public Broadcasting Service** (PBS) to provide the interconnection for television programming. PBS did not create programming; it distributed programming funded and created by others. PBS began live interconnected program distribution in October 1970. In 1973, PBS was reconstituted. No longer a creature of CPB, it was now a station-owned membership organization.

CPB created **National Public Radio** (NPR) in 1970. NPR was to provide programming, as well as interconnection service. NPR began live network operations in May 1971.

Through increased funding and interconnected networking, programming improved and audiences increased. Public television programs such as *America, The Forsyte Saga, The Ascent of Man,* and *Masterpiece Theatre: Upstairs/Downstairs* drew both critical notice and measurable audiences. Public broadcasters paid more attention to ratings, and they offered evening programming that held broader appeal than before 1967.

Viewing patterns for public programming did not parallel those of commercial programming (*PRT,* 7.3). Most public television audience members viewed selectively. Nonetheless, in the mid-1990s, almost 100 million viewers watched public television in an average week. The average PBS household watched public television almost 3 hours a week. Prime-time ratings were typically higher than those of cable networks with similar programs.

### 22.1.4 Problems for Noncommercial Educational Broadcasting

Problems persisted. One involved **struggles among components of the public broadcasting establishment.** Public television stations transferred their resentment from NET to CPB. The stations jealously guarded their own programming power and felt that CPB was trying to force a lock-step commercial-network-style program schedule. CPB and PBS fought over control of programming and the interconnection. The PBS board consisted primarily of station representatives, so the stations sided with PBS. Some noncommercial broadcasters felt that their medium should devote itself primarily to formal instruction and resented moving toward general interest public broadcasting.

A second problem stemmed from **political meddling.** The Carnegie Commission had recommended that the CPB be trust-funded by a dedicated federal excise tax on television sets. This would provide revenue without having to depend entirely on congressional appropriations, thereby insulating the CPB from political interference in programming. To avoid controversy and to get the Public Broadcasting Act passed, this tax was not made part of the legislative package. As the commission foresaw, there was political interference in programming policies both from members of Congress and from the executive branch, beginning with the administration of President Richard M. Nixon.

Nixon fought PBS efforts to build up its news and public affairs programming. He viewed such programming as too liberal and critical of his administration and policies. Clay Whitehead, head of Nixon's Office of Telecommunications Policy, spoke at the 1971 NAEB convention and accused public broadcasting of turning into a fourth network, contrary to the principle of localism. Additionally, newsmen Sander Vanocur and Robert MacNeil had just been hired away from commercial broadcasting at salaries higher than those of members of Congress. Vanocur and MacNeil were also known for stating their opinions, which frequently ran counter to those of the Nixon administration. In 1972, Nixon vetoed a 2-year funding bill for public broadcasting, saying that PBS and CPB both undermined localism. This helped drive the wedge deeper between the stations and CPB.

A third problem involved **money.** For long-range planning and operational stability, public broadcasting needed funding that would continue for longer than 1 year. Congress began multiyear appropriations for CPB in 1975 but attached conditions to the appropriations. One bill, for example, established salary ceilings for CPB, PBS, and NPR employees. And, of course, the appropriations came in the form of matching funds.

Other problems emerged—constant interruption of broadcasts to raise funds led to complaints from viewers; continual reliance on corporate underwriting of programming led to complaints from commercial broadcasters; inadequate programming for attracting large national audiences or meeting special-audience and strictly instructional needs. In response, the Carnegie Corporation announced formation and funding of a new commission in 1977.

The Carnegie Commission on the Future of Public Broadcasting released its report in January 1979. **Carnegie II**[2] called for funding to increase by some 300% to $1.16 billion by 1985. The money was to be derived at least in part from a spectrum-use fee to be paid by commercial licensees. Carnegie II called for further controls to insulate public broadcasting from government control. Congress put some of the proposals into the various attempts to rewrite the Communications Act (*PRT,* 13.4.1). However, as these rewrite attempts failed, none of the Carnegie II revisions took place.

In 1973, CPB and PBS reached a compromise agreement on program control. The CPB programming department would make final decisions on CPB-funded programs, but PBS could dissent from such decisions. A complicated system of joint CPB–PBS committees would referee scheduling of the interconnection and running of programs not funded by CPB that either organization felt were not balanced or objective. An increased portion of CPB funds would flow directly to the stations. This agreement eased the problem of internal feuding, at least temporarily. The problems of lack of money and political meddling intensified.

### 22.1.5 Public Broadcasting's Scramble for Survival

In his campaign for president, Ronald Reagan vowed to cut government spending. After the election, Reagan made clear that one area in which he would reduce spending was public broadcasting. In fiscal year 1983, CPB's appropriation dropped $35 million, a 20% decrease from fiscal year 1982. Public broadcasting stations and organizations scrambled to accommodate the fund cut. Personnel were released, programs cut, and alternative funding sources—even commercials—were explored.

Historically, federal regulation had prohibited public stations from airing advertising of any kind. Corporate underwriting credits could contain only visual and aural identification of the donor, no reference to the business or product. The FCC loosened restrictions somewhat in 1981, permitting use of logos and identification of product lines. That same year, responding to the probability of reduced government funding, Congress passed a bill to allow a few public stations to experiment with limited advertising. The law established a **Temporary Commission on Alternative Financing for Public Telecommunications** (which public broadcasters abbreviated as TCAF). TCAF, in turn, set up an experiment whereby selected public television stations ran advertising between programs.

The experiment began in early 1982 and ended June 1983. Of the stations that completed the experiment, six ran commercials; another two ran enhanced underwriting—clustered underwriting credits. After the experiment, the stations reported overall that they made money and had received little or no negative reaction from their viewers. Several said that pledge drives conducted during the experiment made more money than before. Nonetheless, TCAF's final report said that public TV should not carry advertising. The commission feared the negative impact it might have on subscribers, legislators, and underwriters.

Instead, TCAF recommended that public broadcasters be permitted to air enhanced underwriting announcements. Such announcements could identify program supporters by use of brand names, trade names, slogans, brief institutional-type messages, and public service announcements. The FCC subsequently revised its guidelines for underwriter identification so that public broadcasters could air specific brand names, trade names, and product and service lines of donors and underwriters. A donor acknowledgment could include a logo or slogans that identify but do not promote; locations; value-neutral descriptions of product line or service; and trade names, product, or service listings that aid in identifying the contributor.

Public broadcasters could not air paid announcements for profit-making entities. By 1986, however, some licensees felt they could broadcast general service announcements (GSA). GSAs were local enhanced underwriting announcements that looked like commercials. National underwriters worried that GSAs might obscure national program credits, so PBS wrote guidelines separating GSAs from some fully underwritten national programs.

### 22.1.6 NPR's Year of Tribulation

Of all major elements in public broadcasting, NPR seemed to be in the best shape to generate its own funding. NPR had entered into a number of agreements with communications firms to supply its satellite relay system and the subcarriers of its affiliates for various types of revenue-producing services. In 1983, NPR formed Ventures, a subsidiary to pull together its several joint technological enterprises.

A few weeks later, word went out that NPR was deeply in debt, and that the debt was growing larger. An audit revealed that NPR had not used adequate financial procedures and controls. Soon, it became clear that NPR would have a $9.1-million deficit by the end of the fiscal year. Various rescue plans were put into effect, but none could produce enough money to guarantee the majority of the debt.

The end of July was almost the end of NPR. The network had a payroll due and no money to meet it. Finally, CPB agreed to guarantee a loan. NPR's member stations repaid the loan. NPR survived and instituted fiscal policies and accounting procedures designed to prevent similar problems in the future.

### 22.1.7 More of the Same and More

The problems remained. Squabbles, political meddling, and lack of funding all continued into the 1990s.

Money was probably the basic problem. The Reagan administration continued to resist federal support for public broadcasting. Nonetheless, by fiscal year 1988, Congress had managed to restore CPB appropriations.

Over the years, individual members of Congress tried to establish a permanent trust fund. By the mid-1990s, the major point of dispute for many seemed to be the size of the fund.

The apportioning of federal appropriations shifted. More money went to local stations and less to the national level. This trend had begun earlier but accelerated in the latter part of the 1980s. In 1986, for example, CPB and NPR agreed on **the business plan,** a restructuring of public radio budgeting and operating procedures. Under this plan, programming funds previously allocated to NPR now went to the stations. The stations, in turn, chose whether to pay NPR membership fees for the entire "bundle" of NPR programming. The plan seemed to work well. The stations, however, always arguing for more local control, urged further revision. Two years later, NPR responded by adopting an **unbundling plan.**

Under this plan, stations bought separate packages of programming from NPR. The plan also allowed nonmember stations to purchase NPR programming. In the meantime, Congress worked on proposals to restructure public television along the lines of radio's business plan, and CPB looked toward the possibility of having to narrow the number of activities for which it provided financial support.

Other problems involved cable and independent producers. In the wake of must-carry's uncertainties (*PRT,* 3.5.2.1), some cable systems cut second and third public television stations from their channel lineups. Some system operators shifted public stations from their original cable channels to other, often less desirable, channels. Cable networks competed with public television for programming and audiences (*PRT,* 7.4.2.1). Independent producers felt that CPB and PBS had denied them opportunity to make and air programs. They lobbied Congress for a share of CPB's funding without CPB control.

Battles over funding for public broadcasting accelerated in the mid-1990s. Concern about federal budget deficits brought efforts to restrain government spending, and public broadcasting became a target. Some opposed spending federal money for cultural activities. They argued that public broadcasting reflected a biased political viewpoint, and primarily served an upper middle-class elite that did not need a subsidized broadcast service. In response, public broadcasting showed that its audience is demographically similar to the public at large.

Some argued federal funding for public broadcasting was no longer needed. First, they said that public broadcasting had not capitalized on other available funding sources. These critics pointed especially to the licensing fees earned by products related to such popular programs as *Sesame Street* and *Barney and His Friends.* If public broadcasting would insist on a fair share of these rights payments there would be sufficient revenue to replace federal assistance. Public broadcasting advocates produced data showing that after payment of such expenses as manufacturing and distribution, the amount of licensing money that would actually reach public broadcasting was far less than the traditional amounts of federal support.

A second argument was that there was no longer a need for public broadcasting because cable-delivered services such as A & E, Discovery, Nickelodeon and The Learning Channel were providing sufficient children's, documentary, cultural, and educational programming. Public broadcasters argued that commercial realities prevented the newer networks from providing the diversity of programming or local productions of public broadcasting stations. Further, because broadcast signals reached places unserved by cable, only public broadcasting could bring programming to everyone.

When the Republicans won control of both houses in 1994 their leadership spoke of phasing out federal funding for public broadcasting. After extensive lobbying by the stations and the Clinton administration, the original funding levels were reduced, but not eliminated. Funding levels for subsequent years were below the earlier allocations (Table 22.1).

**TABLE 22.1**

CPB Funding History

|  | *Original Appropriation* | *Rescinded by Congress* | *Final Appropriation* |
| --- | --- | --- | --- |
| FY 1994 | $275 million | 0 | $275 million |
| FY 1995 | $292.64 million | $7 million | $285.64 million |
| FY 1996 | $312 million | $37 million | $275 million |
| FY 1997 | $315 million | $55 million | $260 million |
| FY 1998 | $250 million | 0 | $250 million |
| FY 1999[a] |  |  | $250 million |
| FY 2000[a] |  |  | $250 million |

*Note.* Data from Corporation for Public Broadcasting.
[a]Proposed.

In response to these reductions, CPB imposed new rules governing awarding of station grants. Eligibility requirements for radio were increased to include evidence of minimum audience numbers or minimum listener contributions. CPB phased out funding for TV stations whose signals overlapped. The target was licensees with two or more stations serving the same market.

Efforts accelerated to create a permanent trust fund to replace the annual federal budget subsidy. One proposal would raise funds through the auctioning of spectrum assigned to public broadcasting, but not yet in use. Public broadcasters argued that there was no indication that the market for such spectrum would generate the necessary revenues, nor was there very much spectrum available. In 1996, the FCC did allow WQED in Pittsburgh to sell one of its licenses to a commercial operator to generate revenue.

The second proposal brought opposition from commercial broadcasters. Some Congressional leaders suggested auctioning the spectrum space to be used by commercial stations for Advanced Television Services (*PRT,* 12.5). Such fees would raise enough money to create a public broadcasting trust fund and help to reduce the federal debt.

In late 1997, a group of public-television station leaders called a "convention of stations." The meeting culminated a year-long review of the system's decision-making processes. It confronted such issues as differences in perspective between local stations and the national PBS, and means of exploiting new technologies for the benefit of public television.

## 22.2 PUBLIC BROADCAST PROGRAMMING

Despite the litany of woes just recited, noncommercial broadcasting has progressed. Public radio and television had improved immeasurably since 1960. Programming was often just as slick and professional as that of commercial broadcasting—more so, in the case of the consistently fine dramas from PBS. They demonstrated that high-quality programming could succeed and could attract audiences seeking alternatives to existing commercial programming.

### 22.2.1 National Public Programming

Public broadcasting programming at the national level is largely the responsibility of PBS and NPR. The federally funded CPB provides funds to PBS for network interconnection, to individual production organizations for program production, and to individual stations for programming and other operations. The PBS network schedule consists of those programs whose productions CPB has funded directly, those selected and paid for by the stations as a group, those financed by corporate underwriting or by foundations, those produced by individual stations for local audiences and then selected for national exposure, and those that have been aired previously on the network and have been selected to repeat.

The PBS **National Program Service** includes prime-time, general audience, and children's programs. PBS produces no programs itself, but does distribute programming on the public television satellite system.

Programming sources include PBS member stations, organizations set up especially to produce for PBS, and production organizations from outside the public broadcasting pale. Major producing stations include WGBH in Boston, WNET in New York City, KQED in San Francisco, KCET in Los Angeles, WETA in Washington in DC, WTTW in Chicago, and WQED in Pittsburgh. Probably the best known special public television production agency is Children's Television Workshop (CTW), producer of *Sesame Street* and *Electric Company.* Some commercial production companies also provide programming to PBS. *The Newshour With Jim Lehrer* is produced by TCI's Liberty Media. British television has contributed programming ranging from *Civilisation* to *Red Dwarf.*

NPR provides programming and technical operations for member stations. For a yearly membership fee, qualified stations receive programming and support services, a satellite-delivered communications system, and engineering training and advice. NPR also represents stations' interests before the FCC and Congress.

NPR stations buy programming blocks such as the morning news block or afternoon news block. Following the success of talk radio in commercial radio (*PRT,* 7.2.1.2), NPR began a midday block of talk programs.

Some of the better known regular NPR offerings include news magazines *Morning Edition, All Things Considered,* and *Weekend Edition.* One of the more unusual—yet popular—NPR programs is *Car Talk,* a call-in program broadcast on Saturday mornings. The hosts offer maintenance advice, humor, and snide remarks.

In 1982, representatives of four public radio stations and one regional public radio organization formed American Public Radio. In 1994 the network was renamed **Public Radio International** (PRI). The network complemented NPR by providing additional quality radio programming. For years the best known offering was the Saturday afternoon variety show, *A Prairie Home Companion,* produced by Minnesota Public Radio.

## 22.2.2 Local Public Programming

Public television stations often have a split personality. During daytime, a station may broadcast instructional material for in-school use or for-credit home study. The contracting agency, usually a local school board or college, pays the station for running and often producing this material.

During afternoon and evening hours, the station typically airs general-interest programming. Most will come from PBS, but the station will get some from other sources and produce some itself. Other sources might include free or low-cost programming from regional networks, other public television stations, government agencies, or educational institutions. A public television station may buy programming from commercial syndication sources to put together a classic film festival or to air documentaries, specials, even old entertainment series first broadcast by commercial television.

The quality also varies for locally produced general-interest programming. Lack of funding is often a cause.

Many public radio stations program a fine arts and classical music format. Others program jazz, talk, public affairs, or even Black and progressive rock music. Still others program a little bit for everybody.

Religious stations operating in the reserved portion of the FM band program their messages in a variety of ways. Programming ranges from the subtle approach, featuring classical music and discussion programs to 24 hours of hard-driving preaching, hymns, "Jesus rock," and "beautiful inspirational music."

Many noncommercial radio stations are neither NPR affiliates nor religious stations. Their programming is so diverse as to defy classification, ranging from wall-to-wall classical or progressive rock to straight variety formats; from university student-government playgrounds to radio–television production laboratories. A few actually air courses for credit.

## 22.2.3 Community Stations

One novel programming form is that of **community stations.** Community-station programming represents a radical departure from standard radio fare. Each and all can have access to the station's airwaves. This brings unpopular causes, antiestablishment ideas, and strong language before the microphones. Community-station proponent Lorenzo Milam has described it as "free-form noninstitutional radio." Some of the best known examples of community-station programming come from stations of the Pacifica Foundation (*PRT,* 15.3.5.1).

When the first community stations signed on, the public did not know what to make of them. Community stations depended solely on listener support. Because much of the community felt alienated by their programming, the stations seemed to lurch from financial crisis to financial crisis. Funding was largely dependent on listener contributions and grants from foundations.

## 22.3 PUBLIC STATION LICENSEES

Most noncommercial stations are owned by nonprofit organizations. Beyond this generalization, it is difficult to categorize types of ownership. As of 1997 there were about 350 public television stations and almost 600 NPR affiliates. PBS and NPR affiliates tend to be owned by state educational broadcasting commissions, colleges and universities, school boards and systems, and broad-based nonprofit community corporations. The ownership of noncommercial radio stations not affiliated with NPR is even more diverse—universities, community corporations, school boards, churches, religious groups, seminaries, high schools, college student government associations, cities, counties, and boys' clubs.

Most noncommercial radio stations are in the reserved portion of the FM band. Some licensees, however, operate noncommercial broadcast stations in the AM band. Some nonprofit institutions also operate commercial stations.

Limitations on the number of licensees do not apply to noncommercial broadcasting. Twin Cities Public TV, for example, operates two television stations in St. Paul, KTCA-TV, channel 2, and WTCI-TV, channel 17.

## 22.4 PUBLIC BROADCASTING FUNDING SOURCES

Overall, **public broadcasting gets less than half its money from taxes**, but less than 20% of its money comes from the federal government. Sources of public broadcasting's tax revenues include state governments, CPB, tax-supported colleges and universities, local governments, and federal government grants and contracts. The other half comes from subscribers, businesses, foundations, auction participants, private colleges and universities, and other sources.

In actual dollars, public broadcasting operates on a relatively miniscule budget. In fiscal year 1994, for example, Congress appropriated CPB $275 million. During this same period, the three commercial networks paid an average fee of $1.4 million for each hour of prime-time programming (*PRT*, 7.3.1.1). CPB's total annual congressional funding for 1 year would not quite cover expenses for 3 hours of programming per day for 3 months on one commercial television network.

Congress specifies how CPB should spend its federal appropriation. A small portion may go to CPB's operating expense; the majority, to TV and radio at a ratio of about three to one. For each medium, most money goes for **community service grants** (CSG); the remainder to national programming. A station must apply and meet certain criteria to qualify for a CSG. CPB gives CSGs on a matching basis; the exact amount for each station varies according to a formula. The station may spend the money almost any way it wishes. It uses a portion for programming.

The National Endowment for the Arts (NEA), the National Endowment for the Humanities (NEH), and the U.S. Department of Education provide additional federal funds for programming at both national and local levels. The National Telecommunications and Information Agency (*PRT*, 14.3.1.2) administers the

Public Telecommunication Facilities Program that makes facilities grants for local stations.

PBS derives some of its funding from CPB. This pays for management and operation of the satellite relay interconnection. The remainder comes from the dues PBS charges its member stations, from interest income, and from its program library and other services (Fig. 22.1).

NPR's member stations provide more than 60% of NPR's operating budget with their membership dues. Stations derive funds from their listeners, businesses in their communities, and grants from CPB. NPR also seeks grants and underwriting from corporations, foundations, associations, and individuals.

## 22.5 COMMERCIAL ACTIVITIES OF NONCOMMERCIAL BROADCASTING

The matching funds concept has led public broadcasting to a continual search for nonfederal money. Public stations have engaged in a number of activities to raise money, several of which parallel, or at least bear a resemblance to, advertising.

Many public stations publish and distribute **program guides** to their audiences. These guides often contain advertising. Revenue from guide advertising helps defray publication expense and may even contribute to station operating expenses.

Public stations also broadcast announcements somewhat analogous to the advertising of commercial broadcast stations. These include underwriting announcements, GSAs, pleas for money, and auctions.

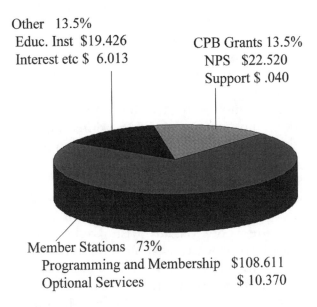

Other   13.5%
Educ. Inst  $19.426
Interest etc $  6.013

CPB Grants 13.5%
NPS   $22.520
Support $  .040

Member Stations   73%
Programming and Membership   $108.611
Optional Services            $ 10.370

**FIG. 22.1. PBS funding sources, fiscal year 1997.** PBS receives funding from a variety of tax and nontax sources. (*Source*: PBS.)

The **underwriting announcement** is probably the most familiar. Many public broadcasting programs are supported by grants from various organizations, including major companies. Local businesses and even individuals support programming on stations. Announcements notify the audience that the program or programming has been underwritten or supported or made possible by a grant from Mobil, Goerings' Book Store, or whomever.

Some public television stations' GSAs resemble commercials. GSAs air between programs, ostensibly to recognize businesses that donate money to the station. In reality, local advertisers pay for them, and they look like advertising spots.

Despite TCAF's failure (*PRT,* 22.1.5) some elected officials, public broadcasters, and others have advocated allowing stations to sell advertising time. Many of these proposals suggest that commercials would be presented only between programs.

One idea has been to create a second public television network that would be commercially supported. Others have advocated allowing program services such as Discovery to buy time for their programs on public stations, and then to sell advertising time within the programs.

Another type of announcement, peculiar to public broadcasting, is the **plea for money.** Stations usually air these pleas during membership drives. Individuals go on the air to ask for donations or subscriptions for the station, often promising gifts or premiums in return. Some public television stations have periodic **auctions** to raise money. Showing and describing the items to be auctioned, together with the names of merchants or manufacturers donating them, would seem to parallel the promotional announcements of commercial broadcasting.

In considering these announcement types, the case could be made that public broadcast stations seem to sell time, much like commercial stations. They sell foundations and businesses on underwriting programs, then mention the underwriters by name before and after the programs. They sell merchants and other retailers on donating goods and services for auctions, then name the businesses and extol the products over the air. Some GSAs look suspiciously like outright commercials.

Many complain about public broadcasting's fund-raising efforts. Stations conduct what seem like almost continual pleas for donations and subscribers, and audiences compare them unfavorably to advertising on commercial broadcasting. *Broadcasting & Cable* magazine has editorialized against commercial-like practices of noncommercial stations on several occasions. Commercial broadcasters generally object to any semblance of advertising in noncommercial broadcasting.

The problem, however, is not that public stations engage in commercial practices or siphon off a few potential advertising dollars. The basic problem is funding. Given that public broadcasting is to continue to provide a high-quality, audience-drawing service, then unless and until some means are found to provide continuing, adequate, full funding—not tied to matching funds and not tied to the appropriations process—public broadcasting will be forced to continue to engage in money-raising schemes.

## 22.6 PUBLIC BROADCASTING ORGANIZATIONS

Public broadcasting seems to be a sea of alphabet soup, thick with the initials of constituent organizations. We have already discussed several of these. The CPB is an important source of funding for stations, programming, and the public television interconnection. CPB is a congressionally chartered, nonprofit corporation, not a branch of the federal government; however, Congress provides its funding.

The primary national noncommercial networks are PBS and NPR. Both were organized by CPB and both have headquarters in Washington, DC. Stations must meet certain minimum criteria to become member stations of either organization.

Neither PBS nor NPR parallels exactly its commercial counterparts. Although PBS arranges for, manages, and sends programs to affiliated stations, it does not exercise absolute control over its own programming. It must share that control with CPB and with the stations it serves. PBS stations can exercise significant choice in scheduling programs.

**The Independent Television Service** (ITVS) was created by Congress in 1988 and began operation in 1990. ITVS' mandate is to fund programming from independent producers who serve diverse audiences and previously underserved groups.

NPR does produce and control its own programming. Member stations, however, pick and choose the programming they wish to pay for and air.

NPR also acts as a station membership and representation organization. Stations join, and NPR uses station dues to provide membership and professional services and to represent the stations' interests before CPB, Congress, the executive branch, and the general public. In other words, NPR functions as a network, as an affiliate association, and as a public broadcasting equivalent of NAB.

Public television stations, however, have split the lobbying and programming functions between two organizations. PBS provides programming and membership services (such as promotion, engineering, and advertising assistance). Lobbying, planning, and research were spun off into a separate organization in 1979, the National Association of Public Television Stations. Today the organization is known as the **Association of American Public Television Stations** (APTS).

Stations may join NPR and PBS only if they meet certain professional, staffing, technical, and operational standards. This excludes many high school and college FM radio stations.

Public Radio International is a private, nonprofit network of public radio stations. PRI produces no programming itself. However, the network nurtures development of radio productions from all over the country and the world. It also provides promotion and marketing services. By the mid-1990s, PRI was distributing more than 300 hours of programming each week. Some stations were affiliated with both NPR and PRI.

The **National Federation of Community Broadcasters** (NFCB) is an organization for non-NPR public radio stations licensed to community organizations. It distributes programs, provides training, and assists groups seeking to develop new stations. NFCB looks out for the interests of its constituent licensees in dealing with CPB, Congress, the executive branch, the FCC, and other agencies in Washington, DC.

NAEB was an influential organization for more than four decades. Originally, its membership consisted of noncommercial broadcast stations. In 1956, it also started admitting individuals. In 1973, the stations pulled out because they now had lobbying organizations outside NAEB. Without station dues, NAEB could not support its array of services and publications. In 1981 it declared bankruptcy and went out of business.

On the other hand, a descendant of National Educational Television still exists. NET was instrumental in assisting New York City's WNDT, channel 13 to get on the air in 1962. NET continued as a major producer of programs for noncommercial television until 1969, when it merged with WNDT. The television station changed its call letters to WNET and assumed a role as one of the primary sources of national programming for PBS.

There are a number of regional and state organizations. Regional groups include the Central Educational Network, Eastern Educational Network (which also operates the Interregional Program Service), Eastern Public Radio, Pacific Mountain Network, Public Radio in Mid-America, Rocky Mountain Corporation for Public Broadcasting, Rocky Mountain Public Radio, Southern Educational Communications Association, and West Coast Public Radio.

Many states have set up central governmental bodies to operate public television stations. Some of these state systems are interconnected. Among the more elaborate networks are those of Alabama, Georgia, Kentucky, Mississippi, Nebraska, North Carolina, and South Carolina. In most states a specially created state agency operates the system; in others a state university or the state department of education runs the network.

## 22.7 PUBLIC BROADCASTING, DEREGULATION, AND NEW TECHNOLOGIES

Public broadcasting has been aggressive in using new technologies. In 1978 PBS became the first network to replace land lines with satellites. Later, it was a leader in the development and application of closed-captioning technologies. Video description service, in which an off-camera narrator describes the visual scene for the sight-impaired, began in 1990 and is offered by more than 100 stations. In 1991 the *MacNeil/Lehrer News Hour* was translated into Spanish and transmitted simultaneously on the second audio program (SAP) channel. Some public radio stations have used their subcarrier authorization (SCA; *PRT,* 11.6) to offer reading services for the blind.

The Telecommunications Act of 1996 allowed telephone companies to offer video services. Public television stations told the FCC that they deserved access to telephone company carriage at preferred rates, and that these services should come under provisions of the must-carry rules as they applied to cable television. Public broadcasters argued that they would be able to exploit the technologies through such uses as distance learning and Internet-based educational applications.

In 1996 the PBS series *Life on the Internet* was made available "on demand" on the Internet. Each episode was stored for 1 week, and could be played in its entirety whenever desired by computer users with the appropriate Internet connections. Text transcripts could be retrieved at any time after broadcast. Generally, public broadcasting organizations at all levels have welcomed the coming of new forms and new uses of radio and television. They see new media not only as alternative delivery systems but also sources for sorely needed funding.

The FCC has also helped by removing some regulations that blocked public stations from generating revenues. For example, the FCC eased restrictions on underwriting announcements, allowed noncommercial FM stations to use their subcarriers for moneymaking ventures, and permitted educational entities to lease unused time on their ITFS channels to MDS programmers.

Public broadcasting organizations now lease programming for use on videocassettes and videodiscs, provide teleconferencing services, rent out unused time on their satellite systems, and cooperate in various schemes to make profitable use of their satellite interconnection and their subcarriers—for example, paging and data distribution.

The mandate of the Telecommunication Act of 1996 that television stations move toward digital broadcasts on a second channel will affect public TV (*PRT*, 12.5.2). Stations will have to buy new production and transmission equipment.

Public TV stations have talked about such applications as simultaneous instructional programs aimed at elementary, secondary, college, and adult audiences. Stations and PBS have also committed themselves to HDTV programs.

The phrase *public broadcasting* may already be dated; we may be witnessing a metamorphosis—a change from stations and station organizations to a group of self-sustaining, nonprofit telecommunication programmers.

## 22.8 INSTRUCTIONAL BROADCASTING

Noncommercial educational broadcasting takes two basic forms. We have discussed one, public broadcasting, in some detail. However, we have merely mentioned the other, instructional broadcasting. **Instructional broadcasting** refers to the use of public airwaves for formal academic instruction.

### 22.8.1 Mostly Television

Instructional broadcasting is done primarily by television. Radio could be used to teach many of the same things for which television is now used and at a fraction of the cost. However, instructional radio is not widely used in the United States, so our discussion deals mainly with instructional television.

The public television station and the instructional television station are often one and the same. The station broadcasts general-interest public programming on evenings and weekends and instructional materials on weekdays. Sometimes the organization that initiates or uses the instructional programming is the station's licensee, as in the case of a station owned by a public school system. Usually, however, instructional programming involves second parties, often school districts. School districts contract with a station to air instructional material, each district paying a share based at least in part on the number of students in that district who use the programming.

### 22.8.2 Uses of Instructional Broadcasting

Some instructional broadcasts are designed for use **in the classroom**. Instructional broadcasting can be used at any and every level of schooling, from kindergarten through college postgraduate. It has come into increasing use to offer freshman-and sophomore-level college courses in the general education area. Instructional broadcasting may be used **to teach an entire subject, to teach part of a subject,** or **to provide supplementary material**. Instructional broadcasting may also be used **to allow study at home**. Community colleges, particularly, use television to offer credit courses in basic requirements.

### 22.8.3 Instructional Television Program Sources

Sources of instructional programming include institutions that sponsor or give credit for the broadcast courses, stations themselves, state and regional organizations, and national production centers and libraries.

In the 1980s, both PBS and CPB took on educational responsibilities. PBS's Adult Learning Service works with public TV stations and local colleges to make television courses available to adult learners nationwide. Its Elementary/Secondary Services provides leadership in the development and distribution of quality instructional TV series and services to stations and school agencies. The PBS National Narrowcast Service delivers video-based training and educational programming to businesses, industry, and colleges by satellite, ITFS, and addressable cable.

A special grant funds CPB development of college-level instructional materials, primarily audio and video courses. Some of the courses have included *Planet Earth, The Africans,* and *Economics USA.* Each academic year, more than 150,000 students enroll in courses offered by over 1,000 colleges. Named for the donating and administering agencies, this Annenberg/CPB Project also funds applications that demonstrate how communications technologies can increase opportunities for higher education.

### 22.8.4 ITFS and Satellite for Instructional Purposes

Some school districts, community colleges, and other educational institutions utilize **instructional television fixed service** (ITFS; *PRT,* 12.8) for wireless distribution of instructional programming.

An institution uses ITFS when it wishes to distribute video educational materials to a number of physically separated units. An ITFS licensee may operate multiple channels, a distinct advantage over broadcast television. ITFS does not cost as much to build and operate as broadcast television, nor does it require a continuous broadcast-style schedule of programming. On the other hand, its line-of-sight transmission characteristic means that distance and transmission paths are critical in setting up an ITFS system. Also, few homes are equipped to receive ITFS, negating its use for home study. In some cases this can be overcome if a cable system agrees to carry the ITFS programming.

### 22.9 CLOSED-CIRCUIT RADIO AND TELEVISION

**Closed circuit** means that signals are distributed in a way that limits access to reception. The uses of closed-circuit television (CCTV) are almost endless. To illustrate CCTV's diversity, let us take one field, education, and look at some of the ways in which CCTV is used there.

Like instructional broadcasting, nonbroadcast television may be used to teach an entire subject, to teach part of a subject, or to provide supplementary material. It can be used to teach almost any number of persons, from one to as many as viewing facilities permit. It is used by public and private schools, colleges, and universities; by industry; by the military; and by every level of government.

### NOTES

1. Carnegie Commission on Educational Television, *Public Television: A Program for Action* (New York: Harper, 1967).

2. Carnegie Commission on the Future of Public Broadcasting, *A Public Trust* (New York: Bantam, 1979).

### FURTHER READING

Collins, Mary. *National Public Radio: The Cast of Characters.* Washington, DC: Seven Locks, 1993.

Engelman, Ralph. *Public Radio and Television in America: A Political History.* Thousand Oaks, CA: Sage, 1996.

Fuller, Linda K. *Community Television in the United States: A Sourcebook on Public, Educational, and Governmental Access.* Westport, CT: Greenwood, 1994.

Hoynes, William. *Public Television for Sale: Media, The Market, and the Public Sphere.* Boulder, CO: Westview, 1994.

Lashley, Marilyn. *Public Television: Panacea, Pork Barrel, or Public Trust?* Westport, CT: Greenwood, 1992.

Looker, Thomas. *The Sound and the Story: NPR and the Art of Radio.* Boston: Houghton Mifflin, 1995.

# 23

## FOREIGN NATIONAL
## AND INTERNATIONAL RADIO
## AND TELEVISION

The world has undergone profound political and economic changes in the last decade. The dissolution of the Soviet Union and the end of the Cold War have altered the environment for telecommunications policies and practices. Telecommunications systems around the world are in a state of flux caused by new technologies and new economic realities.

Greater reliance on market forces has brought U.S.-style commercially supported broadcast services to compete with government monopolies. Between 1987 and 1991 the number of national television channels around the world increased from 354 to 521.[1] New communication technologies have created worldwide program services that cannot be regulated by any single government and, increasingly, national broadcast systems are being decentralized, or are being joined by local or regional services. In many of these systems U.S.-produced programs are a significant portion of the schedule.

In this chapter we examine electronic mass media outside the United States, first, as systems within the boundaries of other countries and, second, as informational products that cross national boundaries. We begin with an analytical model that summarizes operational characteristics of national systems of mass communication. Then we examine the broadcasting systems of four nations. We discuss the growing use of new technologies by other countries, major international organizations related to broadcasting, the flow of programs in the world market, and the phenomenon of foreign media ownership. Finally, we review U.S. international broadcasting efforts.

### 23.1 WELLS' ANALYSIS

Alan Wells[2] noted five key requirements, which he called **dimensions**, that are shared by all national systems of mass communication. For each dimension he listed several options. The options represent methods that he found nations employ to meet these requirements. So if we look at Wells' key dimensions and the options for each, we should have an idea of the variety of national broadcasting systems and the alternatives countries employ to deal with radio and television. Wells' analysis is diagrammed in Table 23.1 and explained in the following.

Wells' dimensions are control, finance, programming goals, target audiences, and feedback mechanisms. Options for control include direct operation by the government; operation by a private corporation in which the government has stock interest; operation by private companies, with government regulation in varying degrees; and operation by sponsoring institutions such as churches, political parties, or listener organizations.

Wells listed five options for finance of systems. Finance options include a tax or license fee paid by owners of receivers, subsidization from general tax revenues, sale of advertising time, subsidization by private organizations or individuals, and subsidization through a combination of advertising and taxation.

Programming goals include one or any combination of six options: entertainment, education, sales, culture, political ideology, or operation as cheaply as possible.

There are three audience options: elite, mass, and specialized. **Elite** refers to the wealthy, the educated, and the literate. An example of a specialized audience could be programming aimed at workers in a particular factory.

**Feedback mechanism** refers to means by which audience response to programming is determined. Wells listed four feedback mechanism options: reports from field workers, audience participation and local control, polls and ratings, and evaluation by critics and sponsors.

## 23.2 NATIONAL SYSTEMS: FOUR EXAMPLES

At this point we go from theory to practice and find how some of these options translate into actual operation. As examples, we examine the electronic mass media systems of four countries—the United Kingdom, China, India, and the

**TABLE 23.1**
Key Dimensions of Media Systems

| Dimensions | Options |
| --- | --- |
| Control | State-operated, public corporation, partnership, private enterprise (with varying degrees of government regulation), institutionally sponsored |
| Finance | License fees, general taxation, advertising and taxation combination, advertising, private subsidy |
| Programming goals | Entertainment, education, sales, culture, political ideology, cheapest possible operation (utilizing foreign material) |
| Target audience | Elite, mass, specialized |
| Feedback mechanism | Reports from field workers, audience participation, polls and ratings, reports from critics and sponsors |

*Note.* From Alan Wells, *Mass Communications: A World View* (Palo Alto, CA: Mayfield, 1974). Used by permission.

Netherlands. These systems do not represent the total spectrum of options across each dimension. They do, however, show how four quite different countries use electronic media to serve specific needs.

As in all national systems of mass communication, each of these four is dependent on the money available for operation. Relatively, India has a much more limited system than the other three countries. Nations in Third World countries do not have money to provide more extensive broadcast service.

### 23.2.1 United Kingdom

The United Kingdom of Great Britain and Northern Ireland is a highly industrialized nation. Great Britain includes England, Scotland, and Wales. In the United Kingdom, broadcast licenses are issued for 10-year periods. Three organizations hold licenses—the **British Broadcasting Corporation** (BBC), the **Radio Authority,** and the **Independent Television Commission** (ITC).

During the 1980s, the government accelerated industry privatization. **Privatization** refers to the transfer of formerly government-run industries and services to private, profit-seeking companies. Privatization included the electronic media.

Although the BBC, ITC, and Radio Authority are independent of direct, day-to-day government control, they do have certain obligations in their programming. For example, programs must be impartial in controversial matters and display balance and a range of subject matter. Codes restrict the violence in television programs, especially during hours when children are likely to be viewing.

*23.2.1.1 BBC.* The BBC was established in 1927 by royal charter. The crown (government) appoints its board of governors. The board sets policy and appoints the board of management headed by a director-general to carry out that policy and to run the corporation.

For years, the BBC had a monopoly. Its noncommercial programming largely reflected the taste of the upper class individuals who set its policy. There was little audience research, and the BBC purposely programmed slightly above the perceived level of the public in an effort to raise taste. However, a number of factors militated against the status quo—a carefully organized campaign to introduce commercial television, offshore radio competition, demand for local service, and sociopolitical activism in Scotland, Wales, and Northern Ireland. As a result, British broadcasting underwent changes in the 1950s and 1960s, beginning with the Television Act of 1954. This legislation created the BBC's first domestic competition in 27 years, then called the Independent Broadcast Authority (IBA).

The BBC's broadcast activities are organized into three English regions (BBC North, BBC Midlands & East, and BBC South) and the Northern Ireland, Scotland, and Wales regions. The regional organizations produce programming for the national networks and programs, especially news, for regional audiences.

The BBC operates about 40 local radio stations, five national radio networks in England, and national services in Scotland, Wales, and Northern Ireland. The local radio stations work with local radio councils to produce a full range of programming by and for their communities. The national radio channels broadcast from high-powered transmitters. Each radio network carries a different type of programming—Radio 1, popular and rock music; Radio 2, "middle of the road" music, light entertainment, and sports; Radio 3, classical music, documentaries, dramas, and speeches; Radio 4, news and public affairs, features, and drama; and Radio 5 Live, news and sports.

BBC's two television channels serve the range of viewer interests. BBC 1 presents more programs of general interest, such as light entertainment and sports. BBC 2 emphasizes minority interests and includes programs such as documentaries, serious drama, and international films. By law, the BBC also provides at least 10 hours of programming each week to the independent Welsh language channel, S4C.

The BBC runs no commercials. Owners of television sets pay annual license fees of about $150 for each color television and about $50 for each black-and-white television. From the license fees Parliament makes grants to the BBC. Parliament exercises no direct control over programming.

BBC International Television represents the BBC in the sale of programming overseas and arranges for coproductions. It also promotes the development of the BBC's international television channels such as World Service Television.

***23.2.1.2 Commercial Broadcasting in the United Kingdom.***    Until 1990 commercial broadcasting was under the supervision of the Independent Broadcasting Association. In that year television was placed under the **Independent Television Commission,** and radio under the **Radio Authority.** The Secretary of State for National Heritage appoints chairs, deputy chairs, and members to the boards of the two organizations.

*U.K. Commercial Radio.*    The Radio Authority is responsible for radio advertising and for selecting licensees for the newly authorized commercial radio. Franchisees for the three national commercial stations are Classic FM, Talk Radio UK, and Virgin Radio (which features popular music). Independent Radio News, a part of Independent Television News, provides news programming for all of the stations. Another commercial broadcaster, Atlantic 252 reaches about two thirds of the United Kingdom from its transmitter in Ireland.

There are also a small but growing number of local commercial stations. For example, in 1996 radio listeners in London could choose from more than 25 radio services.

The commercial sector has increased its audience in recent years. In 1995 the combined audience share for commercial radio exceeded that of the BBC for the first time,[3] although the public stations later regained a small advantage.[4] Clearly the two systems are competitive, but the long-term success of commercial radio may rest with its ability to attract audiences away from the BBC, as overall radio listening in the United Kingdom has not increased in recent years.[5]

*U.K. Commercial Television.*    The ITC is responsible for licensing and regulating commercially funded television. For many years ITC supervised two television channels, channel 3 and channel 4. Channel 3, The ITV Network, is programmed by 15 regional licensees and one national licensee that provides a national morning news program (called **breakfast-time programming**). Licenses were awarded for a 10-year period that began in 1993.

Channel 4 is required to provide education and information programming as well as entertainment. It is expected to appeal to interests not served by channel 3, and to encourage innovative and experimental programming. Channel 4 sells its own advertising and receives financial support from the channel 3 licensees if its revenues fall below a certain level.

In Wales S4C carries many of channel 4's programs, but during prime time it broadcasts Welsh-language programs. Funding for S4C comes from the government and the sale of advertising.

In 1997 a new commercial service, channel 5, began operation. The license was awarded to a consortium including CLT, a European broadcast conglomerate, and two British media firms.

Channel 5 targets its programming at an under-35 audience. Among its programs were *Beverly Hills 90210* and *Melrose Place.* When it went on the air the signal was available only to about 65% of homes in the United Kingdom.

The ITC owns and operates its transmitters but does not broadcast itself. Instead, it chooses independent companies to do the programming. These companies earn profits through the sale of advertising time. The "Rules on Advertising Breaks" have traditionally required that advertising messages were to be carried at the beginning, the end, or natural breaks of programs. However, there has been reconsideration of those policies in light of competition from satellite and cable-delivered services. Program-length infomercials were authorized in 1996.[6]

Divided geographically, each region in the country is served by an independent program company. Several companies share the contract for London. The companies exchange programs, with most exchange-network programming coming from the largest companies. The companies have jointly set up Independent Television News, a nonprofit company that produces news programming they all may use.

ITV is the most popular channel. In 1997 prime time shares averaged 38.8%, compared to 32.3% for BBC 1 and BBC 2. Channel 4 had a 7.8% share, and channel 5 a 3.1%. The various satellite and other services had a combined 8.8% share.[7]

### 23.2.1.3 Educational Broadcasting in the United Kingdom.    Both BBC and ITC transmit educational programming. This programming includes in-school and continuing education material. An individual can earn a degree entirely by television through Open University courses. British broadcasting provides educational radio programming as well as television.

*23.2.1.4 Uses of Other Electronic Media in the United Kingdom.* The United Kingdom pioneered teletext and videotex. In 1974, the BBC introduced CEEFAX, a teletext news and information service (*PRT,* 5.5.3). Shortly thereafter, independent television started its own teletext service, ORACLE. In 1979, the Post Office launched Prestel, an interactive videotex service (*PRT,* 5.5.4). In 1983 cable television was introduced, but growth has been slow. In 1996 cable penetration was only about 20%, and many areas in the United Kingdom had no cable available. Some 80 cable television franchises were originally granted, but by the mid-1990s consolidation and lack of success reduced the number to 12. Some observers expect further consolidation.[8]

Cable television has faced competition from satellite-delivered services. Rupert Murdoch's **BSkyB** (British Sky Broadcasting) began operating in 1990, and serves more than 4 million subscribers. Its program packages reach additional subscribers through arrangements with cable television operators.

Satellite programming includes a variety of channels. Sky One is the most popular, featuring such U.S. Fox network programs as *Beverly Hills 90210* and *X-Files* and original productions of dramatic, documentary, and children's programs. BSkyB also provides subscription movie and sports channels, British all-news, travel, arts, and soap opera program services and the international versions of MTV, The Disney Channel, Nickelodeon, and the Sci-Fi Channel.[9]

## 23.2.2 People's Republic of China

Almost one quarter of the world's human population lives in China. Established as a kingdom over 2,200 years ago, modern China has had a communist political and economic system since Mao Zedong led a military campaign which ousted the Nationalists in 1949.

In recent years the Chinese leadership has steered the economy away from a centrally planned communist system into a more market-oriented system. Balancing the freedoms required for a market economy and a restrictive political system has been difficult for China. These tensions reached a breaking point in 1989, when students led large demonstrations in Beijing's Tiananmen Square. As television transmitted live pictures to the world, the Chinese Army ended the protests in a direct and brutal way.

China has the third largest land area of any country, after Russia and Canada. Mandarin is the official Chinese dialect although others are spoken around China. Cantonese is the dialect of southern China, a region in which the government has granted significant economic freedoms to the populace.

Hong Kong in southern China was a British Crown Colony for more than a century. In 1997 Hong Kong reverted to Chinese control. How China will accommodate itself to Hong Kong's free-wheeling, market-oriented media is a development that bears watching. Hong Kong has been home to STAR, the satellite system owned by Rupert Murdoch that transmits programs throughout Asia. Hong Kong's print and electronic media have operated in a more liberal political and economic system than that of China.

After the Nationalists were defeated in 1949 they fled to the offshore island of Taiwan where they established a new government. Although the Chinese government considers Taiwan to be a province of China, the island has established a successful Western-oriented economy. Media from Taiwan commonly reach the mainland.

### 23.2.2.1 Overview of Broadcast Media in China.

The Chinese broadcast media[10] are expected to serve the goals of the government and the ruling Communist Party, to promote the successes of socialist modernization, help unite the people in terms of language and culture, and to further economic growth. At the same time, the media have moved away from content aimed at political indoctrination toward a more entertainment and service-oriented approach.[11]

Although the Chinese radio and television systems receive direct financial support from the government, sale of advertising time is permitted. Print and broadcast media are expected to serve a watchdog function, helping to ensure that the country advances. Criticism of the political leadership is not tolerated.

Chinese broadcasting is three-tiered, featuring national, regional, and local stations. Authority for broadcasting resides in the Ministry of Radio, Film, and Television. The national radio service is called **Central People's Broadcasting Station** (CPBS) and **China Central Television** (CCTV) is the national television service. By the mid-1990s more than 500 cable systems had been constructed, reaching about 30 million households.[12] The government has authorized additional cable systems. Cable channels are filled with locally produced programming and programs from outside of China. Although individual satellite receivers were outlawed in 1993, enforcement is often lax. Satellite services, such as STAR, are viewed by some Chinese.

An agricultural education radio and television system serves rural China. Many of the programs are educational or designed to improve agricultural techniques.

### 23.2.2.2 Chinese Radio.

CPBS operates five national radio services that reach most of the country. In some areas multiple frequencies carry the same programming. There are areas of China that cannot receive television, so radio is particularly important for educating and informing the people. In addition to the national services, regional and, in major cities, local stations are also available.

Radio programming is a mix of about half entertainment, music, and sports, and half news and educational programs. English and other foreign language lessons are taught by radio. A particularly popular program is a daily summary of reports from China's major newspapers. Among the foreign suppliers of programming to CPBS is the Disney Corporation.[13]

### 23.2.2.3 Chinese Television.

CCTV operates five services, four of which are domestic. CCTV 1 and 3 offer general entertainment; CCTV 2 provides news, information, and education; and CCTV 5 is a sports service. CCTV 4 is an external service described as the "Best of Chinese Programming, beamed via satellite to overseas."[14] The domestic CCTV programs are transmitted from stations and repeaters. As in the United States, satellites link the physical network.

China has a well-established film industry, so most programming is domestically produced. Foreign programs, including American, are also shown. CCTV has entered into arrangements with some Western suppliers to provide programs in return for the right to sell advertising time on the Chinese stations.[15] In 1996, the Ministry of Radio, Film, and Television told stations to limit the amount of overseas films and TV movies to no more than 15% of prime time.[16]

The national evening news program is carried simultaneously on all channels. The first half of the program is devoted to reports of Chinese social and economic progress, and the second 15 minutes to world news.[17]

Under Mao, broadcasting was tightly controlled by the central government. Management of the broadcast media has been increasingly decentralized under the economic policies initiated in the 1980s by Deng Xiaoping.[18] In addition to the national services, there are about 30 province-level regional stations and some 200 city-level stations.[19] These stations enjoy considerable autonomy from the central authority. CCTV establishes general program guidelines, but local and especially regional stations can make programming decisions, buy programs from domestic and foreign sources, and produce their own news programming. Some consider themselves to be competitors of CCTV, even counterprogramming the central service's schedule.[20]

One example is Beijing Television Station (BTV). Serving an audience of more than 20 million, BTV operates three over-the-air channels and one cable channel, with more than 70 hours of daily programming. BTV is supported by advertising sales.[21]

A variety of program services are available by satellite from **Satellite Television Asian Region** (STAR). STAR is a Hong Kong-based service owned by Rupert Murdoch's News Corporation International. Its footprint reaches much of Asia, and includes such services as CNN International, MTV International, and various programs produced in the various Asian languages.

Audience data about China's television services are gathered by a number of companies, including A. C. Nielsen. The first large-scale national rating survey, based on a panel of more than 10,000 viewers, began in late 1996. A French media research company, Sofres, gathered diary information in more than 50 cities, measuring broadcast and cable viewing.[22]

### 23.2.3 India

An influential South Asian country, India is the world's largest democracy, with more than 935 million people. There are 16 official languages, including Hindi, the most widely spoken, and English, which is used for national political and business communication. Much of the population is bound by tradition, economically poor by Western standards, and barely half of the population is literate. One of the goals of broadcasting, especially television, is to help create unity among

India's ethnic and language groups. For example, in the late 1990s, radio and television production facilities were built in northeast provinces as part of a plan to end unrest in that area.[23]

India has one of the largest film production industries in the world, and the country exports programs to other countries, especially in Africa. There are about 115 million radio sets in India, and about 45 million homes have television sets. Cable television has grown rapidly, with some 20 million homes, primarily in major cities, connected to a cable system. The Indian broadcasting system is undergoing significant changes. The previously state-owned **All-India Radio** (AIR) and **Doordarshan India** (Television India) are being spun off into a separate, independent **Broadcasting Corporation of India (Prasar Bharati).** Broadcasting had been controlled by the Ministry of Information and Broadcasting and was financed by Parliamentary grants and by advertising. Until 1984 license fees were also collected on receivers. As elsewhere, new technologies have affected Indian broadcasting. VCRs, satellites, and cable have brought new competition and demands that Doordarshan broaden its programming mix.

### 23.2.3.1 All-India Radio.

AIR has a three-tier system. A national radio program service reaches almost 80% of the population. The National Channel, broadcasting from transmitters around the country, features news and information, sports and popular music, light features, and some commercial advertising. AIR's regional services carry the national program service, produce their own programs, and run programs produced by the individual stations within each region. These regional services broadcast in a number of national or regional languages. Local radio serves a small area. According to AIR, "Local radio is down to earth, intimate and uninhibited. The programs are area specific. They are flexible and spontaneous enough to enable the station to function as the mouth piece of the local community."[24]

Vividh Bharati, or "All-India Variety Program" is a commercial service on 30 stations around the country. The content is largely motion picture music, popular in India, with other forms of popular and devotional music, and spoken word programming. Musical selections are sent from stations around India to the Bombay production center that creates lengthy tapes that are sent back to the stations for broadcast.

In 1994 AIR began satellite distribution of 20 of its channels to Indian cable systems. This service also links station participants and audiences in interactive discussions about important events.

The News Services Division of AIR is one of the largest in the world. It broadcasts 89 news bulletins daily in 19 languages, including English. The regional services broadcast 134 news bulletins daily. Commentaries on the proceedings of Parliament are broadcast from Delhi in English and Hindi. Similar commentaries are broadcast from the state capitals when the legislatures are in session.

### 23.2.3.2 Doordarshan India.

Doordarshan (DDI) is responsible for television broadcasting. In May 1994 there were about 578 transmitters and extensive satellite distribution to reach more than 85% of the population. DDI has 20 television centers and the system is financed through government funds and advertising sales.

DDI programming is largely designed to spur social and economic change, unify the multicultural nation, and accomplish similar social goals. Only about one third of the television programs can be classified as entertainment, although sports programs are also popular. DDI's **Metro Channel** is available in India's major cities. It primarily shows sponsored entertainment programs. DDI's newest service, **DD-3** has carried a significant amount of artistic and cultural programs. Government officials have criticized the cost of the channel, and have suggested that at least half of its programs should be commercially sponsored.[25]

News programs consist of regular bulletins and discussion programs. Most are in English or Hindi. Regional centers also telecast news programs, usually in local languages. When in session, news about Parliament is telecast from Delhi and regional stations telecast reports about their state legislatures.

Most of DDI's news reports come from AIR. It also has news exchange agreements with such international consortia as the Asian Broadcasting Union.

The introduction of new technologies has affected DDI. Although cable television is not officially sanctioned, small distribution systems have been built throughout the country. Many large apartment buildings may have a satellite dish and distribution hardware. In many cases entrepreneurs began by connecting VCRs to the distribution systems to bring movies to viewers.[26]

Satellite services have complicated the Indian television situation. The availability of English and Hindi language programs on STAR eliminated DDI's monopoly and brought Indian viewers a wider variety of entertainment programs than previously available. Indian viewers had two channels at the beginning of the 1990s, but by the middle of the decade those with satellite or cable reception had more than 30. Whereas many Indians decried the cultural invasion, others pointed out that CNN and the BBC World Service provided faster and more complete news coverage than did DDI. DDI entered into a joint venture with CNN, it carries music videos from MTV, and expects to operate its own satellite service in the late 1990s. In May 1996, the Information and Broadcasting Minister declared her intent to make AIR and DDI independent in their programming. She said they would have to develop credibility in a competitive environment, and that new ways would have to be found to protect and glorify India's cultural heritage in the face of "open skies" and foreign television broadcasts.[27]

***23.2.3.3 Indian Educational Broadcasting.***    India uses the broadcast media to help fight against ignorance and illiteracy. Television programs are intended to support developmental activities and the educational system. One example is the use of **prodevelopment soap operas,** which entertain and subtly attempt to convey educational and development themes. Radio is used extensively in schools and for adult and continuing education.

For many years, India encouraged supervised group attendance to radio and television programming. Thousands of villages had community radio receivers for collective listening. Delhi television also transmitted programs especially for farmers' teleclubs. Troubles plagued these projects, however, and the government eliminated them.

India was the first country to make extensive use of DBSs to reach rural populations. In the 1975 SITE Project experiment, the United States loaned a communications satellite to the government of India to transmit educational television programs to 5,000 villages. In 1983, India launched its own Insat satellite for direct broadcast of educational television.

### 23.2.4 The Netherlands

The Netherlands is a small, prosperous European democratic monarchy. The Ministry of Education, Culture, and Science has overall responsibility and broad supervisory authority over broadcasting. For most of its history, Dutch broadcasting was a complex amalgam of public broadcasting organizations; currently there are three television stations and five radio stations in the public service. The Dutch have attempted to modify their system to accommodate changing media conditions.

Commercial broadcasting was authorized in 1988. The Netherlands also has one of the highest penetrations of cable television in the world at about 80%. Dutch cable brings viewers public and commercial services from nearby countries and satellite-delivered services such as CNN International, NBC SuperChannel, EuroSports, and subscription movie channels.

***23.2.4.1 Pillarization.***   The shape of Dutch broadcasting is deeply rooted in the very fabric of Dutch society. The origins of its structure predate the development of broadcasting. At the end of the 19th century, Catholics and Protestants rebelled against the dominance of the secular conservative liberals. The religious groups were successful in winning subsidization for their schools equal to that of the state schools. This success led to pillarization—a separate institutional framework for each denomination. Each had its own political party, church, trade union, schools, newspapers, and even leisure clubs.

The broadcasting system developed in the 1920s and it conformed to this pillarization concept. Four denominational groups and one neutral group divided radio broadcasting time and facilities. With the coming of television in the 1960s, the boundaries between the pillars started to soften. The Broadcasting Act of 1969 provided for access to broadcasting by new groups, and three more organizations emerged. As described below, The Media Act, which took effect in 1988 and was later amended, brought significant changes to Dutch broadcasting.

***23.2.4.2 Broadcasting Associations.***   The seven broadcasting associations represent cultural, religious, or political mainstreams in Dutch society. One association is Catholic (KRO), two are Protestant (EO and NCRV), one is Socialist

(VARA), and three are independent (AVRO, VPRO, and TROS). Smaller organizations are also given some time in the broadcast schedule. For example, RVU produces educational programs for broadcast and videocassette distribution.

The breadth of approaches to broadcasting in The Netherlands is illustrated by statements from two of the associations. The main goal of "the Evangelical Broadcasting Corporation (EO) . . . is to reach the 'unreached' with the Gospel of the Lord Jesus Christ by a wide range of Christian programming including information, education, culture and entertainment."[28] In contrast, "Since its foundation in 1926 the VPRO has achieved loyal supporters as well as fierce opposers. Some of the free-minded programs have resulted in riots, witch hunts and official reprimands, but also in pleasure to many viewers and listeners and to many healthy discussions."[29]

In 1995 the seven broadcast groups were given 5-year "concessions" for the broadcast channels. This represented a change in the Dutch system as program-time allocations had previously been made on a yearly basis. Associations were grouped on the three public channels: AVRO, KRO, NCRV, and spiritual broadcasters on NL1; EO, TROS, and educational broadcasters supplemented by NOS programs on NL2; and NPS, VARA, and VPRO on NL3.

The reorganization was intended to allow the public broadcasting services to compete more efficiently with the commercial services. One member of Parliament complained, "These broadcasters once represented the pillars of Dutch society. Now they are anachronistic. Everyone seems to be watching commercial television."[30] Whereas the broadcast associations were previously the focus of regulation, the TV channels now became central. The Dutch intended to facilitate cooperation among the associations and the channels. For example, the Media Act requires each broadcasting association to devote 20% of its programming to culture and art and 30% to education and information programming. However, the associations on each channel can create a single umbrella organization to facilitate cooperation, in which case the program regulations would apply to the channel as a whole, rather than to each association.

***23.2.4.3 NOS.*** The broadcasting groups work together through **NOS,** the **Nederlandse Omroep Stichting** (Netherlands Broadcasting Foundation). In 1988, the Media Act made significant changes in the role NOS played in Dutch broadcasting. Previously, organizations were required to use NOS facilities for all productions. This was changed to 75%, breaking the NOS monopoly and allowing other producers to provide programs.

In 1995 NOS was split into two organizations. The **Netherlands Program Service** (NPS) creates social and cultural programs for NL3. The NPS has as much airtime as the older broadcasting associations, but at least 40% of its programming must be cultural in nature and at least 15% of the TV programs and 20% of the radio programs must be aimed at ethnic and cultural minorities.

NOS continues as producer of newscasts and live political and social event coverage, including sports, which are carried on all three channels. NOS also is the coordinating body of the national public broadcasting organizations. It also allocates airtime (formerly a task of the National Media Board) and coordinates the three television channels.

### 23.2.4.4 Financial Support of Dutch Public Broadcasting.    Advertising provides about one quarter of the operational funds for broadcasting and license fees provide the remainder. **Stichting Ether Reclame** (STER; Foundation for Advertising Over the Air), a government body, produces and sells all broadcast advertising. Commercial announcements are allowed immediately before and after scheduled news programs and in blocks between programs. All STER profits go back into broadcasting.

### 23.2.4.5 Commercial Broadcasting in the Netherlands.    In 1989 the Netherlands began receiving commercial television broadcasts from RTL 4 in neighboring Luxembourg. In 1992 the Media Act was amended to allow domestic commercial broadcasting in the Netherlands. One public broadcasting association, Veronica (VOO), moved to the commercial sector, forming a partnership with the largest Dutch and European production company, Endemol and the Luxembourg-based commercial channels RTL 4 and RTL 5.

### 23.2.4.6 Dutch Broadcast Programming.    Radio in the Netherlands consists of five national program services, 10 regional services, and a growing number of local services in the larger cities. The broadcast associations and organizations are also given time on Dutch public radio. Dutch public radio stations have been programmed according to format: Radio 1 for news and sports; Radio 2 for light entertainment; Radio 3 for pop music; Radio 4 for classical music; and Radio 5 for discussion, opinion, and special target audiences. NOS produces news and sports programming that is broadcast on all five channels.

Public television consists of three program services. As described earlier, programs are provided by the broadcasting associations. Although some of the nonfiction programming reflects the interests of the respective association responsible for the program time, even the religious associations include popular domestic and imported entertainment programming. NOS programs are broadcast on all three channels, but its sports and live event coverage is found primarily on NL2. Educational programming is prominent in NL3's schedule. The first two services operate 3:00 p.m. to midnight. One is operated by the Catholic, Protestant, and Socialist groups; the second, by the neutral organizations. The third, programmed by NOS, educational broadcasters, and smaller organizations called **minibroadcasters,** operates 6:00 p.m. to 11:00 p.m. Joint television programming accounts for around one fourth of all programming. A portion of each week is devoted to educational programming, primarily on the third channel.

The commercial services primarily program entertainment and sports. Most programs on RTL 4 and RTL 5 are imported series and films, as well as U.S. programs.

*23.2.4.7 Program Responsibility in the Netherlands.*    The Dutch have a reputation for libertarian ideas about human behavior. This is reflected in programming policies. For example, the Netherlands refused to ratify a Council of Europe Convention on Transfrontier Television that prohibited indecent or pornographic programs, or those that gave prominence to violence or would be likely to incite racial hatred. The Dutch argued that their laws already prohibited incitement to racial hatred, and that identifying "prominence of violence" was difficult. Further, Dutch law would not allow for complete prohibitions on indecent or pornographic programs involving adults.[31]

The Dutch expect their broadcasters to know what programming would be acceptable to the public, and grant the audience the freedom to make programming selections. However, the broadcasters are also responsible for the effects of their programming. There are policies designed to deal with potentially harmful effects. Programs not suitable for children younger than the age of 12 cannot be broadcast before 8 p.m., and those for children younger than the age of 16 not before 9 p.m. The ratings for all theatrical films must be announced at the start of the broadcast.

An interesting approach to dealing with the effects of television is **Korrelatie** (correlation), an organization used by the Dutch public broadcasters and Luxembourg-based commercial broadcasters RTL 4 and RTL 5. Korrelatie is used in the case of programs that might incite strong emotional responses, such as those dealing with sexual violence or racism. Korrelatie takes telephone calls after programs, provides psychological help if required, refers callers to other social aid services, or supplies information. The organization's telephone number is included in the closing credits of programs, and is sometimes referred to during the program. Other activities designed to mitigate against harmful effects of television programs include The Ombudsman organization, and STOA, which works with NOS in the representation of minorities in programming.

The Dutch continue trying to improve their public broadcasting system. In late 1996 the Parliament considered the Ververs Commission Report, which called for a public vote every 4 years to select the groups that would participate in the public broadcast system. Any group failing to receive at least 10% of the vote would be removed from the system. The proposal also called for creation of a Programming Council that would take over many of the programming decisions previously made by the public broadcasters.[32]

## 23.3 NEW TECHNOLOGIES: A GLOBAL VIEW

During the 1980s, new technologies became increasingly important throughout the world, just as they did in the United States. The Canadians and the Japanese, for example, produced television programs in HDTV. The French government established Minitel, a national videotex service that provides a variety of news, bulletin boards, and telephone listings. All homes receive a Minitel terminal at no cost.

In the 1990s there was an increase in satellite direct-to-home services, and the introduction or growth of cable television services. The Internet has reached much of the world, and leaders of the industrialized nations have met to discuss a global information infrastructure. International versions of NBC, CNN, ESPN, and MTV have found their way into homes on all continents. The economic and cultural impact of television programs has become so important that the issue almost scuttled a worldwide tariff agreement.

Perhaps the most significant changes have occurred as a result of communication satellites. Although cable television has been used in some countries, growth has been slower elsewhere. In Britain, for example, initial enthusiasm about cable was dashed by the costs of constructing systems in the major cities. In the mid-1990s, cable penetration was still only about 20%. Elsewhere in the world, cable's spread has also been limited by the costs of construction. Many "cable systems" are really SMATV systems serving large apartment buildings.

As described earlier, Murdoch's BSkyB in the United Kingdom and Europe and STAR in Asia have reached millions of homes with ad-supported and subscription services. Programming includes international versions of such U.S. services as ESPN, CNN, and Discovery, as well as movie, news, and general entertainment services. The most successful satellite programming has been produced or dubbed in the local language.

Other satellite television services have been planned or operate elsewhere in the world. In Latin America only Mexico and Argentina have extensive cable television systems. DTH satellite services are becoming increasingly available. Two competing services began in the late 1990s. Galaxy Latin America is a consortium of Hughes Communications, which operates DirecTV in the United States, and broadcast companies in Mexico, Venezuela, and Brazil. Galaxy will mix programs aimed at the entire coverage area with local programming from various countries.

Competition comes from a consortium of Murdoch's News Corporation, TCI, and the largest broadcast companies in Mexico and Brazil. The group plans to use two satellites to transmit separate programs to individual Latin American countries.[33]

**Orbit** is operated by a Saudi Arabian company, The Mawarid Group. Orbit is a digital subscription satellite service providing programming to North Africa and the Arab Middle East. Arabic-language programming includes a 24-hour movie channel, two channels of Egyptian programming, and BBC's Arabic-language news channel. English services include channels featuring highlights of newscasts and entertainment from the major U.S. broadcast networks, Discovery Channel, ESPN International and CNN International. Orbit also features four French-language entertainment services, and 24 radio channels.[34]

A consequence of the new technologies has been to open channel space to private, commercial program services. Previously, where a country had only a small number of channels, government-owned or -subsidized services could easily fill programming needs. Satellites and cable allowed more channels and created an opportunity that commercial services exploited.

Faced with competition from these services, many government-owned broadcasting systems became partly or entirely privatized. The U.S. government supported the moves on ideological grounds but also for economic reasons. The commercialization of media in other countries created an opportunity for U.S. companies to buy commercial time to advertise their products overseas, and production companies to sell programming to the new operators (*PRT,* 23.5). Both helped to reduce the U.S. trade deficit.

## 23.4 INTERNATIONAL ORGANIZATIONS

A number of regional organizations promote cooperation among broadcasters across national boundaries. One of the most important organizations, however, goes beyond both broadcasting and regionalism. This is the International Telecommunication Union.

### 23.4.1 International Telecommunication Union

Founded in Paris in 1865, the International Telegraph Union changed its name to the International Telecommunication Union (ITU) in 1934. In 1947 the ITU became an agency of the United Nations. The ITU deals with all uses of radio waves and includes over 185 nations and more than 350 public and private organizations in its membership. The member nations decide how the frequency bands are to be used and who gets to use them. ITU works with nations to eliminate interference, make the best use of radio frequencies, and foster cooperation among members to keep common carrier rates reasonable. Additionally, ITU helps developing nations to build and improve communications facilities.

In light of such telecommunications trends as convergence, globalization, and deregulation, the ITU underwent significant restructuring in 1992.

At ITU's Geneva, Switzerland, headquarters, a secretary-general heads a permanent staff that deals with day-to-day operations. Member nations meet every 4 years in a **Plenipotentiary Conference** to make long-term ITU policy. Regulations covering radio, telephone, and telegraph are made in **World Conferences on International Telecommunications**. The **ITU Council** is composed of 46 members elected by the Plenipotentiary Conference. Seats are allocated equitably among the ITU's five regions, the Americas, Western Europe, Eastern Europe and Northern Asia, Africa, and Asia and Australasia. The Council considers broad policy issues between Plenipotentiary Conferences.

The ITU carries out its activities in three sectors. For each sector, periodic international meetings develop policy and a permanent staff administers the day-to-day business.

The **Telecommunications Standardization Sector** studies technical and tariff issues with the goal of standardizing telecommunications globally. Every 4 years, or more often if enough members request it, a Telecommunications

Standardization Conference is held to consider proposals from the Advisory Group on Standardization or other special working groups. Those proposals adopted by the conference are called **Recommendations,** because adherence by any nation is voluntary.

The **Radiocommunications Sector** ensures the efficient use of the spectrum by terrestrial and satellite-based services. Given the rapid changes in technologies it is not surprising that the sector holds Radiocommunication Assemblies and Radiocommunication Conferences every 2 years. The Assembly provides the technical basis for the work of the Conference.

The **Development Sector** facilitates and enhances telecommunication activities in the developing nations. It presents policy options and mobilizes resources at the national and regional level, and offers expertise and studies of specific telecommunications projects. One Development Conference and one Regional Conference in each ITU region are conducted in the 4 years between Plenipotentiary Conferences.

### 23.4.2 Regional Broadcasting Organizations

Geneva is also headquarters for the **European Broadcasting Union** (EBU). The EBU consists of active member-broadcasting organizations in countries within ITU's European broadcasting area. There are also associate (nonvoting) members from countries in Africa, Asia, and the Americas. The EBU promotes study of common problems and exchange of information, assists in development of broadcasting, and fosters cooperative production and exchange of news and programs among members. The EBU operates full-time facilities for program distribution and exchanges. A permanent network of 11 satellite channels and terrestrial links forms EBU's **Eurovision.** In 1996 the EBU paid the second highest rights fees (behind NBC in the United States) for the Summer Olympics, and has secured rights to the winter and summer games through 2008 for broadcast on Eurovision. *Euronews,* a daily multilingual news program, is carried by many of the European public broadcast networks. **Euroradio** uses two satellites to relay more than 2,000 concerts, sporting events, and other programs to the national radio networks of EBU members.

In 1993 the EBU's membership was increased by the addition of the former Soviet bloc nations and newly independent republics of the former Soviet Union. These nations had previously belonged to an organization parallel to the EBU, called the International Radio and Television Organization (OIRT). Regional broadcasting associations also exist for Asia, North and South America, the Caribbean, the Middle East, and Africa. Some include very poor countries and some include countries separated by vast distances. For these and other reasons, none has the scope of facilities and operations of the EBU. Nonetheless, all work toward cooperative international program sharing.

Countries near each other make individual agreements concerning use of frequencies. They also band together to make multicountry regional agreements. Normally, such agreements comply with overall parameters set by the ITU.

### 23.4.3 European Union

Although not a regional broadcasting organization, the **European Union** (EU) exemplifies cross-national cooperation that extends to broadcasting. The EU consists of 15 nations that resolved to eliminate tariff barriers to create a single market. They are Austria, Belgium, Denmark, Finland, France, Germany, Greece, Ireland, Italy, Luxembourg, the Netherlands, Portugal, Spain, Sweden, and the United Kingdom. The gross national product of the EU is larger than that of either the United States or Japan. Citizens of EU countries can enter other EU nations without passports, and plans call for a unified monetary system with a single currency by the end of the century. The EU includes a popularly elected European Parliament and administrative functions.

The role of the EU in relation to broadcasting has become more significant with the growth of transborder commercial broadcasting. It has become increasingly difficult for individual countries to impose content regulations on domestic services when competition from outside the borders has no such restrictions. Thus, EU policies have already been established in such areas as advertising of tobacco, alcoholic beverages, and health and medical products. The EU's Eurocourt has ruled that certain business advantages given to the EBU by the EU to secure exclusive rights to sporting events violated the rights of other broadcasters. The ruling increased the ability of commercial services to attract audiences away from the national public services.

Two administrative directorates general are particularly relevant to telecommunication. The first, **Directorate General X** (DG X), is responsible for coordinating and promoting EU activities in **information, communication, culture and audiovisual.** DG X operates production facilities and coordinates activities for journalists covering EU activities. It produces *Europe by Satellite,* a daily feed of news stories and video clips of EU activities. The program often includes the opportunity for live interviews with EU officials.

One of many building blocks for the EU was the TV Without Frontiers directive. It eased barriers to satellite and other TV channels crossing from one European country into others. It included loosely construed quotas on non-European programming, program and advertising content guidelines, and limits on total ad time.

DG X is also responsible for the **Media II Program**, to promote and develop the European audiovisual programming industry through the year 2000. The program includes professional training, financial assistance and technical assistance for the production of programs for theatrical and television audiences, and support for securing distribution of programs. In television, the program focuses on independent production companies.

**Directorate General XIII** (DG XIII) coordinates and promotes EU activities in **telecommunications, information market and exploitation of research.** DG XIII is the primary agency involved in development of networked multimedia and other aspects of **the information society,** the European version of the United States' proposed national information infrastructure (*PRT,* 5.14).

### 23.4.4 International Satellite Communication

The use of satellites for international communication has led to the creation of a number of coordinating and operational organizations. The largest is **Intelsat**, the **International Telecommunications Satellite Organization**. Intelsat develops, builds, and operates a worldwide commercial satellite system. Intelsat membership is open to any nation that belongs to ITU and agrees to follow the organization's rules. Members contribute financially but also receive shares of the organization's revenues. About 140 nations are Intelsat members.

Intelsat has more than 20 satellites positioned in geostationary orbit above the Atlantic, Pacific, and Indian Oceans. They provide a link for intercontinental transmissions. Intelsat carries more than half of all international telephone traffic and virtually all transoceanic television broadcasts.

For many years Intelsat had a monopoly on international satellite traffic. One designated organization from each member nation had exclusive rights to work with Intelsat. In the United States that was Comsat (*PRT,* 5.3.2), whereas most countries designated their government PTT (Post, Telephone, Telegraph) agency. For example, a user who wanted to transmit a television signal from the United States to Germany would arrange with Comsat to transmit to a ground station owned by the German PTT, Deutsch Telecom. Intelsat satellites above the Atlantic would be used to make the link. All three entities would receive fees (Fig. 23.1).

Private firms began to compete with Intelsat in the 1980s. Early in the decade, the U.S. FCC had received applications from companies that wished to offer international communications satellite service. Intelsat and most of its members opposed private competition. The United States took an official stand on the matter in 1984 when President Reagan stated that international communications satellite systems that would operate outside Intelsat "are required in the national interest."[35] Diplomatic and organizational maneuvering by the United States managed to remove Intelsat objections. As a result, Intelsat approved Pan American Satellite Corporation (PanAmSat) to offer **separate satellite services** between the United States and Peru in late 1986. Other competitors to Intelsat such as Columbia Corporation and Orion have followed.

Pressure continues building on Intelsat to privatize its operations to achieve greater efficiencies. Intelsat expects to reach a final decision on restructuring in early 1997.[36]

On a regional level, other organizations exist to coordinate communications satellites. Examples include Eutelsat, a consortium of Western European nations; Asiasat, headquartered in Hong Kong; and Arabsat in the Middle East.

## 23.5 INTERNATIONAL PROGRAM MARKET

Most of us conceive of world trade as the flow across national borders of commodities such as coal, wheat, and automobiles. It also includes sound recordings, motion pictures, television programs, news packages, and even entire

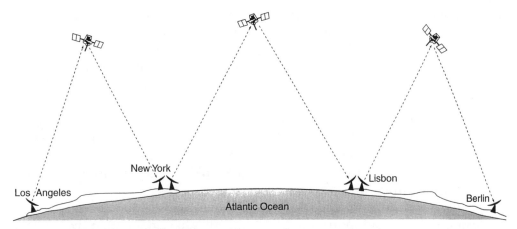

**FIG. 23.1. International satellite feed.** Satellite transmissions between continents require the use of multiple satellites and telecommunications facilities. Here, a transmission goes from Los Angeles by a domestic satellite to New York. From there it is transmitted to Lisbon by an Intelsat satellite over the Atlantic. From Lisbon it is transmitted by a European satellite to Berlin. There are charges for using each of the transmission and receiving sites and for the use of the satellites.

programming services. Entering the 21st century, programming was one of the few product categories in which the United States exported far more than it imported. The economic importance of television and other programming was such that disagreement between the United States and France over programming quotas stalled a worldwide trade agreement in 1993, and the United States and China almost engaged in a full-scale "trade war" over the production of pirated music and videos by Chinese factories.

### 23.5.1 U.S. Programs Sold Overseas

The United States is an important source of programs for many foreign broadcasting services. Almost since the beginning of television, U.S. programs have appeared in other countries. The widespread use of U.S. programs has also been controversial, leading to charges of media imperialism (*PRT,* 23.5.3).

*23.5.1.1 Overseas Syndication Rights for American Programming.* Just as U.S. fast-food restaurants and soft drink companies have spread throughout the world, so, too, have popular U.S. television and radio programs. Off-network and first-run episodes of everything from *Baywatch* to *Sesame Street* to the nightly newscasts of the three major broadcast networks are seen by viewers throughout the world.

Sale of these programs can be an important source of income to producers and syndicators. In 1995, sales of U.S. programs to foreign broadcasters totaled about $3 billion. Almost $2 billion was in sales by the major production studios to over-the-air broadcasters. The remainder represents sales by other producers and the sale of programming to pay services.[37]

The financial and strategic importance of U.S. programming was illustrated by 10-year deals between MCA and two competing German broadcast groups. The contracts, worth about $3 billion, involved the sale of series and specials, feature films, and coproduction agreements. The advertising-supported RTL bought the German rights to every television series and television movie produced by MCA as well as every MCA theatrical film made available for television.

The other German company, The Kirch Group, bought the German-language rights to such theatrical hits as *Apollo 13* and *Twister*. The company used the films as part of its launch of a digital subscription television service. The two contracts by MCA came only 1 week after Time Warner sold The Kirch Group the rights to a package of feature films.[38]

Generally, the most popular U.S. programs shown overseas have been action/adventure, soap operas, and sports. Situation comedies have not done as well, largely because humor seems to be related to culture and language. On the other hand, car chases or seductions seem to have universal appeal, and sports such as basketball and even American-style football have fans in all countries.

### 23.5.1.2 Overseas Distribution of American Program Services.

Technologies that allow multichannel programming, such as cable and satellites, have produced a new trend in the spread of U.S. programs overseas. International versions of CNN, Discovery, ESPN, MTV, and NBC are seen in many countries. In 1996 Westinghouse purchased Telenoticias, an all-news service in Latin America. Joint ventures, such as ESPN's partnership with a Japanese company to operate a 24-hour sports network in the Asian country, are also becoming more commonplace.

### 23.5.2 Foreign Program Suppliers to U.S. Media

For the most part, the flow of programs has been largely from the United States to foreign countries. Few programs have made their way to commercial broadcast stations, and even fewer to the networks. Probably because of similar language and culture, Canadian and British productions have been the rare exception.

In some cases foreign programs have served as models for successful U.S. shows. Such hits as *All in the Family, Three's Company,* and *Sanford and Son* were directly based on British situation comedies. More recently, attempts have been made to produce U.S. versions of *One Foot in the Grave* and *Absolutely Fabulous*.

There are three notable exceptions to the absence of foreign programs on U.S. television. One is PBS. Programs from Britain, ranging from *Masterpiece Theatre* to the medieval mystery *Brother Cadfael,* have been among the most acclaimed in public television history. Individual public television stations have also had ratings and fund-raising successes with British comedies such as *Are You Being Served?, Fawlty Towers,* and *Red Dwarf.*

The second exception is the programming on the growing number of Spanish-language stations and program services in the United States. Latin American and, to a lesser extent, Caribbean and Spanish productions fill much of the airtime of these stations. Especially popular are the **telenovelas**, which combine elements of soap operas and miniseries.

Finally, many of the cable-delivered services have successfully used foreign-produced content to fill program schedules. Arts & Entertainment, for example, has shown such British series as *Inspector Morse* and *Lovejoy*, and Comedy Central has featured British comedies *Absolutely Fabulous* and *Drop the Dead Donkey* and the Canadian series *The Kids in the Hall*. International sporting events are a staple of the ESPN services, and foreign motion pictures are shown on basic and pay-cable services.

### 23.5.3 Consequences of Foreign Use of U.S. Programming

The spread of programming and media from the United States has not been without controversy. Many observers have complained of U.S. media imperialism. Other critics, especially in the Third World, argue that news media in the United States and other Western countries present a distorted view of world events.

#### 23.5.3.1 *Charges of Media Imperialism.*    Some critics argue that many U.S. television and radio programs promote unhealthy values. When these programs are broadcast in other countries this argument becomes even more important. Third World countries battle ignorance, poverty, disease, tribal animosities, illiteracy, and overpopulation. At the same time, they attempt to use radio and television programs to promote a sense of national unity and preserve their cultural heritage. Programs from the United States, produced more slickly and with higher budgets than most nations can afford, often promote such values as sexual attractiveness, wealth, and dominance by any means. Even in industrialized nations, the cultural values of U.S. programs may conflict with indigenous values.

Many countries attempt to limit the influence of U.S. programs. Most restrict the number of imported programs. In Canada, for example, a certain proportion of broadcast programs must be produced by Canadians.

Some individual programs from the United States are prohibited. For example, many Moslem countries do not allow programs that conflict with their religious beliefs. The United Kingdom has established a board with the authority to ban foreign television programs on the basis of "sex, violence, taste and decency." German broadcasters for many years banned or severely edited U.S. programs that referred to the Nazis, or dealt with sensitive issues such as abortion.[39] The attitude of the British toward U.S. programs was expressed by a former vice chairman of the BBC: "The U.S. is a violent country with a violent TV culture, and their TV reflects it."[40]

The spread of communication satellites has complicated the issue of media imperialism. A single satellite signal can cover one third of the earth, crossing numerous borders. Although authoritarian governments can successfully prevent citizens from owning receiving dishes, this is more difficult in democracies. In

Western Europe, for example, many countries have been forced to give up efforts to maintain a media service free of foreign cultural influence.

### 23.5.3.2 New World Information Order.    For more than two decades a concern of many has been the flow of information between developing Third World countries and the industrialized world. They complain that Western news media often present negative images of their countries, concentrating on failures, upheavals, or natural disasters.

The developing countries fought to allow governments to control information flow both within and across their borders. They wished to overcome what they called the West's colonialist domination of international news, to have some control over news reports originating within their countries. Controls would include measures such as licensing of journalists, a government-written code of conduct for journalists, and even censorship.

This desire to control communication ran counter to the Western ideal of a free flow of information. The United States, of course, supports the free flow concept. Both the United Nations and the U.N. Educational, Scientific, and Cultural Organization (UNESCO) supported the free flow of information. However, the developing countries used UNESCO as a forum to discuss their problems and, during the 1970s, succeeded in winning some ground in their fight for information sovereignty. To complicate matters (at least for the United States), the then-Soviet Union and other Communist-bloc nations supported the developing countries.

In 1978, UNESCO commissioned a report by an international committee on what became known as the **new world information order.** Sean McBride, former Irish foreign minister, headed this Commission on International News. In 1980, the McBride Commission released its report, which supported the concept of open information flow. It condemned press censorship and urged that journalists everywhere be allowed to talk with political dissidents. However, it also endorsed the new world information order, and Western media interests viewed a number of its recommendations as encouragement of government censorship.

Nonetheless, the United States supported the report at UNESCO's 1980 biennial general meeting in Belgrade. At the same time, the United States successfully sponsored a proposal for the agency to help Third World countries upgrade their own media to divert UNESCO from efforts to regulate the world press. The International Program for Development of Communications was created as an independent agency of UNESCO to help Third World countries obtain communications equipment—printing presses and broadcasting gear—and training for journalists.

### 23.6 MULTINATIONAL MEDIA OWNERSHIP

As we have seen, the growth of new technologies has led some U.S. program suppliers to develop into multinational organizations (*PRT,* 23.5). As more national communication systems are privatized, U.S. firms may well increase their ownership or program control of foreign media. The reverse—foreign ownership of U.S. electronic media—has also occurred.

U.S. cable operators such as TCI and telephone companies such as U.S. West have built and operated cable systems in other countries since the early 1990s. In many cases these operations are in partnership with local telecommunications companies.

There has also been an increase in the number of multinational media conglomerates. Disney, Time Warner, and News Corporation own production and distribution capabilities, allowing them to reach almost every country in the world (Fig. 23.2).

U.S. law limits foreign ownership of U.S. broadcast stations. However, no such limits exist regarding cable television systems, other electronic media, and program suppliers. Australian-born Rupert Murdoch built a huge communications empire before becoming a U.S. citizen so he could buy the television stations that formed the basis of the Fox network (*PRT,* 3.5.2.7). Most of his media holdings are outside the United States.

Some foreign companies view U.S. production firms as profitable investments. Purchases of U.S. media firms included 20th Century Fox Film by Murdoch's News Corporation (*PRT,* 3.5.2.7) and Columbia Pictures by Sony Corporation for $3.4 billion.

## 23.7 INTERNATIONAL BROADCASTS

As early as World War I, nations used radio to transmit propaganda to other countries. Today, most countries have external services that beam programming to areas beyond their own boundaries. These services have traditionally transmitted in the shortwave frequencies. New technologies and the end of the Cold War have allowed some services to add satellite and cable delivery to their transmission techniques. Some made their programs available on the World Wide Web.

External-service broadcasts often have two aims. First, they provide a way for a nation's citizens living on foreign soil to keep up with events at home. Second, they present the broadcasting nation's views on the news and the world situation directly to citizens of other countries. The BBC World Service has been particularly successful in achieving this latter aim. The United Kingdom's external voice has earned a reputation for comprehensive and objective coverage of international events. As a result, the BBC World Service has built what may be the largest external-voice audience in the world.

There are also a small number of private shortwave stations that broadcast religious or advertising-supported entertainment programs. For example, WRNO in New Orleans broadcasts a format of Top-40 music, sports, and commercials to a worldwide audience. Like most international broadcasters, WRNO uses shortwave frequencies. U.S. law prohibits shortwave broadcasts from U.S. soil intended solely for a domestic audience.

**Time Warner, Inc.**

FILMED ENTERTAINMENT

Warner Bros.; Warner Bros. Feature Animation; New Line Cinema; Castle Rock; Turner Pictures; Turner Feature Animation; Hanna Barbera Prods.; HBO

Independent Prods.; Warner Bros. Television Animation; Witt-Thomas Prods.

LIBRARIES

Warner Bros. films (more than 3,200 titles from studio made 1950 and later, as well as pics from Allied Artists and Monogram); Warner Bros. films (850 titles, pre-1950); MGM (2,200 titles, pre-1986); RKO (700 titles); Hanna-Barbera Cartoons (3,000 half hours); Looney Tunes and Merrie Melodies (3,500 cartoons); Warner Bros. and MGM cartoons (1,050 titles); MGM television (shows such as <u>Gilligan's Island</u>); Warner Bros. television (more than 26,000 episodes).

BROADCASTING

The WB Network; TBS Superstation

CABLE PROGRAMMING

HBO; Cinemax; CNN; CNN Headline News; CNNfn; CNNSI (to be launched); TNT; TBS Superstation; Turner Classic Movies; The Cartoon Network; CNN Airport Network; CNN Radio; CNN Spanish Network; Warner Bros. Pay TV; DreamShop (interactive shopping mall from TW Cable Programming); New York I News (24-hour newschannel from TW Cable).

International ventures include various spinoffs in Europe, Latin America and Asia, including HBO Ole and HBO Asia; CNN International; TNT Latin America; Cartoon Network Latin America; TNT & Cartoon Network Europe; TNT & Cartoon Network Asia.

Combined companies also would have equity investments in Court TV (now 33% owned by Time Warner Entertainment); E! Entertainment Television (58% owned by TWE); Sega Channel (33% owned by TWE); Sport South (44% Turner interest in regional sports network); n-tv (33.1% Turner interest in German-language news network).

CABLE SYSTEMS

Time Warner Cable (11.7 million subscribers covering 20% of U.S. households, 2.2 million more will come from recent mergers and acquisitions); Advance/Newhouse joint venture (1.5 million subscribers); Time Warner Communications (telephone, telephony service)

MUSIC

Warner Bros. Records; The Atlantic Group; Elektra Entertainment Group; Warner Music Intl.; Time Life Music; Warner-Chappell

PUBLISHING

Time Inc. Magazines (including Time, Sports Illustrated, People and Entertainment Weekly); DC Comics; Book-of-the-Month Club; Time Life Books; Sunset Books; Warner Books; Little, Brown; Oxmoor House; Leisure Arts; Time Warner AudioBooks; Turner Publishing; Time Warner Electronic Publishing

CONSUMER PRODUCTS AND RETAIL STORES

Warner Bros. Studio Stores; Warner Bros. Toys; Warner Bros. Interactive Entertainment; Turner Retail Group (four stores in Atlanta, one in Japan, Hanna-Barbera Store in Orlando)

SATELLITE

Primestar (31% owned by TWE)

NEW MEDIA

Pathfinder (Internet venture); Line Runner (cable TV modem service; The Full Service Network (digital interactive network in Orlando, Fla.); Turner New Media

SPORTS

Atlanta Braves; Atlanta Hawks (96% Turner interest); World Championship Wrestling; WB Sports

EXHIBITION

Warner Bros. Intl. Theatres

VIDEO

Warner Home Video; Turner Domestic Home Video; Time Life Video

THEME PARKS

Six Flags (49% owned by TWE); Warner Bros. Movie World (Germany); Warner Bros. Movie World (Australia)

REAL ESTATE

CNN Center (Atlanta office and hotel complex) (*Source*: Time Warner, Turner Broadcasting Co., Reuters/Variety.)

FIG. 23.2. Multinational media conglomerates: Time Warner and Murdoch.

**Rupert Murdoch's Global Reach**

USA ASSETS

MOVIES
Twentieth Century Fox; Fox 2000; Fox Searchlight;
Fox Family Films; Fox Animation Studios

TELEVISION
Twentieth Century Fox Television; Fox Broadcasting
Co.; Fox News; fx Networks; Fox Television
Stations (When News Corp.'s acquisition of New
World closes, the Fox owned-and-operated station
group will have 22 stations, with a reach of nearly
35% of the country); The Golf Channel (30%)

PUBLISHING
HarperCollins (with additional operations in Europe
and the Asia/Pacific region); New York Post
newspaper; TV Guide; The Weekly Standard; News
America FSI, publisher of promotional, free-standing
inserts; Zondervan, publisher of religious books

OTHER
Los Angeles Dodgers baseball team

EUROPEAN ASSETS

SATELLITE AND CABLE
BSkyB satellite service (40%); Leo Kirch-backed
digital platform DF1 in Germany (minority stake);
Vox TV in Germany (49.9%)

PUBLISHING
Five major newspapers, including the Times of
London and the tabloid Sun, and seven magazines,
all in the U.K.

ASIA-PACIFIC ASSETS

MOVIES
UTV production house in India (50%)

SATELLITE AND CABLE
Pan-Asian satcaster Star TV (93%); JSkyB, proposed
Japanese digital satellite network; Asia Today,
broadcaster of India's Zee TV, EL TV and Zee;
Cinema (49.9%); Filipino-language Viva Cinema

ASIA-PACIFIC ASSETS

SATELLITE AND CABLE (continued)
(50%); Chinese-language Phoenix TV (45%); Music
Channel (V) Thailand (50%)

MUSIC
Festival Records; Mushroom Records

PUBLISHING
Minority stake in 22 commercial printing companies
in Australia/Pacific Basin; Chinese electronic
publisher Beijing PDN Xinren Information
Technology Co. (50%)

LATIN AMERICA

SATELLITE AND CABLE
Canal Fox cable channel; Prime Deportiva sports
cable channel (50%); Cinecanal movie channel (joint
controlling interest); Sky Latin America (30%)
proposed DTH satellite service

AUSTRALIAN ASSETS

TELEVISION
14.9% of Seven Network Satellite and Cable; Foxtel
(50%); Sky News (50%); Sky Channel sports and
racing service (50%)

MOVIES
Fox Studios Australia

PUBLISHING
The Australian and other major dailies in Sydney,
Adelaide, Melbourne, Queensland, etc. (65% of total
newspaper market); 15 Australia/Pacific Basin
magazines (minority stakes); Australian Newsprint
Mills (41.7%); Fairfax newspapers (5%)

OTHER
Ansett Airlines (50%); Super League, Australia/New
Zealand rugby league

(*Source*: *Variety*.)

FIG. 23.2 (cont'd.)

The U.S. government operates or finances international broadcast services through the United States Information Agency, Radio Free Europe/Radio Liberty, and the American Forces Radio and Television Service. The **International Broadcasting Bureau** of the **United States Information Agency** (USIA) operates three services, The Voice of America, the Office of Cuba Broadcasting, and Worldnet. Founded in 1942, **Voice of America** (VOA) is the U.S. government's official broadcast voice to the people of other nations. It attempts to gain listeners and credibility with accurate, objective news reporting, presentation of the broad range of U.S. thought and institutions, and presentation and discussion of U.S. policies. VOA is also a source of U.S. music and entertainment, especially for young people. VOA has more than 100 transmitters, two thirds of which are located overseas. Eight high-power AM transmitters are supplemented with shortwave transmitters. VOA broadcasts more than 900 hours of programming each week, in some 47 languages, including English. VOA has an estimated weekly worldwide audience of more than 100 million.

The second service is the **Office of Cuba Broadcasting**, which manages **Radio Marti** and **Television Marti**. Radio Marti was established in 1984 to transmit programs from Florida to Cuba. The initial proposal for Radio Marti drew opposition from U.S. broadcasters who feared that Cuba would retaliate by interfering with U.S. domestic stations. Cuba had, in the past, occasionally turned up the power on its radio transmitters and purposely interfered with U.S. stations. The Cuban government, however, chose not to retaliate for Radio Marti. Radio Marti broadcasts from a 100-KW AM transmitter in the Florida Keys, about 90 miles from Cuba. The AM broadcasts are supplemented by shortwave broadcasts.

**Television Marti** uses a transmitter and antenna in a blimp 10,000 feet above the Florida Keys to enable its transmissions to reach Cuba. Those opposed to spending money for TV Marti have argued that the signals of existing South Florida television stations already reach Cuba, allowing residents to see U.S. news and information.

Finally, the International Broadcast Bureau operates **Worldnet,** an international television and film service. Originally, the purpose of Worldnet was to allow journalists in other countries to conduct video interviews with U.S. officials. It has since taken on additional functions. Available by satellite throughout the world, and used in more than 125 countries, Worldnet distributes regular news and information programs about the United States as well as the weekly "Dialogs," hour-long teleconferences among journalists, newsmakers, and other government officials. U.S. embassies and U.S. Information Service posts receive the programming and disseminate it to local broadcasters. In addition, broadcasters in other countries directly receive the satellite feeds.

There are also plans for a new Radio Free Asia, that would be operated by the International Broadcasting Bureau to reach audiences in China and other Asian nations. By law the USIA is prohibited from disseminating information intended for overseas audiences in the United States.

During the Cold War, **Radio Free Europe and Radio Liberty** (RFE and RL) broadcast primarily with shortwave into the Soviet Union and eastern Europe. Whereas VOA strived for respect as an unbiased and unimpeachable source of information, RFE and RL's programming reflected the foreign policy objectives of the U.S. government, especially with reference to the Soviet-bloc countries. At one time, RFE and RL masqueraded as privately funded organizations when, in fact, they were created and operated by the U.S. Central Intelligence Agency. Today RFE and RL operates from Prague, in the heart of the former Soviet bloc. It provides programming to 19 nations in Eastern Europe and the independent states of the former Soviet Union. Claiming more than 25 million listeners, RFE and RL programming aims to promote democratic ideals and market economics. Funding comes largely from the U.S. government, and RFE and RL uses USIA facilities for most of its transmissions.[41]

American Forces Radio and Television Service (AFRTS) provides information, education, and entertainment to U.S. military personnel and their families overseas. The 1988 film *Good Morning Vietnam* told the story of a disc jockey working at a Saigon AFRTS station in the early days of the Vietnam War.

The AFRTS Broadcast Center at March Air Force Base in California obtains radio and television programs from commercial networks and syndicators, and produces some original material. Selected material includes various music formats, television series, news from national television and radio networks, local news and information, and such talk shows as Rush Limbaugh. Sports are a prominent part of the radio and television schedules. These programs are distributed by satellite to certain overseas AFRTS stations. For others, the material is recorded and mailed.

AFRTS operates radio and television outlets—some closed-circuit some broadcast, and some no more than a VCR and monitor—in about 140 countries. The broadcast stations operate at low power to limit coverage to U.S. bases but can often be received and enjoyed by nationals who live near the bases. In this respect, AFRTS also qualifies as international broadcasting.

## NOTES

1. Michael Tracey and Wendy W. Redal, "The New Parochialism: The Triumph of the Populist in the Flow of International Television," *Canadian Journal of Communication* 20 (1995): 345.

2. Alan Wells, Ed. *Mass Communications: A World View* (Palo Alto: National, 1974) 7–9.

3. Raymond Snoddy, "Medium Comes of Age," *Financial Times* 20 September 1995: 35.

4. Keith Weir, "BBC Reclaims Lead in UK Radio Listening," *Reuters* 17 May 17 1996.

5. Snoddy, "Medium," 35.

6. "Infomercials to Get Wider UK Audience," *TeleSatellite News* 3 July 1996, http://www.TELE-satellit.com/listserver/ts-news/msg00038.html.

7. "ITV," http://www.itv.co.uk/about/popular.html.

8. Erich Boehm, "Mergers Drive UK Cable," *Variety* 18 March 1996: 42, 45.

9. "About Sky Television" http://www.sky.co.uk/about.html 5 July 1996.

10. Much of the description of Chinese radio and television programming in this chapter comes from Joseph S. Johnson, "China," in Lynne Schafer Gross, Ed., *The International World of Electronic Media* (New York: McGraw-Hill, 1995) 277–298; and James Lull, *China Turned On: Television, Reform and Resistance* (London: Routledge, 1991).

11. Du Ruiqing, "Additional Comments," in Gross, Ed., 296.

12. "The People's Republic of China," in Volume 1 of *The Europa World Yearbook 1995* (London: Europa, 1995).

13. Army Archerd, "Disney in China Radio Deal," *Daily Variety* Online Edition, 29 July 1996, http://www.yahoo.com/headlines/
news.

14. Archerd.

15. Archerd.

16. *Satellite Journal International* 1 July 1996: 13.

17. Johnson, 286.

18. Jian Wang and Tsan-kuo Chang, "From Class Ideologue to State Manager: TV Programming and Foreign Imports in China 1970–1990," *Journal of Broadcasting & Electronic Media* 40 (1996): 198–199.

19. Lull, 26.

20. Lull, 26.

21. "BTV Today," http://www.bta.net.cn/csp/tss/btv/btvtoday.htm.

22. Fara Warner, "Sofres Group will Rate China's TV Audience," *The Wall Street Journal* Interactive Edition 1 August 1996, http://www.wsj.com.

23. "Meaningful Initiatives," *National Briefs* 9 March 1996, http://www.indiaserver.com/news/thehindu/030996thehindu/THE01.html.

24. AIR Homepage, http://air.kode.net/glance/tier.htm.

25. DD-3 May Go Commercial," *National Briefs* 6 March 1996, http://www.indiaserver.com/news/thehindu/030696thehindu/THB05.html.

26. Lalit Acharya and Surekha Acharya, "India," in Gross, Ed., 267.

27. "Monopoly in Media Ends, Says Sushma Swaraj," *Business Line* 18 May 1996, http://www.indiaserver.com/news/bline/051896bline/BLFPO8.html.

28. "EO Homepage," http://www.omroep.nl/eo/foreign/whoweare.html.

29. "VPRO English Language Homepage," http://www.vpro.nl/htbin//scan/www/e-server/engelse-home.

30. Marlene Edmunds, "Dutch Dismantles TV," *Variety* 6 November 1995: 52.

31. Child pornography is strictly prohibited by Dutch law. In 1996 the Dutch government established a website designed to identify and locate Dutch distributors of child pornography over the Internet. "Dutch Clamp Down on Internet Child Porn," *Reuters* 21 June 1996.

32. Marlene Edmunds, "Dutch Rub: Broadcast Overhaul Fight Looming," *Variety* 1 July 1996: 29.

33. Karen J. P. Howes, "Direct-to-Home Satellite Services in Latin America," *Via Satellite* March 1996: 14–18.

34. "Orbit Satellite Television and Radio Network," http://www.orbit.net/mark/obprof.htm.

35. "President Extends Free-Market Doctrine to Space," *Broadcasting* 3 December 1984: 37.

36. "Intelsat Debates Restructuring," *Via Satellite* July 1996: 12–13.

37. Elizabeth Guider, "Hollywood Nets $2 Billion from Overseas TV," *Variety* 15 April 1996: 45, 52.

38. "MCA Sets Programming Pacts With Two German Media Firms," *Wall Street Journal* Interactive Edition 30 July 1996, http://www.wsj.com; Judy Dempsey, "German TV Rivals Buy Rights from MCA," *Financial Times* Online Edition 31 July 1996, http://www.ft.com.

39. Erik Kirschbaum, "German TV Yields to Nazi References in Hollywood Films," *Variety* Online 8 July 1996, http://www.yahoo.com/headlines/news.

40. Richard Mahler, "U.S. Producers May Face British Censorship Hurdles," *Electronic Media* 23 May 23 1988: 37.

41. Kevin Klose, "Welcome to Radio Free Europe/Radio Liberty," RFE/RL Homepage http://www.rferl.org/PR/Kevin.html.

## FURTHER READING

Allen, Robert C., Ed. *To Be Continued . . . Soap Operas and Global Media Culture*. New York: Routledge, 1992.

Barnett, Steven, and Andrew Curry. *The Battle for the BBC*. London: Aurum, 1994.

Bourgault, Louise M. *Mass Media in Sub-Saharan Africa.* Bloomington: Indiana University Press, 1995.

Boyd, Douglas A. *Broadcasting in the Arab World: A Survey of the Electronic Media in the Middle East.* 2nd ed. Ames: Iowa State University Press, 1993.

Campbell, Robert W. *Soviet and Post-Soviet Telecommunications.* Boulder, CO: Westview, 1995.

Casmir, Fred L., Ed. *Communication in Eastern Europe.* Mahwah, NJ: Lawrence Erlbaum Associates, 1995.

Dowmunt, Tony, Ed. *Channels of Resistance: Global Television and Local Empowerment.* London: British Film Institute, 1993.

Doyle, Marc. *The Future of Television.* Lincolnwood, IL: NTC, 1992.

Drummond, Phillip, Richard Paterson, and Janet Willis, Eds. *National Identity and Europe: The Television Revolution.* London: British Film Institute, 1993.

Fisher, David I. *Prior Consent to International Direct Satellite Broadcasting.* Boston: Martinus Nijhoff Publishers, 1990.

Fortner, Robert S. *International Communication: History, Conflict, and Control of the Global Metropolis.* Belmont, CA: Wadsworth, 1993.

Frieden, Rob. *International Telecommunications Handbook.* Boston: Artech, 1996.

Gerbner, George, Hamid Mowlana, and Kaarle Nordenstreng, Eds. *The Global Media Debate: Its Rise, Fall and Renewal.* Norwood, NJ: Ablex, 1993.

Gross, Lynne Schafer, Ed. *The International World of Electronic Media.* New York: McGraw-Hill, 1995.

Hachten, William A., and Harva Hachten. *The Growth of Media in the Third World: African Failures, Asian Successes.* Ames: Iowa State University Press, 1993.

Harley, William G. *The MacBride Commission.* Lanham, MD: University Press of America, 1993.

Hilliard, Robert L., and Michael C. Keith. *Global Broadcasting Systems.* Newton, MA: Focal, 1995.

Hodge, Errol. *Radio Wars: Truth, Propaganda and the Struggle for Radio Australia.* Cambridge, UK: Cambridge University Press, 1995.

Hoffman-Riem, Wolfgang. *Regulating Media: The Licensing and Supervision of Broadcasting in Six Countries.* New York: Guilford, 1996.

Horrie, Chris, and Steve Clarke. *Fuzzy Monsters: Fear and Loathing at the BBC.* London: Heinemann, 1994.

Jankowski, Nick, Ole Prehn, and James Stappers. *The People's Voice: Local Radio and Television in Europe.* London: Libbey, 1992.

Johnston, Carla Brooks. *International Television Co-Production: From Access to Success.* Newton, MA: Focal, 1992.

*Journal of Broadcasting and Electronic Media* 40 (Spring 1996). Special Issue on International Media.

Karikari, Kwame. *Independent Broadcasting in Ghana: Implications and Challenges.* Accra, Ghana: Ghana University Press, 1994.

Lull, James. *China Turned On: Television, Reform and Resistance* London: Routledge, 1991.

MacDonald, Barrie. *Broadcasting in the United Kingdom: A Guide to Information Sources.* 2nd ed. London: Mansell, 1993.

Maxwell, Richard. *The Spectacle of Democracy: Spanish Television, Nationalism, and Political Transition.* Minneapolis: University of Minnesota Press, 1994.

McDaniel, Drew O. *Broadcasting in the Malay World: Radio, Television, and Video in Brunei, Indonesia, Malaysia, and Singapore.* Norwood, NJ: Ablex, 1994.

Miller, Nod, and Rod Allen. *Broadcasting Enters the Marketplace.* London: Libbey, 1994.

Mowlana, Hamid. *Global Communication in Transition: End of Diversity?* Thousand Oaks, CA: Sage, 1996.

Negrine, Ralph, and Stylianos Papathanassopoulos. *The Internationalisation of Television.* London: Pinter, 1990.

Noam, Eli M., and Joel C. Millonzi. *The International Market in Film and Television Programs.* Norwood, NJ: Ablex, 1993.

Olechowsa, Elzbieta, and Howard Aster, Eds. *Challenges for International Broadcasting: Identity, Economics, Integration.* Oakville, Ontario: Mosaic, 1994.

Raboy, Mark. *Missed Opportunities: The Story of Canada's Broadcasting Policy.* Montreal, Canada: McGill-Queen's University Press, 1990.

Reeves, Geoffrey W. *Communications and the "Third World."* New York: Routledge, 1992.

Schiller, Herbert I. *Mass Communications and American Empire.* 2nd ed. Boulder, CO: Westview, 1992.

Smith, Anthony, Ed. *Television: An International History.* Oxford, UK: Oxford University Press, 1995.

Walker, Andrew. *A Skyful of Freedom: 60 Years of the British World Service.* London: Broadside, 1990.

Wells, Alan. *World Broadcasting: A Comparative View.* Norwood, NJ: Ablex, 1996.

Wood, James. *History of International Broadcasting.* London: Peregrinus, 1994.

# 24

## CORPORATE VIDEO

You are familiar with CBS, HBO, and MTV. But what about Lobster TV, FedEx TV, or Kodak Business TV? Red Lobster Restaurants, Federal Express, and Kodak are just three of the organizations that produce and distribute video programming to employees, customers and other specially targeted audiences. In fact, more programs are produced by and for organizations than for broadcast distribution to the general public. "New" media applications like multimedia, interactive video, and videoconferencing have moved from the organizational world to the consumer market. Such well-known performers as Robin Williams and John Cleese have "starred" in videos seen only by employees of AT&T or other organizations.

This type of video goes by many names—industrial television, organizational and institutional video, and private video to name a few. Today, the most common name seems to be **corporate video,** and that is the term we use in this chapter. Corporate video has certain characteristics. Generally, **programs are intended for a narrow and specifically defined audience with the purpose of accomplishing a specific organizational objective.**

These programs typically have been distributed on videotape. Organizations also use CD-ROM and other multimedia technologies and conduct videoconferences using satellite networks to distribute live and prerecorded programming.

In this chapter we examine corporate video—history, scope, why organizations use it, types organizations use, production and distribution technologies, production process, organizational factors that affect it, legal issues, and international and multinational uses. We conclude with a look at organizational uses of other media forms.

### 24.1 HISTORY OF CORPORATE VIDEO

Organizations have long used media to communicate with customers, employees, and the public. In the early 1900s businesses, political candidates, and others used the newly developed motion picture to promote products and causes. A major impetus to the growth of corporate video came from the use of training films by the military in World War II. Faced with the task of quickly training millions of recruits, the military turned to Hollywood for help. Classic "motivational" films

**633**

such as Frank Capra's *Why We Fight* series, and training films produced by Walt Disney and other studios featuring such Hollywood actors as Ronald Reagan, showed that the visual media could be effective training and motivational tools. In fact, one of the "founders" of mass communication research, **Carl Hovland,** carried out some of his early research on the mass media by testing the effectiveness of those films for the U.S. Army.

Films are expensive to produce and distribute so relatively little development occurred in corporate video until television became available. In the early 1950s some organizations built large closed-circuit studios, sending live television programming throughout headquarters buildings and other nearby facilities. Universities and other educational institutions made use of live closed-circuit television to help teach the large number of post-World War II students. The invention of videotape allowed organizations to record and distribute video programming outside their live closed-circuit systems. However, few corporate facilities could afford the early 2-inch videotape recorders. The introduction of the small-format open reel and cassette videotape machines in the early 1970s began the explosion of corporate video. With the introduction of inexpensive consumer-level VCRs, and lower cost professional-level production and postproduction equipment, corporate video became a staple of company training and communication.

## 24.2 SCOPE OF CORPORATE VIDEO

Corporate video is used worldwide by many different organizations. The number of people who produce corporate video is hard to pinpoint, but it is well over 10,000. According to one survey, some 12,000 organizations in the United States use video,[1] although not all produce their own programming.

## 24.3 WHY ORGANIZATIONS USE VIDEO

Both profit-seeking and not-for-profit organizations seek to increase revenues and to reduce expenses. Video can help organizations to accomplish those objectives.

### 24.3.1 Increasing Revenue

Using video to increase an organization's revenues is an easy concept to understand: Broadcast advertising has the same goal. However, a manufacturer might also use **point-of-purchase** videos to demonstrate a product in a hardware or department store. A computer purchaser might select one brand over another because it includes a video that explains computer setup and operation.

A food and drug company expanding into a new area sent 250,000 videos to residents living near its 10 new stores. The company found that more than 30% of the people receiving a video visited one of those new stores.[2]

Many not-for-profit organizations show **fund-raising videos** to community groups, employees of large companies, or the general public. United Way has successfully used videos produced as donations by corporate video organizations and others.

### 24.3.2 Reducing Expenses

Measuring the success of a video designed to bring in revenue is relatively simple. Measuring the reduction of expenses is more complicated.

One example is the use of video to reduce training costs. Employees can remain at their home office and view a videotape or satellite feed instead of traveling to a corporate training facility. The company eliminates the costs of transportation, housing, and meals, and making up for their time away from work. IBM has calculated that conducting a centrally located training class costs $375 a day for each of its employee in attendance. A self-paced interactive multimedia package costs only $75 a day.[3]

With video all employees receive the same information presented with equal energy and enthusiasm. Live training may suffer from instructors who have lost their edge repeating the same course many times in many locations. In other cases the difficulties of traveling to a training site may simply make the trainees or instructors too tired to perform effectively.

Corporate video has been used to help improve job safety and increase productivity, thereby saving the organization insurance and worker's compensation expenses. Video designed to improve organizational morale can reduce business costs by increasing productivity or reducing absenteeism. Hewlett-Packard has estimated that the development time for some of its products has been reduced by 30% through the company's use of one type of corporate video, videoconferencing.[4]

## 24.4 WHAT MAKES VIDEO AN EFFECTIVE TOOL?

Any organization makes use of all of its available tools to bring in revenue and reduce costs. The effectiveness of video stems from the evolution of modern business, society, and the attributes of the medium.

### 24.4.1 Modern Society and Corporate Video

One factor in the growing use of corporate video is the existence of **large, widespread organizations.** In the past the owner of a store or factory might have known all of the employees by name. Owners and employees lived in the same town, and economic status aside, usually shared common backgrounds and values. The owner wishing to communicate to the employees could have assembled all of them in one room.

Today, multinational organizations employ tens of thousands of people in hundreds of offices around the world. Video allows executives to deliver messages quickly to all employees. Programs can be used to create a feeling of organizational pride. Many large organizations produce company news programs to tell employees about company operations elsewhere and provide an opportunity to "meet" employees working in other parts of the world.

A second reason many organizations use video is the **increasingly complex nature of technologies.** For example, a large organization must be able quickly and efficiently to teach its employees the latest version of a database or word processing program. Video has proven to be a successful training tool.[5]

The third reason behind the use of video is that organizations must function in an increasingly **competitive economy.** Any advantage, such as a company's better trained sales force or a value-added product like an instructional video, has to be exploited. Rapidly informing a workforce of changes in company policies or procedures can translate into increased profitability. No organization can afford to have its offices in Kansas City using one type of inventory form and its offices in Munich using something different.

Finally, we live in a **visual society.** We have grown up with television and are used to receiving information in this form. Many find reading to be boring or tedious when compared with viewing a slick video presentation and prefer visual teaching. Some workers are functionally illiterate—unable to read well enough to understand training manuals. Video effectively reaches employees lacking reading interest or skills.

### 24.4.2. Strengths and Weaknesses of the Video Medium

Video has some unique strengths that have made it a successful tool for training, employee communication, and other organizational tasks. Close-ups, special effects, and graphics can improve understanding and retention of material. Robot cameras can go to unsafe or inconvenient places.

Video can show the personality of other employees or corporate executives, creating a sense of identity often missing in modern organizations. Executives can use the intimacy of video to rally support and build trust among workers.

Video has its weaknesses, and successful corporate video producers help clients avoid misusing the medium. For example, video does not effectively convey large amounts of facts and statistics. Many people do not have long attention spans when watching a video; the program must be kept short—typically 8 to 10 minutes in length—or provide a great deal of variety of content or style.

Another weakness of video stems from the viewing environment. Distractions can cause information to be missed. Some of the information might be unclear to the viewer. Unless the viewer can stop the program and play back a segment, the material may be lost. In a classroom a student can ask the instructor to repeat something or explain the material in a different way; that opportunity does not exist with a videotape.

Finally, corporate video often has a very brief **shelf life**. Although this is not a problem with a one-time message from the CEO, an expensive training program or a new employee orientation program might soon lose its impact as a result of organizational changes. New managers, new titles, even new buildings can make the program obsolete or confusing. Although employees might be amused by the clothing and hairstyles seen in a rerun of a 1970s sitcom, a training video loses its credibility when the performers look out of fashion.

## 24.5 CORPORATE VIDEO PROGRAMMING

Corporate video programming is used for training, employee communication, and external communication. Special interest videos are another type of corporate video. Each of these are described in the following sections.

Corporate video programming differs in many ways from broadcast programs. First, corporate video programs are not designed to entertain or to capture an audience for advertising. There are no program schedule strategies or ratings. A corporate video program has a specific objective such as to reduce accidents, attract volunteers, or inform employees of new procedures. Although the producers of a corporate video program may use entertaining techniques such as humor to keep the viewer's attention, many objectives can be accomplished in a straightforward, even dull presentation. When learning the material in a training video can mean life or death to a power company lineman, the producer does not need special techniques to keep the viewer's attention.

Because there are no programming strategies or network schedules, programs can be whatever length necessary to accomplish the objective. There is no need to build action to an "act break" so viewers will stay and watch the commercial before the program resumes.

The typical corporate video program is probably 8 to 12 minutes in length. Programs seldom last more than 15 or 20 minutes, because holding viewers' attention for that length of time can be difficult. Some training material is broken into **modules** to better fit the learning capacities of viewers, whereas others might have stopping points to allow discussion of issues raised in the program.

There are many types of programs used in corporate video. Not all organizations need all of these types, and some organizations may use only one type.

### 24.5.1 Corporate Video for Training

According to many surveys, training videos account for the largest proportion of corporate video used in the United States. In some cases these videos stand alone; the employee or trainee views the videotape (perhaps more than once) and carries out the task. More often the video will be part of a training package that might include printed materials and live instruction.

Video is particularly useful for training. Close-ups, split-screen views, animation, or special effects can help the trainee learn the task more easily than in a live classroom. Video gives everyone the same information, increasing training consistency. Finally, by replaying all or portions of the video, the trainee can repeat misunderstood or missed content.

### 24.5.2 Corporate Video for Employee Information

In the United States this is usually the second most common use of video by organizations. Print materials, such as company newsletters, memos, and bulletin boards, keep employees informed of organizational actions, head off unfounded rumors, and provide a sense of organizational identity. Video can also be used in one-time and continuous employee information strategies (Box 24.1). The CEO might want to discuss the impact of a new merger; a live satellite feed to managers delivers that message quickly and with impact. Many organizations produce regular news programs designed to keep employees up to date on activities of the company and employees (Box 24.1).

### 24.5.3 Corporate Video for External Communication

We are most likely to be familiar with an organization's use of video for external communications. External communication, though, ranks below the others mentioned in numbers of video produced.

Video in external communications includes a number of different uses. One example is **customer relations**. Organizations produce videotapes or live satellite feeds to be sure that customers understand new products or procedures or to provide training on products.

Video can also be an important tool for **sales and marketing support**. These might include a video a salesperson takes on a sales call to demonstrate a product or a point-of-purchase video on continuous play in a department store. Some companies provide videotapes to help purchasers use their products. Videos have also become an increasingly important part of sales proposals made to potential clients or to funding agencies. For example, a tourist board might use a video travelogue to lure a convention to its city.

Videos are used as part of lobbying efforts in Washington, DC, and state capitals, as part of corporate presentations to the Wall Street financial community, and as supplements to printed materials, such as corporate annual reports. Many high schools and colleges now produce video yearbooks and colleges often use videotapes to help recruit new students.

### 24.5.4 Video News Releases

Video news releases (VNRs) have become a part of the public relations activities of many organizations. The goal is to prepare a package that looks like a typical

---

### BOX 24.1. HOW TWO COMPANIES USE VIDEO: MOTOROLA AND FLORIDA POWER AND LIGHT

**Motorola, Inc.** created a video to communicate to its 55,000 employees a new company-wide drug-free policy. From focus groups, Motorola executives estimated that at least 30% of people in their work groups were using drugs, a fact that could potentially damage the company's quality standards. Motorola developed a program that put supervisors through formal training to help them learn to communicate with employees; 80 supervisors were trained and they then trained 7,000 to 8,000 other supervisors.

The core of the entire program was a videotaped presentation consisting of five modules. The video provided a consistent presentation of information about the policy, the testing procedures and consequences, and supervisors' roles. In addition to the video, Motorola introduced internal newspaper articles, employee discussion groups, one-on-one discussion sessions between supervisors and employees, and a hot line. The entire effort alleviated employees' fears and alerted them to the consequences of drug use. Motorola estimates it costs between $750,000 and $1,000,000 to operate the program each year, but concludes that not having the program could result in higher costs—both human and financial. (*Personnel Journal,* May 1993)

**Florida Power and Light** (FPL) changed its monthly video magazine, *Close-up* to a daily newscast, *FPL-TV News,* when Hurricane Andrew hit south Florida in 1992. The new program proved to be a critical communication tool for several departments in the following month. *FPL-TV News* is now taped weekly, and distributed via fiber optics to the 70% of employees at sites linked to the network. The remaining employees receive a taped monthly digest.

The program has since been used to help inform employees about personnel changes and cost reductions. During a Tampa Bay oil spill cleanup, news crews shot extra footage to use in federally mandated cleanup training programs.

The news program is cost effective. The initial investment required about $500,000, and monthly production costs run about $1,500. According to FPL, the program gives employees access to critical news and to the company executives, and gives executives the chance to show they are in touch with employees. (*Video Systems,* November 1993)

---

news story but directly or indirectly promotes a product, an organization, an industry, or a particular point of view on an issue. The provider wants to encourage use of the release in a regular news show. Even if the broadcast identifies the release as coming from a corporate source, the material is likely to receive credibility by its inclusion in the news. There are companies that specialize in the production and distribution of VNRs, but this activity sometimes is the responsibility of the corporate video department.

### 24.5.5 Special Interest Video

Increasingly, videos are produced for direct sale. These might include "how-to" tapes on cooking, tennis, or other topics or programs about model trains, horses, or race cars. Although not strictly corporate video, most of these follow a similar format. There is little real difference in the approach a company might use in a training tape targeted to its employees and a how-to program for sale to the public.

## 24.6 CORPORATE VIDEO PRODUCTION PROCESS

The technical steps of creating a corporate video do not differ from a television program. A script must be written; visual material recorded; sound, music, narration, and special effects may be added; and the final program put together in postproduction editing. Because corporate video meets an organizational objective, the process is more like the creation of a commercial than a television program.

### 24.6.1 Role of the Client

With the possible exception of a special interest video designed for retail or direct sale, no corporate video program is ever produced unless a client requests it. The client may be an employee of the same organization as the video department or be seeking the work of an outside production house. In any case, the client typically must approve all elements of the production.

For the video producer, working with some clients can be a challenge. Some clients are placed in charge of a video project but have no real enthusiasm for the task. Rather than read a proposal or a script, they will devote their attention to other tasks, delaying completion of the project. In some cases the client is not the real decision maker in the process. Although the client may agree to a proposal, a script, or even a completed production, the video department might suddenly learn that the client's boss or the CEO or the Board of Directors has its own opinions about the product.

### 24.6.2 Corporate Video Proposal

Most corporate video producers will prepare a proposal for the client's approval (Fig. 24.1). This "front end" work ensures that the producer is creating what the client seeks in terms of budget, approach, and factual information. The client, sometimes with the assistance of others in the organization, provides information about the target audience, how the tape will be used, budget, and deadlines. A **content expert** (often the client) provides the necessary information to the scriptwriter, who is unlikely to be knowledgeable about the subject.

In the proposal, the producer may provide a **treatment,** a narrative description of the program. A treatment does not include detailed dialogue and stage

*ECBI Video
Productions*

**II. Production Purposes**

Your detailed responses to these questions will help us produce a successful video package. Please use additional space to answer these questions

**1. What is the purpose of this production/What organizational problem(s) is it intended to solve?**

_____

_____

_____

**2. What are the goals for the completed production?**

_____

_____

**3. What are the behavioral objectives of the production (i.e., after seeing the production, what should the viewer do, want to do)**

_____

_____

**4. Describe the target audience--please indicate all relevant demographic characteristics (such as age, education, gender)**

_____

_____

_____

_____

**5. What will be the viewing environment for presenting this video? Will it stand alone, or will it supplement a live and/or printed presentation?**

_____

_____

_____

_____

**6. What additional materials (such as pamphlets, workbooks) will be used with this video? Who will be responsible for producing these materials?**

_____

_____

_____

FIG. 24.1. **Production request.** Corporate video producers rely on clients to provide information required to create a properly designed package. (*Source*: ECBI Productions. Used by permission.)

directions, so it is easier for the client to read than a script. Also, if the client rejects the initial approach, the writer will have saved effort by preparing a treatment instead of a complete script. Ultimately, the client should sign an approval of the proposal. This protects the producer: Clients who change their minds, do not provide necessary materials, or do not grant access to locations can delay completion of the production.

In the case of outside production companies, a portion of the production fees may be collected at this point. This helps provide working capital for the company and ensures that the client will not delay payments at the conclusion of the project.

Producing a successful corporate video requires a thorough understanding of the target audience. In corporate video, programs are typically aimed for specific audiences. Network programs might be targeted to women 18 to 49 years old or upper income men 25 to 54 years old. In corporate video, the audience might be the clerical staff of branch offices or wedding photographers. In each case, the writer must write the script for the education, age, and other characteristics typical of that specific audience.

More than one corporate video has failed to meet its objectives because the target audience found elements to be unrealistic. For example, high-school-educated factory workers will reject a training program if the dialogue sounds like the words of an MBA or the characters are improperly dressed or do not behave in a manner typical of that group of workers.

### 24.6.3 Corporate Video Program Formats

Corporate video programs can take any form found in television. The on-camera lecture and the voice-over narration are probably the most common formats, but others are used as well. Such factors as budget, available time, and target audience will affect the choice of format. Popular formats for corporate video include the panel discussion, dramatic role playing, the interview, and take-offs of such standard broadcast programming as quiz shows (which can be useful in training applications) and music videos.

### 24.7 DISTRIBUTION AND PRODUCTION OF CORPORATE VIDEO

As described in *PRT,* 24.4, corporate video has taken advantage of technological advances to become a significant part of the communications world. Today, corporate video encompasses a number of different production and distribution technologies. The use of these technologies will depend on the needs of the organization and budgetary and infrastructure resources. Prerecorded video elements might be used in any of the other media described here.

### 24.7.1 Videotape Copies

Most corporate videos are distributed for use in VHS players. Typically, an organization will produce on its videotape format of choice, dub the tapes to VHS, and duplicate them for distribution.

A large organization may need hundreds or thousands of copies of a tape for distribution to offices or customers. Amway, a home products company, has needed as many as 12,000 tapes each month to send to its distributors.[6] Many organizations use the services of **duplication houses.** These businesses are able to make hundreds of copies of a videotape at one time and can provide packaging and even mailing services.

Once the video is duplicated, the organization can use any means to distribute the videotapes. If speed is required, an overnight delivery service might be utilized. Other methods include the U.S. Postal Service or a company's own transportation system.

### 24.7.2 Teleconferencing

Although video can be effective, videotape has some weaknesses. First, distribution may be too slow for important messages. Videotape is also a one-way medium. The audience cannot react to the content in a timely manner or cannot ask questions. Organizations that desire more rapid distribution or real-time interaction among participants might use one of the **teleconferencing** technologies. When applied to education or training, these technologies are often called **distance learning.**

Terms are often used interchangeably when describing the various forms of teleconferencing. A teleconference might be an **audioconference** (audio teleconference) or a **videoconference** (video teleconference). There are also different technologies within each category, such as multipoint videoconferencing. We use specific terms to describe the various forms of teleconferencing, but be aware of the lack of standardization.

The most common form of teleconferencing is audio only. This might be as simple as a conference call among participants in various offices. The use of a fax machine, an electronic tablet, or other real-time graphics technologies can enhance the voice-only teleconference. This application is usually called **audiographic teleconferencing.**

Another increasingly common form of teleconferencing involves the use of computers. Real-time and e-mail-based conferences have also become popular among users of the Internet and other computer online services. Software and hardware are now available to allow visual as well as audio contact directly from the desktop.

Most video teleconferencing systems in use today are more elaborate than a computer desktop. Generally, we can discuss these forms of teleconferencing as **interactive** and as **point-to-multipoint videoconferencing.**

### 24.7.2.1 Interactive Videoconferences.
In this form, both video and audio are two-way. Participants at the sites can see and hear each other. The cost of linking multiple sites and switching signals and the psychology of keeping track of multiple participants has generally limited these systems to two sites, although some organizations hold three-way interactive videoconferences.

Interactive videoconferences often make use of an organization's dedicated facilities. Special rooms, equipped with proper lighting, audio, graphics generators, cameras, and monitors may be established at two or more important offices of an organization. Companies may use their own satellite facilities, fiber optic or other terrestrial networks, or lease capacity from service providers. Telephone companies and specialized companies also provide facilities for rent.

### 24.7.2.2 Point-to-Multipoint Video.
In this application, audio and video are sent from one point to many receiving sites; audio feeds are made available from the receive sites back to the origination point (often using regular long-distance telephone calls). Audience members can phone in questions or participate in discussions. Point-to-multipoint videoconferencing is also called **business television** (BTV).

BTV has many uses. Some large organizations conduct regular programs linking sites around the United States or even around the world. These are usually dedicated facilities. For example, General Motors transmits regular training programs on auto maintenance and repair to its dealers.

Another type of BTV is the ad hoc or event program. Many professional organizations conduct special seminars for members. In 1995, ITVA distributed a live 2-hour satellite-distributed program to update its members about digital video technologies and their likely impact on the video profession. Members around the United States could phone questions to the expert panelists.

There are also commercial BTV networks. These carry special interest programming and are financially supported through advertising, subscriber fees, or both. Westcott Communications, for example, offers satellite networks to such clients as the law enforcement community, fire fighters, accountants, and auto dealers.

Organizations have embraced teleconferencing technologies because they reduce expenses and improve the efficiency of decision making. Matsushita Corporation of America links its Dallas headquarters with its four largest regional offices. The company estimates a meeting involving employees traveling to Dallas costs more than $1,300 per person for travel, 14 hours of lost productivity at $50 per hour, plus lodging and meals. The entire cost for a videoconference, regardless of the number of participants, is about $1,600.[7]

The money and time saved using videoconferencing can allow more members of the organization to participate. An engineer or accountant who might be needed for only a few minutes is unlikely to travel to an in-person meeting, but can participate in the videoconference.

### 24.7.3 Multimedia and Interactive Corporate Video

The use of computers to combine text, visuals, and sounds has meant an explosion in corporate use of **interactive multimedia.** These technologies are effective for training and information delivery.

In a linear video, the viewer passively watches with no control over pacing or sequence. Interactive technologies allow the user to select the order in which elements will be presented. The user can bypass content in which they have no interest or for which they have no need. In training applications users can be tested with material repeated or restated to improve the learning environment.

Interactive multimedia is expensive to produce and use. Extensive time is required to plan the interactive sequences and ensure that proper links between elements are programmed so that interactivity actually occurs. Videotape is not efficient for interaction because shuttling the tape forward and backward is necessary to move from segment to segment. The video content is digitized and placed with other visual information and the computer program on computer disks or optical disks such as CD-ROMS. Whereas viewing a videotape might only require the user to have access to a VCR and television set, using multimedia requires extensive and expensive computer technology.

### 24.8 ORGANIZATIONAL FACTORS AFFECTING CORPORATE VIDEO

Corporate video departments exist to serve the objectives of their parent organizations. As a result organizational factors affect the functioning and output of the department. These factors, described in the following sections, include the use of in-house and outside production capabilities, the location of the video department within the corporate structure, and budgetary issues.

### 24.8.1 In-House Versus Out-of-House

Originally almost all corporate video was produced by professionals employed by the organization (exceptions might be made for performers or some unusual requirement). The company owned the equipment and facilities and the **in-house** video department served only the parent organization.

Changes in video technology and the conduct of business in the late 1980s and early 1990s led to the downsizing or elimination of many in-house corporate video departments. Despite this action, corporate video use actually increased. The organizations hired outside contractors or production companies, a practice known as **outsourcing.**

Why did in-house departments shrink or disappear? Shareholders began to ask why their company needed to own video equipment and why it needed to have video producers on its staff (they were asking the same questions about such other support functions as the clerical and custodial staffs). At about this same time, sophisticated and expensive postproduction equipment began changing so quickly and so often that few organizations could keep up. Creation of animated graphics and postproduction were increasingly turned over to outside facilities.

As a result, a significant change occurred in the corporate video profession. Many organizations kept only a small staff of video experts, usually producers or writer-producers. Virtually all of the production work was contracted to outside professionals. **Freelance** or **independent** personnel were hired for specific jobs such as script writing, videography, or editing. In many cases these freelancers were the very same employees who had worked for the organization on a full-time basis. Some of these former employees were given long-term contracts under which they essentially worked full time for their former employer.

Production companies have taken over much of the corporate video work. Some production companies specialize in corporate video, but others also produce commercials, music videos, and other products. Some of the larger production companies provide "end-to-end" services, from script writing to tape duplication and distribution; others specialize in one aspect such as postproduction or tape duplication.

Some organizations have kept their in-house capability. For example, in the defense industry, people working on a video must have security clearances. Rather than trying to clear independent personnel for every new production, the organization keeps its own staff.

An in-house staff will be more familiar than outsiders with an organization's culture and procedures. For example, one corporation hired an outside company to produce a video; one corporate policy was to refer to clerical workers as *administrative aides,* not *secretaries.* The production company was unaware of this and at considerable expense and delay had to remake a video that continually referred to secretaries.

An in-house unit is available whenever the executives want it. A successful production house may already be booked when the CEO needs to record a message to employees.

### 24.8.2 Location Within Overall Organization

Most organizations house their video personnel under the supervision of a manager who reports to an executive of a larger unit. Large organizations may give video responsibilities to more than one department in more than one geographic location. These units might share resources and cooperate on projects. For example, the corporate communications department might work with the video services department to produce a company news magazine. In other organizations the various video units may be entirely separate from each other.

The most common departmental locations for corporate video departments include human resources (also called personnel or training), marketing, corporate communications, or public relations. Organizational location can affect the status of the video department, the types of programming it produces, and the qualifications of its employees.

The organizational location of the corporate video department plays an important role in determining the types of programs it produces. For example, a video unit located in the human resources department is likely to devote most of its efforts to producing training videos, videos designed to improve morale or productivity or to reduce absenteeism. If the video department is part of corporate communications, it will probably produce messages from the executives to the employees, VNRs, or videos in support of company meetings.

The type of programming a corporate video department produces will be reflected in employee qualifications. Many professionals, especially writers, directors, and producers, specialize in one or another type of corporate video, such as training or promotion. Others may specialize in a specific industry, such as medicine or financial services.

The part of the organization in which the video department resides will have its own requirements and culture that will be reflected in job descriptions and hiring decisions. For example, a human resources department is probably staffed by people who majored in personnel management, psychology, or education and most of the department's work centers around those activities. Therefore, management might be more comfortable hiring a video professional who has had similar education or experience. The video unit housed in corporate communications, on the other hand, may hire staff members having a journalism, public relations, or advertising background.

### 24.8.3 Budgets, Budgeting, and Economics

The economics of corporate video are somewhat different than the economics of broadcasting or cable. One problem corporate video departments have is demonstrating their contribution to the financial health of the organization. Any large organization's budget must efficiently allocate resources and account for expenditures. In the case of in-house corporate video departments, two budgetary models are commonly used, the **direct budget** and the **chargeback** model.

### 24.8.3.1 Direct Budget Versus Chargeback Systems.

For the in-house video department, funds for production come from within the organization. The mechanism for allocating those funds differs among organizations.

One method of allocating funds is the direct budget. The video department receives an annual sum to pay for personnel, equipment, maintenance, supplies, and so forth. The video unit accepts work from other departments within the organization and pays for production costs from its budget (if there are extraordinary costs, such as hiring professional talent, or special effects, the requesting department may be asked to pay for some or all of those expenses).

One challenge for the video department in the direct budget environment is to prove its worth to the organization. Because departments requesting video productions incur few, if any, costs, productions may be undertaken whether or not a real organizational need exists. Second, the direct budget scenario reduces the need for the video department to maintain a competitive stance to secure work. Because it will receive its annual budget and requesting departments will probably provide enough work to keep the video staff busy, there is little incentive to improve service, technology, or production quality.

In the chargeback system, the requesting department is "billed" for the costs of producing the video (because the video unit and requesting department are working for the same organization, this is usually an accounting transfer). This budget method has a number of advantages for the organization. First, frivolous production requests are reduced or eliminated because expenses are paid from the requesting unit's budget, not the video department's. Second, organizations can more accurately measure the financial effectiveness of productions. The actual costs are detailed in the "bills" sent to the contracting department, which can compare them with benefits received.

Some departments are allowed to go outside the organization if the video department cannot meet cost or quality requirements. Because the video department must compete for work to survive, economic theory says it should operate more efficiently. In some cases the video unit can also solicit work from noncompetitors outside the organization, as long as internal clients are given priority (and often a reduced charge).

### 24.8.3.2 Typical Corporate Video Costs.

Corporate video productions rarely approach broadcast programs in terms of budget. One survey found the median cost of in-house productions to be around $12,000.[8]

Many professionals estimate that the minimum cost for a production of reasonable quality will be at least $1,000 for each finished minute. A program lasting 10 minutes, for example, would have a budget of about $10,000. One organization, 1st Interstate Bank of Washington, reported its videos generally cost

$1,000 to $6,000 per finished minute.[9] Contrast this with a typical network sitcom budget of $800,000 for 22 minutes—in other words, almost $37,000 per finished minute.

Talent costs represent a significant difference in the budgets of corporate video and broadcast programs. Company employees are often used as unpaid "talent" in corporate video productions. Some companies with major budgets occasionally use well-known actors. For example, AT&T hired Robin Williams to perform in a series of management training programs. Commonly, though, corporate video often makes use of beginning professional actors or unpaid volunteers.

Because of the small budgets for a corporate video, small production crews are common, often including only a producer-director, videographer-lighting director and perhaps a production assistant or sound person. Flexibility and the ability to do more than one task are essential skills for working in corporate video production. Corporate video productions often make use of low-cost or public domain stock footage, prerecorded production library music, and low-end computer graphics.

***24.8.3.3 Demonstrating Impact.***    Corporate video departments and professionals must demonstrate the economic impact of their efforts. For the in-house department, demonstrating its effectiveness is critical to survival; the outside unit must have a successful track record to persuade new clients to contract for production services. Producers of an entertainment program can point to ratings, and a commercial producer can use sales figures to demonstrate that revenues exceeded costs, but corporate video producers seldom have such direct evidence.

There are many reasons corporate video departments have difficulties demonstrating effectiveness. First, video is often only one part of a larger training or communications effort. A training video might be included in a course that also includes classroom instruction and practice on a real or simulated piece of equipment. The department must measure how the video contributed to the overall effectiveness of the training.

Second, costs and benefits may be indirect. Reductions in absenteeism or improvements in employee morale are hard to measure against the organization's bottom line.

Although producers and clients often try to evaluate the effectiveness of video projects, the video department seldom has the time or money to undertake systematic evaluation. Unless the client or requesting department provides these resources, the video unit will normally move from finishing one project to completing the next in line.

## 24.9 LEGAL ISSUES IN CORPORATE VIDEO

Because corporate video does not normally use broadcast stations or cable distribution, it is not subject to the same types of regulation as those media. There are important issues that concern corporate video professionals. These include copyright and the rights to use the likenesses of others.

## 24.9.1 Copyright and Corporate Video

Copyright issues are important to all content creators. Unfortunately, because of lack of knowledge, misunderstandings, or even ethical lapses, corporate video producers sometimes use copyrighted music, visual images, or other elements without permission. Although the copyright laws can be complex, generally content may not be used without permission of the copyright owner. The fact that a video is being produced for a not-for-profit organization or will only be seen by employees of a company is irrelevant. This restriction applies to music as well as video clips from movies and television programs. Producers must also take care that they have permission to use music in the production and, separately, for the presentation of the video (these are referred to as the **synchronization rights** and the **performance rights,** respectively).

Ownership of copyright can also be a concern for the producer. Generally, all creative efforts that go into a corporate video, such as the script, original music, or visuals, are collectively considered to be a **work for hire.** This means the contracting organization controls the copyright, not the scriptwriter or other creative personnel. This can be negotiated at the beginning of the production process. The material may not be used in a résumé tape or for other purposes without permission.

## 24.9.2 Privacy, Use of Likeness, and Other Such Issues in Corporate Video

Corporate video producers often include interviews or video clips of company employees, customers, or the general public. People have the right to control use of their likeness. Such protection is not limited to the living. The rights to use the likenesses of deceased celebrities belong to the family or other surviving entity.

**Release forms** are important protection for the organization against later actions. In a release form, permission is given for the use of the voice or likeness, with any compensation spelled out. A signed release form can prevent a disgruntled employee from later halting use of the video, or a performer who later achieves stardom from seeking additional compensation for the work. Parents or guardians must sign release forms for minors.

Corporate logos, trademarks, and similar images are also legally protected. Trademark owners and other businesses are careful to protect the use and protect against exploitation of their properties. Although a video producer might think the company would welcome the "free exposure" in the program, that decision lies with the trademark owner.

## 24.10 INTERNATIONAL AND MULTINATIONAL CORPORATE VIDEO

Production and use of corporate video is not limited to the United States. Many companies are multinational, with branch offices and subsidiaries around the world.

The international and multinational nature of corporate video creates challenges for producers and clients. These include the actual production process and the difficulty of producing an effective program to be seen by employees who may speak different languages and be from very different cultures.

### 24.10.1 Producing Corporate Video Overseas

Multinational organizations may wish to include video segments about their many branches in a program. Even organizations located only in the United States may wish to shoot overseas, perhaps to produce a video documenting customer uses of their product in Europe or Asia. Typically a small crew is sent to the foreign locale to shoot the video.

One problem the crew will face is that there is no world standard for electrical power. Equipment designed to run on the 60-Hz system of the United States will not run properly on the 50-Hz European electrical system. Further, even electric plugs and sockets differ from country to country.

Video scanning systems also differ around the world. A U.S. crew working in Europe must be sure it has a supply of videotapes compatible with its camera.

Producers from the United States working in other countries may have to find crew members who are fluent enough in English to understand verbal instructions or who can adapt to the style and form typical of U.S. productions (*PRT*, 24.10.2). Customs requirements for bringing camera equipment into and out of countries vary, as do work rules related to hiring production crews, tax laws, and the procedures required for securing permits for video production in public locations.

### 24.10.2 Language and Culture in Program Content

Producing corporate video for employees around the world creates particular challenges. First, programs must be translated (or subtitles added) for employees who speak different languages. This would include both audio and graphics. An example comes from the in-house producers of training videos for a European automobile manufacturer. Different versions of the programs have to be prepared for speakers of the major languages spoken in the seven countries in which the company has factories. Different versions were even produced for U.S. and British employees; for example, what U.S. workers refer to as the *trunk* of a car is called a *boot* in the United Kingdom.

Usually corporate video producers send copies of scripts to colleagues in the offices in other countries for translation before beginning production. Different narrators may have to be hired who can read fluently and convincingly in various languages. Program formats are usually limited to voice-over narration because of the need for translation. Translating or dubbing dialogue in a role-playing video can be time consuming and expensive. Subtitles may be required.

Language is not the only issue in producing corporate video for international organizations. Cultures differ over such matters as humor, body language, superior–subordinate relationships, gender status, and even use of color and music. A European automobile company had to reshoot a training video that showed a woman driving into a dealer for service. One of the company's factories was located in a conservative Moslem country where women are not permitted to drive.

## 24.11 USE OF OTHER MEDIA FOR CORPORATE COMMUNICATION

Although we have focused on video in this chapter, many departments produce material for other electronic media. Audiocassettes have become a popular medium for distributing training material, motivational programs, or messages from executives. Employees can listen to the tapes in their cars, at home, or other convenient locations.

Corporate video professionals may also create multiple-image slide presentations and computer-generated graphic presentations. Finally, still photographs and print materials such as brochures and company newsletters often come from corporate video professionals.

## NOTES

1. Bob Filipczak, "Video Budget Growth Continues," *Training* September 1993: 62.
2. Jim Ackerman, "Video Takes to the Mailboxes," *American Salesman* January 1993: 11–15.
3. Connie Guglielmo, "Corporate Training: Cheaper, Better, Snazzier," *New Media* March 1992: 19–21.
4. Andrew Kupfer, "Prime Time for Videoconferences," *Fortune* 28 December 1992: 90–92.
5. Daniel Bissonnet, "The Role of High Technology in Training," *Technology in Higher Education Journal* June 1990: 51–53.
6. Barbara Schwartz, "Inside, Outside: Where Corporations Go to Satisfy Their Video Needs, *Millimeter* June 1990: 81–85.
7. Carl Levine, "Matsushita Supports Videoconferencing," *Video Systems* January 1994: 64–65.
8. Bob Filipczak, "Video Budget Growth Continues," *Training* September 1993: 62.
9. Peter Covino, "Video Plays Growing Role in Corporate Communications Picture," *Presentation Products Magazine* August 1990: 28–32.

## FURTHER READING

Cartwright, Steve. *Secrets of Successful Video Training: The Training With Video Casebook.* Belmont, CA: Wadsworth, 1990.
DiZazzo, Ray. *Corporate Scriptwriting: A Professional's Guide.* Boston: Focal, 1992.
Gayeski, Diane. *Corporate and Instructional Video.* 2nd ed. Englewood Cliffs, NJ: Prentice-Hall, 1991.
Gayeski, Diane. *Corporate Communication Management: The Renaissance Communicator in Information Age Organizations.* Newton, MA: Focal, 1993.
Hanclosky, Walter V. *Principles of Media Development.* Newton, MA: Focal, 1995.

Marlow, Eugene. *Corporate Television Programming: Technique and Applications.* Belmont, CA: Wadsworth, 1992.

Marlow, Eugene. *Electronic Public Relations.* Belmont, CA: Wadsworth, 1996.

Ostroff, David H., J. Arnall Upshaw Downs, and Pamela Franklin. *The Effectiveness of Video in Organizations: An Annotated Bibliography.* Irving, TX: ITVA, 1995.

Richardson, Alan R. Ed. *Corporate and Organizational Video.* New York: McGraw-Hill, 1992.

Van Nostran, William J. *The Scriptwriter's Handbook: Corporate and Educational Media Writing.* Newton, MA: Focal, 1996.

# VII

## Sociopsychological
## Perspective

Obviously, the media play a role in our daily decisions. We now look at the relation between radio–television and human behavior and the impact of one on the other. In chapter 25, we define factors that determine this impact. In chapter 26, we examine the nature of the impact. In chapter 27, we review some of the theoretical structures that attempt to explain the impact. We take into account not only the media, media personalities, and their messages, but also audience members—as individuals, groups, and society.

We have left this topic until last to emphasize its importance. Chances are, you welcome radio and television into your life for several hours many days. The following chapters examine what this means to you and to the society of which you are part. Even more than the last entry on the balance sheet of any media business, this is the bottom line.

# 25

## Factors in Degree of Impact

You have probably heard the argument that television is a powerful vehicle of persuasion. It may be, but over the years researchers have found it difficult to establish that television actually causes persuasive effects. In fact, in 50 years, researchers have identified only a handful of causal relations between a person's exposure to mass media messages and various types of behavior. One example is the early experimental research that showed that people who viewed a violent film segment were more likely to engage in aggressive behaviors.[1] Keep in mind that experimental research is usually conducted in a controlled laboratory setting. Experiments allow researchers to hold constant all factors (e.g., time of day, circumstances of viewing, etc.) except those under study. Still, experimental studies have provided conflicting findings when it comes to the effects of television viewing.

Field studies (*PRT*, 27.1.2) are even less likely to find strong relations between television viewing and particular behaviors. Field studies investigate mass communication where the audience normally receives it—in homes, automobiles, or wherever. Researchers do not tightly control field studies, so other variables are free to mitigate the impact of the message.

You may be aware of it but the process of viewing television involves many factors that researchers call variables, and they can all affect the way you react to a televised message. Let us say, for example, that you are watching television and a beer commercial interrupts the program. Do you inevitably and immediately get a can of that brand of beer, open it, and begin to drink it down? Perhaps you do—if you (a) are thirsty, (b) like that brand of beer, and (c) happen to have it available. However, you probably do not because other factors are involved. You may not even drink alcoholic beverages due to religious or moral convictions. Your family or friends may frown on it. You may be diabetic, on a diet, or allergic to beer. You may not like that particular commercial or beer commercials in general. Your roommate may have drunk all your beer, and you do not feel like going to the store. You may simply dislike the taste of beer. You may not even pay attention to the commercial; you may be so inured to the almost continual flow of television advertising that you automatically tune out commercials or even switch channels.

The point here is that television viewing—or any use of a mass medium—does not occur in isolation. It is part of an environment of factors or variables that affect your behavior. Because of this, researchers will always find it difficult to establish that television causes certain behaviors.

## 25.1 ESTABLISHING CAUSAL RELATIONS

One goal of media research is to fully explain the impact of television on individuals and society. To do this researchers must establish **causal relations among variables**. This means they must identify which variables affect or cause others to change—or even occur in the first place. Suppose a study finds a relation between amount of violence on television and the number of violent crimes in society. Three **criteria of proof** are necessary to establish a cause–effect relation between the two variables: (a) the two variables must be statistically related, (b) the cause must precede the effect, and (c) alternative explanations for the finding must be eliminated.

### 25.1.1 Statistical Relation

This means that as one variable level increases, the other increases or decreases. In our example, a statistical relation is established if the researcher finds that as television violence increases the number of violent crimes increases. Because both increase, this would be a positive relation. A negative relation would be established if the amount of violent crime decreased as television violence increased or vice versa. Finding a statistical relation does not mean that the two variables are causally related. Two other elements of proof must be established.

### 25.1.2. Cause Before the Effect

This is often called **proof of causal priority**. This means that to establish that television caused the effect, the researcher must show that the increase in violence on television occurs **before** the increase in violent crimes.

### 25.1.3. Eliminate Alternative Explanations

In other words, the change in the effect variable must not be caused by anything other than the cause variable. This means there can be no other variables—involved in the study or not—that actually explain the statistical relation. This is by far the most difficult criterion to establish. In our example, the researcher must demonstrate that the increase in violent crime is caused **only** by the increase in violence on television. The researcher must rule out alternative explanations for the increase in crime such as an increase in unemployment, early release of violent criminals due to overcrowded prisons, or changes in the method of reporting crime. If alternative explanations for the statistical relation cannot be ruled out, then a causal relation is not established and we could not conclude that television violence caused the increase in violent crime.

The researcher might still suggest that television played a role in the increase in crime. The fact is that the relation between television and violence in society probably does involve a number of variables. For example, some experts argue that only persons already predisposed to commit a violent crime could be influenced to do so by violence on television.

Television viewing is a complex process that involves a large number of factors. The interaction of these factors determines whether there will be an impact and, if so, what it will be. Some of the more important of these factors include an individual's psychological or mental makeup, other persons, conditions of reception, medium, message, and communicator.

## 25.2 YOU

You, the audience, bring as much to the television viewing situation as does the programming you view, and maybe more. Your attitudes, predispositions, personality, and degree of involvement with the subject matter all figure in your reception of mass media messages and what you do with them.

### 25.2.1 Attitude Formation

You have certain attitudes about things, people, and places. You may believe that capitalism is preferable to socialism. You may feel that police are underpaid in most communities, or you may prefer Snoop Doggy Dogg's music over that of Tom Petty. However, attitudes are more complex than just feelings or beliefs about things. Theorists tell us that attitudes consist of at least four dimensions—social, cognitive, behavioral, and emotional.

*25.2.1.1 Socialization.*    You do not adopt attitudes. You acquire them. You acquire them unconsciously and gradually as a result of your experiences. You are, in large part, the product of all that you have ever experienced. You learn from elements within your environment, and we call this learning **socialization.** Formal agents of socialization include parents, teachers, and religious leaders. Friends and other peers are also agents of socialization. Your environment is especially influential as you mature. Places, things, and even strangers with which you come in contact play a part in attitude formation. Obviously, growing up in Philadelphia can be a much different experience than growing up in Greenville, South Carolina, or Moses Lake, Washington. Playing a game of stickball or johnny-on-the-pony in the Bronx provides a much different experience than playing organized Little League Baseball or red rover in a small Midwestern town.

Regardless of where you spent your childhood, your experiences are different from anyone else's. This means that what you have learned is also different. As a result of this **differential learning,** you have a particular and special-to-you way of making sense of the world, of mentally dealing with the objects, things, persons, messages, and situations that you encounter.

***25.2.1.2 Cognition.***    This making sense and dealing with is called **cognition.** Cognition includes the many processes of assimilating experiences and relating them to previous experiences, of attaching meaning and value to them, and of ordering them into organized patterns of knowledge.

You are not a passive receptacle for a television commercial or any other persuasive message. You do things to the message. You receive the message and put it through the cognitive processes—trim it down, add to it here and there, reshape it to make it fit into your particular system of order and your own individual set of beliefs, values, and attitudes. You even decide what the message means.

Your very **need for cognition** differs from that of anyone else. In other words, you are different from others regarding the extent to which you need and are motivated to learn, think, and deal with your environment. This, too, affects the way you deal with a message.

***25.2.1.3 Behavior.***    Your behavior directly contributes to your attitudes. You may, for example, prefer sweetened tea, in part, because you always drank sweetened tea. You may prefer Democratic political candidates because you previously voted Democratic. Or, you may prefer Snoop Doggy Dogg over Tom Petty because you have listened to his music more. A change in behavior can result in a change in attitude. Experiments have shown that people who are forced to perform a behavior that conflicts with their attitude will actually change the attitude to match the behavior. For example, suppose you think that soccer is boring, but you are forced to tell a group of children how exciting it is. The research shows that your attitude toward soccer may become more favorable so that it better matches what you said. You may even begin to watch or play soccer.

***25.2.1.4 Emotion.***    Attitudes have an emotional component. You may oppose depictions of violence in television and movies because you actually fear being a victim of violence yourself. Research has shown that appeals to emotions such as fear can change attitudes. Rational and logical appeals, however, have proved more effective in bringing about long-lasting changes.

## 25.2.2 Predisposition

The behavior–attitude relation works both ways. Not only does behavior affect attitudes, but attitudes also affect behavior. Both make you susceptible to act certain ways. These susceptibilities are **predispositions,** and they include selective exposure, selective perception, and selective retention.

***25.2.2.1 Selective Exposure.***    Your predispositions help determine what you do with a televised message, including whether you even pay attention to it in the first place. You tend to watch or notice those messages that correspond with your opinions and interests. Message–interests correspondence is called **congruence;** your tendency to pay attention is **selective exposure.**

Suppose, for example, you watch television one evening during the political season. A campaign program comes on featuring the Republican candidate for some office. You may be more likely to watch the program if you are a Republican.

Some studies suggest that you may avoid messages that run counter to your opinions and interests. Suppose you want to purchase a new car. You narrow your choices quickly but have great difficulty in deciding whether to buy a Lexus or a BMW. Eventually you purchase a BMW. If a major car publication then comes out with an article touting Lexus as the "Car of the Year," you may choose not to read it. Research has not consistently supported this avoidance tendency.

### 25.2.2.2 Selective Perception.
The cognition process makes you hear, see, and mentally emphasize some elements of a message and ignore or deemphasize others. This is **selective perception**, and it helps to explain why two people perceive and interpret the same message different ways.

In our campaign program example, a Republican is likely to perceive the Republican candidate's television speech as reasoned, logical, and eloquent. A Democrat might view the same speech as distorted, inconsistent, and pretentious.

**Semanticists,** scholars who study meaning, explain that words contain no meaning in and of themselves. Any **meaning comes from within people**—senders and receivers of messages—who use the words. This is basic to the process of selective perception. When someone speaks a word, **the receiver or listener decides what the word means.** Suppose someone says the word *republican.* On hearing that word, **you assign a personal meaning**, and your meaning does not necessarily correspond to that intended by the speaker. The meaning that we hold for words evolves, again, through differential learning, so people often assign very different meanings for the same words.

Perception can be so selective that an individual may actually interpret a message in a way that is exactly the opposite from its intent. This is the **boomerang effect.** Some people, for example, use the word *bad* to mean good. If such a person told you that the Rolling Stones are really bad, you may incorrectly think they actually hate the Rolling Stones' music. Or, suppose that during a televised speech, a candidate tells a joke to illustrate the absurdity of bigotry. A racially prejudiced supporter might actually interpret the story as advocating bigotry. In 1995 entertainer Michael Jackson was widely criticized because people perceived certain lyrics of his song "They Don't Care About Us" to be anti-Semitic. He claimed the song actually intended the opposite—to demonstrate the ugliness of racism. The controversy became so severe that Jackson changed the lyrics and rereleased the song.

### 25.2.2.3 Selective Retention.
In selective retention, you tend to remember messages that jibe with your opinions and interests and forget those that do not. You are more likely to remember the name of that Republican candidate who spoke on television if you are a Republican.

Selective exposure, selective perception, and selective retention (sometimes referred to collectively as selective perception) are not inevitable; they are tendencies, so you may find yourself paying attention to messages that deal with matters outside your interests or that run counter to your opinions.

### 25.2.3 Personality

Some persons are more persuadable than others, irrespective of issue or type of influence. If you are one of these persons, it is likely that television could affect you more than someone who is not so persuadable. Among the factors that affect persuadability are **self-esteem, intelligence,** and **age.**

Research has shown that if you have a high level of self-esteem and regard for your own abilities, you tend to resist persuasion and propaganda. Intelligence seems to affect not so much the degree of persuadability as the kinds of persuasive appeals that are most effective. If you are highly intelligent, inconsistent and illogical arguments probably do not work as well on you as on persons of lower intelligence. Complex, difficult arguments usually do not work as well on persons of lower intelligence. Younger people are typically more persuadable than older ones.

### 25.2.4 Involvement

Degree of involvement with the message topic also affects persuadability. When you become interested in a particular topic you are more likely to read about it, search out information on it, work on it, and spend time on it. As your involvement grows, your susceptibility to being persuaded on this topic decreases.

## 25.3 OTHERS

The impact any given televised message has on you is determined in part by your relationships with other persons, particularly persons whose acquaintance and opinions you value. In social psychological terms, these persons serve as your **psychological reference group.** A reference group is any group of persons with whom you share a very personal and definite sense of belonging. These groups are not necessarily formal organizations, although they can be. You probably have a number of different reference groups, perhaps even one for each major facet of your life.

The particular reference group that comes into play in any given situation depends on the nature of the situation and on you as an individual. The group can be large, small, inclusive, exclusive, formal, or informal. It can be your family, members of your fraternity or sorority, people who share your religious beliefs, your neighbors, your coworkers, volunteers in your political organization, members of your racial or ethnic group, your Friday afternoon (or Thursday night for many college students) partying buddies, or people you meet in the laundromat. Social scientists have demonstrated that people tend to adopt the group's norms—its behaviors, values, and priorities—as their own. The group, in turn, reinforces and validates their adopted opinions.

The group may perceive, discuss, and evaluate the content of a televised message as consistent or conflicting with its norms. This usually happens informally. For example, suppose you see a political candidate on television advocating passage of a proposed law restricting gun ownership. Reference group influence may be as simple as a discussion of the candidate's remarks among friends after a pick-up basketball game, a discussion condemning the gun control legislation as a violation of your right to bear arms. It may be as elaborate as members of your activist group rallying in favor of the legislation and against gun possession and the high level of crime in your community. You may initially be undecided. However, if your reference group favors the legislation and engages in favorable discussion of the issue, you are more likely to change your attitude or behavior in the direction of the legislator's televised message. Group disapproval lessens that chance.

Even if the group never discusses the legislator's televised message, you may be familiar enough with group norms to know what the group would say. That can influence you, just as though the group had actually discussed it. For example, if you were a member of the National Rifle Association (NRA), you might resolve right then to vote against the candidate, no matter how sound the arguments for gun control. You would assume from past experience the NRA's opposition to the candidate.

Many of our examples in this chapter have involved political issues. The same principles apply to other topics—news, information, entertainment, and advertising. Reference groups play a significant role in whether you would prefer to attend a concert by Boyz II Men, Nine Inch Nails, or the Boston Symphony. Groups play a role in whether we pull for the Boston Red Sox or New York Yankees, whether we prefer body building or aerobic exercises, and even which brand of soft drink we prefer.

Product advertisers make positive efforts to take advantage of the various factors involved in impact. Many television commercials, for example, attempt to provide surrogate reference groups. Thus, you see commercials that feature a young parent telling a slightly younger parent which disposable diaper to use, or a manicurist telling a customer which hand lotion to use.

The young parent and the manicurist represent advertisers' attempts to depict opinion leaders. As originally conceived, the relation between mass media and interpersonal communications consisted of a **two-step flow of communication** (Fig. 25.1). Within the group, certain individuals are thought to be more sensitive to media messages. These individuals, the **opinion leaders**, bring up the messages for discussion by the group. Thus the flow of information and influence goes from media to opinion leaders in a first step, and from opinion leaders to the group in a second step. This two-step model is probably too simple to describe the actual flow of communication. There are many steps and many opinion leaders involved at all levels. Still, researchers have found that **interpersonal communication occurring after a televised message** can have **greater impact** than the initial message.

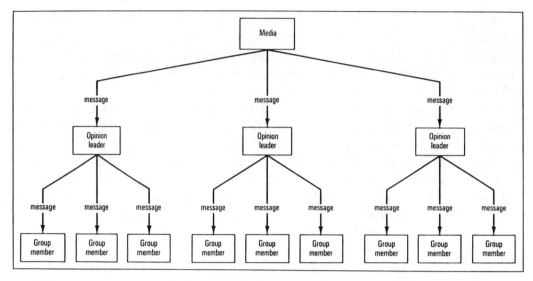

**FIG. 25.1. Two-step flow of communication.** Although the actual process is probably more complex, this early model does illustrate that interpersonal communication and influence affect television's impact.

## 25.4 CONDITIONS OF RECEPTION

Where and how you view affects television's impact. Consider a violent, scary movie on television. It will likely affect you much more if you watch it at home by yourself late at night than if you watch it during daylight hours while carrying on a conversation with friends.

## 25.5 MEDIUM

The medium of television helps determine impact. When you watch television primarily for relaxation and entertainment you switch off your critical faculties. Because you drop your critical guard, you may become more influenced by messages. You may be more vulnerable to intended messages—especially persuasive ones such as commercials. You may also be more vulnerable to **unintended messages,** such as the themes, values, and depictions of society emphasized in programs and commercials. Suppose, for example, your favorite television drama depicts women only as middle managers whereas all top executives are males. The program's writers and producers may not set out to reinforce the so-called glass ceiling or advance stereotypes about women, but may unintentionally do so. This kind of subtle, unintentional message may have a greater impact on how we perceive gender differences than if the program put forth a blatantly sexist, deliberate argument that women cannot handle higher level executive positions.

Your own experience with the medium also bears on television's impact. You know the difference between commercials, entertainment, and information programs. However, the differences are becoming increasingly obscure. Viewers are entertained when frogs croak out the name of a popular beer or Michael Jordan banks basketballs off buildings and around planets for swish shots. Today, **program-length commercials** that seem like entertainment programs promote cosmetics, financial investments, and "amazing" new cleaning fluids. **Tabloid programs** include segments on breaking news but are more concerned with ratings than objective presentation of facts. Religious broadcasters carry their own versions of newscasts designed to look very much like actual newscasts produced by professional journalists.

## 25.6 MESSAGE

The message itself is a factor in television's impact. Suppose a political candidate appears on television arguing that the MTV program *Beavis and Butt-Head* should be banned from television during hours when children might tune in. The candidate concludes the program should air only between midnight and sunrise. Any of the following aspects of the candidate's arguments may affect your reaction to it: whether the arguments are adapted to your interests, amount of discrepancy between your opinion and the opinion advocated by the candidate, whether the message presents one side or several sides of the issues, and whether the message arouses fear.

The message's style of presentation is also important. A speech on the perils of cigarette smoking delivered by the Surgeon General on C-SPAN may have a persuasive impact. But does cigarette smoking in music videos on VH-1 or MTV have an even greater impact? What will be the effect of interactive television? Will increased audience participation in the mass communication process affect the degree of message impact?

## 25.7 COMMUNICATOR

How you perceive the individual who delivers the message affects your reaction to it (Box 25.1). The communicator's **prestige,** your perception of the communicator's **intent** (to sell, to entertain, to report, etc.), how much you **like** the communicator, and the degree to which you **empathize** with or perceive yourself as similar to the communicator all affect the impact of the message.

Television advertisers attempt to use the most effective communicators in commercials. Most advertisements feature persons who are well known and respected and who can communicate a sense of sincerity. For example, Major League Baseball's home run king, Hank Aaron, appeared for some time in commercials promoting a particular brand of television set. Aaron was not selected because he was an expert on television receivers. The company wanted an individual of high character who was well known, liked and respected by a broad

---

**BOX 25.1. YOUR PERCEPTION OF THE SPEAKER AFFECTS
YOUR PERCEPTION OF THE ARGUMENT**

Think about the factors mentioned in the text and rate each of the following—on a scale of 1 to 10—on how much they could influence your attitude toward the dangers of driving while under the influence of alcohol: your favorite local newscaster, your best friend, ABC newscaster Peter Jennings, talk show host Montel Williams, rapper Raphael Saadig, actress Susan Lucci, evangelist Jimmy Swaggart, and Geraldo Rivera. How much would your ratings vary? Would anyone get a perfect 10? How about a 1? Which factors most affected the highest and lowest ratings?

---

range of the viewing audience, and with whom many people could in some way identify. Sometimes actors are chosen for commercials just because they look like what ad agencies think you look like, or what they think you want to look like. The characteristics of the individual delivering the message can have as much impact as the message itself.

## NOTE

1. Walters, R. H., and E. Llewellyn-Thomas, "Enhancement of Punitiveness by Visual and Audio-visual Displays," *Canadian Journal of Psychology* 17 (1963): 244–255. See also, Moliter, Fred, "Children's Tolerance of Real-Life Aggression After Exposure to Media Violence," *Child Study Journal* 24 (1994): 191–207; Bryant, Jennings, and Dolf Zillman, Eds., *Perspectives on Media Effects* (Hillsdale, NJ: Lawrence Erlbaum Associates, 1986).

## FURTHER READING

Brosius, Hans-Bernd. "The Effects of Emotional Pictures in Television News," *Communication Research* 20 (1993): 105–124.

Bem, Daryl J. *Beliefs, Attitudes, and Human Affairs.* Belmont, CA: Brooks/Cole, 1970.

Comstock, George A. *Television and the American Child.* San Diego, CA: Academic, 1991.

Comstock, George A., Steven H. Chaffee, Natan Katzman, Maxwell E. McCombs, and Donald F. Roberts. *Television and Human Behavior.* New York: Columbia University Press, 1978.

Katz, Elihu, and Paul F. Lazarsfeld. *Personal Influence: The Part Played by People in the Flow of Mass Communication.* Glencoe, IL: The Free Press, 1964.

Klapper, Joseph T. *The Effects of Mass Communication.* Glencoe, IL: The Free Press, 1961.

Larson, Charles U. *Persuasion: Reception and Responsibility.* 6th ed. Belmont, CA: Wadsworth, 1992.

O'Keefe, Daniel J. *Persuasion: Theory and Research.* Newbury Park, CA: Sage, 1990.

Skill, Thomas. "Four Decades of Families on American Television," *Journal of Broadcasting and Electronic Media* 38 (1994): 449–464.

# 26

## IMPACT

In the previous chapter we examined major factors in television's impact. Here, we concentrate on the impact itself. We look first at impact on individuals, then on society. We conclude by considering long-range impact.

### 26.1 IMPACT ON INDIVIDUALS

Public concern and research have focused on several areas of television's impact on us as individuals. These include attitudes and values, behavior, and the special case involving children, the subject of considerable research on television's effects.

#### 26.1.1 Attitudes and Values

In *PRT,* 25.2.1, we found that attitudes affect our perception of televised messages. These messages can also affect our attitudes. The effect may take the form of reinforcement, creation, or conversion. Messages may also try to canalize or channel our existing attitudes. They work best in impacting attitudes when they function in a monopolistic communications environment.

*26.1.1.1 Reinforcement.*   Television's role in changing your attitudes and values is governed in large part by your predispositions. As a result, television is more successful at **reinforcing existing attitudes** than changing attitudes. In fact, reinforcement is the most common type of impact. After all, you are more attracted to programming content that is congruent with your existing interests, opinions, and behaviors.

*26.1.1.2 Creation.*   Creation of new opinions is the next most frequent effect, although not nearly as frequent as reinforcement. A televised message is most likely to win you to its point of view **if you have formed no opinion on the subject.**

*26.1.1.3 Conversion.*   Television's rarest effect is conversion. If you are a Republican, television alone will usually not convince you to become a Democrat.

**665**

If you are a rap music fan who detests country and western music, watching a program on The Nashville Network will not convert you into a country and western music fan. Most audience members **actively select** which programs to watch and not watch, so you probably would never have watched The Nashville Network in the first place.

If you do change your mind on a subject after exposure to a televised message, factors other than television probably played a role in the change. Those factors predispose you or "soften you up" for the conversion over a period of time. Television may have triggered the conversion, but you were ready to change.

### 26.1.1.4 Canalization.

Given what you read in the preceding paragraph, it is no surprise that most product advertising does not aim for conversion. Many television commercials do not attempt to convince you to use a particular product. What they try to do—because you probably already use the kind of product they sell—is convince you to use their brand. In other words, they canalize or channel your buying behavior. **Canalization** is most likely to affect decisions that are **not really that important** to us. Household goods provide an excellent example. You probably do not make meaningful, deep-seated cognitive commitments to specific brands of laundry detergent, paper towels, bath soap, and shaving cream. The commercials attempt to canalize or **channel you toward a particular brand.** Again, canalization is most likely when **the choice of a particular brand, company, or store is not very important.**

Not all retail decisions apply. You may feel very strongly about your favorite brand of soft drink, ketchup, or toothpaste. If you strongly prefer Dr. Pepper over Pepsi, television advertising for Pepsi is not likely to change your mind.

### 26.1.1.5 Monopolization.

Television advertisements would stand a much better chance of achieving conversion if an advertiser could dominate the mass media. Monopolization would occur if **all media** (not just television) **would carry commercial messages only about that advertiser's product.** Suppose the telecommunications media, motion picture theaters, newspapers and magazines, and all other forms of media embarked on a massive Pepsi advertising campaign and carried ads only for Pepsi. Research has shown that you would be much more likely to convert to being a Pepsi drinker.

The concept of monopolization was actually developed within the context of political propaganda. If a political regime controls all mass media in a country, it can program the media to carry only its propaganda and affect attitudes in the population.

### 26.1.2 Behavior

Discussion, concern, and research that focuses on television's impact on individual behavior can be divided into four general areas. These include violence; sexual material; life patterns; and inactivity, withdrawal, and escape.

***26.1.2.1 Violence.***    Violence in television has been a major issue since the 1950s. Organizations have protested it. Politicians have investigated it, even proposing government-imposed solutions such as mandatory ratings and a V-chip to lock out violent programming. The assumption is that televised violence causes or contributes significantly to aggressive behavior in viewers—especially younger viewers.

Many approaches attempt to explain the impact of televised violence. The **catharsis theory** suggests that when you watch televised violence, you drain off aggression-causing frustrations. In other words, watching violence on television has a **cathartic effect that purges you of any need to behave violently.** Catharsis theory, therefore, suggests that violent behavior **is actually reduced by television.** This approach has received little support from research.

The **aggressive cues theory** (also called **stimulating effects theory**) assumes that exposure to televised violence increases your level of physiological and emotional arousal. This arousal increases the chance that you will act violently or aggressively.

The **observational learning theory** assumes that you can learn aggressive behavior from television. Under certain conditions, you copy the aggressive behavior of television characters.

**Reinforcement theory** suggests that exposure to televised violence reinforces existing patterns of behavior. If you are normally nonviolent, you selectively perceive a program so that it reinforces your nonviolent norms and attitudes; a violent person would perceive a program to support that inclination.

Research suggests that viewing of televised violence **can lead to aggressive behavior in children.** However, a violence–aggression relation operates **only on children who are already predisposed to be aggressive, and only in some contexts.** The child's level of self-esteem, the amount of parental advice and guidance in viewing, whether the outcome of the violence is favorable or unfavorable, and whether the violence is perceived as fantasy or reality all seem to mediate the effect. In other words, a well-adjusted child who views—while in the company and guidance of parents—a television drama depicting an armed robbery or stabbing is not very likely to copy or model what was seen on television.

A research team headed by George Comstock reviewed some 2,500 reports and research studies into the impact of television. The team concluded that **television may increase aggressive behavior** in three ways. First, it can **teach viewers hostile acts** with which they were previously unfamiliar. Second, it can generally **encourage various ways of using aggression.** Third, it can set off or **"trigger" aggressive behavior**—behavior that imitates that shown on television.

The research of George Gerbner led to development of what he called cultivation theory.[1] This theory asserts that we are exposed to so much television that it creates for us a symbolic world. We are exposed to verbal and nonverbal symbols on television on a continuing, long-range basis. This symbolic world is not real, but the symbols continually affect or cultivate our perceptions of reality.

Television cultivates because it exposes millions of us nationwide, even world-wide, to the same messages. We may assign different meanings to those messages, but we all see and hear the same symbols—or have a **common symbolic experience.** As television shows violence, we are more likely to accept violence as a reality of our environment, even to the extent of overestimating the amount of actual violence that occurs. Light viewers are less likely to be influenced or cultivated. Heavy viewers, meanwhile, may be **mainstreamed** with other heavy viewers into a common view of the world.

**26.1.2.2 Sexual Material.**   By and large, radio and television have stayed free of obscenity, a result of federal law and self-regulation. However, times and programming concepts have changed. On early television Lucy and Desi retired to separate beds. Astronaut Tony Nelson's "Jeannie" had to hide her navel. Today, we have access to adult pay-cable and satellite channels. We can watch R-rated motion pictures on movie channels. Programs on advertising-supported television deal with teenage sex, rape, homosexuality, and transexuality. We hear popular recordings that deal with incest. We can tune in to radio stations that feature sexual conversation—from so-called "therapists" who offer callers love-life advice to radio hosts who syndicate sexually oriented content across the nation.

Exposure to explicit sexual materials seems to bear **no relation to delinquent behavior.** If these findings can be generalized to television, they mean that although televised sexual material may lead to sexual arousal, the material by itself does not produce antisocial attitudes or deviant behavior.

Research has raised concern, however, for more subtle types of effects. For example, one study found that men, after viewing pornographic pictures of women, advocated lighter sentences for convicted rapists.[2] The research suggested that exposure to sexually explicit material may lead some to **trivialize** actual violent, criminal sexual behavior.

Inconclusive research on the effects of sexually explicit programming has not deterred the FCC from enforcing long-standing indecency regulations. The Commission bans indecent programming during hours when children are likely to tune in and issues heavy fines for violators (*PRT,* 15.3.5.2).

**26.1.2.3 Life Patterns.**   Television, by its very existence, affects the way you live. When television appeared in the U.S. home, people adjusted their lives and reduced time spent with magazines, radio, books, movies, and other media. They also reduced nonleisure activities and began to coordinate viewing with meals and routine household duties.

If you are like most persons, you **spend more time watching television than any other activity,** except sleeping and working. Television may **bring your family together physically, but you probably interact or converse little** with each other when watching television because you are all focused on the program. Sometimes, even if you do converse it may be to argue over what to watch or how loud to set the volume. Having more than one television in the home may help prevent such disputes, but multiset households only serve to disperse family members into separate rooms.

### 26.1.2.4 Inactivity, Withdrawal, and Escape.

Some social scientists have contended that television and other media may **cause** you to be inactive, to withdraw attention from contemporary affairs, and to escape from reality. Mass communication researchers refer to these negative implications of media use as **media dysfunctions.** For example, if you watch television news and information programs, you may feel that you are interested and informed. Yet, you may take no action to affect the issues and help solve problems in society—a result, perhaps, of your assumption that, because you know about the issues, someone else must be "doing something" about them. In this case, television works as a narcotic, lulling you into a false "knowing is doing" sense of security. Researchers call this a **narcotization effect.**

Another possible dysfunction is **privatization.** In this case we use this term to mean **a psychological retreat from public to private concerns.** News, by definition, features aberrant behavior; that is, events that deviate from the norm or from what most people believe to be right and true. In privatization, you feel **overwhelmed by all the bad news** and frustrated by your inability to deal with it. Therefore, **you turn away from the affairs** over which you have no control to **focus completely on personal matters** to the exclusion of social, political, and economic reality.

Social scientists say that you sometimes use television for the very purpose of escape. You may watch music videos or a college football game just to get away from daily problems and worries. You may also use television to relax, to stimulate your imagination, for later discussion of programming with others, for emotional release and vicarious interaction, or just to kill time. If you **overuse television for escape, it is a dysfunction.** However, **television's escape function probably helps you,** giving your critical and creative processes a break, allowing your mind to rest, helping recharge your mental batteries.

### 26.1.3 Children

Despite all the furor over the V-chip, program ratings, and the disturbing nature of the material just reported concerning violence, the news is not all bad. In fact, the bulk of research shows that **an emotionally balanced child suffers little, if any, long-lasting negative effects** from television.

On the other hand, **an emotionally disturbed child or one who is predisposed toward antisocial or aggressive behavior patterns may suffer negative effects** from television. Some children are more likely to believe that what they see on television is the norm and what they see in real life is the exception.

Very young children often cannot distinguish between fiction and nonfiction on television. However, even children as young as 6 years old recognize commercials for what they are, and by 8 or 9 years old they are even skeptical about advertising claims. Nonetheless, repeated exposure to a television commercial can move the child from skepticism toward persuasion. Children in homes where television is on constantly tend to suffer more negative effects, even when the television is on largely as background with no one viewing.

Parental interaction with the child concerning television content can counter most such effects. Therefore, in the matter of your child and television, factors of the child's own mental and emotional state, your example and interaction with the child, and the home environment you provide seem to outweigh television as an influence.

## 26.2 IMPACT ON SOCIETY

Society is more than an aggregate of individuals. It is also the customs, morals, values, standards, and institutions shared by those individuals. We now look at the impact of television on society in the United States, impact that involves culture, politics, and social change.

### 26.2.1 Culture, Style, and Taste

At various times, critics have charged that television degrades public taste by pandering to the lowest common denominator. They contend that television could be used to raise the cultural level of the population. However, **taste is much more influenced by social, personal, educational, and family determinants** than by television. You probably come to television with your tastes already formed and seek programming congruent with them. Therefore, if *Rugrats* or professional wrestling is showing opposite *Masterpiece Theatre* or *Nature,* you watch the program that best reflects your customary taste.

There are doubts about television's ability to raise the general cultural level. Despite the BBC's years of monopoly and its attempt to raise taste, large percentages of the U.K. population switched over when other programming sources—foreign, pirate, and British commercial stations—became available. On the other hand, concentrated use of television programming in emerging nations has led many of their citizens to show increased interest in their cultural heritage.

Television can also **bestow prestige and enhance authority.** This comes close to being a tautological situation—that what you see on television must be important or famous because it is on television; the very fact that it appears on television makes it important. Celebrities are used to enhance the effect. Basketball superstar Michael Jordan is considered so influential that he has earned millions of dollars appearing in commercials for a fast-food restaurant, an underwear manufacturer, a sports drink product, a shoe company, and a brand of hot dogs.

Bestowed prestige occurs in other media. In many cases, radio stations (often with help from MTV) can make a music recording popular just by playing it.

Newspapers and magazines have long spread the word on style, taste, and manners. Motion pictures have a long history of influencing style and manners. Recording artists can have an effect. It was on February 9, 1964, that the Beatles were first seen by Americans on the *Ed Sullivan Show*. Soon thereafter, young men went from crew cuts to longer hair and started wearing more diverse clothing. Thirty years later, Madonna influenced millions of fashion followers with her risqué, lingerie-styled clothing.

## 26.2.2 Politics

Politicians have known instinctively for years that television alone will not change anyone's mind. A good political campaigner writes off voters who strongly favor the opposition. No amount of media persuasion will change their minds. Therefore, the campaigner "goes where the ducks are" and **concentrates much advertising on voters who favor the candidate.** The campaigner seeks to reinforce the voters' positive feelings to the point where they will actually go to the polls and vote.

The modern election campaign often features two opposing candidates who have nearly equal support among the active, politically aware portion of the electorate. The balance of power then lies with the **uncommitted nonvoters** who neither know nor care about the campaign. These persons are characterized by high use of one medium above all others—television. To get their vote requires **television advertising.** Expensive political advertising specialists are hired to research public preferences and to create an image of the candidate to meet those preferences. Campaign staff members and paid "spin doctors" are trained to put a positive spin on the candidate's comments and behaviors no matter how negative they may appear. Professionals working for candidates receiving only 8% of the vote "spin" the numbers to claim a victory.

All this presents a rather chilling spectacle—public office available only to those of great personal wealth or beholden to large contributors, who run on slogans and catch phrases, who are packaged and merchandised like soap and dog food, and who owe election to a constituency that does not know and does not care. Luckily, elections do not always work that way. Some of the most expensive campaigns have failed and efforts to reduce campaign spending have been increasingly successful.

Politics are also affected by television's **ability to confer status and prestige.** It can transform regional politicians like Jimmy Carter and Bill Clinton into national political figures and ultimately into presidents. Former entertainers, such as Ronald Reagan, Shirley Temple Black, and Sonny Bono, and athletes such as Bill Bradley and Steve Largent entered politics after gaining fame first through exposure in movies or on television.

Social scientists suggest that the greatest **impact of television on voter preference comes between campaigns**, not during. As discussed in *PRT*, 8.1.5, television news, by its very nature, must select, edit, and order. Even live and on the scene, a camera operator must select specific portions of the scene to send on to us. Therefore television structures what you see by selecting, emphasizing, and interpreting events.

In the 1964 U.S. presidential campaign, for example, the war in Southeast Asia was not an issue. By 1968, **television and other media coverage had made it the most important issue.** Social scientists call this the **agenda-setting function** of the media. The media do not tell us what to think, but they have a **major impact on what we think about.**[3]

**Television campaign coverage and candidate advertising seem to help turn out the vote.** However, researchers have found **some evidence that national television coverage of voter returns influences those who have not yet voted.** Critics had expressed concern that televised reports of presidential returns from early time zones, along with computer-assisted projections of who would probably win, might influence people in later time zones who had yet to cast ballots. For example, estimates are that as many as 800,000 Californians were discouraged from voting because of early network projections of a Reagan victory over President Carter in the 1980 presidential election. The projections were accurate, but the reduced turnout surely affected local elections. The networks, sensitive to criticism and problems created by early projections, agreed in 1985 to refrain from projecting a winner in state elections until the polls in that state are closed.

### 26.2.3 Social Change

Most radio and television outlets and networks try for the largest possible audiences. Therefore, they program material that they hope will be entertaining but will not offend viewers and advertisers. Some cable and large-market radio programming targets more diverse audiences. Network television programming often exposes deviations from established and normal behaviors just to attract interest. Before ABC began airing the program *NYPD Blue* the network carried announcements warning of sexual and violent content. The program resulted in controversy and a few affiliates refused to carry it, but the announcements increased viewer interest. ABC faced even greater controversy when it aired an episode of the program *Ellen* that featured two women kissing.

By bringing deviation to public attention, television may influence people to think about and take a stand on it. The net effect is often to force some kind of public action against what may previously have been privately tolerated. Thus, television programming may **both enforce and expose deviations from accepted attitudes and behavior patterns in society.**

It would be logical to assume that such impact would obstruct social change, promote conformity, weaken individualism, and decrease tolerance of differences. Sometimes it may. But television has played a significant role in, for example, publicizing the problems and inequities experienced by women, children, Blacks, and other minorities. Unfortunately, for years it has also played a significant role in reinforcing ethnic and gender stereotypes.

Television and other media do seem to help new ideas and products gain acceptance. In adopting a new concept, you probably go through five overlapping stages:

1. You become **aware** of the concept.
2. You become **interested**.
3. You **evaluate** information.
4. You **try or test** the concept.
5. You **adopt** it; that is, you make a decision on continued use.

During this process, you talk to other people about the concept, but you also get much information from the media.

This five-part adoption of innovations model also helps to explain how new ideas and concepts spread. A few persons are quick to adopt a new concept; others, slower in varying degrees. This means that as the concept spreads, various groups are going through the five phases of our adoption model. For example, you, as one of the few early adopters, may have been one of the very first to get a CD player or home computer. You may have purchased a modem so you could browse the Internet and set up your own Web page. On the other hand, it may take years before the few laggards—the very slowest adopters—decide to move from cassette tapes to CD players, or even learn to use a computer. Between the few at either end of the scale are the majority of persons.

### 26.2.4 Knowledge Gap Hypothesis

Mass media disseminate information to broad segments of society. One effect of this, however, may be to increase the disparity in knowledge levels among higher social classes. This potential media dysfunction is called the **knowledge gap hypothesis.**[4] According to this hypothesis, all social classes learn from the media, but over a period of time **persons in higher socioeconomic classes will likely accumulate more knowledge** concerning public affairs, science, and current events. Thus, the knowledge gap may grow ever wider.

Researchers have offered several reasons why the knowledge gap phenomenon can occur. First, certain media, including multichannel cable, pay-per-view programming, and magazine subscriptions, are more affordable, and therefore more accessible to higher income households. Second, the mass media may target higher income consumers who are more likely to have greater interest in and more ability to understand certain topics. Persons of higher social status are also more likely to communicate with others of similar status, thus allowing the multistep flow of communication (*PRT,* 27.2.3) to contribute to the knowledge gap.

Developments in information technology including home computer access to the Internet and other online information sources have increased concern that the knowledge gap may widen even faster. However, more recent knowledge gap research has suggested that **highly motivated individuals** are likely to obtain available information regardless of socioeconomic status.[5]

## 26.3 LONG-RANGE IMPACT

Most of the types of impact we have discussed so far are short range. For example, by itself, exposure to a violent murder on a television program normally will not cause someone to go out and commit a murder. Or, by itself, a televised message will not change a person from a liberal to a conservative.

Where we dealt with long-range impact, we used hedge words such as *seem to, likely to,* and *probably.* This is because researchers find it difficult to test for long-range impact. The research studies themselves must be long range and cover a span of months and even years. Researchers then face the difficult task of establishing cause-and-effect relations (*PRT,* 25.1) between television viewing and various types of impact.

We do know that commercial television does not offer what most people believe is an accurate depiction of the world. It emphasizes certain themes and values—those that draw the largest audiences and sell products—violence; sexual innuendo; sexual deviancy; high adventure; absurd situations; sharp demarcation between good and evil; absolute resolution of all problems within a time frame of 30 to 60 minutes; stereotyped roles and behavior for men, women, and various racial groups; and beauty, youth, and sexual desirability as important goals. One need only browse through program listings for television situation comedies, drama, and talk shows to see variations of these themes and more.

We learned in chapter 25 that other factors usually migitate against television having a negative effect on "normal" people. Foremost among these other factors were socialization and interpersonal contact. However, there are situations in which other factors are largely absent. For example, in many families parents use the television set as a combination sitter, companion, and opiate for their young children. The children watch anything they want as long as they keep quiet and out of the way. The parents interact with their children so little that **a high percentage of their total sensory input**—experiences that help form attitudes for life—**comes from television.**

Of course, that cannot happen to you or to your children. You care, and television viewing is monitored and regulated in your home. Maybe, but there are a few facts you should keep in mind. First, one of the conditions that determine impact of television is **exposure pattern**. This means that the more a message (such as a particular set of themes and values) is repeated, the greater its chance to be effective.

Second, as discussed already, U.S. commercial television (including subscription cable services) continually stresses certain themes and values, and we expose ourselves to them for long periods of time. U.S. households average over 45 hours per week of viewing activity, the majority of which is commercial and subscription television. That means the TV set runs over one third of our waking hours, over 2,300 hours per year, exposing us to these themes and values.

Third, **other media stress the same themes and values.** In fact, many of the different types of impact we have attributed to television alone actually apply to that whole group of institutions and products we call mass media.

Fourth, social scientists tell us that the **mass media represent a new force in the socialization process.** As such, the media partially supplant parents, teachers, and other direct authority figures.

True, television and the other media do not mirror society. They focus on the deviant, the aberrant, and the exception. But, of course, neither did *Hamlet* mirror early 17th-century English or Danish society. It, too, is full of violence, greed, immorality, and all that other stuff critics say television carries. Yet, *Hamlet* is held up to us as "good literature." Is that fair? Perhaps not. On the other hand, children do not sit in their living rooms for hours watching *Hamlet!*

## NOTES

1. Gerbner, G., L. Gross, M. Morgan, and N. Signorielli, "The Mainstreaming of America," *Journal of Communication* 30 (1980): 10–29. See also, Gerbner, G., L. Gross, M. Morgan, & N. Signorielli, "Some Additional Comments On Cultivation Analysis," *Public Opinion Quarterly* 44 (1980): 408–410; and Signorielli, N. and M. Morgan Eds., *Cultivation Analysis.* Newbury Park, CA: Sage, 1990.

2. Zillman, D., and J. Bryant, "Pornography, Sexual Callousness, and the Trivialization of Rape," *Journal of Communication* 32 (1982): 10–21.

3. McCombs, M. E., and D. L. Shaw, "The Evolution of Agenda-Setting Theory: 25 Years in the Marketplace of Ideas," *Journal of Communication* 43 (1993): 58–66.

4. Tichenor, P. J., G. A. Donohue, and C. N. Olien, "Mass Media Flow and Differentiated Growth in Knowledge," *Public Opinion Quarterly* 34 (1970): 159–170; and Gaziano, C., "The Knowledge Gap: An Analytical Review of Media Effects," *Communication Research* 10 (1983): 836–845.

5. Severin, W., and J. Tankard, *Communication Theories: Origins, Methods, and Uses in the Mass Media,* 3rd ed. (White Plains, NY: Longman, 1992), p. 245.

## FURTHER READING

Adler, Richard P., Gerald S. Lesser, Laurence K. Meringoff, Thomas S. Robertson, John R. Rossiter, and Scott Ward. *The Effects of Television and Advertising on Children.* Lexington, MA: D.C. Heath, 1980.

Berger, Arthur A. *Essentials of Mass Communication Theory.* Thousand Oaks, CA: Sage, 1995.

Biagi, Shirley. *Media Impact: An Introduction to Mass Media.* Belmont, CA: Wadsworth, 1996.

Bryant, Jennings, and Dolf Zillmann. *Media Effects: Advances in Theory and Research.* Mahwah, NJ: Lawrence Erlbaum Associates, 1994.

Davison, W. Phillips, James Boylan, and Frederick T. C. Yu. *Mass Media: Systems and Effects.* 2nd ed. New York: Holt, 1982.

Dorr, Aimée. *Television and Children: A Special Medium for a Special Audience.* Newbury Park, CA: Sage, 1986.

Frank, Ronald E., and Marshall G. Greenberg. *The Public's Use of Television: Who Watches and Why.* Beverly Hills, CA: Sage, 1980.

Gordon, George. *Erotic Communications: Studies in Sex, Sin, and Censorship.* New York: Hastings, 1980.

Graber, Doris A, Ed. *Media Power in Politics.* 3rd ed. Washington, DC: CQ, 1994.

Harris, Richard Jackson. *A Comparative Psychology of Mass Communication.* Hillsdale, NJ: Lawrence Erlbaum Associates, 1989.

Hiebert, Ray Eldon, and Carol Reuss, Eds. *Impact of Mass Media: Current Issues.* 3rd ed. White Plains, NY: Longman, 1995.

Lang, Annie, Ed. *Measuring Psychological Responses to Media Messages.* Hillsdale, NJ: Lawrence Erlbaum Associates, 1994.

Liebert, Robert M., Joyce N. Sprafkin, and Emily S. Davidson. *The Early Window: Effects of Television on Children and Youth.* 3rd ed. New York: Pergamon, 1988.

Morley, David. *Television, Audiences, and Cultural Studies.* New York: Routledge, 1993.

Rogers, Everett M. *Diffusion of Innovations.* 4th ed. New York: The Free Press, 1995.

*Television and Behavior: Ten Years of Scientific Progress and Implications for the Eighties.* Washington, DC: U.S. Government Printing Office, 1982.

Valdivia, Angharad N., Ed. *Feminism, Multiculturalism, and the Media.* Thousand Oaks, CA: Sage, 1995.

Zillman, Dolf, Jennings Bryant, and Aletha C. Huston, Eds. *Media, Children, and the Family: Social Scientific, Psychodynamic, and Clinical Perspectives.* Mahwah, NJ: Lawrence Erlbaum Associates, 1994.

# 27

# RESEARCH AND THEORY

Mass communication research is the field within which radio and television research is conducted. Mass communication also includes research into advertising, newspapers, magazines, the recording industry, motion pictures, and other media. Note that the singular form is used—mass *communication.* Scholars study the social, historical, and psychological *process,* not the technical aspects of equipment. They believe the plural form *communications* connotes the latter, so they use the singular to describe their field.

## 27.1 RESEARCH

Research begins with a question. Sometimes it asks simple questions such as **how many or what kind of people listened** to a radio station. Other times research asks **what relations exist** between two or more mass communication variables. Often, it asks **what causes** some particular phenomenon.

### 27.1.1 Notion of Science

Scientific research is empirical, objective, and systematic. By **empirical,** we mean the researcher gathers data by direct experience or direct observation. The researcher strives for **objectivity** by using certain methods designed to minimize the effects of personal bias. The researcher ensures that the work will be **systematic** by specifying procedures—the design and methodology—in advance, then following them to the letter. Both Arbitron and Nielsen, for example, publish detailed descriptions of the procedures used to collect and compile radio and television ratings data. Social scientists publish methodologies so detailed that other researchers are able to duplicate and verify their research. In **quantitative** research, the researcher uses statistical techniques to deal with and analyze numerical data. Based on these data, the researcher draws certain conclusions concerning the relation among variables. In **qualitative** research, the researcher analyzes and interprets data—such as statements made during an interview—without assigning numbers to the statements.

We said that research begins with a question. When that question is formally stated, it is often in the form of a **hypothesis.** A hypothesis poses a prediction.

The research tests the hypothesis. The results of the research allow the researcher to accept or reject the hypothesis and, thus, answer the question. The question often asked is, "What, if any, relation exists between two entities?" The entities are **variables**. For example, consider the following two radio variables: amount of news broadcast and morning drive ratings. We might hypothesize that an increase in the amount of news broadcast will result in an increase in ratings during morning drive. Because we are hypothesizing that a change in one variable **causes** a corresponding change in the other, they are **independent** and **dependent** variables, respectively.

In the preceeding example, the researcher's overall goal is to test whether a radio station's news programming **affects** overall station ratings. As we saw (*PRT,* 25.1), we must be very careful, however, before concluding that any variable causes a change in another. Our ratings may have gone up because we ran new promotions for morning drive or gave away contest prizes at the same time that we upgraded our news. Or, our strongest competitor may have changed air personalities or format. If so, we cannot assume a cause-and-effect relation between our two variables.

Hypothesis-testing research is usually **based in theory.** The researcher examines a general principle or theory, then derives a hypothesis from that theory. The **two primary goals of theory-based research** are to evaluate the theory—to determine whether it makes accurate predictions, whether it has limitations, and whether it is correct—and to expand the theory. Much hypothesis-testing research in mass communication is not theory based, one reason being that we still do not have adequate theories addressing many practical concerns of media professionals. However, in formulating any hypothesis or research question, the mass communication researcher should review and take into account previous related research.

### 27.1.2 Research Methodologies

Mass communication scholars use a variety of methods to find answers. In the **historical-critical method,** the researcher examines documents and firsthand reports contemporary with the era, event, or phenomenon under investigation. For example, suppose you wanted to research the root causes of the panic that occurred during and after the 1938 broadcast of Orson Welles' *War of the Worlds* Martian invasion program (*PRT,* 2.2.4.1). You would first review any and all research previously conducted regarding the broadcast. You would certainly need to study a tape of the program itself, its script, newspaper clippings from the days following the broadcast, and FCC records to see what complaints were made and the reaction of the Commission. You would also interview anyone still around who was connected with the program and anyone who actually heard the broadcast.

In the **case study method,** the researcher examines in detail a mass communication situation or a series of such situations for underlying principles. Two classic case studies are those by Warren Breed on social control in the newsroom[1] and David Manning White on the gatekeeper functions (selection of news items) of a newspaper wire editor.[2] Examples of case studies in radio and television include those by Lynch[3] and Ravage[4] on the production of two specific weekly network television series.

Most scholars who investigate impact use some form of **quantitative** research. Here, they literally measure things on a numerical scale—things such as hours of television viewing, aggressive behaviors, or audience perceptions of bloody scenes in a television program (Box 27.1). After measuring, the researcher then attempts to determine if the numbers are significant. For example, results of a study might suggest that people tend to exhibit more aggressive behavior as they watch more bloody scenes on television. The researcher would run statistical tests on the numbers involved to determine if there was a real relation between these two variables or if the numbers (results) could have occurred strictly by chance.

Historical-critical and case study researchers sometimes utilize quantitative methodology. Suppose, for example, that a study proposes some relation between network television prime-time program development effort and series longevity. In this case, the researcher might determine the number of program development projects the major television networks had supported each year over a period of time, then count the total number of episodes of each series that started in those same years.

Two types of research that almost inevitably involve numbers are the field study and the experiment. In the **field study,** the researcher does not alter conditions but studies the mass communication process as it occurs in real life. The researcher goes into a real-world environment, asks questions, and observes behaviors. The data are then examined for relations among variables, for example, between prolonged television viewing and aggressive behaviors among children.

The **experimental method,** on the other hand, is used most often in the laboratory. In one of its simpler forms, the researcher exposes two groups of individuals to conditions that are identical in all respects save one. The researcher then tests both groups to see if any differences show up in the expected areas. For example, a researcher might expose each of two similar groups of children to two

---

**BOX 27.1. ASSIGNING NUMBERS TO MEASURES**

You may be wondering how researchers could measure, using numbers, a variable such as degree of liking of radio formats. Usually, the researcher will ask participants in the study to respond to a series of questions. The researcher then assigns numbers to the answers. For example, the researcher might ask participants "To what extent do you like listening" to various formats, with the following choices: like a lot, like, like somewhat, dislike somewhat, dislike, and dislike a lot. The researcher then assigns numbers to the responses in the following manner: like a lot = 6, like = 5, like somewhat = 4, dislike somewhat = 3, dislike = 2, and dislike a lot = 1. The researcher can use the numbers to calculate average "liking" scores for all participants for each of the formats.

versions of a television program. The programs are identical except that one version contains violence and the other contains no violence. After exposure, the children of each group would be allowed to play, and the researcher could watch and count the number of aggressive acts—for example, one child pushing another. If children in the violent-action-exposure group commit a significantly greater number of aggressive acts (the dependent variable) than those in the other group, the researcher could tentatively attribute the presence of the televised violence (independent variable).

Experimental laboratory research has the advantage over field study research with respect to **control.** In the laboratory, the researcher can use a carefully constructed research design to hold constant—ensure the sameness of—all variables except those under study. Given positive results, and assurance of no significant threats to the validity of the study, our laboratory researcher could conclude, with a fair degree of assurance, that exposure to televised violence increases the number of aggressive acts children commit during play. However, our field researcher—even with results that show a positive relation—cannot draw such an unqualified cause–effect conclusion. There was no control, thus there were probably multiple other variables at work in addition to television—parents, peers, other media, and so on.

Yet the field study has an advantage precisely because of these multiple other variables. After all, they are present in real life. Besides, the laboratory study is a contrived situation.

Still another method combines aspects of both experimental and field studies. In the **field experimental method,** the researcher uses laboratory controls, but conducts research in the real world.

The **survey method** is used extensively in mass communication research. Social scientists and media researchers including the ratings firms use data from samples of a population to make conclusions about the entire population (*PRT,* 18.1.2 and 18.1.5).

### 27.1.3 History of Mass Communication Research

The origins of mass communication as a field for research go back to World War I. Governments of the combatant nations used propaganda to mobilize their populations. They described the enemy as subhumans whose primary aims were to rape, pillage, and kill. These were the first formal, widespread government uses of propaganda in modern times, and they worked. Whole countries threw themselves into the war effort.

After the war, reaction set in. The public began to fear propaganda as some omnipotent force against which they were powerless to resist. As a result, psychologists began to analyze propaganda and to research persuasion by mass media. Research soon spread beyond inquiry into propaganda. Faculty members in university schools of communication and journalism adopted methodologies from the social sciences and launched their own research.

## 27.2 THEORIES OF MASS COMMUNICATION

In our discussion of research we slipped in the term *theory* and brushed by it with a few remarks about usefulness and scarcity. This section first defines theory, then reviews the most important theories relevant to mass communication.

### 27.2.1 Definition and Characteristics of Theory

A simplified definition of theory is **a set of interrelated statements that explain and predict a phenomenon.** One example of a theory would be a set of statements that explain how television commercials affect the audience. Note that theories must go beyond mere explanation or description. They must **predict** phenomena and explain not only what happens but **why and how** the process occurs as well.

Explanations must meet rigorous criteria and serve specific functions before being labeled a theory. However, it is difficult for theories in the social and behavioral sciences to meet these criteria. In most natural sciences—chemistry, for example—a scientist can see the variables and even mix them up in test tubes. The scientist can observe what goes on, can measure precisely the values and quantities involved, and so can account for all occurrences. This is not so in the behavioral and social sciences, where we are dealing with attitudes and behaviors.

For example, two people react to the same television program in different ways. How do we account for the difference? There being no obvious explanation anyone can see, psychologists suggest the existence of **intervening variables.** Two classes of intervening variables seem to play large roles in the effect of message stimuli on people—**psychological makeup** (such as attitudes, beliefs, and values; *PRT,* 25.2.1) and **interpersonal relationships** (*PRT,* 25.3).

Of course no one can see your psychological makeup. It is not an organ, a gland, or a particular part of the brain. It is something psychologists have posited to explain differential behavior. Attitudes cannot be seen or located, so there is no way to measure them directly. Instead, psychologists measure **overt behavior,** under the assumption that the attitude (if it exists) underlies behavior and therefore behavior reflects attitude. They use all kinds of measurements, from pencil-and-paper personality tests to counting the number of times a button is pushed. Keep in mind that a pencil-and-paper test asks respondents to report attitudes. These tests cannot measure the attitude directly. All of these measures are, in fact, **indirect.**

### 27.2.2 Borrowed Theories

Some mass communication researchers borrowed theories from other fields. The information-processing theories, which were developed in psychology, have proven especially interesting to communication researchers. Other borrowed theories used by mass communication researchers have included those that focused on persuasion, attitude change, and reference groups.

### 27.2.3 Effects Theories

Although not really theories in the formal sense, these early formulations served to illustrate developments and changes in the way researchers regarded mass communication and its relation with individuals. The first—and one that has been discredited by social scientists—was the **bullet theory**. According to this theory, media messages were "shot" into people much like a bullet—meaning and all. The bullet theory assumed that the individual was insignificant and socially isolated. A powerful communications stimulus, such as a propaganda message, could reach basic human instincts, and humans would respond. They would all respond the same way because they all shared a common instinctual inheritance. A given stimulus yielded a given response. To get a different response, one had to change the stimulus.

As we will see, this bullet theory was eventually discounted. Some scholars even questioned whether it was ever really accepted by serious mass communication researchers. However, even the very terminology used by researchers seemed to be influenced by this viewpoint. Social scientists investigated the effects of mass communication, the implication being that the **media messages produced an effect on audience members**. The audience members, as individuals, brought nothing to the communication act.

However, research in psychology soon led to the startling conclusion that people are different. The **individual differences** theory suggests that because people vary in their psychological makeup, they each respond differently to media messages. We discussed many of the concepts encompassed by the individual differences theory in *PRT*, 25.2.

Individual differences researchers still assumed that people were essentially passive and responded only to external stimuli, such as televised messages. As a result, research in the area of individual differences was unproductive and virtually abandoned during the 1960s.

**Social categories** theory added a sociological component to the individual differences (psychological) perspective. This theory, too, acknowledged that individuals differ, but it added the notion that people from a particular religious, ethnic, work, and neighborhood environment would tend to think like other people from the same environment. Teenagers raised in New York City would, therefore, have concerns and interests similar to each other but quite unlike middle-aged Minnesota farmers.

The discovery that people, after receiving information from mass media, talked with and influenced one another led to formulation of the **social relationships** theory. During the 1940 presidential campaign, three researchers[5] studied a panel of some 600 residents of Erie County, Ohio. They wanted to find out the impact of the campaign, including its mass media aspects, on voting intentions. However, when they asked their panelists to describe recent exposure to campaign communications, the medium named most often was not radio, newspapers, magazines, or any mass medium. It was **conversation**—talking to other people. From this and other studies we learned the importance of interpersonal relations in mass communication, including the opinion leader process and the two-step flow hypothesis, discussed in *PRT,* 25.3.

The last of this group is the **cultural norms** theory. The assumption here is that mass media, through selective emphasis of certain themes and values, create the impression in their audiences that what they see on television is what "the real world" is really like. The impact on the norms of society can be conscious or unconscious and can either reinforce existing norms or institute new ones. Research seems to indicate that mass media actually have little power to change norms in the short run, but more likely reflect and reinforce trends that already exist. Researchers believe, however, that over the long run, the mass media do act to create and change social norms. See, for example, the discussion of cultivation theory (*PRT,* 26.1.2.1).

The effects theories were never fully developed. Perhaps this was because they were motivated more out of fear of the power of media than out of objective scientific curiosity. Or it may have been due to the faulty assumptions about human behavior. Still, except for certain types of effects, research never established that the media were all powerful.

Eventually, researchers began using a **limited effects** model in their theoretical approaches. They realized that human behavior could not be explained by simplistic, passive, stimulus–response effects models.

### 27.2.4 Uses and Gratifications

The uses and gratifications approach assumes that individuals are cognitively active. It asks **what we use communication for,** rather than what communication's effects on us are. If you think the communication will be useful or will give you satisfaction, you will expose yourself to it; if not, you will try not to expose yourself to it, or you will disregard or forget it.

Charles Wright[6] suggested that the media serve four basic functions for society. These include surveillance, correlation, transmission of culture, and entertainment. In performing the **surveillance** function, mass media provide information for society. This roughly corresponds to dissemination of news, but we get information from all media content, not just formal news. For example, MTV and contemporary hit radio tell us what recordings are popular.

The **correlation** function includes interpretation of information and suggestion for response. Editorial and propaganda messages attempt correlation most directly, but again, we take cues for behavior from all types of content.

In the **cultural transmission** function, audience members pick up cultural cues and norms of behavior from mass media messages. This is education in the broadest sense of the term. Just as *Sesame Street* can teach us the alphabet, so can soft drink commercials teach us that it is "in" to be slim.

The **entertainment** function refers to mass communication messages intended for amusement, irrespective of what other impact they may have. You probably use the mass media for entertainment more than any other reason.

Any one mass media message may serve all four functions for us. For example, we watch television news programs to get information. However, the treatment of news at many television stations has made the entertainment function a very important factor in its presentation. At the same time, we receive cues concerning correlation (what the president says, what people are doing and saying, editorial comment) and cultural transmission (this is what happens to people who disobey the laws of society, this is how the very wealthy or powerful or popular behave, this is what the in-crowd is doing or wearing).

Wright proposed that the role of mass communication in society be analyzed by asking the following 12-element question:

|  | (1) manifest | (3) functions |  |
|---|---|---|---|
| What are the | and | and | of mass communication? |
|  | (2) latent | (4) dysfunctions |  |

(5) surveillance (news)          for the (9) society
(6) correlation (editorial activity)          (10) individual
(7) cultural transmission          (11) subgroups
(8) entertainment          (12) cultural subsystems?

**Manifest** means the functions are there, we are aware of them, and they are intended. **Latent** means that they are hidden, we are not aware of them, and they are unintended. **Functions** are positive uses of media. They work to maintain harmony or progress. **Dysfunctions** are negative consequences. They work against smooth functioning.

### 27.2.5 Agenda-Setting Theory

**Agenda-Setting Theory** suggests that the media, through selective emphasis of certain issues and events, have a significant effect on what the public thinks about. The theory makes no claim that the media influence actual attitudes about issues, people, and events—only that we are more likely to think about what is shown on television, discussed on radio, or written about in the newspaper. The theory grew out of research conducted on the 1968 presidential campaign. First, researchers analyzed the content of media coverage of issues in the campaign. Then, they asked people to name the most important problems in the country. The researchers found a strong relation between issues covered in the media and those named as important problems by the public. Later research indicated a causal link—it was indeed the media coverage that affected perceptions of the importance of issues.

Researchers later referred to the process by which media selectively emphasize some issues and ignore others as **priming**. Priming may have significantly affected the outcome of the 1980 presidential election. Whereas other issues were given less media attention, the Iranian hostage crisis—an albatross for President Carter—was consistently emphasized as voters decided whether to vote for Carter or the eventual winner, Ronald Reagan.

### 27.2.6 Play Theory

**Play theory** distinguishes between work (reality, earning a living) and play (largely unproductive, except for self-satisfaction). According to play theory, the central concern of mass media is to allow people to throw off social control and withdraw into play. Play theory avoids the helpless audience and all-powerful media situation that the word *effects* seems to imply and assumes a psychologically active audience.

### 27.2.7 Dependency Theory

Mass communication researchers De Fleur and Ball-Rokeach introduced the **dependency theory of audience–media–society relations**. They suggested that as society becomes more complex and informal communications channels outside the immediate group begin to be disrupted, people depend more on mass media for information. The degree of dependency varies. As the media serve more information-delivery functions and as social change and conflict increase, people become more media dependent. Under these conditions, the mass media achieve a broad range of cognitive (how we perceive things), affective (how we feel about things), and behavioral (what we do about things) effects.

These effects, however, are not entirely one-way. The relationship among audience, society, and media is actually tripartite. Changes in audience cognitive, affective, and behavioral conditions feed back and, in turn, alter both society and the media.

### 27.2.8 Spiral of Silence

This theory suggests that the mass media are actually quite powerful—more powerful than we are able to ascertain through available methods of research. Elizabeth Noelle-Neumann argued that when individuals perceive their opinions and ideas to be in the minority, they remain silent.[7] The media, by helping create dominant opinions, help form impressions that public opinion is either contrary to or moving away from individual minority positions. Thus, the individuals remain silent, resulting in a **spiral of silence**. As this process continues, minority viewpoints disappear.

Several factors increase media influence on public opinion. First, the media are readily available to the masses. Also, the mass media have a "cumulative" effect on individuals because certain messages or ideas are heard and seen repeatedly on radio and television and in magazines and newspapers. These messages become dominant over those that are less emphasized or not presented by the media. Finally, Noelle-Neumann suggested that the shared perceptions of television networks, newspapers, and magazines help shape majority opinion and contribute to the spiral of silence.

## 27.3 RESEARCH AND THE COMMUNICATION PROCESS

Historically, the bulk of empirical research has dealt with effects—what the mass media do to people. However, as you have seen with uses and gratifications theory, there are other ways to study mass communication.

Claude E. Shannon's 1948 paper "The Mathematical Theory of Communication"[8] opened important new insights on the subject of human communication. In the article, he dealt with communication by analogy. Shannon identified a few key elements and relations present in every communications system—a **model** of the communication process (Fig. 27.1). He focused on mechanical and electronic systems such as telegraphy and telephony, but scholars in the social sciences also found models useful to illustrate and study the process of human communication. Scholars have constructed a number of interesting models that depict their concepts of the process of mass communication.

One of the simpler, more universal models appears in Fig. 27.2. Note that it applies equally well to either interpersonal or mass communication.

A second line of research concentrates on the message. Some scholars use **content analysis,** a research technique that employs scientific methodology to describe the message—for example, number and type of portrayals of ethnic minorities in television commercials. Content analysis might also investigate portrayals of women and minorities on prime-time television or even favorable and unfavorable news coverage of political candidates.

Other research centers around the encoder, for example, media organizations and their personnel. The narrative-style case study has been used most often in describing encoding activities, but researchers also use quantitative methodology. The role of the gatekeeper—the person that decides which encoded messages will be sent through the channel for ultimate reception—has been the focus of considerable media research.

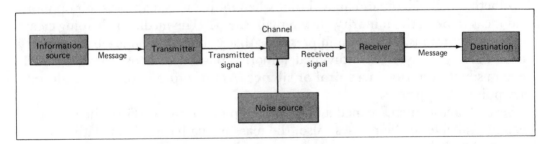

FIG. 27.1. **Shannon's model of the communication process.** (*Source*: Claude E. Shannon and Warren Weaver, *The Mathematical Theory of Communication,* 11th printing, 1967, Urbana: University of Illinois Press, 1964. Copyright 1949 by the Board of Trustees of the University of Illinois. Used with permission of the University of Illinois Press.)

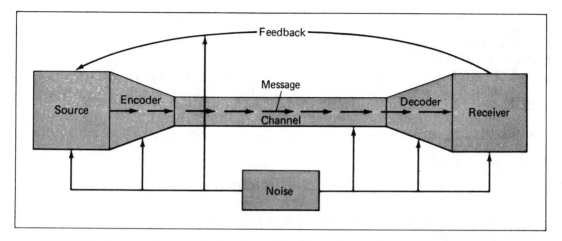

**FIG. 27.2. Communication model.** A model such as this can be used to represent almost any level of communication—for example, the present discussion. I am the source and I have a message about communication models that I want to get to you, the receiver. I encode my message by committing it to writing. It travels through the channels of this book and light rays that enter your eyes as reflected from the printed symbols on this page. Once you decode the message by reading it and your mind assigns meaning to it, communication has occurred. Feedback could be as direct and specific as a letter from you or as general as sales of this book. Noise may enter at any point in the model; my inability to explain, your watching music videos while trying to read, a poor printing job on this page, and so on.

One type of feedback research is part and parcel of the very system of commercial radio and television—the ratings. However, feedback also includes consumer behavior in response to advertising and telephone calls resulting from per-inquiry and direct-response marketing formats. Some content analysis has been done on certain types of feedback to the mass media as well as on media content.

Researchers investigating channels focus on the media themselves. Studies may take the form of surveys designed to determine degree of reliance on a particular medium for news and other information. Media reliance has been compared to other variables such as involvement in community issues, voting behavior, and perceptions of criminal defendants.

### NOTES

1. Warren Breed, "Social Control in the News Room? A Functional Analysis," *Social Forces* 33 (1955): 326.

2. Reported as "The Gatekeeper: A Case Study in the Selection of News," *Journalism Quarterly* 27 (1950): 383.

3. James E. Lynch, "Seven Days with 'All in the Family,'" *Journal of Broadcasting* 17 (1973): 259.

4. J. W. Ravage, "'. . . Not in the Quality Business.' A Case Study of Contemporary Television Production," *Journal of Broadcasting* 21 (1977): 47.

5. Paul F. Lazarsfeld, Bernard Berelson, and Hazel Gaudet, *The People's Choice* (New York: Columbia University Press, 1948).

6. Charles R. Wright, *Mass Communication: A Sociological Perspective,* 2nd ed. (New York: Random, 1975), 8–22.

7. "Mass Media and Social Change in Developed Societies," *Mass Communication Review Yearbook* (Beverly Hills, CA: Sage, 1980) 1: 657–678: and "The Spiral of Silence: A Theory of Public Opinion," *Journal of Communication* 24 (1974): 43–51.

8. Reprinted along with exposition and comment by Warren Weaver in book form as *The Mathematical Theory of Communication* (Urbana: Univeristy of Illinois Press, 1949).

## FURTHER READING

De Fleur, Melvin, and Sandra Ball-Rokeach. *Theories of Mass Communication.* 5th ed. New York: Longman, 1989.

Hsia, H. J. *Mass Communication Research Methods: A Step-By-Step Approach.* Hillsdale, NJ: Lawrence Erlbaum Associates, 1988.

Lindlof, Thomas R. *Qualitative Communication Research Methods.* Thousand Oaks, CA: Sage, 1995.

Lowery, Shearon A., and Melvin L. De Fleur. *Milestones in Mass Communication Research.* 3rd ed. New York: Longman, 1995.

McCombs, Maxwell E., and Lee Becker. *Using Mass Communication Theory.* Englewood Cliffs, NJ: Prentice-Hall, 1979.

McLuhan, [Herbert] Marshall. *Understanding Media: The Extensions of Man.* New York: McGraw-Hill, 1966.

McQuail, Denis. *Mass Communication Theory: An Introduction,* 3rd ed. Newbury Park, CA: Sage, 1994.

Perry, David K. *Theory and Research in Mass Communication: Contexts and Consequences.* Mahwah, NJ: Lawrence Erlbaum Associates, 1996.

Priest, Susanna H. *Doing Media Research: An Introduction.* Thousand Oaks, CA: Sage, 1996.

Severin, Werner J., and James Tankard, Jr. *Communication Theories: Origins, Methods, Uses.* 4th ed. New York: Longman, 1997.

Singletary, Michael W. *Mass Communication Research: Contemporary Methods and Applications.* New York: Longman, 1994.

Singletary, Michael W., and Gerald Stone. *Communication Theory and Research Applications.* Ames: Iowa State University Press, 1988.

Startt, James D., and William David Sloan. *Historical Methods in Mass Communication.* Hillsdale, NJ: Lawrence Erlbaum Associates, 1989.

Tan, Alexis S. *Mass Communication Theories and Research.* 2nd ed. New York: Wiley, 1985.

Wimmer, Roger D., and Joseph R. Dominick. *Mass Media Research: An Introduction.* 4th ed. Belmont, CA: Wadsworth, 1994.

Wright, Charles R. *Mass Communication: A Sociological Perspective.* 3rd ed. New York: Random House, 1986.

# INDEX